What Music Tells Me

What Music Tells Me

Beauty, Truth and Goodness and Our Cultural Inheritance

David Eaton

Dedicated To My Family

Contents

Preface

Art cannot change events. But it can change people.
It can affect people so that they are changed.
Because people are changed by art—enriched, ennobled,
encouraged—they can act in a way that may affect
the course of events by the way they vote, the way they behave,
the way they think.[1]
Leonard Bernstein

Those who are familiar with the third symphony of Gustav Mahler (1860-1911) will undoubtedly make the connection between the title of my book and the various titles that Mahler ascribed to the six movements of that symphony.* For Mahler, nature, angels, humankind and love all had something to say to him—presumably something imbued with beauty, truth and goodness. He would say that it was through the art of music that he could find answers to many of his questions regarding life, love and the pursuit of happiness. Mahler intuited, as did those in ancient cultures, that music

---

* Mahler ascribed the following titles to the six movements of his third symphony: "Pan Awakes, Summer Marches In", "What the Flowers in the Meadow Tell Me", "What the Animals in the Forest Tell Me", "What Man Tells Me", "What the Angels Tell Me", "What Love Tells Me"

wasn't solely about pleasure or aesthetics. Like the philosophers of ancient China and Greece, Mahler believed that music possessed moral and ethical implications and could be a gateway to higher truths and deeper understandings of the human condition. Hebrew and Christian philosophers also shared this perspective and wrote copious treatises regarding the effects of music on self and society. Any examination of our cultural patrimony reveals that the metaphysical, spiritual and axiological aspects of music, and its potential as a change agent in the spheres of politics and public ethics, has been a constant refrain from antiquity to Mahler—and it remains so today.[2] In this context examining our past can be highly elucidating. Edmund Burke cautioned against "deriding the wisdom of the ancients" regarding "the gravity of culture or the immutability of human nature," because understanding the past can be instructive in the quest for knowledge and insight in the pursuit of socio-cultural betterment.[3] The "hyper-presentism" that permeates much of our current socio-cultural dialogue and debate confines us to a decidedly restrictive evaluation of our societal problems and limits our discovery of possible solutions to help us get to a better place. Music and art can be part of the solution as Leonard Bernstein asserted. The music of the past, and the rationales that inspired its creation, can be edifying.

Though our personal tastes and preferences about music are highly varied, for just about everyone, music is something they can't seem to live without.* We know that music can be therapeutic and healing. It arouses emotions and alters consciousness. It can be motivational, informative, inspiring and unifying. For many, music *is* religion. We never tire of its pleasurable effects and those effects on the soul are palpable. Neuroscience tells us that when we listen to music our brain releases dopamine, an organic chemical compound associated with stimulation and reward-motivated behavior—and it's addictive!

Explorations into the origins of music reveal that the cultures of antiquity shared similar perspectives regarding music's ability to address innate human desires in a wordless mode of "heartistic" communication. Our desire for beauty is atavistic—a primal instinct—and great works of art have the enduring capacity to address that desire in powerful ways. Ethnomusicologists and

---

* Søren Kierkegaard considered Mozart to be a musical genius. Pierre Boulez considered Mozart's music to be trivial.

anthropologists note that virtually every culture held the belief that music possessed a spiritual dimension, thus music often accompanied religious ceremonies and rituals. The farther back in time we travel we find scant evidence of notation or sonic theories regarding how the musical components of pitch, rhythm and harmony were organized and presented as musical expression. However, there were attempts in ancient Greece (Damon of Athens, e.g.) to understand the effects of music on our mood and psyche—psychoacoustics, in modern parlance. It was Pythagoras' examination of the mathematical properties of the overtone series, the sonic etymology of all music, that revealed the underlying physics in the natural phenomenon of pitch production.

Theorists and philosophers, from the ancient kings in Mesopotamia to Confucius and Lu Buwei in China, to Pythagoras and Plato in Greece, to Boethius, Kepler and Rameau in Europe, examined this sonic etymology and developed speculative concepts about music's effect on our psyche and what it might be trying to tell us with regard to our pursuit of happiness, as well as to humankind's place in the cosmos. Noted neuroscientist Oliver Sacks asks, "Did song, in fact, precede speech (as Darwin thought); did speech precede music (as his contemporary Herbert Spencer believed); or did both develop simultaneously," as others have speculated?[4] Though we can make educated and inspired guesses about the answers to these questions, nature provides certain clues regarding pitch production.

Due to its linkage with religion and politics, the axiological aspect of music has been the source of continual examination and debate.* The idea espoused by the nineteenth-century French dramatist and literary critic Théophile Gautier of *l'art pour l'art* (art for art's sake) held a great deal of currency in the late nineteenth century because it sought to detach art from any moral or political implications. Yet we know that art and music have not been as disengaged from moral and political concerns as Gautier would have us believe—quite the opposite, in fact.

Musicologist Richard Taruskin observes that from its earliest incarnations opera often traded in political narratives. He notes that opera was "a world where satyrs romped and Eros reigned, where servant girls chastised their

---

* Axiology is the study of the nature, types, and governing criteria of values and value judgments.

masters, where philandering counts were humiliated, and where, later and more earnestly, rabbles were roused and revolutions abetted."[5] To suggest that art cannot encompass moral implications while being aesthetically pleasing, politically provocative and intellectually stimulating ignores a significant facet of art history. Isaiah Berlin refers to this as "value pluralism": the condition in which multiple considerations can be equally valid while being seemingly contradictory. Composers of opera, as Taruskin observes, have the ability to manipulate the audience's emotions and response to music, "and this is the source of music's power … it's the source of music's danger and it is not confined to opera."[6] In this context music has social and political relevance.

Immanuel Kant could not rationally explain the effects of aesthetic experience on our psyche, yet he intuited that those experiences were valid, universal (everyone has them), and could be transcendent—the "archetype of revelation," in fact.[7] Because music is often seen as an agent to promote change and assist in the creation of harmonious relationships, we imagine that music, regardless of its origins, can have the effect of ameliorating antagonisms, building bridges and promoting healing. This narrative has ancient roots.

The creation and appreciation of beauty, as well as our quest to understand its moral and transcendent attributes, are significant aspects of our cultural patrimony. Art historian Camille Paglia contends that historically, "civilization is defined by law and art. Laws govern our external behavior, while art expresses our soul."[8] Postmodernists argue that reality is an entirely subjective creation; as such, there are no "essences," absolute truths or meta-narratives in the human experience; and therefore, reliance on such is futile. This supposition has ties with Nietzsche and existentialism, which also reject the idea of meta-narratives, universal truths and absolute values. But this postmodern view denies (or ignores) the very real and universal human desire to experience beauty in order to satisfy the part of us that is beyond our physical and rational realities. Denying the transformative aspect of music and its ability to console, heal, inspire and inform is decidedly obtuse. When we are stripped of our metaphysical foundations, we shouldn't be shocked when we find ourselves lost in the abyss of chaos, moral confusion, absurdity and a great deal of insipid art. Regarding beauty and its linkage to truth and goodness, British philosopher Roger Scruton avers:

There is an appealing idea about beauty that goes back to Plato and Plotinus, and which became incorporated by various routes into Christian theological thinking. According to this idea beauty is an ultimate value—something that we pursue for its own sake, and for the pursuit of which no further reason need be given. Beauty should therefore be compared to truth and goodness, one member of a trio of ultimate values which justify our rational inclinations.[9]

Despite this particular observation, Scruton often makes the same case as Bernstein and Taruskin that art isn't exclusively about aesthetic pleasure because music can, and does, have profound moral implications in the context of creating an ethical culture. Citing our social development in the context of community, columnist David Brooks asserts, "We are not self-completing creatures. To thrive we have to throw ourselves into a state of dependence—on others, on institutions, on the divine."[10] I concur, but I submit that we *ought* to include a dependence on history—religious and nonreligious—in our quest for greater understanding of who we are, where we are going and how best to improve our socio-cultural environment.

It's important for artists to understand that their creative endeavors have consequences within the communities where they live and work. Artists don't create in a vacuum. Consequently, there are moral and ethical imperatives linked to the gift of creativity. To ignore this, or to think that our creative endeavors are not contingent on these imperatives, would seem to be fundamentally at odds with our quest for betterment. Of course, the pitfall in conflating any artist's personal morality vis-à-vis their art (Richard Wagner, e.g.) can result in disconcerting paradoxes and conundrums that are difficult to unravel without falling prey to self-serving double standards and duplicity. Yet the attempt to disentangle these seemingly intractable inconsistencies is necessary in order to ascertain what might be the most effective way to facilitate social and cultural improvement, and ascertain the role of musicians in that quest.

Discussions about art, religion and politics can be vexing and downright polarizing, however, these discussions are worth having in our attempt to arrive at a consensus as to how we might make our planet a better place for our children—and how we might make better children for our planet! I think of my children a great deal and how my actions and behavior affects them. In the course of writing this book, I received an e-mail message from my eldest daughter, who at the time was attending college and majoring in religious studies.

> Hi Dad. :) I just experienced a moment of "musical epiphany." I was listening to *The Lark Ascending* by Ralph Vaughan-Williams, and when I really just stopped to listen (as I do every once in a while), the music really struck something deep inside. I was struck by the idea that while music, in one, very simplistic sense, is "only" a combination of successive sounds, it is simultaneously so, so much more than that. Indescribable ... at least by me. Just made me think of you, and how I love you so much and how love and music (and therefore, probably God, as well) are actually quite similar on a deep, central, reverberating level. Missing you.

Any exegesis on music and its effects on our being is fundamentally about what my daughter shared in that e-mail message: sound, physics, emotion, intellection, creativity, aesthetics and spirituality—all conjoined in ways that yield meaning and beauty in an artful way. Her epiphany was not unlike the realizations of many others for whom music is an indispensable part of their lives. Eduard Hanslick's description of music as being merely "sonorous forms in motion" seems extremely wanting by comparison and is at odds with Schopenhauer's contention that music is not merely representational, mathematical or symbolic. For Schopenhauer music possessed a phenomenological aspect in that it is the manifestation of the thing in itself—the will. Joyful music *is* joyful and not merely a representation or an exemplification of joy. This is why music impacts us in such enthralling ways.

Another daughter, Anna Mahler, whose father was the aforementioned Gustav, and a distinguished artist in her own right, offered this insight regarding the metaphysical attributes of the arts:

> Through truly great art we can participate in the secret of creation, the whole of creation. The chaos of the so-called reality of everyday life disappears and makes room for a deeper, truer reality, a mysterious ordering ... which transmits, in the most sublime cases of perfection, the almost mystical certainty that the universe makes sense.[11]

I concur with the sentiments of these two daughters and their observations remind me of Albert Einstein's contention that there is beauty in the mysterious.

So, what does music tell *me*? Many things, but above all it affirms the notion that we are both corporeal and incorporeal beings, and as such, music can put us in touch with the entirety of who we are. It also tells me that axiological concerns in the creation and production of art remain important factors in our pursuit of a lasting peace—the hope of all ages. Our identities are determined by what we prioritize, what we treasure and what we love. Values matter; hence, the music we create and listen to has implications beyond aesthetics, intellection, or craft. If art and music can alter consciousness and provide an awareness of problems and solutions to those problems, then artists should not merely be bystanders in the process of change. Music informs me of these things—and more.

Much of what I write about in this book is predicated on my real-life experiences as a professional musician for over fifty years and there are autobiographical aspects in certain chapters. Frequently, I venture into non-musical terrain, specifically with regard to various ideological, philosophical and political realities concerning the religious and the political disputes that now affect our general well-being and our art. I view the emergence of ideologies that are the progeny of either postmodernism or cultural totalitarianism (often referred to as "cultural Marxism"), as being inherently deleterious, illiberal and dangerous.* Moreover, having traveled to Israel many times between 2003 and 2011, I have developed a heightened interest in interfaith issues. For many, interfaith reconciliation is seen as an exercise in futility. However, I am in accord with maestro Daniel Barenboim, who suggests that the path toward any meaningful reconciliation "requires dialogue, which consists of honest speaking and often painful listening," the conditions for understanding without which it is impossible to even imagine peace.[12] As Bernstein asserted, art "can affect people so they are changed," thus, whether artists are "believers" or not, the

---

* The term "cultural Marxism" has taken on an anti-Semitic connotation primarily due to the fact that many of the Frankfurt School neo-Marxists who advocated Critical Theory were Jewish—Max Horkheimer, Erich Fromm, Theodor Adorno, Herbert Marcuse, e.g. Melanie Phillips, who is Jewish, uses the term "cultural totalitarianism" in her critique of the Frankfurt School, and I believe this to be an apt description.

power of art *ought* to be used in ways that can foster positive change in society. The question as to what virtues or universally shared values are necessary to realize positive change is one I attempt to answer throughout this book.

Though I am a person of faith, I am well aware that there is great consternation about utopian prescriptions, whether based on religious or secular convictions. Acknowledging that, my concern is how we can better ourselves in the mode of what Hans Blumenberg referred to as "infinite progress," which makes "each present relative to its future."[13] The framers of the American Constitution had similar perspectives in mind when they envisioned our nation progressing toward, "a more perfect union." I know that my better angels haven't always been front-and-center in my own life in my attempts at becoming a better person and a more responsible artist. Like most everyone else, I fall short of God's glory and I remain in a state of "infinite progress."

Still, I believe that the role of artists in the process of achieving social betterment has great consequence in our continual pursuit of truth, beauty and goodness. The insights that I share in this book are largely predicated on that premise. I offer my perspectives in the spirit of humility: of giving of one's best to one's society in the hopes of deepening our understanding about music and, in so doing, rediscovering the essence of our cultural patrimony as well as discovering the most efficacious path toward attaining a culture of peace.

Nota Bene

If I may quote the aforementioned Roger Scruton: "Some parts of this book started life elsewhere." A number of these essays were published in various periodicals and journals between 1986 and 2015 and have been edited for this publication. Others were posted on the *Peace Music CommUNITY* (PMC) website forum from 2008 through 2014. It was my intention on the PMC website to provide information that both professional musicians and the general public might find insightful. In this respect I am more of a "public writer" than an "academic theorist." Readers will notice that there are redundancies that occur due to cross-referencing of essays that were posted in different places and at different times spanning several decades. Because the chapters of this book were written as standalone essays, there isn't a linear narrative that proceeds from chapter to chapter. There are, however, several "grand narratives" that underscore much of what I offer in these essays. Moreover, because

I intended this book to be as much for the general public as for musicians, I frequently provide footnotes to help contextualize certain issues.

In his cautionary tale, *1984*, George Orwell warned: "Who controls the past controls the future. Who controls the present controls the past."[14] There is a great deal of validity in Orwell's assumption, therefore studying and contextualizing the past in an honest fashion can be beneficial. Cherry-picking certain facts to support a particular narrative isn't really an attempt to fully understand history in relation to our current human condition. On a macro level it is my understanding that human history has been baleful because humankind has continually fallen short of the expectations of God, our Heavenly Parent. I'm a guilty party in that respect.

In my examination of music and its historical place in society, I've been inspired and enlightened by the commentary of many highly informed individuals, including Leonard Bernstein, Denis Dutton, Edward Rothstein, Alex Ross, George Rochberg, Allan Bloom, Kay S. Hymowitz, Leonard B. Meyer, Melanie Phillips, Richard Taruskin, Jonah Goldberg, Roger Scruton, Camille Paglia, Robert R. Reilly, Charles Rosen, Bruce Bawer, Heather MacDonald, Michael Walsh, Dana Gioia, Stanley Crouch, Michael Novak, Russell Jacoby and a host of other essayists, philosophers and artists. Their perspectives on art and culture are cited in the ensuing chapters and they represent conservative, moderate and liberal outlooks. I've also included a list of recommended recordings at the end of each essay in which I have cited various composers, their music and their views regarding their art in the hopes that readers will explore the music that has enriched my life so abundantly.

Endnotes

1   Leonard Bernstein, interview with John Gruen: *Los Angeles Times*, December 31, 1972.

2   Norman Lebrecht, *Why Mahler? How One Man and Ten Symphonies Changed the World* (New York: Anchor Books, 2010), p. 8.

3   Jonah Goldberg, *The Tyranny of Clichés: How Liberals Cheat in the War of Ideas* (New York: Sentinel/Penguin Group-USA, 2012), Kindle Edition.

4   Oliver Sacks, *Musicophilia: Tales of Music and the Brain, Revised and Expanded Edition* (New York: Vintage Books-Ransom House, 2008), p. 264.

5   Richard Taruskin, *The Dangers of Music and Other Anti-Utopian Essays* (Berkeley-Los Angeles: University of California Press, 2010), p. 222.

6   Richard Taruskin, "The Many Dangers of Music," lecture, Graduate Center, City University of New York, 2016, https://www.youtube.com/watch?v=Jiy_xXTjW3k.

7   Roger Scruton, *An Intelligent Person's Guide to Modern Culture* (South Bend, Indiana: St. Augustine Press, 2000), p. 31.

8   Camille Paglia, *Glittering Images: A Journey Through Art from Egypt to Star Wars* (New York: Vintage Books, 2012), p. xi.

9   Roger Scruton, *Beauty: A Very Short Introduction* (New York: Oxford University Press, 2011), p. 2.

10   David Brooks, *The Road to Character* (New York: Penguin-Ransom House, 2015), p. 244.

11   Anna Mahler, *Anna Mahler: Her Work*, Anna Mahler's essays, Introduced by Ernst H. Gombrich (Stuttgart, Germany: Besler-Verlag, 1975), p. 11.

12   Daniel Barenboim, *Music Quickens Time* (London-Brooklyn: Verso Books, 2008), p. 103.

13   Hans Blumenberg, *The Legitimacy of the Modern Age*, translated by Robert M. Wallace (Cambridge, MA: MIT Press, 1983), p. 35.

14   George Orwell, *1984* (New York: Harcourt. Inc., 1949), p. 33.

1

The Journey

The art of writing is the art of discovering what you believe.
Gustav Flaubert

A friend once told me that the first sign of oncoming senility is having the uncontrollable urge to write a book. Well, senility seems to be encroaching because that urge has become rather intense for me over the past few years. The prospect of undertaking such a project seemed more than a bit daunting at the outset, but as I threw myself into the process I realized that my senility might be more acute than I had fully realized. Since our faculties for comprehension can be one of the first things to diminish in our advancing years, I wondered if I could actually pull this off.

I began reading serious analytical commentary on music and composers in my college days at Ohio State University in the late 1960s—Sir Donald Francis Tovey, Harold C. Schonberg, Theodor Adorno, Aaron Copland, Halsey Stevens, Milton Cross and David Ewen being among my earliest reads. During the ensuing years, as I continued to study, discuss and research the art of music and its effects on our psyche, my fascination with these issues became an important aspect of my development as both a musician and a civic-minded person. In the process of writing I have found that there is ample evidence to support Sir Francis Bacon's assertion that "reading makes a full man, conference a ready man and writing an exact man."[1] Gustav Flaubert's assertion that writing is "the art of discovering what you believe," seems inherently correct as well. In the process of writing this book I found that writing is similar to composing music in that it requires many of the same organizational and editing skills. Moreover, like the practice of musical composition, it can be very humbling, for there is a plethora of talented writers and commentators who have honed their craft to extremely high levels in expressing their views about music and culture. The fact that there have been copious books written about music, perhaps thousands, testifies to our fascination and love for this most sublime human endeavor.

Music has been a significant part of my life for the better part of five decades—going on six. I have been blessed with the opportunity to travel the world as a conductor, composer and producer, and through those experiences my faith in the ability of music to work its magic as a harmonizing agent has been validated time and again. In fact, I would say that for many musicians, professional or amateur, this idea lies at the heart of why they pursue the art of music and why it continues to be the source of great joy and satisfaction.

Attending Catholic elementary school in suburban Cleveland, Ohio, I had the good fortune of being in an environment where exposure to music was considered an important facet of the educational process. My father, a World War II veteran, was an electrician and built a "hi-fi" record player from scratch. We were one of the first families in our neighborhood to have a television—because dad made one! I remember the basement workspace where he assembled tubes, wires, speakers and a picture tube into this electronic marvel that allowed us to watch and listen to the Dorsey Brothers and other musical notables of the era. My parents loved big band music and Broadway musicals, and in the early days of the recording industry when long-playing records (LPs) and "high fidelity" were in their formative stages, I was fortunate to live in a home where music was always present on the turntable or the radio—usually too loud for my parents. I started music lessons when I was ten years old and absolutely loved being in my school bands and orchestra. As a trombonist I especially enjoyed the big bands of Tommy Dorsey and Glenn Miller, two of my dad's favorites.

As it did with many teenagers growing up in the 1960s, the emergence of "rock and roll," an appellation coined by Cleveland radio personality Alan Freed (a.k.a. "Moondog" and another trombone player from Ohio State), had profound effects on my decision to pursue music as a career. The so-called "British Invasion" and Woodstock would also play heavily into my life choices, as I played in several popular rock bands between stints as a music student in college. But it was attending a concert by the Cleveland Orchestra when I was a sophomore in high school in 1965 that sealed the deal for me. Hearing that world-class ensemble was a riveting musical experience after which I couldn't get enough classical music. From that point on I spent many a day at the Cleveland Public Library listening to recordings of the music of Beethoven, Tchaikovsky, Sibelius, Copland, Mahler and Shostakovich—scores in hand. One great symphony or concerto led to another, and the sense of discovery with each new piece and each new composer was positively addictive. Attending Cleveland Orchestra concerts was like going to church. Music became my religion.

I made my first visit to New York City in 1966 on a four-day high school field trip that included attending a ballet, a Broadway musical and visits to several museums. The ballet performance by the New York City Ballet included Claude Debussy's *Jeux* and a contemporary piece that incorporated a rock band with an orchestra (I can't recall the title—*Astarte*?). I was completely enthralled by the entire experience. This excursion to the Big Apple also included a performance of *Fiddler on the Roof* with Herschel Bernardi in the role of Tevye and visiting the Metropolitan Museum of Art and the Guggenheim and Frick Museums. This was rather heady stuff for teenage kids from the Midwest and for me an indelible experience that put major wind in the sails of my nascent musical voyage. While having breakfast in the street-level restaurant at the Empire Hotel, overlooking the resplendent, new structures of Lincoln Center, I made a determination: I was going to come to New York and become a symphony orchestra conductor and compose music in the Big Apple. From that day on becoming a composer and conductor in the tradition of Beethoven, Aaron Copland, George Szell and Leonard Bernstein became an obsession. Watching Bernstein's *Young People's Concerts*, produced and televised by CBS, only heightened my aspirations.

After my New York experience my routine of listening to classical music every day intensified, even during my days as a rocker. I studied music theory in high school and at the Cleveland Music Settlement and started composing and arranging music. By the time I finished my freshman year at Ohio State I had composed several tone poems, a symphony and several works for chamber ensembles, symphonic band and mixed chorus—including several atonal works. I did a significant portion of the arranging for the various rock bands and ensembles I performed with and had my first experiences as a songwriter and working in the recording studio at that time as well. The backdrop for all of this was the war in Viet Nam.

The Peace Movement in America

Being in college during the Viet Nam era quickened my interest in philosophy and geopolitics. I vividly recall hearing the news of Bobby Kennedy's assassination and the disturbances at the Democratic National Convention in Chicago in 1968. Like many of us from that generation I had friends and classmates who died in Viet Nam. I had performed at a nightclub in Kent, Ohio with one of my rock bands—the North River Street Rock Collection—just days prior to the Ohio National Guard shootings that took the lives of four Kent State students on May 4, 1970. The antiwar atmosphere on the campus at that time was palpable and when Neil Young's protest song "Ohio" hit the airwaves, I recall how that galvanized the revolutionary attitudes of many of my friends and colleagues.

As Young would recall years later, "It's still hard to believe I had to write this song. It's ironic that I capitalized on the death of these American students. Probably the most important lesson ever learned at an American place of learning. David Crosby cried after this take."[2] Crosby reminisced, "I remember getting nuts at the end of the song, I was so moved ... I was freaked out because I felt it so strongly, screaming, 'Why? Why?'"[3] In the ensuing years Richard Nixon became a despised figure for his political proclivities and for having instituted the draft lottery. The prospect of being drafted into the military and being sent to Viet Nam hung over our generation's heads like a noose at the gallows.

Emanating from the streets of San Francisco, the "hippie" movement was well underway. An article in *The National Review*, published August 8, 1967, suggested that those who gravitated to hippiedom were New Age "secessionists," young people who, cannot stand the constraints, the conventionalities, and the hypocrisies of our society, and so they have determined to secede and establish their own "joy" society in the midst of ours, but inwardly dissociated from it. They are inner expatriates, going off to live their authentic lives, not to Paris or the South Seas, but to the sidewalks, parks, and beaches of our big cities, particularly on the West Coast ... [and] Mayor Lindsay's Fun City.[4]

These "peaceniks" and "flower children" were those of the generation who were caught up in the Aquarian ethos of the late '60s: dissidents expressing their defiant aversion to war and anything relating to the military—and to all things "plastic." Aspiring to a Bohemian lifestyle was seen as a measure of one's authenticity. Conformity was so "nowhere."

Music acted as the soundtrack for that era and for my generation—the so-called "baby boomers." Our love of music became quasi-religious. "Make love, not war" was our credo, sex and drugs were our sacraments and rock 'n' roll was the music that accompanied the liturgy. The spirit of rebellion and defiance was everywhere, especially in music. As the "free love" generation and its music literally rocked the suburban comforts of post-World War II America (and elsewhere), the deconstructionist mindset that engulfed that era questioned traditional attitudes about family, society, authority, sexuality, art, politics, entertainment and religion. Daniel Ellsberg's whistleblowing on the Kennedy, Johnson and Nixon administrations' perfidy regarding the false premises for prolonging the war in Viet Nam only exacerbated the distrust in authority figures. Watergate was fuel on the fire.

It's been suggested that the phenomenon of Beatlemania, and all that it entailed, exerted the most profound effect on the psychology of contemporary culture in the second half of the twentieth century. With the surviving Beatles now approaching their eighties, that supposition is hard to refute. When my father saw how rock music was being used by Madison Avenue to market and sell everything from cars to aluminum siding, he realized (much to his dismay) that it was a cultural force that wasn't going away anytime soon. His realization was not unlike that of many of our parents. Whether from Liverpool, Detroit, Haight-Ashbury or the beaches of California, popular music was making serious waves—and serious money.

In the late '60s I was far from being a *soixante-huitard*, but like many students of that era I was empathetic and supportive of the antiwar movement.* I viewed communism as something inherently bad, but that wasn't because I went through any heart-wrenching introspection. It wasn't much of a stretch to comprehend that Russian hegemony was a very real global threat. In spite of academia's naïve acquiescence to the socialist ideology that championed the "dictatorship of the proletariat," it wasn't difficult to ascertain that much of the Marxist canon was a counterfeit contention: the staggering body counts confirmed as much. How could the advocates of "the dictatorship of the proletariat" act in such an inhumane fashion toward the very constituents they claimed to be championing? The cognitive dissonance for me was rather intense and my distaste for anything Marxist grew irksome.

Though most Americans knew little about Hegel's concept of the dialectic and how that played into the theories of Karl Marx, the advent of the atomic era—along with living through the Cuban Missile Crisis, Sputnik, Nikita Khrushchev's defiant shoe-pounding episode at the United Nations and the Iron Curtain—alerted many Americans to the fact that as a freedom-loving people we had a serious adversary to reckon with. Some were more concerned than others, and the political left exhibited a great deal of empathy toward Marxist revolutionaries such as Fidel Castro and Che Guevara. Totalitarianism of any stripe seemed so inherently wrong and oppressive that I couldn't easily fathom why there was any infatuation with it at all. Why was a racist thug like Guevara, who killed more of his rivals than Mussolini,[5] idolized by so many? It made no sense. Neither did the neo-Marxist ideas of the Frankfurt School alumni Theodor Adorno, Herbert Marcuse and Walter Benjamin. I found Adorno's dialectic views on music to be especially wrong-headed and wrong-hearted.

The nightly news reports from Walter Cronkite, Chet Huntley, David Brinkley and John Chancellor about people being shot as they attempted to escape from East Berlin to the West—replete with video evidence—only confirmed my intuition that communism was something to be condemned in the most

---

* The term *soixante-huitard* originated to describe the French radicals who participated in the civil unrest in 1968.

unequivocal manner.* Cumulatively, these occurrences changed my attitudes about America's role in the world and I found myself becoming even more concerned with geopolitical matters. The Six-Day War in Israel in 1967 and the executions of the Israeli athletes at the 1972 Olympic games in Munich were also serious eye-openers for me. By getting to know Jewish students my perspectives about the Middle East began to go through a metamorphosis as well. As I learned more about the Holocaust, Babi Yar† and the tyrannies perpetuated against artists in the Soviet Bloc—Russian composers Dmitri Shostakovich and Sergei Prokofiev in particular—my attitudes regarding music and the social responsibilities of artists became even more entrenched. Though I remained somewhat liberal on certain social issues at the time, when it came to geopolitical concerns my conscience became ensconced in decidedly conservative and patriotic attitudes. (Playing all those marches by John Philip Sousa in my high school and college bands may have had something to do with my sense of patriotism as well.)

The predilection of many artists in America to embrace a "liberal" worldview dates back to the post-World War I era. Charlie Chaplin, perhaps the most celebrated entertainer of his time, was a serious advocate of socialism. The plight of the common man in the wake of the Great Depression affected Chaplin who had experienced abject poverty growing up in England. Though Chaplin never embraced communism per se, he was nonetheless "an ardent champion of the underdog and as an avowed pacifist … a push-over for the raw trend of Communist thought."[6] Like American composer Aaron Copland, he was an advocate of the American Communist Party leader Earl Browder and considered himself more or less "pro-communist" in terms of seeing communism as a remedy for the injustices perpetuated by capitalist greed. Copland actually campaigned for Browder's presidential bid in 1936.

---

* If you're old enough to remember, NBC's nightly newscast in the late 1960s concluded with the credits being rolled to Nikolai Rimsky-Korsakov's *Procession of the Nobles*.

† Babi Yar was the ravine in Kiev, Ukraine where as many as 150,000 Jews were murdered by the German army in World-War II. Dmitri Shostakovich's 13th Symphony, composed in 1962, is based on a poem by Yevgeny Yevtushenko, in which the poet recalled the forgotten horrors of the tragedy. Yevtushenko would say: "If I were to be able to write music I would have written it exactly the way Shostakovich did. … His music made the poem greater, more meaningful and powerful," Elizabeth Wilson, Shostakovich: *A Life Remembered*.

As film historian Steven J. Ross points out, Chaplin may have had second thoughts about communism after he met Shostakovich and heard firsthand about life as an artist in Russia and how the composer was "forced to compose his music along party lines and receive party approval before making public statements."[7] These oppressive conditions within the communist "utopia" were the norm for artists, academics and members of the media living under the Stalinist regime at that time. As Jonah Goldberg observed:

> When agents of the state and other officials have unilateral authority to change the ideal based upon their own political, aesthetic, or cultural preferences, they are substituting objective standards for their own arbitrary power, their own priestcraft.[8]

> As that catastrophic experiment [Soviet Marxism] demonstrated, whenever you try to replace well-established cultural norms with an abstract new system, you do not open the door to a new utopia; you open the door to human nature's darker impulses.[9]

Those darker impulses could be really dark in the Soviet Union—or Castro's Cuba, Kim's North Korea and Mao's China—as Aleksandr Solzhenitsyn informed the world in his book *The Gulag Archipelago*, published in 1973.

It was also in 1968 that I saw Stanley Kubrick's film *2001: A Space Odyssey*. Of the most impressionable aspects of the film was Kubrick's inclusion of Richard Strauss's symphonic poem *Thus Spake Zarathustra*. This was my introduction to Strauss and to Friedrich Nietzsche, both of whom I knew next-to-nothing about at the time. Nietzsche's *Zarathustra* tome was written between 1883 and 1885, and Strauss's music was composed in 1896. By this time I was no longer a practicing Catholic and I had become quite agnostic about organized religion. Music was my new religion and as I began to explore Strauss's *Zarathustra* music and the literary source that inspired it, I began to observe a connection between Nietzsche, the death of God movement and the advance of Marxism-Leninism, especially the idea of resentment being ginned up as a primary impulse for revolution and ending oppression. Reading *Zarathustra* was quite an intellectual slog for me at the time, but what stuck with me was Nietzsche's use of the term *tarantula* in several passages. Looking back at those passages again in preparing for this book, I realized there was something quite prescient about *Zarathustra* vis-à-vis resentment and Marxism. From *Zarathustra*:

> Thus I speak to you in a parable—you who make souls whirl, you preachers of equality. To me you are tarantulas, and secretly vengeful. But I shall bring your secrets to light; therefore I laugh in your faces with my laughter of the heights. Therefore I tear at your webs, that your rage may lure you out of your lie-holes and your revenge may leap out from behind your word justice. For that man be delivered from revenge, that is for me the bridge to the highest hope, and a rainbow after long storms.
>
> The tarantulas, of course, would have it otherwise. "What justice means to us is precisely that the world be filled with the storms of our revenge"—thus they speak to each other. "We shall wreak vengeance and abuse on all whose equals we are not"—thus do the tarantula-hearts vow. "And 'will to equality' shall henceforth be the name for virtue; and against all that has power we want to raise our clamor!"
>
> You preachers of equality, the tyrannomania of impotence clamors thus out of you for equality: your most secret ambitions to be tyrants thus shroud themselves in words of virtue. Aggrieved conceit, repressed envy—perhaps the conceit and envy of your fathers—erupt from you as a flame and as the frenzy of revenge.[10]

Heavy stuff. Resentment, vengeance, reprobation, abuse: all justified by the purveyors of Marxism in the quest for equality and social justice. Some have argued that rather than being prescient, Nietzsche was merely describing the human condition as it has played out in the course of human history.* As Jordan Peterson points out, hierarchies are natural in an evolutionary sense, but are problematic because human nature has been corrupted and obsessed with power, often under the pretext of compassion, justice and social betterment.† This remains a quandary in the human condition.

---

* Leonard Bernstein expounded on Nietzsche's writings and Strauss's *Zarathustra* symphonic poem during his New York Philharmonic Young People's Concert on November 4, 1971.

† Hierarchy is intrinsic to Western musical syntax and theory.

A New Perspective for Me: Music and Cultural Power

It was at a Cleveland Orchestra concert in 1971 that I first became acquainted with the music of the twentieth-century German composer Paul Hindemith (1895-1963). His life and career, which I chronicle later in this book, remains an edifying narrative for any artist who possesses the inclination to use their creativity in the advocacy of humanitarian concerns. The libretto of his opera *Mathis der Maler*, which deals with the role of artists in the face of a corrupt and tyrannical aristocracy, remains instructive, as does his commentary regarding these issues. The choices that German artists were confronted with during the ascendance of the Third Reich had life-and-death ramifications. Some opted to remain and pursue their artistic careers in Germany, while some thought that to be morally unconscionable and went into exile. Others, according to varying accounts, remained "disturbingly neutral." These choices would have long-lasting consequences.

Several prominent artists of the Austrian-Germanic sphere—soprano Elisabeth Schwarzkopf, composers Richard Strauss and Carl Orff, and conductors Wilhelm Furtwängler, Karl Böhm and Herbert von Karajan—lived with the stigma of having Nazi ties throughout their post-World War II careers. The suspicions surrounding Karajan were especially acute due to the iconic maestro's meteoric rise to prominence in the classical music sphere in the 1950s. Some believed that Karajan, a gifted conductor who became the music director of the Berlin Philharmonic (for life) in 1955, had capitalized on Nazi favoritism to advance his career. Though some of the evidence regarding this allegation is circumstantial, the misgivings surrounding his Nazi connections and his disappearance during the de-Nazification of Europe in the years just after the war never abated.* I remember when, in 1988 Karajan conducted his final New York concerts at Carnegie Hall with the Berlin Philharmonic, there were demonstrators carrying anti-Karajan placards outside the hall, protesting his appearance. The suspicions surrounding his Nazi connections continued until his death in 1989.

The narratives surrounding Hindemith and Karajan in Germany are not unlike our current social reality; therefore, they remain instructive for those

---

* Norman Lebrecht explores Karajan's legacy vis-à-vis the Third Reich at length in his book *The Maestro Myth*.

who live in a pluralistic society as we attempt to attain the proper equilibrium between individual freedom and social responsibility. The freedoms that we are afforded in democratic and republican conditions, where civil liberties and negative rights are thought to be protected by law, allow for behavior and cultural expressions that some may find to be morally objectionable.* In my rock 'n' roll days, being able "to do your own thing" and honoring the code of "different strokes for different folks" seemed to be a completely libertarian mindset and one that anyone under the age of thirty readily embraced. But as we witnessed the deaths of some of our most celebrated cultural heroes—Jimi Hendrix, Janis Joplin, Jim Morrison, Brian Jones, John Bonham, Keith Moon—and saw our friends struggle with addictions and psychological breakdowns, it became all too clear that abuses of freedom could have extremely deleterious consequences. Coming to a mature attitude with regard to our choices required attaining adult sensibilities, and this process seemed to encroach on the unbridled idealism of our youthful mirth. Living as we pleased without taking the requisite responsibilities in relation to the society at large may have seemed like Nirvana, but it was decidedly immature and an indication of arrested emotional development.

As the music industry changed in the decades between 1970 and 1990, it was becoming apparent that the edgy social and political commentary that had been the driving force behind the music of many bands and musicians in the era immediately surrounding Woodstock and Haight-Ashbury was giving way to decidedly commercial concerns. There was big money to be made in pop music, thus rocking the establishment's boat with politically charged music made CEOs and shareholders of entertainment entities uneasy. Soft R&B, MOR (middle of the road) and disco began to rule the airwaves. One of my favorite bands of the late '60s, Chicago, went from being a fairly

---

* Making the distinction between a democracy and a republic is important. Democracy is predicated on the idea that the rule of the people, or the majority, is salient, whereas a republic makes "the law" the primary aspect of society. The word "democracy" does not appear in the Declaration of Independence. James Madison, in The Federalist Papers, was especially contemptuous of "democracy." The founders understood that the essence of freedom necessitated the limitation of government. Madison wrote in Federalist Paper, No. 39: "We may define a republic to be, or at least may bestow that name on, a government which derives all its powers directly or indirectly from the great body of the people, and is administered by persons holding their offices during pleasure, for a limited period, or during good behavior."

progressive outfit producing jazz-rock anti-war jams to a stereotypical "power ballad" group, with front man Peter Cetera crooning romantic tunes like "If You Leave Me Now," accompanied by so much orchestral "sweetening" in the arrangements that it could give you diabetes. Grit was out. Glam was in, and it paid big dividends as the star power of artists like Michael Jackson and Madonna, along with the emergence of the music video, took center stage.* Whereas hyper-intellectualism basically marginalized serious art music, the diminishing intelligence and social relevance of pop music had the effect of reducing pop to a mere commodity.† Quite presciently, the aforementioned neo-Marxist philosopher Theodor Adorno foresaw the problematic aspects of "mass media" and its effect on the commercialization of the arts in the 1940s, and this is one of the few perspectives that we actually share.

As the Cold War droned on, the influence of American popular culture seeped into Asia, South America, Europe, the Middle East and even behind the Iron Curtain. A good friend and colleague, Sasha Mishnaevski, former principal violist in the Detroit Symphony Orchestra, grew up and studied in Leningrad before moving to the United States in 1976. He recounts how Russian students listened to American popular music in the hopes that they would one day be able to experience the freedom that their counterparts in the West enjoyed. Wearing jeans and listening to rebellious American pop music were the fantasies of many young people who were oppressed in the Soviet Bloc. In the 1950s there was a conspiracy theory circulating that held that the CIA had invented rock and roll and used Radio Free Europe to broadcast this "forbidden" music in the hopes of undermining the Soviet authorities. Playing in rock bands in Russia or merely owning records by Western artists could result in beatings or imprisonment.‡

---

* Michael Jackson's "Thriller" video (1983) and Madonna's "Vogue" video (1990) are considered to be among the most important forays of pop music into the visual realm.

† Regarding the effects of the Cold War on serious art music, Richard Taruskin observes: "Amid the kind of chronic anxiety to which the Cold War tensions gave rise, triumphant rhetoric in the arts took on an air of saber-rattling, producing not euphoria but heightened apprehension." [Source: Taruskin, *Music in the Late Twentieth Century*, p. 8.]

‡ The creation of the National Endowment for the Arts by President Johnson in 1965 was a part the United States' response to the Cold War competition with the Soviet Union. Science, space exploration, sports and the arts became various battlegrounds on which to demonstrate superiority between the two superpowers. New Jersey congressman Frank Thompson stated

Still, the allure of the music was irresistible and infectious. So-called "bone music," the making of bootleg pressings on discarded x-rays, was a way that young Russians could listen to music that had been banned in the U.S.S.R. This practice was viewed as subversive by the Soviet authorities because it might promote "insurrectionary tendencies in listeners. ... For teenagers who didn't much fancy joining the Leninist youth brigades of the Komsomol, the lure of the *stilyagi*—a hipper subculture that embraced all things jazz, rock 'n' roll and Hollywood—must have seemed irresistibly exotic."[11] Thus "bone music" was a way for young Russians to get their musical fix. The caveat for them, like several of my Chinese friends who grew up during Mao's Cultural Revolution, was that they had to go about listening to this music in a furtive way. Soviet authorities were highly suspect of what they viewed as the subversive characteristics of Western pop culture; therefore, being surreptitious in one's listening habits was highly prudent.*

In 1974 I had several spiritual experiences that precipitated my conversion to Unificationism. This life choice was quite startling for me, and my family at the time, but to this day I have never questioned that choice. In fact, in the ensuing decades, I've had other spiritual experiences that affirmed that decision and bolstered my faith conviction. My faith has informed many of the issues and choices that have guided my journey as a person and a musician. The concept of "Godism" remains a significant aspect of my life and work.

In 1976, I had the fortuitous opportunity to audition for and become a member of the New York City Symphony.† I had bigger ambitions, and after lobbying the orchestra's music director, Thomas Ludwig, for an occasion to conduct the orchestra for the better part of a year, he gave me an opportunity to conduct a rehearsal of one of his compositions. In 1977 he offered me

---

in 1954, "The sooner we can implement a program of selling our culture to the uncommitted people of the world as a weapon, the better off we are." [Source: Blair Tindall, *Mozart in the Jungle: Sex, Drugs, and Classical Music*, p. 51.]

* The 2017 documentary film *Free to Rock*, produced by Jim Brown (not the American football player), explores popular music behind the Iron Curtain in greater detail.

† The New York City Symphony was founded in 1926 and became a fully professional ensemble in 1956. In 1974, under the auspices of the International Culture Foundation, a cultural organization founded by Rev. Sun Myung Moon and Dr. Hak Ja Han Moon, the orchestra was acquired and supported through the patronage of ICF.

another opportunity to conduct a chamber ensemble comprised of members of the orchestra. My initial concert program consisted of serenades by Mozart (K. 388) and Dvořák (Op. 44) and Igor Stravinsky's *Octet*. I was on my way.

In 1985 I became the orchestra's music director. During my tenure with the orchestra I have produced and conducted concerts at Lincoln Center, Carnegie Hall, the Manhattan Center, the Metropolitan Museum of Art, the United Nations, the Apollo Theater and other important venues in New York City, as well as having toured with the orchestra both internationally and throughout the United States. I also was able to relive my band days in high school and college when I was appointed as the conductor of the historic Goldman Memorial Band in 1998. For three years I had the great joy of conducting the Goldman Band in its summer concert series at the city's historic sites including Coney Island, the Bronx Botanical Gardens and Lincoln Center. Sadly, the Goldman Band disbanded (no pun intended) in 2004 due to financial constraints after presenting thousands of concerts over a span of nearly nine decades. Times were changing and so were the musical tastes of the public at large.

Modernity and Romanticism

Since 1975 I've maintained an active career as a composer and producer having composed and arranged over nine hundred compositions, songs and transcriptions. Computer technology, along with advent of Musical Instrument Digital Interface (MIDI)* and virtual orchestra software, has impacted the art of music-making in ways few could have imagined in the late 1980s. My first experiences with the Synclavier, a cutting-edge, electronic instrument-workstation capable of replicating orchestral sounds via digital sampling, presented a daunting proposition. Was the human element in music under siege? It seemed so at the time. I was far from being a Luddite, yet my first reactions

---

* MIDI (Musical Instrument Digital Interface) "is a protocol—a set of specifications—agreed upon by representatives of computer and synthesizer manufacturers between 1981 and 1983 to standardize their products so that they could all interact (interface) ... this nexus vastly miniaturized and domesticated the hardware required for computer synthesis of music." This "democratization" of computer technology made it affordable to those who previously would not have had access to large mainframe computers found in universities or specialized music laboratories like IRCAM in Paris—and it resulted in huge profits for companies like Apple, Korg, Roland, Steinberg and Yamaha. [Source: Richard Taruskin, *Music in the Late Twentieth Century*, p. 501.]

to computer-generated music left me highly skeptical. Though I now find this technology to be indispensable, it nevertheless has put many fine musicians out of work. MIDI technology revolutionized the realm of computer music by making computer technology readily available to composers and performers at a relatively low cost. As Richard Taruskin explains,

> [this] new musical era was the by-product of industrial innovation in pursuit of profits. It was literally—and directly—created by capitalism, and can stand therefore as a musical triumph of the free market and the world-wide conversion to an "information-based" economy.[12]

The use of electronic media in composition dates back to the pioneering efforts of the early twentieth century by Thaddeus Cahill, Leon Theremin, Olivier Messiaen, Ferruccio Busoni and Edgard Varèse. These composers explored new attitudes, methods and aesthetics regarding musical expression. Recollecting the conversations he had with Busoni, Varèse recalled how they would ponder the direction that musical composition would, or should, take in order to free itself from the "straightjacket of the tempered system."[13] At the beginning of the twentieth century, key-centered, diatonic music born of equal temperament* was seen more and more as being an "exhausted" musical idiom. This perspective was supported by a progressive group of early twentieth-century composers, most notably Arnold Schoenberg, whose revolutionary methods of composing forever changed the landscape of art music.

As I delved into the compositional methods of twentieth-century modernism in my student years, I began to engage in composing using this atonal syntax. This, however, was a short-lived venture. As I continued to work in modern idioms, I couldn't reconcile my "romantic" spirit with the decidedly *contra*-romantic methodologies of atonal serialism. I had this epiphany: if "common practice" tonality was one type of "straightjacket," then surely

---

* Equal temperament is a system of tuning in which any octave is divided into 12 equal semitones, which was a distinct departure from the use of pure Pythagorean intervals. Zhu Zaiyu (1536-1611) of China and Flemish mathematician Simon Stevin (1548-1620) were two of the earliest-known theorists to experiment with equal temperament. However, it was J. S. Bach, who in 1722 published his collection of 24 keyboard works known as *The Well-Tempered Clavier*, who is credited with codifying this tuning system, and in so doing, setting the course of Western music for the next 300 years.

dodecaphonic serialism was another. If I had to choose, I would let my heart lead the way.

It was the German physicist Werner Meyer-Eppler who first introduced the term "aleatory"* into the lexicon of modern composition in the 1950s. The concept of aleatory, "chance" music found new adherents, most notably John Cage, whose "anything goes" musical utterances—breaking glass, ripping paper, radio frequency distortion, pouring water in various containers, randomly dropping cans on the floor, e.g.—bordered on being absurdist to many. For others, the unbridled freedom of the non-traditional musical materials and methods of aleatory music seemed to run counter to the traditional "bourgeois" attributes of order, discipline and coherence—the characteristics of the great musical legacy of the past. Certain ideologues with Marxist tendencies believed this to be a welcome development in art music precisely because it assisted in the takedown of what they viewed to be an unjust and inherently oppressive political structure.

Yet Stravinsky spoke of the necessity of limits as a means to prevent composers from getting "lost in the abyss of freedom." Intuitively, I felt that the "Cage-ian" ethos of source-material overindulgence was a masquerade for lack of craft or downright ineptitude. (Cage admitted that harmonic theory in the tonal syntax "escaped him.") Call me a Philistine in that regard, but that's a distinction I'm happy to make—as are many other professional musicians. Regarding Cage's leap into "the abyss of freedom"—or was it license?—the formalist composer Charles Wuorinen lamented, "How can you make a revolution when the revolution before last has already said that anything goes?"[14]

The Chinese modernist composer Chen Qigang, who was sent to a *laogai* (a forced labor camp) during Mao's Cultural Revolution, immigrated to France, studied under Olivier Messiaen and became a French citizen in 1992. He observed that the near fanatic preoccupation with intellection in contemporary art music resulted in the increased marginalization of the genre. Chen's reasoning for this occurrence:

> In the West, our situation as composers is very sad. ... In the 1950s we lost command of the field, not just because popular composers took over but, because we ceded the terrain. We "developed" to the point where we

---

* From the Latin *alea*, meaning "dice."

no longer knew anything about the art of writing melody. We had a kind of nonexistence in musical life.[15]

This "nonexistence" surely has contributed to the marginalization of contemporary art music and is a sad commentary on the state of serious musical composition. Some argue that this was just a fallow period of creative aridity, but others see a pernicious and determinist mindset at work: a mindset that is the progeny of radical egalitarianism and intolerant multiculturalism, in which characterizing any art as being "superior" to any other is either invidious or an expression of privilege. Even a cursory examination of academia reveals a decidedly neo-Marxist attitude (in the guise of Critical Theory) being in the equation.

Still, in recent decades there are signs that the fog of mid-century modernism is lifting and that art music that speaks to the heart and soul, as well as the mind, is finding its way out of the modernist margins. It's important to note that not all composers in the period between the two World Wars embraced and employed the atonal methods of Schoenberg and his disciples. In fact, the music by composers of that era remains in the active orchestral, opera, ballet and chamber-music repertory—the music of Bartók, Shostakovich, Copland, Britten, Barber, Prokofiev, Hindemith, Janáček, Blacher, et al.—is rooted in the syntax of the common practice, though with atypical syntactical propensities.

Moreover, a fair examination of various cultures reveals that some cultures do certain things better than others, and it is neither an expression of arrogance nor intolerance to make such distinctions. Certain cultures treat women better than others. Certain cultures are better at accepting and assimilating those of differing ethnicities or sexual orientations. Some cultures do agriculture, or oceanic enterprises, or computer science better than others. In an interview with Charlie Rose for CBS's *60 Minutes* on September 27, 2015, Vladimir Putin stated that America's creativity is an attribute that distinctly sets it apart from other nations. He seemed genuinely impressed by this particular "American" trait. Putin's was a familiar refrain that I've heard from my friends and colleagues from Japan, South Korea, China and Taiwan. The cultural DNA of Asian societies has traditionally not been as predisposed to individual expression and innovation as that of the West. The hard-won freedom that we enjoy in the West allows for creativity to flourish in ways that we too often take for granted. How we use that freedom is no small matter.

As we reexamine our cultural legacy, I would hope that political correctness take a back seat to common sense and objective reasoning. My personal journey as an artist reinforces the aforementioned idea that music is, or ought to be, a harmonizing agent in the pursuit of a more enlightened and humane world. As I reach retirement age, I have no plans to retire. As a good friend, Josh Cotter (a fine musician in his own right) recently said to me, "Retire? That just means getting new tires and continuing on life's journey." OK, then, let's go! There's music to be made. The journey continues.

Recommended Recordings

Tommy Dorsey: *Greatest Hits* (RCA)

Glenn Miller: *Greatest Hits* (RCA)

Tchaikovsky: Symphony No. 5, George Szell, Cleveland Orchestra

Sibelius: Symphony No. 2, Sir Colin Davis, Boston Symphony Orchestra

Beethoven: Overtures, Leonard Bernstein, New York Philharmonic

Copland: *The Tender Land Suite*, Aaron Copland, Boston Symphony Orchestra

Mahler: Symphony No. 4, George Szell, Cleveland Orchestra, Judith Raskin, soprano

Shostakovich: Symphony No. 13, *Babi Yar*, Kurt Masur, New York Philharmonic

Debussy: *Jeux*, Jean Martinon, ORTF National Orchestra

Bock & Harnick: *Fiddler on the Roof*, Original Cast Album

Neil Young: *Decade* Album

Beatles: *Anthology* Album

Doors: *Very Best of the Doors* (Rhino)

Janis Joplin: *The Woodstock Experience* (Columbia/Legacy)

U2: *Singles* (Interscope)

Chicago: *A Hit by Varèse* (Chicago V)

Varèse: *Arcana*, Riccardo Chailly, Royal Concertgebouw Orchestra

Rimsky-Korsakov: *Procession of the Nobles*, Eugene Ormandy, Philadelphia Orchestra

Prokofiev: *Romeo and Juliet*, Lorin Maazel, Cleveland Orchestra

Sousa: Marches, Richard Franco Goldman, Goldman Memorial Band

Hindemith: *Mathis der Maler*, William Steinberg, Boston Symphony Orchestra

Strauss: *Songs for Soprano and Orchestra*, Elisabeth Schwarzkopf, soprano

Mozart: Symphony No. 35, Karl Böhm, Berlin Philharmonic

Orff: *Carmina Burana*, Herbert Blomstedt, San Francisco Symphony & Chorus

Brahms: Four Symphonies, Wilhelm Furtwängler, Berlin Philharmonic

Tchaikovsky: Symphony No. 4, Herbert von Karajan, Berlin Philharmonic

Dvořák: Serenade in D-minor, Op. 44, Istvan Kertesz, London Symphony Orchestra

Stravinsky: *Octet for Winds*, Steve Richman, Harmonie Ensemble

Mozart: Wind Serenades, Jack Brymer, London Wind Soloists

Messiaen: *Turangalila-Symphonie*, Myung-Whun Chung, Bastille Opera Orchestra

Busoni: Piano Concerto, Christoph von Dohnányi, Cleveland Orchestra and Chorus

Zappa: *Hot Rats*, Frank Zappa, guitar

Zappa: *A Pig with Wings*, Ensemble Modern, Jonathan Stockhammer

Boulez: Piano Sonatas, Claude Helffer, piano

Bartók: *Concerto for Orchestra*, Fritz Reiner, Chicago Symphony Orchestra

Schoenberg: *Variations for Orchestra*, Herbert von Karajan, Berlin Philharmonic

Wagner: Overtures and Preludes, Sir Georg Solti, Chicago Symphony Orchestra

Britten: *Peter Grimes*, Benjamin Britten, Royal Opera House Covent Garden

Barber: Piano Concerto, St. Louis Symphony, John Browning, piano

Blacher: *Paganini Variations*, Op. 26, Robert Whitney, Louisville Orchestra

Janáček: *The Cunning Little Vixen*, Sir Charles Mackerras, Vienna State Opera

Endnotes

1   Francis Bacon, *The Major Works*, Oxford World Classics (Oxford and New York: Oxford University Press, 2002), p. 81.

2   Neil Young, *Decade*, Liner Notes, Reprise Records, CD-264-037, released 1977.

3   Dorian Lynskey, "Neil Young's Ohio—The Greatest Protest Record," Film & Music, *The Guardian*, May 6, 2010.

4   Will Herberg, "Who Are the Hippies," *National Review*, February 25, 2015, originally published on August 8, 1967, https://www.nationalreview.com/2015/02/who-are-hippies-will-herberg/.

5   Jonah Goldberg, *Liberal Fascism: The Secret History of the American Left from Mussolini to the Politics of Change* (New York: Broadway Books, 2007), p. 194.

6   Steven J. Ross, *Hollywood Left and Right: How Movie Stars Shaped American Politics* (Oxford and New York: University Press, 2011), p. 43.

7   Ibid.

8   Jonah Goldberg, *Suicide of the West: How the Rebirth of Tribalism, Populism, Nationalism, and Identity Politics is Destroying American Democracy* (New York: Crown Forum, 2018), p. 226.

9   Ibid., p. 231.

10 Friedrich Nietzsche, *Thus Spake Zarathustra*, translated by Thomas Common (Germany: Ernst Schmeitzner, Pantiano Classics, 1883-1891), pp. 81-82.

11 Peter Paphides, "Bone Music: The Soviet Bootleg Records Pressed on X-rays," *The Guardian*, January 29, 2015.

12 Richard Taruskin, *Music in the Late Twentieth Century* (Oxford and New York: Oxford University Press, 2010), p. 501.

13 Robert Morse Crunden, *Body and Soul: The Making of American Modernism* (New York: Basic Books, 2000), p. 49.

14 Elliott Schwartz and Barney Childs, editors, *Contemporary Composers on Contemporary Music* (New York: Holt, Rinehart and Winston, 1967), p. 371.

15 Chen Qigang, as cited by Alex Ross, *Listen to This* (New York: Farrar, Straus and Giroux, 2010), p. 168.

2

First Thoughts: Music, Philosophy and Religion

I do not feel obliged to believe that the same God who has endowed us with senses, reason, and intellect has intended us to forgo their use and by some other means to give us knowledge which we can attain by them.[1]
Galileo Galilei

Music was born free; and to win freedom is its destiny.[2]
Ferruccio Busoni

The metaphysical aspects of music and art, as well as their moral and ethical dimensions (axiology), have fascinated philosophers and artists going back a few millennia. The Sumerians believed that music had divine origins and that the gods entertained themselves with songs based on modes with distinct mathematical proportions, some of which were not unlike the diatonic pitch sets and melodies that we find in Western tonal music.* The Chinese of Confucius' time believed that music could be a significant factor in providing order in society, hence, they placed a great deal of importance on the ennobling, aspects of music. Moreover, the Chinese held that music, when aligned with the natural order of the cosmos, possessed therapeutic and healing power. Like the Chinese, the Greeks emphasized the moral and ethical power of the tonal art and its effect on self and society. The Platonic ideal of truth, beauty and goodness, as well as the concept of a "sacred geometry" as it pertained to the "harmony of the spheres," has continued to influence scientific and philosophical thought until this day.

Early Christian philosophers such as Boethius, Augustine and Aquinas were influenced by Greek axiological precepts and viewed beauty and art as vehicles that could improve one's character, as well as fashion a devotional frame of mind whereby one could more easily connect with the Almighty—the supposed source of love and all things good. The *Enneads* of Plotinus, as extrapolated into Christian philosophy by Thomas Aquinas, were based on the assumption "that truth, beauty and goodness are attributes of the deity," through which "the divine unity makes itself known to the human soul."[3] For Aquinas the transcendental aspects of truth, beauty and goodness were "features of reality possessed by all things, since they are aspects of being, ways in which the supreme gift of being is made manifest," and thus properly understood.[4]

Music is considered to be a cultural universal and though we cannot know the exact origins of music, we do know that it has always been realized according to certain quantifiable mathematical properties—frequencies, ratios, intervals, durations, vibrations and decibels. Musician and neuroscientist Daniel J. Levitin has written that when we listen to music, "we are actually perceiving multiple attributes or 'dimensions.'"[5] Sound vibrations can be explicated mathematically according to physical law (the overtone series), and the combinatory utilization of these properties, whether codified in a syntactical fashion or not, point to mathematics as the basis of sound and music on the

---

* Tonality is the codified system of pitch and chord relationships that results in a specific hierarchical syntax that induces aurally perceived stabilities and attractions in music. Also known as the "common practice," it has been the theoretical foundation of almost all Western music since the early eighteenth century.

corporeal level. The arranging of these properties in imaginative and aesthetically pleasing ways can be said to be the basis of the art of music. This begins to explain how something seemingly as abstract and ephemeral as music can be simultaneously aesthetically pleasing (subjective) and intellectually truthful (objective), thereby possessing the ability to speak to our heart and mind— the totality of our personhood. An isolated pitch-event may not evoke an emotional response, but the ordering of multiple pitch-events—melodically, harmonically, rhythmically—in an imaginative and cogent fashion surely does.

Recent studies in the realms of cognitive science and psychoacoustics have revealed how sound, manifested as music, affects the brain in various ways depending on the levels of complexity and relatedness present in the musical materials being heard. A significant reason why diatonic music born of the Western cultural tradition has become a prominent modality is due to its capacity to simultaneously manifest aesthetic beauty *and* elicit deep emotions. Conversely, abstract expressionism born of the atonal techniques of the early twentieth-century modernists failed to gain widespread acceptance due to a distinct absence of aesthetic pleasure, which, in turn, produced scant emotional gratification. Complicated musical utterances that produce aural indeterminacy may equate with intellectual and methodological profundity, but more often than not yield little in the way of aesthetic enjoyment and emotional satisfaction.

Metaphysical Underpinnings

Medieval history scholar Thomas F. Madden observes that the Renaissance in Europe was born "from a strange mixture of Roman values, medieval piety, and a unique respect for commerce and entrepreneurialism," and these circumstances proceeded "to other movements like humanism, the Scientific Revolution, and the Age of Exploration."[6] During the Renaissance, science and religion were not viewed as being mutually exclusive but rather correlative domains that when adjoined and integrated in artistic endeavors could yield sublime expressions of beauty and meaning.

In his treatise on music, *Le Istitutioni Harmoniche,* the Italian Renaissance music theorist Gioseffo Zarlino (1517-1590) posited that the human voice was a gift from God and human intelligence was the gift to "contemplate celestial matters and understand the occult and divine by means of the five senses." Of the five physical senses, Zarlino believed that hearing was the most valuable because it allowed for a full "comprehension of science by intellect." Taking his cue from Pythagoras, Zarlino proffered that nature was the source of the harmony of the spheres, that "everything is depended on the Prime Mover," and that "the order of things ordained by the Creator produces a silent harmony of the universe."[7] Zarlino's insight is the cosmological antecedent of the beliefs of Martin Luther and Johann Sebastian Bach, who believed that music was the most efficacious way to offer praise and gratitude to the Almighty.

Luther considered music to be "a sermon in sound." Bach asserted that the musical technique known as "figured bass" was an effective way to "praise and glorify God" and to "recreate" one's mind and soul. Johannes Brahms, another good Lutheran, considered his relationship with God to be essential in order "to compose something that will uplift and benefit humanity—something of permanent value."[8] Schiller and Goethe considered aesthetic beauty to be a gateway into moral and ethical discernment due to its transcendental aspects. For the European philosophers, art wasn't merely entertainment but was considered a repository of moral knowledge that could provide "aesthetic education." The predilection for aesthetic beauty and the emphasis on "returning to nature" in late nineteenth-century Europe was, in effect, a reaction against the Enlightenment rationale that posited that spiritual and metaphysical concerns were subsidiary in relation to reason, rights and empirical truth. However, we should remember that many composers in Europe at the time of the Enlightenment were "believers" and continued to write copious amounts of liturgical music. It was a time when "the Catholic mass becomes a genre available for concert performances by Protestants," a time "when we listen to scripture because of what Bach wrote rather than because of what St. Matthew wrote."[9] We should remember, too, that the Enlightenment did not put an end to religious belief or to the moral foundations of Christian culture in general. Even in a culture of well-reasoned "knowers," Immanuel Kant could not reject his belief in God, writing in his *Critique of Pure Reason*, "I must, therefore, abolish *knowledge*, to make room for *belief*."[10]

The Skepticism of Modernity

In the seemingly "godless" twentieth century, artists of all disciplines continued to find efficacy in the truth, beauty and goodness paradigm because of the metaphysical underpinnings of its rationale. Though the evisceration of religious tradition that began with Max Stirner, Karl Marx and Friedrich Nietzsche has been pervasive throughout modernity, many contemporary artists continued to place great importance on the spirituality of music and its transformational effect on our souls. Understanding the influence of music on self and society remains an essential aspect of our cultural patrimony. As Roger Scruton avers:

> Nobody can doubt the importance of music in our civilization, both as a source of communal bonding and an object of solitary consolation. People are shaped by the things they listen to and the recreations they enjoy, and Plato was surely right to regard the Corybants* of his time with a measure of suspicion.[11]

It goes without saying that in the postmodern era, absolutes and certainty with regard to matters of morality and ethics—"meta-narratives" in postmodernist jargon—are viewed with great suspicion and derisiveness. Utopian mindsets—be they the result of religious idealism or ideologically-based social engineering—are especially suspect in the aftermath of Hitler's Germany, Stalin's Russia, Mao's Cultural Revolution and 9/11. Russell Jacoby's observation that those who pine for utopian prescriptions in this day and age are "widely considered out to lunch or out to kill," is one that finds a great deal of currency in the new century.[12] As pragmatism and utilitarian concerns dominate our cultural reality, idealism born of messianic or utopian dispositions is scorned, often with good reason. Skepticism *can* play a role in ascertaining what values are necessary for social betterment and thus should not be dismissed in a cavalier fashion as being counterproductive in our pursuit of truth.

Yet, there is great consternation about the dissolution of moral standards and how we've become inured to the horrors that occur on a disturbingly frequent basis. Our national dialogue has become increasingly coarse and vituperative. Our political discourse is more often than not "a carnival of invective," as aptly described by Roger Hodge. Camille Paglia, "the Boadicea of the besieged and mutilated Humanities; a Joan of Arc for the lost and wandering

---

* In Greek mythology the Corybants were dancers who attended the goddess Cybele and were known for their wild and frenzied ritual dances.

liberal arts," * opines that the humanities are ruined and considers the multi-cultural penchant for deriding art created by dead, white, European males on purely ideological grounds to be so much "garbage."[13] American poet Larry Woiwode claims that the detrimental effects of television, "the Cyclops that eats books," has turned our youth into citizens lacking the capacity for critical judgment and moral certitude. Regrettably, these observations are ineluctable.

David Brooks notes that when "moral ecologies" change, we are faced with certain "trade-offs" that require reconciling and compromise. He writes:

> Since legitimate truths sit in tension with one another, one moral climate will put more emphasis here and less emphasis there, for better or worse. Certain virtues are cultivated, certain beliefs go too far, and certain important moral virtues are accidentally forgotten.[14]

Well yes, that's all too true. However, moral virtues have not merely been forgotten. There has been a calculated assault on certain virtues and values that have been historically linked to the idea that there may be universal truths: truths that when understood and implemented have had the effect of mitigating self-centeredness and the proclivities that arise from selfishness, immorality and cynicism. Because postmodernism considers truth to be fungible and subject to a variety of interpretations, morality and ethics today are no longer rooted in universal virtues but are often based on subjective explications. Individualism and the celebration of "the self" have become the predominant cultural concerns. In this scenario, "The self," according to Brooks, "is less likely to be seen as the seat of the soul, or as the repository of some transcendent spirit."[15] Because our spirituality is diminished, our creative endeavors suffer as a result.

Allan Bloom was writing about all this decades ago. His view that romanticism was "a competition for experiencing the most exalted and sublime states" is one that the "romantic" in each of us can easily relate to.[16] However, modernism's rejection of the romantic ethos in favor of hyper-intellectualism, secularism, egoism and nihilism has had the effect of making us less humane and our art more indeterminate, inane, less pleasing, less satisfying, and sadly,

---

* Boadicea was the British-Celtic Iceni queen who led an uprising against the Roman Empire in the first century AD.

44

less relevant. For many, modern art is a scam that insults both their intelligence and their values. By the late twentieth century a plethora of postmodern cultural theorists promulgated the idea that any attempt to ascribe to tonal music certain eternal, absolute or natural justifications was nothing less than a form of cultural determinism born of a decidedly imperialist-colonialist-capitalist mindset. But is that true?

Ironically, the pursuit of empirical and scientific truth flies in the face of openness because absolutism of any kind is interpreted by multicultural deconstructionists as being at odds with unbridled openness to all ideas favored by postmodernists, especially the idea that there may be universal truths. In his takedown of this particular multiculturalist piety, Jacoby sees the "sleight of hand" of duplicity at work, pointing to "mindless relativism" masquerading as some higher virtue: tolerance, diversity, equality, e.g. "Multiculturalism," Jacoby opines, "means embracing whatever comes tearing down the turnpike of history; every truck is dubbed a culture and some even get tagged 'nations'. … Critical thought requires conceptual care and precision; nowadays this has been exchanged for cheerleading and academic bombast."[17]

In his book *Springtime for Snowflakes: "Social Justice" and Its Postmodern Parentage*, New York University professor Michael Rectenwald cites how neo-Marxist philosopher Herbert Marcuse's idea of "repressive tolerance" in academia has had the effect of silencing rigorous debate and skepticism while advocating the indoctrination of students with ideological tropes that are rooted in the postmodernist pablum of the French Nietzscheans like Jacques Derrida and Michel Foucault.* As Rectenwald explains, according to the latest iteration of repressive tolerance, "even classic liberals and idiosyncratic feminists like Christina Hoff Sommers and Camille Paglia are treated as discursive criminals" because they dare to challenge the rationales of Derrida or Foucault, not to mention the "woke" cancel culture warriors.[18] As Israeli Bible scholar and philosopher Yoram Hazony observes, "Liberalism is being expelled from its former strongholds, and the hegemony of liberal ideas, as we have known

---

* French philosopher, Michel Foucault (1926-1984) developed his idea of the "discursive method" as a way to analyze how the social world, expressed through language and practice, is affected by various sources of power. Foucault's ideas have been linked to the neo-Marxist concept of Critical Theory in that both view "traditional ideas" as being complicit in the exercise of power.

it since the 1960s, will end. Anti-Marxist liberals are about to find themselves in much the same situation that has characterized conservatives, nationalists, and Christians for some time now: They are about to find themselves in the opposition."[19] Old-school liberals like Paglia have been citing this trend in academia for decades.

Science has provided modern man abundant knowledge of the corporeal world and along with it certainty, immutable truths, and "absolutes"—all of which are the antithesis of relativism. At face value, the desire to be "open" to new ideas can be seen as being inherently good and beneficial. However, Bloom contends that there are two manifestations of openness: one that promotes *laissez-faire* indifference so as not to be viewed as an arrogant, prideful "knower," and another which encourages the serious examination of knowledge in the context of history and our cultural patrimony, with the intent of discovering that which can make us better people. The former is rooted in a decidedly politically correct mindset that can be extremely disingenuous. As Bloom put it:

> Openness, as currently conceived, is a way of making surrender to what is most powerful, or worship of vulgar success, look principled. It is historicism's ruse to remove all resistance to history, which in our day means public opinion, a day when public opinion already rules. ... If openness means to "go with the flow," it is necessarily an accommodation to the present. ... True openness means closedness to all the charms that make us comfortable with the present.[20]

Bloom viewed this as part of the "romantic dilemma" with regard to morality and ethics. We desire peace. We desire to be free and unencumbered. But freedom requires us to be accountable for our actions in the context of community—for what we "ought" to do in order to foster conditions for the general well-being of the commonwealth (which was also Spinoza's contention). This requires that we examine history in order to find what works well for the benefit of the communities in which we live and work.

In his remarks regarding the threat of radical Islam, President Barack Obama cited the belief that the "moral arc of history" bends toward goodness, and that terrorism as perpetuated by ISIS radicals had "no place in the twenty-first century." However, history's "bending toward goodness" requires responsible actions based on moral codes that were deemed beneficial to a given society or cultural sphere. Predictably, some of those moral codes are now being characterized by contemporary multiculturalists as being untoward due to their connection to Western culture. In responding to the former president's "moral arc" narrative, Jonah Goldberg offered this sagacious, countervailing viewpoint:

> History by definition depends on human action and human interpretation. ... The idea that there is a moral arc to the universe, that history has "sides," is dangerous because it can lead to forgetfulness of this basic fact and absolve us from taking our personal and collective destinies into our own hands. Putting your faith in a dialectically deterministic universe is very different from putting your faith in God, in countless ways—starting with the fact that putting your faith in God also requires asking God to put His faith in you. God asks much of us; a benevolent universal algorithm asks nothing. Obama may be right that the Islamic State has "no place in the 21st century," but if so, it will be because people—not the universe—make it true.[21]

Regardless of one's feelings about Goldberg's political persuasion, religious claims or ideological perspectives, he is essentially correct with regard to the human portion of responsibility in swaying the arc of history.* Whether believers or nonbelievers, by being mere bystanders we run the risk of becoming complicit in the destruction of our collective humanity. As Jean-Paul Sartre opined, choosing to do nothing is still a choice. Doing the right thing requires taking responsibility, although questions remain with regard to "what is right."

Dr. Martin Luther King, Jr., cited the "moral arc" narrative in a number of his speeches; however, it was first attributed to the transcendentalist cleric Theodore Parker in 1857. Parker, a dedicated abolitionist and reformer within the Unitarian church, used the "moral arc" narrative in expressing confidence that the injustice of slavery could not continue in America. His views hearkened back to Thomas Jefferson's perspective regarding justice and the Almighty: "Indeed I tremble for my country when I reflect that God is just, and His justice cannot sleep forever."[22]

---

* Jonah Goldberg decided to title his recent book *Suicide of the West* rather than *Death of the West* because suicide is a choice.

Still, without citizens accepting responsibility and taking action in accordance with godly virtues, it is my contention that goodness will not be realized in any significant fashion. Nietzsche's aversion to the Judeo-Christian ethos, in the estimation of Roger Scruton, was in part based on his desire to be accommodated (especially sexually) without moral restrictions in order "to escape the eye of judgment." Yet, creating a moral and just society requires judgment, and judgment is based on moral codes that are established according to common interests and values, many of which are predicated on religious precepts. The idea of a governmental judiciary in which judgment is assessed according to law goes back to at least ancient Rome.

Our cultural patrimony owes a great deal to moral and ethical precepts that are the progeny of ancient wisdom and insight. Every functional society bases their laws on mutually agreed upon moral codes. In the West, and particularly in America, our laws have been based largely on our Judeo-Christian heritage. In recent decades, we have witnessed a shift toward Darwinist social science with a deep bow to neo-pagan and pragmatic concerns rather than faith-based moral codes—codes that we intuitively perceive as having virtue and merit. Societies that have moved toward the secularist direction have failed miserably, as evidenced by extreme brutality, oppressiveness and body counts. Though radical utopian prescriptions should be suspect, Jacoby suggests that without some hint of utopian idealism being in the cultural equation, utilitarian pragmatism is incomplete and thus ineffective in its quest for social progress.

Too often in the postmodernist vision, surveying the moral codes and cultural attitudes of the past is seen as regressive, invidious and decidedly "bourgeoisie." Is there nothing to be learned from our ancestors? If the rejection of "meta-narratives" means rejecting truth claims of any sort, are we not inviting apathy and radical relativism to metastasize into a cancer that will ultimately degrade and destroy all spiritual values? Should we categorically reject the legacies of the past because the advocates of the truth, beauty and goodness paradigm were, like us, less than perfect? Is the examination of the past merely a skillful ruse "to make the world of the past serve our present-day needs," as contemporary composer Pierre Boulez asserted?[23] Reason would seem to dictate that there is great benefit in the Platonic paradigm of truth, beauty and goodness so long as we remain "open" to its virtues.

Religious Patrimony and Music

History informs us that art and music that embody the attributes of truth, beauty and goodness, have the potential to enrich our lives in profound ways. The birth and development of tonal diatonic music, for instance, owe a great deal to the religious impulses of Western Christendom. The liturgical music born of those impulses is imbued with great beauty and meaning and in many instances was created with the intent of bringing believers into a sacred consciousness. The phenomenon of the Western musical syntax is a result of the sublime organization of corporeal properties (acoustics, frequencies, pitch sets, dynamics, harmony, rhythm, decibels, etc.) that yield aesthetic beauty with decidedly metaphysical implications. Arthur Schopenhauer, who by varying accounts was a decent flutist, accorded music, specifically "absolute music"— music without words or programmatic connotations—a unique status for its ability to express "universal feelings," going so far as to opine that, "to the man who gives himself up entirely to the impression of a symphony, it is as if he saw all the possible events of life and of the world passing by within himself ... every emotion, every striving, every movement of the will."[24]

Schopenhauer and E. T. A. Hoffmann argued that Beethoven's instrumental music possesses "universal" attributes that affect our consciousness in edifying ways. However, I will attest that when my students hear the same piece by Beethoven it conjures a wide variety of responses and feelings—sacred and profane. Our uniqueness as listeners plays heavily into our responses to music, and for many, religious undertones seem far removed from the cultural equation. For some, all music has political or ideological connotations. For others, it's a benign pleasure, nothing more. From an ontological perspective, I see (and hear) music as having implications relating to that which I consider to be cosmic and divine—something transcendent and godly—especially in terms of the harmonization of polar opposites: major modes and minor modes, consonant intervals and dissonant intervals, long tones and short tones, loud and soft, e.g.

Though religious belief has been castigated for being both regressive and repressive throughout most of the twentieth century, in recent decades there has been a renewed interest in spirituality and music with religious connotations. The music of Arvo Pärt (*Berliner Messe*) and Morten Lauridsen (*O*

Magnum Mysterium) draw on Gregorian chant and Eastern Orthodox musical traditions for its inspiration. In his book *By Design: Science and the Search for God*, American author and journalist Larry Witham alludes to a renewed interest in the old metaphor of "reading the Book of Nature," which suggests that there is a chief author and propagator of truth, or "at least a text imbued with meaning" that we might benefit from if we chose to be *open* to its contents.[25]

The innately human inclination to seek beauty and pursue truth and understanding by examining the natural world is not a recent phenomenon. Yet, any theocentric mindset will likely be unsettling to those who possess a secular view of life in which science and reason are sacrosanct. Postmodernists will have none of that as well. Understandably, there are those who remain deeply skeptical, obdurately so, of utopian idealism, especially if that idealism is born of religious conviction. I can see their point. Still, if the tenets of religion can be agents for betterment, and often they are, then they deserve investigation in the context of our creativity and our efforts toward establishing a culture of peace. And shouldn't we be *open* to that?

Endnotes

1 Galileo Galilei, in response to Christina of Tuscany in 1615, as quoted by Perry McAdow Rogers, *Aspects of Western Civilization: Problems and Sources in History*, Vol. II (Upper Saddle River, NJ: Prentice Hall, 1988), p. 53.

2 Ferruccio Busoni, *Sketch of a New Aesthetic in Music*, translated by Theodore Baker, (New York: G. Schirmer, 1911), p. 5

3 Roger Scruton, *Beauty: A Very Short Introduction* (Oxford and New York: Oxford University Press, 2011), p. 3.

4 Ibid.

5 Daniel J. Levitin, *This is Your Brain on Music: The Science of a Human Obsession* (New York: Penguin Group-USA, 2007), p. 14.

6 Thomas F. Madden, "The Real History of the Crusades," *Christianity Today*, May 6, 2005.

7 Gioseffo Zarlino, *Le Institutioni Harmoniche*, translated by Lucille Corwin (Ann Arbor: ProQuest, 2009), pp. 65-66.

8 Arthur M. Abell, *Talks with Great Composers* (Bridgewater, NJ: Replica Books, 1999), pp. 5-6.

9 Alasdair MacIntyre, *After Virtue: A Study in Moral Theory* (Notre Dame, IN: University of Notre Dame Press, 1984), p. 38.

10 Immanuel Kant, *Critique of Pure Reason*, translated by J. M. D. Meiklejohn (London: Henry G. Bohn, 1855), p. xxxi.

11 Roger Scruton, *The Soul of the World* (Princeton, NJ: Princeton University Press, 2014), p. 150.

12 Russell Jacoby, *The End of Utopia: Politics and Culture in an Age of Apathy* (New York: Basic Books, 1999), p. xi.

13 Rex Murphy, "Campus Social-Justice Maoists Dared to Come for Camille Paglia. Big Mistake." *National Post,* May 3, 2019.

14 David Brooks, *The Road to Character* (New York: Penguin Random House, 2015), p. 247.

15 Ibid., p. 252.

16 Allan Bloom, *Love and Friendship* (New York: Simon & Schuster, 2003), p. 260.

17 Jacoby, *The End of Utopia,* p. 61.

18 Michael Rectenwald, *Springtime for Snowflakes: "Social Justice" and Its Postmodern Parentage* (Nashville, TN: New English Review Press, 2018), Kindle Edition, Preface.

19 Yoram Hazony. "The Challenge of Marxism," *Quillette*, August 16, 2020, https://quillette.com/2020/08/16/the-challenge-of-marxism/.

20 Allan Bloom, *The Closing of the American Mind: How Higher Education has Failed Democracy and Impoverished the Souls of Today's Students* (New York: Simon & Schuster, 1987), pp. 41-42.

21 Jonah Goldberg, "Days of Future Past," *National Review*, October 2, 2014, https://www.nationalreview.com/2014/10/days-future-past-jonah-goldberg/.

22 Thomas Jefferson, "Query XVIII," *Notes on the State of Virginia*, as cited in *The Writings of Thomas Jefferson*, edited by Paul Leicester Ford (New York: G. P. Putnam's Sons, 1892-99).

23 Pierre Boulez, IRCAM: U.S. Tour Program Notes (Paris: IRCAM Editions, 1986), p. 10.

24 Arthur Schopenhauer, *The World as Will and Representation*, Volume I, edited by Judith Norman, Alistair Welchman, and Christopher Janaway (Cambridge: Cambridge University Press, 2011), pp. 287-290.

25 Larry Witham, *By Design: Science and the Search for God* (San Francisco: Encounter Books, 2003), p. v.

3

Music for Peace

For peace is not mere absence of war, but is a virtue that springs from force of character: for obedience is the constant will to execute what, by the general decree of the commonwealth, ought to be done.[1]
Baruch Spinoza

Peace Music CommUNITY*

The insightful assertion of philosopher Baruch Spinoza (1632-1677) has resonated with many who have engaged in the process of establishing a more peaceful world—the hope of all ages. Of course, that which "ought" to be done in the context of establishing a culture of peace is predicated in large part on the moral and ethical precepts that are perceived to be most beneficial to the general welfare of a given community. Are there universally shared values and virtues that humanity can abide by? If so, what are those

---

* This essay was written in 2008 for the Peace CommUNITY website. I revised it for this book in 2017. In the original essay I attempted to share a vast array of attitudes about music and art by artists, philosophers and commentators in the hopes of historically contextualizing the influence of music on self and society. This essay was very much "a stream of consciousness" endeavor.

virtues and values and who decides if they are indeed beneficial for "the commonwealth"? Immanuel Kant's vision of "a perfectly constituted state" and a "universal civic society," in which the human potential for goodness could be fully realized was based on the utopian belief that humanity would develop in the same manner as "nature's secret plan."[2]

C. S. Lewis asserted in *Mere Christianity* that "the Law of Human Nature" informs us as to what we "ought" to do in relation to others. However, human nature being what it is, we often behave in ways contrary to that which "ought" to be done. If we aspire to be moral beings we should be mindful of how our actions impact others. Regrettably, the moral atrophy that has befallen humankind with regard to subjugating selfishness for the benefit of the greater good has contributed to a social condition in which moral relativism, situational ethics and "emotivist" rationales have become extremely pervasive. Few will deny the fact that we are witnessing the dissolution of moral and ethical standards in a most pernicious way, or that finding our way out of this social malaise remains a quandary. The "crooked timber of humanity" indicates that humanity is decidedly out of step with "nature's secret plan," and herein lie the cause of many of our failings—individually and collectively.

Edmund Burke, considered by many to be the founding father of modern conservatism, cautioned against the incessant derision of the "wisdom of the ancients" by the Jacobin radicals who believed that the "political religion" of utopianism was the most efficacious way to create an ideal society. It should be fairly evident that familiarizing ourselves with the past can provide us with perspectives (especially with regard to art, literature and music) that can be highly instructive. As Burke asserted, examining the insights and wisdom of ancient civilizations can be of great benefit in our pursuit of knowledge in order to better perceive "the gravity of culture or the immutability of human nature."[3]

Fast-forwarding to the current century, Jonah Goldberg avers that, try as they might, contemporary "social planners cannot straighten the crooked timber of humanity simply by applying some algorithms or imposing really clever taxes." As Goldberg opines, "It is folly to think you know all you need to know about life as long as you have a computer with a good Wi-Fi connection."[4] That may be a bit snarky (and Goldberg can be a "snarxist" of the highest order), but in this era of social media saturation and the bloated blogosphere, where everyone believes that their opinions are sacrosanct, Goldberg's point is well taken. Russell Jacoby put it more succinctly regarding the pervasiveness of hyper-presentism vis-à-vis historical inquiry:

> Today's banalities apparently gain in profundity if one states that the wisdom of the past, for all its virtues, belongs to the past. The arrogance of those who come later preens itself with the notion that the past is dead and gone. ... The modern mind can no longer think thought, only can locate it in time and space. The activity of thinking decays to the passivity of classifying.[5]

Jacoby wrote that in 1975! Goldberg, Jacoby, Jordan Peterson, Camille Paglia, Edward Rothstein, Thomas Sowell—liberals and conservatives alike—understand that "classifying" according to race, gender, sexual orientation or ethnicity is a kind of pseudo-democracy in which individualism gives way to collectivism and groupthink.

So how does all this relate to music and art? I'm often asked if my creative endeavors are affected by my social environment and are thus a reflection of the world around me (a passive modality), or if I seek to affect change in the world through that which I create (an active modality). I believe it is both: a "reciprocity of influence," as Richard Taruskin so nicely put it. Obviously, we are affected by our surroundings, but we are also capable of changing them to varying extents. Musicians must be especially attuned to this concept due to the powerful effect that music can have on our consciousness. Being an activist in terms of using my talent for the greater good is something of great importance for me. It is my contention that artists must be willing to do more in this regard. It's historically and spiritually important to do so. Noting the moral and ethical power of music and its effects on self and society, Plato stated in *The Republic*:

> The care of the governors should be directed to preserve music and gymnastics from innovation; alter the songs of a country, Damon says, and you will soon end by altering laws. The change appears innocent at first, and begins in play, but evil soon becomes serious, working secretly upon the characteristics of individuals, then upon the social and commercial relations, and lastly upon the institutions of the state; and there is ruin and confusion everywhere.[6]

The Greeks placed a great deal of importance on the role of artists and musicians in creating the psychology that could foster conditions for a more enlightened civil society. Damon of Athens, son of Damonides, was one of the first philosophers to study the effects of music on one's mood—psycho-acoustics, in modern terminology. Religious commentator Karen Armstrong observes that Aristotle was likely more attuned to traditional understandings of spirituality than Plato. Aristotle, according to Armstrong, was "not preoccupied with orthodoxy, pointing out that initiates who took part in the mysteries [metaphysics]" did not learn about spirituality by facts or data but through experiencing "certain emotions" and being "put in a certain disposition."[7] This speaks to the importance of one's consciousness in the process of ascertaining what may be the path toward human betterment.

Concerning the issues of tragedy and the terrible events in life, Aristotle believed the emotions one experienced as a result of suffering could evoke a spiritual experience, in which feeling, or *pathein*, rather than thinking could be transformative by turning "our deepest fears into something pure, transcendent, and even pleasurable."[8] Concerning music, Aristotle, as quoted by Hunayn, opined:

> These are the effects of music: It awakes the remote counsel, brings close the stray thought, and strengthens the tired mind. Music, therefore, causes the return of that which was lost; it makes us pay attention to that which was neglected, and that which is turbid becomes clear. He who has been exposed to this beneficial influence participates in every counsel and opinion, and finds the right one without error. He will fulfill his promise without delay.[9]

Confucius held similar beliefs,* going so far as to say: If a person be without the virtues proper to goodness, what has he to do with the rites of propriety? If a person be without the virtues proper to goodness, what has he to do with music?"[10] In the view of the thirteenth-century kabbalist Rabbi Isaac ben Jacob ha-Kohen, those who were proponents of Jewish mysticism likened musicians

---

* There is an oft cited quotation by Confucius that reads: "If one should desire to know whether a kingdom is well-governed, if its morals are good or bad, the quality of its music will furnish the answer." I first came across this quote in David Tame's book, *The Secret Power of Music* in 1984, but I've not been able to find the source text from which it is taken. However, there is quotation by Chinese politician, Lu Bu Wei in his *Spring and Autumn Annals*, that essentially makes the same assertion.

"who properly direct their fingers over the holes and strings of their instruments" were akin "to the high priest who awakens the Holy Spirit through prayer."[11]

The cultures of antiquity understood music to be a potent force in shaping the dispositions of individuals and society in the pursuit of societal betterment. Conversely, art that was not in accord with certain moral and ethical precepts was seen as being potentially enervating. The concept of "Music for Peace" is not new, but my guess is that those ancient cultures might be astonished to see how little our contemporary artistic expressions reflect or express that which is ennobling and morally upright. Echoing the philosophers of antiquity, musicologist David Tame opined that, "music is the releaser into the material world of a fundamental, super-physical energy from beyond the world of everyday experience." There existed a view in the cultures of antiquity that "the voice of the priest within the realm of time and space becomes a vehicle for the energizing Voice of the Creator to manifest its forces through."[12] The idea of "music as God's voice to us" was a mythological premise for many ancient cultures.

In 1990, Mikhail Gorbachev offered the following, and somewhat astonishing observation concerning the need for a different perspective in our attempts at fashioning a better social reality:

> We need a different, conscientious attitude toward work, science, education and the arts, toward a culture in the broadest sense of the word. We need to create conditions whereby all spiritual values will be appreciated in society as a vital necessity for its full-blooded life and progress.[13]

I say astonishing, because here we have the former Secretary General of the Communist Party of the Soviet Union, and an exponent of the godless ideology of Marxism, calling for a mindset that includes a greater necessity for *spiritual* values and awareness.* Many artists are idealists at heart and wish to use their talent for a "higher purpose." Whether one possesses a belief in God or not, I believe it is fair to say that for artists of all disciplines, our state of mind and disposition affects that which we produce. Christianity in Europe,

---

* In 2008, amid reports that Gorbachev was a "closet Christian," his foundation, The International Foundation for Socio-Economic and Political Studies, released a statement affirming that the former Soviet leader remained an atheist, though he acknowledged the important role that religion plays in society. [Source: The Gorbachev Foundation, March 24, 2008].

for instance, had a major influence on music and musicians. Johann Sebastian Bach claimed that the compositional technique known as figured bass was

> the most perfect foundation of music, being played with both hands in such a manner that the left hand plays the notes written down while the right hand adds consonances and dissonances in order to make well-sounding harmony to the Glory of God and the perfect delectation to the spirit; and the aim and final reason, as of all music, so of the figured bass, should be none else but the Glory of God and the recreation of the mind.[14]

Note Bach's reference to the presence of "consonances and dissonances" in the process of producing "well-sounding harmony." This points to the idea of harmonizing opposites in the pursuit of a harmonious end result. Ontologically, music can be viewed as a metaphor that demonstrates or expresses the beauty of harmonious relationships. In his essay, "The Decay of Lying: An Observation," Oscar Wilde opined that, "life imitates art far more than art imitates life,"[15] and that "the energy of life—as Aristotle would call it—is simply the desire for expression, and Art is always presenting various forms through which this expression can be attained."[16] If we take the idea of the "reciprocity of influence" at face value, it could be said that Bach's assertion regarding the harmonization of intervallic opposites is a way that art imitates life, not to mention reflecting the nature of God in an ontological sense.

Throughout the ages, artists, philosophers and cultural commentators have had important and meaningful things to say about peace, music and the responsibility of artists. Gandhi instructed that we must change as individuals before we can expect to see change in the world. When Spinoza asserted that, "All happiness or unhappiness solely depends upon the quality of the object to which we are attached by love,"[17] he was echoing St. Augustine, who suggested that people and societies fail because they choose to love the wrong things. Though he possessed a timorous distrust of music's sensual properties, Augustine nonetheless intuited that music, when applied in a sacred fashion and with virtuous intent, could assist in developing a more devotional frame of mind and that, in turn, could be beneficial in the realization of a more humane society.

Taruskin, in referring to the moral power of music vis-à-vis Richard Wagner's anti-Semitic attitudes, writes:

As long as some music somewhere is considered tref [not kosher], we have not forgotten that music is a powerful form of persuasion that does work in the world, as serious art that possesses ethical force and exacts ethical responsibilities.[18]

The reality of music's "ethical force" can apply to music of any genre. Love is manifested though action. How we act, how we create and how we relate to our fellow citizens becomes our essential trial in our attempts to establish a culture of peace. Our behavior and that which we create has consequences.

Postmodern anti-essentialists would have us believe that there are no meta-narratives and no metaphysical realities to ponder. From their point of view, the Sumerians, Chinese, Greeks, Jews, Indians and the early Christians in Europe were completely daft with regard to music's metaphysical properties and its effects on consciousness and behavior. Were Bach, Schiller, Goethe, Schopenhauer and Brahms delusional in their assertions regarding the potential of the "aesthetic education" that art and music could provide? Postmodernism has given us "radical relativism," thus making any claim of objective truth—moral, aesthetic or intellectual—a specious contention. When composer Arnold Schoenberg suggested that the public needed "to be cured of the delusion that the aim of the artist is to create beauty,"[19] was he being a prophet or a provocateur?

Contemporary Attitudes

In 1967, University of Chicago professor of music Dr. Leonard B. Meyer made the prescient assertion in his book *Music, the Arts and Ideas* that the advance of globalization and new technology would create a "fluctuating stasis" in the realm of art music. This would result in a condition where pluralism, diversity and a "multiplicity of styles" would be the norm: a scenario in which no single, "triumphant" style would dominate the landscape of art music.[20] A random sampling of the music by composers of the last several decades—Thomas Adès, Eric Whitacre, Steve Reich, Jennifer Higdon, Paul Lansky, Max Richter, Arvo Pärt, Elliott Carter and the NOW Ensemble—would prove Dr. Meyer's assertion to be highly perspicacious. It's difficult to imagine a technique, idiom or innovation that hasn't been attempted in the realm of art music. Diversity reigns supreme. Meyer also averred that ideology would shape music in ways that we might not expect, and that "dictatorships, nationalist and ethnic conflicts" and discoveries in the sciences would indicate, "that determinism is a doubtful doctrine." Moreover, modern philosophy, according to Meyer, "called into question the possibility of arriving at ultimate, eternal truths."[21] He cites Robert Heilbroner, who alluded to the "diminution of historical optimism" as the beginning of postmodernist thought. He wasn't wrong.

In a *Time* magazine interview, Bono, lead singer of the hugely popular rock band U2, stated that music has the ability "to make people vulnerable to change." In a nod toward Gandhi, he said, "But in the end you must become the change you want to see in the world."[22] Dr. Martin Luther King, Jr., shared a similar sentiment: "Now the judgment of God is upon us, and we must either learn to live together as brothers and sisters, or we are all going perish together as fools."[23] The Unitarian Universalists have a saying: "More important than the creed is the deed." This is another way of saying "orthopraxy over orthodoxy," or as the apostle James put it in scripture, good deeds justify one's faith. Beethoven and Schiller, like the ancients before them, intuited that the gods needed to be in the peace equation and choosing to ignore them could result in deleterious consequences.

In a piece for the *New York Times* on Valentine's Day in 2013, Gordon Marino spoke to the issue of tenderness and how contemporary art and culture discourages a penchant for feelings and vulnerability—attributes connected to what Allan Bloom called "the gentle hopes of love." As Marino explains:

> Almost by definition, every culture cultivates certain qualities and feelings. In the United States, we lionize resolve, determination and resiliency. Although we have a strong nostalgic streak, we are a hard people who no less than the ancient Romans entertain ourselves with a steady diet of throat slitting and torture images that can only work to pound the tenderness out of us. Of course, our TV tough guys always shroud their violence in some mollifying narratives that render their acts of slaughter righteous and emotionally satisfying. But for the most part in our culture, we leave the feeling of tenderness in a small pot in the mudroom. To feel tenderly is to feel vulnerable and vulnerability is not a favorite American dish.[24]

One may argue the veracity of Marino's contentions, but great art can make us vulnerable to change and in that respect he makes a valid point. Music, especially, has the ability to alter consciousness. As Allan Bloom reminds us, "the gentle hopes of love" have taken a back seat to the ugly cynicism and ego-centric pursuits in our contemporary culture. It doesn't have to be that way. Rather than becoming lost in the abyss of moral relativism, we can choose to aspire to higher virtues in life and art, and thus shape our destiny accordingly.

In the opening chapter of his book *How Music Works*, contemporary musician David Byrne speaks to the issue of creativity vis-à-vis historical context. As Byrne puts it, "context largely determines what is written, painted, sculpted, sung or performed," and this is "exactly the opposite of conventional wisdom that maintains that creation emerges out of some interior emotion, from an upwelling of passion and feeling" that the creative artist draws upon, or an urge that "will brook no accommodation, that it simply must find an outlet to be heard, read or seen."[25] This is the typical romantic telling of the creative story, and one that appeals to us precisely because of its romantic notions. This is not to suggest that emotion doesn't play a significant part in the creative process, but historically a great deal of art has been created for utilitarian purposes, and these purposes have often had spiritual or religious premises. That said, there remains the need to assess art from an axiological perspective as well as aesthetic, technical, intellectual and commercial concerns.

Twentieth-century French philosopher Jacques Maritain asserted that, "Artistic creation does not copy God's creation, it continues it. ... Nature is essentially of concern to the artist only because it is a derivation of the divine art in things, *ratio artis divinae indita rebus*. The artist, whether he knows it or not, consults God in looking at things."[26] In his book *The Responsibility of the Artist*, Maritain writes: "Because an artist is a man before he is an artist, the autonomous world of morality is simply superior to (and more inclusive than) the autonomous world of art. ... In other words Art is indirectly and extrinsically subordinate to morality."[27] This is no small point, but again, it points to the "reciprocity of influence."

When, and if we become vulnerable to change, how will we change, and by what moral codes will we abide? As creative people it is safe to say that we share a certain obligation and social duty to utilize our creative gifts—as Spinoza suggested—in a mode of benevolence. In short, that is what being a "community" is all about: being responsible for our actions in relationship to our fellow travelers on our earthly journey. This can be a daunting proposition because we all have our shortcomings. Human nature guarantees that we will have moral failings and our better angels won't always win the day. Still, doing what "ought" to be done to initiate change in ourselves and in our communities requires that we engage in the process of being the change we want to see in the world.

Gandhi summed it up this way: "We have somehow accustomed ourselves to the belief that art is independent of the purity of private life. I can say with all the experience at my command that nothing could be more untrue. As I am nearing the end of my earthly life, I can say that purity of life is the highest and truest art. The art of producing good music from a cultivated voice can be achieved by many, but the art of producing that music from the harmony of a pure life is achieved very rarely."[28] In that context, creating art that fosters good will remains a significant—and moral—endeavor. We can sing songs of peace, but in addition to singing the songs, we need to live the lyrics!

Recommended Recordings

U2: "Beautiful Day," U2

Beethoven: Symphony No. 9, George Szell, Cleveland Orchestra

Bach: *Christmas Oratorio*, Philippe Herreweghe, Collegium Vocale Gent (DVD)

Thomas Adès: Violin Concerto, Augustin Hadelich, violin

Eric Whitacre: *3 Songs of Faith*, Ronald Staheli, BYU Singers

Steve Reich: "Vermont Counterpoint," Kuniko Kato, percussion

Jennifer Higdon: Violin Concerto, Hilary Hahn, violin

Paul Lansky: *Threads, for Percussion Quartet*

Max Richter: *Retrospective*

Arvo Pärt: *Summa*, Angèle Dubeau, violin

Elliott Carter: Birthday Tribute CD, Various Artists

NOW Ensemble: *Songs from the Uproar*

Endnotes

1   Benedict di Spinoza , *A Theologico-Political Treatise and A Political Treatise* (Mineola, NY: Dover Edition, 2013), p. 314. Based on "Of the best state of dominion," Part 4, *Political Treatise*, translated by A. H. Gosset (London: G. Bell & Son, Ltd., 1883).

2   Immanuel Kant, "Ninth Proposition," *Idea for a Universal History from a Cosmopolitan Point of View*, translated by Lewis White Beck (Indianapolis, IN: Bobbs-Merrill Company, 1963).

3   Jonah Goldberg, *The Tyranny of Clichés: How Liberals Cheat in the War of Ideas* (New York: Sentinel, Penguin Group-USA, 2012), p. 36.

4   Ibid.

5   Russell Jacoby, *Social Amnesia: A Critique of Conformist Psychology from Adler to Laing*, third edition (New York, NY: Routledge, 2017), p. 1.

6   Plato, *The Republic of Plato*, translated by Benjamin Jowett (Oxford: Clarendon Press, 1888), pp. 112-113.

7   Karen Armstrong, *The Great Transformation: The Beginning of Our Religious Traditions* (New York: Anchor Books, Random House, 2006), pp. 391-392.

8   Ibid.

9   Joscelyn Godwin, *The Harmony of the Spheres: The Pythagorean Tradition in Music* (Rochester, VT: Inner Traditions International, Ltd., 1993), p. 95.

10 Confucius, *Confucian Analects*, translated by James Legge (London: Trübner, 1893), Chapter 3, Verse 3, https://china.usc.edu/confucius-analects-3.

11 Stuart Isacoff, *Temperament: The Idea that Solved Music's Greatest Riddle* (New York: Alfred A. Knopf, 2001), p. 112.

12 David Tame, *The Secret Power of Music: The Transformation of Self and Society Through Musical Energy* (Northamptonshire, England: Turnstone Press, Ltd., 1984), p. 24.

13 Mikhail Gorbachev, as cited by Mose Durst, *Unification Culture and the 21st Century* (New York, NY: HSA-UWC, 1991).

14 J. S. Bach, as cited by Karol Berger, *Bach's Cycle, Mozart's Arrow: An Essay on the Origins of Musical Modernity* (Berkeley and Los Angeles, CA: University of California Press, Ltd., 2007), p. 122.

15 Oscar Wilde, *Intentions* (Auckland, New Zealand: The Floating Press, 2009), p. 39.

16 Ibid., p. 40.

17 John Caird, *Spinoza,* Philosophical Classics for English Readers, edited by William Knight, LLD (London: William Blackwood and Sons, 1888), p. 9.

18 Richard Taruskin, *The Danger of Music and Other Anti-Utopian Essays* (Berkeley, Los Angeles and London: University of California Press, 2009), p. 23.

19 Joseph Henry Auner, *A Schoenberg Reader: Documents of a Life* (Yale University, 2003), p. 93.

20 Leonard B. Meyer, *Music, the Arts, and Ideas: Patterns and Predictions in*

Twentieth-Century Culture (Chicago-London: University of Chicago Press, 1994), p. 317.

21   Ibid., pp. 330-331.

22   Josh Tyrangiel, "Can Bono Save the World?" Time 159, no. 9, March 4, 2002.

23   Marian Wright Edelman, foreword to The Trumpet of Conscience, by Dr. Martin Luther King, Jr., (Boston: Beacon Press, 1967), p. ix.

24   Gordon Marino, "Try a Little Tenderness," Op-eds, New York Times, February 14, 2013.

25   David Byrne, How Music Works (San Francisco: McSweeney's, 2012), p. 23.

26   Jacques Maritain, as cited by Peter Kalkavage, "Music in the Modern Age," The Imaginative Conservative, March 3, 2012, http://www.theimaginativeconservative.org/2012/03/music-in-modern-age.html.

27   Jacques Maritain, The Responsibility of the Artist (New York: Gordian Press, 1972), p. 41.

28   Mahatma Gandhi, All Men Are Brothers: Autobiographical Reflections (London and New York: Continuum, 1980), p. 164.

4

Beauty, Truth and Goodness

Only through Beauty's morning-gate, dost thou
penetrate the land of knowledge.[1]
Friedrich Schiller

I t's often been said everyone is a "romantic" at heart. We constantly seek love and beauty in our lives. We are deeply affected by beauty—in nature and art. Musicians compose and sing about "getting back to the garden" and realizing a "universal brotherhood." Poets—often considered idealistic phenomenologists—pen imaginative utterances that provide glimpses into the human soul in search of meaning. Arcadian painters of antiquity and the Renaissance were "Edenic," in that their works often depicted idyllic and utopian views of life. The magnificent art of Asian, African and Middle Eastern cultures reflects a sublime beauty that transcends the time and place of their creation and continues to amaze.

In contemporary society, the artists and producers whom we hold in high esteem are those whose creative endeavors move our hearts and touch our souls, and we pay good money to be so moved. Even in troubling circumstances we try to remain hopeful and envision a better reality—a return home to that Edenic place. All of this suggests that the pursuit of beauty, truth and goodness has been intrinsic to the human experience and remains a significant aspect of our cultural patrimony. In his book *The Art Instinct: Beauty, Pleasure, and Human Evolution,* Denis Dutton writes:

> Artistic masterpieces fuse myriad disparate elements, layer upon layer of meaning, into a single, unified, self-enhancing whole. ... The greatest works of art unite every aspect of human experience: intellect and the will, but also emotions and human values of every kind. ... Psychologically, some of the most staggering moments in aesthetic experience, the ones we may remember all of our lives, are those instants where the events that make up the whole of a vast novel, an opera, or a poem, sonata, or painting fall meaningfully into place.[2]

We might argue that Dutton is referencing a decidedly Western experience, one predicated on what has been referred to as the "masterpiece fixation." Though this "fixation" may be problematic for some, it's not implausible to believe that the innate human desire to create and experience beauty transcends historical epochs, religious belief, ethnicity, cultural spheres, politics and economic status. According to Dutton, the human impulse to create and seek beauty is atavistic. Though art and music affect different people in different ways, there is no quarrel about the validity and universality of their psychic effects or communicative properties. Great art speaks to us in differing but profound ways. For many, the desire for spiritual fulfillment can only be satiated by experiencing beauty—be it in nature or art. Regarding our experience with beauty, philosopher Roger Scruton put it this way:

> We are not, in aesthetic judgment, simply describing some object in the world. We are giving voice to an encounter, a meeting of subject and object, in which the response of the first is every bit as important as the qualities of the second. To understand beauty, therefore, we must gain some sense of the variety of our responses to the things in which we discern it.[3]

British poet William Hazlitt wrote: "The spirit of poetry is in itself favorable to humanity and liberty. ... Poetry dwells in a perpetual Utopia of its own, and is, for that reason, very ill calculated to make a Paradise on earth, by encountering the shocks and disappointments of the world."[4] As skeptical as we might be about utopian idealism in this day and age, there is more than a sliver of truth in Hazlitt's claim, for he made his observation in 1816 and paradise on earth remains a fantasy. In Russell Jacoby's ruminations on the loss of utopian idealism as it pertains to philosophy, politics and art, he posits that truth has become a casualty in postmodernism, a condition in which "balky universals" are considered tools of oppression and control; "discursive violence," as Michel Foucault would have us believe. In defending the "truth" aspect of art (and philosophy), Jacoby cites poet William Wordsworth, who opined that the object of poetry "is truth, not individual and local, but general and operative; not standing upon external testimony, but carried alive into the heart by passion; truth which is its own testimony, which gives strength and divinity to the tribunal to which it appeals."[5] Utopian idealism is often derided, but Jacoby argues that without having "an emphatic idea of freedom and happiness, a better society can scarcely be envisioned; utopia withers," and this results in moral relativism, unbridled subjectivity, misguided multicultur-alism, "murky" political thinking—and some really bad art.[6]

Historically, there have been artists of all disciplines and circumstances who have demonstrated a willingness to use their talents to endorse and contribute to causes that they believed to be conducive to achieving peace and goodwill. Friedrich Schiller, who as a young man possessed a desire to study theology and to pursue a life as a cleric, believed that one's soul state (*Seelenzustand*), was edified through experiencing beauty. For Schiller, "aesthetic education" could be the basis for a moral society that "would help establish the freedom that political revolution conspicuously failed to achieve."[7] Immanuel Kant, who was greatly influenced by Schiller's views regarding aesthetic education, understood that the pleasure we derive from that which we perceive as being beautiful was beyond pure reason, yet those experiences were valid and uni-versal—everyone had them. In his observations of Schiller's influence on Kant with regard to the nexus of aesthetics and morality, Roger Kimball, publisher of *The New Criterion*, observed:

> The feeling of freedom and wholeness that aesthetic experience imparts is thus not merely private but reminds us of our vocation as moral beings. In this context, Kant famously spoke of beauty as being "the symbol of moral-ity" because in aesthetic pleasure "the mind is made conscious of a certain ennoblement and elevation." Thus it is that although taste is "the faculty of

judging an object ... by an entirely disinterested satisfaction" it is also "at bottom a faculty for judging the sensible illustration of moral ideas."[8]

Unlike Schiller, Kant was famously indifferent about music and assigned it a rather low place among the arts, yet he nonetheless viewed music as "the highest among those arts that are valued for their pleasantness."[9] Kant acknowledged that the pleasure derived from artistic beauty was not merely about emotions or affectations but something far more sublime: transcendental, in fact. He cited three types of pleasure in the Platonic sense: that which is agreeable, good and beautiful. Moreover, he proffered that aesthetics should have its own faculty, namely, judgment, which would mediate between the faculties of pure reason and practical reason. But Kant's insistence on "disinterestedness" in the evaluation of art, as well as the idea that artists need not have any "purpose" for creating art beyond the purpose of making it, resulted in his relegating music to a relatively unimportant status due to its abstract and ephemeral properties. In his estimation, music merely aroused sensations and thus didn't "convey propositions" that would cultivate the mind.[10] Kant's idea of "disinterestedness" in evaluating music is especially unfortunate because it tends to minimize any moral or ethical "purposes" that might be attributed to music's creation. Additionally, his relegating music to a subsidiary status in relation to other art forms, indicates a lack of perception regarding music's ability to affirm the significance of the metaphysical features of the human experience.*

Taking a countervailing view of music, Kant's contemporary Johann Gottfried Herder wrote in 1800 of the ability of music to move one's heart and spirit by way of the movement of resonant sound vibrations, be they produced by the human voice or a musical instrument, with "each tone sensing the harmony of all tones." Herder asks, "Might one therefore ask if music, through its inner efficacy, surpasses each art that expresses itself through the visible? It *must* surpass them, just as the spirit surpasses the *body*, for music is

---

* "It is important to recognize that the German word '*interesse*' has a special meaning in eighteenth-century German, and should not be confused with similar sounding English words or even contemporary German words. For Kant, interesse means a kind of pleasure that is not connected with desire; it is neither grounded in desire, nor does it produce it." [Source: Nick Zangwill, "Aesthetic Judgment," *The Stanford Encyclopedia of Philosophy*, edited by Edward N. Zalta, Spring 2019.]

spirit, related to the power of innermost strength, of that *movement*."[11] In a beautifully poetic utterance about the art of music and its effect on our being, Herder writes:

> Every moment is temporary for this art, and so it must be, for it is precisely the ways in which it is shorter and longer, stronger and weaker, more and less, that produces its meaning, its impression. In its arrival and departure, in its becoming and being, therein lies the conquering strength of sound and its perception. In the ways this or that tone combines with others, in the ways tones rise and fall, disappear, or raise and renew themselves on the string stretched by harmony toward eternal, insoluble laws, therein lies my soul, my courage, my love and hope. ... You effervescent spirits of the air, come with gentle tones and flee, move my heart and release me to an eternal longing, through you and to you.[12]

The romantic era of Europe in the nineteenth century emphasized the sincere and authentic pursuit of "inner goals" in the realms of ethics, politics and aesthetics. Beauty was not merely "symbolic" in the Kantian sense; it could be consciousness altering. British political philosopher Isaiah Berlin observed that the romantic era marked a time where attitudes about art and aesthetics were undergoing a philosophical transformation, whereby the "notion of eternal models ... is replaced by a passionate belief in spiritual freedom, individual creativity,"[13] as well as "an effort to return to the forgotten sources of life, a passionate effort at self-assertion, both individual and collective, a search after means of expressing an unappeasable yearning for unattainable goals."[14] The celebration of individual heroism, even failed heroism, was part and parcel of the zeitgeist of the late nineteenth century and remains a significant narrative in the literature and cinema of our contemporary culture.

Romanticism and the Enlightenment

Prior to the emergence of the romantic ethos in nineteenth-century Europe, the Enlightenment, with its predilection for "natural law" and "practical morality" over supernatural religion and metaphysics, constituted a major shift in attitudes regarding music and the arts among intellectuals in eighteenth-century Europe. In some respects, this may be seen as the initial impetus toward the prioritization of scientific inquiry in particular, and the secularization of culture in general. The so-called "differentiation" of truth, beauty and goodness—"the Big Three," as described by American philosopher Ken Wilber—had many benefits, including the ascendancy of liberal democracy, the respect of individual rights, the rise of empirical science and the abolition of slavery and human trafficking. But as Wilber notes, there has been a negative legacy as well. Once differentiation was achieved, there needed to be a balanced integration of the Big Three, and this didn't happen. As Wilber contends:

> So the dignity of modernity began to slide into the disaster of modernity: the Big Three didn't just differentiate, they tended to dissociate! ... Because the Big Three were not harmoniously balanced and integrated—they were ripe for plunder by more aggressive approaches. ... Science began to crowd out consciousness, aesthetics and morals.[15]

Wilber views the disassociation of emotion, values and rationality to be a disastrous cultural blunder. Given the cultural and social malaise that we now find ourselves in, it's difficult to refute his assertion. Understanding the nexus of reason and emotion remains an integral aspect in our pursuits to become moral beings. Every emotion we experience is based on a judgment or assessment, which is an apposition of affect and reason. Our judgments do not simply accompany our emotions, but are essential to them, and these cannot be separated from each other as though they were not contingently connected. The disassociation of the Big Three is problematic because reason is the faculty that allows us to ascertain what is true or false about the various judgments that lie at the heart of an emotion, and thereby determine an emotion to be appropriate, misguided, imprudent and so on. Thus, the disassociation of the Big Three is counterproductive to the process of establishing a proper balance between reason and consciousness in our attempts to become moral citizens, attain morally upright relationships, and achieve a more humane society.

Although reason and affect can be distinguished from one another, to consider our emotions as being merely surges through the mind and body, or as mere affectations, is the kind of disassociation that Wilber cautions against. For instance, if we love someone we assess that person to be worthy of our love. Conversely, if we dislike someone there is a *reason* for that disliking. If we fear someone, there is a *reason* for that fear, and so on through all of our emotions. There is a distinct presence of reason in our emotional responses to people or circumstances, though we may not be wholly conscious of that in the moment when we experience them. Edmund Burke pointed out that we can paradoxically be affected by both love and fear when having an encounter with nature. We simultaneously love the aesthetic aspect of nature—the harmony, the order, the serenity, the grandeur—yet we fear the untamed power of nature, knowing full well that nature can be dangerous: life-threatening, in fact. Both aspects can be "elevating" and can have the effect of lifting us out of our everyday thoughts and experiences.[16]

Neuroscientist Antonio Damasio posits in his book *Descartes' Error: Emotion, Reason, and the Human Brain* that reason and emotion are integrated in ways that were previously thought to be untenable. Damasio offers what he calls the "somatic marker hypothesis," which holds that chemical records, or markers, stored in our brain from previous experiences are either consciously or subconsciously accessed and then used to assist our decision-making. These somatic markers have the effect of overriding pure reason and allow for emotion to direct us to the best choice among a variety of alternative choices. Damasio does not assert that that all of our choices are the result of our emotions dominating reason. He refers to the idea of "high reason" in relation to "choices that are made on the basis of weighing logical considerations, without allowing emotion to interfere with the process."[17] Still, if Damasio's hypothesis is valid, it can be construed that reason and emotion are related in ways that are fundamental to our decision-making process and our behavior. A crime of passion is almost always the result of an imbalance, or a "disassociation" of emotion and reason, and when this occurs we say that a person "lost their mind," or was "out of their mind."

It has been suggested in certain philosophical circles that the emergent romantic spirit of the late nineteenth century was a reaction against the Enlightenment notion that metaphysics was a subsidiary concern and that reason was the preferred conduit to truth. In certain respects, romanticism was a reclamation of that which had for centuries been considered elemental to the creative impulse, as well as our intrinsic desire to experience beauty. In the arts, romanticism was above all a movement that emphasized and celebrated the validity of emotion as an authentic source of aesthetic experience. The romantics didn't reject science and reason, they simply attuned their perspectives in ways that allowed "heart-knowledge" to be more pertinent than "head-knowledge" (Goethe's terms) in the creative equation. The music of the late romantic composers—Tchaikovsky, Strauss, Mahler, e.g.—is steeped in this rationale.

Romantic attitudes about art and beauty encouraged a more active participation in matters of appreciation and understanding as well. British author and theologian Charles Williams stated: "The word Romanticism should not be too narrowly confined to a literary manner. It defines an attitude, a manner of receiving experience."[18] Nietzsche put it this way: "For an event to have greatness two things must come together: The immense understanding of those who cause it to happen, and the immense understanding of those who experience it."[19] Williams conceded that there was a "cheap" and "false" type of romanticism but nevertheless believed that the value of "true" romanticism held a great deal of "intellectual honor."[20]

In his *Letters on the Aesthetic Education of Man*, Schiller makes the case that art has the ability to transcend the practical concerns of our everyday circumstances and is a necessary part of the process in our contemplation and understanding of the entirety of human life. Music historian Donald J. Grout offered a similar insight:

> In a very general sense, all art may be said to be Romantic; for though it may take its materials from everyday life, it transforms them and thus creates a new world which is necessarily, to a greater or lesser degree, remote from the everyday world. ... Music of the Romantic era is constantly thrusting beyond the borders of the rational into the unconscious and supernatural.[21]

Accordingly, it could be said that the spirit of romanticism as it pertains to creativity is as old as humankind itself.

Modernism

In *fin de siècle* Europe, Nietzsche's abnegation of religion had far-reaching implications, one of which was the vilification of certain aspects of the romantic ethos. For avant-garde artists of the early twentieth century, the pursuit of aesthetic beauty came to be viewed as a counterfeit contention—delusional, in fact. Musicologist Richard Taruskin acknowledges that romanticism became an "all-purpose punching bag" that modernists and postmodernists loved to slam in order to justify their philosophical leanings. He also warns of the corruptions of romanticism due to the promulgation of the kind of utopian idealism—replete with body counts—espoused by the likes of Jacoby.[22] That said, the evisceration of the romantic spirit by the avant-garde was a prelude to the pervasive worship of science and technology, and the arts were not exempt from this particular development. The "plundering" that Wilber alluded to was well under way.

In the realm of art music, Arnold Schoenberg was the precursor to what would become a legion of composers in the early and mid-twentieth century who embraced the idea that "formulaic composition" was a historical inevitability and that the public needed to be "cured of the delusion that the artist's aim is to create beauty."[23] This is a specious claim, for it runs counter to the innate humane desire to experience that which is beautiful and pleasing. The deterministic idea that atonal formulaic composition was something that had to happen is, according to Taruskin, "a barefaced pack of lies."[24]

Because a great deal of modern art music in the post-World War II era, with its predilection for doctrinaire intellectualism, often fails to address our desire for beauty, it results in music that is not in any way inviting or aurally ingratiating. Taruskin opines that Schoenberg's "'emancipation of dissonance' ... owes its seductive political vibes to the liberatory rhetoric of the dialectic," and had more to do with emancipating composers than with musical style.[25] Theodor Adorno and other neo-Marxist ideologues were enthusiastic advocates of the "emancipatory" aspects of atonal music, especially as it pertained to the eradication of "bourgeois" attitudes regarding aesthetics—not to mention "old world" attitudes regarding religion, sexuality, politics, morality and ethics.

This is but a perpetuation of the Hegelian narrative that propels Marxist thought. Because most iterations of Marxism demand enemies—the wealthy, the oppressor, the racist—to fuel revolutionary urges, it will manufacture new ones when the old ones become useless and are no longer advantageous for revolutionary purposes. Hegel's thesis-antithesis-synthesis archetype is predicated on the necessity of conflict in order for progress to occur. Thus, resentment, rage, rebellion and retaliation all find their justifications in leftist Hegelian ideology and Critical Theory. Turning Marx's axiom that "religion is the opiate of the masses" on its head, it could be said that resentment is the opiate of ideological left.

In this Hegelian context, consonance and dissonance in music—and in nature—are no longer polar opposites to be adjoined and harmonized in a sublime artistic fashion, but rather are considered oppressing constituencies that are in conflict. Dissonances are outnumbered by consonances in the overtone series—and in the tonal syntax—hence, they must be "emancipated" so that they may take their equal place in the musical firmament. This is why Taruskin and Scruton have ascribed a dialectic premise to the emergence of the "new music" in the early twentieth century.

Though all pitches are created equal, in tonal music these differing aural properties can, and do, have differing attractions, functions and relationships, which evoke different emotional responses. The musical syntax of tonality is distinctly hierarchical, and this runs counter to the idea of egalitarianism that is pervasive in the ideological underpinnings of the political left. Taoism, which emphasizes the ideal of polar opposites, *yin* and *yang*, existing in mutual harmony and relatedness, seems closer to the natural processes of development and progress than Hegel's dialectical theories, precisely because of its emphasis on harmonious engagement and relationships rather than conflict and struggle. In the *Tao Te Ching* of Lao Tzu we read: "That the musical notes and tones become harmonious through the relation of one with another; and that being before and behind give the idea of one following another."[26] In the realm of phonetics in natural languages, are vowels sounds in "conflict" with consonant sounds? Obviously not. In our attempts to reconcile science with faith, or the cognitive with the intuitive, or mind with heart, we would do well to remain "open" to the virtues of every aspect of our existential reality. In this respect, the harmony-relatedness paradigm espoused by Taoism could be said to be in accord with Kant's views regarding human progress, as well as being ontologically in accord with "Nature herself."

The aesthetically unpleasant, cynical and nihilistic artistic expressions that have dominated much of the twentieth century art scene are viewed as being the result of the contra-romantic mindset espoused by Schoenberg, Adorno and other modernists. According to Allan Bloom, the pernicious amalgamation of moral relativism and deconstruction led to the condition where modernism became "a kind of auction in which the victor is the one who has the most terrible things to say about the human condition. Truth began to appear to be whatever was ugliest and most opposed to gentle hopes of love."[27] If the desire to experience beauty is primordial, we might ask: what was the impetus that justified the creation and proliferation of the "successor school" of modernity and its preoccupation with all those "terrible" and "ugly" expressions? The answer lies in the ongoing differentiation of the Big Three.

Ken Wilber, who studied both medicine and Eastern philosophy, should be noted for his attempts to renew the idea of a unified theory of consciousness, in which he posits that there are four domains, or quadrants, of development that define the validity of a particular truth. These are the biological, psychological, cognitive and spiritual—each providing a somewhat different but not unrelated view of truth. He refers to this as "integral theory." From this perspective, empirical science and pure reason are but two factors in our epistemological pursuits. Wilber avers that art, aesthetics and spirituality are additional factors in the pursuit of truth, and as such he recognizes that "a given truth-claim may be valid without being complete; true, but only so far as it goes, and this must be seen as part of other equally important truths," which include, "an interior dimension—one that is subjective and interpretive, and depends on consciousness and introspection."[28] This could be called intuition and is in accord with Kant's ideas regarding aesthetic judgment. The basic concept behind Wilber's integration theory is not exactly new, but it's one worthy of examination in our attempts to find remedies for our injurious cultural proclivities, especially if we consider the integration of the Big Three to be an essential factor in accomplishing that endeavor.

Wilber's assertions reminded me of Leonard Bernstein's Harvard Lectures given in 1973 when the iconic composer-conductor presented a series of talks on music and its evolution in terms of syntax and practice. Citing his Harvard mentor and aesthetician, Professor David Prall, Bernstein recalled how Prall's views regarding the correlation of beauty, analytic method and historical perspective was for him, "a luminous revelation," which led him to the conviction "that the best way to 'know' a thing is in the context of another discipline."[29] Acknowledging that the terms "beauty," "aesthetics," "mind" and "spirit" had become anachronistic in an era when "behavioristic obsessiveness"—not to mention atonal serialism—was all the rage, Bernstein, nonetheless, was making a case similar to Wilber's: namely, that ascertaining any "truth claim" may require forays into multiple disciplines in order to better understand "the whole truth."

As the advance of postmodernism and "emotivist" rationales persist, values become merely subjective and a matter of personal choice, and according to Wilber, they are no longer "anchored in any sort of substantive reality." Once the intrinsic attributes of values, consciousness and virtue are scrubbed from the cosmos, "you should not be surprised if your own lifeworld starts to look completely hollow and empty. To *complain* about this state of affairs is like murdering your parents and then complaining you're an orphan."[30] That's a bit harsh, but it points to the necessity of juxtaposing "the Big Three" and honoring science, morality and aesthetics, and not, as Wilber states, simply "reducing one to the other in an orgy of theoretical violence."[31] Postmodernism is especially guilty of perpetuating this particular orgiastic reality, and now biological universals are considered anathema to social progress. When "impartiality" or "coherence" are considered "tools of power in history" or modes of "discursive violence" by postmodern political theorists, we are lost in the abyss of Foucauldian banalities and cynicism.[32]

Biological universals are now considered fascist because they "impose" truth claims that run counter to the politically correct position that gender is a social construct.* But as Jordan Peterson astutely pointed out, if gender is socially constructed, then it can be socially deconstructed, or one can be talked out of their gender identity, or one can change their mind about it, possibly multiple times—whenever it may be to one's economic, social or political benefit. In this scenario, coherence and rational thinking are reduced to nonfactors in the pursuit of objective truth and we end up in a "post-truth" era.

The Goodness Factor

In what was a retributive diatribe aimed at Richard Wagner's concept of "the total art work (*Gesamtkunstwerk*), and particularly the juxtaposing of art

---

* In a recorded video discussion with Jordan B. Peterson, Camille Paglia asserts that one of the first things that any women's studies curriculum should have included was biology. She recalls how she "almost got into fist fights" with certain people in university women's studies programs who insisted that biology was not to be part of any women's studies curriculum, due to a definite ideological perspective that rejected the scientific basis of gender, [Source: "Modern Times: Camille Paglia & Jordan B. Peterson," October 2017, https://www.youtube.com/watch?v=v-hIVnmUdXM&ab_channel=JordanBPeterson.]

and religion (Wagner was once thought to be a religious sage of sorts), Igor Stravinsky queries in his autobiography, "But is it at all surprising that such confusion should arise at a time like the present, when the openly irreligious masses in their degradation of spiritual values and debasement of human thought necessarily lead us to utter brutalization?"[33] This was but one composer's contentious critique of another regarding the issue of whether or not music should have moral connotations as well as aesthetic ones. Still, it points to an important question with regard to the purpose, or purposes, of music, and Stravinsky was making this query in the era when the evisceration of religious belief was becoming increasingly strident.

Stravinsky wrote his autobiography in 1936 after "the Great War." At the time, Germany was seen by many as an emerging global menace, despite its splendid musical legacy and religious heritage. He expressed distress about the influence of "the openly irreligious masses" and the potentially deleterious consequences of abandoning faith in favor of science and intellection and how this became a central narrative of the twentieth century, arguably the most brutally inhumane century ever. The issue of art and morality continued to be an important concern for the early twentieth-century composers, and as Taruskin points out, there is a cost in promulgating the idea that artistic considerations should always be "front and center in any discussion of art, and to resist—indeed, to disdain—consideration of any other kind."[34]

This was an especially pertinent issue with regard to Stravinsky himself, due to some of his "gratuitously vulgar and malicious" comments about Jews in the years just after the Holocaust. Is it ethical to look the other way because Stravinsky was among the most highly regarded composers of his time, or do we need to call out artists for their morally questionable indiscretions? Taruskin asks, "how ethical are such ethics, if they cause us to value the integrity of works of art above humane concerns?" And finally, how ethical is an ethic "that holds artists and art lovers to be entitled, by virtue of artistic commitment to moral indifference, and that *the greater the artist the greater the entitlement?*"[35] If artists become unassailable for their serious moral lapses simply because of their talent or some "abstract musical worth," then we have become enablers in our moral demise. To paraphrase Lord Acton's admonition regarding absolute corruption, there is no worse heresy than to sanctify a great artist merely because of his or her great artistry.* The *goodness* aspect of the Big Three *ought* to be in the artistic equation, regardless of the status of the art or the artist.

Friedrich A. Hayek proffered that the development of knowledge and the growth of civilization were similar "only if we interpret knowledge to include all the human adaptations in which past experience has been incorporated." All that constitutes a particular cultural sphere, "our habits and skills, our emotional attitudes, our tools, and our institutions," in other words, that which we assess to be productive and beneficial based on the experience of trial and error, "are as much an indispensable foundation of successful action as is our conscious knowledge."[36] This includes the religious underpinnings of morality, for without considering these pillars of morality any assessment is incomplete. For Hayek, conscious knowledge was a given, but knowledge needed to be validated by experiences that demonstrated that a particular truth claim was, in fact, true and thus beneficial. By assessing our cultural patrimony in the context of our experiences in the present, we can begin to arrive at a more comprehensive understanding of how we have benefited from the legacies of the past—socially, economically, spiritually and artistically—and how we might continue to benefit from those legacies.

Our perpetual desire for love and beauty is a defining aspect of who, and ontologically, what we are. Romantic idealism remains deeply ingrained in our psyches—individually and collectively. In the arts, we see and hear it in popular music, the cinema and to varying extents in the fine arts, art music and literature of recent vintage. It's important to note that not all composers of the early twentieth century embraced the "new formalism" espoused by Schoenberg and his acolytes. The music of Béla Bartók, Dmitri Shostakovich,

---

* In his oft-quoted comment regarding the corrupting aspect of power, Lord John Dalberg-Acton wrote: "I cannot accept your canon that we are to judge Pope and King unlike other men, with a favourable presumption that they did no wrong. If there is any presumption it is the other way, against the holders of power, increasing as the power increases. Historic responsibility has to make up for the want of legal responsibility. Power tends to corrupt, and absolute power corrupts absolutely. Great men are almost always bad men, even when they exercise influence and not authority, still more when you superadd the tendency or the certainty of corruption by authority. There is no worse heresy than that the office sanctifies the holder of it." [Source: John Emerich Edward Dalberg-Acton, *Historical Essays and Studies*, edited by John Neville Figgis and Reginald Vere Laurence (London: Macmillan & Co., 1907), p. 504.]

Sergei Prokofiev, Ralph Vaughan Williams, Benjamin Britten, Aaron Copland and Samuel Barber, to name but a few, does not completely break with the tonal syntax of the common practice. Notable composers working in the new century such as John Adams, Arvo Pärt, Tobias Picker, Paul Moravec, Jennifer Higdon, Max Richter, Morten Lauridsen and Osvaldo Golijov have also eschewed the crabbed mannerisms of atonal serialism and have reintroduced quasi-tonal properties into the contemporary compositional lexicon. Their music enjoys a relatively healthy popularity as a result.

Like many artists, I have come to the study of philosophy through my art. Having been a professional musician for more than five decades, I have had the good fortune to perform in Russia, Israel, Canada, across Europe, Asia, Central and South America and throughout the United States. From these experiences I have witnessed the power of music as a transformational agent of change. That power is very real and potent; thus, using it with a sense of moral responsibility remains essential in our attempts to foster conditions that can promote social betterment. To some, that may seem to be the perspective of a hopeless "romantic," but I believe that it is in the pursuit of beauty, truth and goodness in an integrated fashion that we have an opportunity to transform our "fallen" reality and hopefully find our original, truer selves. This isn't about being to the left or right on socio-cultural issues, but rather seeking a higher love, a higher truth and overcoming that which leads us to an "endarkened" reality. In this way we can all be considered "romantic" heroes and heroines in our transformative quest.

Recommended Recordings

Tchaikovsky: Orchestral Suite No. 3, Neeme Järvi, Detroit Symphony Orchestra

Strauss: *Ein Heldenleben*, Vladimir Ashkenazy, Cleveland Orchestra

Mahler: Symphony No. 1, Mariss Jansons, Royal Concertgebouw Orchestra

Schoenberg: Chamber Symphonies, Orpheus Chamber Orchestra

Bartók: Concerto for Orchestra, Fritz Reiner, Chicago Symphony Orchestra

Shostakovich: Symphony No. 5, Yakov Kreizberg, Russian National Orchestra

Prokofiev: *Romeo and Juliet*, Lorin Maazel, Cleveland Orchestra

Vaughan Williams: *The Lark Ascending*, Hilary Hahn, violin

Barber: Essay No. 2 for Orchestra, David Zinman, Baltimore Symphony Orchestra

Copland: *The Tender Land Suite*, Aaron Copland, Boston Symphony Orchestra

Adams: *Grand Pianola Music*, Ransom Wilson, Solisti New York

Pärt: *Tabula Rasa*, Angèle Dubeau, La Pietà

Moravec: *Autumn Song*, Marya Martin, flute

Richter: *Recomposed, Vivaldi: The Four Seasons*, Konzerthaus Kammerorchester Berlin

Britten: *Simple Symphony*, Iona Brown, Norwegian Chamber Orchestra

Higdon: *City Scape*, Robert Spano, Atlanta Symphony Orchestra

Golijov: *Lua Descolorida*, Dawn Upshaw, soprano

Lauridsen: *O Magnum Mysterium*, Jeffrey Budin, The Bay Brass

Picker: *Old and Lost Rivers*, Christoph Eschenbach, Houston Symphony Orchestra

Ives: *The Unanswered Question*, Leonard Bernstein, New York Philharmonic

Stravinsky: *Les Noces,* Karel Ancerl, Czech Philharmonic Orchestra, Prague Philharmonic Chorus

Endnotes

1   Friedrich Schiller, *Friedrich Schiller: Poet of Freedom, Vol. II* (Washington, D.C.: Schiller Institute, 1988), p. xxvii.

2   Denis Dutton, *The Art Instinct: Beauty, Pleasure, and Human Evolution* (Oxford and New York: Oxford University Press, 2009), p. 237.

3   Roger Scruton, *Beauty: A Very Short Introduction* (Oxford and New York: Oxford University Press, 2011), p. 61.

4   *Selected Writings: William Hazlitt*, edited by Jon Cook (Oxford and New York: Oxford University Press, 1991), p. 47.

5   William Wordsworth, preface to *Lyrical Ballads*, in *William Wordsworth*, edited by Stephen Gill (Oxford: Oxford University Press, 1986), pp. 604-605.

6   Russell Jacoby, *The End of Utopia: Politics and Culture in an Age of Apathy* (New York: Basic Books, 1999), pp. 136-137.

7   Roger Kimball, "Schiller's Aesthetic Education," *The New Criterion*, March 2001, https://newcriterion.com/issues/2001/3/schilleras-ldquoaesthetic-educationrdquo.

8   Ibid.

9   Immanuel Kant, *Critique of Judgment,* reproduction of the original by J. H. Bernard (Norderstedt, Germany: Books on Demand GmBH, 2020), p. 150.

10 Richard Taruskin, "The Many Dangers of Music," lecture, Graduate Center, City University of New York, 2016, https://www.youtube.com/watch?v=Jiy_xXTjW3k.

11 Johann Gottfried Herder and Philip V. Bohlman, *Song Loves the Masses: Herder*

on Music and Nationalism (Oakland, CA: University of California Press, 2017), p. 257.

12 Ibid.

13 Isaiah Berlin, *The Crooked Timber of Humanity: Chapters in the History of Ideas*, edited by Henry Hardy (John Murray, 1990), pp. 56-57.

14 Ibid., p. 92.

15 Ken Wilber, *A Brief History of Everything* (Boston, MA: Shambhala Publications, Inc., 2000), p. 115.

16 Scruton, *Beauty*, p. 61.

17 Michael Dunn, "The Relationship Between Emotion and Reason," theory-ofknowledge.net, May 9, 2013, https://theoryofknowledge.net/tok-2015/ways-of-knowing/emotion/.

18 Charles Williams, *The Figure of Beatrice: A Study in Dante*, reprint (Cambridge: D. S. Brewer, 2000), p. 14.

19 Friedrich Nietzsche, *Untimely Meditations: Wagner in Bayreuth,* as cited by Carl Pletsch, *Young Nietzsche* (New York: Simon & Schuster, 1991), p. 189.

20 Williams, *The Figure of Beatrice,* p. 14.

21 Donald J. Grout, *A History of Western Music* (New York: W. W. Norton & Company, Inc., 1960), p. 493.

22 Taruskin, *The Danger of Music*, p. xv.

23 Joseph Henry Auner, *A Schoenberg Reader: Documents of a Life* (Yale University Press, 2003), p. 93

24 Taruskin, *The Danger of Music*, p. 7.

25 Ibid., p. 317.

26 *Tao Te Ching: A New English Version,* translated by Stephen Mitchell (Perennial Classics, 2006), p. 9.

27 Allan Bloom, *Love and Friendship* (New York: Simon & Schuster, 1993), p. 260.

28 Tony Schwartz, foreword to *A Brief History of Everything*, by Ken Wilber (Boston, MA: Shambhala Publications, Inc., 2000), p. xv.

29 Leonard Bernstein, *The Unanswered Question: Six Talks at Harvard* (Cambridge, MA: Harvard University Press, 1976), p. 3.

30 Wilber, *A Brief History of Everything*, p. 119.

31 Ibid., p. 120.

32 Jacoby, *The End of Utopia*, p. 143.

33 Igor Stravinsky, *Chronicle of My Life* (London: V. Gollanzc, 1936), p. 70.

34 Taruskin, *The Danger of Music*, p. 439.

35 Ibid., p. 441.

36 Friedrich A. Hayek, *The Constitution of Liberty* (Chicago, IL: Chicago University Press, 1960), p. 26.

5

From the Heart

Where words leave off, music begins.
Heinrich Heine

Is music a "universal language" as Longfellow suggested? Or is this merely a platitude, easily debunked as a truism rather than an immutable "truth"? As Heinrich Heine,* Franz Schubert and Felix Mendelssohn observed, music possesses a unique ability to reach places in our soul and psyche that words seemingly cannot. Music is ephemeral, nonrepresentational and possesses ineffable properties; that is why it is impossible to quantify "meaning" or aesthetic characteristics of a particular musical utterance. Consequently, beauty and meaning in music will remain in the ears of the beholder, or as it is sometimes said, "*De gustibus non est disputandum*": In matters of taste there can be no disputes.

We all sense that music "speaks" to us and possesses the ability to convey and express emotions in powerful ways. It stirs deep feelings and passions. It affects our heart and our psyche. Though we may consider music a language,

---

* Heinrich Heine was a notable German poet whose poems were set to music by Robert Schumann and Franz Schubert.

the way in which it speaks to us remains mysterious and enigmatic. Mendelssohn, a composer whose music exhibits great lyricism and warmth, suggested that music is more specific about what it expresses than words written about it could ever be as it "fills the soul with a thousand things better than words."[1] That may be true; however, the same piece of music will often *say* different things to different people. Why this happens remains a mystery, but Albert Einstein—who played the violin and loved the music of Mozart—believed that there was beauty in the mysterious, and perhaps that's why we find music to be so enchanting, so enticing.

The origins of Western tonal music date back to the liturgical music of the early Christian church in Italy and the Middle Ages. As such, a fervent religious impulse underscored the evolution of tonality into the early Renaissance and on into the seventeenth and eighteenth centuries. During the Enlightenment it became fashionable to question the rationale behind religion and the relevance of God, as the pursuit of pure reason became the central ethos and primary attitude with regard to the creation of a more humane society. Nevertheless, many composers of that era continued to hold strong religious convictions and composed music for the church, as evidenced by Mozart and Haydn, who both composed many wonderful settings of the Catholic Mass and other liturgical works.

Ludwig van Beethoven was a "believer" and once confided in his friend Bettina von Arnim, "I know that God is nearer to me than to other artists. I associate with Him without fear; I have always recognized and understood Him and have no fear for my music."[2] At one point in the *Heiligenstadt Testament*, a document in which he bears his soul about his art, the emotional devastation of his deafness and thoughts of suicide, Beethoven gives us a glimpse into his heart in relation to God and his art: "Almighty God, who looks down in my innermost soul, you see into my heart and you know that it is filled with love for humanity and desire to do good."[3] On the opening page of the score of his great D Major Mass, Beethoven inscribed the words, "*Von Herzen. Möge es wieder—zu Herzen gehen*": "From the heart. May it in turn go to the heart." As we know, the pugnacious Beethoven was an intensely passionate individual, and his music reflects that passion in significant measure, not to mention a certain optimism and supreme confidence. These qualities are conveyed through his music in coruscating flashes of glory, joy and pathos, and remain a significant reason why his music continues to "speak" to us long after its creation.

In a very real sense, Beethoven was a child of the French Revolution, and as such, he harbored great hope for what humankind might achieve once individual freedom and civil liberties were afforded to all people. Beethoven is considered the compositional bridge between the so-called "Classical Period" of Mozart and Haydn and the nineteenth-century romantics.* His music created a vortex in the musical waters of nineteenth-century Europe, as the great composers of the romantic era—Schubert, Mendelssohn, Chopin, Schumann, Brahms, Liszt, Tchaikovsky, Wagner, et al.—were profoundly influenced by the heightened emotional aspect of musical expression that Beethoven's music embodied. The underlying *zeitgeist* regarding music emphasized the expression of emotion as an authentic source of aesthetic experience, and Beethoven was the impetus for that particular rationale.

As the *raison d'être* of musical composition went through a significant metamorphosis in the early twentieth century, composers sought new modes of expression, which resulted in a plethora of new techniques and methodologies. The romantic ideals of the nineteenth century gave way to new discoveries and experimentation that rejected the rationales of the previous centuries. Moreover, the emphasis on "heartistic" expression was increasingly viewed as anachronistic. In fact, the pursuit of aesthetic beauty in music was no longer a primary rationale for many contemporary composers.

Arnold Schoenberg's early forays into the realm of atonality (he preferred the term "pantonality") gave rise to music that was primarily concerned with intellectual processes and formulaic methodologies. The post-World War II era saw an explosion of what might be termed "left-brain music" as the *de rigueur* methodologies of atonal serialism became dominant, almost tyrannically so. Composing music "by the numbers" was viewed as being concomitant with advances in science and technology, and as such, the "parochial" syntax of tonality was thought to be "exhausted" as a viable musical practice.

Though it was Schoenberg who launched the move away from traditional musical syntax, Igor Stravinsky, too, would eventually adopt a formalistic,

* As Richard Taruskin has pointed out in his book *Text and Act*, Beethoven would not have known what one meant by "the Classical Period" since this was "a fictive term and concept produced by romantic historiography" in the late nineteenth century.

anti-metaphysical rationale, stating that composition should be done "under the stern auspices of order and discipline."[4] This move to "back to Bach" neoclassicism and the "new objectivity" in composition, was seen by some as having a decidedly ideological bent: a reaction against the "old contracts" of Judeo-Christian Europe with its distinctive spiritual underpinnings. Aesthetic and metaphysical concerns became subsidiary to formal ones, but there were problems with this mindset as Richard Taruskin points out:

> Directing attention resolutely away from content and focusing entirely on form is hardly an "immediate" response to art. It is no one's first response. (Why else, after all, is a taste for "absolute music" the most notoriously "cultivated" of all artistic tastes?) It is a learned response—learned from Stravinsky. It has its costs.[5]

The Advocacy of the "New Music"

In 1974, French composer and conductor Pierre Boulez—"the arch-apostle of modernism," as Dmitri Shostakovich described him—put forth the following statement at an international press conference for the opening of the *Institut de Recherche et Coordination Acoustique/Musique* (IRCAM), on the new horizons of musical composition in the late twentieth century:

> Our age is one of persistent, relentless, almost unbearable inquiry. In its exaltation it cuts off all retreats and bans all sanctuaries; its passion is contagious, its thirst for the unknown projects us forcefully, violently into the future; it compels us to redefine ourselves, no longer in relation to our individual functions, but to our collective necessity. Despite the skillful ruses we have cultivated in our desperate effort to make the world of the past serve our present-day needs, we can no longer elude the essential trial: that of becoming an absolute part of the present, of forsaking all memory to forge a perception without precedent, of renouncing the legacies of the past to discover undreamed of territories.[6]

Here we have a leading figure of contemporary music saying that past traditions have little or no value in contemporary life. Moreover, Boulez considered it a "skillful ruse" to attempt to make the past seem important, and that "forsaking all memory" is a desirable condition for humankind. This mindset is what has been driving a great deal of the postmodern attitudes in academia, in which "hyper-presentism" has the effect of diminishing any attempt to learn from the past while reducing our cultural patrimony to being merely the residue of a bourgeois culture.

In the aftermath of the French Revolution, Edmund Burke cautioned against renouncing the legacies of the past and deriding "the wisdom of the ancients." For Burke, the idea of creating a better system or better ideology, while dismissing the beneficial aspects of our cultural patrimony, meant unnecessarily "acquiescing to ideological fanaticism."[7] Burke's reverence for the "inheritance of the past" was directed to mitigate radical attempts to alter and diminish the wisdom of past cultures in their movements toward a better future. Being grateful for what had come before was a way to repay the debt of past generations "through responsible stewardship for the sake of the unborn." When we only live in the present, we neither honor the past nor protect the future.[8] To the conservative mind, gratitude for the good things of the past is always in the equation.*

We shouldn't forget that the "progressive" theories of Marx, Engels and the Young Hegelians were rooted in their disdain for God and religion. Their predilection for a "scientific" view of history—or "scientism," as Hayek described it—was an attempt to dismantle traditions, especially those rooted in theological premises. Predictably, the result of the modernist mindset as articulated by Boulez and his acolytes has led to the inexorable marginalization of art music in the post-World War II era. As the art of musical composition became steeped in hyper-intellectualization, this created the condition in which music born of past traditions was not only considered archaic but unimportant and irrelevant. Boulez, for instance, considered Mozart to be trivial.

Not everyone embraced this supposition. Cultural commentator Denis Dutton reminds us that great works of art "possess a relentless capacity to arrest attention and excite the mind, generation after generation. Their nobility and grandeur also flow from their ability to address deep human instincts. They will live as long as we do."[9] The perspectives of Boulez and his modernist

---

* Conservative commentators Roger Scruton and Yuval Levin have written extensively on the issues of gratitude and obligation in the context of conservative thought. See Scruton's essay, "A Righter Shade of Green," published June 16, 2007 by *American Conservative*, and Levin's remarks on the occasion of his receipt of the Bradley Prize, delivered June 12, 2013.

disciples have had the effect of diminishing the very attributes that make great art so alluring by virtually ignoring the "deep human instincts" that Dutton alluded to. Twentieth-century American composer George Rochberg, whose compositional style evolved away from atonal modernism and toward a decidedly "romantic" and accessible syntax, offers a view that is in accord with that of many music lovers: "There can be no justification for music ultimately if it does not convey eloquently and elegantly the passions of the human heart."[10] I'm with George.

Daniel Barenboim argues that it was necessary in the 1970s for Pierre Boulez "not to see the beauties" in tonal music "because he was fighting causes that were to him much more important" at that time.[11] This may be so, but to be fixated on the technicalities and intellectual aspects of the art of composing, at the expense of the emotive aspects, results in the deemphasizing—or eliminating—of one of music's most essential elements altogether. In this context, Boulez's manifesto on modern music may be more of a *truism* than a *truth*. Music that fails to evoke or convey emotion can be said to be inhumane on one level, for emotion and spirituality have a fundamental primacy in the human experience.

Igor Stravinsky once opined that music was essentially powerless to express anything but that skilled composers *could* elicit various emotional responses in listeners by using the requisite musical materials (intervals, chords, pitch sets, rhythms). Yet in letters to friends and colleagues regarding his groundbreaking ballet score, *The Rite of Spring,* he referenced the expressive abilities of music. "In *The Rite of Spring,*" he writes, "I wished to express the sublime uprising of Nature renewing itself—the whole pantheistic uprising of the universal harvest."[12] Not only was he admitting to music's expressive characteristics, he, like Richard Strauss—a composer whose music he found to be "treacly"—was using music to create a sonic picture in order to conjure and convey a specific narrative.

Writing in the *Washington Post,* music critic Anne Midgette observed, "The problem—for many if not most composers—is that dramatic expression is scary, and not at all hip."[13] In an interview she conducted with the 2007 Pulitzer Prize-winning composer, David Lang, one of the co-founders of the "new music" ensemble Bang on a Can, the composer remarked on the condition of contemporary art music: "One of things that's been forgotten in music for a long time is the ability to be nakedly emotional."[14] Lang wasn't wrong, and this is one reason why popular music remains so ... popular.

Having lived through the era of atonal supremacy, I have often seen that compositions wrapped in the integument of intellection and rigid formalism rarely find life after their premiere performances. The acerbic music composed by mid-century modernists that failed to touch our hearts has also failed to find its justification, and enthusiastic audiences. Though there are some who would give me serious grief for having the temerity to state the obvious, it's not difficult to acknowledge that so much of the "new music" composed according to the aesthetics of the Second Viennese School is largely ignored due to its lack of perceivable dramatic expression and "heartistic" confluence.

I'm not aware of Pierre Boulez's attitudes about God, faith or religion. I do know that he was an extremely gifted musician and in his early career was an extreme ideologue, defiantly so when it came to his advocacy of new music. However, I suspect that as he grew older (he passed in 2016), he may have recalibrated his thinking, arriving at views in greater accord with those of Beethoven and Rochberg, to varying extents. During the last two decades of his career Boulez began performing and recording the symphonies of the supreme arch-romantic, Gustav Mahler. If the past can serve no present-day need and is merely a "ruse," as Maestro Boulez and others who share that view have argued, then why bother with Mahler at all? More importantly, why does the music of Beethoven and Mahler continue to "speak to us" and to find enthusiastic adherents?

Much has changed since 1974, when Maestro Boulez delivered his IRCAM manifesto, as there has been an evolution in our perspectives regarding life and art. New musical styles have emerged that are "rediscovering" the viability of the tonal idiom, as evidenced by the music of Arvo Pärt, Eric Whitacre and the NOW Ensemble. Some consider the reemergence of tonality or pantonality to be merely a marketing ploy aimed at a broader, upscale audience with disposable income. But that's just being cynical. That's not to say that composers don't want to get paid for their work, but it belies the idea that something more humane and aesthetically pleasing is once again in the compositional equation and that audiences are hungry for music that speaks to the totality of who they are.

The integration of mind and heart, for so long a measure of successful musical achievement, is finding favor once again. Musicologist Susan McClary views the emergence of organizations such as Bang on a Can, the Ethel String Quartet, the NOW Ensemble and other "downtown" musical enterprises, to be a reaction to the "uptown" academics of the Juilliard School and Columbia University—and a positive development. McClary suggests that the new music of the downtown arts scene is the work of "traditionally marginalized" artists, those who were "defined by the mainstream as noise." Consequently, they were in a position "to observe the oppressive nature of the reigning order," of those who, in the determinist machinations of the "institutional framework," viewed the "downtowners" as being nothing more than purveyors of lowbrow pastiche. McClary views the "downtowners" as being "dedicated to injecting back into music the noise of the body, of the visual, of emotions, and of gender."[15] In this respect, she is not unlike Camille Paglia, who has always been an advocate of the sensory and sensual aspect of art. Whether or not the "uptown" academics were *de facto* "oppressors," Boulez and his epigones could be quite caustic in their diatribes against composers who didn't comport with their formulaic orthodoxies.

Responding to the assertions of McClary and Midgette regarding the growing popularity of these new styles of composition that "challenge the ideology of the rigorous, autonomous, elitist" mid-century modernists like Mr. Boulez and his acolytes, Taruskin posits:

> On one hand there is a music, increasingly under attack, that makes its appeal exclusively to the cerebral cortex. On the other hand there is music increasingly successful, that speaks, if I may put it so, directly to the medulla and the ganglia. Is there any music being written today that addresses an integrated personality, a whole human being?[16]

Taruskin made this query in 1989. Since then we have witnessed a burgeoning interest in art music composers who actually seem to care if we listen. Leonard B. Meyer presciently observed in 1967 that our "cosmopolitan world culture," in which globalization and technology would become more dominant, would give rise to a wave of diversity and pluralism in art music. Part of that pluralism has led to the reintroduction of tonal, diatonic syntax in contemporary art music. This development has validated the idea that the desire for aesthetic beauty is primal and humane. Commenting on the future of contemporary art music, Rochberg contends:

> The hope of contemporary music lies in learning how to reconcile all manner of opposites, contradictions, paradoxes; the past with the present, tonality with atonality. That is why, in my most recent music, I have tried to utilize these in combinations that reassert the primal values of music.[17]

Those "primal values" are the progeny of the "deep human instincts" that Denis Dutton cited—values that may, in fact, be "universal." David Hume, in the fourth of his *Four Dissertations* (1757), averred that history demonstrated that "the general principles of taste are uniform in human nature," and that certain works of art might have attributes that could be considered "eternal" because they've been admired across generations and cultures.[18] Postmodernists who are hooked on the opiate of anti-essentialism will disagree, but Rochberg's assertion that music that effectively "conveys the passions of the human heart" will find its justification seems inherently correct—provable, in fact. That justification is linked to music's ability to "speak" to us in profound ways. Echoing the notions of Rochberg and Dutton, Roger Scruton considers the human desire for beauty as something that fulfills our intrinsic "metaphysical condition ... as free individuals, seeking our place in a shared and public world." Citing Plato and Kant he opines that, "the feeling for beauty is proximate to the religious frame of mind, arising from a humble sense of living with imperfections, while aspiring towards the highest unity with the transcendental."[19]

In the final chapter of his bestselling book *This Is Your Brain on Music*, neuroscientist Daniel J. Levitin speaks to the idea of music's capacity to enhance long, productive and loving relationships. Citing the "multiple, reinforcing cues of a good song—rhythm, melody, contour," Levitin asserts that when these cues "stick in our heads," we are predisposed to the kind of social interaction, including courtship, that make us human. As he put it:

> That is the reason that many ancient myths, epics and even the Old Testament were set to music in preparation for being passed down by oral tradition across the generations. As a tool for activation of specific thoughts, music is not as good as language. As a tool for arousing feelings and emotions,

music is better than language. The combination of the two—as best exemplified in a love song—is the best courtship of all.[20]

Music, the mysterious language of heart, remains universal in its ability to move us, to change our consciousness and touch our soul, when it adheres to or integrates the principles of tonality to significant degrees. Forsaking the past seems inherently unwise—even obtuse. Alex Ross suggests that there are no "globally consistent signifiers of emotion" in music,[21] yet in the tonal syntax, major and minor modes do, in fact, impart or elicit definite, contrasting moods—and have done so for centuries.

In his Norton Lectures at Harvard in 1973, Leonard Bernstein cites Noam Chomsky's concepts of a universal grammar, also known as monogenesis, and makes a persuasive case that just as there are common phonological traits in languages, like consonants and vowels, so too there are common phonological traits in all music, "preordained by nature": consonances and dissonances born of the overtone series. Consistently regular sound vibrations—"energy in vibratory motion," as physicists describe it—are the phonetic basis of all music regardless of the means of production or the culture of origin.[22] When these phonetic elements are ordered and adjoined in a particular fashion, music with distinct emotional features is the result. Bernstein rhetorically asks: Do these phonetic signifiers in music, signifiers born of polar opposites interacting in a harmonized fashion, have universal communicative or expressive potentialities? We might answer that the emotions we experience when we perceive ordered musical sound-energy are real—transcendent, in fact—and not merely imagined.

Research into psychoacoustic phenomenon, reveals that it is not unreasonable to conclude that the relationship between the physical and the metaphysical is stimulated when we hear music. Music that "speaks" to the entirety of my personhood tells me that Bernstein, Dutton, Longfellow and others are essentially correct in their assertions regarding the innate desire for beauty and how music satiates that desire and addresses deep human instincts, especially the primal instinct to communicate and relate to others in ways that can foster harmony, cooperation and unity. I believe Mendelssohn had it right in referring to music's communicative attributes, when he suggested that music "fills the soul with a thousand things better than words." Though we may differ on just how, or in what fashion music "speaks" to us, we can easily agree that the communicative aspect of music, no matter how ephemeral or incorporeal it may be, is nonetheless perceptible and real.

Recommended Recordings

Beethoven: *Missa Solemnis*, John Eliot Gardiner, English Baroque Soloists

Haydn: Symphony No. 91 & 92, Rene Jacobs, Freiberg Baroque Orchestra

Mozart: The Symphonies, Sir Charles Mackerras, Prague Chamber Orchestra

Schubert: Symphony No. 9, George Szell, Cleveland Orchestra

Chopin: Piano Concerto No. 1, Philadelphia Orchestra, Emanuel Ax, piano

Liszt: *Hunnenschlacht*, Zubin Mehta, Berlin Philharmonic

Schoenberg: String Quartets, LaSalle String Quartet

Brahms: Symphony No. 4, Leonard Bernstein, New York Philharmonic

Tchaikovsky: Symphony No. 6, Christoph von Dohnányi, Cleveland Orchestra

Wagner: Prelude, *Parsifal*, Herbert von Karajan, Berlin Philharmonic Orchestra

Boulez: *Notations for Orchestra*, Pierre Boulez, Lucerne Festival Academy Orchestra

Stravinsky: *The Rite of Spring*, Pierre Boulez, Cleveland Orchestra

Mahler: Symphony No. 1, Seiji Ozawa, Boston Symphony Orchestra

Rochberg: *Transcendental Variations*, Christopher Lyndon-Gee, conducting

Lang: "Wed," Ethel String Quartet

Pärt: *Da pacem Domine*, Andrey Boreyko, Hilliard Ensemble

Whitacre: *Alleluia*, Eric Whitacre, Eric Whitacre Singers

Reich: *New York Counterpoint*, Bang on a Can

NOW Ensemble: *NOW*

Shostakovich: Symphony No. 10, Kurt Sanderling, Berlin Symphony Orchestra

Mendelssohn: Symphony No. 5, Charles Munch, Boston Symphony Orchestra

Schumann: *Liederkreis*, Op. 24, Dietrich Fischer-Dieskau, Jörg Demus

Schubert: *Schwanengesang*, D. 957, Dietrich Fischer-Dieskau, Gerald Moore

Endnotes

1   Felix Mendelssohn, as cited by R. Larry Todd, *Nineteenth-Century Piano Music* (New York and London: Routledge, 2004), p. 193.

2   Alexander Wheelock Thayer, *Thayer's Life of Beethoven* (Princeton, NJ: Princeton

University Press, 1949), p. 494.

3   Ibid., pp. 304-305.

4   Igor Stravinsky, as cited by Richard Taruskin, *The Danger of Music and Other Anti-Utopian Essays* (Los Angeles, Berkeley, and London: University of California Press, 2010), p. 397.

5   Ibid., p. 425.

6   Pierre Boulez, IRCAM: U.S. Tour Program Notes (Paris: IRCAM Editions, 1986), p. 10.

7   Jonah Goldberg, *The Tyranny of Clichés: How Liberal Cheat in the War of Ideas* (New York: Sentinel, Penguin Group, 2012), p. 33.

8   Patrick J. Deneen, *Conserving America? Essays on Present Discontents* (South Bend, IN: St. Augustine's Press, 2016), p. 147.

9   Denis Dutton, *The Art Instinct: Beauty, Pleasure, and Human Evolution* (New York: Bloomsbury Press, 2009), p. 7.

10 George Rochberg, *The Aesthetics of Survival: A Composer's View of Twentieth-Century Music* (Ann Arbor: University of Michigan Press, 1984), p. 237.

11 Daniel Barenboim, *Music Quickens Time* (London and New York: Verso, 2008), p. 146.

12 Igor Stravinsky, *Music in the Western World: A History in Documents*, edited by Piero Weiss and Richard Taruskin (Schirmer, Wadsworth Group, and Thomson Learning, Inc., 1984), p. 439.

13 Anne Midgette, "When Opera Is New and Unproved," *Washington Post*, September 7, 2008.

14 Ibid.

15 Susan McClary, afterword to *Noise: The Political Economy of Music*, by Jacques Attali, translated by Brian Massumi (University of Minnesota, 1985), pp. 157-158.

16 Taruskin, *The Danger of Music,* p. 15.

17 Joan DeVee Dixon, *George Rochberg: A Bio-bibliographic Guide to His Life and Works* (New York: Pendragon Press, 1992), pp. 86-87.

18 David Hume, "Of the Standard of Taste," *Four Dissertations* (London: 1757), p. 232, https://quod.lib.umich.edu/e/ecco/004806396.0001.000?view=toc.

19 Roger Scruton, *Beauty: A Very Short Introduction* (Oxford and New York: Oxford University Press, 2011), pp. 145-146.

20 Daniel J. Levitin, *This Is Your Brain on Music: The Science of a Human Obsession* (New York, NY: Penguin Group-USA, 2006), p. 267.

21 Alex Ross, *Listen to This* (New York: Farrar, Straus and Giroux, 2010), p. 27.

22 Leonard Bernstein, *The Unanswered Question: Six Talks at Harvard* (Cambridge, MA: Harvard University Press, 1976), pp. 3-53.

6

Confucius Says

If a person be without the virtues proper to goodness
what has he to do with the rites of propriety?
If a person be without the virtues proper to goodness,
what has he to do with music?
Confucius

Does music possess secret power?

In his insightful book *The Secret Power of Music: The Transformation of Self and Society through Musical Energy*, British author David Tame explores the attitudes of the ancient cultures of China, Greece, India and the West regarding music and its effects on their respective cultures. Tame's insights are highly perspicacious, especially with regard to the axiological assessment of art and music. Axiology is the study of the nature, types and criteria of values and of value judgments, especially in the realm of ethics. Many have argued that assessing music and art in an axiological manner is highly problematic, invidious, in fact. However, music historian Richard Taruskin refers to this as a "poietic fallacy": the penchant for assessing music solely on the basis of compositional methodology while disavowing or ignoring aesthetic and ethical concerns.* Whether one agrees with Taruskin's view or not, the ancients recognized the importance of the axiological examination of the tonal arts, and the ancient Chinese perspectives about music and its "power," remain highly instructive.

Reading Tame's book in 1985 was my first encounter with Confucius' attitudes and ideas regarding the art of music. Chinese musical philosophy reveals a highly developed system of theory and mysticism that was prescient in its attitudes about music. The Chinese attached a great deal of importance to the transcendent and therapeutic power of sound and music. Individual pieces of music were believed to possess an "energy formula," which in turn had the ability to exert powerful influences over those who listened to it. This metaphysical concept of music, with its attendant spiritual connotations, held that moral and ethical implications in musical creativity, production and performance were not to be minimized. As Tame observes, for the Chinese, motivation and intention were salient factors, and they believed that the components of music—rhythm, melody, harmony, instrumentation—could yield mystical influences when ordered in a harmonious fashion. Though they considered music to be a natural phenomenon, the Chinese "understood the power within music to be a 'free energy,' which each man could use or misuse according to his own free will."[1] Consequently, Chinese philosophers and educators directed a great deal of attention toward music and freedom, and the correlation of both with responsibility.

Because the Chinese understood that music was not composed or performed in a social vacuum, there existed significant social implications in the creation and presentation of music. As a result of this awareness, music that was merely a form of entertainment was seen as having little redeeming social value. Music that endeavored to express or convey universal truths, which in turn could benefit the development of a person's character and thereby make that person an asset to society, was music that was considered good and beneficial. Conversely, music that was deemed to be overtly sensual or exotic

---

* Richard Taruskin coined the term *poietic fallacy* to describe the modernist rationale which proffers "the conviction that what matters most (or more strongly yet, all that matters) in a work of art is the making of it, the maker's input." The etymology of the term *poietic* is from the Greek, *poiein*, which means "to make." [Source: *The Dangers of Music and other Anti-Utopian Essays*, p. 305.]

was seen as being immoral and was thought to have negative effects on one's spirituality and character. Confucius states in *The Analects*, 16.5:

> There are three types of delights that improve you, and three types of delights that diminish you. To delight in li and music, to delight in speaking of others' good points, to delight in having many worthy friends—these improve you.* To delight in arrogant pleasures, to delight in idle wanderings, to delight in banquet parties—these diminish you.[2]

Consider Confucius' remarks about the music of certain composers of his time: "The music of Cheng is lewd and corrupting, the music of Sung is soft and makes one effeminate, the music of Wei is repetitious and annoying, the music of Ch'i is harsh and haughty."[3] It is intriguing to note Confucius' highly subjective views vis-à-vis the moral, and possibly corrupting, aspects of the music on the citizenry. His views reveal an explicit concern about the effects of music on one's character. Confucius says:

> The noble-minded man's music is mild and delicate, keeps a uniform mood, enlivens and moves. Such a man does not harbor pain or mourn in his heart; violent and daring movements are foreign to him.[4]

> If a person be without the virtues proper to goodness, what has he to do with the rites of propriety? If a person be without the virtues proper to goodness, what has he to do with music?"[5]

In his *Spring and Autumn Annals,* Chinese politician Lu Bu Wei (291-235 BC) offers similar views:

> The will of people living in an area can be known by examining the customs prevailing there. And their virtues can be known by examining their will. Whether a state will become prosperous or face its downfall, whether its sovereign is sensible or unworthy, and whether a person is honorable or base, can all be known by the music they enjoy.[6]

> Music is a product of the heart. When the heart is moved, the feelings can also be reflected by euphonious sounds. And when a euphonious tune

---

* In Confucian terminology li refers to propriety, ritual or rites.

is heard, the heart can also be touched by it. Hence, the customs of an area can be known by examining its tunes. The will of people living in an area can be known by examining the customs prevailing there. ... When their virtues are well cultivated, they can compose music. If the tunes compose are harmonious, they will resonate euphoniously, and they can edify and direct the common people to pursue Tao.[7]

It becomes clear that the two primary aspects of the ancient Chinese philosophy regarding music were the effects of music on one's psyche and the issue of freedom vis-à-vis social responsibility. When compared to the rationales and motivations of artists of the modern age, the Chinese ideal of music-making seems highly enlightened. If individuals were affected by music, it stood to reason that society as a whole could be influenced—positively or negatively—as well. Confucius understood that cultivating the conditions necessary for developing a humane culture mitigated the propensity to behave according to our "animal spirits," and treat others merely as objects.

Other ancient Chinese texts offer corroborative views regarding music: its usage, its ethical connotations and its origins. The ancient Chinese text *The Memorial of Music* states:

> Therefore it is, that when music is generally taught, the duties of the five relations [as defined by Confucian thought] are thoroughly comprehended; the ears and eyes are quick and penetrating; the animal spirits and the emotional nature are in perfect calm; public manners and customs are reformed, and the whole empire enjoys profound tranquility.[8]

The connection of the tonal arts with the ordering principles of physical laws and metaphysical ideals was considered important due to the belief that the same laws and principles contained within music and sound production were present in the celestial order that governed the entire universe. Those of us who possess even a cursory understanding of the Chinese philosophical tome the *I Ching* understand that the Taoist axiom of harmonizing the polarities of *yang* and *yin* is one of its central tenets. The fusion of Taoist principles and Confucian ethics would give rise to the various rationales that guided the Chinese in matters of art and social governance.

Confucianism is an ethical and sociopolitical philosophy that emphasizes the importance of humane relationships in establishing an ethical culture. The

Five Relations—of sovereign and subject, father and son, elder brother and younger brother, husband and wife, and friend and friend—were to be based on the attributes of humanism and social responsibility. Chinese philosophy scholar Herbert Fingarette refers to Confucianism as an attempt to view what is "secular" in a more "sacred" fashion. Confucianism is not a religion, per se, but acts as a social contract in an attempt to fashion an ethical society.[9]

The cosmology of *yang* and *yin* is germane to both Confucian and Taoist doctrine and was considered elemental in humankind's pursuit of harmony and peace. Taoism promotes the concept of seeking a mystical identification with the patterns of the natural world, "the impersonal Tao," through meditation and trance. With its emphasis on the individual's harmonization with nature in a pliant fashion, it stands as a complementary philosophy to Confucianism's strenuous efforts to mold society according to social archetypes and ethical standards. Since harmonization is a central goal in both of these philosophies it is easy to understand the importance the Chinese placed on the role of music as a potential harmonizing agent. Moreover, there existed a belief that music should embody and integrate the attributes of truth, beauty and goodness in a sublime balance of content and form. Again, the moral and ethical aspects of that equation were not to be minimized. Selflessness was seen as a high virtue. The *Tao Te Ching* supports this contention:

> The heavens endure; the earth is very old. Why? Because they do not exist for themselves, they therefore have long life. The truly wise are content to be last, they are therefore first. They are indifferent to themselves; they are therefore self-confident. Perhaps it is because they do not exist for themselves that they find complete fulfillment.[10]

Truth and beauty could be manifested when the complementary opposites of intellectual and emotional, masculine and feminine, metaphysical and physical were well harmonized. If one could be harmonized in mind and body, such a person would be able to achieve inner peace and tranquility and become one with the cosmos, thus attaining a "perfected" state—a condition of harmonized relatedness to the world in which one exists.* Lu Bu Wei gives further insight into these precepts:

---

* This is also a central tenet of Buddhism.

Music has a very long history. It is composed according to precise rules based on *Tao*. *Tai Yi* develops *Two Yi*. *Two Yi* develops *Yin* and *Yang*. *Yin* ascends and *Yang* descends constantly, thus, everything in the world is created by the interaction of these two forms of vitality. They exist in chaos. Sometimes they combine together, but at other times they are separate from each other, and this is the *Tao* of Heaven. ... All things of the world are based on *Tao* and generated by the cooperation of *Yin* and *Yang*. When the youngest shoot starts to germinate, Yin and Yang will condense inside it, and it can thus develop a form. And when it has a fixed form, it must also occupy some space and it can also make a sound. The sound can be euphonious only when it is harmonious, and euphony can be created only when it is moderate. Ancient kings gave their tunes harmony according to the rules of harmony and moderation.[11]

The emphasis on harmony and relatedness and their genesis from "the great One" is underscored countless times in Chinese writings. Tame alludes to the ancient text the *Li Chi* and its view that "the harmony and sacred proportion of heaven is viewed as entering the earth through the mediation of music and ritual." The *Li Chi* states:

Music is the harmony of heaven and earth while rites are the measurement of heaven and earth. Through harmony all things are made known; through measure all things are properly classified. Music comes from heaven; rites are shaped by earthly design.[12]

According to ancient Chinese custom, manifesting balance, harmony and relatedness was to be the motivation and purpose of a musician's work. By bringing these attributes into a performance it was thought that the musician was interfacing spiritually with the cosmic forces of heaven and thus was personifying celestial order. For Confucius the harmony-relatedness paradigm was important in that "ceremony established the correct manner of physical movement in man, while music perfected man's mind and emotions."[13] The moral inculcation of a person's character and the development of an ethical society are continually linked to the Confucian view of music. The ancient Chinese postulate of "music as a microcosm" would be echoed by Pythagoras and early Christian philosophers centuries later by Greek and early Christian philosophers. According to the Greeks and their Christian followers, there existed cosmic relationship between mathematics and music. Love, divine order, music and mathematics were considered branches of the same cosmic tree. Attaining harmony in all human endeavors was thought to have cosmic meaning in the development of one's psychological disposition.

An intriguing side effect of the harmony-relatedness paradigm was the intolerance in classical Chinese music for anything that was a result of chance or improvisation. These practices were considered antipodal to the reverence for order and balance. Consequently, spontaneity and its unruly cousin, impetuousness, were highly suspect. The intimate relationship between music and universal, cosmic order was not to be left to chance; therefore, discipline and proficiency became hallmarks of the classical Chinese musical tradition. To a society that was based largely on the philosophy of balance and harmony, the notion of expressive freedom would almost certainly be viewed as threatening and possibly corrupting. Innovation has challenged the status quo of all cultures, and in ancient China this was considered especially vexatious due to the belief in the transformative power music. Yet as Tame points out, virtually every major civilization of antiquity held this view. As Tame notes:

> The wise among them were therefore very much aware of the pitfalls of either extreme in music—over-rigidity or over-innovation—and sought to achieve a balance between the two. An unwise degree of innovation or a condition of outright musical anarchy could prove deadly to the State. But, on the other hand, complete inflexibility could cause music to stagnate.[14]

It would be incorrect to view Confucius as a "timid conservative" who espoused "servile conformity" in matters of ethics and morality. As Karen Armstrong points out, far from being "preoccupied with liturgical minutiae," Confucius was a revolutionary with an egalitarian bent who "gave a new interpretation to the customary *li*." These rites and ceremonies "were not designed to enhance a nobleman's prestige, but to transform him by making the practice of self-forgetfulness habitual." For Confucius, taking egotism out of ritual "brought out profound spiritual and moral potential," thus making it possible for even the common man to become a *junzi*—a "gentleman" or a "superior man"—who had developed to his fullest capacity.[15] Peimin Ni echoes this contention in his discourse on Confucian views on music, ritual and governance, noting that music could "transform the people and society without visible force" in such a way that citizens "would not even notice the existence of their government, much like when shoes fit, one does not feel them."[16]

Yet as history informs us, the dichotomy between traditional modes of discipline and expressive freedom that concerned the Chinese has been a topic of debate in virtually every culture for eons. Jonah Goldberg reminds us that the Chinese were "pathbreaking scientific (and bureaucratic) innovators, but they couldn't relinquish their political monopoly, and eventually snuffed out technological progress in the name of imperial hegemony."[17] The desire for societal control and tribal protectionism has been a long-standing feature of the human condition. Art and music that might threaten the imperial tribe was obviously a concern of the Chinese ruling class. That said, one wonders what Confucius might say regarding the social implications of our contemporary musical culture. My guess is that he'd be astonished about how little importance is placed on the axiological aspects of music and creativity, and how stunted our development in these matters has been. He might have a difficult time finding many *junzi* among us.

Endnotes

1   David Tame, *The Secret Power of Music: The Transformation of Self and Society through Musical Energy* (Northamptonshire, England: Turnstone Press, Ltd., 1984), p. 34.

2   *The Analects of Confucius: An Online Teaching Translation*, translated by Robert Eno, (Robert Eno, 2018), p. 91, https://chinatxt.sitehost.iu.edu/Analects_of_Confucius_(Eno-2015).pdf.

3   Tame, *The Secret Power of Music*, p. 34.

4   Curt Sachs, *The Rise of Music in the Ancient World* (New York: Norton, 1943), p. 106.

5   Confucius, *Confucian Analects*, translated by James Legge (London: Trübner, 1893), chapter 3, verse 3, https://china.usc.edu/confucius-analects-3.

6   Lu Bu Wei, *The Spring and Autumn of Lu Bu Wei*, Book I (Guangxi, China: Guangxi Normal University Press, 2005), p. 242.

7   Ibid., p. 244.

8   "Notions of the Ancient Chinese Respecting Music: A Complete Translation of the YOK-KYI, or Memorial of Music, according to the Imperial Tradition," translated by Dr. B. Jenkins, *Journal of the North-China Branch of the Royal Asiatic Society, Volumes 4-5* (Princeton: Princeton University Library, 1868), p. 43.

9   Herbert Fingarette, *Confucius: The Secular as Sacred* (Long Grove, Il: Waveland Press, 1998).

10   *Tao Te Ching*, translated by Frank J. MacHovec, *The Feminine Tao* (website), http://earlywomenmasters.net/tao/ch_07.html.

11   Lu Bu Wei, *Spring and Autumn*, p. 242.

12   Tame, *The Secret Power of Music*, p. 40.

13   Ibid.

14   Ibid., p. 41.

15   Karen Armstrong, *The Great Transformation: The Beginning of Our Religious Traditions* (New York: Anchor Books, Random House, 2006), p. 249.

16   Peimin Ni, *Understanding the Analects of Confucius: A New Translation of Lunyu with Annotations* (New York: SUNY Press, 2017), p. 380.

17   Jonah Goldberg, *Suicide of the West: How the Rebirth of Tribalism, Populism, Nationalism, and Identity Politics is Destroying American Democracy* (New York: Crown Forum, 2018), p. 100.

7

American Music

*The new music of America was democratic and global,
able to defeat any rival simply by its refusal to believe in rivalry,
happily appropriating every sound that could be reissued as a song.*
Roger Scruton

In a very real way American music is world music. Because America is an immigrant nation, those who came from other lands brought their distinct musical traditions with them. As a result, American music is a rich amalgam of highly varied styles and influences. Some of the earliest musical expressions in America were Christian hymns that were sung in churches and schools utilizing the technique known as "shape note" singing.* Many of these hymns were eventually published in 1835 in the hymnal known as

---

*. Shape note singing is a musical practice and tradition of social singing from music books printed in shape notes. Shape notes are a variant system of Western musical notation whereby the note heads are printed in distinct shapes to indicate their scale degree and solmization syllable (fa, sol, la, etc.). Since 1801 shape notes have been associated with American sacred music, specifically with singing schools, with musical conventions, and with all-day gatherings known as "singings." Denounced by critics as uncouth, the simplified notation has persisted in the rural South, where it continues to form the basis of strong traditions of church and community singing. [Source: Encyclopedia Britannica]

Southern Harmony, including a tune known as "New Britain," which John Newton used as the melodic basis for his song "Amazing Grace."

As a young musician growing up in suburban Cleveland, I played in Jazz combos, big bands, symphony orchestras, concert bands, marching bands, Broadway show orchestras, Rock bands, Jazz fusion bands, brass choirs, a Blues band and even a funk-Motown review outfit. Like most young people of my generation, listening to the "Top 40" on the radio—which offered a highly varied musical menu—was a daily ritual and I loved the music of the Beatles, the Stones, the Supremes, the Four Seasons, the Kinks, Deep Purple and the Staples Singers as much as I did Tommy Dorsey, Glenn Miller, Rodgers and Hammerstein, and Beethoven—music my parents had introduced to me. In every ensemble that I played in there was music composed by American composers: Duke Ellington, Aaron Copland, Leonard Bernstein, Miles Davis, Laura Nyro, John Philip Sousa, George Gershwin, Stan Kenton, James Brown, Sly Stone, Ferd "Jelly Roll" Morton and more.

It's often said that Jazz is "America's classical music." Jazz has its roots in a variety of traditions: Caribbean melodic elements, European harmonic syntax, African and Latin rhythms, African-American spirituals, field hollers, Ragtime and Blues. Cross-fertilization is everywhere in the origins of Jazz. In his seminal book on the history of Jazz, Marshall Stearns posits that the genesis of the Jazz idiom was the result of the synthesis of the musical traditions of Europe and West Africa that took place over three centuries.

Stearns points out that both musical traditions employed the diatonic scale and diatonic harmony as significant aspects of their musical materials, especially in the music for the African kora, a 21-stringed instrument from West Africa. There are a number of theories regarding the arrival of "blue notes" in Jazz and the juxtaposition of the diatonic and pentatonic scales. Leonard Bernstein suggests in his Harvard lectures of 1973, that the naturally lower, or flat, sixth partial in the overtone series may have been a significant factor in the use of "blue notes" within the diatonic scale.

The synthesis of European harmony—predicated on equal temperament—and African drumming that found its way to the

Caribbean, were the prime elements in the evolution of Jazz. Based on his study of Haitian culture, Harold Courlander averred:

> On the plantations and off, the Negros never forgot the drum rhythms of their own countries, nor their ancestors and deities. They never forgot how to make fine drums. And whether the drum was of a Congo pattern, or Ibo, or Arada, all men listened to it, and danced in the light of smoking oil lamps.

Another key figure in the origins of Jazz, was the talented pianist and composer Louis Moreau Gottschalk (1829-1869). Born into a Creole family in New Orleans, Gottschalk developed a formidable pianistic technique that landed him in front of Frederic Chopin and Franz Liszt, who were impressed with his abilities. Gottschalk would eventually travel to the Caribbean and South America, where, upon hearing the music of those cultures, he began to incorporate the syncopated rhythms of Latin music into his "serious" compositions. Much of Gottschalk's music was quite popular and was widely known and this is likely one of the ways these rhythmic devices eventually found their way into the rags of Scott Joplin (1868-1917) as well as the music of Ragtime pioneers James Reese Europe (1881-1919), Jelly Roll Morton (1890 c.-1941) and Will Marion Cook (1869-1944). Morton referred to the Latin rhythms in Ragtime as "the Spanish tinge." In an interview with Alan Lomax in 1938 for the Library of Congress, Morton offered this observation regarding the Spanish influence in his music:

> I heard a lot of Spanish tunes. I tried to play them in correct tempo, but I personally didn't believe they were perfected in the tempos. Now take the habanera "La Paloma," which I transformed in New Orleans style. You leave the left hand just the same. The difference comes in the right hand—in the syncopation, which gives it an entirely different color that really changes the color from red to blue. Now in one of my earliest tunes, "New Orleans Blues," you can notice the Spanish tinge.

Though the Gottschalk-Latin connection seems fairly obvious, certain musicologists debate the issue. Stearns doesn't give Gottschalk any mention in his book. Reid Badger, in his authoritative biography of James Reese Europe, barely mentions Gottschalk but references the fact that Gottschalk was probably the first American composer to compose a tango. Others see Gottschalk as a pivotal figure, including the preeminent Jazz pianist Dick Hyman, who, in his survey of Jazz pianists, cites Gottschalk as the precursor to Joplin and other Ragtime icons.

Novelist and film director Rupert Hughes wrote in *The Boston Musical Record* in 1899 that Ragtime was often derided by scholarly "serious musicians" for its unsophisticated vulgarity; but he nonetheless presciently opined that "none of these reproaches have ever succeeded against a vital musical idea," and that Ragtime "will be taken up and developed into a great dance-form to be handled with respect, not only by a learning body of Negro creators, but by the scholarly musicians of the whole world."

Will Marion Cook, who studied with the iconic Czech composer Antonín Dvořák and the brilliant Hungarian violinist Joseph Joachim, proclaimed, "There will one day come a black Beethoven, burned to the bone by the African sun." Joplin studied piano with German-born piano teacher Julius Weiss as a young boy growing up in Texarkana, Texas and would eventually compose dozens of Ragtime compositions, a ballet and two operas. His opera *Treemonisha* is considered one of his most important works, and according to his wife, Lottie, was somewhat autobiographical, especially with regard to the heroine Treemonisha and her advocacy of education as a means to earn respect and achieve stature in society.

The music of James Reese Europe would become the favorite music of dancers Vernon and Irene Castle—the Fred Astaire and Ginger Rogers of the early twentieth century—who inspired a major ballroom dance craze that swept through America at that time. James Reese Europe played the violin, mandolin and piano and became one of the most influential musicians in New York City prior to World War I. A highly regarded music director, arranger and a successful cabaret pianist, he was a key figure in developing black musical theater in the city, as well as the founder of the first black musicians union in the United States.

Dvořák taught at Jeannette Thurber's National Conservatory of Music in New York City from 1892 to 1895, and it was his contention that it would only be a matter of time before America would find a unique voice in the music world. It's likely that Dvořák envisioned an "American style" that was closer to the Central European model of symphonic composition but with influences of uniquely American music—gospel, African-American spirituals, Appalachian folk music and Ragtime. His intuition proved to be correct. Hughes, writing in *The Etude* magazine in 1920, echoed Dvořák's contention:

> American Ragtime or 'Jazz,' which is Ragtime raised to the Nth power, is scorned as fit only for the musical wastebasket. Naturally much that 'Jazz' has brought has been hopelessly cheap and artificial, but behind it all there is a germ of something very wonderful, which the composer with ears made in America will build into the master-music of tomorrow.

The prescience of Dvořák and Hughes was wholly justified, as Jazz evolved into a vital and uniquely American musical genre that would eventually find ardent enthusiasts in Europe, South America, Africa and Asia. The pioneers of Ragtime predated the great Delta and Chicago Blues musicians—John Lee Hooker, Robert Johnson, Muddy Waters, et al.—by a generation. Political columnist and Jazz historian Stanley Crouch avers that Jazz, which emphasizes spontaneous composition via improvisation, may be one of the highest art forms ever created.

African-American composer William Grant Still (1895-1978) wrote several symphonies that predated George Gershwin (1898-1937) in the use of Blues, Bazz and Ragtime elements in a symphonic guise. Born in Mississippi, Still studied violin as a young boy and would eventually receive a scholarship to attend the Oberlin Conservatory of Music in Ohio. His composition teachers included George Whitefield Chadwick and Edgard Varèse. Still's *First Symphony*, which he titled, "Afro-American," was composed in the late 1920s and is punctuated with elements derivative of early Jazz, Blues and spirituals (not to mention one thematic idea that likely influenced Gershwin's iconic song, *I Got Rhythm*). Still's first symphony received its world premiere by the Rochester Philharmonic in 1931, making it the first symphony composed by a black composer to be performed by a major American symphony orchestra in the United States. George Gershwin's music owes a great deal to Still's Classical-Jazz synthesis.

Commenting on his landmark composition Still stated, "I knew I wanted to write a symphony; I knew that it had to be an American work; and I wanted to demonstrate how the blues, so often considered a lowly expression, could be elevated to the highest musical level." Other African-American musicians were similarly interested in the idea of combining popular and Classical styles. Duke Ellington's forays into the realm of "composed Jazz" with works such as his symphonic Jazz suites *Black, Brown and Beige, Three Black Kings* and *The River* are among the finest early examples of the Classical-Jazz merge.* The Duke Ellington-Billy Strayhorn arrangement of Tchaikovsky's *Nutcracker* ballet remains a classic for its bold attempt to merge the genres of the European Classical style and Jazz.

Perhaps no American composer was as eclectic as the New England transcendentalist Charles Ives (1874-1954). Though his music found few advocates during his early years, Ives's polyglot style was revolutionary in many respects as it was a precursor to the innovations that more notable, twentieth-century European composers would be credited with developing. He was the classic "mad scientist" in that no style or influence was off-limits in his compositional palette — church music, hymns, patriotic marches, folk songs, European art music, polytonality, polyrhythms, quarter tones, tone clusters, aleatory elements, parlor ballads — were all fair game to Ives as source material. In retrospect it may not be farfetched to suggest that Ives may have been the Frank Zappa of his time. It could be said that Ives's eclecticism was emblematic of how American music is a pluralistic convergence of a multitude of genres and idioms.

The trend towards musical cross-fertilization has been even more prevalent in the current age of globalization and technology. This is also highly evident in twentieth-century "art music," as Western culture has undergone a transformation that few could have envisaged a century ago. This condition has led to a scenario in which, according

---

*. The three kings that Duke Ellington honored in his composition of the same name were Balthasar, the black king of the Maji, King Solomon in the Old Testament and Dr. Martin Luther King. Jr. I conducted Ellington's *Three Black Kings* suite at the Apollo Theater in a Black History Month concert with the New York City Symphony in 1990.

to ethnomusicologist Mark Slobin, "We are individual music cultures ... [coexisting in a] ... fascinating counterpoint of near and far, large and small, neighborhood and national, home and away." Some four decades earlier, Dr. Leonard B. Meyer referred to the condition in contemporary music as a "fluctuating stasis" in which a plethora of musical styles coexist in an increasingly diverse world.

> Our culture—cosmopolitan world culture—is, and will continue to be, diverse and pluralistic. A multiplicity of styles, techniques, and movements, ranging from the cautiously conservative to the rampantly experimental, will exist side by side: tonality and serialism, improvised and aleatoric music, as well as jazz with its many idioms, and popular music. ... Through paraphrase borrowing, style simulation, and modeling, past and present will, modifying one another, come together not only within culture, but within the oeuvre of a single artist and within a single work of art.

Meyer made this observation in 1967, and as prescient as he was, one wonders if he envisioned the dramatic impact of digital technology, through which sampling, synthesizing and sound modulation would become enormous factors in the cross-fertilization process. The result of this diversity and pluralism is that there no longer exists a singular, "triumphant" style in the realm of "classical" or serious art music, a condition that should not be considered either negative or undesirable. In the stylistic milieu that exists within the contemporary music sphere, it is worth noting that tonality remains a viable musical syntax and has never really gone out of fashion. Journalist and music critic Harold C. Schonberg observed that the first decade of the twentieth century witnessed "a series of convulsive changes in human thought": changes that were so radical and unprecedented that their impact and influence on the human condition was not fully comprehended for decades. The discoveries and innovative methodologies of Freud, Planck, Einstein, Kandinsky, Stravinsky, Varèse and Schoenberg were revolutionary in their effects on their respective disciplines—effects that continue to reverberate in our current age.

Of course, while Freud, Kandinsky and Schoenberg were busy in Europe, composers like Joplin, J. R. Europe, Cook, Ives and

Morton were doing their cross-fertilization thing in places like New Orleans, New England, Chicago and Harlem. The American spirit of ingenuity and creativity was producing a musical landscape that was as varied as it was innovative. The dark underbelly of American society, specifically racism, also played a significant role in the development of early American music. The normal career tracks that were readily available to white musicians, especially in Classical music, were not available to musicians of color. James Reese Europe, Will Cook and other non-white musicians had to find other ways to "make it" in the music business.

Cook formed the Southern Syncopated Orchestra and performed both Ragtime and concert music. In what is considered to be one of the first reviews of a Jazz concert, the notable Swiss conductor, Ernest Ansermet wrote of his high praise for one of Cook's players, who in his performance of the Blues "gave the idea of a style" that was "gripping, harsh, with a brusque and pitiless ending like that of Bach's second *Brandenburg Concerto*. I wish to set down the name of this artist of genius; as for myself, I shall never forget it—it is Sidney Bechet." Ansermet was equally impressed with the invention, richness and the "force of accent" that the musicians in Cook's orchestra displayed.

In 1910, the enterprising James Reese Europe organized the Clef Club, a society for African-Americans in the music industry. In 1912, the Clef Club made history when it presented a concert at Carnegie Hall for the benefit of the Colored Music Settlement School in New York City. The Clef Club Orchestra was the first Jazz ensemble to play at that esteemed venue. It is hard to overstate the social importance of the Carnegie Hall concert in the history of Jazz in the United States. It was twelve years before the Paul Whiteman and George Gershwin concert at Aeolian Hall and twenty-six years before Benny Goodman's famed concert at Carnegie Hall.

In the opinion of Jazz historian and composer Gunther Schuller, James Reese Europe "had stormed the bastion of the white establishment and made many members of New York's cultural elite aware of Negro music for the first time." Jazz legend Eubie Blake called Europe "the savior of Negro musicians in a class with Booker T. Washington and Martin Luther

King." The Clef Club's Carnegie Hall concert was particularly significant in that it demonstrated the power of art and music to assist in the process of overcoming the barriers of race and class. David Mannes — concertmaster of the New York Symphony Orchestra at the time, and director of the Music Settlement School, the concert's beneficiary — possessed a staunch belief in the idea that music was a universal language and as such could serve as a catalyst in bridging racial divides.

Mannes's view was echoed by the notable ethnomusicologist and civil rights activist Natalie Curtis Burlin — an in-law of Col. Robert Gould Shaw, who commanded the 54th Regiment of Massachusetts in the Civil War, the first regiment to enlist African-Americans. Burlin studied with pianist, Ferruccio Busoni in Europe, admired the operas of Richard Wagner and was greatly interested in the music of the Native American and African-American cultures. Burlin, who was influenced by her uncle, the noted transcendentalist journalist, George William Curtis, believed that "if anything can bring harmony from the present clashing of the two races during this difficult period of problems and adjustment, it might as well be the peace-giver, music." She was a firm advocate of the promotion of African-American music and the idea that this music could be a factor in promoting American cultural development and "the spirit of Democracy for which we fought in Europe." Despite this high-mindedness, ticket sales for the Clef Club concert were initially very slow, and it took an editorial in the *New York Evening Journal* just weeks before the concert to ensure a good response at the box office.

Notwithstanding the trepidation and anxiety surrounding the social implications of the occasion, the historic concert sold out and proved to be a great success as the interracial audience responded with "applause that became a tumult." David Mannes' vision had paid off, as the concert raised $5,000 for the Colored Music Settlement School. He remarked that, "a wedge in opening the public halls and theaters to colored people had been made." James Reese Europe assured Burlin that the concert would be a great success despite the orchestra's rather unusual instrumentation. He correctly predicted that once people experienced the "swing" of the music, "they'll eat it right up." Commenting on the orchestra's performance, Mannes stated the orchestra's playing was "very imposing and seductively rhythmic" and described Europe as "an amazingly inspiring conductor … always dominating this strange assemblage before him with quiet control." Based on the success of their initial concert, the Clef Club Orchestra retuned to Carnegie Hall for concerts in 1913 and 1914. J. R. Europe's commitment to the black musician in a society dominated by whites was one of his great contributions to the social betterment of American culture at large. He was quite vocal about this discrimination but did not allow bitterness or resentment to deter his efforts on behalf of his fellow musicians. As he stated:

> I have done my best to put a stop to this discrimination, but I have found that it is no use. The music world is controlled by a trust, and the negro must submit to its demands or fail to have his compositions produced. … I am not bitter about it. … It is, after all, but a slight portion of the price my race must pay in its at times almost hopeless fight for a place in the sun. Some day it will be different and justice will prevail.

After joining the army, Europe would eventually form a regimental military band that performed throughout France during World War I, bringing his syncopated rhythms to the "old world." His 369th Army Regiment, known as "the Harlem Hellfighters," served with distinction in "the Great War" and was revered for demonstrating uncommon valor and bravery in battle. His new band won the admiration of the French people, although regrettably, it never garnered the same praise and distinction in the United States. In battle Europe distinguished himself as a courageous leader. In music he was pioneer and "savior." His is not a name that comes to mind when discussing the origins of Jazz, yet he was a seminal figure in the birth of American music. The evolution of musical tradition in the United States has been shaped by the undeniable talent and diversity of all of America's people and we are certainly richer for that.

Another socially important aspect of American popular music is how it represents the life and times of "the common man." With the emergence of the middle class after the Industrial Revolution, the distinctions between "highbrow" and "lowbrow" musical expressions were mitigated by the increased democratization of American life. As social conditions changed, music—and people's response and expectations of it—also changed. Initially, popular music didn't receive the same critical analysis that Classical music did. It was, more or less, to be enjoyed in a way that was free from any intellectual or elitist gaze. Commenting on this condition, Roger Scruton observed that American popular music is "democratic and global … able to defeat any rival simply by its refusal to believe in rivalry, happily appropriating every sound that could be reissued as a song." Assimilation has been the American way.

The academic ideologues of the twentieth century who professed — with a decidedly determinist bent — that the tonal idiom of the past was irrelevant and could only result in producing kitsch and music dripping with a sanguine sentimentality, didn't fully understand that American culture was born of a spontaneity intrinsic to the American lifestyle. It's undeniable that Jazz and American popular culture are among America's most influential cultural exports. As Scruton asserted: "One conclusion to draw from the history of American popular music is that we should take the word 'popular' seriously. … This music was not imposed upon the American people by an unscrupulous 'culture industry,'" which was the neo-Marxist supposition of Theodor Adorno. As Scruton noted, "It arose 'by an invisible hand' from spontaneous music-making, with a large input from Afro-American music, both secular and religious."

As such, it was music very much *of the people, by the people and for the people*. This development caused some consternation among the intellectual class, whose tendency to promote the "sacralization" of high art as something of a higher or nobler cast, led to the practice of making distinctions between "highbrow" and "lowbrow" tastes in music. The spirit of the American Revolution was motivated by a desire for equality and democratic ideals, and as such, attitudes about art and music became more egalitarian as well. Scruton points out that this was due to the fact that American music was the product of common interests, and "it gets up the intellectual nose, precisely because it seems to leave no opening for the would-be 'priesthood.'" Intellectuals on the political left, those who typically advocate greater degrees of state control, "have never been able to accept that the spontaneous choices of ordinary people might be the *final explanation* of their social world."

The fact that popular music is given to "common sentiment" in the manner of the folk music of Europe or South America should not necessarily be taken as an indicator of "bad taste" or poor craftsmanship. Many composers of the American songbook possessed solid foundations in music theory and piano technique, as Harold Arlen's sublime use of harmonic invention in "Over the Rainbow" (all those heart-tugging chromatic voicings) or Barry Mann's clever use of sequential suspensions and resolutions in James Ingram's hit song "Just Once" (produced by Quincy Jones), attest.° Even though we don't make critical analysis of pop music in the manner we would of Classical compositions, it is clear that there have been many extraordinary songwriters and lyricists at work in the American music arena—individuals who possessed a great deal of musical knowledge and craft.

Still, many have derided popular music for its shallowness and for how Madison Avenue has used it to fetter consciousness in order to sell us everything from cars to fast food. One of the first serious critics of popular culture was Frankfurt School philosopher Theodor Adorno, whose concerns about the effects of "mass culture" date back to the 1940s. Scruton observed that Adorno's disdain for American popular culture was not solely about its artistic "banality," but also, and perhaps more salient, about his disdain for anything that promoted the idea of free-market capitalism. Music that dissuaded the public from considering the virtues of socialism was viewed as a mitigating factor in the historical inevitability of a socialist modality. Scruton notes:

> Adorno wanted to show that the freedoms seemingly enjoyed by the American people are illusory freedoms, and that the underlying cultural reality is one of enslavement—enslavement to the fetishes of the market and the consumer culture, which by placing appetite above long-term values lead to the loss of rational autonomy. Popular music was not, for Adorno, something that Americans had been liberated *to*, but something that they must be liberated *from*.

Debates regarding the value, or lack thereof regarding popular culture and music, have been raging since Plato first wrote about the effects

---

*. Quincy Jones was among many American musicians who studied in France with Nadia Boulanger who was considered the leading authority on Western music theory.

of music in *The Republic*. In recent decades these debates have taken on decidedly ideological underpinnings, reflecting the emerging attitudes of culture warriors, especially in the United States. Adorno and those of like mind viewed popular culture as an affront to their determinist ends precisely because of its commercial appeal and marketability. This, in turn, fostered the capitalist tendencies that the Frankfurt School neo-Marxists detested. That said, it's hard to argue that Mick Jagger and Keith Richards didn't strike some seriously resonant chords, metaphorically speaking, when they wrote their amazing song, "Sympathy for the Devil." Though John Lennon considered the Beatles' *Sgt. Pepper* album to be "the biggest load of shit we've ever done," it still ranks as one the most creative examples of pop culture ever produced, Paul Mc-Cartney's "granny music shit" which Lennon detested notwithstanding. Yet, it was the Beatles' imaginative attempt to create something daringly original that secured *Sgt. Pepper*'s place in the annals of popular music as a groundbreaking achievement. We shouldn't forget Lennon's declaration in his song "Revolution": "If you go carrying pictures of Chairman Mao/You ain't gonna make it with anyone anyhow."

In the prologue of his influential book *Highbrow/Lowbrow: The Emergence of Cultural Hierarchy in America*, Lawrence W. Levine recalls several instances in which his friends and colleagues took him to task for not making qualitative distinctions between American artists Buster Keaton and Norman Rockwell and their "more serious" European counterparts. In contemplating this all too familiar assessment regarding art and music—and our ongoing reverence for all things European when it comes to art—Levine cites *San Francisco Chronicle* columnist Gerald Nachman, who suggested that we "take for granted all things quintessentially American. I thought that we were over that but it's too ingrained; we're patriotic about everything but our art." As Levine, Scruton, Nachman and others have opined regarding American popular music, there is much to be patriotic and inspired about. In spite of its detractors, the legacy of American music and its creative pioneers remain vital and is worth celebrating.

Postscript

According to current multiculturalist views rooted in politically correct pieties, American patriotism is a form of supremacy that protects the status quo. Conversely, appreciating or assimilating cultures of "the other" is a mode of "cultural appropriation." European composers who were enamored with Jazz and incorporated certain aspects of the idiom into their compositions—Darius Milhaud, Paul Hindemith, Boris Blacher, Igor Stravinsky, Dmitri Shostakovich—would be accused of appropriation by the progressive leftists who view all things "white" or European as intrinsically racist.

I've composed music that merges Classical styles with Rock, Jazz, Reggae, Gospel, Folk music (oriental and occidental), and Hip-Hop. The artists working in these genres with whom I've collaborated—Black, Asian, Latino—did not recoil in horror over the idea of performing with a European-style symphony orchestra. They were all enthusiastic partners in the creative process. Many prominent artists of color have appeared with the Boston Pops orchestra and other symphonic ensembles. Jeri Lynne Johnson, founder of the Black Pearl Orchestra in Philadelphia, developed her ensemble with the intent to create opportunities for a diverse assemblage of musicians. If the Classical music tradition is so untoward, why have many musicians from Asia and Latin America pursued careers in this realm?

As Natalie Curtis Burlin said in the aftermath of the aforementioned Carnegie Hall concert in 1912, "If anything can bring harmony from the present clashing of the two races during this difficult period of problems and adjustment, it might as well be the peace-giver, music."

Recommended Recordings

Ellington: *Black, Brown and Beige Suite*, JoAnn Falletta, Buffalo Philharmonic
  Ellington: *Three Black Kings Suite*, Maurice Peress, American Composers Orchestra

Nyro: *Eli and the Thirteenth Confession*

Beatles: *Abby Road*

Davis: *Birth of the Cool*, Miles Davis, trumpet

Zappa: *Uncle Meat*

Morton: "Dead Man Blues," Jelly Roll Morton, *The Best of Ken Burns Jazz* (PBS)

Holiday: "Solitude," Billie Holiday, *The Best of Ken Burns Jazz* (PBS)

Brown: *Love, Power, Peace: Live at the Olympia, Paris, 1971*

Ives: Symphony No. 4, Christoph von Dohnányi, Cleveland Orchestra

Gottschalk: Selected Piano Works, Cecile Licad, pianist

Ruggles: *Sun-Treader*, Christoph von Dohnányi, Cleveland Orchestra

Dvořák: Symphony No. 9, Eugene Ormandy, London Symphony Orchestra

Joplin: *Treemonisha*, Gunther Schuller, conductor

Cook: Overture, *In Dahomey*, Rick Benjamin, conductor

Europe: *Castle Perfect Trot*, Rick Benjamin, conductor

Still: *African-American Symphony*, Neeme Järvi, Detroit Symphony Orchestra

Chadwick: Symphony No. 2, Neeme Järvi, Detroit Symphony Orchestra

Gershwin: *Porgy and Bess*, Simon Rattle, conductor

Stravinsky: *Petrushka*, Pierre Boulez, Cleveland Orchestra Milhaud: *La creation du monde*, Orchestre De 19 Soloistes

Schoenberg: Chamber Symphony No. 1, Orpheus Chamber Orchestra

Varèse: *Ameriques*, Christoph von Dohnányi, Cleveland Orchestra

Bernstein: *Prelude, Fugue and Riffs*, New York Philharmonic, Benny Goodman, clarinet

Sousa: Marches, Frederick Fennell, Eastman Wind Ensemble

Tchaikovsky-Ellington-Strayhorn: *The Nutcracker Suite*, The Duke Ellington Orchestra

Chopin: Preludes for Piano, Claudio Arrau, pianist

Koite: *Senegambia: Music for Kora* (Keytone Label)

Beatles: *Sgt. Pepper's Lonely Hearts Club Band*

Rolling Stones: *Beggars Banquet*

References

1   Harold Courlander, *Haiti Singing* (Chapel Hill, NC: The University of North Carolina Press, 1939), p. 5.

2   Alan Lomax, interview with Jelly Roll Morton, (Washington, D.C., Library of Congress), 1938.

3   Will Marion Cook, as cited by Maurice Peress, *Dvořák to Duke Ellington: A Conductor Explores America's Music and Its African-American Roots* (Oxford and New York: Oxford University Press, 2004), p. 153.

4 Rupert Hughes, *The Etude*, May 1920, as found in *American Quotations* (New York: Portland House, 1988), p. 391.

5. Lorenzo Candelaria and Daniel Kingman, *American Music: A Panorama* (Boston: Schirmer, Cengage Learning, 2004), p. 261.

6 Richard Taruskin, "Nationalism: Colonialism in Disguise?" *New York Times*, August 22, 2008.

7 Leonard B. Meyer, Music, the Arts, and Ideas: Patterns and Predictions in *Twentieth-Century Culture*, second edition (Chicago and London: University of Chicago Press, 1994), p. 317.

8 Harold C. Schonberg, *The Lives of the Great Composers* (New York and London: W. W. Norton & Co., 1981), p. 595.

9 Ernest Ansermet, as cited by William Benzon in *Beethoven's Anvil: Music in Mind and Culture* (New York: Basic Books, 2001), p. 248.

10 Gunther Schuller, *The Musical Worlds of Gunther Schuller* (New York: Da Capo Press, 1999), p. 37.

11 Vivian Perlis and Libby Van Cleve, *Composers' Voices from Ives to Ellington: An Oral History of American Music* (Yale University Press, 2005), p. 61.

12 Michelle Wick Patterson, Natalie Curtis Burlin: *A Life in Native and African American Music* (Board of Regents of the University of Nebraska, 2010), p. 308.

13 James Weldon Johnston, *Black Manhattan* (Cambridge, MA: Da Capo Press, 1991), p. 124.

14 David Mannes, *Music Is My Faith: An Autobiography* (W. W. Norton & Co., Wakeman Press, 2007), p. 219.

15 Reid Badger, *A Life in Ragtime: A Biography of James Reese Europe* (Oxford and New York: Oxford University Press, 1995), p. 67.

16 *Ibid.*

17 *Ibid.*, p. 121.

18 Roger Scruton, *Understanding Music: Philosophy and Interpretation* (London and New York: Continuum International Publishing Group, 2009), p. 216.

19 *Ibid.*

20 *Ibid.*, p. 217.

21 Roger Scruton, *The Soul of the World* (Princeton, NJ: Princeton University Press, 2014), p. 152.

22 Geoff Emerick and Howard Massey, *Here, There and Everywhere: My Life Recording the Music of the Beatles* (New York: Gotham Books, New York, 2006), p. 243.

23 Lawrence W. Levine, *Highbrow/Lowbrow: The Emergence of Cultural Hierarchy in America* (Harvard University Press, 1990), p. 2.

24 Patterson, *Natalie Curtis Burlin*, p. 308.

8

How Deep Is Your Love?

I think one's art goes as far and as deep as one's love goes.
I see no reason for painting but for that.[1]
Andrew Wyeth

Andrew Wyeth passed away today. He was 91.*
For those who view artistic creativity as an act of love, the iconic American artist's motivation for painting seems especially meaningful.

Wyeth's paintings made him one of the most popular American artists of the twentieth century. We can intuit that his popularity was linked to his realist style at a time when abstract expressionism ruled the art world. To the cultural elitists of the late twentieth century, being a "popular" artist often meant "selling out" to conservative, middle-class, bourgeoisie values and attitudes. To many in the art world this made Wyeth an anachronism—or worse. But many others enjoyed how his paintings made them *feel*, his traditionalist style notwithstanding. His critics found him to be merely "illustrative" and given to sentimentalist tendencies. This made him somewhat of a controversial figure in the art world, not because he was a practitioner of modernist techniques

---

* This essay was originally written on January 16, 2009 and expanded in 2020.

but because he eschewed them. Preferring to work in a more conventional mode, albeit in a highly individual style, he didn't aim to be a provocateur. The dismissive views of Wyeth and his art are not unlike those directed toward twentieth-century composers who shunned the atonal-serialist trends of post-World War II modernism in favor of more conventional idioms.

In reporting of his death, the *New York Times* observed, "Mr. Wyeth behaved contrary to the cliché of the bohemian artist. He was also a vocal patriot, which endeared him to some quarters during the Cold War and dovetailed with a general sense that his art evoked a mythic rural past embedded in the American psyche."[2] Wyeth's rural subject matter was a matter of some consternation among those who belonged to the modernist school of art and art criticism. Commenting on the populist aspects of Wyeth's work, former *New York Times* art critic Brian O'Doherty wrote in 1974:

> Modernist art is urban art. ... While it accepts the urban view of the landscape ... it will not accept the rural view, nor is it equipped to read it, or perceive in it anything more than clichés identified with forms of nationalism troubling to the liberal spirit. ... Thus Wyeth, the only genuine rural artist of the slightest consequence, is attacked with a violence far beyond the usual etiquette of critical disagreement.[3]

Writing for *National Review*, Jonah Goldberg makes a poignant point regarding the modern artist's penchant for creating art with the express intent of impressing other artists rather than pleasing the general public. Goldberg cites the realm of architecture as an example of this particular modernist predilection:

> The average intelligent person goes to the Louvre in France and marvels at the beauty of the 17th-century buildings. The average architecture critic yawns at the musty old antiques and gushes over I. M. Pei's glass pyramid. I don't hate the glass pyramid. ... But I don't go to Paris to see a structure that I could see at a relatively upscale suburban mall. ... Modern art caters to popular tastes just as little as architecture. A great deal of performance and installation art strikes most normal people as a colossal joke or a straight-up con. And please don't tell me that my failure to appreciate three squares and a triangle or a blob of paint on a canvas is my shortcoming. If something isn't aesthetically pleasing or interesting, or doesn't require skills I do not have,

and makes a stupid point stupidly, I don't appreciate it as art. That doesn't make me a philistine. It makes me a non-rube.[4]

Goldberg speaks for many art and music lovers for whom modern artists and art critics tend to dismiss as unsophisticated or naïve. That said, the criticism of Wyeth's work on ideological grounds is altogether confounding considering that at the time of the Great Depression many artists sympathized with the plight of the common man, especially those living in rural America who suffered severe economic hardship. A number of well-known artists of that era believed that socialism was a necessary antidote to the toxic aspects of capitalist greed. Charlie Chaplin, perhaps the most celebrated entertainer of his time, was enamored with the idea of socialism and the belief in economic fairness, and he often advocated socialist ideas. It would seem that Wyeth's paintings, which often celebrated the lives of those of humbler means, would resonate with the liberal ethos of fairness and egalitarianism. Alas, this was not the case. To those of the contemporary politically correct mindset, Wyeth's populism and patriotism seemed to be at odds with fairness, justice and the welfare of the masses.

Too often there is a perception that patriotism is the sole province of conservatives and as such should be derided as a manifestation of jingoism, colonialism and neo-conservative conquest. This is an unfortunate perspective and one that is not entirely accurate. Because all people and nations have flaws, one's love of country—not to mention one's spouse, children, friends and relatives—requires that we find it in our hearts to love that which is imperfect. We can certainly find defects in the American experience, but there is much good as well. Roger Scruton points out that in a "culture of repudiation" great things are difficult to build but easy to destroy. Striving toward betterment entails grappling with our deficiencies—individually and collectively—while resisting the temptation to destroy or dismantle what has provided so many with a better lot in life. Daniel Schwammenthal, former editorial page writer for *Wall Street Journal Europe*, notes: "History and evolutionary biology teach us that the normal course of human affairs is tribalism, oppression and poverty. The emergence of liberal democracies isn't the inevitable endpoint of supposedly linear Western progress but an aberration—and a rather fragile one at that."[5] With that in mind, we should heed Scruton's cautionary contention regarding "repudiation" and the destruction of that which has value.

Style

Wyeth's iconic painting *Christina's World* reflects the type of direct expression that is characterized by what the British *Times* art critic Rachel Campbell-Johnston called "a haunting realism." That realism was the result of a decidedly "less-is-more" approach in his paintings. Wyeth once remarked, "It's what you take out of a picture that counts. There's a residue. An invisible shadow."[6]

Another Wyeth painting, *Wind from the Sea* (1947) displays a level of craft and brilliance that confirms the impression that he was an immensely gifted artist. When I see that painting, I find myself in a state of wonderment. I find myself asking, "How did he do that?" The mystery of how he achieved the translucent effects in this painting is undoubtedly what creates the emotionally alluring aspect of much of his art. The "less-is-more" characteristic of Wyeth's style reminds me of Einstein's perspicacious assertion regarding the mysterious:

> The most beautiful emotion we can experience is the mysterious. It is the fundamental emotion that stands at the cradle of all true art and science. He to whom this emotion is a stranger, who can no longer wonder and stand rapt in awe, is as good as dead, a snuffed-out candle. To sense that behind anything that can be experienced there is something that our minds cannot grasp, whose beauty and sublimity reaches us only indirectly: this is religiousness. In this sense and in this sense only, I am a devoutly religious man.[7]

I confess that I knew little of Andrew Wyeth's views and perspectives about art, religion, politics and life, but his "love" comment immediately caught my attention, especially in the context of his attitudes about the Cold War. In my formative years as a musician in college, I was somewhat torn over the issues of Viet Nam and the Cold War. It wasn't difficult to be opposed to the Viet Nam War, or war in general, but having learned about the tyrannies perpetuated against artists in the Soviet Bloc—from the testimony of composers Dmitri Shostakovich and Sergei Prokofiev in particular—I understood that there was a fundamental hypocrisy in Marxist ideology. How could Joseph Stalin and the exponents of the "dictatorship of the proletariat" be so brutally inhumane to the very constituency they purported to be championing?

We can extrapolate that Wyeth may have come to a similar understanding of the scourge of Marxism and the designs of Soviet communism. His patriotic feelings vis-à-vis the Cold War could easily be attributed to the experience of witnessing the inhumane treatment of one's fellow man in the name of a reprehensible, godless ideology. The Cold War certainly affected me in that fashion. As much as I could identify with the liberal antiwar sentiment, I could also identify with the idea that there was a moral imperative to oppose communist tyranny.

In his book *The Rest Is Noise: Listening to the Twentieth Century*, Alex Ross describes the propagandistic Cultural and Scientific Conference for World Peace held at the Waldorf Astoria Hotel in New York in 1949. Shostakovich, perhaps Russia's most celebrated composer at the time, attended the conference as a cultural icon of the Soviet regime. At Stalin's prodding, Shostakovich delivered a highly anticipated speech in which he apologized for departing from populist themes in favor of the more formalized musical utterances that the Soviet cultural authorities found objectionable; themes that did not comport with party orthodoxy. Taking his cue from the Soviet authorities, Shostakovich criticized Arnold Schoenberg, Paul Hindemith and his countryman Igor Stravinsky, for their forays into formalist compositional methodologies.* However, as the conference proceeded, media attention was directed towards left-leaning American artists, including the notable composer Aaron Copland, who had been naively sympathetic to communist-socialist causes in the 1930s. As Ross notes, Copland often made statements that "showed lamentably little awareness of what life inside the Soviet Union was really like."[8]

Artists like Copland and Chaplin were careful to make the distinction between communism and fascism for fear of being associated with Hitler's rise to power in Germany. However, as Friedrich Hayek observed in *The Road to Serfdom*, there were more similarities than actual differences between the two ideologies, starting with fact that both had totalitarian intentions. Fascism may have been to the right of communism, but only by inches, not miles. As economist Bill Flax notes:

> In the Thirties, intellectuals smitten by progressivism considered limited, constitutional governance anachronistic. The Great Depression had apparently proven capitalism defunct. The remaining choice had narrowed

---

* Shostakovich's five thousand-word speech was delivered by an interpreter in the composer's presence at the Waldorf conference.

between communism and fascism. Hitler was about an inch to the right of Stalin.[9]

Individual liberties and pluralism were anathema to these totalitarian-utopian prescriptions and political dissent was not tolerated. Hayek cites British foreign correspondent F. A. Voigt, who covered politics in Europe in the 1930s. Voigt believed that there were scant differences between Hitler and Lenin and wrote, "Marxism has led to Fascism and National Socialism, because, in all essentials, it is Fascism and National Socialism."[10]

Pulitzer Prize-winning political journalist Walter Lippmann arrived at a similar conclusion regarding the diminution of freedom in centralized governments, stating that, "the generation to which we belong is now learning from experience what happens when men retreat from freedom to a coercive organization of their affairs. ... As the organized direction increases, the variety of ends must give way to uniformity."[11] Whether under Hitler or Lenin, human suffering increased exponentially because individual liberties and volition were thwarted. Uniformity of thought (groupthink) becomes the necessary modality for preservation in these political regimes and this results in a mindless obedience to the state. George Orwell foresaw this in his book *1984* when he wrote: "In fact there will be no thought, as we understand it now. Orthodoxy means not thinking – not needing to think. Orthodoxy is unconsciousness."[12]

Though Copland never joined a political party, he nevertheless openly supported Communist Party presidential candidate Earl Browder in 1936 and even composed what he called "my communist song," a little ditty titled "Into the Streets May First," based on a poem by Alfred Hayes.[13] Hayes's poem was an unabashed communist paean that included the lines:

> Out of the shops and factories,
> Up with the sickle and hammer,
> Comrades, these are our tools,
> A song and a banner!

Copland, like Chaplin and other artists of that time, shared the notion that a communist-socialist alternative to capitalism was in the best interests of "the common man." In the 1940s Copland composed the film score for the pro-Communist propaganda film *The North Star*. These overt flirtations with communism landed the composer in front of Senator Joseph McCarthy during one of his hearings on Un-American Activities in 1953. Moreover, a performance of his *Lincoln Portrait*, which was to be featured at Dwight Eisenhower's inaugural ceremony, was canceled due to the objections of some in Washington who were convinced that Copland was a communist sympathizer.

One can easily presume that Shostakovich must have been confounded by the American artistic community's dalliance with anything Marxist. Having experienced treachery under Stalin's iron fist firsthand, Shostakovich must have experienced serious cognitive dissonance given the fact that many American artists were naively enamored with the spurious fantasy of socialism. In his memoirs, which he dictated to Solomon Volkov,* Shostakovich expressed a deep suspicion of the West for not being morally outraged at the plight of all those who had been brutally oppressed in the name of communism.

When confronted with the predilection for communist tendencies among the American arts community, one wonders if Shostakovich didn't view artists of that era as being "useful idiots" for their advocacy of Soviet communism. Knowing all too well that the civil liberties afforded to artists in the United States would have been forcibly revoked by the authorities in Russia, it's no wonder that Shostakovich recoiled from such naïveté. Playwright Arthur Miller, who witnessed the composer's appearance in New York recalled, "God knows what he was thinking … what splits ran across his spirit."[14] Shostakovich's colleague, the émigré composer Nicolas Nabokov, who attended the conference in the hopes of exposing the lack of freedom of artists under Soviet rule, observed that Shostakovich "seemed like a trapped man, whose only wish was to be left alone, to the peace of his own art and to the tragic destiny to which he, like most of his countrymen, had been forced to resign himself."[15]

Shostakovich's life under the communist regime made him profoundly empathetic toward others who suffered under the yoke of totalitarianism. His late compositions, often dark and somber utterances, represented his way of honoring those who died and suffered under dictatorial circumstances. He would say:

---

* The veracity of Volkov's book has come under intense scrutiny. See the postscript at the end of this essay.

The majority of my symphonies are tombstones. Too many of our people died and were buried in places unknown to anyone, not even their relatives. It happened to many of my friends. Where do you put the tombstones for Meyerhold or Tukhachevsky? Only music can do that for them. I'm willing to write a composition for each of the victims, but that's impossible, and that's why I dedicate my music to them all.[16]

Richard Taruskin—who has written extensively on Russian composers, their music and the political realities in which they lived and worked—cautions against engaging in hagiography when assessing Shostakovich's alleged "martyrdom." Taruskin explains: "To see Shostakovich as a passive pawn in Stalin's clutches at the Waldorf does scant justice to a man whose collisions with power had taught him to play a complicated game with exceeding, self-concealing skill. ... No one makes a successful career anywhere without learning and executing an intricate social dance."[17] That might have been especially true in communist Russia, where being politically correct was literally a life-and-death proposition.*

It's not hard to fathom why Andrew Wyeth, or any altruistic soul, might have a disdain for the conditions that many artists suffered under in totalitarian regimes—and still do. Too often music and art became vehicles for propaganda under the Soviets, and the forced alignment with Marxism could have dire consequences As the utopian Marxist dream morphed into a ghastly nightmare, Hungarian composer György Ligeti stated, "So many people believed in this utopia, and then they were so completely disappointed—more than disappointed."[18] In retrospect, why American artists of that era were purblind to the tragic reality of Shostakovich's circumstances, as well as to those who were murdered by the brutal communist regime, continues to confound. This irony is one that I too find especially vexatious. Yes, war is bad, but the treachery of advancing any totalitarian rule by violating civil liberties and human dignity is equally reprehensible, perhaps more so. Being an advocate

---

* In a 1992 article for *Women's Review of Books* titled, "A Short History of the Term 'Political Correctness,'" MIT professor Ruth Perry notes that the term "politically correct" was initially coined by Leon Trotsky to refer favorably to those whose views remained in accord with the ever-shifting Bolshevik Party line. The term has also been attributed to Italian Marxist Antonio Gramsci and to Mao Zedong. It should be noted that the term was also in the lexicon of political speech in the United States in the eighteenth century, though in a different context.

for civil liberties and freedom is an important first step toward achieving peace and is a measure of our humanitarian concern for others.

Wyeth and Modernity

Apart from geopolitical and purely ideological concerns, another socio-logical drama was being played out in the later years of Wyeth's career. As noted previously, abstract expressionism in art and music were increasingly viewed as having little to do with traditional "American" middle-class values as "historical antecedents." Modern art, with its predilection for subjectless, nonrepresentational content—and the attendant snobbish or nihilist attitudes of the artists and appreciators of modernism—was seen as being anti-populist and elitist. This contributed to the so-called "cultural gap" between the art-ists and the masses, and as Lori Lyn Bogle observes, this engendered feelings among middle-class citizens that "esthetically they had not yet arrived after all—and, indeed, might never make it." As Bogel put it:

> The art of the abstract expressionists was also perceived as functionless when function was a quality that Americans had traditionally demanded in the visual arts. ... Unlike an Andrew Wyeth painting with its photographic rendering of each blade of grass, a Mark Rothko or a Jackson Pollock com-municated no evidence of hard work. And as one art critic has noted, respect for hard work amounts to an "esthetic prejudice" in America.[19]

Because many Americans considered nonrepresentational abstractionism in art to be degenerate and not at all in accord with American virtues and values, it was not uncommon to associate modern art with the subversive activities perpetrated by communist sympathizers and anti-capitalist revolu-tionaries during the Cold War era. Subscribing to the idea that the rationale for creativity meant that "the gesture on canvas was the gesture of liberation from Value—political, esthetic, moral,"[20] modern artists, perhaps unwittingly, were creating according to a decidedly Nietzschean perspective. Consequently, this was antipodal to the American psyche that valued hard work and the development of a sense of community and equality. Self-absorbed, bohemian individualism was not popularly viewed as the path to altruism and social harmony. It's also important to acknowledge that "meritocracy," the by-prod-uct of a serious work ethic, is now considered by the "woke" left to be an expression of white supremacy and privilege and a mode of either oppression or maintaining a racist status quo.

It would seem that artists ought to have a depth love for their fellow travelers in their life's journey. Wyeth's remarks about love, life and his art in the context of humanity's current dilemmas—in Asia, the Middle East, South America and beyond—remain especially relevant. His views on love and his vocation are reminiscent of those of another great artist, Vincent van Gogh who wrote, "But I think the best way to know God is to love many things,"[21] and,

> I believe people are wrong who think love prevents one from thinking clearly, for it is then that one thinks very clearly and is more active than before. There is the same difference in a person before and after he is in love as between an unlighted lamp and one that is burning. The lamp was there and it was a good lamp, but now it sheds light too, and that is its real function. And love makes one more calm about many things, and so one is more fit for one's work.[22]

For many artists, their creative endeavors are, in fact, expressions of love and a mode of spiritual fulfillment. Poet and playwright Julia Cameron opines: "Creativity is an experience … a spiritual experience. It does not matter which way you think of it: creativity leading to spirituality or spirituality leading to creativity."[23] Though Goethe averred that there is "no patriotic art,"[24] Andrew Wyeth's views about creativity remain highly instructive for those who believe in the importance of love as a motivating impulse for any artistic endeavor, especially when such endeavors pertain to the pursuit of a better society, nation or world. We might not identify this pursuit as being necessarily patriotic but rather as desirous of—and working toward—a more civil society and a culture of peace, something beyond national identity.

Postscript

The veracity of Solomon Volkov's assertions about Shostakovich's political views has come under intense scrutiny since the publication of his book *Testimony* in 1979. Questions regarding Volkov's book were initially raised in 1980 by musicologist Laurel E. Fay. She discovered passages in several of the chapters of Volkov's book that duplicated material almost verbatim from articles published as Shostakovich's between 1932 and 1974. This resulted in an acrimonious debate over Volkov's relationship with Shostakovich and the validity of the conversations upon which his book is based.

Supporters and detractors of Solomon have been engaged in less-than-scholarly invectives since, including Norman Lebrecht, who compared Fay "to a Holocaust revisionist."[25] Malcolm Hamrick Brown considered this a low blow by Lebrecht. Brown cites Shostakovich's daughter, Galina, who endorsed Volkov, saying, "I am an admirer of Volkov. ... There is nothing false in [*Testimony*]. ... It represents, fairly and accurately, Shostakovich's political views."[26] The composer's son, Maxim, however, offers a countervailing assessment, stating that he was far less convinced of Volkov's integrity. Brown's *A Shostakovich Casebook* chronicles the ongoing charges and countercharges in greater detail. Richard Taruskin cites Elizabeth Wilson's book *Shostakovich: A Life Remembered* (1994), which, according to Taruskin, "presents a great gabble of conflicting viewpoints from which we are invited to draw our own conclusions."[27] He points out that though Volkov's book has been discredited in the United States, it still holds great currency in Germany.

Recommended Recordings

Shostakovich: Symphony No. 5, Leonard Bernstein, New York Philharmonic (1959)

Shostakovich: Symphony No. 5, Yakov Kreizberg, Russian National Orchestra

Prokofiev: Piano Concerto No. 3, Martha Argerich, piano

Copland: *Lincoln Portrait*, Aaron Copland, conducting, Henry Fonda, narrator

Hindemith: Viola Sonatas, Christian Euler, viola, Paul Rivinius, piano

Schoenberg: Trio for Strings, Op. 45, Goeyvaerts String Trio

Stravinsky: *Requiem Canticles*, Robert Craft, Simon Joly Chorus, Philharmonia Orchestra

Endnotes

1   Richard Meryman, *Andrew Wyeth: A Secret Life* (New York: HarperCollins, 1996), p. 11.

2   Michael Kimmelman, "Andrew Wyeth, Painter, Dies at 91," *New York Times*, January 16, 2009, p. A1.

3   Meryman, *Wyeth: A Secret Life*, p. 424.

4   Jonah Goldberg, "Sports vs. Art," *National Review*, December 2, 2011, https://www.nationalreview.com/g-file/sports-vs-art-jonah-goldberg/.

5   Daniel Schwammenthal, "To America, From a Worried European Friend," *Wall Street Journal*, July 28, 2020.

6   Meryman, *Wyeth: A Secret Life,* p. 297.

7   Walter Isaacson, *Einstein: His Life and Universe* (New York: Simon & Schuster, 2007), p. 387.

8   Alex Ross, *The Rest Is Noise: Listening to the Twentieth Century* (New York: Farrar, Straus and Giroux, 2007), p. 406.

9   Bill Flax, "Obama, Hitler and Exposing the Biggest Lie in History," *Forbes*, September 1, 2011.

10   F. A. Voigt, *Unto Caesar* (New York: G. P. Putnam's Sons, 1938), p. 95.

11   Walter Lippmann, as cited by Friedrich Hayek, *The Road to Serfdom* (University of Chicago Press, 2007), pp. 79-80.

12   George Orwell, *1984* (Boston: Houghton Mifflin Harcourt, 1983), p. 50.

13   Ashley Pettis, "Mayday: Marching with a Song," *New Masses*, May 1, 1934, https://www.marxists.org/subject/mayday/articles/song.html.

14   Ross, *The Rest Is Noise*, p. 410.

15   Ibid.

16   Solomon Volkov, *Testimony: The Memoirs of Dmitri Shostakovich* (New York: Limelight Books, 1979), p. 156.

17   Richard Taruskin, "Was Shostakovich a Martyr? Or Is That Just Fiction?" *New York Times*, August 26, 2016.

18   Paul Griffiths, *György Ligeti* (London: Robson Press, 1983), p. 11.

19   Lori Lyn Bogle, *The Cold War: Cold War Culture and Society* (New York: Routledge, 2001), p. 300.

20   Harold Rosenberg, *Tradition of the New* (New York: Horizon Press, 1960), p. 30.

21   Irving Stone, *Dear Theo: The Autobiography of Vincent van Gogh* (New York: Penguin Group, 1937), p. 45.

22   Ibid., p. 183.

23   Julia Cameron, *The Artist's Way: A Spiritual Path to Higher Creativity* (New York: J. P. Tarcher, Penguin Group, 2002), p. 2.

24   George R. Marek, *Beethoven: Biography of a Genius* (New York: Funk & Wagnalls, 1969), p. 151.

25 Malcolm Hamrick Brown, *A Shostakovich Casebook* (Bloomington, IN: Indiana University Press, 2004), p. 314.

26 Ibid.

27 Taruskin, "Was Shostakovich a Martyr?"

9

The Folklore of "the Other"

Peace for Israel means security and that security must be a reality.
I solemnly pledge to do my utmost to uphold the fair name of the Jews,
because bigotry in any form is an affront to us all.
Dr. Martin Luther King, Jr.

Having traveled to Israel on numerous occasions since 2003, it's heart-breaking to see what is happening there yet again as the bombings and reprisals for such are plaguing the Holy Land.* There are many wonderful people being affected, and so many lives are being impacted by the ongoing impasse. The political and cultural bifurcation that one experiences in Jerusalem is highlighted when one travels into East Jerusalem and encounters the security wall: the drab, grey, graffiti-laced concrete structure that is both an eyesore and a heartache for those who live there.

The wall means different things to different people living in Israel. Ask a Palestinian about it and you'll get an earful of resentment about the historic injustices that have been perpetuated against the Palestinian people by the interloping "occupiers" who have displaced them and now run the country.

---

* This essay was written in 2009 and revised in 2012.

Ask an Israeli about the wall and you get a terse, sobering response: it saves lives. The seemingly intractable issue of sovereignty is never far from the hearts and minds of those who live in this otherwise beautiful and historic land.

In 2008 I met Kitty Cohen, director of The Folklore of the Other Institute, an interfaith organization in Israel that seeks to create conditions for understanding and respect for people of various faith traditions. Kitty has been working at this for over twenty years. She explained that in her early experiences of doing interfaith work she produced seminars and conferences but quickly realized that these types of events had little effect in ameliorating historical antagonisms. The polarizing aspects of religious and political convictions were far too ingrained to be resolved merely through dialogue. As she explained, dialogue often led to greater misunderstandings and created deeper chasms. She changed her focus to social action—service projects, music, art and sports. This change of focus toward project-based initiatives demonstrated that when people work together for a common cause, the barriers of religion, ethnicity and race disappear more rapidly and become subsidiary concerns.

Cohen was especially laudatory of Daniel Barenboim's work with the West–Eastern Divan Orchestra, an ensemble comprised of young instrumentalists from Israel, Egypt, Syria, Lebanon and Jordan. Maestro Barenboim and his orchestra have garnered major media attention for their efforts to promote understanding and reconciliation through music, including performing concerts in the West Bank. Dr. Bernard Sabella, a member of the Palestinian Legislative Council, wrote of Maestro Barenboim's initiative:

> I was impressed with his emphasis on music as a joiner of hearts and transformer of personality, even of inherited culture. I was also impressed with his belief that music can soften the unbridgeable political gulfs that separate peoples in conflict. ... But ... I felt sad in the heart as I was torn by the question of how could music and other forms of art and culture, even when shared by musicians and artists of the two sides of the political divide, overcome inherent inequities and injustice in systems of dominance and separation?[1]

Obviously, Dr. Sabella was not fully convinced that intercultural ventures such as the West–Eastern Divan Orchestra could transform the situation in Israel, and many share his skepticism. He went on to say, "The danger in 'peace music,' and I am sure that Barenboim is aware of this, is that it could become a complacent piece of the unjust system as represented by the political, social and economic status quo of the occupier–occupied."[2] This may well be a serious caveat, yet I would argue, as does Kitty Cohen, that any effort to foster understanding and respect is better than no effort at all.

There is a DVD of the Divan Orchestra's concert in Ramallah, where the ensemble was enthusiastically received. Regrettably, and somewhat predictably, there was an attempt to politicize the concert. Barenboim addressed the audience and appealed to their humanity by paraphrasing Dr. Martin Luther King, Jr., saying that any attempt at trying to get along and seek peaceful solutions is a far better option than "drawing knives."

It is interesting to note that Israelis hold Dr. King in very high regard and that Israel is one of several countries apart from the United States that honors Dr. King's birthday as a matter of national importance. (Canada and Japan also have observances.) In recent years the Israeli consulate in New York has produced concerts in Dr. King's honor, usually in conjunction with a prominent African-American church. I have attended several of these events, and in 2010 the annual concert took place at the Apollo Theater in Harlem and featured my dear friend and colleague David D'Or, one of Israel's preeminent vocal artists. After singing for Dr. Martin Luther King III at an interfaith conference in Tel Aviv in 2008, David was invited by Dr. King to appear at the 2009 commemorative concert in Harlem that was produced by Dr. King's Realizing the Dream Foundation, at which President Bill Clinton was the keynote speaker. The fact that many in the Jewish community marched with Dr. King during the Civil Rights Era obviously plays into this historic relationship.

Given Dr. King's views regarding Israel and his commitment to nonviolent solutions for peace and justice, it's worth noting his views regarding the conflicts faced by those who reside there. Writing for the *Israel National News*, Yonatan Sredni cites comments that Dr. King made regarding Israel just prior to his death.

> On March 25, 1968, less than two weeks before his tragic assassination, he spoke out with clarity and directness stating, "peace for Israel means security, and we must stand with all our might to protect its right to exist, its

territorial integrity. I see Israel as one of the great outposts of democracy in the world, and a marvelous example of what can be done, how desert land can be transformed into an oasis of brotherhood and democracy. Peace for Israel means security and that security must be a reality."[3]

On another occasion he said: "I solemnly pledge to do my utmost to uphold the fair name of the Jews—because bigotry in any form is an affront to us all."[4]

I attended the aforementioned interfaith conference in Tel Aviv in the spring of 2008, at which Dr. Martin Luther King III was the keynote speaker. His views that day echoed those of his father as he stated that courage in the face of brutal oppression is the first attribute needed in the attempt to fashion nonviolent solutions for peace. Participants from the various faith traditions who attended the conference were in accord with Dr. King's assertion, but I wondered who among them would exhibit the necessary courage to confront the enmity that has plagued the Holy Land for eons.

Music as Mediator

Maestro Barenboim explains that the name of the West-Eastern Divan Orchestra was derived from a collection of poems written between 1814 and 1819 by Johann Wolfgang von Goethe after the iconic essayist and writer was introduced to the Qur'an. Goethe was one of the first European intellectuals to take an interest in non-European cultures and studied Arabic late in his life. The fourteenth-century Persian poet Hafez had written a collection of poems, *Divan*, about the importance of understanding "the other" and Goethe was duly impressed with his writings on the subject. His own poems, compiled in the collection *West–Eastern Divan*, express his thoughts and attitudes regarding understanding "the other." "To merely tolerate," he would say, "is to insult; true liberalism means acceptance."[5] Obviously, there are certain issues and cultural practices that are not easily accepted by those of other cultural spheres. When impasses occur, alternative options to develop relational harmony must be implemented, and here is where the sacred application of music can be highly efficacious.

Some have argued—including Maestro Barenboim's controversial collaborator in the Divan Orchestra project, the Palestinian scholar Edward

Said—that one cannot fairly criticize any oppressed people unless one has experienced that people's suffering in the same manner or to the same degree. Though there may be some credibility in that supposition, we can ascertain that one would not necessarily have to live through any particular horror—be it the situation in Gaza, or the Holocaust, or living behind the Iron Curtain, or under the brutality of Mao's Cultural Revolution—to either empathize with or critique these situations from a purely humane perspective. For many, regardless of culture, justification of the use of terror is indefensible because terror violates the basic human right to life and creates conditions for moral equivocation. Our intuition tells us that this mode of recourse inherently inhumane. Moreover, most will agree that seeking paths to peace and understanding via art, sports and other mutually beneficial endeavors is better than warmongering. On the other hand, unilateral disarmament when your "brother" is both speaking and acting like he wants to kill you could be construed as being suicidal. Hence, we get security walls.

Maestro Barenboim concedes that there are limitations to what the Divan Orchestra can actually accomplish in the pursuit of peace. The orchestra has not been able to perform in several of the countries where its young musicians hail from, and as Barenboim observes, the orchestra has been both highly praised and heavily criticized. Still, he believes the effort of bringing these musicians together can, in his words, "create the conditions for understanding without which it is impossible even to speak of peace. It has the potential to awaken the curiosity of each individual to listen to the narrative of the other and to inspire the courage necessary to hear what one would prefer to block out."[6] Perhaps building bridges is the best one can hope for in this type of effort, but without a willingness to cross a bridge the journey toward peace remains an impossibility. Barenboim points out that the process of coming to a better and more enlightened understanding requires "sensitive talking and often painful listening,"[7] not to mention compassion and forgiveness.

When Israeli Prime Minister Yitzhak Rabin and PLO Chairman Yasser Arafat shook hands on the White House grounds at the conclusion of their peace talks in 1993, many Israelis wondered how their prime minister could offer his hand to someone who in their view had the blood of so many Jews on his. Rabin reminded his fellow Israelis that when attempting to make peace and reconcile historical resentments, you are not doing so with your historical

friend, but rather with your historical enemy. Forgiveness may in fact be conditional, but without these initial, conditional steps—in this case, a mutually
agreed upon set of principles as well as that historic handshake and a willingness to forgive and move forward—there could be no opportunity to move
toward reconciliation.

In my travels to Israel I have encountered choirs, bands and dance ensembles that were comprised of Christians, Muslims and Jews. At a large interfaith
rally for peace that I coproduced at Independence Park in downtown Jerusalem in 2003, the well-known Israeli band Gaya featured five accomplished
Jewish instrumentalists and two Arab rappers who fronted the band on several
songs and rapped for peace—in English! Music as a vehicle for change is a
concept that many artists in Israel consider to be paramount. David D'Or has
been using his music for interfaith and intercultural efforts in Israel for years.
He considers this a sacred calling and is always seeking opportunities to work
with "the other." The peace cantata that we composed together, *Halelu: Songs
of David*, is our contribution to the process of peacebuilding.*

At a conference of the American Symphony Orchestra League in 1988,
Leonard Bernstein shared his experiences from a recent trip to Israel and made
an impassioned plea for love to be at the heart of any attempt to ameliorate
historical antagonisms. In the aftermath of the assassination of President John
F. Kennedy, Bernstein also offered the following remarks in a speech given at a
United Jewish Appeal benefit event:

> It is obvious that the grievous nature of our loss is immensely aggra-
> vated by the element of violence involved in it. And where does this violence
> spring from? From ignorance and hatred—the exact antonyms of Learn-
> ing and Reason. Learning and Reason: those two words of John Kennedy's
> were not uttered in time to save his own life; but every man can pick them
> up where they fell, and make them part of himself, the seed of that ratio-
> nal intelligence without which our world can no longer survive. This must
> become the mission of every artist, of every Jew, and of every man of good-
> will: to insist, unflaggingly, at risk of becoming a repetitive bore, but to insist

---

* Excerpts of the *Halelu* cantata can be viewed on Youtube, e.g.: "Hope of All the Ages,"
https://www.youtube.com/watch?v=13yOUjk-vnI&ab_channel=nycsym.

on the achievement of a world in which the mind will have triumphed over violence.

We musicians, like everyone else, are numb with sorrow at this murder, and with rage at the senselessness of the crime. But this sorrow and rage will not inflame us to seek retribution; rather they will inflame our art. Our music will never again be quite the same. This will be our reply to violence: to make music more intensely, more beautifully, more devotedly than ever before.[8]

This is a credo of sorts, and one that resonates with many idealistic musicians. As mentioned previously, Dr. King instructed that the first attribute needed to accomplish any nonviolent approach to peace was courage. As musicians and artists we would do well to take the advice of Bernstein and Dr. King to heart with great alacrity and to be serious advocates of altruism in our creative endeavors.

As we consider the scenario facing Israel it is gratifying to know that folks like Daniel Barenboim, Kitty Cohen, Gaya, David D'Or and others are committed to using their talents and resources to promote peace, understanding and respect of "the other." No effort is too small or insignificant.

Peace, Shalom, Salaam Alaykum.[*]

Recommended Recordings

Barenboim: *Live in Ramallah*, West–Eastern Divan Orchestra (DVD)

Bernstein: Overture, "Fancy Free," *Candide,* New York Philharmonic

David D'Or: *In Concert with the Israel Philharmonic*

Eaton-D'Or: *Halelu: Songs of David*, David Eaton, Ra'anana Symphony Orchestra

Endnotes

1   Dr. Bernard Sabella, "If Music Be the Soul," *Een Ander Joods Geluid*, April 21, 2006.

2   Ibid.

3   Yonatan Sredni, "Thoughts for Martin Luther King Day," *Israel National News*, January 15, 2012, https://www.israelnationalnews.com/Articles/Article.

---

* To see more of the work being done to foster peace in the Middle East through the arts and music, visit the Facebook group, "Peace, Shalom, Salaam," https://www.facebook.com/Peace-Shalom-Salaam-117516891637338/.

aspx/11131.

4   Ibid.

5   Daniel Barenboim, *Music Quickens Time* (London and Brooklyn, NY: Verso, 2008), p. 60.

6   Ibid., p. 59.

7   Ibid., p. 103.

8   Leonard Bernstein, *Findings* (New York: Anchor Books, 1982), p. 220.

10

"David, forget the neo."

Whether one calls oneself conservative or revolutionary,
whether one composes in a conventional or progressive manner,
whether one tries to imitate old styles or is destined to express new ideas ...
one must be convinced of the infallibility of one's own fantasy
and one must believe in one's own inspiration.
Arnold Schoenberg

A number of years ago as I was contemplating various programming concepts for a concert season for the New York City Symphony, a colleague suggested that I consider the idea of featuring piano concertos by American composers. I thought this was an intriguing idea, and as I began the task of surveying the concertos of many gifted composers, I came across two fine works in the genre by Lee Hoiby (1926-2011). At the time, I was not at all familiar with Mr. Hoiby's work, but I discovered that he had studied composition with Gian Carlo Menotti and was a friend of the notable American composer Samuel Barber. Upon hearing a recording of his two concertos I decided to program the second concerto, composed in 1979, as part of the orchestra's concert season at Lincoln Center.

Having made my decision, I contacted Mr. Hoiby's publisher to inquire about obtaining the music and to my delight, I was informed that Mr. Hoiby would be willing to come to New York to be the soloist in what would be the New York premiere of his concerto. Prior to the rehearsals I traveled to Lee's residence in central New York to discuss the music, and as we spoke about his concerto, his relationships with Menotti and Barber, and his penchant for writing in a decidedly tonal and "romantic" style, I asked, "Lee, do you consider yourself a to be a neo-romantic? "He smiled and replied, "David, forget the neo."

Like many of us, Lee possessed an affinity for music steeped in the spirit of the romantic tradition of central Europe in the nineteenth century: music that speaks to the heart and mind and, as such, possesses the ability to speak to the totality of who we are. He obviously made a choice to compose in a romantic style at a time when it wasn't in vogue, but his having the talent and craft to convincingly do so made performing his music a wonderfully rich artistic experience. Lee considered composing to be analogous to archaeology:

> It requires patient digging, searching for the treasure … the ability to distinguish between a treasure and the rock next to it and recognizing when you're digging in the wrong place. The archaeologist takes a soft brush and brushes away a half-teaspoon at a time. Musically, that would be a few notes, or a chord. Sometimes the brushing reveals an especially lovely thing, buried there for so long.[1]

My encounter with Lee reminded me of the aforementioned remarks of Arnold Schoenberg (1874-1951) regarding the art of composition and the necessity of being "convinced of the infallibility of one's own fantasy," as well as believing in one's own inspiration.[2] Schoenberg's assertion seems inherently correct. Most artists would agree that being convinced in one's inspiration is the prerequisite for creating any meaningful work of art. This view comports with that of Aldous Huxley, who opined that all art must be sincere and that it's imperative for artists to be true to themselves as they go about their creative endeavors. The "rightness" of Schoenberg's view in this case, however, is completely at odds with the "wrongness" of many of his other views regarding music, art and aesthetics—views that influenced several generations of modern composers and, in the estimation of many, sent serious art music to the extreme margins of contemporary culture with seemingly no road to recovery in the second half of the twentieth century.

Schoenberg's forays into the realm of atonal serialism—with an assist from fellow Austrian Josef Hauer—at the outset of the twentieth century were predicated in large part on the post-romantic attitude that the public needed to be "cured of the delusion that the artist's aim is to create beauty."[3] This contra-romantic impulse was rooted in a scientific, materialist and non-metaphysical mindset that was derivative of the ideological premises of Marx and Nietzsche: premises that permeated philosophy, social commentary and art in the early part of the twentieth century and continue to have far-reaching effects in our contemporary culture. Schoenberg conceded that his atonal method of composing—known as 12-tone or "dodecaphonic" music—would have a difficult time finding enthusiastic adherents but he contended that with greater familiarity, music predicated on "the emancipation of dissonance" would eventually supplant the "tired clichés" of tonal, key-centered music. "My music is not lovely,"[4] he would say, but he nevertheless remained a serious advocate of this rather cold-hearted and decidedly un-romantic idiom.*

The Ethos of Modernity

In his collection of essays, *The Roots of Romanticism*, Isaiah Berlin points out that the notion of idealism that the Romantics celebrated in the late nineteenth century was not idealism in the philosophical sense but rather a contemporary and "ordinary" sense of the term, whereby "the state of mind of a man who is prepared to sacrifice a great deal for principles or for some conviction, ... who is prepared to go to the stake for some something which he believes" was to be admired and emulated.[5]

With this attitude as the underlying rationale of romanticism, the arts, especially musical composition, adopted a correlative mindset, or perhaps more precisely, a correlative "heart-set." Musical composition became much more than work commissioned for a specific occasion; rather the expression of

---

* Arnold Schoenberg's 12-tone method of composing is predicated on the idea that when creating a melody—or "tone row," as he termed it—none of the 12 pitches within the octave (A-A#-B-C-C#-D-D#-E-F-F#-G-G#) can be repeated until all the other pitches are utilized in the "row." This method is a decidedly human construct, in which no particular pitch is given supremacy over another pitch.

personal feelings and convictions became the sources of inspiration, resulting in the idea that "art is the expression of somebody, it is always a voice speaking." As Berlin notes, the romantic view of a work of art "is the voice of one man addressing himself to other men ... the expression of the attitude to life, conscious or unconscious, of its maker."[6]

The contra-romantic rationale that permeated art of the early twentieth century often resulted in works of extreme abstraction and indeterminacy. It goes without saying that certain types of music, or more accurately, musical syntaxes, are more pleasurable and communicative than others. This has a great deal to do with how "naturally" the mathematical properties of a given piece of music are organized and presented to the ear. As a result, the degree to which the organization of various musical materials embodies that which is "natural"—ontologically speaking—corresponds to the degree of pleasurable and emotional satisfaction in the listening experience. Conversely, complicated musical syntaxes that impart aural indeterminacy and sonic confusion often fail to move us and thus find little or no prevalence among larger segments of society. Allan Bloom proffered that whereas romanticism...

> ...was a competition for experiencing the most exalted and sublime states, its successor school [modernism] was a kind of auction in which the victor is the one who has the most terrible things to say about the human condition. Truth began to appear to be whatever was ugliest and most opposed to gentle hopes of love.[7]

According to the postmodernist, anti-essentialist ethos, attempts at creating or celebrating beauty as expressions of heart and transcendence were seen as being so much romantic "foolishness" and naiveté: in fact, a deception. The justification for the ugliness of twentieth-century art was that it was an expression or reflection of the ugly realities that engulf us. The revolutionary mindset of the avant-garde induced artists to view the ideals of the "old world" as impotent and no longer effectual in providing solutions to our seemingly intractable problems. This rationale fostered new ideas about art, thus embracing the new meant discarding the old. Former director of the Voice of America, Robert R. Reilly echoes Bloom's observation: "The source of much 'originality' in modern art has not been in creation, but in destruction: a process of taking away what has been given not only by tradition, but by Nature itself."[8]

Moreover, the unfortunate and disturbing ascendance of identity politics, neo-Marxism and social deconstructionism—thanks to Derrida, Foucault, Rorty, Adorno—vis-à-vis the "horrors of Western culture" resulted in art music that is valued primarily for its polemics and intellection rather than having an alluring aesthetic. Art historian Camille Paglia has been especially contemptuous of assessing art from a set of *a priori* abstractions that are predicated on politically correct multiculturalism masquerading as humane egalitarianism, while rejecting the social, political and cultural circumstances in which the art was created.

Yet in our contemporary culture, the spirit of romanticism seems to be alive and well in the realms of cinema, pop music, jazz and world music, as well as in certain schools of painting, sculpture, literature and art music of recent vintage. In the immediate aftermath of World War II, however, the romantic spirit as it pertained to musical composition tended to be considered anathema to progressivism. Hyper-intellectualism, born out of a deep-seated veneration for scientific discovery and experimentation remained stubbornly ensconced as the prevailing mindset—especially in the academy. That said, the realm of art music has been undergoing a metamorphosis over the past several decades, resulting in a far more diverse compositional landscape with no "triumphant" style ruling the day.

Since the human experience remains largely an experience of heart, emotion and spirituality, it stands to reason that those who compose music that reflects or embodies those facets of our being in significant measure, will find enthusiastic listeners. Conversely, the composer whose music eschews these attributes—often purposely so—will find far fewer adherents, and this in turn will foster the continuing marginalization of serious art music.

Most reasonably informed people will recognize names such as J. K. Rowling, Martin Scorsese, Stanley Kubrick, David Mamet, Steven Spielberg, Quincy Jones, Wynton Marsalis, Sting or Andrew Lloyd Webber—artists and producers of significant achievement in their respective fields. Wolfgang Rihm, Chen Yi, Sofia Gubaidulina, Kaija Saariaho, Thomas Adès, Melinda Wagner—do these names ring a bell? Not likely, yet these are among the most celebrated art music composers currently on the world stage and include Pulitzer Prize winners, a MacArthur Genius Grant awardee and a Charles Ives Living Award winner. Adès has been likened to a messianic savior of serious composition. So why does the music of these composers remain largely unknown to the public? A well-reasoned extrapolation would suggest that due to the prioritization of intellection and methodology over aesthetic concerns, their music does not speak to the passions of the human heart, nor to the spirituality of the human experience. Bereft of the aesthetic properties that stir our passions, their music doesn't relate to, and doesn't convey anything associated with, our heart and soul in meaningful ways; hence, it's largely ignored.

We understand that certain cosmological aspects of romanticism are in accord with the ancient concept of macrocosmic relatedness. Romantic art, musicologist Donald J. Grout contends, "aspires to transcend immediate times or occasions, to seize eternity, to reach back into the past and forward into the future, to range over the expanse of the world and outward through the cosmos."[9] Romanticism celebrates metaphor, ambiguity, suggestion, allusion and symbol. As a result, instrumental music—which was originally shunned by the early Christian Church—eventually became favored over music with text in the romantic era due to its "incomparable power of suggestion" and mystery. Richard Wagner considered the wordless utterances of the orchestra to be the vehicle best suited to conjure the atmospherics of primal and sub-conscious feelings. As contemporary vocalist and composer Meredith Monk put it: "Music, itself, is such an evocative medium. It's very openhearted. And I don't like the idea that people have to work through the screen of language … a screen in front of the emotion and the action. I like the idea of a direct communication that bypasses that step."[10]

In his Norton Lectures at Harvard, Leonard Bernstein averred, "in any sense that music can be considered a language … it is a totally metaphorical language."[11] Citing the etymology of the term "metaphor"—*meta* meaning "beyond," *pherein* meaning "carry"—Bernstein reminds us that music possesses the ability to carry us beyond the physical realm and into the inner realm of spirit and heart. It could be said that the invisible, vibratory world of instrumental music corresponds to the unseen, vibratory incorporeal realm that is associated with religious belief. The mysteriousness of that realm fascinates and many are intuitively drawn to it. Schopenhauer, who had many intriguing insights regarding the metaphysical aspects of music, believed that music stood alone, quite cut off from all the other arts. In it we do not recognize the copy or repetition of any Idea of existence in the world. Yet it is such a great and exceedingly noble art, its effect on the inmost nature of man so powerful, and it is so entirely and deeply understood by him in his inmost consciousness as a perfectly universal language, the distinctness of which surpasses even that of the perceptible world itself.[12]

The cultural attitudes of nineteenth-century romanticism regarding creativity, as Isaiah Berlin averred, were largely predicated on the idea that the stimulus of one's innermost feelings and moods—be they the result of joy, suffering, melancholy, pathos, desire, hope, love—were elemental to the creative process: an occurrence in which that stimulus, according to Wagner, "usurps his whole being at the hour of conception."[13] These feelings and moods engender the allegorical stuff of the myths, legends and fables of every culture. For the romantic composer they were a trove of inspirational source materials, that when expressed through one's craft and technique in efficacious ways, resulted in music representing a sublime balance of heart and emotion, the subjective, with syntax and form, the objective.

One wonders about the "fantasies" and "inspirations" of the more recent generations of composers who have tended to eschew "romantic" rationale at all costs. Of course, many modernists would claim that they are in touch with their inner spirituality, but they reason that the resources born of the diatonic syntax have been "exhausted" and that new paradigms of composition are both necessary and inevitable. Why, they ask, compose in ways that have been done before? In this context, innovation, experimentation and originality trump all other concerns—all the time! The past becomes useless and has no meaning. Popular music remains "popular" because it addresses the human desire for aesthetic beauty.

Speaking to the significance of the past, especially with regard to myth and the occult vis-à-vis scientific rationale, twentieth-century American composer George Rochberg makes the following observation regarding the hyper-intellectualization of modern thought and its disdain for past traditions and rationales:

Modern man may view with disdain his primitive forebears for propitiating the gods as a means of defense and protection against the unseen and unknown—but it is doubtful he would even be here to practice this disdain had his ancestors practiced the modern variety of science. Rationally it is probably not demonstrable that man has survived through fantasy, but intuitively one knows we are still here today only because of that faculty for the fantastic, only because of our innate passion for images, symbols, myths, metaphors.[14]

Rochberg's perspicacious commentary suggests that modernism's discarding of the spiritual and mystical in music, and its predilection for abstraction, intellection and formulaic processes, undermines what may be the intrinsic attribute of music; namely, the ability to move the human heart and thus to put us more closely in touch with our inner, spiritual selves. Even the atheistic Hitchens-Dawkins-Harris crowd doesn't argue the legitimacy of spiritual experience, though they would never acknowledge its connection to an invisible, omniscient and omnipotent "Supreme Being." Ironically, even Schoenberg would admit that the formulaic atonal syntax that he championed had significant deficiencies with regard to "moving" people in an emotional way due to its "unnatural" syntactical premises.

As mentioned previously, the underlying rationale behind modern composition of the post-World War II era was based on the ideas that tonality had exhausted its potentialities and that the philosophical tenets of romanticism no longer held intellectual honor. As such, the contra-tonal methodologies that were being developed by Schoenberg and his acolytes were seen, in a determinist manner, as being historically inevitable.

Twentieth-century Hungarian composer, György Ligeti found himself creatively incarcerated by the quasi-tyrannical and intolerant attitudes of the avant-garde. He considered this to be a highly distressing condition in which to carry out his creative work. He would say:

> When you are accepted in a club, without willing or without noticing you take over certain habits of what is in and what is out. Tonality was definitely out. To write melodies, even non-tonal melodies, was absolutely taboo. Periodic rhythm, pulsation, was taboo, not possible. Music has to be a priori. ... It worked when it was new, but it became stale. Now there is no taboo; everything is allowed. But one cannot simply go back to tonality, it's not the way. We must find a way of neither going back nor continuing the

avant-garde. I am in a prison: one wall is the avant-garde, the other wall is the past, and I want to escape.[15]

Ligeti, who grew up under a totalitarian regime in Eastern Europe, was highly allergic to controlling influences. He compared the situation within the compositional landscape of the late twentieth century to the conflict between Nazis and Communists. Citing the attitudes of modernist composers and academics, he observed, "True, there were no people being liquidated … but there was certainly character assassination."[16] Self-confessed cultural bully, Pierre Boulez could be especially nasty in hectoring those who didn't advocate or embrace the rationale and methodologies of "new music." Boulez, in an especially chilling manifesto titled "Schoenberg Is Dead"—published in 1952 when memories of Nazi perfidy were still fresh in the minds of many—went as far as to say: "Since the Viennese discoveries, any musician who has not experienced—I do not say understood, but truly experienced—the necessity of the dodecaphonic language is USELESS. For his entire work brings him up short of the needs of the time."[17]

Polemics aside, it's interesting to note Boulez's use of the term "discoveries." Was the emergence of Schoenberg's formulaic 12-tone system a de facto "discovery" in the manner of Pythagoras' elucidation of the mathematical properties of the overtone series, or Isaac Newton's explications of the laws of gravity, or Johannes Kepler's findings regarding planetary motion? There is a decidedly determinist bent to Boulez's claim that is analogous to Marx's idea that we are on an inevitable path to socialism—historical determinism—in that Schoenberg's system was seen as something that had to happen; a logical step in the evolution of musical syntax, something quintessentially "natural." But as Richard Taruskin notes, "Boulez's rhetorical model was the Communist journalism of his day,"[18] a model very much the by-product of the Marxist rationale promulgated by Theodor Adorno. The 12-tone method was a human construct *that may not have appeared* had Hauer or Schoenberg not made conscious efforts to create it. Calling it a "discovery" is simply untrue, but the term served to reinforce Boulez's determinist and supercilious attitudes regarding musical composition.

That which for eons had been the primary components of music—melody and rhythmic pulsation—was shunned by the modernists, and this obliterated what had been previously acknowledged as the most natural impulses of musical expression: namely, the human desire to sing and dance. Music that purposely avoids these two fundamentally human impulses in favor of intellectual formalism could be considered aberrant. Commenting on the preponderance of intellection in art music, British conductor Sir Colin Davis cites Austrian novelist Hermann Broch (1886-1951), whose trilogy of novels, *The Sleepwalkers*, is based on humankind's increased predilection for intellectualism. Davis avers:

> Broch analyzes the disintegration of Western values from the Middle Ages onward. After man abandoned the idea that his nature was in part divine, the logical mind assumed control and began to try to deduce the first principles of man's nature through rational analysis. The arts followed a similar course: each art turned in upon itself, and reduced itself further and further by logical analysis until today they have all just about analyzed themselves out of existence.[19]

From this perspective it would seem that we have become victims of the "paralysis of analysis," lost in the abyss of information overload in which our left brain all but obliterates our right brain. There is no integration. Spirituality and mystery, and perhaps most importantly, heart, have become subsidiary concerns to the modern artist and composer. That which reinforces our divinity is diminished; the romantic spirit dies.

It has been suggested that the advent of the compositional style known as Minimalism—with its penchant for perpetual patterning by way of omnipresent ostinatos and copious consonance—has ushered in a new era of accessibility. As a result, it is alleged that the resultant spirituality in this particular genre of art music is due to the purposeful avoidance of intervallic and harmonic dissonance. (The emancipation of consonance!) However, American composer John Adams, a leading exponent of early Minimalism, acknowledged that the overly and overtly static and jejune melodic and harmonic properties characteristic of the minimalist style often result in the creation of "grand prairies of non-event."[20] Though consonance is once again fashionable, it is the polar relationship of consonance and dissonance in music that yields the cathartic experiences that are highly evident in the tonal idiom. It is the ebb and flow of perceivable polar opposites in the tonal syntax that gives it its emotional properties. Composing in a way that avoids either consonance or dissonance, or conversely contains a preponderance of one or the other, often results in music that is rather soulless and decidedly non-romantic—music lacking emotional catharsis and a "heartistic" confluence between composer and listener. Still, Minimalism has provided an opening for music that speaks to the heart.

It's interesting to note that the renewed emphasis on "romanticism" in composition is not a new reality. In 1986, John Rockwell, citing the influence of Minimalism in relation to the "severe rationalism" and "the obsession with intellectual virtuosity" of mid-century modernism, observed:

> Tonal, emotional symphonic music lost fashionable favor for a couple of decades, at least in Germany and France and those American cities whose intellectuals paid heed to the latest European trends. But in Russia, Scandinavia, Britain and the outback of America, composers continued to write Romantic music, and now suddenly they find themselves in favor again. ... We should all—composers, critics, casual listeners and historians present and future—concentrate more on the actual music that has been and is being composed, and less on the polemics and justifications and well-meaning program notes that surround it.[21]

The so-called "new music" (all music is "new" at the time it is first created) composed by the mid-century modernists, music that willfully eschewed any aesthetic that might yield a sympathetic response from the public at large, spawned the decidedly unsocial subculture of professional creators whose music had little relevance outside of their insulated coterie. Increasingly, professional composers sought to impress other composers and, with the validation of their peers made grant-seeking their main priority. Yet, even within that professional subculture there has been a sobering realization that the stature of art music and those who compose it have little impact or influence in the world outside their small sphere of associates and colleagues. Taruskin notes that whether music was the result of highly formulaic processes or extemporaneous randomness, much "new music" was the progeny of "automatism," a rationale based on "the resolute elimination of the artist's ego or personality from the artistic product," a dehumanized goal of music and art "pushed to a hitherto unimaginable extremity."[22] Whereas Schoenberg sought to emancipate dissonance via formalism, John Cage was looking to emancipate noise via extemporal means.[23] Either way, indeterminacy was the consequence, and the general public generally recoiled from it.

I'm reminded of Dana Gioia's insightful essay on the condition of poets and poetry in the late twentieth century. As Gioia, former chairman of the National Endowment of the Arts, put it:

> Decades of public and private funding have created a large professional class for the production and reception of new poetry comprising legions of teachers, graduate students, editors, publishers, and administrators. Based mostly in universities, these groups have gradually become the primary audience for contemporary verse. Consequently, the energy of American poetry, which was once directed outward, is now increasingly focused inward. Reputations are made and rewards distributed within the poetry subculture. To adapt Russell Jacoby's definition of contemporary academic renown from The Last Intellectuals, a "famous" poet now means someone famous only to other poets. But there are enough poets to make that local fame relatively meaningful. Not long ago, "only poets read poetry" was meant as damning criticism. Now it is a proven marketing strategy.[24]

These concerns regarding the increasing irrelevance of poetry as articulated by Gioia are not unlike those in the arena of art music. The highly specialized and arcane methods of the post-Schoenberg Darmstadt* era failed to attract large enthusiastic audiences. What is indisputable is that the allure of tonal and quasi-tonal syntaxes remain ineluctable as evidenced by the emerging popularity of composers Eric Whitacre, Jennifer Higdon and Arvo Pärt. These composers, and others who value and comprehend the importance of the theoretical and aesthetic attributes of tonality, will possess the ability to address the "romantic" aspects of the human experience in profound fashion. Music that embodies and engenders these attributes, music that sings and dances—as Hoiby's does—will surely find sympathetic adherents and audiences because it's natural. It's human. As Schopenhauer suggested, it's the stuff of life itself.

Forget the neo—indeed!

---

* The Darmstadt International Summer Courses for New Music began in 1946 with the intention of re-establishing Germany as a locus for modern art music. For several decades after World War II, the Darmstadt courses attracted the most highly regarded composers in Europe, including Pierre Boulez, Luciano Berio, Luigi Nono, Hans Werner Henze and Karlheinz Stockhausen, as well as American modernists Elliott Carter and Milton Babbitt.

"David, forget the neo."

Recommended Recordings

Hoiby: Piano Concerto No. 2, Robert Stankovsky, piano

Menotti: *The Saint of Bleecker Street*, Richard Hickox, Spoleto Festival USA Orchestra

Barber: *Second Essay for Orchestra*, David Zinman, Baltimore Symphony

Yi: *Fengyang Song*, Nan H. Washburn, conducting

Rihm: String Quartets, Doelen Quartet

Saariaho: *Du Cristal*, Esa-Pekka Salonen, Los Angeles Philharmonic

Golijov: *Last Round*, Eric Jacobsen, The Knights

Gubaidulina: *Canticle of the Sun*, London Symphony Orchestra, London Voices

Schoenberg: Piano Concerto, Cleveland Orchestra, Mitsuko Uchida, piano

Ligeti: *Atmospheres*, Jonathan Nott, Berlin Philharmonic

Adams: *Shaker Loops*, Ridge String Quartet

Whitacre: *Lux Aurumque*, Schola Cantorum Reykjavík

Bernstein: Overture, *Candide*, Leonard Bernstein, New York Philharmonic

Rochberg: String Quartets, Concord String Quartet

Adès: *Living Toys*, Markus Stenz, London Sinfonietta

Boulez: Piano Sonatas, İdil Biret, piano

Higdon: Viola Concerto, Nashville Symphony Orchestra, Roberto Diaz, viola

Pärt: *Nunc dimittis*, Schola Cantorum Reykjavík

Wagner: Overtures & Preludes, James Levine, Metropolitan Opera Orchestra

Wagner, Melinda: Concerto for Flute, Strings and Percussion, Paul Lustig Dunkel, flute

Endnotes

1   Zachary Woolfe, "Lee Hoiby, 85; Composed Operas and Songs," *New York Times*, March 30, 2011, p. A24.

2   Arnold Schoenberg, *Style and Idea: Selected Writings of Arnold Schoenberg*, edited by Leonard Stein (Berkeley, CA: University of California Press, 1975), p. 218.

3   Joseph Henry Auner, *A Schoenberg Reader: Documents of a Life* (Yale University Press, 2003), p. 93.

4   Theodor W. Adorno, *Can One Live after Auschwitz?: A Philosophical Reader*, edited by Rolf Tiedemann (Stanford, CA: Stanford University Press, 2003), p. 371.

5   Isaiah Berlin, *The Roots of Romanticism*, edited by Henry Hardy (Princeton, NJ:

Princeton University Press, 1999), p. 9.

6   Ibid., p. 59.

7   Allan Bloom, *Love and Friendship* (New York: Simon and Schuster, 1993), p. 260.

8   Robert R. Reilly, "Reaching the Transcendent," *World & I Magazine,* January 1990.

9   Donald J. Grout, *A History of Western Music* (New York: W. W. Norton & Co., Inc., 1960), p. 493.

10 William Duckworth, *Talking Music: Conversations with John Cage, Philip Glass, Laurie Anderson, and Five Generations of American Experimental Composers* (New York: Da Capo, 1999), p. 359.

11 Leonard Bernstein, *The Unanswered Question: Six Talks at Harvard* (Cambridge, MA: Harvard University Press, 1976), p. 139.

12 Arthur Schopenhauer, *The World as Will and Idea, Vol. I,* translated by R. B. Haldane and J. Kemp, third edition (Boston: Ticknor and Company, 1888), p. 330.

13 Roger Scruton, *Understanding Music: Philosophy and Interpretation* (London and New York: Continuum International, 2009), p. 125.

14 George Rochberg, *The Aesthetics of Survival: A Composer's View of Twentieth-Century Music* (Ann Arbor, MI: University of Michigan Press, 1984), p. 141.

15 Alex Ross, *The Rest Is Noise: Listening to the Twentieth Century* (New York: Farrar, Straus and Giroux, 2007), p. 506.

16 Ibid., p. 508.

17 Pierre Boulez, *Stocktakings from an Apprenticeship,* translated by Stephen Walsh (Oxford: Clarendon Press, 1991), p. 113.

18 Richard Taruskin, *Music in the Late Twentieth Century* (Oxford and New York: Oxford University Press, 2010), p. 19.

19 Robert R. Reilly, "Musings on Minimalism," *World & I Magazine,* July 1989, pp. 179-180.

20 John Adams, *Harmonium,* liner notes, Telarc Recording, Cleveland, Ohio, 1995, CD 80365, (Liner notes).

21 John Rockwell, "A Century Hence, Our Music Won't Sound the Same," *New York Times,* January 12, 1986, p. H25.

22 Taruskin, *Music in the Late Twentieth Century,* p. 55.

23 Ibid., p. 56.

24 Dana Gioia, "Can Poetry Matter?" *The Atlantic,* May 1991.

Retro Is Cool

If a playwright, novelist or filmmaker fails so utterly to reach an audience,
we call it failure; why in music do we call it success?
Max Raimi

Retro is cool. Look at all those kids wearing Converse All Stars, the basket-ball shoes that predated Nike, Adidas and Reebok. I'm "old school," too. I love the music of the '60s—especially the 1760s and the 1860s!

A few years ago my two daughters and I were watching a documentary on the life and work of the famed Japanese animator Hayao Miyazaki. My girls are part of a legion of children who count Miyazaki's films among their favorites. According to my eldest daughter, Miyazaki is "very cool." I mentioned that Miyazaki's work was a bit "old school" when compared to the state-of-the-art, digitally animated films that are now being produced by Disney-Pixar and other digital animation production companies. My daughter responded, "Retro is cool, Dad."

The Miyazaki documentary featured a panel discussion that included several American animators who had traveled to Japan to visit Miyazaki and tour his production facilities. When asked why Miyazaki's films had such a broad international appeal, one of the Disney-Pixar animators stated without hesitation that it was because Miyazaki's work "expressed so much heart." I was struck by this response, because "heart" is a description one rarely encounters in critiques or reviews about contemporary art music. It certainly is a significant attribute in Miyazaki's films, one that makes them so endearing to so many. In the context of the contemporary art music scene, "heart" may be considered "retro," but it continues to be the attribute that we find so alluring in the music that continues to find favor with contemporary audiences.

In 2005 I attended a concert by the Cleveland Orchestra at Carnegie Hall, in which the ensemble performed *Four Seasons*, a new work by the contemporary Chinese composer Chen Yi. Chen is one of the most celebrated and most performed composers before the public today, with both a Pulitzer Prize and a Charles Ives Living Award to her credit.

In his review of the concert, *New York Times* music critic Bernard Holland described the music as consisting of "buzzing strings, rippling mallet percussions, nervous brass figures, big timpani and high-pitched wind chords,"[1] among other things. To be sure, Chen's *Four Seasons* is nothing like Vivaldi's much-beloved chestnut of the same name, since her music offers a deep, reverential bow to the compositional legacy of post–World War II modernists while attempting to juxtapose traditional Chinese stylistic elements in the same vein as her colleague, Tan Dun.

What Holland might have said was that Chen's new piece was akin to hundreds of other contemporary pieces composed in the international, indeterminate, atonal school that has dominated contemporary art music in the post–World War II era. In many ways the "new" techniques that Chen employs have become predictably routine—conventional anti-conventionality, so to speak. (Cluster chords, a preponderance of percussion, violins playing *glissando* tremolos—*sul ponticello*, of course!) Chen's *Four Seasons* was the prototypical contemporary utterance, displaying a facile command of technique and orchestral color, but with a deep bow to the aesthetics of mid-twentieth century modernism.

No doubt this is what Chen intended. Perhaps, along with a legion of other modern composers, Chen feels that music that "sings" or expresses "heart" is too passé, too anachronistic, too "romantic" and must be avoided at all costs—a disposition that is all too prevalent in modern art music. The fact that the music of early twentieth-century composers such as Benjamin

Britten, Samuel Barber, Béla Bartók, Aaron Copland, Dmitri Shostakovich and Sergei Prokofiev still finds far more favor with contemporary audiences than the music of modernists like Chen speaks to the innate human desire for music that actually "speaks" to us, or perhaps more appropriately, "sings" to us.

In his book *Why Classical Music Still Matters*, Fordham University music professor Lawrence Kramer asserts that a primary characteristic of modernism is "a principled hostility to all traditions, including the tradition of person-hood."[2] This is a characteristic that has become all too prevalent in much modern art music, in which identifiable melodies are basically nonexistent. A non-musician friend upon hearing music by contemporary composer Iannis Xenakis asked me, "Why is he so pissed off?" Well, one could say that there's a great deal in the world to be pissed off about, but my friend's comment is not unlike the attitude that many laypeople, even educated and cosmopolitan laypeople, have regarding atonal, athematic music born out of the aesthetic of the Second Viennese School. The atonal and abstract nature of this musical syntax often leaves people cold and uninvolved. The compositional rationale that emerged from the twentieth-century Viennese methodologies was decid-edly impersonal and predicated on mathematics and intellection, resulting in what Richard Taruskin aptly described as "algorithms produced [by] sound sequences that could not be parsed as relationships by a listening ear, only by an inquiring mind."[3] The stripping away of emotion, feelings and "expressive intention," all those human elements that Pierre Boulez referred to as "accu-mulated dirt," was an attempt by modernists to diminish "personhood" and ego in order to "find a way of composing that would stamp out the artist's puny person and allow something 'realer' to emerge. And what could be realer than number?"[4] This may be considered an oversimplification by some, but not by much.

Melody in the traditional sense, all but disappeared from most modern music in favor of coloristic and timbral concerns, textures, exotic orchestra-tion, pure sound, theoretical experimentation, formulaic conceptualization, algorithms and rhythmic complexity for complexity's sake. Melodies and motivic gestures were supplanted by "tone rows," "pitch sets" or "sound atoms" (Stockhausen's term). Kramer acknowledges the potential richness of these elements but argues very persuasively that "they remain a subplot," and that even in our postmodern world, "melodic drama more than held its own,"[5] just not in a great deal of new art music. The irony, if not hypocrisy, of the Darmstadt School modernists was that in their attempt to "democratize" pitch and "emancipate" dissonance in the quest of a new, universal and completely impersonal musical language, one that freed itself from the old, bourgeoisie mannerisms of romantic excesses, they created a new, elitist class of artists. Their fixation on technical skill and methodology—how music was made—rather than aesthetic or social concerns was rooted in the mindset that by being highly esoteric, this music could not be "commandeered for purposes of propaganda."[6] The resulting aesthetic was unambiguously antisocial. Theodor Adorno referred to serial methodology as the "dialectics of loneliness."* Serialism's trueness in trumping all other concerns and eschewing all "decorative elements," was geared toward "the negation of illusion and play ... a force which prohibits music from offering comforting consolation."[7] This was not intended to be music for the masses.

The past thirty years has seen a shift in compositional rationale as many composers have moved away from the crabbed mannerisms of total serialism and the dark, impersonal aspects of the Darmstadt reasoning. It's been suggested that the Minimalism of the 1980s—the music of Steve Reich, Philip Glass, John Adams—ushered in the "emancipation of consonance," and as a result, "accessibility" is no longer viewed as selling out to the conventions of the eighteenth and nineteenth centuries. Other "accessible" modes of composition are finding greater currency as well. As *Washington Post* music critic Anne Midgette observes, "Stylistic mélange alone is now taken as investing some measure of contemporaneity. What a few decades ago was slammed as lowbrow pastiche is today heralded as a visionary merging of disparate traditions (think Osvaldo Golijov)."[8] Golijov's music is infused with a variety of musical influences that demonstrate the "contemporaneity" that Midgette alluded to. Hardcore modernists may still consider the Golijov model "lowbrow pastiche," but audiences find his music engaging, for good reason.

The advent of electronic music in the early twentieth century was seen by some as a harbinger of the destruction of traditional orchestral music, yet

---

* Developed in the twentieth century, serialism is a method of composition predicated on a formulaic technique in which pitches, rhythms, dynamics or harmonic rhythms are used in fixed, mathematical sequences constructed by the composer. Arnold Schoenberg's 12-tone method is perhaps the best-known example of this style.

others viewed it merely as progress and the natural evolution of composition. Edgard Varèse, considered one of the forefathers of electronic music, opined that the initial reaction was an exaggeration, saying:

> Our new liberating medium—the electronic—is not meant to replace the old musical instruments, which composers, including myself, will continue to use. Electronics is an additive, not a destructive factor in the art and science of music. It is because new instruments have been constantly added to the old ones that Western music has such a rich and varied patrimony. ... Musical principles remain the same whether a composer writes for orchestra or tape.[9]

Though we might agree with Varèse regarding his claim that the medium of electronic sound production can be an "additive," his choice of musical materials demonstrates that he was an influential figure in the promulgation of the very non-traditional and non-hierarchical "musical principles" that sent melody to the hinterlands.

Taruskin skeptically views "the impulse to dehierarchize musical styles and genres, and the concomitant proliferation of eclectic practices" as the not-so-beneficial and not-so-healthy cultural trend that we now call "postmodernism." Citing the "punk-attired" Kronos Quartet, Taruskin reminds us that "the music biz stands ready as ever to co-opt anyone's success, and the academy stands ready as ever to turn today's counterculture into tomorrow's orthodoxy."[10] It's hard to argue with Taruskin's contentions, but should we be surprised about where our culture now stands?

In the epilogue of his book *Music, the Arts, and Ideas*, which was first published in 1967, University of Chicago musicologist Leonard B. Meyer, presciently asserted that at the turn of the century there would be tremendous diversity in composition as the advance of technology and globalism would give rise to a condition in which a multiplicity of musical styles and influences would coexist within art music, even within a single work.[11] The music of Tan Dun, Arvo Pärt, Einojuhani Rautavaara, Harrison Birtwistle, Wolfgang Rihm, Sofia Gubaidulina, Paul Moravec, Pierre Boulez, Kaija Saariaho and John Adams, to name but a few contemporary composers, attests to that diversity. No single "triumphant style" rules the compositional landscape the way tonality did for several hundred years or, for that matter, the way atonal serialism did for a good part of the latter half of the twentieth century.

Though none of the aforementioned composers' music will be confused with that of Brahms or Mahler, questions remain: Can lyrical music rooted in tonal principles of the "common practice" be viewed as relevant or important in a postmodern cultural environment? Will any such music be dismissed and disdained as being hopelessly outdated, without consideration of its emotive power or compositional integrity? Is the idea of "personhood" in music, vis-à-vis heart, and its great emotive vehicle—melody—irrelevant in art music? I ask these questions as a concerned musician who has witnessed the extreme marginalization of the music that represents, among other things, one of the crowning achievements of the human experience.

One of my recent compositions, the cantata *Halelu: Songs of David*—a collaborative effort with Israeli vocalist, David D'Or—has found a number of ardent admirers.* Several of them have in turn assisted in the production of the music as a DVD, a CD and several concerts—no small accomplishment in light of the considerable resources needed to mount such endeavors. Their admiration of *Halelu* can be directly attributed to the music's "heartistic" attributes—attributes that are the result of utilizing a tonal syntax and the melodic richness of the music. In a conversation that we had as we worked on the piece, David and I wondered what critiques might be levied at *Halelu* in light of its unabashedly romantic expression. To be sure, this is "old school retro" music, music that is aesthetically closer to that of Brahms and Britten than Boulez or Birtwistle. I anticipated that the music would in all likelihood, be viewed by the music press and other "serious composers" as being dated, sanguine, unoriginal, anachronistic, treacly, cliché, kitsch or "lowbrow pastiche." David didn't care. Neither did I.

What was important to us was creating something of artistic integrity that people actually would want to listen to—music that would speak to the condition of "personhood." We didn't want to be like the proverbial orator who has an important message to convey but uses a language so arcane, complex and

---

* You can find videos of the Belgrade performances of the *Halelu* cantata on Youtube: "The Hope of All Ages," https://www.youtube.com/watch?v=13yOUjk-vnI&ab_channel=nycsym, and "All Holy Children Sing," https://www.youtube.com/watch?v=-zKZwgLKmyI&ab_channel=nycsym.

specialized that cognition and communication are all but impossible. After all, the emotive power of art is what most people find appealing about it. In a very significant way this remains art's *raison d'être.*

Recall the controversy surrounding the Pulitzer Prize for Music being awarded in 1992 to Wayne Peterson for his composition *The Face of the Night, the Heart of the Dark.* In an unprecedented editorial action, the governing board of the Pulitzer committee rejected the choice of the Pulitzer music panel, Ralph Shapey's *Concerto Fantastique,* and instead awarded Peterson the prize. The reason given for the override was that the Pulitzer's governing body felt that Peterson's music was more "accessible" than Shapey's. Of course, the music panel rankled over the interference of individuals who lacked compositional expertise for making this kind of subjective assessment, and such a parochial one at that. Disenchantment with the Pulitzer Prize Board was expressed in the music press in nearly every quarter, especially in the *New York Times* as exemplified by Edward Rothstein:

> One board member, Walter Rugaber, publisher of The Roanoke Times and World News, countered, saying that the board should take into account "the layman's or consumer's point of view." Since these compositions will be performed for a public, he continued, "it is not inappropriate for people who are not professional musicians, composers or performers to listen to the best that the professionals recommend, and to express an opinion that one is more interesting than the other."
>
> This comment invokes the rift that has haunted music in this century between the disgruntled public, often unhappy with new works, and composers who are seen to award grants to one another with utter disregard for unwashed nonprofessionals. The Peterson work was used to assert listeners' rights in this battle.[12]

In the aftermath of that infamous override, Max Raimi, a member of the Chicago Symphony Orchestra, the ensemble that performed the world premiere of Shapey's composition, sent a letter to the editor of the *New York Times* concerning the Pulitzer fuss. Speaking to the issue of "listeners' rights," Raimi remarked that in his tenure with the CSO he had never witnessed such a negative reaction to a new musical work and offered the following response to Rothstein:

Consider three 1991 Pulitzer Prize winners: Neil Simon, John Updike and Shulamit Ran. Any well-educated American might reasonably be expected to have some opinion of the work of the first two. But if you ask several hundred random college graduates for an opinion on the music of Shulamit Ran and one of them comes up with an answer, I suggest you immediately buy a lottery ticket while your luck holds. (I mean no disrespect to Ms. Ran; substitute just about any recent music Pulitzer winner.)

I wish Mr. Rothstein could have joined me on stage for the premiere of Mr. Shapey's Concerto Fantastique and looked out at the faces of the audience. It was a scene of suffering out of Dante. After each movement there was an exodus from the hall unprecedented in my experience. The listeners were not provoked or challenged—this was no Sacre du Printemps. They were merely enduring a prison sentence.[13]

Raimi may have been guilty of some hyperbole here, but he then put forth what I believe to be a most perspicacious query regarding the Pulitzer flap and the condition of modern art music: "If a playwright, novelist or filmmaker fails so utterly to reach an audience, we call it failure; why in music do we call it success?"[14] Why, indeed? A follow-up question might be: why, for the better part of two generations, did we continue to present prestigious awards and large commissions to composers of Shapey's ilk, knowing that we'd likely get more of the same? For some, Raimi's question may be seen as philistinism run amok, but Raimi is a professional working in a major symphony orchestra, he's not some uniformed rube.

Dutch composer John Borstlap observes that when major symphony orchestras program "new music" that is the progeny of a compositional syntax with little or no aesthetic appeal, it is mostly "the result of an isolated feeling of obligation, mixed with a bit of heroic image making—fighting for the new."[15] This is characterized as being courageous and progressive, without much thought given to performers or the audience. Too often in the post-World War II era, ideology-based determinism dictated the compositional rationale of modern art music in a specious deference to the academy. In effect, the mid-century modernists turned their backs on the concert-going public. Should "the rights of listeners" be a factor in this scenario?

Theodor Adorno's assertion that in the hands of talented composers the expressive power of atonal music can be as effective as tonal music remains unconvincing. Swiss conductor Ernest Ansermet regarded atonal music as having limitations in its expressive-emotive abilities due to what he referred to as its "faulty aesthetic." If the contention is true that history has a way of sorting itself out in terms of what is relevant in artistic style, we can now ascertain that Ansermet's claim may have been correct, as the music of most atonal composers gets relatively few performances and is shunned by the greater concert-going public. Obviously, composers must be "true to themselves" and avoid overt "pandering" to public tastes, but those who remain obdurate in their attitudes regarding "listeners" will likely be ignored.*

In the case of *Halelu*, David D'Or created melodies of great lyricism and passion, music through which a "heartistic" communication with audiences can easily be achieved. As a singer whose musical roots are steeped in Western classical tradition, Middle Eastern and North African folk music, liturgical music and popular song, David's musical ideas reflect the stylistic diversity that Meyer alluded to. In this respect, the sincerity of David's expression trumps formal or syntactic concerns, and this seems to be the starting point of any meaningful artistic endeavor. Arnold Schoenberg's assertions regarding the importance of being "convinced of the infallibility of one's own fantasy and ... one's own inspiration" seems especially relevant.[16]

When I first heard David's thematic ideas for *Halelu*, I was immediately captivated by the melodic richness of his music. It would have been an artistic incongruity for me as his collaborator to utilize anything but a syntax that was rooted in tonality in developing this music. David's melodic ideas echoed those of nineteenth-century European tradition as well as traditional Hebrew song. It seemed very natural to work in the style of these traditions, and the decision to utilize a tonal framework allowed me to work in accord with my own "fantasy." And this particular fantasy is one that continues to speak to humanity in powerful ways.

Kramer's assertions regarding what he refers to as "the fate of melody," in the context of our cultural patrimony, seems inherently correct. The musical traditions that continue to speak to our humanity remain viable precisely

---

* As of this writing (November 2021), recordings of the aforementioned works of Ralph Shapey and Chen Yi do not seem to be commercially available. Wayne Peterson's Pulitzer Prize-winning composition, *The Face of the Night, the Heart of the Dark*, has recently been recorded by the Boston Modern Orchestra Project, some thirty years after its premiere.

because they allow for significant degrees of emotional expression and communication to occur. Melody seems directly related to the "fantasies" of those on the other end of the musical spectrum—the listeners. Diversity in musical composition is now the norm; therefore, employing the tonal syntax as a means to express or convey "heart" in music is just one part of a pluralistic musical milieu.

To look at it another way: tonality is "retro" and "retro" is cool. At least that's what my daughters keep telling me.

Recommended Recordings

Chen: Concerto for Percussion, Lan Shui, Singapore Symphony Orchestra

Vivaldi: *The Four Seasons*, Fabio Biondi, Europa Galante

Varèse: *Déserts*, Pierre Boulez, Chicago Symphony Orchestra

Britten: *Simple Symphony*, Sir Neville Marriner, Academy of St. Martin in the Fields

Barber: Violin Concerto, Gil Shaham, violin

Bartók: *The Miraculous Mandarin*, Jean Martinon, Chicago Symphony Orchestra

Copland: *El Salon Mexico*, Leonard Bernstein, New York Philharmonic

Shostakovich: Symphony No. 11, Leopold Stokowski, Houston Symphony Orchestra

Prokofiev: *Alexander Nevsky Cantata*, Neeme Järvi, Royal Scottish National Orchestra

Reich: *New York Counterpoint*, Alain Damiens, clarinet, Franck Rossi, electronics

Glass: Violin Concerto, Christoph von Dohnányi, Vienna Philharmonic

Adams: *Fearful Symmetries*, John Adams, Orchestra of St. Luke's

Moravec: *Tempest Fantasy*, Trio Solisti

Golijov: *Oceana*, Robert Spano, Atlanta Symphony Orchestra and Chorus

Pärt: *Tabula Rasa*, Gidon Kremer, Lithuanian Chamber Orchestra

Rautavaara: *Angels and Visitations*, Leif Segerstam, Helsinki Philharmonic

Xenakis: *Phlegra*, Pierre Boulez, Paris Orchestra Ensemble InterContemporain

Rihm: *Dithyrambe*, Jonathan Nott, Arditti Quartet

Saariaho: *Graal Théâtre*, Esa-Pekka Salonen, BBC Symphony Orchestra

Brahms: *Haydn Variations*, George Szell, Cleveland Orchestra

Mahler: Symphony No. 8, Eliahu Inbal, Frankfurt Radio Symphony

Gubaidulina: *Offertorium*, Charles Dutoit, Gidon Kremer, Boston Symphony Orchestra

Shapey: *Three for Six*, Robert Black, New York New Music Ensemble

Rimsky-Korsakov: *Scheherazade*, Ernest Ansermet, Suisse Romande Orchestra

Schoenberg: Five Pieces for Orchestra, James Levine, Berlin Philharmonic

Martynov: *Schubert–Quintet (Unfinished)*, Kronos Quartet

Peterson: *The Face of the Night, the Heart of the Dark.*, Boston Modern Orchestra Project

D'Or-Eaton: *Halelu: Songs of David*, David Eaton, Ra'anana Symphony, Philharmonia Chorus of Israel

Endnotes

1   Bernard Holland, "Familiar Brahms and an Unaccustomed *Four Seasons*," Classical Music Review, *New York Times,* October 19, 2005.

2   Lawrence Kramer, *Why Classical Music Still Matters* (Berkeley and Los Angeles, CA: University of California Press, Ltd., 2007), p. 69.

3   Richard Taruskin, *Music in the Late Twentieth Century* (Oxford-New York: Oxford University Press, 2010), p. 39.

4   Ibid., p. 43.

5   Kramer, *Why Classical Music Still Matters*, p. 70.

6   Taruskin, *Music in the Late Twentieth Century*, p. 17.

7   Theodor Adorno, *Philosophy of Modern Music* (London-New York: Continuum, 2007), p. 29.

8   Anne Midgette, "When Opera is New and Unproved," *Washington Post*, September 7, 2008.

9   Edgard Varèse, as cited by Elliott Schwartz, Barney Childs, and Jim Fox, *Contemporary Composers on Contemporary Music* (New York: Da Capo Press, 2009), p. 202.

10   Richard Taruskin, *The Dangers of Music and Other Anti-Utopian Essays* (Berkeley and Los Angeles, CA: University of California Press, 2009), pp. 13-14.

11   Leonard B. Meyer, *Music, the Arts, and Ideas*, second edition (Chicago and London: University of Chicago Press, 1994), p. 317.

12   Edward Rothstein, "In the Fracas Over a Prize, No One Won," Classical View, *New York Times*, April 19, 1992.

13   Max Raimi, letter to the editor, "Who's Listening?" *New York Times*, May 10, 1992.

14   Ibid.

15   John Borstlap, *The Classical Revolution: Thoughts on New Music in the 21ˢᵗ Century*,

revised edition (Lanham, MD: Scarecrow Press, Inc., 2017), p. 5.

16 Arnold Schoenberg, *Style and Idea: Selected Writings of Arnold Schoenberg*, edited by Leonard Stein (Berkeley, CA: University of California Press, 1975), p. 218.

Arts in the Aftermath of 9/11

*Our notions of profit and value could be adjusted to allow for a greater
degree of artistic questioning without an implication that such actions would
automatically have adverse economic consequences.
Artists could hold themselves to a higher standard of honesty.*
Paul Simon

As Americans continue the long recovery from the shock and anguish caused by the terror attacks of September 11, 2001, many questions linger in the haze of that ill-fated day. In the aftermath of 9/11 book sales about Islam and the Qur'an skyrocketed as Americans sought answers and insights in their attempts to make sense of the heinous acts that changed their lives in unthinkable ways.* A question that many Americans were asking was, "Why do they hate us?" Though that question may have faded from our national consciousness it remains a question in need of answers.

---

* This essay was originally written in 2003. In 2011 I had the opportunity to conduct the New York City Symphony at the United Nations as part of the U.N.'s commemorative program for the tenth anniversary of 9/11. I edited and expanded this essay after that concert and again in 2015 after I conducted another concert at the United Nations for the U.N.'s 70th anniversary celebration.

As we learned more about Islam and the various resentments that many in the Arab world directed toward the West, it became apparent that a serious point of contention among Muslims—fundamentalists and moderates—was the pervasive influence of Western popular culture in the Muslim world. This resulted in a spate of collective soul-searching as the motivations of artists, producers and production entities were called into question in ways that had rarely been experienced previously. Weighed against American foreign policy vis-à-vis Israel, or other Western economic or geopolitical influences, it is difficult to ascertain the degree to which Western cultural and artistic endeavors prompted the resentments that motivated the planners, and celebrators, of the 9/11 attacks. Yet it cannot be denied that the influence of certain cultural expressions produced by our commercially oriented and highly secularized entertainment industry have contributed to the antagonism that Arab Muslims feel toward the West in general and the United States in particular.

In his 1951 tome *Milestones*, the Muslim Egyptian scholar Sayyid Qutb wrote extensively about what he viewed to be the hypocrisies of Western Christian culture, especially with regard to racism and sexual immoderation.* Qutb's indictments of the West, especially the secularization, immorality and its "pagan ignorance and rebellion against God," became a primary source behind a great deal of radical Islamic resentment. In *Milestones* he wrote:

> Mankind today is on the brink of an abyss, not because of the danger of complete annihilation which is hanging over its head ... because humanity is devoid of those vital values which are necessary not only for its healthy development but also for its real progress. Even the Western world realizes that Western civilization is unable to present any healthy values for the guidance of mankind. It knows that it does not possess anything which will satisfy its own conscience and justify its existence. ... Islam is the only system which possesses these values and this way of life.[1]

Furthermore:

---

* Sayyid Ibrahim Husayn Shadhili Qutb was perhaps the most prominent Muslim activist in Egypt in the post-World War II era. He was also the most well-known member of the Muslim Brotherhood. He was executed in 1966 by Gamal Abdel Nasser's regime after he was implicated in a failed assassination attempt against Nasser.

The Islamic civilization can take various forms in its material and organizational structure, but the principles and values on which it is based
are eternal and unchangeable. These are: the worship of God alone, the
foundation of human relationships on the belief in the Unity of God, the
supremacy of the humanity of man over material things, the development of
human values and the control of animalistic desires, respect for the family,
the assumption of the vice-regency of God on earth according to His guidance and instruction, and in all affairs of this vice-regency the rule of God's
law (al-Shari'ah) and the way of life prescribed by Him.[2]

Other Muslims have echoed Qutb's critiques about Christian culture.
However, because the views Qutb expressed in *Milestones* were based on his
two-year visit to the United States just after World War II, his assessments
were seen as being highly credible. In another publication, *The America I Have
Seen*, he expresses disdain for just about everything in America, from sexual
attitudes to the cinema, football, gravy, barbershops, clothing and jazz, which
he characterized as "music that the savage bushmen created to satisfy their
primitive desires."[3] Due to his outspoken derision of American culture, Qutb
is considered by many to be the intellectual godfather of the Muslim Brotherhood,[4] as well as radical jihad.

As our world community seeks ways to mollify the antagonisms that have
created resentments among many in the Arab world, discussions inevitably
turn to the cultural expressions of the West and those responsible for producing them. The debate regarding the entertainment industry and how it may
need to come to terms with itself in a climate of heightened anger, resentment
and rage is now in full cry.

Appropriate Responses

Opinions from the arts community about this issue were as diverse and impassioned as the artists themselves, some more well-reasoned than others. In the
weeks following the 9/11 attacks, the *New York Times* solicited opinions from
artists representing a variety of disciplines about what an appropriate response
might be from those who create, produce and perform in the American cultural arena. In a provocative *Times* essay, songwriter Paul Simon called for "a
higher standard of honesty" and an "artistic and spiritual rebirth" in our society. He also called for a move away from corporate, bottom-line motivations

and encouraged that we reexamine ourselves as a people and a culture. Simon opined:

> The nihilism and violence that are often found in our music and film should be recognized as the cynical entertainment that they are when contrasted with the reality of September 11. The firefighters and police who worked 24-hour shifts were real-life heroes, completely alien to the popular culture's idea of heroism. Artists should feel comfortable with this non-show-biz reality, and let it be reflected in their work. The marketplace can accommodate these truths without losing money. Our notions of profit and value could be adjusted to allow for a greater degree of artistic questioning without an implication that such actions would automatically have adverse economic consequences. Artists could hold themselves to a higher standard of honesty.[5]

HBO producer Tom Fontana opined that the events of 9/11 meant "figuring out where the United States fits in the global family ... examining the roots of intolerance, of fanaticism, of hate. This means understanding the importance of neighbors, co-workers, relatives, friends and faith."[6] Offering a countervailing perspective, *Time* magazine contributing editor Lance Morrow characterized those seeking root causes for the attacks as being "too philosophical for decent company."[7] Perhaps the most unfortunate comments about the tragedy came from composer Karlheinz Stockhausen, who referred to the attack on the World Trade Center as "the greatest work of art that is possible in the whole cosmos ... something in one act ... we couldn't even dream of in music."[8] Needless to say, this was a very disturbing analogy and one bereft of any credibility.

Music historian David Tame observes that all civilizations have been confronted with the choices between art and music that denigrate or "encourage the contemplation of the eternal verities." Those choices are, in some ways, a microcosm of the history of civilization itself. He points out that when corrupting or degrading music appears within a culture, it happens very suddenly and with almost cataclysmic results. Destructive music, according to Tame, "attains to a position of power and of widespread popularity with the masses within just a few years or decades; and its influence upon society in general is often similarly sudden, bringing swift and negative change in philosophies, politics, morals and lifestyles."[9] We need only to look at popular cultural in our own era to see evidence of this. In the context of current popular art forms, George Carlin's comedy routine citing the "seven dirty words that you can never say on television" now seems like a quaint aphorism. We hear these "forbidden" words with greater frequency in popular culture and this results in normalizing crudeness, coarseness and incivility. *Huffington Post*, for instance, now runs a culture and arts feature called "Good Shit." Where does it end?

In light of Paul Simon's comments, any honest assessment requires an admission that a culture that considers desensitizing disaster films depicting massive carnage (and the attendant violence and destruction), or the sexually graphic programming that saturates cable TV and the Internet, or the vile lyrics of certain music, or reality TV, as being merely forms of benign entertainment cannot be considered a culture having a high degree of moral integrity—or common sense. The erosion of our moral and ethical perspectives as well as our insensitivity toward others has led to a moral relativism that many in our world community see as contemptible—or worse. Perhaps Qutb's observations should have been a wake-up call for the West.

The Role of Artists

Questions remain: What roles do the arts and artists play in creating a moral and ethical society? Do creators and producers bear any responsibility for the antagonism that causes resentment and hatred in our world community? Should art be exempt from any moral assessment? Do "absolute" moral and ethical truths that could be applied to an artistic enterprise actually exist? Is "art for art's sake" a concept that absolves artists from civic responsibility?

There is a notion among some in the arts community that freedom of artistic expression is sacrosanct and, as such, attempts to ascribe certain tenets of morality, which can be subjective, should not given much credibility regarding moral culpability. Richard Taruskin refers to a fixation with craft and technique as a "poietic fallacy": a condition in which art is assessed exclusively by methodological concerns—how art is made—without regard to its moral implications or aesthetics. It is as foolish to think that art is above any moral scrutiny as it is reprehensible not to condemn radical extremists for their acts of vengeance. Of course, arriving at a consensus about how a civilized society applies axiological considerations to art can be highly subjective and a seriously vexatious endeavor. Whose values should we apply in this assessment process? Perhaps a more appropriate question would be: what values do we consider to be beneficial? The idea that there may be universally shared values that can be ascertained and expressed in art is worth considering in our attempts to arrive at a consensus about how we might achieve cultural betterment.

At the outset of the twenty-first century it is undeniable that the more depraved aspects popular culture are pervasive, and that the values they engender have had a corrosive and dehumanizing effect on society. In fact, the word "art" has been greatly trivialized as the lines between trend and tradition, the profound and the superficial, truth and cliché, have become increasingly indistinct. This is due in large part to the corporate, bottom-line motivations that Simon alluded to. Questions regarding the motivation behind the creative process have been asked throughout history and having passionate views about the moral and ethical aspects of art and music have not been the sole franchise of philosophers of antiquity, classical artists or clerics.

Of course, the issue of censorship is quickly raised in any discussion about artistic freedom. Following the September 11 attacks, the Boston Symphony Orchestra (BSO) canceled a scheduled performance of excerpts from John Adam's controversial opera, *The Death of Klinghoffer*. The opera is based on the murder of an American Jew, Leon Klinghoffer, by Palestinian terrorists aboard the cruise ship *Achille Lauro* in 1985. The management of the BSO felt it was prudent "to err on the side of being sensitive" in the emotional climate of the moment.[10] Adams was upset with the BSO's decision. Commenting on Adams's *Klinghoffer* opera in relation to the 9/11 attacks and the decision by the orchestra's management to cancel the performance, Richard Taruskin cited a morally questionable aspect of the opera's libretto in which the motivations of the terrorists are characterized as being justified. He offered this perspective on the importance of forbearance and honesty in the moment:

> The Death of Klinghoffer trades in the tritest of undergraduate fantasies. ... If the events of September 11 could not jar some artists and critics out of their habit of romantically idealizing criminals, then nothing will. But isn't it time for artists and critics to grow up with the rest of us, now that the unthinkable has occurred? If terrorism ... is to be defeated, world public opinion has to be turned decisively against it. ... Censorship is always

deplorable ... but the exercise of forbearance can be noble. Not to be able to distinguish the noble from the deplorable is morally obtuse.[11]

Taruskin's perspective points to the importance of freedom and its correlative partner, responsibility. Accountability is a prerequisite in the establishment of a truly benevolent society. Giving no quarter to terrorist intentions and acts requires steadfastness in order to maintain a civil society. Robert Spano, who was scheduled to conduct the BSO performance of the *Klinghoffer* music, empathized with Adams's feelings of distress regarding the BSO's decision but understood that there were greater sensitivities to be considered in the immediate and painful aftermath of the 9/11 attacks.

> John is angry, and I feel terrible that this has hurt him. ... I'm a big supporter of his music. I perform it all the time, and I will continue to, and I'm sorry he took offense. But I don't agree with him that we did the wrong thing. I, as a person, am deeply wounded, as so many people are, and I think we're being sensitive to that. The fact that these choruses were performed recently in Amsterdam is one thing, but we should realize that the situation is different in New York and Boston. I don't think this is about being escapist. It's about being inappropriate.[12]

Spano's assessment regarding the appropriateness of the BSO's executive board seems correct. The board wasn't making a censorious judgment but rather an empathetic plea for an understanding of the moment. In essence, the BSO's decision was about timing, not about curbing artistic expression. If we desire or demand sensitivity for *our* artistic concerns, we must be willing to reciprocate in kind. This seems eminently fair. Holding the moral high ground, however, must be more than talking the talk. Echoing Gandhi, superstar singer Bono of U2 commented in a 2002 *Time* magazine article:

> When you sing, you make people vulnerable to change in their lives. You make yourself vulnerable to change in your life. But in the end, you've got to become the change you want to see in the world. I'm actually not a very good example of that—I'm too selfish, and the right to be ridiculous is something I hold too dear—but still, I know it's true.[13]

Although it may be our "right" to act in a ridiculous fashion, in a humane, caring and just society it may not be our right to absolve ourselves for ridiculous behavior if it adversely affects others. Not taking the feelings of others into account is childish. Adults who don't understand this become tyrants. To manifest real change requires more than high-minded rhetoric; rather it requires significant doses of moral courage and adult behavior. The "honesty" that Paul Simon called for requires the arts community to take a hard look at itself and to be willing to implement the necessary steps to facilitate its own reformation. There has been much talk about the need for Islam to reform itself from within, but a mature assessment leads to the realization that reformation *ought* to go both ways. The pervasiveness of much of the West's depraved and nihilistic popular culture, combined with the "hyperbolic and aggressive selling" of such,[14] makes holding a position of moral integrity difficult, if not impossible. Moreover, it's important to make distinctions between freedom and license. Changes are necessary, but change is a process, not an event, though events like 9/11 can dramatically impact the process. We must begin the process in earnest. Taruskin again:

> If terrorism—specifically, the commission or advocacy of deliberate acts of deadly violence directed randomly at the innocent—is to be defeated, world public opinion has to be turned decisively against it. The only way to do that is to focus resolutely on the acts rather than their claimed (or conjectured) motivations, and to characterize all such acts, whatever their motivation, as crimes. This means no longer romanticizing terrorists as Robin Hoods and no longer idealizing their deeds as rough poetic justice. If we indulge such notions when we happen to agree or sympathize with the aims, then we have forfeited the moral ground from which any such acts can be convincingly condemned.[15]

Condemnation may be an appropriate starting point, but taking responsibility and holding violators accountable for their perfidy is a necessary aspect of the endgame as well. Holding ourselves accountable as artists and producers is also a *sine qua non*.

The Hope of All Ages

As the accountability debate continues, it is troubling to see that any scrutiny of art and artists conjures cynicism or ridicule from both sides of the political spectrum. On his visit to Rome shortly after the 9/11 attacks, Cardinal Edward

Egan of New York suggested that Americans might do a little "soul-searching" in the aftermath. Regrettably, but somewhat predictably, those of a liberal mindset attempted to characterize Egan as an intolerant fundamentalist, while conservatives thought his remarks were "unpatriotic." The polemics regarding motivation in matters of art and religion related to the 9/11 attacks seem unending. Yet it remains apparent in Western societies that scurrilous, low-est-common-denominator motivations and bottom-line corporate mentalities are now juxtaposed in very coercive ways. This gives rise to cultural expressions that are impossible to defend in any honest assessment of moral integrity. Shouldn't we now explore and move toward "higher-common-denominator" motivations?

In an interview with John Stossel of Fox News, former editor for *Rolling Stone* magazine Kurt Loder was questioned about the concerns that religious leaders in other countries have about the "loose" sexual standards that are so pervasive in American popular culture—the gist of Qutb's critique. When asked if this was a legitimate grievance, Loder responded, "Well, screw 'em ... the people who dislike American popular culture are not fun people ... why should we care?"[16] How myopic. The merits, or demerits, of American popular culture notwithstanding, one wonders how Loder might feel if he had neighbors whose behavior offended him, and after asking them to modify their behavior to assuage his discomfort they told him to screw off. My guess is that he'd consider his neighbors not to be very "neighborly" but rather insensitive, self-centered and arrogant. He'd have a point.

When Loder made his "screw 'em" remark, there was laughter from the studio audience. But is this really a laughing matter—a joke? British philosopher Roger Scruton contends that though laughter is an expression of amusement, it in no way means that laughter is purely subjective "in the sense that 'anything goes,' or that it is uncritical of its object." Jokes, as Scruton observes, can be the "object of fierce disputes" and are often offensive. In the West we may joke about burqas and headscarves, but this is can be offensive to Muslims.

A joke in "bad taste" is not just a failure: it's an offense, and one of the most important aspects of moral education is to teach children not to commit that offense. Think about this, and you will quickly see that, however difficult it may be to define such notions as "judgment" and "taste," they are absolutely indispensable to us.[17]

To not joke about, or to not "make light of," the feelings or customs of others is an indication of maturity and sensitivity, as well as a display of forbearance. No one is suggesting that we should "cut off from our emotion and feeling" as MTV's Lisa Kennedy indignantly claimed in Stossel's panel discussion. Nor is exercising a bit of forbearance and sensitivity taking a step toward "becoming like North Korea," as Kennedy opined. (Was she being just a bit *extremist*?) It is arrogant and hypocritical to absolve ourselves for behavior that others find abhorrent and offensive while demanding others modify their behavior for our benefit, judging them—or laughing at them—if they don't.

In Stossel's program, Matt Welch, co-author of the book *Declaration of Independents*, argued that most of the world loves us but dislikes our government, citing the fact that many "ape" our popular culture. This is a shallow generalization at best, for it ignores many of the difficult questions vis-à-vis art, behavior and responsibility that arise in the context of a global community in which artists and producers are citizens—not to mention that a fair amount of popular culture doesn't amount to much artistically. Welch, ignoring the perfidious cocktail of obscene lyrics and misogynist attitudes that are pervasive in rap music, argued that hip-hop is much loved by young people in Morocco and other countries, as if this is some important measure of what American artists can offer the world. Welch should be reminded that there are more than a few folks in America, including many prominent members of the African-American community—Oprah Winfrey, Stanley Crouch, Melba Moore, Dionne Warwick, John McWhorter, the editors at *Essence* magazine and the late C. Delores Tucker—who consider much of what constitutes the hip-hop culture to be highly exploitative and a bane for urban youth. The aggressive glorification and marketing of urban thuggery and misogyny is not necessarily an export we should be touting if we wish to take the moral high ground in this debate. As McWhorter tells it, "rap took a dark turn in the early 1980s, as this 'bubble gum' music gave way to a 'gangsta' style that picked up where blaxploitation left off. Now top rappers began to write edgy lyrics celebrating street warfare or drugs and promiscuity."[18]

Perhaps more than any objectionable artistic content, it is the unapologetic attitude of the West that evokes contempt from our global neighbors. In a *Chicago Tribune* article, C. Delores Tucker, an iconic civil rights pioneer, took the media conglomerate Time Warner to task for what she viewed as corporate irresponsibility vis-à-vis hip-hop culture. She asked, "How long will Time Warner continue to put profit before principle? How long will it continue to turn its back on the thousands of young people who are dying spiritually and physically due to the violence perpetuated in these recordings?" Tucker, who protested at a Time Warner board meeting, decried the fact that "these images of black young kids acting like gangstas go all around the world."[19] Perhaps Welch, Loder and Kennedy need to rethink their attitudes because it's not just irritated Muslims who view certain aspects of our popular culture as being detrimental to a society's moral ecology.

The hope of all ages has been a world of peace: a world free from hostilities and prejudices. Most artists I know identify with that ideal, some more passionately than others, to be sure. Still, many believe that art should manifest qualities of altruism and humanity and that artists should be at the forefront of any "moral revolution." Calls for censorship are not the answer because censorship is inimical to a pluralistic, democratic society. Defending civil liberties and freedom of expression is imperative in cultivating a healthy society, for freedom is fundamental in the practice of love and peace. The only form of censorship that is necessary or acceptable is self-censorship—a condition in which individuals assess what they create through a filter of altruism. This attitude would seem to place the onus of moral and ethical responsibility squarely on the shoulders of creative individuals and performers. Pluralism cuts both ways, thus calling for a more humane creative ideal should not be considered an expression of oppression or intolerance, but rather a call to becomes less "endarkened" and more enlightened. Without discretion and forbearance we end up with licentiousness, bad behavior and questionable art.

Though I find most of Theodor Adorno's views on modern music to be highly questionable, in his *Essays on Mass Culture* published in 1944 he cautioned that the "fettering of consciousness," that is all too often the result of the pervasive influence of commercial mass media, could lead to conditions that would not be beneficial to maintaining civilized society. For Adorno, not questioning and evaluating cultural expression was decidedly undemocratic and immature, whereas having requisite adult sensibilities enabled any society to take a hard look at itself in relation to what was truly beneficial and ethical to the society at large. Though he viewed music largely through the prism of the Marx-Hegel dialectic, his insights with regard to the effects of "mass culture" do have some veracity and this is one of his perspectives that I find myself agreeing with him about.

Adorno, not unlike Qutb, saw "the new American music as the enemy of autonomous thought, a kind of captivating addiction that resulted in the enslavement of its devotees."[20] David Tame averred that modernity's predilection for materialism and reductionism has led us "into the trap of regarding music to be a nonessential and even peripheral aspect of human life." The philosophers of antiquity not only regarded this mindset as being "irrational, *but also, ultimately, suicidal.*"[21] (Emphasis is Tame's.)

In the aftermath of the tragedy of 9/11, a window of opportunity is now open that might allow for a serious period of more sober and enlightened examination as we assess the roles of art and artists in creating a culture of peace. As Taruskin asserted, "The promise not to censor is a promise to critique. ... It's not that musical ethos has been refuted and we no longer believe in it. Rather, it has been exorcized and we no longer assent to it."[22] Becoming anesthetized to the relevance of examining artistic expressions in the context of social and cultural betterment can create conditions that hinder the process of attaining that betterment. To paraphrase Tom Fontana, this may well mean coming to an acute awareness of how artists can best fit into the global family. It's undeniable that artists will have a significant role to play in the process of change, but how we play that role remains every artist's challenge. Why settle for less than what is beneficial to one's society? Why create art that denigrates our collective humanity?

Artists—and audiences!—have choices to make, and the raising of consciousness among the arts community is one way to begin the process of ascertaining what a morally upright and humane cultural perspective might be. The proposition that we would do well to *share* what we create and to produce in the spirit of goodwill and altruism seems especially relevant in the aftermath of 9/11. This would seem be in accord with Paul Simon's advocacy of artists holding themselves "to a higher standard of honesty."

Recommended Recordings

Simon: *Rhythm of the Saints*

Adams: *The Death of Klinghoffer*, Kent Nagano, Lyon Opera Orchestra

Stockhausen: *Kontra-Punkte*, Rupert Huber, Ensemble Recherche

Endnotes

1   Sayyid Qutb, *Milestones* (India: Islamic Book Service, 2006), p. 1.

2   Ibid., p. 71.

3   Sayyid Qutb, "'The America I Have Seen': In the Scale of Human Values," translated by Tarek Masoud and Ammar Fakeeh (Kashf ul Shubuhat), Third Episode, https://www.cia.gov/library/abbottabad-compound/3F/3F56ACA473044436B-4C1740F65D5C3B6_Sayyid_Qutb_-_The_America_I_Have_Seen.pdf.

4   Omar Sacirbey, "The Muslim Brotherhood's 'Intellectual Godfather,'" *Washington Post,* February 12, 2011.

5   Paul Simon, "Look Beyond Commerce," Music: The Aftermath, *New York Times*, September 23, 2001.

6   Tom Fontana, "A Time to Ask, 'Why?'" Television/Radio: The Aftermath, *New York Times*, September 23, 2001.

7   Lance Morrow, "The Case for Rage and Retribution," *Time*, September 12, 2001.

8   Anthony Tommasini, "The Devil Made Him Do It," *New York Times*, September 30, 2001.

9   David Tame, *The Secret Power of Music*: *The Transformation of Self and Society through Musical Energy* (Northamptonshire, England: Turnstone Press, Ltd., 1984), p. 189.

10   Anthony Tommasini, "John Adams, Banned in Boston," *New York Times*, November 25, 2001.

11   Michael K. Bohn, *The* Achille Lauro *Hijacking: Lessons in the Politics and Prejudice of Terrorism* (Washington, D.C.: Potomac Books, Inc., 2004), p. 182.

12   Allan Kozinn, "*Klinghoffer* Composer Fights His Cancellation," *New York Times*, November 14, 2001.

13   Josh Tyrangiel, "Can Bono Save the World?" *Time*, March 4, 2002, p. 69.

14   Simon, "Look Beyond Commerce."

15   Richard Taruskin, "Music's Dangers and the Case for Control," *New York Times*, December 9, 2001.

16   "Nick Gillespie and Matt Welch Join Stossel on *The Declaration of Independents*," June 23, 2011, http://reason.com/reasontv/2011/07/01/

nick-gillespie-and-matt-welch-1.

17 Roger Scruton, *Culture Counts: Faith and Feeling in a World Besieged* (New York: Encounter Books, 2007), p. 7.

18 John McWhorter, "How Hip-Hop Holds Blacks Back," *City Journal*, Summer 2003, https://www.city-journal.org/html/how-hip-hop-holds-blacks-back-12442.html.

19 Monica Fountain, "Crying Foul," *Chicago Tribune*, November 10, 1996, https://www.chicagotribune.com/news/ct-xpm-1996-11-10-9611100411-story.html.

20 Roger Scruton, *The Soul of the World* (Princeton, NJ: Princeton University Press, 2014), p. 150.

21 Tame, *The Secret Power of Music*, pp. 14-15.

22 Richard Taruskin, "The Many Dangers of Music," lecture, Graduate Center, City University of New York, 2016, https://www.youtube.com/watch?v=Jiy_xXTjW3k.

13

Listen

Wherever God revealed Himself to human beings, He was heard.
He may have appeared as a light, but in order to be understood,
His voice had to be heard. "And God spoke" is a standard sentence
in all holy scriptures. The ears are the gateway.[1]
Joachim-Ernst Berendt

I learned very early why God gave us two ears and one mouth,
because you're supposed to listen twice as much as you talk.[2]
Quincy Jones

The five words that changed the music industry: "What does she look like?"
Brian Hardgroove

In the years from 1988 through 1991 I had the opportunity to attend several arts conferences sponsored by Artists Association International, the central themes of which included the spiritual aspects of the arts and the role of the artist in creating a culture of peace. Notable artists, journalists and producers representing the realms of dance, music, literature, the fine arts and the news media offered various perspectives on the matter of art in the pursuit of peace.

In a rather perspicacious witticism on the issue of spirituality, sound and music, American pianist Lorin Hollander cited the biblical verses John 1:1 and 1:14: "In the Beginning was the word, ... and the word became flesh." Hollander hypothesized that since "words" are manifested as sound, the Almighty may have used sound to carry out the task of creation. Hollander suggested that if we follow this hypothesis to its logical conclusion, then it could be argued that instead of the Big Bang having been the primary energy force that initiated the creation of the cosmos, it may have been the Big Twang!

Historical Precedents

In ancient China music and sound vibrations were thought to have moral and ethical connotations as well as healing power when proper harmony was achieved. The remarkable text *The Memorial of Music* provides a telling commentary on just how significant music was viewed by the ancient Chinese culture, especially with regard to their cosmology and Confucian ethics. The following are just a few excerpts from the text that are worth noting:

> As music comes from within, it is peace-inspiring. ... When music prevails, then all reproaches cease. ... The harmony of music is like that between heaven and earth. ... It is because of harmony that beings do not perish.[3]

> In the visible world there are rites and music, and in the unseen world there are spirits of the dead, and the spirits deified. Such being the case, if music and the rites prevail in the empire, every body is respectful and affectionate ... Music is an imitation of what the heavens originate.[4]

> So, music attunes and harmonizes the emotional nature of man—it combines the virtues and nourishes them—and thus it flourishes. ... Benevolence is akin to music, for it unites and harmonizes.[5]

> When the transformation of heaven and earth are untimely, then there is no birth. When the requisite distinctions between male and female are lost sight of, then confusion is complete. So, when music is untimely, harmony

is violated; and when the rites fail to make the relative distinctions of duty, disorder results.[6]

As these passages illustrate, the importance of music in Chinese culture vis-à-vis the harmony of heaven and earth, the incorporeal and corporeal realms, male and female, and the mind and body was a serious concern.

Greek concepts of the "harmony of the spheres" and the "harmony of the world" played heavily into the idea of the interconnectedness of the cosmos. Daniel Barenboim reminds us of Aristotle's assertion that "the eyes are the organs of temptation and the ears the organs of instruction."[7] Aristotle also had keen insights about the effects of music on the human psyche. In his explanations of the philosophy of Greek music theoretician Aristoxenus, Henry Stewart Macran argues that, "the principles of musical science rest, not on the presuppositions of hearing in general, but on the evidence of the developed and cultivated ear."[8] For Aristoxenus, understanding music in its fullest measure meant following "the *process* of its melody with ear and intellect."[9] How well a person cultivated their listening capabilities was essential in attaining the complete understanding of the composition at hand, not to mention how one might better ascertain the mysteries and secrets of the cosmos. It's interesting to note that Apollo was the Greek god of music, dance and medicine and his son, Asclepius was a god of medicine who was thought to use music as a vehicle for healing.

Tibetan culture espoused the belief that the sacred sound of *Om* was a primal energy force. Lama Anagarika Govinda instructed:

> Tibetan ritual music is not concerned with the emotions of temporal individuality, but with the ever-present, timeless qualities of universal life, in which our personal joys and sorrows do not exist. To bring us in touch with this realm is the purpose of meditation as well as of Tibetan ritual music, which is built upon the deepest vibrations that a human voice can produce: sounds that seem to come from the womb of the earth or from the depth of space like rolling thunder, the mantric sound of nature, which symbolizes the creative vibrations of the universe, the origin of all things.[10]

Sufis referred to music and sound as *Ghiza-i-ruh*, food for the soul. According to Sufi teaching, "All occult science, all mystical practices are based upon the science of the word or sound."[11] Most of the world's religions—Judaism,

Zen Buddhism, Islam, Christianity, Sufism, Hinduism—have utilized music and sound within the context of their ritualistic practices and ceremonies. The writings of the mysterious Islamic order known as the Brethren of Purity, or Ikhwan al-Safa, explained music and its spiritual properties in this way:

> Music is at once a spiritual and a corporeal art, according to the Ikhwan. It is corporeal insofar as it is an art practiced with the hands. Thus its matter is composed of natural bodies, and all its products are physical forms. But music also has for its matter that which is entirely spiritual, and that is the soul of the listener. Its effects on the soul of the listener, at least the immediate effects, are all spiritual manifestations. ... Music as a repository of meaning, gives its meaning as form, to the soul as its matter. ... The different character of each piece of music, or of each passage, gives its character to the soul of the listener.[12]

Early Christian philosophers, religious figures and musicians often expounded on the power of music and sound. The writings of sixth-century Christian philosopher Anicius Manlius Severinus Boethius (c. 480-524 CE) were among the earliest essays written from a Christian perspective on the issue of music and the relationship between the corporeal and incorporeal realms. Influenced by Pythagoras' theories, Boethius' treatise *De institutione musica* stood as an authoritative source of understanding for theorists of medieval times with regard to the harmonization of the physical world *(musica mundana)*, the mind and body *(musica humana)* and tones, or within instrumental music, itself *(musica instrumentalis)*. Boethius wrote:

> Now the first type, that is the music of the universe, is best observed in those things which one perceives in heaven itself, or in the structure of the elements, or in the diversity of the seasons. ... Thus there must be some fixed order of musical modulation in this celestial motion. ... Now, one comes to understand the music of the human being by examining his own being. For what unites the incorporeal existence of reason with the body except a certain harmony and, as it were, a careful tuning of low and high pitches in such a way that they produce one consonance?[13]

Baroque composer Johann Mattheson (1681-1764) asserted: "The most important and outstanding part of the science of sound is the part that examines the effects of well-disposed sounds on the emotions and the soul."[14] For Italian philosopher Giuseppe Mazzini, "Music is the harmonious voice of creation; an echo of the invisible world; one note of the divine concord which the entire universe is destined one day to sound."[15]

Moreover, contemporary philosophers and musicians have had a great deal to say about music and its effects on the human condition. Allan Bloom writes in his compelling commentary on the state of higher education, *The Closing of the American Mind*:

> Music is the medium of the human soul in its most ecstatic condition of wonder and terror. Nietzsche, who in large measure agrees with Plato's analysis, says … that a mixture of cruelty and coarse sensuality characterized this state. … Music is the soul's primitive and primary speech … without articulate speech or reason. It is not only not reasonable, it is hostile to reason.[16]

Eminent neuroscientist Oliver Sacks makes a similar observation regarding "non-reasonable" aspects of music when he asserts that music is unique among the arts in that it is "both completely abstract and profoundly emotional." For Sacks, music has no ability to represent anything particular or corporeal, yet it has "a unique power to express inner states or feelings. Music can pierce the heart directly; it needs no mediation."[17] This is perhaps why Sacks and others involved in the field of neuroscience find music to be intriguing from both psychological and therapeutic perspectives.

The use of music as a mode of healing therapy in China can be traced to the earliest Chinese medical text, *The Yellow Emperor's Classic of Medicine*, published 2,500 years ago. Renowned psychic Edgar Cayce believed, as did the Chinese, that sound could be used for medicinal purposes. There are five notes in ancient Chinese music, namely, *gong, shang, jue, zhi* and *yu*. Each of these notes is also matched with an element from the Five Elements of earth, metal, wood, fire and water, and the pitches comprise a pentatonic scale (C, D, E, G, A). Speaking to music's spiritual influence on the origins of science and religion, American contemporary composer George Crumb observed:

> Music is tangible, almost palpable, and yet unreal, illusive. Music is analyzable only on the most mechanistic level; the important elements—the spiritual impulse, the psychological curve, the metaphysical implications— are understandable only in terms of the music itself. I feel intuitively that

music must have been the prime cell from which language, science and religion originated.[18]

Eyes vs. Ears

In our video-oriented contemporary society, the act of listening has diminished, and this is our collective loss. British musicologist Joscelyn Godwin provides an arresting commentary on the importance of being active listeners in our pursuit of truth, beauty and goodness.

> Above all, I hope that more attention and respect will be paid to the act of listening. The listener is just as important to the making of music as the composer and performer, and unlike theirs, the listener's skill is something that everyone can practice and develop consciously. John Cage has taught us to listen to every sound and its encompassing silence; the Sufi in ecstatic audition "hears" from every object in the universe. How different would be a civilization in which hearing, not sight, became the primary sense, and in which we dwelt more in the inner space of tone than in the illusion of the exterior world.[19]

Developing our listening faculties is essential in the process of understanding music to its fullest extent. Nietzsche's dictum that the profound understanding of the one who experiences a particular work of art was as important as the profound abilities of the creators of art is highly credible. Barenboim averred that sound vibrations "change the body directly and deeply, more so than the patterns of light that lead to vision." Citing the early development of ears in the womb (the eyes are developed much later in the gestation period), Barenboim contended that contemporary culture's penchant for prioritizing seeing over hearing belies the importance of hearing as it relates to the art of music, both as a performer and listener.

> The importance of the ear cannot be overestimated. One of its functions is to help us remember and recollect, which means that it is not only an essential link to memory, but it forces us to do so with thought. ... Auditory memory can function on the basis of the subconscious ... and a great deal of analysis and comprehension of the underlying [musical] structure is necessary in order to develop a solid memory of an entire piece. This is what I refer to as recollection: the completion of auditory memory by rational effort.[20]

Our ability, or inability to listen to music has evolved with the advent of technology. The preponderance of recorded music has made us different listeners than our parents and grandparents. In many ways we are no longer critical, active listeners, but rather passive and uncritical. Theodor Adorno, whose disdain for American popular music and jazz could be quite caustic, considered the musical components of popular music—it's melody, harmony, rhythm and structure—to be undemanding, thus contributing to a regression of listening. This regression, according to Adorno, led to the condition where more complex musical utterances were marginalized in favor of music that was superficial and trite—kitsch. This preference had ramifications that extended beyond the musical sphere, including the diminution of our capacity for enlightenment via the arts—what Schiller referred to as "aesthetic education." As Roger Scruton acknowledged:

> The rise of new mass culture has not happened in the realm of music only. Vast social and political changes can be read into this transition, and Adorno was surely right to notice this. ... The process that began in his day has continued, to the extent that it is often unclear today whether music is to be listened to or merely overheard, or maybe even just looked at, as the sound effects fill the background of a gripping video.[21]

In his illuminating book *The World Is Sound: Nada Brahma*, published in 1983, German music journalist Joachim-Ernst Berendt puts forth an intriguing analogy regarding sight and sound. As Berendt opines, sight, with its direct, immediate and unforgiving properties, possesses distinctly masculine attributes, whereas sound, with its amorphous, ethereal and vibratory properties, is more feminine. Alluding to Chinese philosophy, Berendt posited, "the eyes constituted a *yang* type of sense organ: male, aggressive, dominating, rational, surface-oriented, analyzing things. The ears, on the other hand, are a *yin* sense: female, receptive, careful, intuitive and spiritual, depth-oriented, perceiving the whole as one."[22]

In Western music of the nineteenth century, there was a predilection for fantasy and mythology as opposed to the demonstrations of classical formalism in previous eras. Music historian Donald J. Grout has suggested that instrumental music's "incomparable power of suggestion," mystery and irrational experience is what makes it so alluring. The music of the romantic era exemplifies this notion. It is in the metaphysical realm of evocation and imagination that music works it magic on our emotions. It is not in the immediate realm of sight, but rather in the ephemeral realm of sound and music that our imaginations and fantasies are stimulated to heightened degrees.

With the advent of television and video in contemporary culture, our capacity for hearing—and active listening—has been diminished. Berendt, in a nod towards Adorno, writes:

> Human beings with their disproportionate emphasis on seeing have brought on the excess of rationality, of analysis and abstraction, whose breakdown we are now witnessing. In the age of television, seeing people have allowed themselves to be led ad absurdum. No longer do we see the world, we see its images—and unbelievably enough, we are content with that, content with looking at moving pictures. Living almost exclusively through the eyes has led us to almost not living at all.[23]

Hence the emergence of couch potatoes!

According to Berendt, humankind's collective spirituality has become compromised due to the secularization of culture and the deterioration of our ability to listen. Becoming "eye people" as opposed to "ear people" has had the consequence of our culture becoming increasingly desensitized to God and all things spiritual. "Wherever God revealed Himself to human beings," Berendt notes, "He was heard. He may have appeared as a light, but in order to be understood, His voice had to be heard. 'And God spoke' is a standard sentence in all holy scriptures. The ears are the gateway."[24] Berendt argues that any deeper change in consciousness can only occur when we more fully learn to utilize the gift of hearing. Again, it's a question of balance, because seeing things from a proper perspective will also be part of any equation that can bring about a harmonious and unified reality. Goethe asserted that, "the eye of the spirit must see in unison with the eyes of the body, for otherwise there is the danger that one will see something and yet look past it."[25] For non-believers, Berendt's contentions about God and religious narratives are wanting, yet there is something to be said about the importance of hearing with respect to music and spiritual enlightenment.

Advances in the study of cognitive psychology and psychoacoustics reveal that the brain may be "hardwired" to hear a certain way and thus complicated musical utterances, whether melodic, rhythmic or harmonic, are not easily assimilated in ways that can be easily comprehended. If our comprehension of pitch relations, rhythmic patterns and harmonic progressions is impaired due to a complicated or arcane musical syntax, our cognition is hampered, and music is thus reduced to being unpleasant noise without meaning. This complaint has been made about the music of mid-century modernism in which acerbic harmonies, atonal melodies and rhythmic complexity has resulted in the indeterminacy that characterizes so much contemporary art music.

The research of composer Fred Lerdahl of Columbia University and Ray Jackendoff, a linguist at Tufts University, regarding the cognitive constraints of various nonhierarchical compositional syntaxes is highly instructive. Lerdahl and Jackendoff argue that there is a difference between compositional grammar and listening grammar. They have posited that the cognitive processes of sorting out highly complicated musical sound properties—pitch, rhythm, harmony, structures—no matter how well organized, result in aural constraints that yield little in the way of communicative ability and emotional satisfaction. This indeterminacy is a significant reason why a good deal of contemporary art music falls on deaf ears—or perhaps more accurately, confused ears.

Lerdahl argues that the compositional grammar of tonality is not unlike the grammar of natural language, in that natural languages are born out of a spontaneous, subconscious impulse to communicate, whereas artificial grammar not born out of the subconscious is "a conscious invention" lacking any underlying "deep structure" or meaning.* He differentiates between music that is complex, J. S. Bach, for example, and music that is complicated, such as the music of Elliott Carter. Lerdahl proffers that complication produces a condition in which cognitive processes are challenged beyond their natural and physiological capacities. He contends that complex music is based on

---

* The concepts of deep structure and surface structure were developed by the noted linguist, Noam Chomsky. In his theories regarding "generative grammar," Chomsky posited that deep structures of language provide the true meaning of what appears externally. At a deep level of thought, a person has full knowledge of what he wants to communicate to others. For Chomsky, "deep structure" is the core of the semantic relations of a sentence. Two sentences may be structured differently (surface structure) but mean essentially the same thing (deep structure). For example, "Bob threw the ball," and, "The ball was thrown by Bob," have identical meanings though expressed differently.

a "hierarchical structural richness" that results in a perceptible, communicative syntax (tonality is ontologically such), whereas complicated music tends to neutralize and even obliterates hierarchical properties due to "numerous non-redundant events per time unit" that tend to hinder the cognitive process and violate certain psychoacoustic realities.[26] In this sense, listening grammar is no small matter, for it may have everything to do with our preferences in what we choose to listen to.

The Eyes Have It

With the advent of video technology in the final decades of the twentieth century our cultural expressions have been increasingly dominated by the visual realm. Many in the music industry feared that with the advent of MTV and the music video, radio—which had been the primary source for many to discover new artists—would become extinct. There was also a concern that the overemphasis on visuals would eviscerate the magic of music by impinging on our imaginations. As art historian Camille Paglia has cautioned, our brains are over-stimulated by "all-pervasive mass media and slavishly monitored personal electronic devices," and all those screens contribute to sensory overload and contribute to a lack of "*focus*, the basis of stability, identity and life direction." As she correctly notes: "The exhilarating expansion of instant global communication has liberated a host of individual voices but paradoxically threatened to overwhelm individuality itself."[27]

Michael Jackson's groundbreaking music video, "Thriller," released in 1983, is considered an unprecedented achievement in the annals of pop culture. The 14-minute video, directed by John Landis, sold over nine million copies and may have forever changed the way music is experienced—and marketed. In retrospect it is not unreasonable to speculate if this was really a good thing for music, for the overemphasis on visuals since has had the effect of turning us into passive listeners. Like Chauncey Gardiner in the satirical film based on Jerzy Kosiński's novel *Being There*, it seems that rather than listen, we like to watch.

The preponderance of video in the realm of popular music has led to a condition in which it is no longer enough to be a great singer or instrumentalist. In fact, in our contemporary cultural milieu, being telegenic has become a higher priority than musicianship. Being able to actually perform well has become subsidiary to having high cheekbones, an athletic or sexy physique, or looking good in fashionable attire. The MTV-VH1 culture that was spawned by the advent of the music video is predicated on shallow surface realities in the extreme. Brian Hardgroove, bassist in the band Public Enemy, once told me that in his opinion the five words that changed the music industry (and not for the better) are, "What does she look like?"

The hyper-emphasis on "eye culture" is what drives most of popular entertainment. Think of how many screens are in our daily lives—computers, cell phones, tablets and televisions. The realm of visual media is extremely pervasive and the resulting prioritization of sight over sound has had a profound impact on the music industry.

Brian Hardgroove's sentiment regarding the ascendance of sight as a seductive agent in the music industry was presciently noted by C. S. Lewis decades ago. In his book *The Screwtape Letters*, published in 1942, Lewis's protagonist, Screwtape, the senior devil from the "Lowerarchy," asserts: "It is all fake, of course; the figures in the popular art are falsely drawn. ... As a result we are more and more directing the desires of men to something which does not exist—making the role of the eye in sexuality more and more important and at the same time making its demands more and more impossible. What follows you can easily forecast!"[28] And that forecast is decidedly dreary for those who contend that "ear culture" needs to be fortified.

Paglia views the over-saturation of artificial, computer-generated imagery as having negative effects in the process of developing impactful art programs in the educational system. Speaking on the importance of introducing young students to the intrinsic value of art education, she stated:

> My idea is to expose them to art history ... at an early age. So they have something in their minds, images that counterbalance the images that are coming at them from ads and special effects. The special effects have gotten out of control—computerized special effects. Now you have movies that are nothing but special effects, overwhelming sound, which is a great sensation, but character acting and script development, social realism—these things are actually declining.[29]

Regarding the pervasiveness of video culture and its inherent emphasis on external realities, Allan Bloom observed:

As it now stands, students have powerful images of what a perfect body is and pursue it incessantly. But deprived of literary guidance, they no longer have any image of a perfect soul, and hence do not long to have one. They do not even imagine that there is such a thing.[30]

Bloom acknowledges that the tyranny of sight is difficult to overcome. It is, after all, sight that imposes the reality of the proverbial first impression in such an unforgiving fashion. He observes that on certain college campuses "lookism" is now considered a vice similar to racism, sexism and homophobia. "Yet," he also stated, "eros begins, sad but true, in preferences founded in the first place on what is seen with the eyes, founded on ideals of bodily beauty. Nobody seriously ever suggested that this is where it ends, but if this essential beginning is suppressed, farewell eros."[31]

Because images are fixed and without variation, repeated viewings of a particular object can have the effect of desensitizing our imagination. Seeing a movie repeatedly eventually induces the law of diminishing returns as our expectation level declines due to over-familiarization. Music, especially instrumental music, being temporal and ephemeral—and invisible—allows our imagination to conjure limitless possibilities in terms of how we react to it. It is in the realm of these potentialities that music can forever work its magic on our psyche. Listening to music can invite a more active participation in the process of assimilation and appreciation. From a purely musical perspective, I maintain that the ability to actually perform with the highest sense of musicianship is more important than looking good on camera. Yet we have continually succumbed to the allure of the video lens—to our collective loss. Dominic Strinati, in his book *An Introduction to Theories of Popular Culture*, goes a step further regarding the fetish of images: "Media images encourage superficiality rather than substance, cynicism rather than belief, the thirst for constant change rather than security of stable traditions, the desires of the moment rather than the truths of history."[32]

Seventeenth-century mathematician, astronomer and astrologer Johannes Kepler held that a central set of harmonies governed the cosmos, including the production and realization of sound via scales and harmonic principles. This idea has its roots in Greek philosophy, but its reiteration by Kepler demonstrates that the concept of the macrocosmic interconnectedness of astronomy, sound, physics, mathematics and spirituality is one that has found credence for thousands of years dating back to the Sumerian culture of Mesopotamia. Kepler writes in his treatise, *Harmonices Mundi:*

> Now there is need, Urania, of a grander sound, while I ascend by the harmonic stair of the celestial motions to higher things, where the true archetype of the fabric of the world is laid up and preserved. Follow me, modern musicians, and attribute it to your arts, unknown to antiquity: in these last centuries, Nature, always prodigal of herself, has at last brought forth, after an incubation of twice a thousand years, you the first true offprints of the universal whole. By your harmonizing of various voices, and through your ears, she has whispered of herself, as she is in her innermost bosom, to the human mind, most beloved daughter of God the Creator.[33]

Our ears as the gateway to the divine and to higher consciousness—how sublime!

Postscript

I confess that I wasn't the biggest fan of Michael Jackson, but like anyone who has had any exposure to American culture I recognized that he possessed immense talent and was a major influence in popular culture. There are a few of his songs that I always enjoy, "Never Can Say Goodbye," being one. His collaboration with Quincy Jones resulted in songs that can be categorized as "pop classics." Both artists demonstrated uncommon taste and consummate musicianship in their partnership. Regardless of one's view of popular culture, it's always gratifying to experience someone who is in their element and performing at the pinnacle of their career, and when Jackson was on his game he could be a "thriller."

I have a colleague who has been very close to the Jackson family and upon hearing of Michael's death I called him to get his take on the untimely passing of the "King of Pop." My colleague was obviously saddened and recalled his experiences with Michael, saying that the one thing that people overlooked in remembering his life, was his generosity, altruism and humanitarian spirit. According to my colleague the sentiment expressed in the song "We Are the World" was something close to Michael's heart. His Heal the World

Foundation was born out of a deep desire to use music as a harmonizing and healing agent.

I was also informed that Michael loved, and was quite knowledgeable about, classical music. In a 1992 interview for *Ebony* regarding his *Dangerous* album, Jackson confided: "I wanted to do an album that was like Tchaikovsky's *Nutcracker Suite*. So that in a thousand years from now, people would still be listening to it. Something that would live forever. I would like to see children and teenagers and parents and all races all over the world, hundreds and hundreds of years from now, still pulling out songs from that album and dissecting it. I want it to live."[34] The *Dangerous* album's hit song, "Black or White," generated millions of dollars for Jackson's Heal the World initiative.

Regrettably, in the aftermath of his untimely death, the focus has been on other aspects of Michael's life (the cosmetic surgery, finances, lawsuits, drug problems, etc.). This is indicative of the pervasive shallowness of our popular culture. Writing in the *New York Daily News*, columnist and jazz historian Stanley Crouch offered this insightful take on Michael Jackson's life vis-a-vis pop culture:

> Because overblown entertainment has come to replace deep feeling—or spiritual recognition and satisfaction—a man like Jackson became a product of every technological trick available to the recording and video industries. As a whole, they could give him what amounted to an aural or visual facelift. What was done to him became a central part of the dehumanization common to our popular culture in which imagination is less important than contrivance and we find ourselves caught in an era of protracted adolescence.[35]

The dehumanization and contrivance that Crouch alludes to has a great deal to do with the shift in musical priorities from our ears to our eyes. That said, there is great satisfaction and joy derived from becoming mature, but too often attaining maturity is viewed as being stodgy, old and "un-hip." Growing up and becoming more mature is part of life's design. One hopes that as a father to his children, Michael Jackson was able to find the joy and satisfaction that may have eluded him as a pop-music icon. If, as Quincy Jones said, that God gave us two ears and one mouth so that we might listen more than we speak, we ought to hone our listening skills to hear what the Almighty might be saying to us regarding our priorities and the values necessary to attain maturity, both as musicians and appreciators of music.

Recommended Recordings

Chopin: Waltzes for Piano, B 164/Op. 64, Lorin Hollander, piano

Mattheson: *Die Heilsame Geburt, Magnificat*, Michael Willens, Cologne Academy

Crumb: *A Haunted Landscape*, Thomas Conlin, Warsaw Philharmonic Orchestra

Cage: Works for Percussion, Vol. 6, Amadinda Percussion Group

Beethoven: Piano Concertos, Daniel Barenboim, Staatskapelle Berlin

Michael Jackson-Quincy Jones: "Thriller"

Endnotes

1   Joachim-Ernst Berendt, *The World Is Sound: Nada Brahma* (Rochester, VT: Destiny Books, Rochester, 1987), p. 26.

2   Quincy Jones, "Quincy Jones Reflects on Career, Michael Jackson and Why He Wouldn't Work with Elvis," interview with Seth Abramovitch, *The Hollywood Reporter*, May 20, 2021.

3   "Notions of the Ancient Chinese Respecting Music: A Complete Translation of the YOK-KYI, or Memorial of Music, according to the Imperial Tradition," translated by Dr. B. Jenkins, *Journal of the North-China Branch of the Royal Asiatic Society, Volumes 4-5* (Princeton: Princeton University Library, 1868), p. 34,

4   Ibid., pp. 34-35.

5   Ibid., p. 37.

6   Ibid., p. 38.

7   Daniel Barenboim, *Music Quickens Time* (London and New York: Verso, 2008), p. 21.

8   *The Harmonics of Aristoxenus*, edited and translated with notes by Henry S. Macran (Oxford: Clarendon Press, 1902), p. 258.

9   Ibid., p. 269.

10 Lama Anagarika Govinda, *The Way of the White Clouds* (London, UK: Random House, 1966), p. 29.

11 Joachim-Ernst Berendt, *The World Is Sound: Nada Brahma* (Rochester, VT: Destiny Books, Rochester, 1987), p. 34.

12 Fadlou Shehadi, *Philosophies of Music in Medieval Islam* (Leiden, The Netherlands: Brill, 1995), p. 46.

13 *Music in the Western World: A History in Documents*, selected and annotated by

Piero Weiss and Richard Taruskin (New York: Schirmer Books, 1984), pp. 33-35.

14 Ibid., p. 217.

15 Giuseppe Mazzini, as cited by Richard Alan Krieger, *Civilization's Quotations: Life's Ideal* (New York: Algora, 2002), p. 289.

16 Allan Bloom, *The Closing of the American Mind* (New York: Simon & Schuster, 1987), p. 71.

17 Oliver Sacks, *Musicophilia: Tales of Music and the Brain* (New York and Toronto: Knopf, 2008), p. 329.

18 David Ewen, *American Composers: A Biographical Dictionary* (New York: G. P. Putnam's Sons, 1982), p. 157.

19 Joscelyn Godwin, *Harmonies of Heaven and Earth: Mysticism in Music from Antiquity to the Avant-Garde* (Rochester, VT: Inner Traditions International, 1995), pp. 109-110.

20 Barenboim, *Music Quickens Time*, pp. 22-24.

21 Roger Scruton, *The Soul of the World* (Princeton, NJ: Princeton University Press: 2014), pp. 149-150.

22 Berendt, *The World Is Sound*, p. 5.

23 Ibid. p. 6.

24 Ibid.

25 Ibid., p. 7.

26 Fred Lerdahl, "Cognitive Constraints on Compositional Systems," *Generative Processes in Music: The Psychology of Performance, Improvisation, and Composition*, edited by John Sloboda (Oxford: Oxford University Press, 1992), pp. 231-59. Reprinted in *Contemporary Music Review* 6, no. 2 (1992), pp. 97-121.

27 Camille Paglia, *Glittering Images: A Journey through Art from Egypt to Star Wars* (New York: Vintage Books, 2012), p. vii.

28 C. S. Lewis, *The Complete C. S. Lewis Signature Classics* (New York: HarperCollins, 2002), p. 243.

29 Camille Paglia, interview by Robert Birnbaum, *The Morning News*, August 3, 2005, http://www.themorningnews.org/article/camille-paglia.

30 Bloom, *The Closing of the American Mind*, p. 67.

31 Allan Bloom, *Love and Friendship* (New York: Simon & Schuster, 1993), p.15.

32 Dominic Strinati, as cited by John Storey in *Cultural Theory and Popular Culture: A Reader* (Birmingham, UK: Harvester Wheatsheaf, 1994), p. 438.

33 Johannes Kepler, *Harmonices mundi*, translated by E.J. Aiton, A.M. Duncan and J.V. Field (Philadelphia, PA: The American Philosophical Society, 1997), p. 441.

34 Robert E. Johnson, "Michael Jackson: Crowned in Africa, Pop Music King Tells Real Story of Controversial Trip," *Ebony*, May 1992.

35 Stanley Crouch, "Boy Who Never Grew Up Became the Man Who Will Never Grow Old," *New York Daily News*, June 28, 2009.

14

The Divine Nexus of Music and Mathematics

*Music employs number both in its harmonic foundation and its
metrical presentation in time. … The universal aesthetic experience
of mankind, as ancient as the earliest known cave paintings,
seemed to cohere with the composition of the heavens,
through the application of perceptible harmonic ratios.*[1]
David P. Goldman

*Music creates order out of chaos; for rhythm imposes unanimity upon
the divergent, melody imposes continuity upon the disjointed, and harmony
imposes compatibility upon the incongruous. Thus, a confusion surrenders
to order and noise to music, and as we through music attain that greater
universal order which rests upon fundamental relationships of geometrical
and mathematical proportion, direction is supplied to mere repetitious time,
power to the multiplication of elements, and purpose to random association.*[2]
Yehudi Menuhin

The concept of divine order vis-à-vis a tangible relationship of music and mathematics is one that has resonated with philosophers, theorists, academics and artists dating back to the Sumerian culture of Mesopotamia, to Confucius and to the philosophers of ancient Greece. The Greek concept of the quadrivium—the four realms of mathematical study as outlined by Plato, namely, arithmetic, geometry, music and astronomy—has long been considered an integral part of a comprehensive liberal arts education. As the neo-platonic philosopher Proclus (412-485 CE) explained:

> The Pythagoreans considered all mathematical science to be divided into four parts: one half they marked off as concerned with quantity, the other half with magnitude; and each of these they posited as twofold. A quantity can be considered in regard to its character by itself or in its relation to another quantity, magnitudes as either stationary or in motion. Arithmetic, then, studies quantities as such, music the relations between quantities, geometry magnitude at rest, spherics [astronomy] magnitude inherently moving.[3]

The music-math nexus has been expounded on in the treatises of Pythagoras, Ptolemy, Augustine, Boethius, Rameau, Kepler, Euler, Kayser and Einstein. The explications of French composer and theorist, Jean-Philippe Rameau regarding the "directional pull" of tonal harmonies were so convincing that he was dubbed "the Isaac Newton of music."[4] Prior to the Greeks, the Sumerians of Mesopotamia utilized a tonal-arithmetical system—it was a sexagesimal system, based on the number 60—that linked specific pitches to numerical properties and specific gods. In medieval times, the notion that there were seven planets and seven metals that corresponded to the seven pitches in the diatonic scale and the harmonies they produced was germane to the mythological belief that there was a "luminous celestial realm," the final destiny of one's soul, where "living spiritual powers presided over by angelic beings," sirens, according to Plato, and "where God in majesty sat on his triune throne."[5]

The idea that sound and music have mathematical properties as well as a spiritual dimension should not be considered merely the residue of ancient mythologies, however. In Europe the Renaissance was a time when creating art and music based on religious convictions and scientific principles was celebrated as a reflection of humankind's ability to realize its fullest potential—the settings of the Catholic Mass by Josquin des Prez or Brunelleschi's dome of the Florence Cathedral, for example. Religion and science in the Renaissance were not considered mutually exclusive entities, but rather were seen as correlative facets of the human experience that when conjoined and harmonized in artistic endeavors could yield sublime artistic expressions of great beauty and meaning. In his exegesis on the history of musical tuning systems, Stuart Isacoff posited that "music's prized proportions permeated not only the inner sanctums of the church, but the workshops of great artists," thus becoming "entangled in the world of scientific inquiry."[6]

Sound vibrations may be invisible, but they are mathematically quantifiable. With present-day advances in science and technology we now understand that the idea that the vast expanse of the cosmos is "the epitome of silence," a place of "utter stillness," is untenable. In his exhaustively well-researched book, *The World Is Sound: Nada Brahma*, Joachim-Ernst Berendt averred that in their respective eras the concepts of the "music of the spheres" as espoused by Plato, or the "harmony of the world" as posited by Pythagoras and Kepler, were likely understood metaphorically. Now, however, we are finding that these concepts are proven by scientific discovery. Cosmic sound actually exists. As Berendt observes, "In the prologue of *Faust*, Goethe wrote, 'The Sun intones in ancient tourney, With brother-spheres, a rival song.' Goethe suspected that the sun 'intones'; today we know it."[7]

It can be said with reasonable certainty that in the wake of advances in science, modern humankind's diminished capacity—or unwillingness—to perceive things in a spiritual way has resulted in our becoming obtuse in recognizing the *causal* dimension, oblivious to the primordial aspects of the phenomenal world. Yet this was not always the case. Philosophers and theoreticians of antiquity placed a great deal of importance on these issues, and their polemics regarding the cosmic origins of the created world often resulted in vitriolic debates and heated invective.

Whereas certain philosophers and physicists of antiquity argued that air, water or fire were the primordial elements of the cosmos, Pythagoras asserted that the basis of the physical universe was something quite apart from these "earthly" things. It was something more refined but having very definite attributes: "beyond sense, but a fulfillment of all man's perceptions. Through it, the hidden structure of the world became transparent." For Pythagoras this "primordial" stuff of the universe was mathematics—numbers.[8] His theories and insights regarding the production of sound and pitch relations have influenced theoreticians, composers, instrument builders, kings and the clergy from his time to this day.

In the truest sense, the overtone series (the physical phenomenon of vibratory energy producing definite pitches), represents the sonic etymology of all music. The notion of "music as math" has a long history, as articulated in the ninth-century speculative treatise on music *Scolica enchiriadis*:* "Notes pass away quickly; numbers, however, though stained by the corporeal touch of pitches and motions, remain."[9] Pythagoras' epiphany about numbers being "the stuff of the universe" was proven to be correct and opened the doors for physicists and theorists to understand the "secrets" of the created world with greater clarity and vision.

In his essays on romanticism, British political philosopher Isaiah Berlin has pointed out that Greek culture in the classical age was based heavily on mathematics and the belief that there were absolute, unbreakable "axiomatic truths … from which it is possible by severe logic to deduce certain absolutely infallible conclusions."[10] Because "numbers don't lie," the Greeks believed that the cold realm of mathematics could lead to absolute wisdom and knowledge, which in turn could be used to order society in ways that could alleviate suffering, doubt, injustice, ignorance and vice.

Though civic virtue was given high priority by the Greeks, their path of attaining virtue was quite distinct from the Judeo-Christian ethos: an ethos predicated on faith, filial piety, charity, the brotherhood of man, a sense of duty, superiors and subordinates, transgression, sin, atonement and salvation via a messiah figure. This worldview, according to Berlin, would have been "totally unintelligible" to the Greeks.[11] Though the Judeo-Christian tradition places importance on numerology, it is not the primary premise from which that tradition takes its cue.

Some two millennia after Pythagoras the observations of Johannes Kepler and Jean-Philippe Rameau regarding universal harmony and universal

---

* *Scolica enchiriadis* is an anonymous ninth-century music theory treatise and a commentary on singing technique, ornamentation of plainchant, and polyphony in the style of organum. The text draws upon ideas about music articulated by Augustine and Boethius, with an emphasis on mathematical properties in music vis-à-vis the quadrivium.

mathematics were especially notable. Kepler's theories were among the first to give scientific credence to what previously had been largely a matter of faith and mythology. Yet, there is something deeply spiritual in his pursuit of a unified, all-encompassing cosmic theory. In describing the precepts of harmonic proportions in his seminal work on the topic, *Harmonices Mundi*, Kepler acknowledged that these proportions are infinite but also asserted that there was a way to "polish them" and "attach names to them." This was an attempt to "construct from them the splendid edifice of the harmonic system, or musical scale." As Kepler put it: "Its construction is not arbitrary, ... not a human invention ... but entirely rational, and entirely natural, so much so that God Himself the Creator has given expression to it in adjusting the heavenly motions to each other.[12] The notion that our ears are the "gateway" to our heart and soul is not an untenable proposition.

Musicologist Julius Portnoy observed that, "wherever gods reign, be they one or many, the physical character of music is indeed based on mechanics and explained by mathematics, but its origin is in heaven."[13] Is music God's voice speaking to us? Beethoven and many others have believed that. In fact, our ears are remarkable sense organs. In recent decades, much has been ascertained with regard to hearing, cognition, neuroscience and psychoacoustics, as researchers have advanced many insightful perspectives regarding music and its effect on our psyche.* Music theorist Hans Kayser has pointed out that our ears are able "to perceive numerical *quantity* as well as numerical *value*," and this perceptive capability is fundamental to the listening experience as it pertains to music. As Kayser explains:

> The ears not only recognize exact numerical proportions, that is, numerical quantities like 1:2 as an octave, 2:3 as a fifth, 3:4 as a fourth, etc.; at the same time they hear ... values that they perceive as C, G, F, and so on. So the tone value fuses two elements into one unit: the element of sensing—the tone, that is—with the element of thinking, of numerical value. ... In this way sensation controls deliberation—or to put it differently: Our soul is thus capable of deciding on the correctness or incorrectness of an intellectual quantity. Conversely, the phenomenon of tone value also gives us the

---

* The fifth-century BCE Greek musicologist Damon of Athens is said to be among the first to study the effects of different types of music on people's mood.

opportunity to develop proportions and numerical values in the realm of the psyche.[14]

Kayser also maintained that many of the things we find to be aesthetically beautiful, in nature and in art, are predicated to varying degrees, on the mathematical properties of the Golden Section: a geometric ratio that fascinated the Greeks and was believed to be a godly design concept. Some musicologists believe that Mozart may have used this formulation in several of his works. Hungarian musicologist Erno Lendvai published two books that attempted to ascribe the Fibonacci sequence to various compositions of his countryman Béla Bartók, though his extrapolations have not gained much acceptance. Certain compositions of Erik Satie and Claude Debussy are thought to be predicated on the mathematical properties of the Golden Section as well.*

Expounding on the concept of "sacred geometry," the seventeenth-century mathematician Gottfried Wilhelm Leibniz considered music to be "a hidden arithmetic exercise of the soul, which does not know it is dealing with numbers." Still, the soul senses that it is being affected by this "hidden arithmetic" and feelings of "well-being" or "discomfort," which is the result of this "unnoticeable forming of numbers."[15] What's remarkable is that all of this "tone value fusing" and cognitive processing happens instantaneously, with the effects resulting in sensations imparted by music on the psyche in an immediate fashion. Moreover, biochemistry reveals that music that appeals to us releases the pleasure-producing neurotransmitter dopamine into our bodies, and this provides an addictive sensation that results in our craving for more musical stimulation. Though we are not fully aware of this phenomenon as it is occurring, the sensations from the stimulation of hearing music are more real than imagined.

The potential liability of focusing primarily on the formulaic and mathematical aspects of music can have the effect of diminishing music's ultimate justification, but the idea that our ears are "hearing numbers" is a fascinating concept. Speculating on the mechanics of string theory in relation to the vibratory aspects of sound and music, futurist and theoretical physicist Michio

---

* The commercial drum manufacturers Pearl Drums and Tama have done research on the Golden Ratio and have incorporated their findings into their design concepts in order to create a favorable acoustic resonance in their percussion instruments.

Kaku suggests that the theory has quasi-musical properties that are similar to "musical notes on a tiny vibrating string," and that the inner workings of the universe could be "a symphony of vibrating strings."[16] To Kaku, these observations are more than mere analogies, but have some scientific basis, and are not unlike Einstein's speculations about God, music and cosmic geometry. Citing Kaku's assertions, contemporary physicist and jazz musician Stephon Alexander rhetorically asked, "And then what is the mind of God that Albert Einstein eloquently wrote about for the last thirty years of his life? We now, for the first time in history, have a candidate for the mind of God. It is cosmic music."[17]

Numerology

Historically the study of numerology has been associated with the occult, astrology, astronomy, the paranormal, the divinatory arts and "New Age" spirituality. However, the scriptural teachings of Judeo-Christian theology are inextricably linked to numerology: the Trinity, Jesus' 40-day fast, Jacob's 21 years in Haran, the 40-day flood judgment, God rested on the 7th day, the 8 Beatitudes, Jesus' 12 apostles and 72 disciples, the 12 gates of heaven, Jesus' 3 temptations, the 12 tribes of Israel, the 3 archangels, the 3 wise men, Peter's 3 denials, e.g.

It is intriguing to note that these scriptural numbers are multiples or combinations of the number 3 and 4. Certain Christian doctrines refer to the number 3 as being representative of heaven (the Trinity, Jesus resurrected on the third day, e.g.), while the number 4 is representative of earth and nature (the four seasons, the four trade winds, the four directions). Jewish prayers are often repeated in sequences of 3 and 7. Pythagoras believed that the number 3 was more significant than the number 2 due to the implication of a beginning, middle and end—three stages of development. The prime number 5 also has distinct musical implications in the context of the "circle of fifths" in Western tonal theory. Perhaps not so coincidentally, devout Muslims offer prayers five times each day.

Whereas Pythagoras considered the number 3 to be of prime importance, ancient Chinese philosophy emphasized the relationship between polar opposites; hence, the number 2 was significant. The concept of polarity is also highly evident in nature and music. A central tenet of ancient Chinese philosophy is that beauty is realized when any complementary opposites—e.g., *yang* and *yin*, intellectual and emotional, masculine and feminine, corporeal and incorporeal—exist in a harmonized fashion.

If an individual could be harmonized in mind and body, such a person would be able to achieve inner peace and tranquility. This in turn would be a way to achieve "oneness" with the Godhead, "the Great Ultimate," and with the cosmos, thereby attaining a "perfected" state: a state of harmonized relatedness to the world in which one exists. The I Ching speaks to the design of the created world as being predicated on the harmonious relationships of polar opposites: male and female, physical and metaphysical, mind and body and content and form, to name but a few.*

The Chinese text *The Spring and Autumn Annals*, written by Lu Bu Wei, offers further insight into this concept:

> Music has a very long history. It is composed according to precise rules based on *Tao*. *Tai Yi* develops *Two Yi*. *Two Yi* develops *Yin* and *Yang*. *Yin* ascends and *Yang* descends constantly, thus, everything in the world is created by the interaction of these two forms of vitality ... all things of the world are based on *Tao* and generated by the cooperation of *Yin* and *Yang*. When the youngest shoot starts to germinate, *Yin* and *Yang* will condense inside it, and it can thus develop a form. And when it has a fixed form, it must also occupy some space and it can also make a sound. The sound can be euphonious only when it is harmonious, and euphony can be created only when it is moderate. Ancient kings gave their tunes harmony according to the rules of harmony and moderation.[18]

This insightful verse touches on three important aspects of sound production from the ancient Chinese perspective: origin, polarity and harmonization. For the ancient Chinese, the importance of relatedness, as it pertained to the realization of any harmonized condition, was its origin in a first cause: "the Great One." Chinese cosmology viewed mathematics, astronomy, astrology and science as being interconnected and as such placed great importance on proper relationships. If Confucianism is about anything, it's about proper relationships.

---

* Consider the word, "individual": literally, an undivided duality—the harmonized duality of one's mind and body, i.e.

There are those who consider numerology to be pseudo-mathematics, but nature tells us otherwise. Einstein—who played the violin and the piano—posited that the laws of gravity are predicated on the idea that there exists a geometric link to time and space. Music occurs over time and sound vibrations move through space. The acoustic principles of sound production are defined by mathematical ratios, and as philosophers and theorists of antiquity would eventually realize, mathematics was intrinsic to virtually every aspect of the natural world, including music—all music.

Plato's poetic myth of "the music of the spheres," with its implications of a universal, interconnected cosmic geometry—as well as the Pythagorean concept of "music as a microcosm"—was not unlike the philosophical tenets of Confucius, who posited that the underlying principles of music and sound production were governed by the same scientific and mathematical laws that governed the cosmos. Einstein proffered that these relationships were elemental and essential in the quest of "spreading moral and cultural understanding" in the pursuit of freedom. Though his perspective was disputed, often in the most hostile fashion, the "sacredness of the goal" was not.

> All religions, arts and sciences are branches of the same tree. All these aspirations are directed toward ennobling man's life, lifting it from the sphere of mere physical existence and leading the individual toward freedom. ... Both churches and universities—insofar as they live up to their true function—serve the ennoblement of the individual.[19]

With the decline of Rome and the ascendance of Christianity in Europe during the third and fourth centuries, the seeds that would blossom into the great art of the Western world were planted deeply into the fertile soil of religious faith and practice. Arnold Toynbee's assessment that the Church was "the chrysalis out of which our Western society emerged ... [the] germ of creative power"[20] attests to the role that Christian thought played in the development of Western culture, in general, and of musical theory, aesthetics and axiology, in particular.*

---

* In philosophy, axiology is the study of values, which has a significant bearing on morality and ethics.

A central tenet of Greek philosophy, which came to the early church via Rome, specified that music was a medium connected to the forces of nature and that it possessed the power to affect human thought and conduct. This precept was assimilated into early Christian culture and reiterated in the writings of several Christian philosophers, most notably Boethius (c. 480-524 CE), St. Augustine (354-430 CE) and Thomas Aquinas (1225-1274 CE).

The evolution of music and its integration into liturgical practice throughout the Middle Ages gave rise to new attitudes about music and its purpose and function: most notably the idea that music was to be the "servant" of religion. The church elders of early Christianity deemed music to be good only when it "opens the mind to Christian teachings and disposes it to holy thoughts."[21] The church in the Middle Ages was highly concerned with the potentially corrupting elements of music and as a result, certain factions within the church hierarchy were inimical to music in the church. Yet the aesthetic beauty of music and its beneficial effects on the soul could not be denied.

Alluding to Augustine and the underpinnings of music's divine and mathematical properties, David P. Goldman notes:

> Music employs number both in its harmonic foundation and its metrical presentation in time. But what sort of number is it? In the sixth book of his De Musica, Augustine asserted the existence of a higher order of number that in some way stands above the senses, the numeri iudiciales or "numbers of judgment" which "come from God" and enable the mind to judge what it perceives and remembers, as well as what it expects. Augustine's assertion is arresting in all three of its parts: first, that neither our sense perception nor even our memory explains how we hear music; second, that the faculty by which we judge the numbers (rhythms or harmonies) of music is also a kind of number; and third, that this higher-order number comes from God.[22]

The Christians of medieval Europe believed that the aspirations of spiritual fulfillment and redemption could possibly be hindered or obstructed by the pagan or pleasurable aspects of music, and this troubled even the most enlightened practitioners of the faith. St. Augustine's concern and distrust of music notwithstanding, the church would eventually see (or hear!) the benefit of music, acting as an efficacious mediator between heaven and earth.

Tonality as Revelation

In musical parlance "tonality" refers to the codified system of pitch and chord relationships that results in a specific hierarchical syntax that induces *aurally perceived* stabilities and attractions. How various pitches relate and function is the essence of the Western tonal syntax, not unlike how phonetics and words provide meaning in natural languages. As in the evolution of natural languages, the "rules" that govern the musical grammar of the tonal syntax grew out of the subconscious and were abstracted after usage, not before.

As composers in Europe during the Renaissance began to write music with greater linear complexity (polyphony), the natural by-product of this process was a vertical alignment of tones that possessed definite harmonic modalities.* Experiments in tuning and interval modification by Flemish mathematician Simon Stevin and Chinese theorist Zhu Zaiyu, along with the evolution of harmonic syntax though the fifteenth and sixteenth centuries in Europe, led to the development of specific tonal theories, which in turn gave rise to an ordered system of major and minor key centers. This can be seen as a musical manifestation of the *yang* and *yin* properties of polar opposites found in nature. Stevin asserted that mathematical evidence demonstrated that the division of the octave into twelve equal intervals was "the *only natural tuning*" and other tuning systems contained too many faults to be considered "natural."[23]

In his Harvard Norton Lectures in 1973, Leonard Bernstein referred to the major pentatonic scale as being "humanity's favorite" scale. This 5-note scale, "handed to us by nature," is based on the first five different pitches in a given overtone series, and is common to the music of Asia, Ireland, Eastern Europe and Africa. Diatonic tonality, predicated on a 7-note scale, evolved as a musical syntax from the monophonic music of the early Christian church in Europe, and although this type of tonal centricity can also be found to varying degrees in the folk music of Asia, Africa and the Middle East, including in *maqams* (7-note Arabic scales), it came to its full flowering in Europe. As

---

* David P. Goldman, classical music critic at *Tablet* magazine, writes: "At the University of Padua, Prosdocimus de Beldemandis showed in 1425 that Pythagorean calculations could divide the octave into twelve half-tones, identifying all the accidentals required to build a scale starting on any tone. Nicholas of Cusa studied at Padua at the time and surely knew Prosdocimus. The trouble was that Pythagorean arithmetic produced intervals that sound audibly out of tune." [Source: *First Things* Magazine, April 2012.]

musical theory developed in the West, the numerological properties governing the musical organization of sound and rhythm serendipitously reflected the numerology found in scripture. Was this purely coincidental, or was there an implicit mathematical design in the tonal equation?

The development of a tuning system in which "natural" intervals were modified proportionally into twelve equal parts within the aural span of an octave allowed for greater innovation in the realm of composition. The resultant tuning system, known as equal temperament, allowed composers to create music rich in melodic and harmonic variation in their attempts to be more expressive. Here again is a scenario in which mathematics affects the production of art in a significant fashion, resulting in a creative "explosion, that immense boom of music in the Western world that numbers among the greatest phenomena in the cultural history of humankind."[24]

The diatonic major and minor scales, based on a specific sequence of intervals, along with the use of triads (three pitches sounding either simultaneously or in a sequence based on each note of a scale) became the fundamental properties of Western tonality. When certain triads establish a subject-object, or *yang-yin*, relation within a given harmonic progression, an aural base or "home" key center becomes aurally perceptible. How does all this relate to numerology? Consider the following numerological and relational properties in Western tonality.

There are two basic modalities: major and minor. The octave in Western music is divided into 12 equal parts (semitones). There are 7 pitches in the diatonic scale, with the 8th pitch being the start of a new octave—a "new beginning," as referenced in the Bible. (Circumcision in the Hebrew tradition was also to be done on the 8th day after the male child's birth). There are 7 "flat" major keys and 7 "sharp" major keys, and each major key has its relative minor key (C major-A minor, G major-E minor, e.g.). These relative minor scales are started on the pitch located a minor 3rd below its major antecedent. (The pitch A is a minor 3rd lower than C, e.g.)

As previously noted, the basis of Western harmony is the triad—a vertical organization of 3 pitches. Tonality is also hierarchical and relational in that the aural center of a particular modality can be determined only when two or more pitches or triads exist in a relationship.[*] In the tonal syntax, a G major triad (consisting of the pitches G-B-D), for instance, can serve one of four functions depending on the context in which it occurs. Those functions can be either primarily subjective (tonic or dominant) or objective (subdominant or submediant.) Here, multiples of the numbers 3 and 4 are intrinsic to triadic function—a single 3-note chord (triad) being able to serve in four distinct functions based on its position within a specific key center. Dominant chords and secondary dominant chords also exist in a subject-object relational mode.

Musical architecture and form were also influenced by the evolution of the tonal syntax. Sonata form, a musical structure that was prominent in the eighteenth and nineteenth centuries, is a musical form that encompasses a dual-key tonal framework and has three distinct sections: the exposition, the development and the recapitulation. This tripartite musical structure reflects Pythagoras' views regarding the number 3.

Examples of polarity, harmony and relatedness, as expressed in the afore-mentioned ancient Chinese verse by Lu Bu Wei, are highly evident in Western tonal music, including the polarity of major and minor keys, major and minor triads within those keys, tonic and dominant harmonies, consonant and disso-nant intervals, whole tones and semitones and diatonicism and chromaticism. In addition to these tonal properties there are other polar opposites that come into play when creating or performing music: fast and slow tempos, long and short durations, high and low pitches, adjacent and nonadjacent tones, loud and soft volume (dynamics), getting louder (crescendo) and getting softer (diminuendo), tempo acceleration (accelerando) and tempo deceleration (ritardando), bright timbres and dark timbres, parallel motion and contrary motion, duple meters (2/4, 4/4, 2/2) and triple meters (3/4, 6/8, 9/8), sym-metrical meters (2/4, 4/4, 2/2) and asymmetrical meters (5/4, 5/8, 7/8).

When these polar characteristics are organized in a harmonized fashion, music begins to reflect attributes that embody a divine expression ontolog-ically. St. Paul noted in Romans 1:20 that God's invisible nature and deity

---

[*] In Leonard Cohen's iconic song "Hallelujah," he sings: "I heard there was a secret chord/That David played and it pleased the Lord." Since I have proffered that the concept of polarity has divine origins, perhaps it was the relationship between two or more chords, rather than a single, isolated chord, that truly pleased the Lord.

can be clearly perceived in the created world; hence, music that embodies the characteristics found in nature can be said to have "godly" attributes.

Ontological Matters

There exists a common misconception that tonal music refrains from the use of dissonance, when in fact it is the interplay between consonant and dissonant intervals that creates, conveys and evokes emotion in tonal music. Phonetically, these two different, qualitative characteristics are akin to consonants and vowels in all natural languages, in that they are common and necessary. The overtone series, the sonic etymology of all music, contains intervals that are both consonant and dissonant. It is the relational modality between those intervals (and the chords in which they exist), within the syntax of tonality—through tension and resolution—that gives tonal music its emotive and communicative power. Hegel noted that though music was "nonrepresentational," it nevertheless possessed definite structural and mathematic properties that served its expressive function: "Music is architecture translated or transposed from space into time; for in music, besides the deepest feeling, there reigns also a rigorous mathematical intelligence."[25] Hegel might have viewed these various polar opposites as being in "conflict" with one another, but while Hegel emphasized conflict as the mode of attaining progress, the Chinese emphasized harmony and relatedness.

Eduard Hanslick, the notable nineteenth-century music critic and aesthetician, argued against "aesthetics of feeling" in his influential book *The Beautiful in Music*. It was his supposition that emotion does not exist in the materials of music, itself (pitch sets, rhythms, harmonic progressions, e.g.). Though beauty arouses emotion and can "awaken feelings" in the listener, Hanslick, like Hegel, contended that music is "nonrepresentational" in that musical materials have no emotional aspect to them. His attitude would seem to be at odds with Arthur Schopenhauer (and Richard Wagner), who argued that music "does not express this or that individual or particular joy, this or that sorrow or pain or horror or exaltation or cheerfulness or peace of mind, but rather joy, sorrow, pain, horror, exaltation, cheerfulness and peace of mind as such *in themselves*, abstractly, as it were, the essential in all these without anything superfluous."[26] In other words, joyful music isn't merely a representation of joy, but *it is* joyful.

Hanslick's view that individual musical materials (an isolated pitch or chord, e.g.) in and of themselves contain no inherent emotional aspect may have some veracity. Music, however, is all about the sum of its parts and the effect on our psyche when those constituent parts are ordered in an artful fashion. Therefore, the juxtaposing of mathematical properties—frequencies, ratios, durations, velocity, decibels, meter—according to a specific syntactical codification of said properties, causes sensory stimulation resulting in a manifestation of beauty and meaning in music.

When we consider the ontological aspects of the created world, specifically the macrocosmic dualities that fascinated the ancients, as well as the microcosmic interactions that Max Planck brought to light via quantum physics, it is readily apparent that there is a design that governs the way in which the universe operates. In music, the evolution of tonality and the establishment of equal temperament have been viewed by some as artificial and "mathematically constructed," apart from natural or divine concordance. Music theorist Ross W. Duffin argues that equal temperament has had injurious effects on music and that most musicians have been inured to the deleterious effects that its near universal acceptance has caused. He attributes this scenario to "the recent evolutions in musical performance and teaching, the result of decades of delusion, convenience, ignorance, conditioning and oblivion."[27]

Taking Duffin's reasoning at face value it could be extrapolated that Bach, Mozart, Beethoven, Wagner, Debussy and Mahler were all duped by the spurious concoction of temperament. But as Berendt construed, the division of the octave (a *macro*-interval) into twelve equal "subspaces" (*micro*-intervals) reflects Planck's quantum mechanics, in that "effects can be produced only as a multiple of a smallest unit no longer open to further division."[28] J. S. Bach put the finishing touches on the development of equal temperament in 1722, and the resulting concordance of science and imagination toward an aesthetic end was in no small measure why the aforementioned "explosion" of tonal music occurred in Christian Europe.

Microtonal music divides music into smaller sonic intervals. The music of many non-Western cultures such as those of Indonesia, Japan, China and Korea (Pansori) employ microtonal intervals and pitch bending to significant degrees. The contemporary Chinese composer Tan Dun uses the microtonal influences of Peking opera in his compositions. European composers such as

Italian Renaissance theorist Nicola Vicentino—a student of Adrian Willaert, an early tuning experimentalist—employed a 36-note scale in his music and built a specialized keyboard instrument with six rows of keys that he called the *archicembalo* to realize his music. Twentieth-century American composer Harry Partch divided the octave into as many as 43 intervals based on "just intonation" (as opposed to equal temperament) that required the creation of custom-made instruments and specialized notation to realize his compositions. Though microtonal music is fairly common in non-Western cultures and in experimental modern music, it has not globally supplanted tonality as a preferred syntax. This may be due to the aural properties of its quasi-dissonant modality, a modality that may not yield enough of a perceptible differentiation of tones, thereby creating aural indeterminacy, which in turn fails to yield an aesthetic that would be considered ingratiating, beautiful or satisfying by most listeners.

Cosmic polarity—"stars and elementary particles, plants and marine animals, crystals and leaf forms, the male and female bodies and sexuality, cathedrals and cloisters, the structure of the earth"—provides evidence that the enlightened souls of antiquity and their modernist counterparts were on the right track as they contemplated the primordial stuff and grand design of the universe.[29] The ontological premise that asserts that the harmonization and connectedness of various polar opposites, along with the numerological properties found in nature, are what yield beauty and meaning in music, and in life, seems fundamentally correct. Moreover, numerology plays a significant role in matters of creation and of restoration, and the nexus of music and mathematics could be considered a reflection of intelligent design.

Stephon Alexander reminds us that contemporary physicists are "very aware that their beautiful mathematical models fall short of describing what they see." Though Alexander concedes that these models fail to explain many of the eternal questions that we still seek answers to, especially with regard to aesthetics, spirituality and the purpose of life, he nonetheless asks a perspicacious question: "Could the cosmos, in fact, be a vast harmonic realization of vibrations?"[30] Recognizing that the concept of cosmic math vis-à-vis music has credibility, the answer could be: Yes!

Isacoff suggests that there are times when calls for reason "are no match in the human psyche for the potency of numbers, which over time become invested with hopes, dreams, and convictions until they are no longer mere numbers but narratives heavy with meaning."[31] We intuit that that which is observable via science does not completely satisfy our internal or spiritual needs. Love, beauty and truth can fulfill those needs when understood according to their proper positions and proportions.

Because scripture stipulates that love and beauty are in the subject position in relation to the objective realities of law and science, it's important to understand what ought to be prioritized in the pursuit of a principled culture. The tendency of the human condition to gravitate toward that which satisfies our emotional and spiritual longings, rather than to study law and science, is an innate desire. This not meant to diminish the significance of the physical realm, but to better understand this particular ontological actuality. Numbers matter to the extent that they help ascertain the physical, objective properties of the cosmos. The divine nexus of music and mathematics can be seen as evidence of God's love as expressed through the beauty of music, and God's truth as manifested through the lawfulness of mathematics.

A divine nexus, indeed.

Postscript

Throughout the history of Western musical development and the search for standardizations of tuning and compositional syntax, there have been numerous attempts to find common ground with regard to the most efficacious or natural modes for tuning musical instruments. Finding a mutually agreed upon "concert pitch"—a pitch preference that all instruments in a given ensemble are tuned to—has been an ongoing process for centuries. Currently, the accepted standard is A (above middle C on the grand staff) at 440 hertz.*

In Europe during the 1800s the hertz measurement could be as low as A at 400 or as high as 450. Seventeenth-century German composer Michael Praetorius reported that tuning as high as 450 hertz put enormous strains on singers in their upper tessituras. Modern orchestras in the United States and

---

* Hertz (Hz) is a unit of frequency. It is defined as the number of complete cycles per second. It is the basic unit of frequency in the International System of Units (SI) and is used worldwide in both general-purpose and scientific contexts. The term "hertz" is named after the German physicist Heinrich Hertz (1857–1894), who made important scientific contributions to the study of electromagnetism.

Europe are known to use tunings close to A at 440 hertz, though there is some degree of variation depending on the ensemble.

Scientific pitch, also known as "Verdi tuning," uses a lower pitch standard of middle C at 236 hertz (or A at 430.52). Recently there has been a renewed interest in tuning A at 432 hertz, which is considered to be in accord with cosmic harmony and is said to have healing powers due to its vibratory properties, which are said to have a relationship with the double helix in DNA replication.

Recommended Recordings

Bach: Unaccompanied Cello Suites, Yo-Yo Ma, cello

Mozart: *Antretter Serenade*, K. 185, Christopher Hogwood, Academy of Ancient Music

Beethoven: *Kreutzer* Sonata, Yehudi Menuhin, violin, Wilhelm Kempff, piano

Wagner: Orchestral Music, Klaus Tennstedt, Berlin Philharmonic

Mahler: Symphony No. 3, Jascha Horenstein, London Symphony Orchestra

Partch: *U.S. Highball*, Jack McKenzie, Gate 5 Ensemble

Satie: *Sonneries de la Rose + Croix*, Cristina Ariagno, piano

Willaert: *O magnum mysterium*, Marco Gemmani, Cappella Marciana

Debussy: "Reflets dans l'eau", *Images, Book 1*, Ivan Moravec, piano

Bartók: *Music for Strings, Percussion and Celesta*, Iván Fischer, Budapest Festival Orchestra

Endnotes

1   David P. Goldman, "The Divine Music of Mathematics: How Music Theory Proves What Ancient Mathematics Though Impossible," *First Things*, April 2012.

2   Yehudi Menuhin, *Theme and Variations* (New York: Stein and Day, 1972), p. 9.

3   Proclus, *A Commentary on the First Book of Euclid's Elements*, translated by Glenn Raymond Morrow (Princeton, NJ: Princeton University Press, 1992), pp. 29-30.

4   Stuart Isacoff, *Temperament: The Idea that Solved Music's Greatest Riddle* (New York: Alfred A. Knopf, 2001), p. 11.

5   Joseph Campbell, *Myths to Live By* (London: Penguin Books, 1993), pp. 4-5.

6   Stuart Isacoff, *Temperament*, p. 7.

7   Joachim-Ernst Berendt, *The World Is Sound: Nada Brahma* (Rochester, VT: Destiny Books, 1987), pp. 59-60.

8   Isacoff, *Temperament*, p. 29.

9   *Scolica enchiriadis*, translated by Lawrence Rosenwald, as cited in *Music in the Western World: A History in Documents*, edited by Piero Weiss and Richard Taruskin, second edition (Belmont, CA: Thomson/Schirmer, 2008), p. 34.

10   Isaiah Berlin, *The Roots of Romanticism*, edited by Henry Hardy (Princeton, NJ: Princeton University Press, 1999), p. 2.

11   Ibid., p. 3.

12   Johannes Kepler, *The Harmony of the World*, translated by E. J. Aiton, Alistair Matheson Duncan, Judith Veronica Field (American Philosophical Society, 1997), p. 158.

13   Julius Portnoy, *Music in the Life of Man* (New York: Holt, Rinehart and Winton, 1963).

14   Hans Kayser, as cited by Berendt, *The World Is Sound*, pp. 135-136.

15   Berendt, *The World Is Sound*, p. 67.

16   Michio Kaku, as cited by Stephon Alexander, *The Jazz of Physics: The Secret Link between Music and the Structure of the Universe* (New York: Basic Books, 2016), pp. 51-52.

17   Ibid.

18   Lu Bu Wei, *The Spring and Autumn Annals of Lu Bu Wei* (Guangxi, China: Guangxi Normal University Press, 2005), p. 151.

19   Albert Einstein, *The Einstein Reader* (New York: Citadel Press, 2006), p. 7.

20   Arnold Toynbee, as cited by Donald J. Grout and Claude V. Palisca, *A History of Western Music* (New York: W. W. Norton & Company, 1960), p. 32.

21   Ibid., p. 31.

22   Goldman, "The Divine Music of Mathematics."

23   Isacoff, *Temperament*, p. 145.

24   Berendt, *The World Is Sound*, p. 116.

25   G.W.F. Hegel, as cited by Willey Francis Gates, *In Praise of Music* (Philadelphia: Theodore Presser, 1898), p. 110.

26   Arthur Schopenhauer, *The World as Will and Representation*, Volume I, edited by Judith Norman, Alistair Welchman, and Christopher Janaway (Cambridge: Cambridge University Press, 2011), pp. 287-290.

27   Ross W. Duffin, *How Equal Temperament Ruined Harmony (and Why You Should Care)* (New York and London: W. W. Norton & Company, 2007), p. 16.

28   Berendt, *The World Is Sound*, p. 116.

29   Ibid., p. 76.

30 Alexander, *The Jazz of Physics,* pp. 83-84.

31 Isacoff, *Temperament,* p. 146.

15

Arrested Development

Adolescent energy is usually mistaken for vitality
and our social vision is corrupted
by the limitations of overgrown children.
If Barack Obama were to create actual change
we can believe in, he would first urge the country
to grow up and not deny the new era
that is the result of its freedom from the fear of past stereotypes
and its impassioned optimism, which is most
important when wedded to reason.[1]
Stanley Crouch

Like many Americans, I viewed January 20, 2009 as a significant day in American history. Upon hearing President Barack Obama's inaugural speech on that day, I was taken by his call for maturity in a time of uncertainty and deep trepidation. His reference to scripture and the need to "grow up" had a particular resonance for me in light of the cultural milieu in which we live.

We remain a young nation. But in the words of Scripture, the time has come to set aside childish things. The time has come to reaffirm our enduring spirit; to choose our better history; to carry forward that precious gift, that noble idea passed on from generation to generation: the God-given promise that all are equal, all are free, and all deserve a chance to pursue their full measure of happiness. …

What is required of us now is a new era of responsibility—a recognition, on the part of every American, that we have duties to ourselves, our nation, and the world; duties that we do not grudgingly accept, but rather seize gladly, firm in the knowledge that there is nothing so satisfying to the spirit, so defining of our character than giving our all to a difficult task.

This is the price and the promise of citizenship. This is the source of our confidence—the knowledge that God calls on us to shape an uncertain destiny.[2]

Life, liberty and the pursuit of happiness—the American ideal—our shared patrimony; and at the heart of that ideal lies an understanding that answering to a higher authority is part of the process of achieving true fulfillment.

We know that there are many ways through which we can attain happiness. President Obama's call for accepting our responsibilities with the requisite alacrity was especially meaningful. His was a call for a deep-seated happiness, based on a mutual sacrifice, predicated on a God-centered ideal. It would seem that most citizens, though not all, would embrace that call given the religious underpinnings of American culture. In spite of our nation's many flaws, we have made great sacrifices towards the cause of preserving peace and defeating tyranny. One would hope that President Obama's call for selflessness and living for the sake of one's nation would continue to be looked on as a necessary civic responsibility.

The civil rights movement demonstrated uncommon courage in the face of domestic tyranny. Commenting on civil rights pioneer Dr. Joseph Lowery—who delivered the benediction at President Obama's first inaugural—*New York Daily News* columnist and jazz historian Stanley Crouch alluded to both Obama's message regarding adult sensibilities and Lowery's paraphrase of the lyrics to Big Bill Broonzy's song "Black, Brown and White." Crouch commented:

Howell Raines expressed surprise that [comedian] Jon Stewart and his writing crew did not know Lowery was playing off the historic couplet about discrimination based on skin color that Lowery made fun of at the end of the benediction. [White will be alright, brown will stick around, yellow will be mellow, etc.]

Why would they know it? Those men specialize in "enlightened" frat-boy humor, which is why John McCain, who has actual wit, walked all over Stewart whenever he appeared on his show. That was not the intention, there is just a big difference between a frat boy and a man.

Barack Obama has the presence and creates the effects expected of adults. He is not a frat boy or an ethnic bad boy. It is well past the time when Americans should show their pride in this country by moving as swiftly as they can away from the adolescence that our nation has been progressively overcome by since the Berkeley Strike of 1964, the slogan of which was, "Don't Trust Anyone Over 30."

Adolescent energy is usually mistaken for vitality and our social vision is corrupted by the limitations of overgrown children. If Barack Obama were to create actual change we can believe in, he would first urge the country to grow up and not deny the new era that is the result of its freedom from the fear of past stereotypes and its impassioned optimism, which is most important when wedded to reason.[3]

Crouch gets it right here. The jejune qualities that constitute what is fashionable in terms of art, music and our social consciousness are too often the result of arrested emotional development. "We have a popular culture," Crouch has averred, "that misleads the young as it bolsters their commitment to narcissism and opposition to authority. The mentality of the American adolescent is that he or she has a right to be respected no matter how offensive what is done might seem to others."[4] This mentality can ultimately be destructive.

The freedom to dissent, offend and speak one's mind is part of American pluralism. However, offending others can have consequences. Respect for "the other" in the society in which one lives is a sign of a mature expression of egalitarian ideals. It will take adult sensibilities to pull the country out of the severe tailspin it now finds itself in. Young people who channel their energy and talent into responsible actions are badly needed. Many young people in the military are making important life choices, and the Jon Stewarts of the world need to get that. The adolescent sensibilities that tend to permeate contemporary culture are not helpful in an era of global and societal crisis. It's been suggested that Stewart's comic sensibilities would not necessarily play well in places outside the liberal bastions of Manhattan or Hollywood.

The penchant for making light of serious issues or circumstances has fostered a creeping cynicism in our national dialogue. Dana Gioia, former chairman of the National Endowment for the Arts, offered a troubling but accurate perspective concerning the shallowness that has become so pervasive in our culture. Speaking to the 2007 graduating class of Stanford University on the superficiality of the "celebrity-industrial complex" (my appellation) and its effects, he stated:

> I'm not forgetting that politicians can also be famous, but it is interesting how our political process grows more like the entertainment industry each year. When a successful guest appearance on the Colbert Report becomes more important than passing legislation, democracy gets scary. No wonder Hollywood considers politics "show business for ugly people." ...
>
> Distinguished graduates, your support system is about to end. And you now face the choice of whether you want to be a passive consumer or an active citizen. Do you want to watch the world on a screen or live in it so meaningfully that you change it?[5]

If our citizenry needs to grow up, then perhaps we need more musical expressions that assist in that process. Much of the commercially oriented realm of popular culture contributes to the condition of fettering the development of adult consciousness, in that it is based on a lowest-common-denominator rationale rather than higher and nobler aspirations. Composers, producers and artists of all disciplines bear a certain responsibility in our nation's growth process.

In the natural progression of growth and maturity, developing a parental heart in dealing with life's challenges seems concomitant with President Obama's clarion call. Adults who behave in an adolescent manner, as Crouch suggests, cannot offer much that is constructive in the process of shaping our shared destiny. Arrested development is antipodal to the necessary national psyche that President Obama endorsed, therefore artists ought to be a part of the national growth process. As we seek solutions that will enable us to become more responsible and more sensitive to the needs of our families, communities and nation, we might start with heeding President Obama's call to action and examine our sensibilities vis-à-vis what is truly important and necessary for our growth and maturation—individually and collectively.

Expressions of art and music that are the progeny of frat-boy humor, or MTV and sitcom mentalities with regard to sexuality, acceptance, relationships, race and love, will not get us to a better place. We can do better. The fate of our nation and its role in the world hang in the balance. That might seem to be a bit hyperbolic, but it's hard to deny that our cultural identity, as it relates to what we value, is too often manipulated or influenced by the worst of what we are rather than by the best of what we are. The collective arrested development that President Obama alluded to does not serve us well, and the world is taking note.

In a provocative essay for *City Journal*, Manhattan Institute Fellow Kay S. Hymowitz identified a number of the conditions that contribute to the immature attitudes of single young men (SYM) in their 20s and 30s. Among these include the aforementioned "frat-boy" attitudes about sex, women, music, entertainment and relationships in general. She points to the influence of the "Frat Pack" actors and comedians whose movies perpetuate a predilection for adolescent themes—Adam Sandler, Ben Stiller, Vince Vaughn, Owen Wilson, e.g. The entertainment market is saturated with "gross-out humor," "gleeful juvenility," "self-humiliation," "stupid fun" and even "low-level sadism." A staple of David Letterman's show was "Stupid Human Tricks," which could bee considered a gratuitous display of "low-level sadism." And then there is the video game culture. As Hymowitz notes:

> Nothing attests more to the SYM's growing economic and cultural might than video games do. Once upon a time, video games were for little boys and girls—well, mostly little boys—who loved their Nintendos so much, the lament went, that they no longer played ball outside. Those boys have grown up to become child-man gamers, turning a niche industry into a $12 billion powerhouse. Men between the ages of 18 and 34 are now the biggest gamers.[6]

The video game culture is especially coercive considering the violent and debased nature of many of the biggest sellers—*Grand Theft Auto*, e.g. Young men have become increasingly inured to the inhumane subject matter of these video games, and this contributes to a state of nihilistic desensitization. This desensitization has become alarmingly pervasive.

One of my sisters has been an elementary school teacher for decades. She often laments the condition of many of her students who lack basic social skills. As she tells it, she loves to teach but spends much of her time trying to teach her students how to be good human beings and how to relate to her and their fellow classmates in a respectful manner. She sees how family breakdown has led to the scenario where teachers have become surrogate parents rather than facilitators of knowledge. Because children are not being inculcated with good and responsible behavior in their families, they simply do not function well in the classroom. The link between parental responsibility and academic achievement cannot be overlooked or underestimated.

As Americans continue to fall behind other countries in academics and scholastic achievement, there seems to be no abatement in the dumbing down of American culture. America's role in the world is also of no small signif-icance. Yet Roger Scruton, though a non-American, still sees America as a symbol of hope for other nations and peoples who aspire to the civil liberties we sometimes take for granted—or abuse. Scruton notes:

> It is because of America, its success, its conflicts, and its symbolic impor-tance in the world, that the question raised by Spengler is still with us: the question of Western identity. Take away America, its freedom, its optimism, its institutions, its Judeo-Christian beliefs, and its educational tradition, and little would remain of the West, besides the geriatric routines of a now tooth-less Europe. Add America to the discussion, and all the dire prophecies and mournful valedictions of the twentieth century seem faintly ridiculous. Yet, precisely because the West now depends upon America ... Western identity has become an urgent matter of debate.[7]

That dependency comes with a price. As Scruton has pointed out, the tri-umph of America has fostered a great deal of opprobrium, born out of "a bitter and destructive envy." Many of America's harshest critics are also among the world's biggest hypocrites. Listening to tyrants in Venezuela, China or Iran chide the United States for its problems is laughable yet tragic; especially tragic for the good citizens in those places where human rights are continually trampled upon. Historically, dictatorships have been built on the suffering of the masses.

Will we make choices that will actually help us to grow up and be part of the solution? That is no insignificant question. Artists and producers especially need to find mature answers, and hopefully those answers will result in more mature artistic expressions. The answers may not come in an instant, but without mature citizens examining our problems in the context of "a new era of responsibility," there is just no way to get beyond the pathologies that continue to plague of families, and by extension, our nation.

Postscript

Regrettably, much of the promise of President Obama's first inaugural speech did not come to fruition. In fact, as a nation we've become even more polarized, with seemingly little measurable progress in our attempts to find common ground and symbiosis. Our political divide seems intractable. Political violence seems inevitable, especially with the ascendency of militant leftist activism. Writing for *National Review*, Ian Tuttle offered this commentary on militant activism in earlier times:

> Sophisticated justifications for violence were part and parcel of this fever. Leftist radicals were immersed in revolutionary literature—Lenin, Mao, Che Guevara, Malcolm X's Autobiography—and those texts were candid. In 1963, Frantz Fanon published The Wretched of the Earth, the first sentence of which read: "National liberation, national reawakening, restoration of the nation to the people or Commonwealth, whatever the name used, whatever the latest expression, decolonization is always a violent event."[8]

One would have hoped that the election of President Obama would have ushered in an era of greater civility and "rightly ordered affections" rather than "destructive political passions."[9] But alas, that didn't happen. Arrested development remains a bane for our culture at a time when adult sensibilities are so badly needed. Stanley Crouch may have been more earnest in his calls for maturity than President Obama. The ascendance of identity politics and progressive-oriented political correctness in recent years has brought the United States to a place where calls for civil discourse are characterized as a means to perpetuate privilege and supremacy. As a result, invective and vituperative rhetoric are excused in order to advance social justice, but much is lost in these diatribes and any chance for better relations becomes futile.

If I may cite scripture in the manner of President Obama, I would turn to Galatians 3:27-28 in which we read: "Those of you who were baptized into Christ have been clothed with Christ. There is no Jew or Greek, slave or free, male and female; since you are all one in Christ Jesus." In one fell swoop St. Paul wipes away the ideas of race, class, gender and oppressor and oppressed as controlling identities. Not everyone believes in God, and in these turbid times the idea of a transcendent morality is often eviscerated by those who see religion as being more of a problem than a solution.

Conversely, not everyone agrees with politicians like President Obama that politics can solve problems that are cultural in nature. Still, without adult sensibilities being in the socio-cultural calculation, we shouldn't expect that we can magically get beyond the self-centeredness and individualism that hinder our quest to fashion a society in which justice, equality and overall betterment are attained. In the months prior to the 2020 presidential election, the former president called out those who engage in "cancel culture" saying that illiberal behavior of that sort wasn't real activism.

In his book, *The Fractured Republic: Renewing America's Social Contract in the Age of Individualism*, Yuval Levin asserts that an alternative to the "perilous mix of over-centralization and hyper-individualism" exists, and it begins "in loving family attachments." Levin posits that this modality can provide a basis for "a national identity that among its foremost attributes is dedicated to the *principle of the equality of the entire human race.*"[10] (Emphasis added.) If we take the view that we are all God's children, we ought to relate to each other as if that were so. This mindset can and should be inculcated within families, and ideally mature parents can inculcate their children in ways that will accelerate the maturation process.

Endnotes

1   Stanley Crouch, "Barack Obama's Helping Hands: New President Traveled Road Paved with Civil Rights Heroes, not Race," *New York Daily News*, January 25, 2009.

2   Barack Obama, First Inaugural Address, January 21, 2009, https://obamawhitehouse.archives.gov/blog/2009/01/21/president-barack-obamas-inaugural-address.

3   Crouch, "Barack Obama's Helping Hands."

4   Stanley Crouch, "Eric Adams Is Right: Young Black Men Mistake Dehumaniza-
    tion for Authenticity," *New York Daily News*, May 23, 2010.

5   Dana Gioia, "Trade Easy Pleasures for More Complex and Challenging Ones,"
    commencement address, *Stanford Report*, June 17, 2007. http://news.stanford.
    edu/news/2007/june20/gradtrans-062007.html.

6   Kay S. Hymowitz, "Child-Man in the Promised Land," *City Journal*, Winter
    2008, https://www.city-journal.org/html/child-man-promised-land-13063.html.

7   Roger Scruton, *Culture Counts: Faith and Feeling in a World Besieged* (New York:
    Encounter Books, 2007), p. viii.

8   Ian Tuttle, "Everyone an Enemy: The Vague and Dangerous Ideology of Leftist
    Violence," *National Review*, May 29, 2017.

9   Ibid.

10 Yuval Levin, *The Fractured Republic: Renewing America's Social Contract in the Age
    of Individualism* (New York: Basic Books, 2016), p. 4.

16

Instant Gratification

*For the last five centuries, ever since Gutenberg's printing press
made book reading a popular pursuit, the linear, literary mind
has been at the center of art, science, and society.
As supple as it is subtle, it's been the imaginative mind
of the Renaissance, the rational mind of the Enlightenment,
the inventive mind of the Industrial Revolution, even the subversive
mind of Modernism. It may soon be yesterday's mind.*
Nicholas Carr

'm not sure where the term "instant gratification" originated in the contemporary lexicon of behavioral studies, but Aristotle was highly critical of
a culture that prioritized immediate gratification in its pursuit of happiness,
and Freud spoke of "impulse control" and "immediate gratification" in his
discourse on human psychology. Notable psychiatrists such as Aaron T. Beck
and Stephen Strakowski contend that an outsized need for gratification can
be a symptom of having bipolar disorder.* The term has become one of the

---

* See Stephen M. Strakowski, "Impulsivity Across the Course of Bipolar Disorder," https://
onlinelibrary.wiley.com/doi/abs/10.1111/j.1399-5618.2010.00806.x, for instance.

most ubiquitous catchphrases in contemporary culture.

In the run-up to the 2009 Grammy awards, National Public Radio music commentator Tom Moon wrote a column for the *New York Daily News* on the current state of the record album. The term "album" has come to be understood as the compact disc, the CD: a collection of songs performed or written by a person or ensemble. The premise of his column was as follows: Though the album and the CD are now viewed by many as being as "fossilized" as vinyl or cassette tape, the viability of the album as an art form remains relevant. As such, the Grammy category for "Album of the Year" still has currency even though most people these days purchase individual songs as downloads.

Moon pointed to several recent albums as being "gems," yet acknowledged that there now exists an overriding preference for the "single-track approach" as opposed to the "start-to-finish aural experience" of the CD. He alluded to the challenge of listening to music over a long span of time in an age where attention spans have become increasingly diminished. His view, one that I wholeheartedly share, is that investing oneself into a prolonged listening experience can yield great satisfaction and can be a "galvanizing, life-changing thing."[1] Of course, the assertion that the desire for "instant gratification" shortchanges any attempt at having that deeper "life-changing" experience is not exclusive to music.

The irony for me is that as a lifelong lover of classical music—in which symphonies can last as long as forty or fifty minutes, and in the case of the symphonies of Gustav Mahler and Anton Bruckner, even longer—the lament of Tom Moon about popular music has now come full circle.* I have often argued that the desire for instant gratification in our contemporary and increasingly commercialized society was inimical to the classical music experience and a significant reason why serious art music is largely ignored. Now, according to Moon, popular music is succumbing to the same dilemma due to shortened attention spans and the desires of an emotional quick fix.

Advances in technology play into this as well. In his book *Music Quickens Time*, conductor and pianist Daniel Barenboim alluded to this scenario:

---

* The first of Havergal Brian's thirty-two symphonies has a performance time of nearly two hours, which is still much shorter that most operas and ballets.

The great advances in technology and communications media in our time have, in many ways, led to a general tendency to be satisfied with slogans, which are not just poor substitutes but aberrations of the ideas they claim to represent. This shorthand version of knowledge, when accepted at face value, can lead to mental laziness. Information is presented on television and on the Internet in a way that does not allow enough time for reflection and comprehension, thus turning powerful and potentially very positive inventions into the ideal tools for the manipulation of the general public.[2]

Our old thought processes of linear thinking are undergoing changes as we become more reliant on the quick-hitting, information-gathering dynamics of the Internet. We may have more knowledge at our disposal, but we are not necessarily more knowledgeable. In this regard, Marshall McLuhan's well-known axiom "the medium is the message" has become a self-fulfilling prophecy on steroids. It's important to remember that McLuhan's axiom was a *caveat* about being seduced by technology's transformational effects at the expense of our cognitive abilities vis-à-vis long-term thinking. Speaking to this phenomenon, Pulitzer Prize nominee Nicholas Carr observed:

> For the last five centuries, ever since Gutenberg's printing press made book reading a popular pursuit, the linear, literary mind has been at the center of art, science, and society. As supple as it is subtle, it's been the imaginative mind of the Renaissance, the rational mind of the Enlightenment, the inventive mind of the Industrial Revolution, even the subversive mind of Modernism. It may soon be yesterday's mind.[3]

Carr's assertion is analogous to Maestro Barenboim's and Tom Moon's, in that technological advances, combined with hyper-commercialization and a penchant for instant gratification, contribute to the continual dumbing down—or "knowing down," as William Safire described it—of our collective intellectual and emotional sensibilities. This, in turn, has created a condition where emotional intelligence is not nurtured in any significant fashion. Consequently, the benefits of great art, literature and music have become increasingly marginalized, thereby reducing the potential for greater understandings about life, love and our humanity. Citing the emergence of "the private writer" and "the attentive reader," Carr also noted that prior to the Internet there was "a burst of experimentation" that expanded both vocabulary and syntax, and this resulted in greater degrees of expressiveness and deep thinking. Conversely, as social media, with its 144-characters-per-text limit and shortened attention spans, have become more prevalent, "writers seem fated to eschew virtuosity and experimentation in favor of a bland but immediately accessible style."[4] Carr notes that there are those who believe that this trend is a good thing, including New York University digital-media scholar Clay Shirky, who opined in 2008 that, "we shouldn't waste our time mourning the death of deep reading—it was overrated all along."[5] It goes without saying that this mindset leads to a condition in which intellectual laziness becomes pervasive. In a piece for *Smithsonian Magazine*, Camille Paglia weighed in on the deleterious aspects of the digital domain:

> As a 40-year veteran teacher in art schools, I am alarmed about the future of American art. Young people today, immersed in a digital universe, love the volatile excitement of virtual reality, but they lack the patience to steadily contemplate a single image—a complex static object such as a great painting or sculpture. The paintings of their world are now video games, with images in febrile motion; their sculptures are the latest-model cell phone, deftly shaped to the hand. ... The current malaise in the fine arts is partly due to the rote secularism of the Western professional class, who inhabit a sophisticated but increasingly soulless high-tech world.[6]

Cultural commentator Thomas Chatterton Williams, in another *New York Daily News* editorial, alluded to the pernicious effects of too much "TV time" on the African-American family:

> To be sure, television watching is far too high across the board in this country. We are, as the media theorist Neil Postman pointed out in 1985, "amusing ourselves to death." The ability to think critically and with nuance and sophistication, Postman argues, is grossly undermined by the passive nature that is part and parcel of the television-viewing experience. Reading, by way of contrast, is inherently interactive and dialectical, requiring an intense amount of mental engagement.
>
> What is even more decisive, though, is the nature of what's on the tube: Because television is programmed according to ratings, its content is dictated overwhelmingly by its commercial appeal, and not by the quality of the ideas

it presents. That's why for Postman, television, as we consume it, does not and cannot "satisfy the conditions for honest intellectual involvement."[7]

This is old news to be sure, but it is encouraging that some are taking the problem more seriously. Perhaps Williams was taking a cue from former president Barack Obama, who, in his 2011 State of the Union address, called for more parental involvement in the supervision of children in their schoolwork and a limitation of access to television as ways to achieve better scholastic results. Clearly, President Obama, like Williams, saw the correlative relationship between the kind of mind-numbing, lowest-common-denominator entertainment that has become all too pervasive in American households, as well as a precipitous decline in academic achievement. However, as Williams correctly points out, the "TV problem" is not exclusive to the African-American community.

Allan Bloom presented a serious critique of the condition of higher education as it pertains to these issues over thirty years ago. Among the more trenchant of his charges was that the aforementioned hyper-commercialization, combined with moral relativism and a disdain for deferred gratification, produced a condition in which students no longer desired to seek greater truth and understanding through the experience of great literature, art or music. To Bloom, these historical sources of enlightenment have become casualties of a decidedly market-driven culture in which commercial and sexual pursuits outweigh all else, a condition that desensitizes the mind and soul to the eternal verities that great art can so effectively elucidate.

It was no surprise that Bloom's book triggered a spate of highly charged debates in the realms of academia and social science—a debate that continues to have relevance. According to Bloom, the superficiality of much of our contemporary popular culture is a direct result of hypocritical pretensions about freedom and liberation. Not surprisingly, those of a politically correct mindset alleged that Bloom was guilty of perpetuating the traditional attitudes (and art) of dead, white, European males. His assessment was considered to be somewhat "reactionary" by the progressive multiculturalists in the academy. Yet Bloom's understanding of music in particular reveals a perspective that transcends any particular cultural or ideological association:

Music is the soul's primitive and primary speech and it is alogon without articulate speech or reason. It is not only not reasonable, it is hostile to reason. Even when articulate speech is added, it is utterly subordinate to and determined by the music and the passions it expresses.[8]

Though music is comprised of *perceptible* components of melody, harmony, rhythm and form—components that when organized in a particular fashion produce a musical syntax—these components can have the effect of altering consciousness. Consider Arthur Schopenhauer's contention regarding music: "[Music] stands quite apart from all the others [arts]. ... [We] must attribute to music a far more serious and profound significance that refers to the innermost being of the world and of our own self."[9] Schopenhauer's listening experience with music was the canon of eighteenth- and nineteenth-century European art music—the sonatas and concerti of Beethoven and Mozart, the symphonies of Schubert and Schumann, the piano repertories of Chopin and Liszt; no three-minute, three-chord songs here! One had to invest one's time into the comprehension and appreciation of music on this level. If one were willing and able to make an intellectual and emotional investment into the listening experience, the emotional rewards and intellectual insights could be epiphanic, and this is still the case.*

The issue of desensitization also lies at the heart of Theodor Adorno's *Essays on Mass Culture*, published in 1944, in which he portended a demise in social consciousness due to the "fettering" of adult sensibilities vis-à-vis making informed choices based on life experience. Speaking to the issue of making informed choices, we might do well to remember Edmund Burke when he stated, "Example is the school of mankind, and he will learn at no other."[10] Burke was promulgating the idea that actual experience can be highly instructive, desirable, in fact, in the pursuit of ascertaining better ways of doing things. Musicians, for instance, often seek out experienced practitioners of their craft and take "master classes" with accomplished conductors, composers, singers and instrumentalists who have the benefit of experience—artists who've learned from their own successes as well as their failures.

The desensitizing effects of "mass culture" that Adorno alluded to—and Bloom corroborated decades later—cannot be easily dismissed. Their

---

* Schopenhauer was a flutist.

observations underscore the assertions of Carr, Moon and Barenboim, in that the impact of commercialization and technology, though not without certain benefits, has not served us particularly well in terms of inculcating young people with the capacity to develop their emotional intelligence. Instead we are confronted with a state of arrested emotional development and a general lack of intellectual curiosity—not to mention unhealthy desires for fast food, reality TV, pop music and a chattering class of talking heads that more often than not, has no deeper frame of reference than the common perspectives they share.

Why question whether sugary soft drinks or fast food loaded with trans fats may be bad for you? Madison Avenue and all those celebrity endorsers say it's all good, cool and hip. Don't think, don't assess, don't apply adult sensibilities; just buy and consume. The conflicting messages created by Madison Avenue regarding what is good or bad for us was recently highlighted when ESPN sports personality Chris Berman was simultaneously a pitchman for the Nutrisystem diet regimen and Applebee's Neighborhood Grill and Bar. We want it all. We want to be thin and trim, but we want those burgers and fries. (OK, salads are on the menu at Applebee's too.) We wish to be considered spiritual but engage in behavior that is anything but. We understand the importance of cultivating adult sensibilities but too often give in to adolescent desires.

How often have we lamented the fact that our political discourse has been reduced to a series of sound bites fashioned to dominate the current 24-hour news cycle as opposed to a well-reasoned, protracted discussion on salient issues of the day? The financial crises in the United States in 2008 can also be attributed in large measure to "instant gratification" and the desire to experience pleasure and comfort in an immediate fashion at the expense of long-term planning or goals. This scenario can have deleterious consequences. Consider the situation that unfolded in Ukraine in the aftermath of the Sochi Olympics, which gave rise to the absurd notion that the U.S. State Department could use a Twitter "hashtag" campaign to somehow alter the geopolitical calculus behind the aggression of Vladimir Putin. That seems crazy, but that's what happened.

Commenting on the predilection for instant gratification in relation to the pursuit of higher education and an enlightened society, political essayist Victor Davis Hanson observed:

Why do we cling to the arts and humanities in a high-tech world in which we have instant recall at our fingertips through a Google search and such studies do not guarantee sure twenty-first-century careers? ... Without citizens broadly informed by humanities, we descend into a pyramidal society. ... A growing mass below lacks understanding of the present complexity and the basic skills to question what they are told. ... The more instantaneous our technology, the more we are losing the ability to communicate with it. Twitter and text-messaging result in an economy of expression, not in clarity or beauty.[11]

Hanson shares the concerns of Bloom and Paglia regarding the ability of future generations to make decisions according to adult sensibilities: a condition that even the neo-Marxist Adorno understood to be necessary for developing a "democratic" society; Adorno's specious concept of a democratic society, notwithstanding. In very real ways technology is hampering cognitive development and, ironically, even pop music is feeling its effects.

"Heavenly Length"

Conductor George Szell opined that several of Gustav Mahler's symphonies were "hypertrophic and beyond salvation" due to their exceedingly long performing times. Yet Franz Schubert's C Major Symphony No. 9 is often lauded for it's "heavenly length." Beethoven's Ninth Symphony takes about an hour to perform and is a far cry from the earliest symphonies of Mozart, which are often no longer than eight or nine minutes. But can you imagine a pop song lasting eight or nine minutes? Jimmy Webb's "MacArthur Park" comes in at 7 minutes and 30 seconds, but that's a rarity, as is Queen's "Bohemian Rhapsody" or several of the classical-rock merge compositions of Emerson, Lake & Palmer or the early songs of Chicago.

I recently pulled out my *Sgt. Pepper's Lonely Hearts Club Band* CD and the journey through the thirteen tracks remains as satisfying and inspiring as ever. The final song, "A Day in the Life," has a distinctive poignancy after having listened to the previous twelve songs. As a stand-alone track the emotional impact isn't quite as profound. The same holds true when listening to a complete symphony or concerto as opposed to one of its individual movements. When the full measure of the composition is experienced, the emotional impact is often far more cathartic. This holds true in cinema and literature too. We generally accept the idea that attending a movie or reading a novel requires a significant time commitment in order for full appreciation and enjoyment to be realized, yet our unwillingness to invest our time into our listening experiences with music reveals an impatience that shortchanges cathartic experiences.

Deferred gratification when engaging art and music can provide the opportunity for deeply gratifying and intellectually arresting experiences. Instant gratification contributes to the fettering of consciousness and mental lethargy, conditions that are not helpful in the pursuit of a culture of peace. Cultural commentator and author Denis Dutton would concur: "We've lost contact with the deepest springs of our aesthetic interests in a world that compels the passive consumption of entertainment, rather than encouraging the creative development of our human skill and perception."[12] This echoes Carr's contention that in our increasingly web-saturated culture, outfits like Google are predicated on quick-hitting forays onto websites that work against long-term thinking. Because more "hits" generate more ad dollars, shorter visits help the bottom line. For a company like Google, it's clearly a business incentive to diminish prolonged visits to read or gain substantive knowledge. "The last thing the company wants is to encourage leisurely reading or slow, concentrated thought. Google is, quite literally, in the business of distraction."[13]

At the 2007 commencement address at Stanford University, former National Endowment for the Arts chairman Dana Gioia, a Stanford alumnus, alluded to the crisis in American contemporary culture of decreasing attention spans and the effects of technology.

> Everything now is entertainment. And the purpose of this omnipresent commercial entertainment is to sell us something. American culture has mostly become one vast infomercial. ... But we must remember that the marketplace does only one thing—it puts a price on everything. The role of culture, however, must go beyond economics. It is not focused on the price of things, but on their value. And, above all, culture should tell us what is beyond price, including what does not belong in the marketplace. A culture should also provide some cogent view of the good life beyond mass accumulation. In this respect, our culture is failing us. ...
>
> The purpose of arts education is not to produce more artists, though that is a by-product. The real purpose of arts education is to create complete

human beings capable of leading successful and productive lives in a free society.[14]

Gioia's commentary recalls Oscar Wilde's play *Lady Windermere's Fan*, in which we read, a cynic is "a man who knows the price of everything, and the value of nothing."[15] And yet, what we value as a society is of no small concern at a time when cultural attitudes are too often defined by inane artistic expressions like reality TV and certain types of puerile and dehumanizing pop music. Because Madison Avenue views the human desire to "want things" as a primary aspect in developing ad campaigns, the so-called "pleasure principle" drives entrepreneurs and producers to create products that will result in quick profits. This is surely one of the negative effects of capitalism.

It is interesting to note that at the beginning of Gioia's Stanford speech, he acknowledged that his being selected to speak at the commencement exercises was somewhat controversial. This was not because Gioia was necessarily a polarizing figure, but because certain members of the student body felt that he lacked the requisite "celebrity status" for the occasion. The intelligent and thoughtful person that he is, Gioia used the "controversy" to fashion the narrative of his speech, aptly titled, "Trade Easy Pleasures for More Complex and Challenging Ones." Citing Roman emperor Marcus Aurelius' contention regarding the importance of not settling for "easy pleasures" in life, Gioia emphasized the importance of the arts in relation to the shallowness of celebrity.

> Marcus Aurelius believed that the course of wisdom consisted of learning to trade easy pleasures for more complex and challenging ones. I worry about a culture that bit by bit trades off the challenging pleasures of art for the easy comforts of entertainment. And that is exactly what is happening—not just in the media, but in our schools and civic life. …
>
> Art is an irreplaceable way of understanding and expressing the world— equal to but distinct from scientific and conceptual methods. Art addresses us in the fullness of our being—simultaneously speaking to our intellect, emotions, intuition, imagination, memory, and physical senses. There are some truths about life that can be expressed only as stories, or songs, or images.[16]

It's gratifying to see that the enlightened perspective of Dana Gioia is gaining credence. President Obama's website included a portion of Gioia's Stanford commencement address. Arts advocacy by individuals like Gioia can go a long way toward promoting the benefits of prioritizing emotional intelligence and delayed gratification as they pertain to producing more "complete human beings" and, hopefully, better artists.

Recommended Recordings

Mahler: Symphony No. 8, Georg Solti, Chicago Symphony Orchestra and Chorus

Bruckner: Symphony No. 8, Bernard Haitink, Royal Concertgebouw Orchestra

Brian: Symphony No. 1, *The Gothic*, Sir Adrian Boult, BBC Symphony Orchestra

Wagner: Overtures, Georg Solti, Chicago Symphony Orchestra

Schubert: Symphony No. 9, George Szell, Cleveland Orchestra

Beethoven: Symphony No. 9, Herbert von Karajan, Berlin Philharmonic (1963)

Schumann: Symphony No. 4, Daniel Barenboim, Staatskapelle Berlin Orchestra

Mozart: Piano Concertos Nos. 20 & 27, Mitsuko Uchida, Cleveland Orchestra

Liszt: Piano Concertos, Sviatoslav Richter, London Symphony Orchestra

Chopin: Piano Concertos, Alexis Weissenberg, Paris Conservatory Orchestra

Beatles: *Sgt. Pepper's Lonely Hearts Club Band*

Queen: *A Night at the Opera*

Chicago: *Chicago II*

Emerson, Lake & Palmer: *Works, Volume I*

Endnotes

1   Tom Moon, "The Album Isn't Dead, It's Just Spinning at a Different Speed," *New York Daily News*, February 6, 2009.

2   Daniel Barenboim, *Music Quickens Time* (New York: Verso, 2009), p. 41.

3   Nicholas Carr, *The Shallows: What the Internet Is Doing to Our Brains* (New York: W. W. Norton & Company, 2010), p. 10.

4   Ibid., p. 107.

5   Ibid., p. 111.

6   Camille Paglia, "Is the Rise of Secularism Behind the General Malaise in the Fine Arts?" *Smithsonian Magazine*, November 2012, http://www.smithsonianmag.com/arts-culture/why-camille-paglia-is-alarmed-about-the-future-of-art-79905670/?no-ist.

7   Thomas Chatterton Williams, "The TV Set vs. Black Families: African Americans

Must Quit Their Terrible 7-Hour-a-Day Diet," *New York Daily News*, April 21, 2011.

8   Allan Bloom, *The Closing of the American Mind: How Higher Education Has Failed Democracy and Impoverished the Souls of Today's Students* (New York and London: Simon & Schuster, 1987), p. 71.

9   Barbara Hannan, *The Riddle of the World: A Reconsideration of Schopenhauer's Philosophy*, (Oxford: Oxford University Press, 2009), p. 111.

10   Edmund Burke, *Thoughts on the Prospect of a Regicide Peace: In a Series of Letters* (London, 1796), p. 63.

11   Victor Davis Hanson, "How Not to Save the Liberal Arts," *New York Post*, December 18, 2010.

12   Denis Dutton, review of *What Good Are the Arts?*, by John Carey, *The Press*, September 9, 2006, http://denisdutton.com/carey_review.htm.

13   Carr, *The Shallows*, p. 157.

14   Dana Gioia, "Trade Easy Pleasures for More Complex and Challenging Ones," commencement address, *Stanford Report*, June 17, 2007, https://news.stanford.edu/news/2007/june20/gradtrans-062007.html.

15   Oscar Wilde, *Lady Windermere's Fan* (Mineola, NY: Dover Publications, 1998), p. 38.

16   Gioia, "Trade Easy Pleasures."

17

Trends and Traditions

In English writing we seldom speak of tradition,
though we occasionally apply its name in deploring its absence.[1]
T. S. Eliot

We're the robber barons of rock 'n' roll.[2]
Donald Fagen

Albert Einstein is alleged to have said, "The secret to creativity is know-ing how to hide your sources," yet there is scant evidence to prove that Einstein ever made that assertion. The statement can be attributed to English commentator and radio broadcaster C. E. M. Joad, who in 1926 said, "The height of originality is skill in concealing origins."[3]

Was Einstein given to hiding his sources regarding his groundbreaking theories? In his book *Albert Einstein: The Incorrigible Plagiarist*, Christopher Jon Bjerknes provides evidence that the iconic physicist relied on a plethora of research done by others in the field in his development of his theory of relativity. Bjerknes claims that Einstein "did not originate the special theory of relativity in its entirety, or even in its majority." He goes on to say that "many others … slowly developed the theory, step by step, and based it on thousands of years of recorded thought and research."[4]

Bjerknes does not allege that Einstein appropriated all of his insights and discoveries.* However, Bjerknes points out that Einstein's theory was likely the result of a continuum of scientific thought, research and study. To be sure, almost no one starts from "square one" in the pursuit of scientific inquiry or artistic production. It's safe to say that no scientist or artist possesses so complete an understanding of their discipline as to have fully digested the copious amounts of data needed to arrive at new conclusions in their fields of expertise. We all have forbearers who laid the foundations upon which we stand to carry out our respective endeavors. It shouldn't be surprising that Einstein had scientific precursors.

Those who are involved in any creative endeavor generally understand that they are not creating completely apart from a cultural patrimony. There is a tacit understanding that we are part of a continuum of traditions and stylistic evolution. Whether we are aware of it or not, most of those traditions have their roots in religious and ritualistic practice. As Alex Ross puts it: "Composers are genius parasites; they feed voraciously on the song matter of their time in order to engender something new."[5] When we examine the history of Western music, for instance, it is clear that there has been an evolution of style and syntax dating back to the early chants and plainsong of the Roman Catholic Church. Accordingly, our musical heritage encompasses both religious and spiritual influences as well as methodological and stylistic influences.

The music of Scott Joplin, Harold Arlen, Miles Davis, Robert Johnson, the Beatles, Steely Dan and Usher (any "key-centered" music based on the diatonic scale and its variants) stems from the sacred music of Gregorian chant and the early Flemish composers. In fact, it is difficult to cite examples of true iconoclasts in music—artists who were or are completely detached from a previous musical era or style. Edgard Varèse, Frank Zappa or Charles Ives may

---

* On page 4 of Bjerknes we read, "This book is intended solely for entertainment purposes. Due to the possibility of mechanical or human error, this book may contain substantial errors, both typographical and as to content." It seems that the author, for whatever reason, is not enamored with Einstein's claims or methods. Critics of Bjerknes point to evidence that the author relied on claims found in official Nazi propaganda that sought to diminish Einstein for ideological reasons.

have been daringly innovative, but their music is the progeny of the history of notated music in the Western tradition.

Perhaps the two Austrians who developed the non-tonal musical idiom of 12-tone or dodecaphonic music in the early twentieth century—theorist Josef Hauer and composer Arnold Schoenberg—qualify as true pioneers of a compositional syntax that was quite detached from previous traditions. Yet that idiom failed to supplant tonality as a preferred mode of musical expression, and any claims of triumph by composers who employed that idiom remain seriously contested. Schoenberg's now infamous prediction that achieving greater familiarization with non-tonal musical syntaxes through repeated listening would ensure its acceptance has not materialized. Through the lens of current musical history it now looks as though atonality may have run its course. Contemporary composers have turned their backs on the rationale of dodecaphonic, serialist methodology due to its inability to be aesthetically alluring, emotionally satisfying and spiritually uplifting. So divorced was this methodology from the aesthetics of Bach, Mozart, Beethoven, and even the early twentieth-century utterances of Bartók and Stravinsky, that it has failed to find even moderate acceptance or appreciation, despite an abundance of recordings of the music by even the most marginal atonal composers. Schoenberg's "familiarization" dictum has not found any currency.

Tradition and its counterpart, innovation, are both essential to the creative process, for it is against the historical backdrop of tradition that innovation and originality are measured. The ancient cultures of China and Greece were suspicious of innovation due to its potentially destabilizing effects. To societies that were based largely on the philosophy of balance and harmony, the notion of expressive freedom would almost certainly be viewed as threatening and possibly corrupting. David Tame points out that virtually every major civilization of antiquity possessed a timorous distrust of innovation. "An unwise degree of innovation or a condition of outright musical anarchy could prove deadly to the State," as Tame states; but conversely, "complete inflexibility could cause music to stagnate."[6] Plato lamented "unmusical anarchy," and the "thinking that there was no right or wrong in music," which was anathema to traditional Greek thought and thus could be potentially threatening to the process of maintaining an ethical society.[7]

In his review of Richard Taruskin's *Oxford History of Western Music,* esteemed musicologist and pianist Charles Rosen puts forth a cogent commentary about observing musical history and its development.

> What is needed is an investigation of how the music functioned in society and the culture of the time, the individuals who played it, financed it, and listened to it. Above all, one must realize that society can inflect and influence the development of style, but only within limits: the musical language of the previous generations, the weight of its history, is a check on any new development, and at the same time a stimulus and inspiration to what can be accomplished in the future. Musical style is not a passive material that can be molded at will, but a system that both resists and inspires change.[8]

Understanding the "culture of the time" (contextualization) in which art is produced gives us a glimpse into the inner world of a creator and their creations. It also enables us to examine the stylistic evolution of music within various cultural spheres. Musical tastes evolve and the inevitable drift of time factors into the equation. In Puccini's day, for instance, there was little or no popular enthusiasm for the motets of Carlo Gesualdo. There was, however, great enthusiasm for contemporary opera. Market forces and popular tastes mattered a great deal.

A commentary on trends and traditions by former *New York Times* arts editor Edward Rothstein echoes Rosen's viewpoints:

> Artists work within a tradition; they are nestled by it, challenged by it, oppressed by it, but they cannot fully discard it. Trends nestle nobody. Tradition can be cautious to a fault; trends can be reckless to a fault. Tradition demands an active creator who tries to mold it for new purposes; trends create passive participants. Tradition requires dedication: "If you want it," wrote T. S. Eliot, "you must obtain it by great labor." A trend is almost always a cliché, always something that is widely accepted, requiring no proof; it attracts followers rather than leaders, crowds rather than individuals.[9]

In his critique of poet Percy Bysshe Shelley, T. S. Eliot opined that when assessing and evaluating art profundity and sincerity were prime considerations. Glib superficiality results in works of art that do little to nurture the human spirit or impact our consciousness in a positive fashion. In these instances we are left with surface expressions (simulacrum) that rarely probe the soul or elicit an emotional catharsis to any significant degree. As Rosen asserts, the forces of economics, religion, science and politics have all played significant roles in the evolution of musical style and traditions. For instance, in the period preceding and including the Renaissance, there were concerns regarding the use of certain intervals when composing liturgical music, including the tritone, called the *diabolus in musica*, the raised second or seventh, and even the major sixth.* These concerns about using certain intervals were intended to mitigate licentiousness in the process of composing music intended to praise God.†

The establishment of equal temperament in the early eighteenth century also resulted in the ongoing evolution of compositional style and syntax.‡ Moreover, as equal temperament became the standard tuning mode in Europe in the early eighteenth century, instrument construction and manufacturing evolved accordingly, and this too had a significant impact on compositional style. Furthermore, performance issues such as dynamics, articulation, phrasing and tempo gradations—once the interpretive province of performers—increasingly became the province of the composer in the nineteenth century. Unlike the scores of Mozart and Haydn, which had relatively few performance instructions by the composers beyond those of dynamics,

---

* The term *diabolus in musica* is Latin for "the Devil in music." Myth has it that the term has been used since pre-Renaissance times to describe the interval of the tri-tone, a dissonant sounding interval that results when two pitches that are six semitones apart occur in music. However, the initial use of term is attributed to composer, Joanne Josepho Fux, (1660-1741).

† In the sixteenth century, when Henry VIII was ensnared in a conflict with Rome over the issue of his divorce from Catherine of Aragon, anti-Catholic sentiment grew so extreme that it progressed into an anti-organ movement, to the point where these noble instruments were being removed from cathedrals and destroyed throughout England because they were considered "superstitious monuments" and "illegal in the worship of God." [Source: Stuart Isacoff, *Temperament: The Idea that Solved Music's Greatest Riddle.*]

‡ As the evolution of music continued throughout Europe, composers explored new and inventive ways to express a wider range of emotions though their music. This evolution eventually led to the development of equal *temperament* and the great classical tradition of Christian Europe. Equal *temperament*—dividing the octave into 12 equal sonic intervals according to Johann Sebastian Bach's tuning procedure—allowed composers to explore highly varied modes of harmonic expression that had previously not been available to them. In fact, without equal *temperament* we would not have jazz, gospel, Broadway or modern pop music as we know it—let alone the music of Beethoven, Wagner or Mahler.

articulation and tempo, the scores of Mahler, Strauss and Debussy are profuse with designations as to how their music should be executed. In the scores of Mahler there seems to be a performance requirement or designation in every other bar.

Another significant change in the realm of art music in the late twentieth and early twenty-first century, has been the influence of indigenous, non-Western cultures and their music. There have been numerous attempts to juxtapose European classical elements with folk elements, going back to the times of Mozart and Beethoven, and even earlier. Nationalism in music, the practice of using folk songs and folkloric narratives as source material, flourished in the late nineteenth century. Contemporary composers of art music such as Osvaldo Golijov, Tan Dun, Avner Dorman, Michael Torke, Louis Andriessen and Lou Harrison, for example, have incorporated folk and pop music influences in their "serious" compositions.

The pioneering ethnomusicological research of Hungarian composers Béla Bartók and Zoltan Kodály in the early twentieth century led to the advancement of collecting and studying the oral traditions of folk music of indigenous peoples of non-Western cultures. As Bartók gathered and documented the folk music of his cultural heritage, he began to incorporate the characteristics of this music into his compositions. This was accomplished not by merely integrating existing folk melodies into his music, but was far more elemental in that he would construct original thematic material, rhythmic patterns and harmonic progressions that were predicated on the intervallic, rhythmic and harmonic properties of actual Hungarian folk music. In an essay on the influence of folk music on composers, Bartók explained his views regarding the various processes used to assimilate these particular musical elements.

> We may, for instance, take over a peasant melody unchanged or only slightly varied, write an accompaniment to it and possibly some opening and concluding phrases. This kind of work would show a certain analogy with Bach's treatment of chorales. ... Another method by which peasant music becomes transmuted into modern music is the following: the composer does not make use of a real peasant melody but invents his own imitation of such melodies. There is no real difference between this method and the one described first. ... There is yet a third way. ... Neither peasant melodies nor imitations of peasant melodies can be found in his music, but it is pervaded

by the atmosphere of peasant music. In this case we may say, he has completely absorbed the idiom of peasant music which has become his musical mother tongue.[10]

When examining the process of how musical styles evolve, it is important to note that there have been both oral and written traditions that have been passed on from generation to generation. In Western art music since the Renaissance—music of the written-notated tradition—it is apparent that Johann Sebastian Bach influenced just about every composer of repute of the eighteen and nineteenth centuries due to the fact that many composers performed and studied his music. The great symphonic lineage of central European composition is very much the progeny of Bach's vast musical output. In a very real sense Bach begat Mozart and Haydn, who begat Beethoven, who begat Schubert, Schumann, Mendelssohn, Brahms, Dvorák, Tchaikovsky, Mahler, Bruckner, Sibelius, Vaughan-Williams, Rachmaninoff, Shostakovich and Prokofiev. The symphonic lineage went through numerous modifications and innovations, but the basic structural premise of the eighteenth-century symphony, as well as the tonal idiom as employed and expanded by Bach, endured well into the twentieth century.

The development of recording technology has offered new opportunities for exposure to music that was previously unattainable as well. In the United States the traditions of the blues, gospel music, Native American ritual chant and folk music have been passed on and preserved via a strong oral tradition. However, with the development of notation, recording and publishing, these traditions are now more easily preserved, disseminated and assimilated.

In contemporary pop music, Paul Simon's collaboration with Ladysmith Black Mambazo on his *Graceland* album is a classic example of a successful cross-fertilization of differing musical traditions.* The collaboration between

---

* In the 1980s Paul Simon was criticized for his work with South African musicians who were victims of apartheid. Yet, he maintained that he felt he did the right thing. In an interview for the Guardian (April 19, 2012), Robin Denselow cites Simon: "Personally, I feel I'm with the musicians, … I'm with the artists. I didn't ask the permission of the ANC. I didn't ask permission of Buthelezi, or Desmond Tutu, or the Pretoria government. And to tell you the truth, I have a feeling that when there are radical transfers of power on either the left or the right, the artists always get screwed. The guys with the guns say, 'This is important,' and the guys with guitars don't have a chance. … I haven't said that before." [Source: Robin Denselow, "Paul Simon's

Miles Davis and Gil Evans on their groundbreaking album *Sketches of Spain* remains an example of merging American Jazz and traditional Spanish music. Rock bands such as Emerson, Lake & Palmer, Yes and Procol Harum infused stylistic elements from classical music into their music. James Pankow wrote a rock ballet for his band, Chicago, stating that Bach's *Brandenburg Concerti* were among his influences. The fusion of jazz with pop, rock, African and Latin elements, began in earnest in the 1970s and continues to influence talented musicians and bands such as Steely Dan, Pat Metheny, Keith Jarrett and Richard Bona. The "ambient" music of Brian Eno and the "electronica" stylings of Imogen Heap also point to decidedly innovative juxtapositions of old and new.

As mentioned previously, musical cross-fertilization has been going on for centuries, but with the advent of recording technology global exposure to cultures of "the other" has given rise to unprecedented understandings and appreciation of musical expressions beyond what has been the norm for many people. Regarding these influences on modern art music, *Washington Post* music critic Anne Midgette observed, "Stylistic *mélange* alone is now taken as investing some measure of contemporaneity. What a few decades ago was slammed as lowbrow pastiche is today heralded as a visionary merging of disparate traditions."[11] Regrettably, multiculturalists of the politically correct mindset now view this type of stylistic juxtaposition as being a form of "cultural appropriation," with racist or colonialist underpinnings. But is it?

The artistic challenge for composers is how to formulate a unique style that conveys or evokes beauty and meaning without being derivative. The presence of the past is always an influential aspect in creativity and admittedly, it is not easy to shake. To merely shock or disrupt the status quo is not necessarily the mark of genius or expertise. Roger Scruton asserts:

> The most original works of art may be genial applications of well-known vocabulary. ... They may be all but unnoticeable amid the fanfares of contemporary self-advertisement. ... What makes them original is not their defiance of the past or their rude assault on settled expectations, but the

---

Graceland: The Acclaim and the Outrage," Guardian, April 19, 2012] https://www.theguardian.com/music/2012/apr/19/paul-simon-graceland-acclaim-outrage.

element of surprise with which they invest the forms and repertoire of a tradition.[12]

Mozart stood apart from his contemporaries precisely due to his ability to "surprise" the listener with ingenious twists of harmonic invention and inventive melodies. In the opening recitative of his concert aria *Ch'io mi scordi di te?* (K. 505), the ever clever and innovative Mozart visits several tonal centers (A-flat major, G minor, back to A-flat major and then B-flat major) within the first twenty bars of the piece before settling into the main aria's home key of E-flat major. The shifting tonal centers create a wondrous sense of aural movement and displacement. The late string quartets of Beethoven, the late piano works of Brahms or the ballet scores of Stravinsky do not completely break away from the musical traditions on which they are predicated as much as they venture into the extreme peripheries of their respective idioms and syntaxes.

It is the element of "surprise" that awakens us to new possibilities and potentialities and in so doing quickens our curiosity and imagination. Neuroscientists tell us that the "surprise" element in music causes the release of dopamine, and this is what gives us pleasure. Valorie Salimpoor, a neuroscientist at McGill University in Montreal, conveyed the following in conversation with Emily Sohn of the Discovery Channel:

> "You're following these tunes and anticipating what's going to come next and whether it's going to confirm or surprise you, and all of these little cognitive nuances are what's giving you this amazing pleasure. ... The reinforcement or reward happens almost entirely because of dopamine. ... This basically explains why music has been around for so long," she added. "The intense pleasure we get from it is actually biologically reinforcing in the brain, and now here's proof for it."[13]

Music can elicit a variety of emotions, but whatever the specific emotion may be, the feelings we experience are often triggered by the "cognitive nuances" that produce the "surprise" element in music. Anne Midgette's referencing "stylistic *mélange*" and cross-fertilization as part of contemporary music's compositional terrain, points to both the possibilities and problems of juxtaposing non-Western cultural expressions with the European "common practice" tradition. In his early compositions, contemporary Chinese composer Tan Dun, taking a cue from Bartók, attempted to combine the stylistic elements of Peking opera with Western modernism. I had the opportunity to conduct several of Tan's works in a Lincoln Center concert that included the world premieres of his Violin Concerto and Third Symphony. Bernard Holland, writing in the *New York Times*, made the following query in his review of the concert:

> And why, in the first place, should we bother to bring Chinese and Western music together? Homogeneity rarely doubles our pleasure. More often than not it weakens or subverts—like pouring good wine into good beer. For all of Mr. Tan's skills, his Chinese gestures emerge bruised and battered from their orchestral setting. Trying to distinguish them through this haze of bombast was indeed a frustrating experience—despite the careful and sympathetic performances here.[14]

Tan went on to win an Academy Award for his score for Ang Lee's film *Crouching Tiger, Hidden Dragon*, as well as to compose a new opera for the Metropolitan Opera. In these more recent scores he seems to have merged the diverse musical elements of East and West with greater success. The creative challenge lies in how one harmonizes diverse musical elements into a cogent, personal musical expression—admittedly no easy task.

In the development of pop music in America there has been a rich tradition of assimilation through the shared experience of performance and jamming.* Guitarist Walter Becker of Steely Dan attested: "I'm a self-taught musician aside from what I've been able to pick up from other players. ... My primary influences were the best Jazz players from the '50s and '60s and later some of the pop people from the same time period along with the better of the well-known blues musicians."[15]

Steely Dan band members Becker and Donald Fagen admitted that they looked heavily to other songwriters and composers for source material. (They were sued by Keith Jarrett for copyright infringement on one occasion.) Regrettably, however, the marketplace can have a significant and derogatory effect on creativity in popular music. When the Beatles hit it big in the United States, an onslaught of British bands followed, looking to cash in on the new market that the "Fab Four" had so thoroughly dominated. We have seen

---

* As defined in *The Free Dictionary*, in music a "jam session" is an informal gathering of musicians to play improvised or unrehearsed music.

similar phenomenon recently with the emergence of hip-hop. Many artists have tried to imitate the originators of the genre as we have seen numerous times, but marginally talented individuals typically attempt to promote their music without the fresh appeal of the originals.

In the opinion of songwriter Don McLean (*American Pie, Vincent* (aka *Starry, Starry Night),* a primary reason why there aren't many great songs being written is because young songwriters don't listen to the great songs of the past. Not familiarizing oneself with the artistic legacies of the past can be antithetical to the process of developing any art form and this may be why there seems to be a paucity of music commensurate to the great pop music standards of bygone eras. Young songwriters would do well to immerse themselves in the songs of McLean, George Gershwin, Laura Nyro, Joni Mitchell, Paul Simon, et al., in order to develop their craft and gain a greater understanding of the fine tunes that came from some extraordinarily talented artists not so long ago.

It's no secret that the pop music industry has worked in a highly imitative way since its inception. When a unique artist hits the scene there are inevitably numerous "copycat" artists lined up hoping to capitalize on the moment. In this environment originality and the element of surprise become victims of crass commercialism. The latest, greatest fad generally fades out until "the next big thing" emerges to take the public by storm, creating yet another marketing frenzy. This is surely the downside of how modern market principles affect creativity, since lowest-common-denominator rationales tend to permeate the marketplace. (Theodor Adorno's constant lament.) It is an illusion to believe that just by acquiring or consuming things we can attain happiness and fulfillment.

In our modern, technological age, music has increasingly become a commodity, and this has had the effect of diminishing its intrinsic value. Popular music has too often become a kind of emotional "junk food" used to satisfy an immediate and superficial desire—ear candy. In the cinema, computer-generated special effects too often supplant the important skills that used to be a measure of successful filmmaking, namely, acting and writing imaginative screenplays. We see this in music as well. Crafting melodies and harmonic progressions that are deeply affecting has given way to esoteric orchestration, computer-based sound generation and extreme abstraction. Though aurally interesting, much new music fails to move the heart and mind in a transformational way. The tradition of creating a meaningful narrative in music, one that has the ability to address deeper human instincts and moral truths, has been supplanted by a "commodity fetish" (Marx's constant lament), by which music is objectified and thus relegated to being nothing more than merchandise.

Consider the perspective of former chairman of the National Endowment for the Arts, Dana Gioia on this issue:

> Entertainment promises us a predictable pleasure—humor, thrills, emotional titillation, or even the odd delight of being vicariously terrified. It exploits and manipulates who we are rather than challenges us with a vision of who we might become. A child who spends a month mastering Halo or NBA Live on Xbox has not been awakened and transformed the way that child would be spending the time rehearsing a play or learning to draw.
>
> If you don't believe me, you should read the statistical studies that are now coming out about American civic participation. Our country is dividing into two distinct behavioral groups. One group spends most of its free time sitting at home as passive consumers of electronic entertainment. Even family communication is breaking down as members increasingly spend their time alone, staring at their individual screens.[16]

I confess, this happens in my household all too often (my wife's constant lament). The condition of individuals and families, vis-à-vis civic participation, should be the concern of those who believe that culture and art play important roles in the positive development of our societies. As Gioia suggests, the balance between introspection and public-mindedness is a necessity if we are to progress in a truly humanitarian fashion, for being out of balance in anything is rarely a good thing. When I'm asked what music I enjoy, my standard response is: "I like the music of the '80s, especially the 1780s and 1880s." The past may seem unimportant and irrelevant to younger generations of musicians; however, understanding our musical heritage and the great artists of the past seem to be essential aspects in developing our personal styles. Moreover, issues of craft or commercial concerns cannot satiate our innermost desires, especially the desire for a society that embodies the ideals of compassion, understanding, justice and benevolence. Roger Scruton reminds us:

Although the aesthetic experience is central to high culture, it is not the only source upon which a culture draws. … When a common culture declines, the ethical life can be sustained and renewed only by a work of the imagination. And that, in a nutshell, is why high culture matters.[17]

Scruton is no philistine when it comes to popular music. He fully understands that "American music was the product of the common man," and because "it gets up the intellectual nose … it seems to leave no opening for the would-be 'priesthood.'"[18] Still, not surrendering to the trends of our highly superficial contemporary culture can be an important factor in the pursuit of both our artistic and humanitarian concerns. We would do well to keep those concerns, especially the "hunger" for community and social betterment, in the forefront of our artistic pursuits. Artists can feed that hunger but only if they cultivate a taste for art that can truly nourish and replenish the mind, heart and soul.

Postscript

A word about the Korean K-pop band BTS, also known as the Bangtan Boys. The seven-member South Korean boy band arrived on the Korean music scene in 2013 by way of the South Korean production company Big Hit Entertainment. BTS has amassed a huge international fan base known as the "ARMY." Their recordings and videos are slick, well-produced affairs and their lyrics often touch on social issues. In spite of BTS's high-end production values, one can easily trace their musical style and choreography to Michael Jackson's work of forty years ago. It's not really new or innovative. They imitate "the King's" music and expressions extremely well, but it's not groundbreaking.

The same can be said of a great deal of modern art music that continues to be composed in the atonal style of Arnold Schoenberg and his epigones. The sonic utterances of much of this music are based on methods that are now a century old. These methods are neither new nor innovative; as such, the aforementioned "surprise" element that Roger Scruton alludes to is absent and this results in the stultifying condition of much serious art music today.

Recommended Recordings

Laura Nyro: *Eli and the Thirteenth Confession*
Chicago: *Chicago II*

Don McLean: "Vincent (Starry, Starry Night)"

Steely Dan: *Gaucho*

Miles Davis-Gil Evans: *Sketches of Spain*

Paul Simon: *Graceland*

Keith Jarrett: *The Köln Concert*

Pat Metheny: *Orchestrion*

Joni Mitchell: "Both Sides, Now"

Beatles: White Album

Usher: *My Way*

Johnson: *The Centennial Collection*

Emerson, Lake & Palmer: *Works, Volume I*

Bona: *Scenes from My Life*

Arlen: "The Wizard of Oz," John Mauceri, Hollywood Bowl Orchestra

Scott Joplin: *The Complete Rags of Scott Joplin*, William Albright, piano

Schoenberg: Chamber Symphony No. 1, Orpheus Chamber Orchestra

Bach: *The Musical Offering*, Reinhard Goebel, Musica Antiqua Köln

Mozart: *Ch'io mi scordi di te*, Elly Ameling, soprano

Haydn: Symphony No. 104, Roger Norrington, London Classical Players

Beethoven: Symphony No. 3, Claudio Abbado, Berlin Philharmonic

Schubert: Symphony No. 8, George Szell, Cleveland Orchestra

Puccini: *La bohème*, Riccardo Chailly, Milan Teatro alla Scala Orchestra and Chorus

Gesualdo: Madrigals, William Christie, Les Arts Florissants

Schumann: Symphony No. 4, Daniel Barenboim, Staatskapelle Berlin Orchestra

Mendelssohn: Symphony No. 3, Christoph von Dohnányi, Cleveland Orchestra

Brahms: Symphony No. 2, Riccardo Chailly, Royal Concertgebouw Orchestra

Dvořák: Symphony No. 7, James Levine, Chicago Symphony Orchestra

Tchaikovsky: Symphony No. 6, Seiji Ozawa, Boston Symphony Orchestra

Sibelius: Symphony No. 1, Leonard Bernstein, New York Philharmonic

Mahler: Symphony No. 2, Ivan Fischer, Budapest Festival Orchestra

Bruckner: Symphony No. 4, Karl Böhm, Vienna Philharmonic

Vaughan-Williams: Symphony No. 6, Sir Adrian Boult, Philharmonia Orchestra

Rachmaninoff: *Symphonic Dances*, Vladimir Ashkenazy, Royal Concertgebouw

Orchestra

Prokofiev: Symphony No. 1, Neville Marriner, Academy of St. Martin in the Fields

Shostakovich: Symphony No. 10, Kurt Sanderling, Berlin Symphony Orchestra

Bartók: *Dance Suite*, Pierre Boulez, Chicago Symphony Orchestra

Kodály: *Háry János Suite*, George Szell, Cleveland Orchestra

Varèse: *Density 21.5*, Pierre Boulez, Ensemble InterContemporain

Tan Dun: *Crouching Tiger, Hidden Dragon* (Soundtrack)

Golijov: "Night of the Flying Horses," Yo-Yo Ma, Silk Road Ensemble

Dorman: Piano Concerto, Eliran Avni, Metropolis Ensemble

Gershwin: *Porgy and Bess*, Lorin Maazel, Cleveland Orchestra

Torke: *Ecstatic Collection*, David Zinman, Baltimore Symphony Orchestra

Stravinsky: *Symphony in Three Movements*, Leonard Bernstein, Israel Philharmonic

Endnotes

1   T. S. Eliot, "Tradition and the Individual Talent" in *The Sacred Wood: Essays on Poetry and Criticism* (London: Methuen & Co., 1920), p. 42.

2   Walter Becker and Donald Fagen, interview by David Breskin, *Musician Magazine*, March 1, 1981, transcript republished by *The Steely Dan Reader*, http://steelydanreader.com/1981/03/01/steely-dan-interview/.

3   Robert Little, "Raspberries from England," review of "The Babbitt Warren" by C. E. M. Joad, *The New Republic*, March 9, 1927, p. 74.

4   Bjerknes, *The Incorrigible Plagiarist*, p. 7.

5   Alex Ross, *Listen to This* (New York: Farrar, Straus and Giroux, 2010), p. 5.

6   David Tame, *The Secret Power of Music: The Transformation of Self and Society through Musical Energy* (New York: Destiny Books, 1984), p. 59.

7   Ibid., pp. 188-189.

8   Charles Rosen, "From the Troubadours to Sinatra: Part II," review of *The Oxford History of Western Music*, by Richard Taruskin, *New York Review of Books* 53, no. 4, March 9, 2006.

9   Edward Rothstein, "Trend-Spotting: It's All the Rage," *New York Times*, December 29, 1996.

10 Béla Bartók, *The Influence of Peasant Music on Modern Music*, as cited in *Tempo*, No. 14, Second Bartók Number, Winter 1949-1950, p. 20.

11 Anne Midgette, "When Opera Is New and Unproved," *Washington Post*, September 7, 2008.

12 Roger Scruton, *Modern Culture* (London: Continuum Books, 2005), p. 45.

13 Emily Sohn, "Why Music Makes You Happy," *Discovery News*, January 10, 2011.

14 Bernard Holland, "Concert: New York City Symphony," *New York Times*, February 9, 1988.

15 Walter Becker, interview for *America Online*, November 17, 1994, transcript republished by *The Steely Dan Reader*, http://steelydanreader.com/1994/11/17/interview-with-walter-becker-on-america-online/.

16 Dana Gioia, "Trade Easy Pleasures for More Complex and Challenging Ones," commencement address, *Stanford Report*, June 17, 2007. https://news.stanford.edu/news/2007/june20/gradtrans-062007.html.

17 Scruton, *Modern Culture*, pp. 45-46.

18 Roger Scruton, *Understanding Music: Philosophy and Interpretation* (London and New York: Continuum Books, 2009), p. 217.

18

Music and Sex

But classical music does tend to be higher in this sense.
What it wants to achieve or what it wants to say about
the human condition is, I think, rarefied—
and I'm attracted to that.
Sting

If I am asked where the most intimate knowledge of that inner essence
of the world, of that thing in itself which I have called the will to live,
is to be found, or where that essence enters most clearly into
our consciousness, or where it achieves the purest revelation
of itself, then I must point to ecstasy in the act of copulation.
That is it! That is the true essence and core of all things,
the aim and purpose of all existence.
Arthur Schopenhauer

OK, now that I have your attention. …

Recently a complimentary issue of the classical music magazine *Listen* arrived in my mailbox.* This was somewhat surprising because most periodicals about classical music and classical recordings are either on the endangered species list or have become extinct altogether. That a new publication of this sort is now making an attempt to thrive and survive in what is obviously a dying market is a noble endeavor. *Listen*, a quarterly publication, is published in conjunction with ArkivMusic, one of the largest online sources for classical music CDs and DVDs, and one that I visit frequently.

Of particular interest was the fact that the cover story was not about a current firebrand on the classical music scene, such as the dynamic young conductor Gustavo Dudamel or soprano Anna Netrebko, nor was the cover story about an iconic figure of the past; no Leonard Bernstein or Herbert von Karajan or Maria Callas. The cover boy was none other than the pop music icon, Sting. On one level this was not surprising because "crossover" projects by classical artists such as Yo-Yo Ma, Renee Fleming and Anne-Sophie Mutter have topped the classical charts for years. That a pop music idol would cross over to the classical realm is in keeping with current musical preferences. The days when recordings by Bernstein, Karajan, Abbado or Rattle topped the classical charts seem long gone as crossover artists like Andre Rieu and Il Divo rule the day.

Anyone familiar with Sting's musical career knows that he has been venturing into the realm of classical music for some time. His performance in the role of Joseph, the soldier in Igor Stravinsky's *The Soldier's Tale*, with Kent Nagano conducting the London Sinfonietta, dates from 1988. In recent years he has recorded the music of the English Renaissance composer John Dowland and he is attempting to master the lute, Dowland's primary instrument and the precursor to modern guitar. He has recorded orchestral covers of songs from his Police days with the Royal Philharmonic Orchestra (*Symphonicities*, released in 2010).

In his interview for *Listen*, Sting refers to the lives and music of Robert and Clara Schumann, perhaps the most famous musical couple in the annals of Western classical music history. Both Robert and Clara were talented

---

* This essay was originally written in 2010 and edited and expanded in 2021.

composers and pianists. Sting and his actress wife, Trudie Styler, played the roles of these musical lovers in the film *Twin Spirits*. Sting's familiarity with Robert Schumann (1810-1856), who was among the most "romantic" of the romantic composers, eventually led him to the discovery of the fine songs that Clara Schumann (1819-1896) had composed. In the interview, Sting cites a letter by Robert in which the composer refers to music as being "nothing more than resonant light." Sting observes: "I think 'resonant light' is exactly right; scientifically, it's a waveform just as light is, just a different part of the spectrum. I don't know whether he knew that or whether it was just a poetic intuitive image but certainly it's true scientifically."[1]

Speaking to the metaphysical and spiritual aspects of music he states, "If I have a spiritual life, [it] is one of music. I seem to be, through music, in touch with something bigger than myself or bigger than the material world ... it's a spiritual path."[2] On this trajectory I'm sure that many of us are in accord with Sting. Music can put us in touch with our higher selves and in so doing has the effect of bringing about a change in our consciousness. Yet we know that music and the music industry can have negative effects as well.

A bit later in the interview, Sting discusses his views about classical music:

> I think it's really about the higher emotions, about the heart and the intellect at a very high level. It's not really about the lower chakras, it's not really about humping your girlfriend—and there's nothing wrong with that, there's a place in music for that. But classical music does tend to be higher in this sense. What it wants to achieve or what it wants to say about the human condition is, I think, rarefied—and I'm attracted to that.[3]

For me, this observation reflects a rather unfortunate perspective about love and sex in relation to music, not to mention our divinity and the spirituality of sexuality. Though it has become commonplace to relegate sexuality to lower strata in the human experience, I would suggest that sexuality is sacred when motivations and intent are in line with higher virtues and the "higher emotions" that Sting alludes to. The muladhara chakra, according to Hindu tradition, represents sexual energy. Yoga scholar Hans David explains that the energy of the muladhara chakra is vital in that it can affect how one deals with life in general, especially with regard to feelings of freedom in expressing love (and lovemaking). Conversely, when this energy is blocked, misguided or misused it can cause "neurotic disturbances" that result in the inability to express feelings and a "'freezing' of psychosomatic functions."[4]

The theories of Sigmund Freud and Alfred Kinsey regarding sexuality have had deleterious effects in a number of ways. Objectifying sex and equating it with mere physical desire has become a predominant viewpoint in contemporary society. Not understanding sexuality in the context of emotion, intentionality, spirituality, love and godliness is the bane of modern "sexology," and this misunderstanding gives rise to the objectification of sexuality. British philosopher Roger Scruton considers Freud's objectification of sex and equating it to a mere "animal" instinct that needs to be satiated, like hunger, as fundamentally inhumane—even pornographic. Commenting on the moral and intentional aspects of sex, Scruton avers:

> An excitement which concentrates upon the sexual organs, whether of man or of woman, which seeks, as it were, to bypass the complex negotiation of the face, hands, voice and posture, is perverted. It voids desire of its intentionality, and replaces it with a pursuit of the sexual commodity, which can always be had for a price.[5]

Gone is the concept of love and mutual respect. Sex as a commodity leaves us with indiscriminate behaviors that are justified as being normal, even healthy. But as Scruton observes, when morality and intentionality are removed from the equation, we are left with a condition in which sexual conduct is "profoundly demoralized." As he notes:

> In redescribing the human world in this way, we also change it. We introduce new forms of sexual feeling—shaped by the desire for an all-comprehending permission. The sexual sacrament gives way to a sexual market; and the result is a fetishism of the sexual commodity.[6]

Allan Bloom's observation that in contemporary culture the legacy of romanticism has been reduced to "the centrality of sex, but sex without ideals," echoes Scruton's assertions. Bloom refers to American society as one built on the family unit: "a nation of households." In assessing contemporary American attitudes about sexuality in literature, Bloom was of the opinion that as the topic of sex entered the mainstream, writers wrote about sex in ways that were not directed "toward the sublime." Instead, authors gave us "indiscriminate liberation, or therapy to cure our hang-ups, or … psychological engineering to complete the project of equality, which had stopped short at the door of the family."[7] This condition is similar to what Christian author Dick Keyes refers to as "the New Romanticism," wherein the Holy Grail of spontaneity trumps reason and morals, thereby becoming the highest authority by which people make decisions and form their identities. An unfortunate by-product of this particular moral ecology is the rise of sexual objectification and an ego-driven identity. If it feels good, do it. As Keyes puts it, "the absence of a true sense of identity has put great weight on human sexuality to support the unsteady human ego."[8] Moreover, psychologist Rollo Reece May asserts that sex has become "something to do when we can think of nothing more to say to each other," and the body is asked to "compensate for the abdication of the person."[9]

Looking back to ancient perspectives regarding sexuality we find Confucius saying, "I have yet to see a man who loves virtue as much as sex."[10] In Aristotle's *Politics*, the opening chapter cites the importance of governing the human appetites for food and sex: two of the most "elemental human desires" that require cultivating and civilizing customs. Patrick J. Deneen, citing Aristotle's opinions, avers that "for food, the development of manners that encourage a moderate appetite and civilized consumption, and for sex, the cultivation of customs and habits of courtship … and finally marriage" were essential to control the "combustible" desires necessary to attain a cultivated and civilized society. Deneen notes that Aristotle posited that those who do not curb these appetites become "the most vicious of creatures, literally consuming other humans to slake their base and untutored appetites."[11] This attitude often results in the nadir of human selfishness.

I would proffer that when two individuals are conjoined in love, physically, emotionally and spiritually, they have achieved a dimension of divinity. Genesis speaks of male and female being the image of God—the incarnation of God's original masculinity and original femininity. The Hindu philosophy of Tantra reinforces this idea. David Gordon White of Princeton University offers the following definition of Tantric philosophy:

> Tantra is that Asian body of beliefs and practices which, working from the principle that the universe we experience is nothing other than the concrete

manifestation of the divine energy of the godhead that creates and maintains that universe, seeks to ritually appropriate and channel that energy, within the human microcosm, in Creative and emancipatory ways.[12]

The sexual act in Tantric tradition is seen as a way to achieve a cosmic balance between male and female and the process through which human beings can connect with and become one with the Godhead. In Tantric sexual rituals, balancing sexual energies to experience a higher ecstasy is the desired outcome. The concept of creativity as a spiritual gift is one that has been expounded upon for ages. Experiencing sexual ecstasy as a way to meet or experience God, or to achieve our personal divinity, is but another aspect of the human creative impulse.

Of course, the idea of sexuality as a path to the Godhead has not always been a favored viewpoint. In early Christian culture the sins of the flesh were to be avoided because the temptations of the physical body were often seen as having deleterious effects in the pursuit of "holiness." Sacrifice—from the Latin *sacri*, "holy," and *facere*, "to make"—has been considered the more pure path to attain spiritual fulfillment and maturity. Consequently, at various points in Christian history sexual fulfillment has been viewed as inimical to the pursuit of godliness.

Moreover, overcoming one's fleshly desires and remaining chaste became a test of one's faith conviction and a way to attain a higher spiritual condition. But it should be remembered that mandatory celibacy in the medieval church was considered to be an effective hedge against nepotism and a vehicle to ensure that land owned by the church "stayed in ecclesial possession rather than passing down to the children of clergymen." Writing on the issue of celibacy in the ecumenical magazine *First Things*, Grant Kaplan notes the line of reasoning of one such argument: "Since the imposition [of celibacy] was both unnatural and lacked clear theological warrant, many Catholic men who would have otherwise chosen the priesthood decided against it."[13] Though "clerical celibacy" has been viewed as a spiritual discipline, the origins of this practice were not necessarily in accord with the tenet of Genesis 1:28, that humans should "be fruitful and increase in number."

Music too was often seen as being somewhat prurient in this regard as it was often associated with pagan cultures and pagan rituals in medieval Europe.

The early church fathers understood that music possessed a sensual aspect and as such could not easily reconcile music with attempts to foster "rarefied" or higher emotions and thoughts. Still, the aesthetic beauty and effects of music on one's soul state could not be denied. The medieval Christian concept that spiritual fulfillment and redemption were somehow hindered or obstructed by pleasurable things like music is one that troubled even the most enlightened practitioners of the faith. Consider St. Augustine's observations on this dilemma:

> When I call to mind the tears I shed at the songs of Thy Church … I then acknowledge the great utility of this custom. Thus vacillate I between dangerous pleasure and tried soundness; being inclined rather … to approve of the use of singing in the church, that so by the delights of the ear the weaker minds may be stimulated to a devotional frame. Yet when it happens to me to be more moved by the singing than by what is sung, I confess myself to have sinned criminally, and then I would rather not have heard the singing.[14]

The sensuality that is part and parcel of the musical experience need not cause such cognitive or spiritual dissonances. If creativity is the progeny of a sacred covenant with God, then what is needed is a more enlightened viewpoint—one that justifies sensuality within the context of attaining our divinity and a higher love. In his writings on the issues of sexuality and art, philosopher Arthur Schopenhauer viewed sex as actually having metaphysical attributes.

> If I am asked where the most intimate knowledge of that inner essence of the world, of that thing in itself which I have called the will to live is to be found, or where that essence enters most clearly into our consciousness, or where it achieves the purest revelation of itself, then I must point to ecstasy in the act of copulation. That is it! That is the true essence and core of all things, the aim and purpose of all existence.[15]

The noted Wagner scholar Bryan Magee observes that Schopenhauer believed that "orgasm is not only the ultimate experience, but a quasi-mystical one that carries us to the very center of life's mystery, even if, in the nature of things, the experience of it is a very short one compared with the sustained transports of the mystic."[16] According to Magee, Schopenhauer came to a realization that, "the fullest expression of the individual personality is in a loving sexual relationship, in which, perhaps paradoxically, the barriers and limitations of selfhood are transcended," and in this relational state of mutual reciprocation, "the individual loses his sense of self and experiences oneness with the other in the sexual act."[17] Schopenhauer's views greatly affected Richard Wagner and the composer's late works often deal with the narrative of the redemptive power of love. Wagner adopted Schopenhauer's ideas about the metaphysical aspects of love, sex and music in relation to realizing the universal truths that lie in the deepest realms of our subconscious, and these became a basis for several libretti of Wagner's finest operas.

However, Wagner was far from being a pillar of virtue when it came to sexual relations. (Many of us fall short in that regard.) A serial adulterer, he and his promiscuous friend Friedrich Nietzsche were precursors to the Freudian mindset that considered sexual restraint intrinsically unnatural—repressive, in fact. To the romantics of that era, "order, self-restraint, discipline and the crushing of any kind of chaotic or anti-legal factors," were considered "poison" and at odds with freedom and self-expression.[18] Wagner was significantly influenced by Schopenhauer's attitudes about life and sexuality, but to a lesser extent by his attitudes about music.* In his early days as a revolutionary in Dresden in 1848 (a time when the ideas for his Ring cycle were being formulated), Wagner was on a course that would attract Nietzsche as a fellow revolutionary in the assault on traditional sexual mores. For Nietzsche, liberating sexuality from the "false consciousness" of Judeo-Christian culture could lead to the takedown of the repressive gestalt of that particular culture. Sexual licentiousness could then bring about the transvaluation of all "bourgeoisie" morals and values.

In a very real way Wagner and Nietzsche were also the precursors to Frankfurt School alumnus Herbert Marcuse, who posited (in typical Marxist dialectical fashion) that there was an irreconcilable conflict between human biological instincts and one's conscience; therefore, the need to be emancipated from this repression, and the guilt and shame it engendered, was necessary in order for people to be fully liberated and attain happiness. Marcuse's book *Eros and Civilization* is influenced by Freud, who argued that the conflict between

---

* In Wagner's view, all components in the production of opera—music, libretto, dance, etc.—were equal, whereas Schopenhauer ascribed to music a more prominent status.

individual freedoms and civilization's demand for conformity—and the laws that ensure a certain conformity—has the effect of restricting happiness and gratification. Paul Kengor, a leading authority on communism and its ideological underpinnings, writes in his book *Takedown: From Communists to Progressives, How the Left Has Sabotaged Family and Marriage,* that the extreme leftists of Marcuse's ilk have long attempted to "weaponize" sexuality in their attempt to subvert traditional moral attitudes for revolutionary purposes.

Freud posited that sex was basically amoral and without any spiritual essence, and therefore all people are bisexual by nature. The Frankfurt School neo-Marxists eagerly juxtaposed Freud's concepts with Marxist-Hegelian rationale and promulgated the idea that rage, jealousy, resentment and revenge against "traditional" values could be justified because these values, after all, were based on the same traditions of the bourgeoisie, patriarchal culture that caused slavery, imperialism, colonialism and sexual oppression in the first place. Sexual liberation was the way through which Marxist activists could strike back at all that. These "revolutionaries" viewed the power of twisted sexual behavior as a serious weapon in the fight against the "old world" and its values. As Kengor notes, this sexual rebellion "is as old as the Old Testament, even as communists had a new, perverse rebellion in mind. ... The far left has remained undeterred, faithful to its rebellious roots ... hell-bent on taking down the family."[19]

Michael Walsh, in his book *The Fiery Angel: Art, Culture, Sex, Politics and the Struggle for the Soul of the West,* elaborates further on the mindset of the Frankfurt School philosophers:

> No wonder the Marxists historians of the Frankfurt School and their descendants made the study of history one of their prime targets, framing the events of the past within a bastardized dialectic in order to shape or stifle the future, and to impart the propaganda necessary to bring their glorious, atheistic, and fundamentally anti-human new world into being—ironically in the guise of humanism. That it cannot—can never—come to being except at the price of millions of human lives, matters to them not one whit.
>
> In short, they wish to steal our history from us—the primary purpose of Critical Theory—and replace the same set of facts with a different, comprehensive interpretation. They do this in the most intellectually dishonest way possible, by reducing complex tales to a simple anti-narrative, in which our

heroes are the villains, in which our accomplishments are history's schandes (disgrace), and in which our future is headed for the dustbin. Stripping away nuance, subplots, character development, and anything else that does not immediately serve their political purposes, they would present us with the Worst Story Ever Told.[20]

Sex, history, race, culture, ethnicity; all are used by the Critical Theory advocates as cudgels to assault Western Judeo-Christian values.

Musical Orgasm

When considering whether to conduct a reconstructed version of Mahler's "Tenth Symphony,"* Leonard Bernstein famously asked a colleague, "I have one question. Will it give me an orgasm?" The metaphorical quip says a great deal about how music and sex are often conflated. Bernstein, ever the romantic, simply wanted to know if the music would arouse the senses in a cathartic fashion. The fact that he used a sexual context to make his point underscores the emotive and cathartic power that we expect and long for when experiencing great music. The tension and resolution experienced in the aural relationship of consonant and dissonant intervals, or tonic and dominant harmonies in tonal music, create emotional and intellectual sensations akin to the physical sensations in sexual activity. The reciprocity and harmonization of yin and yang elements within the aural spectrum of tonal music is what stimulates our "higher mind" and in so doing can generate a "musical orgasm." Studies in neuroscience point to the release of dopamine, an addictive chemical neurotransmitter that is associated with aesthetically pleasurable experiences, such as cathartic moments in music—and sex. This a way of achieving a "natural high."

The composers of the romantic era—Beethoven, Tchaikovsky, Liszt, Wagner, Mahler, e.g.—would often prolong and sustain the dominant chord (in the object position) at a given climatic point in their compositions in order to heighten aural tension so that when the tonic chord (in the subject

---

* Gustav Mahler died before finishing his tenth symphony, but he left musical sketchbooks that revealed certain ideas as to how he might have completed it. Several composers have attempted to complete a reconstructed version of the symphony based on these materials.

position) arrived the sense of resolution would result in a highly charged emotive catharsis.

In his observation of the music of French twentieth-century composer Olivier Messiaen, *New Yorker* magazine music critic Alex Ross observed:

> God spoke to Messiaen through sounding tones, whether the mighty roar of the orchestra or the church organ, the clattering of exotic percussion, or the songs of birds. The Lord could manifest Himself in consonance and dissonance alike, though consonance was His true realm.[21]

In the context of polarity this is a confounding assessment. It's like saying that the Almighty prefers men to women, or positive valences to negative valences, or sperm to the egg, or vowels to consonants. The nature of Nature is one of balance and harmony between polar opposites. If nature reflects God's image in substance ontologically, then we can extrapolate that God's "true realm" in music is one where the aural interplay between consonance and dissonance is manifested in a sublime union. Both consonant and dissonant intervals are present in the overtone series—the sonic etymology of all music. The creative sexual act is the union of two equally important aspects in which if one aspect were to be missing, procreation and catharsis could not occur. In tonal music, dissonance plays a vital role. It is intrinsic to the tonal syntax and allows the fullest range of emotional expression to be realized when it is proportionally balanced with consonance.

If, as Biblical scripture avers, the image of God is reflected in the harmonized attributes of masculinity and femininity, then the union of these polar opposites can be considered to be a manifestation of God's invisible deity (Romans 1:20). This perspective may be seen by some, as the attempt to anthropomorphize God—ascribing human attributes or characteristics to the Almighty—but rather, it is an attempt to discover, or recover, our human divinity. In music it is the attraction and harmonization of polar opposites that elicits the emotive power that can result in the orgasmic catharsis that Bernstein alluded to.

The idea that God loved us as a parent to such a degree that we were bequeathed the gift of creativity as an expression of that love is a distinct feature of Christianity. This narrative gave rise to the idea of agape love—the highest expression of love between God and humankind. Though eros is associated with the sensual and carnal aspects of love, the idea that sexual love is not "godly," or is without transcendent potentialities, is seen as an incomplete view of sexuality from a Christian perspective. Having sexual relationships in accordance with godly virtues and principles is the path to true love and lasting peace. Sexual probity cannot be underestimated in this regard.

Alluding to Messiaen's faith vis-à-vis his compositional rationale and his *Quartet for the End of Time*, Ross acknowledges a parallel between agape love and eros:

> For Messiaen, the end of time also meant an escape from history, a leap into an invisible paradise. ... Messiaen always took joy in skating between the mundane and the sublime. He loved God in terms that were sensual, almost sexual. Human love and divine love were not opposites, as they are for so many close readers of the Bible, but stages in an unbroken progression.[22]

Though we should be cognizant of the divine aspect of sexual love, we should remember, too, that according to various theological interpretations in Christianity, it was the misuse of sexual love that led to the human fall and the resulting human suffering. As Rev. Phillip Thomas of the Black Hebrew Church of God and Saints of Christ* (and former lead singer for the New York-based R & B group, the Crown Heights Affair) quipped, the fall of man wasn't about the apple in the tree, it was about "the pair on the ground."

We should give Sting and other high-profile artists high marks for using their celebrity for the advocacy of humanitarian issues. He has been a serious advocate for protecting the natural resources and the sustainability of our planet via his activism for environmental concerns, especially regarding Brazil and the Amazon rainforest. Kudos! Yet if we think about "human resources" in the context of sustainability, it could be said that love and the human energy expended through acts of loving are perhaps our most precious human resources. If we consider sexual energy to be the most precious and organic human resource, we should think long and hard about how we engage in sexual behavior. The abuse of sexual love, more often than not, results in tragedy, heartbreak and social pathologies that require inordinate

---

* The Black Hebrew Church of God and Saints of Christ was founded in Lawrence, Kansas in 1896 by William Saunders Crowdy.

resources—emotional and economic—to heal and rectify. Immature attitudes about love and sex contribute to the conditions that lead to divorce and family breakdown, which in turn result in higher crime rates, lower educational achievement, increased drug addiction and increased suicides among young people.

These attitudes also contribute to increased cases of unwanted pregnancies and sexually transmitted diseases—conditions that not long ago created great alarm (and shame), but now are so common that they hardly cause a ripple of concern. Manhattan Institute Fellow Kay Hymowitz cites another troubling trend:

> Sexual intercourse, once considered a pleasure reserved for adults, has become commonplace among kids and has led to dramatic increases in the rates of out-of-wedlock childbirth, welfare dependency, fatherlessness, and abortion. Even though the percentage of teens having sex has decreased somewhat in recent years, sexual activity has trickled down to ever-younger ages.[23]

Hymowitz points to a *New York Times* article in which columnist Jane Brody encourages parents to begin teaching girls how and when to say "no" or "yes" about having sex as early as nine years old. As the subtitle of Hymowitz's cautionary book, *Ready or Not* suggests, "treating small children as adults endangers their futures—and ours." The data regarding social pathologies in the context of sexual promiscuity are irrefutable. Any discussion about human sustainability should include the issue of how our sexual energy is best channeled. The highly suggestive, in-your-face sexual atmosphere that is pervasive in popular culture reeks of permissiveness and moral relativism, and is far removed from a virtuous spiritual reality. If, as Sting sings in the old Police song, "we are spirits in the material world," it becomes imperative to nurture our spirituality according to the practice of true love and a more enlightened view of sexuality.

Roger Scruton is in accord with Hymowitz in pointing out that contemporary popular culture, with its preoccupation with youth and "sexual liberation" (a term coined by Frankfurt School theorist Wilhelm Reich), promotes various "experiences, which can be obtained without undertaking the burdens of responsibility, work, child-rearing and marriage." The removal of commitment in sexual relations undermines the basic structure of a society. Scruton observes that in the scenario where sex is divorced from long-term commitment, it becomes a simulacrum in which there is "no cost in terms of education, moral discipline, hardship or love ... which has the added advantage that it shuts out the adult world completely, and replaces it with a cloud of wishful dreams, the very same wishful dreams that float across the screen of MTV."[24]

In 1934, English anthropologist J. D. Unwin published his book *Sex and Culture* which is based on an exhaustive study of 86 cultures and tribes going back five thousand years. In his research, Unwin found that in every case where sexual mores became skewed, these cultures devolved due to moral decay and eventually disappeared. Unwin's undertaking was an attempt "to test the Freudian notion that civilization is a byproduct of repressed sexuality."[25] Unwin wasn't thrilled with his findings, but in the spirit of anthropological integrity, he published them anyway, saying that his intent was not to advance a particular moral or ideological agenda.

Unwin's research is difficult to refute. He stated: "I offer no opinion about rightness or wrongness. ... In human records there is no instance of a society retaining its energy after a complete new generation has inherited a tradition which does not insist on pre-nuptial and post-nuptial continence."[26] Sexual liberation can be diagnosed as the causal aspect of our current cultural malaise. Will we take the findings of Unwin's historical survey to heart? Scruton provides coruscating insight, as usual:

> Normal desire is an interpersonal emotion. Its aim is a free and mutual surrender, which is also a uniting of two individuals, of you and me— through our bodies, certainly, but not merely as our bodies. Normal desire is a person to person response, one that seeks the selfhood that it gives. Objects can be substituted for each other, subjects not. Subjects, as Kant persuasively argued, are free individuals; their non-substitutability belongs to what they essentially are. ... Free beings must treat each other as ends in themselves.[27]

Restoring sexuality to its divine and sacred place remains an important aspect of our culture's recovery from the morass of moral relativism and abject nihilism that plagues our current social condition. It is through the harmonization of polar opposites—male and female, mind and body—that we experience truth and in so doing become our complete and truer selves. In the process, we become creators, parents, artists—and in this context sexuality becomes a manifestation of a divine and higher love. This, in turn, allows us to become "individual truth bodies" as co-creators with God. The lower chakra is then harmonized with a higher emotion and elevated to the status of divine energy. Sex becomes more than merely "humping." It attains its true beauty, meaning and goodness. Orgasm becomes godly—the apotheosis of conjugal love. Add some great music to the mix and we just may find ourselves on that stairway to heaven.

Postscript

In this essay I referenced Paul Kengor's book *Takedown: From Communists to Progressives, How the Left Has Sabotaged Family and Marriage*. It is important to note that the founders of the Black Lives Matter organization have Marxist inclinations. Observing the violence in the United States that occurred in the aftermath of George Floyd's death, I went to the BLM website and found this statement under the heading, "What We Believe" (the web page has since been taken down):

> We disrupt the Western-prescribed nuclear family structure requirement by supporting each other as extended families and "villages" that collectively care for one another, especially our children, to the degree that mothers, parents, and children are comfortable. … When we gather, we do so with the intention of freeing ourselves from the tight grip of heteronormative thinking, or rather, the belief that all in the world are heterosexual (unless s/he or they disclose otherwise).[28]

Moreover, one of the co-founders of BLM, Patrisse Cullors has admitted (it's on video) that BLM uses Marxist-organizing tactics. We might all agree that racism and social inequities ought to be resolved as quickly as humanly possible. However, Marxism has never proven to be a viable solution to these problems, whether implemented in Russia, China, Cuba, Eastern Europe, North Korea, Africa or Central and South America. In fact, the corruption, human rights violations, and staggering body counts in these places makes it incumbent on sane and moral people to engage in a moral "disruption" of the

Marxist enterprise wherever it rears its perfidious head, especially when there is an attempt to "take down" the family and to weaponize sexuality in that effort.

Perhaps Shelby Steele said it best when he opined that defunding the police, or spending millions of dollars for police sensitivity training will do nothing to solve the problem of family breakdown and absentee fathers in the African American community. I concur.

Additionally, Kengor reports the following regarding President Obama's long-time political advisor, David Axelrod:

> In his long-awaited and just-released memoirs, Axelrod wrote about Obama's early views on gay marriage. Editor and columnist George Neumayr has carefully compared what Axelrod has reported and Obama's various statements and positions. In all, it paints an intriguing and disturbing picture. Contrary to Obama's claims that he is only a recent convert to gay marriage, it looks as though he supported gay marriage as far back as the mid-1990s, when he was an aspiring Chicago politician ... Obama apparently supported legalization two decades ago, but publicly suggested otherwise (meaning he lied) in order to get votes, especially from African Americans who rejected gay marriage in higher numbers than white Americans.[29]

Recommended Recordings

Robert Schumann:

Symphony No. 1, George Szell, Cleveland Orchestra

Symphony No. 2, James Levine, Berlin Philharmonic

Symphony No. 3, Bernard Haitink, Royal Concertgebouw Orchestra

Symphony No. 4, Daniel Barenboim, Staatskapelle Berlin

Piano Concerto, Van Cliburn, piano, Chicago Symphony

Manfred Overture, Leonard Bernstein, Vienna Philharmonic Orchestra

Genoveva Overture, Roger Norrington, London Classical Players

Kreisleriana, Op. 16, Martha Argerich, piano

Carnival, Op. 9, Wilhelm Kempff, piano

Clara Wieck Schumann:

Piano Concerto, Francesco Nicolosi, Alma Mahler Sinfonietta

Complete Songs, Stephan Loges, Susan Gritton

Piano and Chamber Music, Micaela Gelius, Sreten Krstic, Stephan Haack

Sting: *Songs from the Labyrinth*, featuring music by John Dowland

Igor Stravinsky: *A Soldier's Tale*, Kent Nagano, The London Sinfonietta

Mahler: Symphony No. 10, Simon Rattle, Berlin Philharmonic Orchestra

Wagner: Music from *The Ring of the Nibelungs*, George Szell, Cleveland Orchestra

Endnotes

1   Sting, "A Rock Star in Winter," interview by Ben Finane, *Listen*, November/December 2009, https://www.listenmusicculture.com/interviews/sting-interview.

2   Ibid.

3   Ibid.

4   Hans David, *Die Welt des Yoga*, as cited by Hans Cousto, *The Cosmic Octave: Origin of Harmony* (LifeRhythm, 2000), p. 48.

5   Roger Scruton, *An Intelligent Person's Guide to Philosophy* (New York: Penguin Books, 1999), p. 132.

6   Ibid., p. 134.

7   Allan Bloom, *Love and Friendship* (New York: Simon & Schuster, 1993), pp. 264-265.

8   Dick Keyes, *Beyond Identity: Finding Your Self in the Image and Character of God* (Destinee Media, 2012), p. 29.

9   Rollo Reece May, *Psychology and the Human Dilemma*, as cited by Keyes, *Beyond Identity*, p. 29.

10   *The Analects of Confucius: An Online Teaching Translation*, translated by Robert Eno, (Robert Eno, 2018), p. 43, https://chinatxt.sitehost.iu.edu/Analects_of_Confucius_(Eno-2015).pdf.

11   Patrick J. Deneen, *Why Liberalism Failed* (New Haven, CT: Yale University Press, 2019), p. 68.

12   David Gordon White, *Tantra in Practice* (Princeton, NJ: Princeton University Press, 2000), p. 9.

13   Grant Kaplan, "Celibacy as Political Resistance," *First Things*, January 2014, https://www.firstthings.com/article/2014/01/celibacy-as-political-resistance.

14   *The Confessions of Saint Augustine,* translated by J. G. Pilkington, http://www.logoslibrary.org/augustine/confessions/1033.html, Book X, Chapter 33.

15   Arthur Schopenhauer, *Manuscript Remains* Vol. III, as cited by Bryan Magee in *The Tristan Chord: Wagner and Philosophy* (New York: Henry Holt and Company, 2000), p. 170.

16 Magee, *The Tristan Chord*, p. 170.

17 Ibid.

18 Isaiah Berlin, *The Roots of Romanticism* (Princeton, NJ: Princeton University Press, 1999), p. 113.

19 Paul Kengor, *Takedown: From Communists to Progressives, How the Left Has Sabotaged Family and Marriage* (Washington, D.C.: WND Books, 2015), Kindle Edition.

20 Michael Walsh, *The Fiery Angel: Art, Culture, Sex, Politics and the Struggle for the Soul of the West* (New York-London: Encounter Books, 2018), p. 32.

21 Alex Ross, *The Rest Is Noise: Listening to the Twentieth Century* (New York: Farrar, Straus and Giroux, 2007), p. 486.

22 Alex Ross, "Revelations: Messiaen's *Quartet for the End of Time*," *New Yorker*, March 22, 2004, republished, https://www.therestisnoise.com/2004/04/quartet_for_the_2.html.

23 Kay S. Hymowitz, *Ready or Not: Why Treating Small Children as Adults Endangers Their Futures—and Ours* (New York: The Free Press, 1999), p. 2.

24 Roger Scruton, *An Intelligent Person's Guide to Modern Culture* (South Bend, IN: St. Augustine's Press, 2000), p. 115.

25 Philip Yancey, "The Lost Sex Study," *Christianity Today*, December 12, 1994, https://www.christianitytoday.com/ct/1994/december12/4te080.html.

26 Ibid.

27 Roger Scruton, *Beauty: A Very Short Introduction* (Oxford and New York: Oxford University Press, 2011), p. 133.

28 "What We Believe," Black Lives Matter, https://blacklivesmatter.com/what-we-believe/, removed.

29 Paul Kengor, *Takedown*, p. 148.

19

Spiritual Food, Physical Food

From pure sensation to the intuition of beauty, from pleasure
and pain to love and the mystical ecstasy and death—
all the things that are fundamental, all the things that,
to the human spirit, are most profoundly significant,
can only be experienced, not expressed.
The rest is always and everywhere silence.
After silence that which comes nearest to expressing
the inexpressible is music.[1]
Aldous Huxley

In a 1994 interview in *Rolling Stone* magazine, former general secretary of the Soviet Union's Communist Party Mikhail Gorbachev, was asked about life after ruling the Soviet empire. In that interview he mentions that one of his new preoccupations was listening to music. He would say:

> It's wonderful to have a chance to listen to good music. I believe that the greatest achievement of humankind, other than growing grain, is symphonies, classical music. There is a sphere where there is no need for words but where the human feelings are expressed in the highest philosophical way.[2]

Grain and symphonies—physical food and spiritual food—are human-kind's greatest achievements? Actually, I believe Gorbachev is onto something. Nietzsche asserted that life would not be worth living without music, and most of us would agree with him. It is part of the human experience to seek spiritual nourishment, and for many people music has been their favorite dish—or their religion. It certainly was religion for me in my formative years as a young music student. Beethoven was my "messiah" and his symphonic disciples—Schubert, Schumann, Mendelssohn, Brahms, Dvořák, Tchaikovsky, Bruckner, Mahler—were speaking "the gospel." For many of my generation the Beatles were in the messianic mix as well. John Lennon went as far as to suggest that the Beatles had become "more popular than Jesus."[3]

The word religion stems from the Latin *ligare*: to bind. Religion literally means to rebind, as in the rebinding of God and humankind. In this context, music, with its acknowledged spiritual properties, possesses a "religious" aspect in that it can serve as a vehicle to reconnect us to the divine. Implicit in this assertion is that humankind was at one time connected to God, but lost that connection, hence religion's *raison d'etre*—its justification. Music, being invisible, vibratory and an expression of heart, corresponds to the incorporeal or spiritual realm, which is also invisible, vibratory and a realm of heart. Music's ability to change consciousness and to make us vulnerable to change is one of its most important characteristics. Perhaps no other art form so powerfully evokes emotion and heart, and as such, plays an important part in cultivating a culture based on heart and love.

With respect to the symphonic music cited by Gorbachev, it's interesting to note that Richard Wagner placed a great deal of importance on the use of the orchestra in his operas precisely due to the power of purely instrumental music to speak to the subconscious. Through the use of the orchestra, he would say, "the primal urges of creation and nature are represented. What the orchestra expresses can never be clearly articulated, because it renders primal feeling itself."[4] Wagner's contention was antithetical to that of his nemesis Eduard Hanslick, who proffered that the elements of music were non-referential and therefore could not express anything because, "there is no *causal nexus* between a musical composition and the feelings it may excite."[5] Obviously, Hanslick's assertion is refuted by many for whom music is something that elicits and evokes feelings via its emotive power.

Igor Stravinsky consigned to the "dynamic power of the orchestra" the task of *expressing* a plethora of primordial emotions in his ballet score *The Rite of Spring*. These emotions, according to Stravinsky, would include the "the obscure and immense sensation of which all things are conscious when Nature renews its forms," as well as the "profound uneasiness of a universal puberty," and "the fear of nature before the arising of beauty, a sacred terror at the midday sun."[6] In his explanation regarding the ballet's opening episode, Stravinsky was quite specific about the timbre of his instrumental choices in relation to how he intended various sounds to convey his poetic images.*

The nineteenth-century English art critic Walter Pater famously asserted: "All art constantly aspires toward the condition of music."[7] It is the direct, "wordless" communicative aspect of music that many find appealing, and that, in Pater's estimation, was a highly desirable condition for art in general. In a very real way, music suspends rational thought and momentarily puts us in an altered state of consciousness. Music's direct and immediate effect on the listener confirms the idea that it possesses profoundly spiritual potentialities. Aldous Huxley echoes Pater in his comment regarding music's ability to "express the inexpressible."[8]

Late in his life, conductor Bruno Walter developed a keen interest in the philosophical realm of anthroposophy, the study of the incorporeal world as it pertained to the development of the inner self. Developed by Hungarian philosopher Rudolf Steiner, this esoteric branch of metaphysics attracted many adherents who believed in the spiritual properties of art and science and that "knowing higher worlds" was central to attaining the fullest understanding of the human experience. For Walter, Steiner's theories were especially relevant to the human condition and the art of music. As Walter explains:

> Unending light poured forth from Rudolf Steiner's thoughts on the cosmos, earth, and mankind, on the physical and the spiritual world. ... In our epoch of dark materialism, it signified an invaluable enriching to my old age: finally a solid foundation under my feet.[9]

---

* In 1913 Stravinsky wrote an essay for the Parisian arts journal *Montjoie!*, in which he provided his explanation of the "expressive" aspect of *The Rite of Spring*, especially the opening episode. According to the essay, the composer's avoidance of stringed instruments was calculated so as to avoid "cheap expressivity" and any evocation of the human voice. [Source: Richard Taruskin, *Stravinsky and the Russian Traditions: A Biography of the Works through Marva, Volume II.*]

Materialism has fascinated mankind (but) it is not the materialistic which makes life worthwhile. Anything beyond the material things of life brings us to the sense of life. Music—the most sublime—is in this category. ... Music ... is a bridge to God.[10]

It's interesting to note Walter's reference to the "epoch of dark materialism," for this observation was made in 1962. It seems that lamentation about the hyper-materialism that plagues our contemporary culture was already being expressed decades ago. Walter believed that there was a "magic power" in "the deeper meaning of music," and this was like the "pure fresh air" that one finds on a "high mountain top" as one ascends up and away from the dark materialism that permeated much of our modern-day culture.[11] Given that he lived well into the era of post-World War II modernism, with its predilection for atonality and abstraction, Walter's perspectives were especially relevant with regard to the idea that tonal music was a corrective to formulaic and abstractionist trends in musical composition.

In that sense, Walter was a prototypical romantic in that he espoused the idea that music possessed the ability to transform one's life and to take one to a higher plane, and in so doing could make the world a more humane place. Walter believed that atonal music was inimical to the process of attaining a "morally uplifting experience." According to Walter's biographers, Erik Ryding and Rebecca Pechefsky, the conductor "had specific ideas about how it [music] achieved this ennobling effect on human beings. Above all, Walter felt that dissonance in music—though it could abound freely—must ultimately resolve into consonance." They allude to Walter's writings and cite this commentary:

The spiritual excitement created by such delays and hindrances—their emotional effect—depends precisely on the fact that dissonance strives for consonance, and unrest strives for repose, which will be withheld from it through the course of the composition and achieve fulfillment only at the conclusion.[12]

Walter's perspectives owe a certain debt to Schopenhauer, but he was far from being alone in extolling the "virtues" of tonal music in the context of moral and ethical considerations. Ryding and Pechefsky point out that he was not so naive as to suggest that just by listening to music, especially classical music rooted in tonality, one would become a better person; but Walter nonetheless believed that "regular contact with music could, in some cases, actually improve a person's character."[13] Ryding and Pechefsky also point out that Walter's public views criticizing atonal music were somewhat "injudicious," since they were made at the same time when Hitler and the Nazis were also condemning new music, going as far as banning Paul Hindemith's music and labeling him a "cultural Bolshevik."[14] Guilt by association was something that many artists of that era feared, and with good reason.

The composers of the symphonic repertory that Gorbachev referred to often spoke of the religious and spiritual aspects of their art. Speaking to the communicative aspects of music, Felix Mendelssohn remarked, that the music he admired "expresses thoughts to me that are not too *imprecise* to be framed in words, but too *precise*."[15] Alluding to music's effects on the states of one's soul (*Seelenzustände*), Beethoven believed that, "Music is the one incorporeal entrance into the higher world of knowledge,"[16] and could be "the mediator between the spiritual and sensual life."[17] This echoes the concept of *musica humana* (the harmonization of the spirit and body) that the Greeks, Boethius and Rudolf Steiner found to be highly efficacious in their explanations of metaphysics and music.

Beethoven's epic Ninth Symphony, composed in 1824, with its call for a universal brotherhood, remains a musical manifesto of sorts to those who view this music as a noble and godly expression of universal love and truth. The text in the final movement, written by Friedrich Schiller and Beethoven, cites God and Heaven:

> *Joy, lovely divine spark,*
> *Daughter of Elysium,*
> *Drunk with fire, we enter,*
> *Heavenly one, your shrine!*
> *Your magic spells reunite*
> *What convention has rough sundered.*
> *All men will become brothers,*
> *At the gentle touch of your wing. …*
> *Embrace, you millions!*
> *This kiss is for all the world!*
> *Brothers, up there in the star-filled vault*

A loving father surely dwells. . . .
Do you humbly bow down, ye millions?
World, do you feel your Creator?
Seek him up there in the star-filled vault!
He surely dwells among the stars.[18]

A defining feature of romanticism in the late nineteenth century was the exploration of the mysterious and mythology in relation to the human experience. Most composers of the nineteenth century were acutely aware of the spiritual aspects of their art. An overriding narrative in much of Gustav Mahler's music was the poetic idea that the contradictions between the ideal and the reality of life, and the difficulties that ensue as a result of those contradictions, are a part of the human experience that will only find ultimate redemption in a final allegiance to God. His effulgent *Resurrection Symphony*, composed seventy years after Beethoven's Ninth, concludes with a choral exhortation with explicit religious connotations:

O Pain, thou piercer of all things,
From thee, I have been wrested!
O Death, thou masterer of all things,
Now, art thou mastered!
With wings which I have won me,
In love's fierce striving,
I shall soar upwards
To the light to which no eye has soared!
I shall die, to live.
Rise again, yea, thou wilt rise again,
My heart, in the twinkling of an eye!
What thou hast fought for,
Shall lead thee to God! [19]

For both Beethoven and Mahler a connection to the Almighty seemed necessary in order for humankind to overcome its earthly chains. Twentieth-century composers were not completely alien to the spiritual dimensions of their art, in spite of the hyper-intellectualization that permeated much of the century. Stravinsky alluded to the impulses that foster brotherhood, community and a communion with God in relation to music, saying:

> How are we to keep from succumbing to the irresistible need of sharing with our fellow men this joy that we feel when we see come to light something that has taken form through our own action? ... Thus the consummated work [composition] spreads abroad to be communicated and finally flows back toward its source. The cycle, then, is closed. And that is how music comes to reveal itself as a form of communion with our fellow man—and with the Supreme Being.[20]

Alluding to music and its effects on our psyche, David Tame, opines: "music is more than a language. It is the language of languages. It can be said that of all the arts, there is ... none other that more powerfully moves and changes the consciousness."[21] This, of course, is an understanding that most music lovers easily acknowledge. In Harvard lectures in 1973, Leonard Bernstein contends that the phonetic etymology of music is akin to "natural language." Citing Noam Chomsky's theories of linguistics, specifically Chomsky's theory of "universal grammar," Bernstein makes a convincing case that there exist certain universal and innate aspects in tonal music in much the same way that there are universal aspects in language.

Chomsky asserted that the underlying principles of language are genetically transmitted and that all humans share the same linguistic heritage. For Chomsky, language is a process of "free creation, unconstrained by linguistic rule except insofar as such rules govern the forms of words and the patterns of sounds."[22] Though languages are predicated on fixed grammatical laws and principles, the manner in which the principles of generation are used is free and infinitely varied, provided that they result in an effective mode of communication. Appropriating that theory, Bernstein applied it to the process of creating music according to tonal theory, in which the basic components of music—melodies, chords, rhythm—are used in a variety of ways but within a codified set of laws and principles. Meaning in music, however, is more abstract and metaphorical than in natural languages, thus the same music will often have different meanings to different people. Moreover, a given piece of music may have a different meaning, or conjure a different emotional response to the same person depending on the emotional state of the person at a given time.

Analyzing the elemental properties of music—sound, organization and meaning—properties that correspond to phonology, syntax, and semantics in natural language, Bernstein, like Mendelssohn, averred that music, though metaphoric, can nonetheless be very specific in its communicative power with regard to "meaning" and "beauty."[23] The tonal syntax, like any natural language, has well-established rules. Yet "free creation" within the rules of the tonal syntax yields infinite possibilities, just as any natural language yields infinite possibilities in the use of its vocabulary. Having five thousand words at one's disposal when writing or speaking provides greater variety of expression and meaning than having only five hundred words.

Columbia University professor and composer Fred Lerdahl points out that music and language share certain attributes in that both domains consist of organized sound and time, both are culturally universal, both are uniquely human, both employ rhythm and contour, both are hierarchical, both are used in poetry and song, and both generate infinite output from finite principles. However, Lerdahl cautions that these similarities only go so far, and that both domains have significant differences as well. Music, for instance, doesn't have parts of speech (nouns, verbs, adjectives, etc.), nor does it have semantics in the linguistic sense. Language doesn't have anything analogous to pitch sets, scales, harmony or counterpoint, nor does it have the tonal tension and attraction that is intrinsic to tonal music. The two domains are similar but have differences.[24] In Western music the technique of counterpoint is the practice of composing two or more independent melodic lines that are presented simultaneously in relation to a specific harmonic progression. This technique works in music but in language when two or more individuals are saying different things simultaneously, the result is confusion and a lack of communication.

The Spiritual Dimension

The spiritual dimension of music and its nourishing properties are linked to its ability to communicate and take us to that "higher" understanding that Steiner alluded to, albeit in a nonverbal fashion. Bernstein also purported that there was an underlying similarity in music and natural language with regard to the subconscious need to communicate. Communication—like Gorbachev's grain—is necessary for survival. It is, in fact, a primal necessity.

Jesuit philosopher Walter J. Ong's comparison of artificial computer languages and natural language is instructive. Computer languages, Ong writes, "do not grow out of the unconscious but directly out of consciousness … the 'rules' of grammar in natural human languages are used first and can be abstracted from usage and stated explicitly in words only with difficulty and never completely."[25] Bernstein articulated a similar view in his explanation of Schoenberg's atonal 12-tone theories, stating that they were not "based on innate awareness, on the intuition of tonal relationships. They are like rules of an artificial language, and therefore must be learned." This, according to Bernstein, is "form at the expense of content—structuralism for its own sake."[26] With regard to chord grammar, the relational aspect in the tonal syntax cannot be underestimated when assessing its emotive power. Two chords (C major and G major, e.g.) will have distinct functions and differing poetic "meanings" when they are heard in the sequence of C proceeding to G or, conversely, G proceeding to C. In the tonal idiom any major chord can have four different functions depending on the key-center in which it exists—tonic, dominant, or subdominant in major keys, or subdominant in a minor key.

The drive for liberation of the grammatical relational constraints within the tonal idiom by the advocates of atonality, was a quest for total unanimity of pitch and chord relationships—a kind of musical androgyny that would allow for every possible relationship to be considered equal and to become "fully adequate to the musical imagination," according to Richard Taruskin. This liberation led to what Schoenberg called "the emancipation of dissonance," whereby dissonance would have its own justification apart from any syntactical need for resolution. This was antithetical to the grammar of tonality. Taruskin explains:

> The essence of counterpoint [in the tonal idiom] has always been its "dissonance treatment." That, and that alone, is where skill is required and displayed. What makes Bach's *Musical Offering* or The Art of Fugue such astonishing tours de force is not just the complexity of the texture, but the fact that that complexity is achieved within such exacting harmonic constraints. Take away the constraints, and you have rendered the tour de force entirely pointless.[27]

Tonal music in Western culture developed in much the same way as natural language. The rules governing the theories of music composition were abstracted after usage, not before. To varying extents the desire and necessity to communicate with greater efficiency lies at the heart of musical evolution. Music theory, equal temperament, instrumental development, harmonic invention and structural innovation can be said to be progenies of the desire to communicate in more efficacious and meaningful ways. The need to communicate is atavistic and causal, whereas the aforementioned modernist formulaic developments in musical theory and practice in the early twentieth century were resultant phenomena. In this respect, the attributes of tonal music as they pertain to spirituality and creativity take on deeply meaningful and anthroposophical connotations, resulting in a *causal nexus* of sorts.

In 1989 I had the opportunity to visit the National Palace Museum in Taipei, Taiwan. A significant portion of the art on display had been brought to Taiwan from mainland China by Chiang Kai-shek in 1949. I was astounded by the beautiful artworks created centuries ago, including jade and ivory sculptures, tapestries, paintings—amazing art by any measure. My first inclination as a Westerner was to know who created these magnificent artworks. I was astonished (and dismayed) to find that in almost every case the artist was simply identified as "Anonymous." My tour guide informed me that in Oriental societies where Confucian relational modalities are central, the emperor, king or a particular dynasty is acknowledged for having been the source of inspiration (or the source of the artist's commission) rather than the creator of the artwork. The artist was merely considered an artisan who would carry out their creative endeavors in a fairly utilitarian, workaday fashion in service to their liege.

Coming to an understanding about relationships in Confucian cultures, as well as the ethics that those relationships are predicated on, I couldn't help but make the distinction between oriental, Confucian thought and occidental, Judeo-Christian thought vis-à-vis the importance of creativity. Whereas the king or the emperor is considered to be most high—the untouchable potentate whom all must obey and bow to—in an imperial culture, the Judeo-Christian ethos is predicated largely on the ideal that we are, in fact, sons and daughters of the Almighty God and as such have been endowed with the gift of creativity. This gift was given as an expression of God's love as a heavenly parent. As

God's children we rejoice in that love and work together as co-creators with God in our creative endeavors and with a grateful and loyal heart. Through this relationship our creative endeavors allow us to attain our own divinity, and God, as a proud heavenly parent is only too happy to see us receive accolades and appreciation for our endeavors. In this sense, parentalism is an important aspect of the religious experience.

In the West, artists are not relegated to the status of nameless artisans but are routinely exalted for their contributions to the society in which they live and work. To make this point to friends and colleagues, I often ask them if they know who the monarch was where Beethoven lived in 1807. Few can provide the answer. But upon hearing the first notes of Beethoven's Fifth Symphony (composed in 1807), a relatively high percentage of people recognize that motif and know who created it.*

Some believe that in the West we place far too much importance on celebrity when we acknowledge the work of creative individuals, and the celebrity-industrial-complex can surely be held accountable for this on a number of levels. I have many oriental friends who view celebrity worship—and the voyeuristic tendencies that it engenders—as being somewhat obsessive and puerile. Yet, as Edward Rothstein opines, the "old and perfectly defensible habit of our culture to treat great composers and performers as if they were otherworldly beings from the pantheon of the gods" is a habit that is part of our Western cultural DNA. Still, music has moral and ethical dimensions, and when we ignore that, as Rothstein also suggests, "listening becomes focused on mere pleasure or cultish devotion," thereby leading to a condition where "great music has become relatively unimportant … we have filtered out the aspects of music that connect it to creator and culture on any deeper level than 'music appreciation.'"[28] Musical "meaning" in this context remains an important consideration, one that has ramifications that are equally as significant as craft and aesthetics.

In spite of our shortcomings, the idea of human creativity as it pertains to our divinity and spirituality cannot be easily discounted. As American painter George Inness (1825-1894) averred, "Of course, no man's motive can be

---

* Beethoven was living in Vienna at the time of the Fifth Symphony's creation, a time when the Napoleonic Wars were causing continual shifts in political leadership in Europe, so my query was a bit of a trick question.

absolutely pure and single. His environment affects him. But the true artistic impulse is divine."[29] The ability of music to connect us to that which is other-worldly, is a unique and powerful characteristic of the tonal arts. In his famous review of Beethoven's Fifth Symphony, E. T. A. Hoffman extols the suggestive power of instrumental music and echoes Gorbachev's contention regarding its metaphysical aspect.

> Music reveals to man an unknown realm, a world quite separate from the outer sensual world surrounding him, a world in which he leaves behind all feelings in order to embrace an inexpressible longing.[30]

Biblical scripture cites Genesis 1:28 as God's "blueprint" to establish an ideal world through the fulfillment of the three blessings: to be fruitful, to multiply, and to take dominion over the creation. The second and third blessings encompass the attribute of creativity. In this respect the Creator endowed humankind with perhaps the most elemental aspect of his/her Deity—the ability to be a co-creator. Accordingly, artistic endeavors can be considered a manifestation of one's divine character as a son or daughter of God, our Heavenly Parent, when our motivation and intentions comport with godly virtues. Music that contributes to the condition of creating oneness with God can be said to have fulfilled its truest purpose. This can be seen as a decidedly anthroposophical perspective, and perhaps we would do well to view everything in this way.

Gorbachev may not have been aware of all of the spiritual attributes and theoretical considerations inherent in the symphonies of Beethoven, Mahler and other great symphonists when he referenced the significance of symphonic music, but his intuition about the deep philosophical aspects of the music seems inherently correct. The spiritual nourishment that this music provides can satiate our deepest spiritual needs. That's a significant reason why musicians and audiences continue to find "meaning" in performing and listening to these important and meaningful artworks.

Recommended Recordings

Beethoven: Symphony No. 9, Simon Rattle, Vienna Philharmonic

Schubert: Symphony No. 8, Leonard Bernstein, Royal Concertgebouw Orchestra

Schumann: *Kreisleriana*, Op. 16, Vladimir Horowitz, piano

Schoenberg: *Six Little Piano Pieces,* Op. 19, Peter Serkin, piano

Mendelssohn: Symphony No. 3, Christoph von Dohnányi, Cleveland Orchestra

Brahms: Symphony No. 3, Bruno Walter, Columbia Symphony Orchestra

Dvořák: Symphony No. 8, George Szell, Cleveland Orchestra

Tchaikovsky: Symphony No. 3, Riccardo Muti, Philharmonia Orchestra

Bruckner: Symphony No. 7, Riccardo Chailly, Berlin Radio Symphony Orchestra

Mahler: Symphony No. 2, Bruno Walter, Columbia Symphony Orchestra

Wagner: *Parsifal*, Daniel Barenboim, Berlin Philharmonic Orchestra

Stravinsky: *Rite of Spring,* Pierre Boulez, Cleveland Orchestra

Beethoven: Symphony No. 5, Osmo Vänskä, Minnesota Orchestra

Endnotes

1   Aldous Huxley, "The Rest Is Silence," *Music at Night and Other Essays* (London: Chatto & Windus, 1957), p. 19.

2   Mikhail Gorbachev, "The World According to Gorby," interview by Alan Cranston, *Rolling Stone*, no. 689, August 25, 1994, p. 52.

3   Geoff Emerick and Howard Massey, *Here, There and Everywhere: My Life Recording the Music of the Beatles* (New York: Gotham Books, 2006), p. 76.

4   M. Owen Lee, *Wagner: The Terrible Man and His Truthful Art* (Toronto, Canada: University of Toronto Press, 1999), p. 24.

5   Eduard Hanslick, *The Beautiful in Music: A Contribution to the Revisal of Musical Aesthetics* (London and New York: Novello, Ewer, and Co., 1891), p. 25.

6   Peter Hill, *Stravinsky: The Rite of Spring* (Cambridge, UK: Cambridge University Press, 2000), p. 94.

7   Walter Pater, *The Renaissance: Studies in Art and Poetry* (Berkeley and Los Angeles, California: University of California Press, 1980), p. 106.

8   Aldous Huxley, "The Rest Is Silence," p. 19.

9   Erik S. Ryding and Rebecca Pechefsky, *Bruno Walter: A World Elsewhere* (Lincoln, NE and London: University of Nebraska Press, 2006), p. 331.

10 Ibid., p. 353.

11 Ibid.

12 Ibid., p. 244.

13 Ibid.

14 Howard Hartog, *European Music in the Twentieth Century* (London: Routledge &

Kegan Paul, 1957), p. 68.

15   Lawrence Kramer, *Interpreting Music* (Los Angeles and Berkeley: University of California Press, 2011), p. 85.

16   Alexander Wheelock Thayer, *Thayer's Life of Beethoven, Volume 1*, revised and edited by Elliot Forbes (Princeton, NJ: Princeton University Press, 1992), p. 496.

17   Bettina von Arnim, *Goethe's Correspondence with a Child, Volume III* (London: Longman, Orme, Brown, Green and Longmans, 1838), p. 392.

18   Esteban Buch, *Beethoven's Ninth: A Political History*, translated by Richard Miller (Chicago and London: University of Chicago Press, 2003), pp. 103-105.

19   Deryck Cooke, *Gustav Mahler: An Introduction to His Music* (New York: Cambridge University Press, 1980), p. 59.

20   Igor Stravinsky, *Poetics of Music in the Form of Six Lessons*, translated by Arthur Knodel and Ingolf Dahl (Cambridge, MA: Harvard University Press, 1970), pp. 141-142.

21   David Tame, *The Secret Power of Music: The Transformation of Self and Society through Musical Energy* (New York: Destiny Books, 1984) p. 151.

22   Noam Chomsky, *Language and Mind*, third edition (New York: Cambridge University Press, 2006), p. 18.

23   Leonard Bernstein, *The Unanswered Question: Six Talks at Harvard* (Cambridge, MA and London, England: Harvard University Press, 1976), p. 8.

24   Fred Lerdahl, as cited by Stephen Davies, *Musical Meaning and Expression* (Ithaca, NY: Cornell University Press, 1994), pp. 2-3.

25   Richard Taruskin, *The Danger of Music and Other Anti-Utopian Essays* (Berkeley and Los Angeles, CA: University of California Press, 2009), p. 47.

26   Bernstein, *The Unanswered Question*, p. 283.

27   Taruskin, *The Danger of Music*, p. 321.

28   Edward Rothstein, "Karajan: The Nazi Recordings," *The New Republic*, November 7, 1988, pp. 30-31.

29   George Inness, Jr., *Life, Art, and Letters of George Inness, Volume 3* (New York: The Century Company, 1917), p. 17.

30   E. T. A Hoffman, edited by David Charlton, translated by Martyn Clarke *E. T. A. Hoffmann's Musical Writings: Kreisleriana, The Poet and the Composer, Music Criticism* (Cambridge, UK: Cambridge University Press, 2003), p. 96.

20

The Beat Goes On

I have found a paper of mine among some others,
in which I call architecture 'petrified music.[1]
Johann Wolfgang von Goethe

That which is, already has been;
and that which is to be has already been;
and only God can find the fleeting moment.
Ecclesiastes 3:15

There exists a common perception held by many, that classical music is rhythmically uninteresting and not all that exciting. This is actually a misperception. I can't tell you how many times people have said to me: "classical music has no rhythm." This tells me that many people haven't listened to much classical music, especially the music of the second half of the nineteenth century and the early twentieth century, or that they are not articulating their perception in an accurate fashion. Since all music transpires over time, all music possesses rhythmic properties, be they simple or complex.

Rhythm in music is the subdivision of time into temporal units of measure—durations. Rhythmic patterns can be agitated and frenzied, or placid and staid, but all music has rhythmic properties. In any musical ensemble, the issues of tempo (*tactus*) and beat (*ictus*) are important factors in presenting a unified performance. In their co-authored book, *The Rhythmic Structure of Music*, University of Chicago professors Grosvenor Cooper and Leonard B. Meyer posit, "To study rhythm is to study all of music. Rhythm both organizes, and is itself organized by, all the elements which create and shape musical processes."[2] As the aforementioned biblical verse states, time may be fleeting, but in music we get to perceive its movement aurally.[*]

The Grammy Awards ceremony in 2003 at Madison Square Garden featured the New York Philharmonic performing orchestral excerpts from Leonard Bernstein's score to *West Side Story*. Bernstein's music, infused with elements of Latin music and jazz, crackled with rhythmic energy and intensity. The orchestra then accompanied the band Coldplay in one of their songs, *Politik*. The rhythmic differences were striking. Whereas Bernstein's score was rhythmically varied and highly syncopated with boundless energy, the Coldplay tune plodded along in a humdrum, foursquare (and typically four-chord) fashion. Granted, Bernstein's score is not a typically "classical" composition in the manner of Beethoven (whose music often possesses a dynamic rhythmic vitality—listen to his Opus 109, at times it's downright jazzy!); but it nevertheless illustrated with coruscating clarity that rock music doesn't corner the market of rhythmic variation and excitement—it's not close.

In his book, *Music, the Brain, and Ecstasy: How Music Captures Our Imagination*, Robert Jourdain makes several insightful observations on the polemics of rhythm in various styles of music—pop music and classical in particular:

> Rhythm wars. On one side, devotees of meter protest that [classical] art music is missing an entire dimension, robbing the listener of a kind of rhythmic pleasure that has for many become music's mainstay. On the other side, the devotees of classical music complain that the obsession with beat trivializes everything it touches, appealing to our lowest instincts, like greasy

---

* This version of Ecclesiastes 3:15 was translated by the nineteenth-century rabbi and polymath Michael Friedländer, as cited by David P. Goldman in "The Divine Music of Mathematics," *First Things*, April 2012, https://www.firstthings.com/article/2012/04/the-divine-music-of-mathematics.

food. Where one side sees musical opportunity in metrical patterns, the other finds an idiot's metronome, an unceasing racket that makes no more artistic sense than drawing on graph paper. Where one side finds ultimate musical bliss in the architecture of large form, the other complains of effete over-intellectualization.

As Western pop music floods the world, with its drum machines and giant bass speakers in tow, the advantage is now with those who celebrate meter (usually in a trivial form). Enthusiasts of phrase and form, or just of an old-fashioned melody, are often found cowering with fingers in their ears, their sole consolation in reflecting upon a tradition that has lasted centuries and survived greater assaults. The battle is far from over.[3]

Having grown up performing and listening to jazz, rock, R&B and classical music, I can relate to both perspectives. The rhythmic inventiveness found in the music of Rachmaninoff, Bartók, Stravinsky, Schuman, Copland, et al. is quite compelling and highly syncopated. Brahms created wonderful "aural illusions" in his music and Mahler's "large forms" that span long stretches of time can be exhilarating when fully comprehended. The rhythmic propulsion in much of Beethoven's music drives the music with a furious energy that sweeps the listener along in a whirlwind of corybantic excitement. R&B, rock, gospel and jazz are often characterized by "funky" syncopations and driving beats, but so is the music of Tchaikovsky.*

What people who prefer pop music often listen for is a steady, perceptible "beat," usually the function of the drummer. To say that the music of Haydn, Beethoven, Brahms or Mahler lacks a beat (*ictus*) is not accurate. Clearly, there are beats and metric pulsation in their music; however, the realization of the beat is manifested in a fashion different than that of a drummer, percussionist, digital drum machine or a hip-hop beat-boxer (vocal percussionist). As Cooper and Meyer note, when considering the components of music—melody, rhythm, harmony and structure—rhythm may be the most basic component due to the fact that any musical expression, no matter how simple, is predicated on the linear subdivision of time. Any musical structure—a song, a symphonic movement, a chant, a tango—is the result of a

---

* The first movement of Tchaikovsky's Fourth Symphony contains numerous syncopated rhythms and irregular accents, which results in the perception of strong and weak beats occurring in surprisingly off-kilter places.

perceptible subdivision of time into units of measure. Melodies and harmonic progressions are predicated on rhythmic pulsation.

Musicologist Joseph P. Swain asserts that composers in the twelfth century were aware of harmonic rhythm (the pace at which chords change), but it wasn't until much later that music theoreticians began to study and write about its effects on musical structure. Swain cites American composer, Walter Piston's definition of harmonic rhythm as being "the rhythmic life contributed to music by means of the underlying changes of harmony. The pattern of the harmonic rhythm of a given piece of music, derived by noting the root changes as they occur, reveals important and distinctive features affecting the style and texture."[4] Edgard Varèse, who was a major influence on Frank Zappa, prioritized timbre and rhythm over melody or harmony to build his musical structures. Varèse viewed rhythm as something more than just metrics and patterning. Like Piston, he considered rhythm a "generator of form." As Varese explains:

> Rhythm is too often confused with metrics. Cadence or the regular succession of beats and accents has little to do with the rhythm of a composition. Rhythm is the element in music that gives life to the work and holds it together. It is the element of stability, the generator of form. In my own works, for instance, rhythm derives from the simultaneous interplay of unrelated elements that intervene at calculated, but not regular, time-lapses. This corresponds more nearly to the definition of rhythm in physics and philosophy as "a succession of alternate and opposite or correlative states."[5]

The use of *ostinato* (from the Italian for "obstinate" or "persistent"—a repetitive rhythmic pattern) was a device often employed by classical composers to provide a definable pulse on which they could construct their melodic and harmonic ideas. For classical composers the rhythmic characteristics of dance forms such as waltz, polka, sarabande, gavotte, minuet, habanera, bolero, farandole, sousedská tarantella, furiant, saltarello, gigue and ländler often served as the basis for the rhythmic underpinnings of their compositions. The same can be said of pop and jazz vis-à-vis dance beats and groves such a shuffle, swing or disco.

Any etymological study of rhythm as it pertains to the evolution of jazz (and eventually pop music) almost certainly begins with the gifted American composer and pianist Louis Moreau Gottschalk (1829-1869). Gottschalk, whose virtuosity as a pianist greatly impressed Frederic Chopin and Franz Liszt, was a native of New Orleans and traveled extensively throughout South America and the Caribbean. Upon hearing the music of these Latin cultures, he incorporated the rhythmic syncopations of Latin dance music into his compositions. His first symphony, *A Night in the Tropics* (composed in 1859) is an effective juxtaposition of Latin rhythms and European harmony and counterpoint. These syncopated rhythmic influences would give birth to the rhythmic characteristics of ragtime and Dixieland in the early twentieth century.

The use of polyrhythms—different rhythmic patterns being performed simultaneously—can be traced to the music of fourteenth-century Europe, though it is likely that polyrhythms were evident in the music of Africa and the Middle East long before that. The use of asymmetrical meters (5/4, 5/8, 7/8, 11/8, 5/16, 3+2/8+3, etc.) can be found in the dance music of Turkey, Macedonia and Bulgaria, and these rhythms eventually found their way into the more cosmopolitan realms of classical music and jazz.* Polyrhythms can be found in the folk music of Europe and Africa and in the European music of the Renaissance. Brahms, Schumann and Dvořák frequently used crossrhythms and *hemiola*—the rhythmic alteration of two notes in the place of three or three in place of two—in their compositions. Tchaikovsky composed the second movement of his Sixth Symphony entirely in 5/4 time. The pioneering work in the realm of ethnomusicology by Hungarian composer Béla Bartók (1881-1945) also had a significant impact on the rhythmic landscape of early modernism. Many of Bartók's works are infused with the rhythmic elements of Hungarian folk music, particularly the parlando—an accented, speech-like style that is characteristic of Hungarian folk songs. Bartók's ballet score *The Miraculous Mandarin* and his first piano concertos, both premiered in 1927, contain numerous examples of the asymmetrical rhythms that would become commonplace in early twentieth century classical music. Czech composer Leoš Janáček (1854-1928) also assimilated the rhythm and inflections of his "mother tongue" to create pitch contours and inflections in the vocal melodies of his operas.

---

* Ron Myers' composition *Turkish Bath* (made famous by Don Ellis) and Dave Brubeck's *Blue Rondo à la Turk* are notable examples of incorporating Turkish dance rhythms into the jazz idiom.

American composer Charles Ives (1874-1954) incorporated polyrhythms and polymeters (poly-everything—Ives knew few limitations) to great extents in his music. Stravinsky's groundbreaking ballet scores, especially *Rite of Spring* (1913), ushered in an era where rhythmic variation and invention took on greater importance. As jazz became a prominent musical style, European composers such as Paul Hindemith, Igor Stravinsky, Boris Blacher, Darius Milhaud and Dmitri Shostakovich used jazz-oriented syncopation in a number of their works. Aaron Copland's Clarinet Concerto was commissioned by Benny Goodman in 1948 and is strongly influenced by jazz characteristics—rhythmically, melodically and harmonically. The music of post-World War II modernists, especially the minimalist school (Philip Glass, John Adams, Steve Reich, et al.) places great emphasis on rhythmic pulsation or patterning as a means to propel their music.

Eventually, jazz and classical composers began utilizing asymmetrical rhythms in their music to greater degrees. Paul Desmond and Dave Brubeck's iconic piece, *Take Five* (in 5/4 time), is perhaps the most notable example; however, other jazz composers were far more adventurous in their use of asymmetrical rhythms. Stan Kenton, Don Ellis, Miles Davis and fusion groups such as John McLaughlin's Mahavishnu Orchestra, Chick Corea's Return to Forever and Joe Zawinul's Weather Report took rhythmic invention to new levels. In a bold attempt at serious stylistic fusion, arranger Don Sebesky composed a jazz version of Bartók's *Concerto for Orchestra* that included a jazz quintet in the scoring. His version is based on an imaginary meeting between Bartók and Charlie Parker: serious fusion, indeed.

As composers of modern art music became increasingly infatuated with the scientific advances of the modern age, their music became exercises in formulaic writing, in which rhythmic complexity had the effect of obliterating perceptual pulsation and patterning. Whether this was an unintended consequence or not, the absence of any perceptible beat pattern may have been one of the primary reasons why their music failed to connect with the greater public.

Advances in the study of cognitive psychology and psychoacoustics reveal that the brain may be "hardwired" to hear a certain way and thus complicated musical utterances, whether melodic, rhythmic or harmonic, are not assimilated in ways that can be easily perceived and understood. Consequently, this diminishes one's pleasure in the listening experience. If our ability to comprehend the relationships of pitch, rhythmic patterns and harmonic progressions are impaired due to a complicated and arcane musical syntax, cognition is hampered, and music is thus reduced to being perceived as unpleasant or confusing. This has certainly been the complaint about mid-century modernism, the acerbic harmonies, atonal melodies (or the absence of melody altogether) and rhythmic density of which have contributed to the indeterminacy that characterizes a great deal of modern art music. Columbia University composer and researcher Fred Lerdahl asserts that *complex* music based on "hierarchical structural richness" results in a perceptible, communicative syntax, whereas *complicated* music tends to neutralize or obfuscate hierarchical properties due to "numerous non-redundant events per time unit."[6]

I recently had the experience of sharing some music by twentieth century composers and hip-hop artists with my friend and colleague Brian Hardgroove, who was the bass player in the band Public Enemy for over a decade. As I explained to him how modern composers assigned mathematical formulas to the rhythmic, melodic and harmonic components of their music, his demeanor changed and he snarled, "That's bullshit!" For most people music is an experience of heart and emotion. Anything that short-circuits that experience in a fundamental way is viewed as antithetical to the human condition. In relegating any musical experience to a primarily intellectual, left-brain activity, a significant aspect of the musical experience is lost. Music that is the progeny of a decidedly left-brain modality often fails to win over listeners who seek emotional and spiritual fulfillment from music. From this point of view, I could understand Brian's reaction completely.

Brian was equally contemptuous of pop music that eliminates the human element in music-making. Citing the way many pop artists now produce their music, he referred to how a single musician—usually a keyboard player—programs the piano part, the bass part, the drums and percussion, the synthesizer parts using sequencing software, and then "flies in" all the vocals, often recorded completely apart from the instrumental aspects of a given track. This too contributes to a dehumanization of the musical experience and creativity. Music becomes more stilted, more mechanized and less emotional as a result. Brian and I both lament the predominance of MIDI computer sequencing over musicians playing together in order to achieve a rhythmic groove. We prefer a real band.

Goethe referred to architecture as "petrified music."[7] But music is all about movement, tempo gradation and pulsation. It's not static. Those who heard Beethoven perform his piano works wrote about how much *rubato* (the temporary disregarding of strict tempo) he infused in his performances. This type of tempo variation, commonly known as phrasing, is based on ones' emotive rendering of a given work at a given time. In this respect no two performances of the same composition by the same performer will be exactly alike. Achieving a balance between the components of melody, rhythm and harmony—the components that result in the manifestation of a musical structure (architecture)—would seem to be the primary task of any composer. Because music is predicated on time and rhythm, it is ephemeral. Jourdain considers rhythmic perception to be a left-brain activity, and views harmonic perception as being a right-brain activity. He posits that both aspects of the brain work in a unified fashion to allow us to fully understand and comprehend music, which in turn allows us to experience moments of ecstasy and fulfillment.

As noted previously, the claim that classical music lacks rhythmic vitality and energy is simply not true. The cross-rhythms and syncopation in the music of Schumann, Brahms and Dvořák, the jazzy syncopations in the works of Bartók, Blacher and Hindemith, the copious examples of dance rhythms found in pieces like Bizet's *Farandole*, Rachmaninov's *Symphonic Dances*, Mahler's symphonic ländler and the pulsating rhythmic invention in the music of the minimalists suggest that rhythmic vitality in classical art music is alive and kickin'—and always has been. In some ways, beats in dance music, disco and certain popular music can seem very monotonous when compared with the highly varied rhythmic properties in Stravinsky's *Rite of Spring* or William Schuman's *American Festival Overture*.

Whether one prefers jazz, or pop, or hip-hop, or classical music is a matter of personal taste and acculturation. Yet the ways in which we hear and perceive music, its melodic, rhythmic and harmonic properties, are universal. Singing and dancing are primal human activities: perhaps the most natural of all human activities. Johann Gottfried Herder long ago observed that music moves us, physically and emotionally. The rhythms of life are ever present, and as Anthony Storr reminds us:

The effect which music has upon repetitive physical actions is predominantly rhythmic. Rhythm is rooted in the body in a way which does not apply so strikingly to melody and harmony. Breathing, walking, the heartbeat and sexual intercourse are all rhythmical aspects of our physical being.[8]

Developing different preferences in music requires the willingness to explore and sample genres that may be outside of our normal listening experiences. Sampling the wonderfully varied musical menu that is part of our world community opened my eyes and ears to new possibilities as a composer, arranger and producer. I'm currently sketching ideas for a symphony in which I will employ rhythmic elements of jazz and hip-hop. Ascertaining what may be the best choices for the rhythmic aspect of this piece will be a significant aspect of the compositional process. The beat goes on.

Recommended Recordings

Haydn: Symphony No. 88, Bruno Weil, Tafelmusik

Beethoven: Symphony No. 5, Carlos Kleiber, Vienna Philharmonic

Schumann: Symphony No. 3/Bernard Haitink, Royal Concertgebouw Orchestra

Brahms: Symphony No. 3, Georg Solti, Chicago Symphony Orchestra

Dvořák: *Slavonic Dances*, Op. 46 & Op. 72, George Szell, Cleveland Orchestra

Chopin: Ballades, Murray Perahia, piano

Bizet: *L'Arlésienne Suite No. 1*, George Szell, Cleveland Orchestra

Tchaikovsky: Symphony No. 4, Lorin Maazel, Cleveland Orchestra

Rachmaninov: Symphony No. 2, Vladimir Ashkenazy, Royal Concertgebouw Orchestra

Mahler: Symphony No. 1, Michael Gielen, South West German Radio Symphony Orchestra

Hindemith: *Symphonic Metamorphosis*, Herbert Blomstedt, San Francisco Symphony

Blacher: *Orchestervariationen*, Op. 26, Herbert Kegel, Dresden Philharmonic

Stravinsky: *The Rite of Spring*, Pierre Boulez, Cleveland Orchestra

Janáček: *Sinfonietta for Orchestra*, Karel Ancerl, Czech Philharmonic Orchestra

Ives: *Three Places in New England*, Michael Tilson Thomas, Boston Symphony Orchestra

Varèse: *Ecuatorial*, Pierre Boulez, Ensemble InterContemporain

Bartók: Piano Concerto No. 3, Zoltán Kocsis, piano

William Schuman: *American Festival Overture*, Leonard Bernstein, Los Angeles Philharmonic

Barber: *Medea's Dance of Vengeance*, Leonard Slatkin, St. Louis Symphony Orchestra

Copland: Clarinet Concerto, Aaron Copland, conductor, Benny Goodman, soloist

Prokofiev: Symphony No. 5, James Levine, Chicago Symphony Orchestra

Bernstein: *Candide* Overture, Leonard Bernstein, Los Angeles Philharmonic

Bartók-Sebesky: *Concerto for Orchestra*, Don Sebesky, Royal Philharmonic Orchestra

Andriessen: *M is for Man, Music, Mozart*, Jurgen Hempel, Orkest de Volharding

Boulez: *Répons*, Pierre Boulez, Ensemble InterContemporain

Steve Reich: *Music for 18 Musicians*, Steve Reich, conductor

John Adams: *Short Ride in a Fast Machine*, Edo de Waart, San Francisco Symphony

Public Enemy: *It Takes a Nation of Millions to Hold Us Back*

Stan Kenton: *Artistry in Rhythm*

Weather Report: *Heavy Weather*

John McLaughlin-Mahavishnu Orchestra: *Birds of Fire*

Chick Corea: *Like Minds*

Miles Davis: *Birth of the Cool*

Dave Brubeck Quartet: *Time Out*

Gottschalk: *A Night in the Tropics*, Richard Rosenberg, Hot Springs Music Festival Symphony Orchestra

Endnotes

1   Johann Wolfgang von Goethe and John Peter Eckermann, *Conversations of Goethe with Eckermann and Soret, Volume II*, translated by John Oxenford (London: Smith, Elder & Co., 1850), p. 146.

2   Grosvenor Cooper and Leonard B. Meyer, *The Rhythmic Structure of Music* (Chicago: University of Chicago Press, 1960), p. 1.

3   Robert Jourdain, *Music, the Brain, and Ecstasy: How Music Captures Our Imagination* (New York: Avon Books, 1998), p. 154.

4   Joseph P. Swain, *Harmonic Rhythm: Analysis and Interpretation* (New York: Oxford University Press, 2002), p. 6.

5   Edgard Varèse, as cited in *Contemporary Composers on Contemporary Music*, edited by Elliott Schwartz, Barney Childs, and Jim Fox (New York: Da Capo Press,

1998), p. 202.

6   Fred Lerdahl, "Cognitive Constraints on Compositional Systems," *Generative Processes in Music: The Psychology of Performance, Improvisation, and Composition*, edited by John Sloboda (Oxford: Oxford University Press, 1992), pp. 231-59. Reprinted in *Contemporary Music Review* 6, no. 2 (1992), pp. 97-121.

7   *Conversations of Goethe with Peter Eckermann*, translated by John Oxenford and edited by J. K. Moorhead (New York: Da Capo Press, 1998), p. 303.

8   Anthony Storr, *Music and the Mind* (New York: Ballantine Books, 1993), p. 33.

21

Art, Ethics and Politics

This life in and with music, being essentially a victory
of external forces and a final allegiance to spiritual sovereignty,
can only be a life of humility, of giving of one's best to one's fellow man.
This gift will not be like alms passed on to the beggar;
it will be the sharing of a man's every possession with his friend. [1]
Paul Hindemith

A common theme found throughout the essays in this book has been creativity in relation to ethics, morality and establishing a culture of peace—axiology, in philosophical terms. Any such discussion can be vexing due to the sensitivities around morality, religion, politics and personal choice. This is especially the case in a social climate where hyper-egalitarianism mixes with pervasive moral relativism and deconstructionist attitudes. The intermingling of art, politics, religion and ideology has been present in cultural spheres for eons and will likely continue long after we depart from this fair earth. Those in pursuit of political power have always known that art has the power to influence and persuade. Consequently, attempts to commandeer artistic power by those who aspire to influence or control a particular society for political gain has often been seen as a necessity.

Historically there have been two primary strains of political power: one that seeks to maintain the status quo and one that seeks to challenge the status quo. Art has been used by both camps in order to influence and promote change. With the advent of the Internet, cable news networks, the blogosphere and information technology, American politics has become especially rancorous: "a carnival of invective," as described by the former editor of *Harper's* magazine Roger Hodge. This scenario has contributed to the ongoing debate regarding the role of art, media and culture in shaping psychologies and social mores.

In his Academy-Award-winning film *The Lives of Others* (2006), writer and director Florian Henckel von Donnersmarck, probes the issue of politics and art and how those who wield power have disquieting suspicions regarding artists and their potentially "subversive" views. The film chronicles the life and activities of a member of the Stasi, the East German police force that monitored and controlled (often in brutal fashion) the lives of artists living behind the Iron Curtain during the final years of the Cold War. The film's protagonist, a Stasi operative, Captain Gerd Wiesler (Ulrich Mühe), is assigned to investigate and monitor the dealings of an accomplished, popular East German author and playwright, Georg Dreyman (Sebastian Koch) who is alleged by the Stasi to be engaged in subversive political activities. As Wiesler carries out his investigation he begins to develop a certain admiration for Dreyman and his fellow artists. Why this change of heart? Wiesler experiences the transformational power of their art.

Wiesler's suspicions of the alleged charges against Dreyman diminish as he listens to music that Dreyman plays after one of his colleagues commits suicide. (Wiesler hears the music via surveillance microphones that were planted in Dreyman's residence.) The music, as well as the sincere honesty of Dreyman and his fellow artists in the pursuit of their art, affects Wiesler in profound ways, and the power of art and beauty gradually ameliorates Wiesler's cold-hearted intentions. (Spoiler alert!) In an act of moral courage near the film's conclusion, our protagonist assists the subject of his investigation in exposing the treachery of the East German authorities. A central narrative of the film is that art can have the effect of changing one's consciousness and in so doing assist in the process of creating conditions conducive to altruism and goodwill.

Of course, this interpretation can be easily assailed as being simplistic and a romantic contention of a bygone era. Several of von Donnersmarck's critics took exactly that view, arguing that the director's narrative regarding the transformational power of art was naïve or wishful thinking at best. Those who took issue with the premise of Donnersmarck's film will inevitably point to the Nazis and communists who listened to Wagner, Tchaikovsky and Beethoven by night but ran death camps and gulags by day; or mafia dons who love Italian opera yet plotted and carried out vicious crimes against society and each other. Moreover, there is the interesting case of the "Mad Mullah of Somalia," Mohammed Abdullah Hassan, who wrote beautiful poetry about the glories of nature yet was a brutal and despotic warrior.

In the cataclysmic aftermath of World War I, artists in Germany, a nation whose legacy included the great tradition of central-European music, became apostates regarding notions "of transcendence, permanence and lasting value … the romantic esthetic of the Sublime."[2] Nationalism bred separatism and suspicion of anything relating to the metaphysical in art, and artists of all disciplines were affected by the ethos of this ideological shift.

If art is so powerful in its transformational effects, how can it be that certain admirers and practitioners of great art can be vile and perfidious? Part of the answer lies in what individuals value. Purveyors of various inhumane ideologies have effectively used art as agitprop to advance their respective visions, values and political agendas, aesthetic concerns notwithstanding. Noted American psychiatrist Allen Wheelis opined, "Values determine goals, and goals define identity. The problem of identity, therefore, is secondary to some basic trouble with values."[3] Certain values can be troubling, especially if they result in suffering and oppression. Gandhi asserted that to bring about significant and positive changes in the world, we must become the change we want to see. For Gandhi, "walking the walk" was more than a pithy bromide. However, it's important to note that Gandhi's nonviolent method could only take place where a civil, liberal society—as provided by the British in this case—was securely in place. In a very real sense, British values made Gandhi possible. Who were the Gandhi figures in Mao's China, or Stalin's Russia, or Hitler's Germany, or Kim's North Korea? We'll never know because dissent of any kind was not tolerated.

Political commentator David Brooks reminds us that Leo Tolstoy believed that "it is the everyday experiences of millions of people which organically and chaotically shape the destiny of nations—from the bottom up."[4] If Tolstoy's supposition was correct, each individual has a portion of responsibility in determining the direction and outcome of one's community. In the American political process, we have a one-person, one-vote system, and that vote's power is derived from ideological values that hold civil liberties sacrosanct.

"The Hindemith Affair"

I have, from time to time, alluded to twentieth-century German composer Paul Hindemith (1895-1963) in my essays because his life story is germane to many of the issues regarding art, ethics and politics.* Coincidentally, 1995 marked the centennial of Hindemith's birth as well as the fortieth anniversary of the end of the Second World War, the events of which had a profound impact on the lives and work of many of Germany's most celebrated artists. Hindemith's centennial year saw a reemergence of interest in his music and provided the opportunity to reassess the legacy of one of the twentieth century's most prodigiously gifted musicians.

The events that shaped Germany's political and cultural destiny in the decade of the 1930's had grave and far-reaching impacts upon German artists of every discipline. Like his contemporaries, Hindemith's life and work were being profoundly affected by the political ascent of the Third Reich. By 1934 Adolph Hitler and the Nazi party had attained a political power few would have imagined only a decade earlier. In the 1930s, the iconic Richard Strauss was the only German composer held in higher esteem by the international music community than Hindemith, but as his prestige grew internationally, Hindemith came under increased pressure to proclaim loyalty to the Nazi party. Like many Germans in the post-World War I era, he initially possessed a favorable view of Hitler's vision for restoring German dignity and national pride. He proposed a serious music education program for German youth, conducted concerts for the Nazis and composed music for the *Luftwaffe* in an attempt to remain in good graces with party operatives. At the time, he characterized it as "an opportunity not to be missed."[5]

---

* In 1995 I wrote an article for *World & I* Magazine on Paul Hindemith during the centennial year of his birth. In looking back at that article I must admit I was not fully aware of certain circumstances regarding Hindemith and the Third Reich, especially about his post-World War II essays on art and morality. This new essay is an attempt to clarify Hindemith's life and work in the context of a more historically accurate perspective.

It was not long, however, before he would find himself falling in and out of favor with the Nazi officialdom. Hindemith's early works were influenced by the avant-garde attitudes of the early twentieth century, and this prompted the German cultural authorities to label him "a standard-bearer of decadence" and not fit to represent German culture. As the perfidious nature of the Nazis became more apparent Hindemith was confronted with a moral decision as to how he could justify any participation in party affairs. Several notable German artists sought to gain the trust of the Nazi hierarchy with the express intent of advancing their careers. For others, this was a moral and ethical impasse. Having a Jewish wife made the situation particularly difficult for Hindemith and with charges of "cultural Bolshevism" already being levied at him, his prospects of achieving a successful career in Germany under the iron fist of the German Chamber of Culture seemed increasingly remote.

It was under these conditions that Hindemith composed perhaps his most significant work, his fourth opera, *Mathis der Maler*. The circumstances surrounding the creation and production of the opera led to what would become known in Germany as "The Hindemith Affair." The opera's libretto, Hindemith's own, uses the Peasant's War of 1524 as its historical backdrop with its central character, Renaissance painter, Matthias Grunewald (c. 1475-1528), ensnared in a conflict between the peasants and the church. A central narrative of the opera deals with the moral and ethical responsibility of the artist at a time of social upheaval. Should artists involve themselves in socio-political matters, or should the devote themselves solely to their art? In the opening scene of the opera, Mathis is asked the question about the role of the artist in society.

> Have you fulfilled the task that God laid on you?
> Is what you shape and paint enough?
> Are you not intent only on your own advantage?[6]

As the opera proceeds Mathis experiences difficulty in coming to terms with these issues in the context of the greater human struggle before him. Hindemith would eventually, if belatedly (some say conveniently), come to the understanding that the moral and ethical responsibility of artists is eminently important, and in the final analysis being an artist "by no means absolves the artist from a share in the common responsibility."[7] This view, which Hindemith espouses in his 1951 book *A Composer's World: Horizons and Limitations*, was developed, as Richard Taruskin observes, in his later years, when Hindemith and other German artists "developed an exacting social conscience."[8] Not all German artists were forthright in their moral choices prior to *Kristallnacht* in 1938.*

Given the perilous circumstances that artists like Hindemith faced at the time his response to Nazi perfidy is somewhat understandable. Other notable German artists (Richard Strauss, Carl Orff, Karl Böhm, Herbert von Karajan, Wilhelm Furtwängler, Elizabeth Schwartzkopf) were more inclined to acquiesce to Nazi demands for party loyalty. Taruskin considers Hindemith's *A Composer's World* to be "a merciless polemic against his own younger self ... a timid housebroken estheticism he nevertheless tried to pass off as the 'everlasting values' and the 'moral power' of the ancients."[9]

Though we can't know what Hindemith's post-war thought process entailed when writing *A Composer's World,* it was clear that within the Nazi hierarchy some viewed *Mathis der Maler* as a thinly veiled and subversive attempt by Hindemith to fan the flames of dissent, and some believed that the composer was depicting himself as the protagonist in the opera. The Nazis were further aggravated when Wilhelm Furtwängler, then the director of the Berlin State Opera and Germany's most celebrated conductor, agreed to stage the work, thus causing an uproar that subsequently made Hindemith's relationship with the authorities even more problematic. Though Furtwängler attempted to defend the composer, he was nonetheless pressured by the Nazi officials to abort the project. Not to be deterred by this rejection, Hindemith proceeded to compose a three-movement symphony based on the score of the opera. Using the eleven-panel Altarpiece that Grunewald had painted in the Church of Saint Anthony at Isenheim as a source of inspiration, Hindemith's three-movement *Symphonie-Mathis der Maler*, remains one of his most often performed works. The premiere of the symphony (purely instrumental music,

---

* *Kristallnacht* ("Night of Broken Glass") was a pogrom against Jews carried out by the Nazi Party's paramilitary forces and civilians throughout Nazi Germany in November 1938. The German authorities looked on without intervening. The term *Kristallnacht* comes from the shards of broken glass that littered the streets after the windows of Jewish-owned stores, buildings and synagogues were smashed. The pretext for the attacks was the assassination of the German diplomat Ernst vom Rath by Herschel Grynszpan, a 17-year-old German-born Polish Jew living in Paris.

free from any "subversive" text) was conducted by Furtwängler with the Berlin Philharmonic on March 12, 1934 and was an unequivocal success.

Energized by the public's response to Hindemith's brilliant score, Furtwängler initiated new attempts to have the opera produced. However, political pressures mounted once again and in an attempt to mollify the authorities, Furtwängler came to the composer's defense in a letter published in *Deutsche Allgemeine Zeitung*, he testified to the noble Germanic qualities of Hindemith's work:

> [O]ne would be obliged to portray him, whose blood is also purely Germanic, as an outspoken German type; German in the high quality and straightforwardness of his craft, as in the chastity and restraint of his relatively rare outbreaks of emotion. The latest work of his to appear, the symphony from the opera Mathis der Maler, has only confirmed this impression.[10]

Furtwängler's reference to Germanic "blood" notwithstanding, his efforts to ameliorate the situation only exacerbated the vexatious relationship between Hindemith and the Nazis, and Hitler himself issued an order to desist any and all attempts to produce the opera. Furtwängler incurred the wrath of the Nazi party and was discharged from his position as director of the Berlin State Opera and remained in musical exile for a year. Hindemith's opera eventually received its premiere in Zurich in 1938 and was first staged in the United State in Boston in 1956. The first German production of *Mathis* took place in 1946.

Vilified by *Dur Fürher*, his music banned, and relieved of all his duties at the Berlin Academy of Music, Hindemith was now confronted with the dilemma facing all artists living in Germany during Hitler's nefarious reign; either join the Nazi party in order to further one's artistic ambitions or suffer the consequences of incarceration, exile or worse. In 1935 Hindemith spent time in Turkey to reinvigorate that country's music education system, a venture that was highly successful. It has been suggested that this was a move orchestrated by the Nazis to get Hindemith out of the picture in a calculated but uncontroversial manner. Hindemith clearly had opportunities afforded to him given his international stature, but given his wife's Jewish ancestry and the troubling aspects of Nazi ambitions, he chose to leave his native Germany and pursue his creative endeavors elsewhere.

Noted Hindemith scholar, David Neumeyer considered Hindemith guilty of what he called the" Switzerland syndrome;" a condition of disturbing neutrality. Citing the protagonist of *Mathis der Maler*, Neumeyer suggests that like Mathis, Hindemith understood the severity of the struggle, "but still retired from it because he doubted the efficacy as a combatant."[11] But again, given the treacherous nature of the Nazis, discretion may have been the better part of valor for many artists living in Germany at that time. Conductor Herbert von Karajan and soprano Elizabeth Schwarzkopf, two Germany's most esteemed musicians of the post-World War II era, were members of the Nazi Party and the accusations of having advanced their careers due to their Nazi associations haunted them throughout their professional lives. Furtwängler was accused by exiled composer Hanns Eisler for being a willing accomplice to "murder, arson, robbery, theft, fraud, torture of the defenseless, and above all, silencing the truth."[12] Because music was considered to be an expression of German superiority and was an important propaganda tool for the Reich. As such, prominent German musicians were potentially important players in the Nazi ascent to power. Their moral and ethical choices had far-reaching consequences. Norman Lebrecht cites the moral dilemma facing Furtwängler at that juncture in German history.

> In Furtwängler, the Nazis retained an interpreter who performed German music with undiminished conviction while genocide was committed in its name. By opting to remain [in Germany] he endowed the Nazis with cultural respectability at a crucial moment in their ascent, and in wartime gave moral sustenance to their cause. In his confrontations with tyranny, Furtwängler proved a feeble adversary who was all too easily maneuvered into outright collusion. The humanity he expressed in music was traduced and travestied by his paymasters. His legacy as a performer may well be among the most significant in the annals of conducting, but his conduct under political pressure compromised the very profession on which he wielded so formative an influence.[13]

This judgment also followed Hindemith to a certain degree. After a brief time in Switzerland, Hindemith made his first visit to the United States in the spring of 1937 where he made his American debut at the Coolidge Festival in Washington, D.C. performing his *Sonata for Unaccompanied Viola*. In the following years he returned to teach composition at the Boston Symphony's Berkshire Music Center (the Tanglewood Music Institute) and in 1940, with war imminent in Europe, he moved to the United States where he promptly received an appointment to join the music faculty at Yale University. His first major composition after coming to the United States, the *Symphony in E-flat*, received its premiere by the Minneapolis Symphony Orchestra under the direction of Dmitri Mitropolis on November 21, 1941. The piece received its New York premiere at Carnegie Hall in a concert by the New York Philharmonic on Christmas Day under Mitropolis's direction.

It is not hard to extrapolate that this powerful symphonic statement—with its terse fanfares and incessant martial character in the outer movements, its somber, dirge-like second movement, the frenzied scherzo and heroic finale—was the expression of the composer's deeply felt emotions about the circumstances surrounding his exile and the plight of his native Germany as hostilities broke out across the European continent. It's interesting to note as well, that his new symphony shares the same key (E-flat major) as Beethoven's *Eroica* Symphony and Richard Strauss' *Ein Heldenleben*, two works that have palpable references to heroism and the ultimate triumph of righteous idealism.

Firmly rooted in the fabric of American musical life, Hindemith became an American citizen in 1946 and continued to compose and teach in the United States serving as a Charles Eliot Norton Lecturer at Harvard University in 1950. His aforementioned book, *A Composer's World: Horizons and Limitations*, was published in 1951 and speaks very compellingly to the issues of the responsibility of the artist in contemporary society. Though Taruskin and others chide Hindemith for his moral lapses vis-à-vis the Nazi connection, as well as the disingenuous nature of his Harvard lectures, other artists in Germany enjoyed significant careers, despite the Nazi taint. Taruskin notes that Carl Orff, who perhaps was more disingenuous regarding his Nazi associations, in recent years has been given a pass for similar transgressions, although Orff was, "an obvious beneficiary of the regime" and was a granted "a full military exemption from Goebbels' propaganda industry," not to mention the lies and "half-truths" that he fed to the denazification interrogators of the Allied forces after the war in order to be exonerated from any wrongdoing.[14] We might ask why? Is the guilty pleasure we derive from his *tour de force* composition, *Carmina Burana* just too seductive and too appealing for us to expand our own social conscience to hold Orff accountable? Hindemith's best works—the *Mathis* Symphony, the *Symphonic Metamorphosis*, the *Nobilissima Visione* suite and the E-flat Symphony for instance—remain in the active orchestral repertory because the music is well crafted, is rooted in functional tonality, and imparts a pleasurable aesthetic experience. For those who know nothing of the political climate of the era in which they were created, the music is all that matters.*

Cold War Realities

The Hindemith case is but one of any number of historical instances where art, politics and morality intersected in profound ways. Russian artists such as Dmitri Shostakovich and Aleksandr Solzhenitsyn were greatly affected by the regime under which they lived and worked, as have been many artists who have had the misfortune to live under tyrannical dictatorships. In the early years of the Cold War when nuclear disarmament was a heated topic, British philosopher, Bertrand Russell opined that living under communist rule was a better alternative than extinction via nuclear war. Russell is attributed with coining the slogan, "better red than dead," and though he attributed it to others he nevertheless agreed with the sentiment and adopted the phrase as the motto of his Campaign for Nuclear Disarmament. Solzhenitsyn took issue with Russell's pernicious view, stating:

> All my life and in the life of my generation, the life of those who share my views, we all have one standpoint: better to be dead than a scoundrel. In this horrible expression of Bertrand Russell's there is an absence of all moral criteria. Looked at from a short distance, these words allow one to maneuver and to continue to enjoy life. But from a long-term point of view it will undoubtedly destroy those people who think like that. It is a terrible thought.[15]

---

* In a concert review in the *New York Times* (October 7, 2016), Zachary Woolfe opines: "The key for contemporary listeners is to keep not just our ears open, but also our eyes. There is no such thing as apolitical culture—Ravel's *La Valse*, for one thing, lurches like the nauseating World War I hangover that it is. And there should be no such thing as apolitical culture consumers." I must confess that having listened to Ravel's brilliant score more than one hundred times, I never once made an association with the piece and World War I, nor did I ever become nauseous when hearing it.

Cold War warriors in the West (Reagan, Thatcher, Kristol, Buckley, Kirkpatrick, et al.) believed that there was a moral imperative to defeat communism. As the Cold War saw increased competition between the emerging superpowers of Russia and the United States, the arts soon became an important vehicle in the ensuing ideological clashes. Though the U.S. held certain advantages in the realms of technology and industry, the Soviets boasted of their superiority in the realms of sports and the arts. New Jersey Congressman, Frank Thompson believed that culture was something not to be overlooked in the worldwide struggle for democratic ideals saying in 1954, "The sooner we can implement a program of selling our culture to the uncommitted people of the world as a weapon, the better off we are."[16]

American politicians of the era soon bought into the idea that art and culture could be used for political and ideological advancement. Apart from the Works Progress Administration (WPA) established by President Franklin D. Roosevelt, there was little interest in government support of the arts in the United States. In fact, the government was often suspicious of the arts scene and that suspicion was one of the factors that resulted in the creation of the House un-American Activities Committee. This was the time when artist's motivations and their political agendas came under intense scrutiny by the government. Still, many politicians held a favorable disposition regarding the arts, and with the election of John F. Kennedy, whose highly cultured wife, Jacqueline Bouvier Kennedy—a strong advocate of promoting the arts—the aura of the era was changing concerning artistic achievement and its influence.

The National Endowment for the Arts (NEA) was established during the Lyndon Johnson administration. At the groundbreaking ceremony for the Lincoln Center for the Performing Arts several years earlier, President Dwight D. Eisenhower declared that the venue would be "a mighty influence for peace and understanding throughout the world."[17] President Nixon, a trained pianist, believed that the arts could serve an altruistic purpose in the attempt "to heal divisions among our people and to vault some of the barriers that divide the world."[18] Yet, some artists remained skeptical about the government being engaged in the arts in any way for fear of politicizing something they viewed as being sacrosanct. Their apprehension about government control and possible censorship was rooted in their trepidation about creeping McCarthyism, a troubling chapter in American history that had a chilling effect on Hollywood and the entertainment industry in the 1950s.

In 2009 there was controversy over an alleged attempt by Yosi Sergant, who was the communications director for the NEA at the time, to politicize the National Endowment of the Arts.[19] It had come to light that Sergant, who eventually resigned from his NEA post, participated in a conference call and encouraged both grant recipients and prospective grant recipients to use their creative endeavors to promote specific policy initiatives (education, health-care, environment, e.g.) of President Obama. This was seen as a brazen and quite possibly illegal *quid pro quo* that violated the Hatch Act.* The NEA was established to be an independent organization with the express purpose of being free from influence peddling, lobbying, or any endorsement of a particular political or ideological agenda. The attempt to politicize the NEA in this fashion created a firestorm as both conservative and liberal artists and arts administrators questioned the judgment of the Obama administration in pursuing such action.

These scenarios demonstrate how powerful people who wish to bring about political or sociological change, recognize the power of art and artists in assisting their causes. The celebrity-industrial-complex in the West has been especially effective in aiding or abetting any number of causes, from the elec-toral process to AIDS awareness, cancer awareness, world hunger, women's rights, education and global warming. Obviously, having attained celebrity status, many artists seek to promote causes that they feel are important to advance their view vis-à-vis creating a more just and humane world. Having an altruistic mindset is an important factor in developing a culture of peace, thus the fortuitous circumstances that have made celebrities so influential ought to be utilized for the betterment of the human condition. Conversely, misusing or abusing one's notoriety can create conditions leading to moral relativism and ethical compromise—conditions that are antipodal to altru-ism. My intention here is not to equate President Obama with Hitler, the East German Stasi, Soviet Communists or Senator McCarthy, but rather to

---

* The Hatch Act is a federal law passed in 1939 that limits certain political activities of federal employees, as well as some state and local government employees who work in connection with federally funded programs.

elucidate the importance of artists having moral and ethical clarity in their choices regarding how they use their art and celebrity.

Consider the current dilemma for the Venezuelan, super-star conductor Gustavo Dudamel and the ongoing political crisis in his home country. The remarkable success of the Venezuelan youth orchestra initiative (*El Sistema*) was largely due to the largesse of Hugo Chavez's socialist government. With the country on the brink of collapse, there have been calls from both the citizenry and the artistic community in Venezuela for maestro Dudamel to use his enormous cache of celebrity status to speak out against government corruption and advocate for the people who are suffering as a result of that corruption. His tepid response to the crisis drew ire from pianist Gabriela Montero who took him to task on social media saying, "Many Venezuelans are deeply disappointed that he isolated musicians as preferential members of society, once again, by insisting that the only important question to ask, in the midst of an unprecedented humanitarian crisis, is 'Can Venezuela save *El Sistema*?'"[20]

We imagine that art and artist can make a difference in society, but as we've seen artists can be selective in their moral and political stances. Citing the dilemma that both artists and audiences face when confronted with vexatious political and economic realities, Zachary Woolfe writes:

> There are no easy answers, either for Mr. Dudamel or for us, to these kinds of ethical quandaries. And this is hardly the first time we've had to check our moral compasses as classical listeners. Mr. Dudamel has strained to remain above the partisan fray. But what are we to make of the more overt, unapologetic political activity of the Russian conductor Valery Gergiev, a very public booster for Vladimir V. Putin, who was advocating anti-gay laws and squeezing any political dissent as he remains a crucial ally of Mr. Gergiev's Mariinsky Theater? When Soviet artists toured America during the Cold War, were they thawing a conflict, or were they whitewashing human-rights violations?[21]

In an earlier essay, "Music for Peace," I cited Baruch Spinoza, whose perspectives on the development of a more enlightened and humane society are worth noting once again.

For peace is not mere absence of war, but is a virtue that springs from force of character: for obedience is the constant will to execute what, by the general decree of the commonwealth, ought to be done.[22]

What "ought to be done," of course, can be a topic that fosters heated debates that results in the aforementioned "carnival of invective." Certainly, justice is an important factor in any attempt at achieving a meaningful peace, but more importantly benevolence—the inclination to be kind, loving, compassionate and generous—stands as a fundamental attribute in any attempt at ameliorating injustice and overcoming fear and hatred. Historically, religion was that which provided moral and ethical guidance by way of doctrine, ritual, parables and myth. The development of good character requires educating our heart as well as informing our intellect. Accordingly, living for the sake of others becomes an essential virtue in creating a more humane society and culture. Philosopher Roger Scruton suggests that "we should see culture as Schiller and other Enlightenment thinkers saw it: the repository of emotional knowledge, through which we can come to understand the meaning of life as an end in itself. Culture inherits from religion the 'knowledge of the heart' whose essence is sympathy."[23] Art can play a central role in the process of inculcating values. This is what Schiller referred to as "aesthetic education."

It is interesting to note that in Beethoven's (and Schiller's) call for universal brotherhood in the composer's Ninth Symphony, he identifies the importance of having God, "a loving Father," in the equation. If all people are to become brothers and sisters it's natural to assume that having a benevolent, loving parent(s) to guide us on our path to peace would be considered a desired scenario. The disposition for altruistic ideals that Beethoven aspired to can easily be co-opted into a secular humanist worldview absent the moral and ethical standards born out of certain religious convictions. As Scruton further asserts:

We should not expect from culture what religion and morality fail to provide in our times of trial. What we can expect is that culture should conserve, through whatever troubles, the message of something higher; the image of a world of feeling which is also a proof of human worth. We pass on culture, therefore, as we pass on science and skill; not to benefit the individual, but to benefit our kind, by conserving a form of knowledge that would otherwise vanish from the world.[24]

To be sure, religion has been as divisive and polarizing as it has been harmonizing and beneficial. Yet certain tenets of the world's religions—love your neighbor, do unto others, turn the other cheek, love your enemy, pray for those who persecute you, honor and respect humanity and the natural world—should not be dismissed or considered unimportant in any peace-making effort. These various manifestations of benevolence are vital in building harmonious relationships, be they in a family or the greater society and world. Throwing the proverbial baby out with the bathwater is never a good thing.

The United States' Constitution begins:

> We the people of the United States, in order to form a more perfect union, establish justice, insure domestic tranquility, provide for the common defense, promote the general welfare, and secure the blessings of liberty to ourselves and our posterity, do ordain and establish this Constitution for the United States of America.

If we are to take the premise of "inalienable rights ... endowed by the Creator" at face value, we simply must reexamine the role of religion and spirituality in the context of attaining a universal brotherhood. If the realization of "One Human Family Under God" is something to strive for, (as we hear in the lyrics of "We Are the World"), we would do well to ascertain what religious values or ideals can contribute to the realization of that vision. In his farewell address to the nation in 1789, George Washington asserted, "Of all the dispositions and habits which lead to political prosperity, religion and morality are indispensable supports. In vain would that man claim the tribute of patriotism, who should labor to subvert these great pillars of human happiness, these firmest props of the duties of men and citizens."[25] Washington was alluding to the precepts of Judeo-Christian teachings. Defining the values and virtues that comport with godliness is a *sine qua non*—and absolute requirement.

In an essay for the Catholic periodical, *First Things*, Thomas Joseph White cites Aleksander Solzhenitsyn's somewhat controversial commencement address at Harvard in 1978 in which he states:

> [R]eligion can subsist without democracy, but democratic polity in its modern form becomes hollow and fragile without religious transcendence. The capacity to name evil and seek the good requires a moral code. A culture that cannot name God also cannot name evil for what it is, and it cannot

name the ultimate good that can unite the aims of human beings to one another."[26]

Hindemith, Shostakovich and their peers were living and working in decidedly totalitarian and anti-religious cultures. F. A. Hayek, in his seminal book, *The Road to Serfdom*, alludes to the "spirit of totalitarianism" in which any activity must be assessed in relation to how it aids abets the state. "Science for science's sake, art for art's sake," he writes, "were abhorrent to the Nazis, our socialist intellectuals and the communists." If these activities did not derive their justification "from a conscious social purpose;" namely the advocacy of state and its leader class, there could be adverse political consequences for those in the arts and sciences. Moreover, "spontaneous, unguided activity," could be considered suspect or subversive if it did not comport with "the plan" of the entrenched authorities. As Hayek put it: "Once science has to serve, not truth, but the interests of a class, a community, or a state, the sole task of argument and discussion is to vindicate and to spread still further the beliefs by which the whole life of the community is directed. ... The word 'truth' itself ceases to have its old meaning."[27] In this context, the sciences, the arts and sports become mere vehicles for propaganda and indoctrination.

As with Spinoza's comments regarding peace, we see in the United States Constitution a call for justice and the promoting of conditions conducive to the general welfare (benevolence) as being necessary to attain freedom and liberty. Theologian, Dr. Lonnie McCloud observed that the phase "more perfect union" is grammatically incorrect. Perfection is the highest degree of attainment in any endeavor. Something is either perfect or it is not. Dr. McCloud extrapolates that the framers of the Constitution were likely intuiting that attaining liberty is a process through which the continual growth, education and development of our individual and collective consciousness is necessary. Change is a process, not an event. Therefore, as we evolve on our way to "becoming" better individuals we can hopefully achieve a better, "more perfect" union.

As well, change *ought* to be accomplished in accordance with freedom of choice and liberty—the right to choose. Our Constitution was the attempt to limit the power of government in order for freedom and liberty to be relatively unencumbered in our "pursuit of happiness." With greater regularity, the government is seen as a facilitator (or enforcer) of change, especially when change is cloaked in the garb of equity and social justice. Those of the liberal persuasion see this as a necessary function of government, but we should not be deluded to think that "the state" can deliver justice without abuses of power. David Mamet points to the problem with this particular liberal orthodoxy.

> Contemporary Liberal sentiment endorses the abrogation or elaboration of law to ensure that no one suffers, but the first and most important task of law in a democracy is not to right individual wrongs, but to ensure that no one suffers because of the State. And the simple, tragic truth is that this may be accomplished not by a Czar or a committee, or by reorganization, or by accession to office of the Benevolent or Wise, but only by limiting the State's power.[28]

In this context, the role of artists becomes paramount. That which we produce, create and put before the public has ramifications on any number of levels. How we use our creative freedom is no small matter. I've never met an artist who advocates for "the state" to become arbiters of what is "proper" or "subversive" in one's creative endeavors. As the baleful histories of China, Russia, Eastern Europe, Cuba, Nazi Germany or any authoritarian regime regarding the treatment of artist reveals, there ought to be vigilance in protecting artistic freedom. Conversely, artists need to be aware of the "ethic power" of their art and seek to use their talents in ways that can foster conditions for sociological improvement. Paul Hindemith's views on this issue coruscate as much now as they did decades ago. Hindemith avers that here are composers

> who flatly deny the ethic power of music, nor do they admit any moral obligation on the part of those writing. For them, music is essentially a play with tones, and although they spend a considerable amount of intelligence and craftsmanship to make it look important, their composition can be of no greater value, as a sociological factor, than bowling or skating.[29]

Referring to composers who understand the "sociological factors" of their art, he opines that these composers

> will then know about musical inspiration and how to touch validly the intellectual and moral depths of our soul. All the ethic power of music will be at his command and he will use it with a sense of severest moral

responsibility. His further guides will be an inspiring creative ideal and the search of its realization; an unshakable conviction in the loftiness of our art; a power to evoke convincing and exalting forms and to address us with the language of purity. A life following such rules is bound to exemplary persuade others to become associated. This life in and with music, being essentially a victory of external forces and a final allegiance to spiritual sovereignty, can only be a life of humility, of giving of one's best to one's fellow man. This gift will not be like alms passed on to the beggar; it will be the sharing of a man's every possession with his friend.[30]

Hindemith's "disturbing neutrality" during the rise of Hitler has caused angst among his detractors. Yet his enlightened comments here affirm important truths regarding art and the role of artists; individuals who possess enormous potential to influence the societies in which they live and work. Understanding the "portion of responsibility" that artists bear in relation to the overcoming of external forces and aligning with a "spiritual sovereignty" can go a long way towards the realization of the universal brotherhood that Beethoven and other idealistic artists have long sought. Creative individuals can contribute to the realization of the peace dream in dynamic ways if they fully understand the moral and ethical responsibility that Hindemith cites, even if they're latecomers to the necessary epiphanies that might make us more humane.

Taruskin reminds us that when we speak of art and politics we need to contextualize our views and not be given to generalizations, because when it comes to politics "it is a question of which politics; the politics of power or the politics of contention. Art can serve either one." As well, "In a open and mobile polity, art and its possible meanings, like all things public, are subject to endless appropriation and negotiation."[31] Taruskin, Neumeyer and others remain skeptical of Hindemith's belated realizations regarding his art, ethics and politics, considering them part of the composer's "new ethos of preservation-cum-obligation." Their skepticism is justified. Yet, we all evolve on our various life paths, some for the better, some not. As for Hindemith's belated epiphanies regarding art and morality, it's an unfortunate story, but hard lessons often come at a cost and learning from them can hopefully help our collective evolution towards betterment.

In the aforementioned Harvard speech by Solzhenitsyn in 1978, he references the problems with socialism and the perpetual drive for control via laws and regulations imposed by the state apparatus. As he put it: "Voluntary self-restraint is unheard of; everyone strives toward the further expansion to the extreme of legal frames."[32] When individual liberties are curtailed due to increased "legal frames," freedom is diminished. Without freedom, there can be no love. The government can't love us and we shouldn't pretend that it can. The importance of the American constitution is its attempt to limit government and allow for individuals to make choices that are rooted in religious idealism, those "great pillars of human happiness" that Washington alluded to. It's been said that good government begins with self-government.

If we might imagine a maxim that could be a summation of what Washington and Solzhenitsyn wrote about in their politically oriented speeches that were presented 200 years apart, it might be the lyrics of the iconic song "America the Beautiful": "Confirm thy soul in self-control."

Recommended Recordings

Hindemith: Symphony in E-flat, Leonard Bernstein, New York Philharmonic

Orff: *Carmina Burana*, Herbert Blomstedt, San Francisco Symphony and Chorus

Eisler: Two Elegies, Roswitha Trexler, soprano, Jutta Czapski, piano

Mozart: Late Symphonies, Karl Böhm, Berlin Philharmonic

Strauss: Lieder, Op. 43, Elisabeth Schwarzkopf, George Szell, Berlin Radio Symphony

Beethoven: Symphony No. 3, "*Eroica*," Herbert von Karajan, Berlin Philharmonic

Beethoven: Symphony No. 9, Wilhelm Furtwängler, Berlin Philharmonic (1954)

Shostakovich: Symphony No. 1, Leonard Bernstein, Chicago Symphony Orchestra

Hindemith: *Mathis der Maler* (Opera), Rafael Kubelik, Bavarian Radio Symphony

Hindemith: *Symphonie: Mathis der Maler*, William Steinberg, Boston Symphony Orchestra

Endnotes

1   Paul Hindemith, *A Composer's World: Horizons and Limitations* (Cambridge, MA: Harvard University Press, 1951), p. 220.

2   Richard Taruskin, *The Danger of Music and Other Anti-Utopian Essays* (Los Angeles, CA: University of California Press, 2010), p. 392.

3   Allen Wheelis, *The Quest for Identity* (New York: W. W. Norton and Co., 1958),

p. 174.

4 David Brooks, "Heroes and History," *New York Times*, July 17, 2007, p. A21.

5 Alex Ross, *The Rest Is Noise: Listening to the Twentieth Century* (New York: Farrar, Straus and Giroux, 2007), p. 319.

6 Paul Hindemith, *Mathis der Maler*, liner notes, translation by Bernard Jacobson (London, UK: EMI Classics, 1995, CD-5-55237-2).

7 Howard Hartog, *European Music in the Twentieth Century* (New York: Routledge & Kegan Paul, 1957), p. 68.

8 Taruskin, *The Danger of Music,* p. 162.

9 Ibid., p. 398.

10 Wilhelm Furtwängler, "Der Fall Hindemith," *Deutsche Allgemeine Zeitung*, Berlin, November 25, 1934, liner notes by James Goodfriend (Deutsche Grammophon, LP 2530 246), http://www.furtwangler.net/inmemoriam/data/bio_en.htm.

11 Taruskin, *The Danger of Music*, pp. 64-65.

12 Norman Lebrecht, *The Maestro Myth* (UK: Simon & Schuster, 1991), p. 91.

13 Ibid.

14 Taruskin, *The Danger of Music*, p. 162.

15 Aleksandr Solzhenitsyn, *Warning to the West* (The Bodley Head, 1976), p. 119.

16 Blair Tindall, *Mozart in the Jungle: Sex, Drugs, and Classical Music* (London: Atlantic Books, 2005), p. 54.

17 Ibid.

18 Ibid., p. 56.

19 Jeff Zeleny, "Agencies Instructed to Separate Politics from Grant Awards," *New York Times*, September 22, 2009, p. A21.

20 Zachary Woolfe, "Fiddling while Venezuela Starves? Bolívar Symphony Opens Carnegie Season," *New York Times*, October 7, 2016.

21 Ibid.

22 Baruch Spinoza, *Political Treatise*, translated A. H. Gosset (London: G. Bell & Son, 1883), html edition by the Constitution Society, 1998.

23 Roger Scruton, *Culture Counts: Faith and Feeling in a World Besieged* (New York: Encounter Books, 2007), p. 41.

24 Ibid., p. 44.

25 John Avlon, *Washington's Farewell: The Founding Father's Warning to Future Generations* (New York: Simon & Schuster, 2017), p. 275.

26 Aleksandr Solzhenitsyn, as cited by Thomas Joseph White, "The Metaphysics of

Democracy," *First Things*, February 2018, pp. 29-30.

27 F. A. Hayek, *The Road to Serfdom*, edited by Bruce Caldwell (London and Chicago: Routledge, 2007), pp. 177-178.

28 David Mamet, *The Secret Knowledge: On the Dismantling of American Culture* (New York: Penguin Group USA, 2011), p. 103.

29 Paul Hindemith, *A Composer's World*, p. 64.

30 Ibid., p. 220.

31 Taruskin, *The Danger of Music*, p. 219.

32 Aleksandr Solzhenitsyn, as cited by Patrick J. Deneen, *Why Liberalism Failed* (New Haven and London: Yale University Press, 2019), p. 83.

David Eaton's Carnegie Hall debut concert in 1989 with the New York City
Symphony in conjunction with the Turkish Consulate in New York.

New York City Symphony at the Apollo Theater at the Black History Month
concert in 1990, featuring William Warfield; music by Duke Ellington, Joseph
Schwantner and Ludwig van Beethoven.

Violinist Lakisha Gonzalvez with David Eaton and the New York City Symphony at the Apollo Theater in 2006 in a benefit concert for the Harlem School of the Arts.

David Eaton, David D'Or and Seiko Lee perform the world premiere of the peace cantata, *Halelu: Songs of David*, at the Sava Center in Belgrade, Serbia on May 19, 2007.

David Eaton and David D'Or share a bow with members of the Evergreen Symphony Orchestra as part of a peace concert in 2013 sponsored by the Tzu Chi Foundation, a Buddhist humanitarian organization in Taiwan.

David Eaton and soloists who performed at the United Nations as part of the United Nations' 70th Anniversary Concert on June 30, 2015.

International performers join Seiko Lee, David Eaton and the New York City Symphony at the United Nations in the grand finale song, *One World of Peace*, composed by Kevin Pickard, June 30, 2015.

David Eaton with members of the Little Angels of Korea in concert at the Hyo Jeong Cultural Center in South Korea in 2018.

22

Brahms, not Bombs

The Divan [Orchestra] is not a love story, and it is not a peace story.
It has very flatteringly been described as a project for peace.
It isn't. It's not going to bring peace, whether you play well or not so well.
The Divan was conceived as a project against ignorance.
Daniel Barenboim

"Brahms, not Bombs."

I saw this slogan on an anti-war placard being carried by a member of the Cleveland Orchestra during a labor dispute during the Viet Nam war era. Because music is generally considered to be a harmonizing agent and a vehicle to build bridges, thereby creating conditions for mutual understanding and respect, musicians tend to be decidedly idealistic and "dovish" when it comes to matters of war and peace.

Conductor/pianist Daniel Barenboim has attempted to bring a measure of idealism into practice through the important (but controversial) work he has done with the West-Eastern Divan Orchestra. The orchestra's name is taken from a collection of poems by Johann Wolfgang von Goethe that were influenced by the poems of the Persian poet, Hāfez.* A central narrative in Goethe's "West-Eastern" poetry deals with the idea of differing cultural and religious spheres—Orient and Occident, Christian and Muslin, Persian and Latin—finding common ground and mutual respect. Barenboim's ensemble is comprised of young musicians from Egypt, Israel, Jordan, Syria and Lebanon who assemble annually to make music. Barenboim's effort has garnered high praise for its courage and vision. However, the Argentine-Israeli conductor concedes that there are limits in terms of what this particular initiative can actually accomplish. In an interview in *The Guardian*, Barenboim stated:

> The Divan [Orchestra] is not a love story, and it is not a peace story. It has very flatteringly been described as a project for peace. It isn't. It's not going to bring peace, whether you play well or not so well. The Divan was conceived as a project against ignorance. A project against the fact that it is absolutely essential for people to get to know the other, to understand what the other thinks and feels, without necessarily agreeing with it. I'm not trying to convert the Arab members of the Divan to the Israeli point of view, and [I'm] not trying to convince the Israelis to the Arab point of view. But ... I'm trying to create a platform where the two sides can disagree and not resort to knives.[1]

The intriguing aspect of the Divan orchestra is that individuals of differing faith traditions, cultural customs and political views have come together for a common effort in the spirit of cooperation and respect. The predisposition to create conditions for peace must encompass benevolence, justice and understanding. As Barenboim reminds us, ignorance can be a significant obstacle in developing the predisposition for peace. Benevolence and understanding, on the other hand, are essential. Peace means different things to different people, and as such, there have been attempts to politicize the Divan effort, and as we know all too well, the politicizing of art and music is not a new phenomenon.

In his book, *The Rest Is Noise, Listening to the Twentieth Century*, Alex Ross chronicles the more recent history of Western art music, its creators and practitioners, vis-à-vis the political climate of the times in which they lived and worked. For better or worse, the juxtaposition of art, politics and ideology seems

---

* The *West-Eastern Diwan* (or divan) is a collection of lyrical poems written by Goethe between 1814 and 1819 and inspired by the Persian poet, Khwāja Shams-ud-Dīn Muhammad Hāfez-e Shīrāzī (1315-1390).

to have been a constant in the narrative of human history. Consider the plights of Richard Strauss, Wilhelm Furtwängler, Paul Hindemith, Carl Orff and Elizabeth Schwarzkopf in Germany, or Dmitri Shostakovich, Sergei Prokofiev and Alexander Solzhenitsyn in Russia. All faced political pressures to conform to the ideological tenets of Nazism and Communism respectively because they were expected to use their creative endeavors to promote the political and ideological views of the state, often under the threat of retribution if they didn't comply. In the early twenty-first century art and artists continue to be embroiled in political and ideological issues as evidenced by the situation in China with artist-activists such as Ai Wei Wei and Liu Xiaobo, or in Cuba with rapper, Angel Yunier Remon—better known as "El Critico del Arte."[2]

In the late nineteenth century, there existed a heated debate among the European intelligentsia that pitted Richard Wagner, the progressive innovator, against Johannes Brahms, the archconservative classicist. For many, Brahms was the keeper of the flame of the musical traditions revered by the old guard, choosing to work in classical forms such as theme and variation, sonata, concerto and the symphony. He wrote no operas or symphonic poems—the highly popular musical forms of the late romantic era. Conversely, Wagner was considered a pioneering innovator, a composer whose operas looked forward to new vistas of harmonic syntax and dramatic invention. Brahms was often the target of derision by many in the Wagner camp who thought of him as being merely an academician.

Brahms and Wagner also represented divergent and antipodal views concerning religious attitudes. Early in his life, Wagner, a political revolutionary, aligned himself philosophically with the decidedly anti-Christian views of Friedrich Nietzsche (they were friends at one point). Brahms was far more religious by comparison. Brahms and Wagner were also very different personalities. Whereas Wagner was given to bouts of megalomania, Brahms was far more temperate in character. He once confided to Clara Schumann, "Art is a republic. ... Do not confer a higher rank upon any artist, and do not expect the minor ones to look up to him as something higher, as consul."[3]

Brahms's biographer, Jan Swafford averred that for Brahms, "the final court of any musician was the ears, hearts and minds of listeners—above all the cultivated Austro-German music lovers, who in the later nineteenth century made up a large and remarkably sophisticated audience," at a time of "unprecedented music-making in Europe." Swafford contends that, "music was Brahms's religion—but music as a private spiritual and intellectual quest, a shared undertaking ... a communal undertaking to exalt the individual mind and heart and soul."[4] This is not unlike the view of another German, Lutheran composer, Johann Sebastian Bach, who believed that the goal and end aim of music (specifically, the technique of figured bass) was to praise and glorify God and recreate the mind.

The issue of Brahms's faith conviction can be confounding. Some considered him to be agnostic in matters of faith due to his reticence to speak publicly about it. Brahms, according to Clara Simrock (the wife of his publisher Fritz Simrock), "was no churchgoer, yet he was of deeply religious nature" and maintained a measure of interest in scripture and Christian thought throughout his life. Daniel Beller-McKenna points out that Brahms, like most German artists in the nineteenth century, was heavily influenced by Lutheran tradition and cultural thought," yet he was, nonetheless, "a typical product of the post-romantic secularization of German culture."[5] Beller-McKenna notes that in Brahms's comments late in life there is "nothing to suggest that Brahms ever betrayed [his] formative religious training." Brahms may have rejected or questioned certain Christian dogma (he admitted that his reading of Schopenhauer had something to do with that), but he maintained his religious convictions and possessed a keen knowledge of the Bible throughout his adult life, easily quoting scripture when the occasion warranted. As Beller-McKenna notes:

> Brahms and his German contemporaries inherited a culture in which it was possible to be "religious" in a broad, non-dogmatic sense, without holding to the particular tenets of Christianity. For German artists and intellectuals, Lutheranism became as much a cultural tradition as a system of faith, Whatever his beliefs in a deity, Brahms strongly identified with this secularized brand of Lutheranism. ... For the romantics, however, the abandonment of dogma did not mean a renunciation of religion, or, necessarily, of Christianity.[6]

Brahms recalled how in the Protestant tradition, he had "learned the Bible by heart" as a child, but like most children, he didn't comprehend the meaning of what it meant to be a Christian in the fullest sense. As he matured the deeper meanings of scripture seemed to play a greater role in his life, according to Beller-McKenna. At the time of Robert Schumann's death, Brahms recalled how Schumann requested the Bible. "People just don't understand," Brahms would say, "that we North Germans crave the Bible and do not go a day without it."[7] He would say that even in the dark of night in his study he knew where his Bible lay.

Historically, various faith traditions have utilized music for ceremonial and ritualistic purposes and as such, valued music as a way to assist in the process of connecting to God and the incorporeal realm. St. Augustine initially had serious trepidation about music in the church, but eventually ascribed to the notion that it had positive effects, stating that he could "approve of the use of singing in the church, that so by the delights of the ear the weaker minds may be stimulated to a devotional frame."[8] The Roman Catholic Church eventually intuited that our spiritual senses could be stimulated by our physical senses and utilized music, incense, architecture, painting and stained glass windows to enhance the celebration of its liturgy to great effect.

Brahms's *German Requiem,* which had its premiere performance in 1868, is considered one of his greatest works and given his high regard for his Lutheran Bible it is not hard to imagine that the composer's deeply held reverence for scripture ignited the spark for his creative impulse. Late in his life, in a series of interviews with American journalist Arthur M. Abell, Brahms attributed much of his creative inspiration to consciously seeking a spiritual connection to God. Abell's interviews with Brahms (which were given in the presence of Joseph Joachim) are not well known and were published decades after Brahms's death. The delay in publication was, according to Abell, at the composer's request. Swafford does not cite the interviews in his biography of Brahms (Beller-McKenna does), but has questioned their veracity based on the fact that Brahms was not openly religious. However, the characterization of Brahms being agnostic about religious matters may not be entirely accurate, his reticence to speak about his faith notwithstanding.

As noted by Beller-McKenna, Brahms was said to have been highly knowledgeable in matters of scripture throughout his adult life and he based some of his music on liturgical texts. In this context, Brahms's comments about his faith and spirituality in the interviews with Abell, are seemingly expressions of a deep-seated faith conviction. When asked by Abell about connecting to God, Brahms would say that it cannot

> be done merely by will power working through the conscious mind, which is an evolutionary product of the physical realm and perishes with the body. It can only be accomplished by the soul-powers within—the real ego that survives bodily death. Those powers are quiescent to the conscious mind unless illuminated by Spirit. Now Jesus taught that God is Spirit, and He also said, "I and my Father are one" (John 10:30). ... When I feel the urge I begin by appealing directly to my Maker and I first ask Him the three most important questions pertaining to our life here in this world—whence, wherefore, whither (woher, warum, wohin)?
>
> I immediately feel vibrations that thrill my whole being. These are the Spirit illuminating the soul-power within, and in this exalted state ... I feel capable of drawing inspiration from above. ... I realize at such moments the tremendous significance of Jesus' supreme revelation, "I and my Father are one." Those vibrations assume the forms of distinct mental images, after I have formulated my desire and resolve in regard to what I want, namely, to be inspired so that I can compose something that will uplift and benefit humanity—something of permanent value.
>
> Straightaway the ideas flow in upon me, directly from God, and not only do I see the distinct themes in my mind's eye, but they are clothed in the right forms, harmonies and orchestration. I have to be in a semi-trance condition to get such results—a condition when the conscious mind is in temporary abeyance and the subconscious is in control, for it is through the subconscious mind, which is part of Omnipotence, that inspiration comes.[9]

If we take these comments at face value, it's fascinating to note that the flowing of distinct harmonic, melodic, textural and structural components came to Brahms in a straightforward fashion, apparently without interference when he was able to connect to the spiritual realm. This is in accord with Einstein's contention that "when the solution is simple, God is answering." However, we know that Brahms worked on his first symphony for over twenty years. If musical ideas flowed to him "straightaway ... directly from God," as he stated in the interview, we must speculate that perhaps there is bit of poetic license in Abell's reportage, or that Brahms may have been a bit lax in his prayer life at that time. That said, for religious believers, it is not hard to imagine that if Brahms was a channel for divine inspiration, his motivation "to compose something that will uplift and benefit humanity—something of permanent value," was consistent with godly values and virtues in relation to his creative endeavors.

Because Brahms did not often speak publicly with candor or enthusiasm about his faith in the context of his of creative endeavors, it's understandable that there might be skepticism about the veracity of Mr. Abell's interviews. Still, knowing what we know about his faith, it's not difficult to extrapolate that what Brahms supposedly shared with Abell had some measure of credibility. Beller-McKenna goes into great detail citing various sources, including the composer's friends, especially Robert Schumann, Rudolf von der Leyen and Richard Heuberger regarding Brahms's faith and knowledge of scripture. It was Heuberger who recalled Brahms's comment about how the composer praised the manner in which young Protestants "learned the Bible by heart, without understanding any of it."[10]

In a 1947 essay titled, "Brahms the Progressive," Arnold Schoenberg provides an analysis of Brahms's Fourth Symphony in which he asserts that being lucky in composition is a "heavenly gift," something "equivalent to talent, beauty, strength, etc. It is not given for nothing—on the contrary, one must deserve it."[11] This is in accord with Goethe's assertion (as well as T. S. Eliot's), that genius is often the result of a highly industrious work ethic. Given Brahms's attitudes about musical inspiration as cited by Mr. Abell, he would likely attribute the composer's inspirations to either a highly focused work ethic or the Almighty, rather than merely being lucky. Schoenberg acknowledged that, "One can only express what one possesses inwardly."[12] As Brahms attests in the interview with Abell, his "inward" condition had a significant impact on his creative process. Legendary baseball executive, Branch Rickey (who was instrumental in bringing Jackie Robinson to the Major Leagues), once opined that, "luck is the residue of design." Brahms might agree.

One suspects that Schoenberg's views on Brahms's progressiveness was due in part to Schoenberg's advocacy of his own design model in which the developmental processes of germinal materials via inversion, retrograde, retrograde inversion, combinatoriality, etc., was a high priority. Brahms was working in the tradition of Germanic symphonic composition (no pun intended) and was considered by Schoenberg as a purveyor of "motivic saturation" and developmental style. As such, Schoenberg may have viewed Brahms (the progressive) as his compositional antecedent. Moreover, for Schoenberg, Brahms's harmonic grammar, especially the stretching of the tonal syntax in his late piano works (Op. 116-119), legitimized his contentions regarding the organization of musical materials. Richard Taruskin suggests that Schoenberg aligned himself to Brahms in this regard because Brahms's late music "is the lifeline to tradition that is presumed to maintain the possibility of musical intelligibility in the absence of degree functions and directed harmony. It is what made the atonal practice theoretically viable and legitimate."[13]

As any composer knows, there can be diminishing expressive returns when formalism becomes too dominant. Alluding to the penchant to over-emphasize craft and technique at the expense of unbridled spontaneity, Damian Thompson writes:

> There's a supremely professional evenness about late Brahms that, alas, really is prophetic. The cult of craftsmanship is the curse of modern classical music. Brahms can't take all the blame for it; 20th-century composers didn't want to ape his unsexy mannerisms—yet, without realizing it, they inherited his cast of mind.[14]

We most certainly cannot hold Brahms accountable for the cult of serialism that became ensconced as the primary mode of composing among twentieth century modernists. History points to other protagonists in that particular drama. Whereas Schoenberg and his modernist progeny became staunch adherents of the left-brain predilection of musical composition, Brahms seemed to be willingly open to spiritual influences, which was antithetical to modernism's predilection for intellection. In this matter, Brahms was closer to the Renaissance composers of liturgical music and Bach, than the practitioners of formulaic atonality. No doubt that Brahms's late excursions into the far reaches of the tonal spectrum were calculated and his craft is exceptionally refined, but he never fully broke with the tonal tradition.

It seems that Brahms's attitude regarding divine influence on the creative process was similar to that of Richard Strauss. In Strauss' interview with Arthur Abell, he states:

> Composing is a procedure that is not so readily explained. When the inspiration comes, it is something of so subtle, tenuous, will-o-the-wisp

nature that it almost defies definition. When I'm in my most inspired moods I have definite compelling visions involving a higher selfhood. I feel at such moments that I am tapping the source of infinite and eternal energy from which you and I and all things proceed. Religion calls it God.[15]

I am not far enough advanced in my evolution to presume to define such a Cosmic Force, but I know that I can appropriate it to some extent and that after all is the main consideration for us mortals here in this world. I can tell you, however, from my own experience, that an ardent desire and fixed purpose combined with an intense resolve brings results. Determined concentrated thought is a tremendous force and this Divine Power is responsive to it. I am convinced that this is a law and that it holds good in any line of human endeavor.[16]

Again, we are left to consider whether Arthur Abell interviews are credible. Yet, the spiritual essence of music can raise our consciousness and in so doing it creates the possibility of allowing us to see, feel and understand more about the conditions needed to attain a true and lasting peace. In my estimation, music born out of a deeply spiritual impulse can contribute in this effort. So, I'm with those musicians from the Cleveland Orchestra and Daniel Barenboim and his Divan ensemble. "Brahms, not Bombs", is always the more desirable option.

Recommended Recordings

Brahms: Symphony No. 1, George Szell, Cleveland Orchestra

Brahms: Symphony No. 2, Nikolaus Harnoncourt, Berlin Philharmonic

Brahms: Symphony No. 3, Herbert von Karajan, Berlin Philharmonic (1978)

Brahms: Symphony No. 4, Carlos Kleiber, Vienna Philharmonic

Brahms: *German Requiem*, John Eliot Gardner, Monteverdi Choir

Brahms: Late Piano Works, Op. 116-119, Hélène Grimaud-piano

Bach: *Ascension Oratorio*, BWV 11, Ton Koopman, Amsterdam Baroque Orchestra

Schoenberg: *Verklarte Nacht*, Herbert von Karajan, Berlin Philharmonic

Wagner: *Gotterdammerung*, James Levine, Metropolitan Opera

Carl Orff: *Catulli Carmina,* Vaclav Smetacek, Prague Symphony Orchestra

Richard Strauss: *Four Last Songs*, George Szell, Elizabeth Schwarzkopf, soprano

Prokofiev: Symphony No. 1, Orpheus Chamber Ensemble

Beethoven: Nine Symphonies, Daniel Barenboim, West-Eastern Divan Orchestra

Hindemith: *Symphonic Metamorphosis on Themes of Carl Maria von Weber*, Herbert Blomstedt, San Francisco Symphony Orchestra

Dmitri Shostakovich: Symphony No. 7, *Leningrad*, Leonard Bernstein, Chicago Symphony Orchestra

Endnotes

1   Ed Vulliamy, "Bridging the Gap," Part Two, *The Guardian-The Observer*, July 12, 2008, http://www.guardian.co.uk/music/2008/jul/13/classicalmusicandopera. culture.

2   Opinion, "Jay-Z Ignores Cuban Rapper Wasting Away in Prison," *New York Post*, November 6, 2013.

3   Alex Ross, *Listen to This* (New York: Farrar, Straus and Giroux, 2010), p. 318.

4   Jan Swafford, *Johannes Brahms: A Biography* (New York: Random House, 1999), p. 181.

5   Daniel Beller-McKenna, *Brahms and the German Spirit* (Cambridge, MA: Harvard University Press, 2004), p. 38.

6   Ibid., p. 32.

7   Ibid., p. 38.

8   Saint Augustine, *Confessions*, translated by Henry Chadwick (Oxford, England: Oxford University Press, 1991), p. 208.

9   Arthur M. Abell, *Talks with Great Composers* (Bridgewater, NJ: Replica Books, 1999), pp. 5-6.

10 Beller-McKenna, *Brahms and the German Spirit*, p. 38.

11 Arnold Schoenberg, "Brahms the Progressive," *Style and Idea*, edited by Leonard Stein (Berkeley, CA: University of California Press, 1975), p. 406.

12 Ibid., p. 409.

13 Richard Taruskin, *The Danger of Music and Other Anti-Utopian Essays* (Berkeley, Los Angeles and London: University of California Press, 2009), p. 368.

14 Damian Thompson, "Late Brahms is Wonderfully Crafted—Which Is Why It's so Dull," *The Spectator*, November 21, 2015.

15 Abell, *Talks with Great Composers*, p. 86.

16 Ibid., p. 108.

23

Thoughts on Conducting

*What more miraculous creation of mankind is there than
the symphony orchestra—a hundred musicians collaborating
flawlessly in the creation of a single sonority from moment to moment,
under the guidance of a single and singular mind who conveys
the sound image of another's tonal imagination, and carrying
with it a single listener as it carries a thousand or two thousand?
We tend to take for granted the skill and sensitivity of such
a performing organism, and we should take time to marvel afresh
that such a joint effort is possible for human beings so rich
in communication, beauty and meaning.*

I'm often asked: What does the symphony conductor do besides wave their arms around in front of the orchestra? Do conductors actually make a difference? Are all of those gestures really important? Do the musicians in the orchestra really follow the conductor's lead? These are good questions because most people have little understanding of the role of the person standing in front of an orchestra with his back to the audience. Baton technique is but a single aspect of the conducting art, and even within the profession, there are varying opinions about its importance. Leonard Bernstein believed that one could be taught baton essentials in a single coaching session, yet German conductor, Max Rudolf wrote a 450-page book on the topic. Violinist, Isaac Stern proffered that eye contact was supremely important in order for conductors to maintain control of the orchestra in any given performance, yet Herbert von Karajan, perhaps the most celebrated conductor of the post-World War II era, often conducted with his eyes closed.

Though conductors can seem self-assured and *uber*-confident on the podium, they are known to have serious insecurities about the practice of their craft. As Norman Lebrecht puts it, "That agony of self-doubt has been experienced by everyone who ever raised a baton above an open page and a seated mob. I have heard variations on it from Tennstedt and Solti, Jansons and Gergiev, Muti and Abbado. It's an occupational wail."[1] This anxiety can be the result of any number of reasons, not least of which is the process of convincing other talented musicians to agree to a particular way (the conductor's interpretation), of how a given composition should be presented to the audience in a way that is in accord with the composer's intentions. There is a social aspect to that process. Former music director of the New York Philharmonic, Kurt Masur, spoke of how the conductor-orchestra relationship worked best when it was viewed as a musical partnership. Composer John Cage detested what he considered the dehumanizing relationship of conductor and orchestra musicians whereby the musicians sacrificed their personal artistic integrity and dignity in succumbing to the will of an autocratic personality. Terry Riley likened an orchestra to "the army. ... You've got this general sitting in his chair, then the lieutenants, and so on down to the privates ... which I find to be pretty disagreeable as a way to make music together."[2] Incongruities abound.

In describing the art of conducting, certain practitioners of the art can go into long discourses on the mysteries of music-making, how sublime and nuanced the entire process is, and how the conductor was responsible for every aspect of a given performance. British conductor, Sir Thomas Beecham saw it differently. "Conducting is no mystery at all," he would say. "You just hire great musicians and let them play." Having been in the profession for about forty years I would say that there are elements of truth in both perspectives.

As for conductors "making a difference," veteran *New York Times* music critic, Bernard Holland sheds some light on the subject.

For all the justifiable cynicism surrounding the conducting trade, the right arms waving in the right way make wonderful things happen. As a reviewer of orchestra concerts, I am as convinced of as I am baffled by the ability of a powerful guest conductor to change the sound of an unfamiliar orchestra in the space of three rehearsals. Incontrovertible proof rests in the career of Leopold Stokowski, who managed to pack his dessert-like, one-of-a-kind sonorities into a suitcase and carry them from city to city.[3]

Obviously, having talented musicians to work with is a major advantage, but fashioning a cohesive, exemplary performance with any large ensemble—instrumental or choral—requires a collaborative effort with insightful and experienced leadership being part of the equation. Making music in this context is a very *social* experience requiring scholarship, an agreed-upon aesthetic vision and benevolence—a juxtaposition of truth, beauty and goodness.

In the history of Western musical tradition, the evolution of symphony orchestra into its modern form can be seen as the apotheosis of instrumental music. As composers sought the means for greater expression in their compositions, the orchestra provided them with a powerful vehicle through which they could achieve a multitude of expressive utterances. As the technical expertise of modern musicians developed exponentially, composers were afforded the opportunity to write music in new and innovative ways. The resulting compositions became more complex, thus the role of the conductor took on greater significance in terms of realizing a cohesive performance. Beyond the gestural aspect of conducting, other significant matters include scholarship, score-reading ability, and developing a keen musical ear. Having a strong foundation in composing, music theory, and orchestration is important as well. After all, as a conductor you are dealing with musical compositions, hence having the ability to think like a composer can be a distinct advantage.[*]

Experience is a significant factor in the development of the conductor's art, and gaining experience can only take place when either rehearsing or performing mode. Think about it; a singer or instrumentalist can practice in their

---

[*] In a conducting class that I attended at the Tanglewood Institute of Music during the summer of 1988, Gustav Meier, who oversaw the conducting program at Tanglewood from 1980 to 1996, was asked if being a pianist or a string player was more advantageous for becoming a conductor. Meier, affectionately known by the legion of his students as "Gusty," said that being either a pianist of string player was subsidiary to being well-versed in the art of composition.

home or studio to perfect their craft, but a conductor can't take the orchestra home. The only way to gain the necessary experience of conducting is to be in front of an ensemble working through the various performance issues—tempo, phrasing, articulation, dynamics, etc. In a master class I attended with Herbert von Karajan in 1977, he stated that one never really knows a piece of music until one has actually rehearsed and performed it. Truer words have never been spoken. I can't tell you how many times problems arose while rehearsing a composition that I never expected, often in the most innocuous passages. You simply never know how or where problems will occur. It's the conductor's job to identify and solve them.

Among the more intriguing aspects of the new technologies that drive the world of the Internet, personal computers and digital audio-video production (and their attendant pathologies), is how the *new* has fostered interest in the *old*; namely the great music and conductors of the past. With the advent of digital sound reproduction, classical music has been a beneficiary of the binary bonanza as historic recordings of bygone eras, enhanced to varying degrees by digital processing and re-mastering techniques, have elicited a fresh curiosity from historians, scholars, aficionados and stereophiles alike. This phenomenon has generated a rising interest in conductors of the so-called "Golden Age," as old video footage and heretofore "unlistenable" recordings can be found in ever-burgeoning quantities.

The issue of who has "golden" status may mean different conductors to different people. As a baby-boomer growing up in Cleveland, George Szell, music director of the Cleveland Orchestra from 1947 to 1970, and his contemporaries Jacsha Hornstein, Bruno Walter, Otto Klemperer, Herbert von Karajan, Rudolph Kempe, Charles Munch, Fritz Reiner, Sir Adrian Boult, Carlos Kleiber, Igor Markevitch, Sergiu Celibidache, Yvgeny Mravinsky, Karel Ancerl, Klaus Tennstedt, Eugene Ormandy, Kirill Kondrashin, Rafael Kubelik, Leopold Stokowski, and Leonard Bernstein were among the names that I most associated with the "Golden Age" of conductors.

To the generation of music-lovers between the two great wars, other names would most likely come to mind: Wilhelm Mengelberg, Richard Strauss, Wilhelm Furtwangler, Felix von Weingartner, Serge Koussevitzky, Fritz Busch, Leopold Stokowski, Eric Kleiber (Carlos' father), Dmitri Mitropoulos and Arturo Toscanini. These were surely the "Golden" maestros to those of my parent's and grandparent's generations. Going even further back the names Hans Richter, Theodore Thomas, Arthur Nikisch and Felix Mottl might also jog a few "golden" memories.

Interpretation

Simply put, the conductor's task is to bring concord, cohesiveness and "oneness" to a given piece of music. The modern conductor is the final arbiter of musical matters regarding tempo, articulation, phrasing, dynamics, textural clarity and other performance-related concerns. Collectively, these decisions result in an "interpretation" of the music at hand. The interpretive aspect of music-making—a subjective enterprise—is no small matter in the presentation of a particular composition. Different choices of tempo and phrasing can elicit a great deal of debate among highly opinioned aficionados as some conductors often take great liberties with these particular performance matters.

The fourth movement of Gustav Mahler's fifth symphony provides interesting comparisons.* Some conductors will choose a tempo (an interpretive choice) that allows this movement to be performed in just over eight minutes, while others will opt for a much slower pace in which the same music will take twelve to thrirteen minutes to perform. Mahler's designations in the score contribute to these interpretive incongruities. *Adagio* means "slow" in Italian, thus an *Adagietto* (a "smaller" or "lesser" *adagio*) would dictate employing a slightly faster tempo than a full *Adagio*. However, Mahler also uses the German term, *Sehr langsam* (very slow) as an indicator of the general pacing of the music. This gives credibility to the decision to opt for a slower tempo. There is more than a three-minute difference in the performance times of Herbert von Karajan's recording (11:56) and Michael Geilen's (8:30) of Mahler's *Adagietto*, yet both could be construed as being in accord with Mahler's designations. As Gilbert Kaplan notes, Mahler "often complained that conductors tended to

---

* This movement was a musical "love letter" from Mahler to his future wife, Alma Schindler. As Gilbert Kaplan notes, "The Dutch conductor Willem Mengelberg, in his personal copy of the Fifth Symphony, wrote: 'This Adagietto was Gustav Mahler's declaration of love for Alma! Instead of a letter, he sent her this in manuscript form; no other words accompanied it. She understood and wrote to him: He should come!!! (both of them told me this!).' Mengelberg's own description of the Adagietto was 'love, a love comes into his life'" [Source: Gilbert Kaplan, "A Dirge? No. It's a Love Song," *New York Times*, July 19, 1992, Section 2, p. 19.]

'exaggerate and distort' his indications—the largo too slow, the presto too fast.' But in the case of the *Adagietto*, he left room for some confusion."[4]

Most conductors will perform the final movement of Tchaikovsky's Sixth Symphony in nine to ten minutes. Yet in his recording just prior to his passing in 1990, Leonard Bernstein brings the movement in at over eighteen minutes. In the introduction of his symphony, *Mathis der Maler*, Paul Hindemith designates the metronome marking at 66 beats per minute, yet in the recording of the piece with Hindemith himself conducting, he opts for a slower tempo of 55 beats per minute. A close examination of the recordings of Igor Stravinsky conducting his own works reveals many similar occurrences.

In a recent experiment, I listened to the opening five bars of Beethoven's Fifth Symphony—perhaps the most recognizable musical phrase ever written—as performed by twenty different conductors and orchestras. Not surprisingly, there were a variety of interpretive choices. There were differences in tempo, in articulation, in the lengths of the sustained notes, in the lengths of the pauses between two phrases and even tuning, as several realizations by "period" orchestras utilized a lower tuning than the customary A=440 Hz. used by most orchestras.[*] Herbert von Karajan's rendition is characterized by the Berlin Philharmonic tuning at A=443 Hz. Roger Norrington, who is considered to be a leading exponent of "historically performed" interpretations, uses a lower tuning and he adds a diminuendo in the first sustained note (E-flat), and then a crescendo and diminuendo on the second sustained note (D). Another "period" conductor, Nikolaus Harnoncourt, incorporates diminuendos on both sustained notes. Beethoven wrote no such designations in the score. One conductor holds the first sustained note slightly longer than the second, which is exactly the opposite of what Beethoven notated in the score.[†]

Extra-musical aspects of a composition often play into interpretation as well. Mahler believed that: "A symphony must be like the world. It must contain everything."[5] Some conductors go to great lengths in the attempt to

---

[*] Hertz (symbol: Hz) is a unit of frequency. It is defined as the number of complete cycles per second. It is the basic unit of frequency in the International System of Units (SI), and is used worldwide in both general-purpose and scientific contexts.

[†] Hear several examples here: https://soundcloud.com/d-michaele/beethoven-5ths.

discover the intent or a specific source of inspiration that might assist them in gaining insight as to how to "interpret" a given composition. Bernstein was known to have read the literature that composers whose music he was preparing to conduct were reading in order to gain deeper insights into their compositions. Conversely, other conductors focus on the purely musical attributes of the score. Arturo Toscanini was once asked if when conducting the first movement of Beethoven's *Eroica* Symphony he thought of Napoleon (to whom Beethoven initially dedicated the music). Citing Beethoven's designation of the work's first movement, the legendary Italian maestro (ever the literalist) replied, "For me, it's simply *Allegro con brio*."[6]

One thing that orchestral musicians appreciate in a conductor is consistency. If in a performance a conductor deviates from the tempi or phrasing that had been established in rehearsals, this can cause great angst among musicians in the orchestra. Musicians don't appreciate surprises or spontaneous changes that in the heat of the moment could lead to shoddy ensemble, imprecision, missed entrances and embarrassment.

Historically Informed Performances

When, in 1987, Roger Norrington, performed and recorded the nine symphonies and various overtures of Beethoven with the London Classical Players as part of his "Beethoven Experience," he initiated a renewed interest in what is known as "historically informed" or "period" performance practices. His concerts in England along with his EMI recordings drew high praise from the classical music press and this resulted in him becoming a ubiquitous presence on the international conducting and lecturing circuits advocating the "period" gestalt.

The premise of Norrington's interpretive approach was that Richard Wagner's influence on the art of conducting was antithetical to what had been the norm in actual performance practice at the time of Mozart, Haydn, Beethoven and early romantic composers. Removing the "false patina" of Wagnerian excess—all those "meretricious tricks and the thick encrustation of the interpretive nuances that had been piling up for decades,"[7] as described by George Szell—and restoring the performance practices of "the period" in which music was composed has been carried out with missionary-like zeal by Norrington and other "period" practitioners, including Franz Brüggen, Trevor Pinnock,

John Eliot Gardiner, Roy Goodman, Nikolaus Harnoncourt and Christopher Hogwood. In the aftermath of Norrington's highly acclaimed "Beethoven Experience," the performance practices that had yielded wonderful performances from Karajan, Reiner, Szell, Kleiber, et al., performances that had been hailed as being "definitive," were now being critiqued for their "uninformed" status. (All that continuous vibrato—pshaw!)

Performance issues regarding tempo, bowing, articulation, use of vibrato, phrasing, dynamics, size and configuration of ensembles, were being scrutinized under the microscope of "period" practice. The types of instruments used in "period" ensembles (the "hardware" issue) was also of great concern as there evolved a dogmatic insistence on using natural horns and trumpets, wooden timpani mallets, calfskin drumheads, wooden flutes, alto trombones (when called for) and gut strings in the quest for "authenticity." The degree of "authenticity" (the so-called "A-word") in the presentation of a particular work became the litmus test by which Classical music performance was increasingly being assessed. In the 1990s this counter-revolution regarding performance practice was in full sway.

I attended several of Norrington's master classes while at the Tanglewood Institute in 1988 as well as his rehearsals and concerts with the Boston Symphony and the Tanglewood Festival Orchestra. His interpretive ideas were often insightful and his performances of Beethoven's Second Symphony with the BSO and Haydn's *London* Symphony with Tanglewood Orchestra were as bracing as they were illuminating. The brisk tempos that he opted for in the outer movements of both the Beethoven and Haydn symphonies were quite apart from "traditional" tempos that had become the norm. Even his choice of tempi in the "slow" movements, were somewhat faster than those that had become the norm. His penchant for emphasizing dancing as it pertained to tempo and rhythmic considerations in the symphony's inner movements was quite revealing and effectual. At one point in our conducting class, he and his wife danced to a Mozart minuet to demonstrate how he would arrive at certain tempo and phrasing decisions in symphonic movements predicated on specific dance forms.

Several years later I attended a forum on the piano concerti of Mozart held at the University of Michigan in which Norrington conducted several of Mozart's concerti using the *pianoforte* (the precursor to the modern concert grand piano) to replicate the sound perspective of these works when played by Mozart. He also employed very small instrumental ensembles, sometimes with as few as ten musicians standing around the piano accompanying the soloists, as a way to re-create conditions that were likely a common practice in Mozart's time. All of this was an attempt to attain a reasonable facsimile of the performing environments and practices that could be considered "historically informed."

The Norrington phenomenon led to a spate of "period" ensembles being created and this was a boon to the classical music recording industry as the music of the late eighteenth and early nineteenth-century composers was being re-examined and recorded under the banner of "reconstruction." I found many of Norrington's views to be quite illuminating, especially in matters of articulation and bowing, however, I wasn't wholly convinced that his *every* assertion regarding "period" practice was in the best interest of achieving the most musical results. There is just too much evidence to the contrary as the wonderful performances (and recordings) that I grew up with attested. At a Cleveland Orchestra concert I attended just after George Szell's passing in 1970, the noted Czech conductor, Rafael Kubelik appeared as a guest conductor and he opened the concert with Handel's Concerto Grosso, Op. 6, No, 3. When asked in an interview why he eschewed the use of a smaller string section in the "period" manner of the Baroque era in favor of the full 60-member string section of the Cleveland ensemble, he blithely responded, "Why not? They play so beautifully."

Notable music historians have taken issue with the "authenticists" on several fronts. Richard Taruskin, perhaps the most outspoken of these critics, posits that "historically informed" performance practice is a decidedly modern invention and one that has more than a little speciousness in its claims of "authenticity." In a fascinating and highly "informed" essay, oxymoronically titled, "The New Antiquity," Taruskin cites a comment by a member of the Hanover Band in which the musician claimed that "for the first time it is possible to present the orchestra music of Ludwig van Beethoven to the listening public of today in a form which he would recognize."[8] Taruskin sees the incongruity in this perspective for what is and asks: "Does it imply that Beethoven wouldn't know his own music in other renditions? Or that he would not admit their validity?" Doubling down on his argument, Taruskin continues, "Or, simply, that he [Beethoven] would acknowledge, 'Yes, that's how we did it.' Any way you slice it, the Hanover Band is claiming privilege. It is claiming Beethoven's approval."[9]

This claim also implies, somewhat fallaciously, that any "authentic" or "historically informed" performance is "more edifying," thus superior to performances that do not fully adhere to the re-constructionist rationale of the "period" practitioners. It suggests something that is simply not provable; that Beethoven would unequivocally prefer performances of his works that adhere to the "period" model as defined by the Hanover Band, et. al., rather than modern renditions. There is no way to know that. We can extrapolate, for instance, that Beethoven would likely have preferred modern instruments, with their inherently better construction and intonation, to their "period" counterparts.

With regard to tempi, Beethoven added metronome markings to his symphonies when Johann Maelzel introduced the composer to his new mechanical device in 1817. This was after the premieres of eight of his symphonies and begs the question: Which version of the score is the "authentic" (*urtext*) version; the first manuscript or the manuscript with the metronomic designations that the composer himself, added? We can also extrapolate that prior to the addition of the tempo designations, Beethoven himself might have opted for slightly varied tempos based on his mood or other conditions. Furthermore, it has been suggested by some "authenticity" enthusiasts that a militating factor in ascertaining tempos, especially the idea that the fast tempos in Beethoven's time were a bit slower than what is the norm today, was due to the advances in instrument construction. A close comparison of the metronome designations in Beethoven's symphonies and what has become the modern practice suggests the opposite. There is also the issue of Beethoven's metronome. Historians have speculated it could have been faulty due to the well-known fact that the composer's living habits were extremely untidy. Needless to say the issue of tempi remains especially vexatious.

Taruskin, who has been highly laudatory of the "inspired literalism" in Norrington's Beethoven recordings, also considers the idea of extrapolating what Beethoven might have approved or preferred on the basis that it is somehow "self-evident" is a specious contention. "Self-evidence," he avers, "is a product of a contemporary and very suspect ideology."[10] It is also very subjective. If the first performance of a given work is assigned the status of "authentic," then every succeeding performance of that work might be considered inauthentic because no two performances are ever the same. The imprimatur of "authenticity" loses its credibility in this context. There is also no way to ascertain if the circumstances surrounding the premiere of a particular composition—the size of the ensemble, the acoustics of the venue, the quality of the players and their instruments, the variations in tempo, e.g., actually fulfilled the composer's wishes in the first place. Hence, to claim that a particular performance practice is what the composer "intended" is quite tendentious. As Taruskin (by way of Faulkner) posits, "There is no unmediated access to the past. All 'pasts' are constructed in the present."[11] Realizing the veracity of this assertion puts a decidedly modern face on the "period" movement.

In the final analysis, the musicality of a given performance is what provides satisfaction for the "listening public." In 2006 I attended a Lincoln Center performance by the Camerata Salzburg Orchestra conducted by Norrington and was profoundly disappointed. The strict avoidance of vibrato of any kind by the strings in the slow movement of Beethoven's Fifth Symphony and the tender episodes in the incidental music from *Egmont*, turned the music into a sterile, unaffecting affair. The breakneck speed in the opening movement of the Fifth symphony (speed for speed's sake?) resulted in numerous occasions of shoddy ensemble playing (and a few furrowed brows in the first violin section)—and this from an ensemble that presumably specialized in "historically informed" performance practices! There was a distinct lack of *rubato* as everything was presented in a rather four-square manner without any hint of *elastischer tact* (elastic time) that often characterized early romantic performance practice.

According to those who had heard Beethoven play the piano, the use of excessive *rubato* was a common characteristic in his performances. This was nowhere in evidence, and on this night, Norrington's music-making was rather perfunctory. The affecting musicality of my Boston and Michigan experiences listening to Norrington was largely absent. The entire concert seemed more a lesson in "period" didacticism rather than an experience of enthusiasm and inspiration. This is not to say there is no merit in what scholarly research can bring to the interpretive process, but as conductors and performers, we need to remember that it should be a means to a musically fulfilling end and not an end in itself.

Baton Technique, Retouching and EQ

Ralph Black, long-time vice-president of field operations for the American Symphony Orchestra League, once surveyed several individuals who were initiating a conductor search for a particular American orchestra. His query to the members of the search committee was simple: What is the most important attribute that they would like to see in their new conductor? The president of the board of directors responded by saying that having a responsible citizen in the community was an important factor. The head of the orchestra women's volunteer committee wanted someone charming who could interact well in social gatherings. The director of development wanted someone willing to assist in fund-raising efforts. The principal clarinetist wanted "someone with a clear beat!" For musicians the issues keeping time (*tactus*) and showing a clear incisive beat (*ictus*) are no small matters in presenting a unified performance. Hence, "showing the music" via one's baton technique is an important factor.

Attending the conductor's program at the Tanglewood Music Institute in the summer of 1988 provided many insights into the conductor's art. Over the two months, several important conductors came to instruct the young conductors, including the BSO's music director, Seiji Ozawa and a Tanglewood mainstay. Leonard Bernstein believed that having a facile baton technique was essential to communicate effectively on the podium. Maestro Ozawa, who could mimic the gestures of other noted conductors quite well, spoke of the importance of developing the ability to "show the music" through one's gestures. He also instructed that there are times in a given piece of music that the mode of conducting can be either "dictatorial or democratic" and the conductor's job is to know when one has to be a dictator and when you can step back and just "let them play." Or, as Bernard Haitink sagaciously cautioned, "The musicians are very busy with playing. You should not distract them."[12]

I recall a Carnegie Hall concert in the late 1980s in which Bernstein didn't lift a finger to conduct the *Scherzo* of Brahms' Fourth Symphony with the Vienna Philharmonic. He merely stood on the podium and offered suggestions and cues with the sleight nod of his head or a shrug of his shoulders.* Richard Strauss had "Ten Golden Rules" of conducting which included the importance of having the awareness that when conducting one is not doing so to amuse oneself but rather to "delight the audience" by realizing the best possible performance. Szell, a Strauss protégé, echoed his mentor saying, "Conductors must give unmistakable and suggestive signals to the orchestra, not choreography to the audience."[13] That said, audiences adored Bernstein for his excessive podium theatrics. Showmanship made Lenny and big star. Strauss, whose conducting gestures could be minuscule, likely would have admonished Lenny citing one of his Golden Rules: "The conductor should never perspire, only the audience should get warm."

Another essential aspect of the profession is the understanding of how to relate to the musicians whom you are working with. Contrary to the assertion of Isaac Stern and others, there is simply no way that one person can know as much as the collective knowledge of dozens of fine musicians in a large ensemble. It could be easily argued that a conductor who had been a string player before taking up the baton (Maazel, Marriner, Koussevitsky, e.g.), would likely be much more knowledgeable about bowings than a non-string player. Respecting that collective knowledge is an important ingredient in achieving results. In the era prior to the emergence of a more powerful musician's union, conductors had the ability to hire and fire, thus fear could be a great motivator. But in the end, splenetic authoritarianism (Toscanini, e.g.) alone is no longer enough to foster a musical partnership conducive to the highest level of music- making. In certain respects an orchestra is very social, hence getting along well with one's colleagues is fundamental in establishing an *esprit de corps*. A conductor's comportment is no small matter and one's EQ (emotional intelligence) is now regarded as important as their IQ.

Being prepared is another salient point. One of my first conducting teachers always taught that successful conducting is 25% inspiration and 75% preparation. There is no better way to gain the respect of the musicians than having a firm grip of the music at hand. If the orchestra senses that you know your stuff, that you're well prepared, and that you make your points in

---

* There exists a YouTube video of Bernstein doing this with the Vienna Philharmonic in a performance of the finale of Haydn's Symphony No. 88.

rehearsal without rancor and vituperation, they will generally play their hearts out for you. An innate feature of human nature is to aspire to success, thus the conductor's job is to create conditions conducive to attaining musical success.

In many ways, it is in rehearsals that conductors prove their mettle. Szell claimed (much to the irritation of his contemporaries) that his orchestra in Cleveland started rehearsing where other orchestras finished rehearsing. A fastidious taskmaster, he would have the orchestral parts of the music he was preparing to perform meticulously marked with his designations regarding dynamics, articulation and phrasing at the first rehearsal, thereby eliminating the need to take time to explain his intentions. This, in turn, allowed for more time for rehearsing and executing his interpretive requests. Szell also insisted that his musicians listen to each other in much the same way that a chamber ensemble operates. Russian violinist, Boris Belkin, once told me that rehearsing with the Cleveland Orchestra was a remarkable experience because they listened so well. There was a wordless communication that made the entire music-making process a remarkable experience. "If I played a passage with a very specific articulation, the entire string section would immediately respond in kind. It was amazing."

Szell was also among a number of conductors who believed that "re-touching" the orchestration of certain scores was part of the conductor's duty to present the best possible realization of a given piece. Many conductors have "re-touched" the scores of Robert Schumann due to the perception that his choices of instrumentation and dynamics did not allow for the textures or thematic elements of his music to be heard in the most effective fashion. Mahler re-orchestrated the symphonies of Beethoven and Schumann. Though this practice is considered *verboten* by purists, conductors do engage in "retouching" scores to varying extents. (I confess. I have done it.)

A case in point: In the first movement of Antonín Dvořák's Seventh Symphony (Op. 70) when the main theme is presented in its first full *tutti* (bar 55), Dvořák makes a miscalculation that any conductor will need to adjust for the full drama of the music to be realized. At this juncture in the score, Dvořák has the main theme played *fortissimo* by the winds in horn fifths (the bassoons an octave lower than the flutes, oboes and clarinets), while the brass and strings intone a sustained interval of a perfect fifth, (the timpani on a pedal D) also *fortissimo*. There is simply no way for the normal compliment of eight wind players to compete sonically with the sixty to eighty other instruments. The theme just cannot be heard well. A conductor has several options; adjust the volume of the brass and strings to *forte* or *mezzo forte* (which lessens the dramatic impact of the moment), or, as Szell opts to do, have the first and second trombones double the bassoons, thereby giving the theme greater weight and prominence. In either case the conductor "re-touches" Dvorák's score to maximize the musical drama. In the coda of the symphony's finale, some conductors add either horns or trumpets on the theme (scored for the oboes, clarinets, bassoons and the second violins) to give it greater prominence. Several conductors alter the voicing of the symphony's final three D-major chords, opting to have either the first trumpet or first trombone play an F-sharp (the third of the triad as James Levine does) as opposed to the written D-natural. Szell, who also retouched the scores of Schumann and Schubert, was not alone in this practice.

There are times when conductors make actual cuts in certain pieces, but for dogmatists this is considered sacrilegious. Szell made a huge cut (from bars 426 to 555) in the finale of Béla Bartók's *Concerto for Orchestra* and his 1965 recording with the Cleveland Orchestra includes that cut. Eugene Ormandy, who conducted several premiere performances of Serge Rachmaninoff's compositions, cut sections from the composer's Second Symphony in an attempt to make it structurally more concise. I asked the long-time program annotator for the Cleveland Orchestra, Klaus George Roy, if he knew the circumstances that had prompted Szell to make the cut in Bartók's piece. He related a story about how Szell had visited Bartók in New York just before the composer's death to ask permission to make that particular edit, and Bartók consented. Although this was Szell's account of what happened, according to Mr. Roy there doesn't seem to be any corroborating evidence to support or refute Szell's claim. Does any conductor have the "right" to make such wholesale changes in the printed score? We know that composers in the eighteenth and nineteenth centuries often performed movements of the symphonies and concertos piecemeal, but wholesale cutting? The jury is still out on that.

To those of a more dogmatic mindset, something as seemingly benign as not taking the repeats in a particular movement is considered a serious display of disrespect of the composer's wishes. Like most interpretive concerns, it becomes a matter of personal taste and discernment. In his nearly 600-page book *The Compleat Conductor*, noted conductor, composer and author, Gunther Schuller, makes his case for full allegiance to the printed score as a prime standard by which conductors should be judged. He cites copious examples of how even the most esteemed conductors have "sinned" against maintaining fidelity to the printed text in the name of interpretive license. Curiously, in the midst of his admonitions, he praises maestro Carlos Kleiber for precisely the "questionable musical habits" he reviles others for; including the habit of "crescendoing much too early", or not attaining precise dynamics, excessively driving the orchestra to climaxes and several other proclivities that he finds objectionable in the music-making of other well-respected conductors. But why does maestro Kleiber, who was greatly admired by many of his conducting colleagues, get a pass from Mr. Schuller? Intellect; sublime intellect.

> But whatever he does, he does with consummate control, gesturally and intellectually, and with such a joy of music-making, ranging from complete confidence building relaxation in front of an orchestra to passionate, almost ecstatic outbursts, that one can only be compelled to admire in awe—even if one does not always agree with every aspect of his performances. Kleiber is a virtuoso in the best sense, a virtuoso with a mind.[14]

So, is it fair to ask: When other acknowledged virtuoso musicians—Szell, Rubinstein, Heifetz, Rostropovich, Oistrakh, Richter, Horowitz, Fischer-Dieskau—strayed from strict adherence to the text, were they refraining from using their minds? Did they stray from textual adherence due to capricious whims apart from any informed or scholarly decision-making? How does maestro Schuller (or anyone) know that Kleiber's decisions and interpretive choices were based solely on intellect and not an emotional impulse or a personal preference? He doesn't. Schuller is merely making a subjective assessment based on *his* personal tastes. That's fine. We all do it. As an interpreter, I make certain choices regarding tempi, articulation, phrasing or dynamics, and even "retouching" in the hopes of presenting the music that I'm conducting in a way that the audience will find to be stimulating and satisfying. Most, if not all performers engage in this practice.

Mahler proffered that conductors were within their rights to edit his scores. Norman Lebrecht reminds us that Mahler, whose scores contain voluminous performing directions, once stated that his symphonies should be revised every five years and that conductors could be rather free in their editing. Mahler would say, "the music is not to be found in the notes."[15] So much for the composer being the last word on the score. Jean Sibelius was also tolerant of interpretive license in performances of his music as long as conductors were fully confident of their choices. There are three editions of Anton Bruckner's third symphony, for instance, due to the composer making structural changes and editing the orchestration.

Like Schuller, Stravinsky inveighed against "interpretive" excess, insisting that music be performed as written. This was, of course, in keeping with his objective, neoclassic view of music in general. The scores of Bach, Mozart and Haydn contain very few specific expressive indications, thus if one performs them without any expressive gestures—dynamic variance, agogic accents, gradations of tempo or vibrato, phrasing, etc., they become unaffecting affairs. Ornamentation and improvisation in the Baroque era were measures of a performer's abilities and their informed musical "tastes." Yet it was all very personal. Two conductors who I do not particularly enjoy, Toscanini and Furtwangler, are polar opposites in terms of their approaches. Toscanini's literalism often leaves me cold, Furtwängler's excesses infuriate. For me, neither "serves" the music particularly well. Sir Colin Davis can be both highly inspirational in his accounts of the Sibelius symphonies, but decidedly earthbound in his accounts of several of the late Haydn symphonies. But again, it's all very personal.

The great conductor-orchestra relationships of the past have produced a rich and varied history of music-making and more than a few controversies. In many ways, it's the "joint effort" that is central to making great music in any ensemble. In the context of the larger ensemble, the individual "sacrifices" their individual interpretive preferences for the sake of the greater good. This, of course, is an important first step in achieving the realization of a great orchestral performance, not to mention better human relations.

Richard Strauss' Ten Golden Rules of Conducting

1. Remember that you are making music not to amuse yourself, but to delight your audience.
2. You should not perspire when conducting: only the audience should get warm.

3. Conduct *Salome* and *Elektra* as if they were Mendelssohn: Fairy Music.

4. Never look encouragingly at the brass, except with a brief glance to give an important cue.

5. But never let the horns and woodwinds out of your sight. If you can hear them at all they are still too strong.

6. If you think that the brass is not blowing hard enough, tone it down another shade or two.

7. It is not enough that you yourself should hear every word the soloist sings. You should know it by heart anyway. The audience must be able to follow without effort. If they do not understand the words they will go to sleep.

8. Always accompany the singer in such a way that he can sing without effort.

9. When you think you have reached the limits of prestissimo, double the pace.

10. If you follow these rules carefully you will, with your fine gifts and your great accomplishments, always be the darling of your listeners.

Recommended Recordings

Puccini: *Arias*, Eileen Farrell, Max Rudolf, Columbia Symphony Orchestra

Delius: *Florida Suite*, Sir Thomas Beecham, Royal Philharmonic Orchestra

Mahler: Symphony No. 5, Herbert von Karajan, Berlin Philharmonic

Mahler: Symphony No. 5, Michael Gielen, Southwest German Radio Symphony

Mahler: Symphony No. 1, Seiji Ozawa, Boston Symphony Orchestra

Handel: Concerto Grosso, Op. 12, Rafael Kubelik, Bavarian Radio Symphony

Tchaikovsky: Symphony No. 6, Leonard Bernstein, New York Philharmonic

Tchaikovsky: Violin Concerto, Boris Belkin, violin, Vladimir Ashkenazy, conductor

Tchaikovsky: *Capriccio Italien*, Kirill Kondrashin, RCA Victor Symphony Orchestra

Hindemith: Symphony *Mathis der Maher*, Paul Hindemith, Berlin Philharmonic

Beethoven: Symphony No. 2, Roger Norrington, London Classical Players

Beethoven: Symphony No. 3, *Eroica*, Arturo Toscanini, NBC Symphony (1939)

Beethoven: Symphony No. 7, Carlos Kleiber, Vienna Philharmonic

Beethoven: Symphony No. 4, Georg Solti, Chicago Symphony Orchestra

Brahms: Symphony No. 4, Leonard Bernstein, Vienna Philharmonic

Beethoven: Incidental Music to *Egmont*, George Szell, Vienna Philharmonic

Dvořák: Symphony No. 7, George Szell, Cleveland Orchestra

Bartók: *Concerto for Orchestra*, Fritz Reiner, Chicago Symphony Orchestra

Bartók: *Concerto for Orchestra*, George Szell, Cleveland Orchestra

Strauss: *Der Rosenkavalier*, Richard Strauss, Berlin State Opera Orchestra

Brahms: Symphony No. 1, Wilhelm Furtwangler, Berlin Philharmonic

Bach: Orchestral Suite No. 3, Musica Antiqua Cologne, Reinhard Goebel

Haydn: Symphony No. 104, *London*, Antal Dorati, Philharmonia Hungarica

Haydn: *Lord Nelson Mass*, Sir Neville Marriner, Dresden Staatskapelle

Schumann: Symphony No. 2 (Mahler's version), Aldo Ceccato, Bergen Philharmonic

Brahms: Symphony No. 4, Bernard Haitink, Royal Concertgebouw Orchestra

Rachmaninoff: Symphony No. 2, Leonard Slatkin, Detroit Symphony Orchestra

Mozart: Symphony No. 36, *Linz*, Christopher Hogwood, Academy of Ancient Music

Mussorgsky: *Night on Bare Mountain*, Serge Koussevitsky, Boston Symphony Orchestra

Bruckner: Symphony No. 3 (Nowak edition), George Szell, Cleveland Orchestra

Brahms: Symphony No. 3, Nikolaus Harnoncourt, Berlin Philharmonic

The Art of Conducting: Volumes 1 & 2 DVD (Teldec Classics)

Video: Haydn-Bernstein: http://www.youtube.com/watch?v=xIv6ZkiJHcM

Endnotes

1   Norman Lebrecht, "Carlos Kleiber: Not a Great Conductor," *La Scena Musicale*, July 30, 2004, http://www.scena.org/columns/lebrecht/040730-NL-kleiber.html.

2   Terry Riley, as cited by Richard Taruskin in *Music in the Late Twentieth Century* (Oxford and New York: Oxford University Press, 2010), p. 365.

3   Bernard Holland, "Making Music through Sleight of Hand and Eye," *New York Times*, August 13, 1995.

4   Gilbert Kaplan, "A Dirge? No. It's a Love Song," *New York Times*, July 19, 1992, Section 2, p. 19.

5   Donald Mitchell, *Gustav Mahler, Volume II: The Wunderhorn Years: Chronicles and Commentaries* (London: Faber and Faber, 1975), p. 286.

6   Harold C. Schonberg, *The Great Conductors* (New York: Simon and Schuster, 1967), p. 254.

7   Ibid., p. 252.

8   Ibid.

9   Ibid., p. 204.

10   Ibid.

11   Ibid, p. 218.

12   Justin Davidson, "What Does a Conductor Do?", *New York Magazine*, December 26, 2011.

13   Carl Bamberger, *The Conductor's Art* (New York: Columbia University Press, 1995), pp. 117-118.

14   Gunther Schuller, *The Compleat Conductor* (Oxford: Oxford University Press, 1997), p. 194.

15   Norman Lebrecht, *Why Mahler?: How One Man and Ten Symphonies Changed Our World* (New York: Anchor Books, 2011), p. ix.

24

Woodstock's Golden Agers

If you think the world is all wrong,
remember that it contains people like you.
Mahatma Gandhi

We are stardust, billion-year-old carbon.
We are golden, caught in the devil's bargain.
And we've got to get ourselves back to the garden.
Joni Mitchell

Two iconic photos—before and after. One depicting a sea of humanity reveling in the music of their idols on Max Yasgur's farm in upstate New York, the other revealing the horrible mess of mud and refuse that was left behind.* Juxtaposed, these two images might be emblematic of a generation that grew up on rock and roll, loved to get high, party hard, and indulge in "free love," often with reckless abandon. Living the Bohemian lifestyle

---

* This essay was originally written in 2009 and revised in 2020. The lyric by Joni Mitchell is from her song, "Woodstock."

of carefree license, unfettered by so-called "traditional" values, became the fantasy of an entire generation, and music was at the vortex of that counter-culture revolution. In retrospect, Woodstock may have turned out to be more of a moment rather than a movement, and as that "after" photo suggests, the Woodstock generation has been rather messy in the ensuing decades with regard to love, life and its pursuit of happiness. The summer of 2019 marked the 50th anniversary of Woodstock.

A central ethos of the "summer of love" and the social consciousness that was an overriding zeitgeist of that era, was the outright disdain for authority figures. "Don't trust anyone over thirty," became a popular mantra of the Woodstock generation as the groundswell of liberal populism permeated everything from politics to the media the entertainment industry.* As a generation, we waxed poetic about peace, love and universal brotherhood. Music was thought to be a force at the forefront of ushering in a Utopian era in which greed, selfishness and all manner of "plastic" values would be negated. John Lennon and Yoko Ono implored us to "give peace a chance." The hopes and dreams of an Aquarian Age, in which we would "study war no more," and "love would steer the stars," would become a reality—or so we thought.

A rebellious mindset was very much at the heart of rock and roll music in that era. As many of us of that generation are now in our 60s and 70s, a look back at the ramifications of the "free love" generation reveals many unfortunate circumstances due to a plethora of missed opportunities and "sellouts" to the very hypocrisies we decried. In retrospect, the naïve idea that life without restrictions and responsibilities was the path to Nirvana now seems imprudent in the extreme, and there are "messes" everywhere as a result. As we question why the world seems so hopelessly lost some ten decades later, it is Gandhi who provides sagacious insight into our query: "If you think the world is all wrong, remember that it contains people like you."[1] You, me, them—us! "I am he/as you are he/as you are me/and we are all together," according to a tripped out John Lennon.[2] Well yes, we all had a hand in creating this mess and we all bear some responsibility as grown-ups to clean it up. Jonah Goldberg insightfully notes:

---

* University of California, Berkley environmentalist and free speech advocate Jack Weinberg, is credited with coining the phrase, "Don't trust anyone over thirty," in an interview for the *San Francisco Chronicle* in 1964.

It is no coincidence that the post-World War II era of peace, prosperity, and conformity largely created the idea of the teenager. The buttoned-down 1950s gave adolescents something to rebel against. Similarly, the peace and prosperity of the post-Cold War world created the adolescent forty-year-old. The comfort of prosperity leads … to a cultural backlash against the established order and bourgeois values.[3]

Our liberation, especially sexual liberation, was seen as a cosmic coming of age where we would be free from the inhibitions that were put upon us by our parents and their respective catechisms. Decades earlier Nietzsche and his sexual revolutionary acolytes were advocating similar ideas with regard to sexual liberation long before Woodstock.[*] In the 1950s Hugh Hefner's pornographic *Playboy* fantasies were purported to be a liberated model by which young men and women could free themselves from the puritanical principles of that era. But by the late 1960s even Hef's attitudes seemed a bit quaint when compared to the revolutionary, and often hedonistic, psychology that was touting free sex as the ultimate "high" and a rebuke of prudential constraints on sexual behavior. We were into Tantric sexuality but without spirituality. So, how has that worked out?

An editorial in the *Washington Times* on the specious justifications of Hefner's attitudes that succored the "free love" generation, described the condition of the "sexually liberated" malaise in which we now find ourselves, in a perspicacious fashion:

> All the sweet nothings promised by the sexual revolution backfired. Instead of a free-love utopia, the Age of Aquarius is responsible for skyrocketing rates of abortion, venereal disease, broken marriages, out-of-wedlock births and the poverty that comes hand-in-hand with social decay. Although more intangible, it's not coincidental that people also became less courteous. After all, it's not possible to respect and objectify someone at the same time, a rule which ultimately undermines Mr. Hefner's carefully crafted myth of himself as a kind of highbrow gentleman pornographer. Diminishing virtue leaves us all more coarse.[4]

---

* The term "sexual liberation" was coined by the neo-Marxist philosopher, Wilhelm Reich.

All of this coarseness and angst; wasn't all that transcendental meditation, free sex and drug use supposed to enlighten us (Open your mind, man!), and help us avoid the trappings and proclivities that made the world such a mess in the first place? And wasn't music—sweet, sweet music—going to soothe all the savagery and supplant the alienation that made living in this world "such a bitch" with something more humane and decent? American writer and philosopher Elbert Hubbard believed that all music was sacred and that musicians were the priests to lord over this sacred realm. He would say, "music is the only one of the arts that cannot be prostituted to a base use."[5] Well, Hubbard made his assertion way back in 1923 and regrettably he wasn't nearly as prescient as I'm sure many of his contemporaries had hoped.

Because musicians were thought to possess a more high-minded and progressive view of life's great mysteries, what they composed and sang about was increasingly viewed as an expression of contemporary social gospel. Anti-establishment expression in music wasn't the sole province of rock or soul music. Eventually, Broadway would get into the act with the production of that paean to tribal love and counter-culture ethics, *Hair*. Leonard Bernstein's *Mass*, commissioned by Jacqueline Kennedy for the opening of the Kennedy Center for the Performing Arts in Washington, D.C. in 1971, provided an aura of establishment legitimacy to Aquarian ethos as one of Classical music's most iconic and beloved figures joined the parade of progressive, anti-Establishment antagonists. *Mass*, which employs a rock band in the scoring, is decidedly more musical theater than highbrow art music, but it created quite a buzz for its unabashed foray into the realm of popular art. Politics, of course, was never far from the surface when it came to music that might challenge the status quo.

In 1970 Bernstein came under severe political scrutiny due to his encounter with the Black Panthers at a fund-raising event that his wife organized at the couple's New York apartment. The funds were to used to assist members of the Panthers who had been spuriously jailed attain the necessary bail in order to be released.* The gathering at Bernstein's apartment was attended by journalist Tom Wolfe, who according to Bernstein's daughter, Jamie, was an

---

* At the time, twenty-one members of the Black Panthers were awaiting trial for what turned out to be false accusations involving allegations of bomb plots throughout New York City. The trial was eventually dismissed due to unsubstantiated evidence.

uninvited interloper. It was Wolfe who famously coined the term, "radical chic" in referencing Bernstein's Black Panther encounter. This ensnared Bernstein in a public-relations nightmare that put him in the crosshairs of many who felt that he had politically crossed the line. As his daughter explains:

> To most white Americans at the time, the Black Panthers were scary. The group had come into being to protest race-based police brutality, but the Panthers gained greater notoriety for being socialist; for advocating black empowerment "by any means necessary"; and for being anti-Zionist, which had particularly negative resonance in New York City. ... The word "shit-storm" had not yet been coined, but that is what the situation now became. My parents were condemned and mocked in the press. Their own friends criticized them for "siding" with the Panthers. The louder the volume grew, the more misunderstood the event became.[6]

Bernstein, who could be quite the provocateur, was given to supporting progressive causes, and as the good liberal he was, he stood with the New York Philharmonic musicians and American Federation of Musicians Union during the orchestra's labor negotiations while he was the orchestra's music director—a management position. At the time of Black Panther flap, some thought he was biting the hand that allowed him to pocket his New York Philharmonic salary, the princely fees for his guest conducting appearances, recording dates and a host of other income- generating activities; fees that were made possible by the largesse of the very corporate culture that progressives and the Black Panthers condemned.*

The continual objectification of that which has intrinsic spiritual dimensions has had deleterious effects and this became antipodal to our Aquarian fantasies. Music and sexuality were casualties in this regard. As the aforementioned Washington Times editorial astutely observes, objectifying someone is a form of disrespect and belittlement and has little to do with love in its truest realization. The shallowness of this reality is typified in Stephen Still's ode to sexual objectification, "Love the One You're With":

---

*. Major symphony orchestras in the United States receive significant funding from the corporate sector. For many orchestras, this amounts to tens-of-millions of dollars annually.

Don't be angry, don't be sad, and don't sit cryin'
Over good times you've had.
There's a girl right next to you,
And she's just waitin' for something to do.
And there's a rose in the fisted glove,
And the eagle flies with the dove,
And if you can't be with the one you love, honey,
Love the one you're with, love the one you're with,
Love the one you're with, love the one you're with.

Well yeah, that was us. Love the one you're with, no matter what the consequences; how *unenlightened*. Regarding the *zeitgeist* of the era, author James Howard Kunstler recalls:

> You have no idea what a fantastic bacchanal college was in the 1960s. Let the sunshine in! The great anti-war protests gave us a chance to pretend we were serious, but believe me, it was much more about finding someone to hook-up with at the teach-ins and the street marches. The birth control pill was a fabulous novelty. We ignored the side-effects—especially the social side effects that led later on to an epidemic of divorces and broken families.[7]

What's troubling is that we are still as self-centered now as we were then and our socio-cultural messiness continues to have profound ramifications. Evidence suggests that very little has changed, and in fact might be worse, as brothers continue to sell their brothers up the river to make a buck. The excesses of a materialistic and highly commercialized culture have wreaked havoc upon the social fabric of our nation—and a few other nations along the way. As David Brooks notes in his book, *Bobos in Paradise*, in the post-Woodstock era many of the Bohemian idealists of the 1960s who derided corporate culture and the Protestant work ethic as being anathema to the promises of the Aquarian ethos, have become the new free-market entrepreneurial class. Brooks observes:

> The hedonism of Woodstock mythology has become domesticated and now serves as the management tool for the Fortune 500. Americans haven't even adopted European-style vacation schedules. Instead, they pull all-nighters at Microsoft and come in on weekends at Ben & Jerry's. And the people

who speak most devoutly about smashing order and instituting perpetual revolution—the capitalists of the corporate world—are the ones who strive most earnestly for success. ... They have transformed work into a spiritual and intellectual vocation, so they approach their labor with the fervor of artists and missionaries.[8]

Some might view this scenario as a "sellout" to the 60s mindset that increasingly viewed all modes of capitalism as being abhorrent. The pursuit of material wealth couldn't be more of a betrayal to the Bohemian spirit. This is reminiscent of the Angela Davis-type character in Paddy Chayefsky's brilliant film, *Network*; a died-in-the-wool progressive communist who at the beginning of the film rails against the greed of the oppressive corporate machine, but once she becomes a reality TV star of the docudrama series, *The Mao Tse-Tung Hour,* fights tooth-and-nail to make sure she doesn't get stiffed for her residuals.* Money, as we know is just as important to anti-capitalist revolutionaries as it is to the capitalists who they vociferously disdain.

Chayefsky's film was produced just a decade after Woodstock and pointed to the continual decline in American intellectual and moral integrity. Music, as well as television, was succumbing to lowest-common-denominator values that were driven by the desire for commercial success. (Theodor Adorno's observation). Speaking to Chayefsky's "prophetic" outlook, Devin Faraci comments:

> He truly saw where it was all going; raging against how that medium had become debased, stupid and pandering. Everything he says about TV—the way it flatters the viewer, the ways it stultifies and the way it over-magnifies minor things—is absolutely applicable to the age of Buzzfeed. Chayefsky saw our downward slope, the one we're still on.[9]

If rock groups honestly raged publically against the capitalist machine, why wouldn't they eschew instruments made by corporate-oriented companies like Marshall, Fender, Shure or Gibson, companies that participate in the free market? The fact that rockers travel to their gigs on Boeing-manufactured jets and Mercedes Benz limousines that are fueled by big oil corporations like

---

* Chayefsky's prescience is astonishing in his film, *Network*. Among other things, he foretells the phenomenon we now know as reality TV. The *Mao Tse-Tung Hour* in his film was precisely that.

Exxon, Shell or Mobil, would seem to be an affront to their anti-capitalist convictions. Do they really have anti-capitalist convictions, or is it all a pose? It's all very inane and duplicitous because they are part of the machine and either don't know it, or they know it and are willing co-conspirators who are only too happy to pad their bank accounts as professional "ragers."

Most big rock acts are managed by large-scale corporate agencies such as Live Nation, John Scher's Metropolitan Entertainment or AEG Entertainment. Rock is big business and extremely corporate. Selling "merch" at concerts (tee shirts, caps, CDs) is part of the rock concert. Personally, I'm OK with that. Free markets are way cool! Musicians should be paid for their art, but the insipid rants about being against the very mechanism that pays for your instruments, your recording gear, your studio time, your travel and roadies come across as a puerile whine. So much for rock music being the harbinger of Aquarian love, free from the taint of corporatism.

The Record Business Is a "Business"

Is all this a "sellout" to corporate culture? Much to our dismay, the music industry has contributed to the social malaise that Woodstock's "golden agers" helped to create. There is a ton that could be said about the problems of the record industry, but Michael Jackson's death illustrated the sad fact that forty years after "the mother of all rock concerts" back in Bethel, greed and selfishness are rampant in the music industry, and many tried to cash in on the "King of Pop's" passing. That the pop music industry has prioritized business over artistic concerns is not breaking news. Composers of the eighteenth and nineteenth centuries were often embroiled in nasty financial contretemps with their publishers and patrons.

With the increased commercialization of the music business, where billions of dollars are at stake in the global marketplace, the business of music is often conducted without any concern for the human capital that is expended in creating the product that it exploits. When CEOs, lawyers and accountants get paid more than artists, something's amiss—but then again, it is a business and those running the business will always be looking out for their bank accounts first and foremost. The aspirations of artists—especially in the realm of folk music, where dissent and alternative worldviews regularly challenged the establishment—to use their creativity for positive social change, were in effect, hijacked. As Fred Goodman, former editor of *Rolling Stone Magazine*, chronicles in his book, *The Mansion On the Hill: Dylan, Young, Geffen, Springsteen, and the Head-on Collision of Rock and Commerce*, the contradictory relationship between art and commerce was never far from the center of disputations among those in the music business.

> When Dylan and others created folk-rock, those aspirations were transformed to electric music, and the results proved far more popular and profound for the mass culture than folk [music] had ever been. The most influential rock albums were made by people who took themselves quite seriously—as did their listeners. Just a few decades ago rock was tied to a counterculture professing to be so firmly against commercial and social conventions that the notion of a "rock and roll business" seemed an oxymoron.
>
> What I find most troubling is that the scope and reach of the business often makes it impossible to tell what is done for art and what is done for commerce—which calls into question the music's current ability to convey the artistic intent that made it so appealing and different to begin with.[10]

Moreover, there are some who never believed that rock music had any redeeming social or artistic value in the first place and therefore viewed its subjugation by corporate interests as inevitable. That said, many artists were—and still are—idealistic about music being an agent of social change. I continue to be among them.

Most, if not all, popular culture, whether it's the music industry, television, radio and Hollywood, has had its share of bad actors and greedy opportunists as the #me too movement has revealed. One is reminded of Hunter S. Thompson's caustic observation of the television industry: "The TV business is uglier than most things. It is normally perceived as some kind of cruel and shallow money trench through the heart of the journalism industry, a long plastic hallway where thieves and pimps run free and good men die like dogs, for no good reason."[11] My good friend and wonderful Gospel singer, Mzuri Moyo Aimbaye, often refers to television as "tell-a-lie-vision," and with good reason. Too much of what has become the norm in the entertainment industry is downright vile and antithetical to the ideals necessary to create the culture of peace and love that we "imagined" decades ago. Perhaps we were too naive to expect that our music, that which we thought to be pure and beautiful and beyond the baleful intentions of greedy corporate types, would be not corrupted by the "thieves and pimps" Thompson alluded to. But it has. The proclivity to ignore or purposely disregard the spiritual attributes of music with the express intent of turning it into a commodity—to objectify it—is in a sense, pornographic.

The adolescent predilection for instant gratification in our live-for-the-moment culture, combined with crass commercialism, has led to a condition where a good deal of popular music has become coarse and without much in the way of any redeeming social value. (Miley Cyrus as a salacious paramour, gangsta rap, e.g.) What's worse, any objection to the destructive effects of popular culture is often met with charges of intolerance or insensitivity, as if there is no legitimate or rational concern about how popular music often succumbs to our most base instincts. The censoriousness regarding moral and ethical concerns that too often permeates the progressive mindset has the effect of becoming a buffer against legitimate skepticism and any corrective sensibilities, and too often any critique is met with charges of racism, intolerance or bigotry.

Regrettably, thievery and piracy in the music business are not endemic to the post-Woodstock era. Charles Wright (who wrote the soul classic, *Express Yourself*) and other black musicians in the early days of popular music tell stories of rip-offs and scams that left many gifted musicians virtually penniless while lawyers, talent agents and publishers cashed in on their clients' successes. The stories of such are as heartbreaking as they are copious and as we have seen, the rap and hip-hop moguls who now rule the entertainment industry are not any better than their counterparts of a few decades ago in this regard. Black artists such as Wright, Little Richard, Otis Redding, Chuck Berry and Sam Cooke saw their careers flounder while white artists like the Beatles and Rolling Stones and Elvis recorded their tunes and made fortunes.

More recently, Grammy award-winning singer, Dionne Warwick has taken Radio One president, Cathy Hughes, to task for not paying royalties to black artists when Hughes' stations program their songs as part of its playlists. Hughes, who is black, cites the struggling economy, but Radio One has dozens of stations in its stable and earned over $300 million in 2009. In a *Huffington Post* article, Warwick cites the fact that Hughes paid a $10 million bonus to Radio One CEO, Alfred Liggins, who is Hughes' son. At a time when many musicians are struggling, this smacks of the same corporate greed and malfeasance that we get from Wall Street hedge fund operators.

Commenting on government legislation that is needed to close legal loopholes that allow radio stations to circumvent royalty payments to artists (HRH 848, The Performance Rights Act), Warwick stated, "The struggling musicians who need the Civil Rights for Musicians Act don't want a handout from Cathy Hughes or Clear Channel or the National Association of Broadcasters, which is the mouthpiece of big — largely white — corporate radio. They just want to be paid for their work."[12] As a fellow musician, I'm with Ms. Warwick on this issue. The House Bill would require radio stations that make $1.25 million annually to pay only $5,000 for royalties. Several reports indicate the United States, Iran, China and North Korea are among the very few nations that do not pay artists radio royalties. A visit to the House of Representatives website reveals that this legislation has been on the docket since 1995.

In 2018, Smokey Robinson appeared before the U.S. Senate and testified that some of his songs are streamed 50,000 times each day via digital media. He argued that songs composed and recoded before 1972 should be included in the Music Modernization Act that was passed in the House of Representatives. This bill, which has broad support, would help older artists who are in need of financial support in their retirement years. In Robinson's testimony, he stated, "We have lost our entire middle class of songwriters, they're gone," explaining that the outdated way songwriters are compensated has allowed writers to be paid "fractions of pennies on the dollar" for their work.[13]

In the aftermath of Don Imus being fired from CBS-owned WFAN Radio in 2007 after he made disparaging comments about the Rutgers University women's basketball team, there was a spate of discussion on the issues of race and the influence of rap and hip-hop music on America's urban communities. Oprah Winfrey, who has had run-ins with hip-hop artists, allocated two days on her daily broadcast to advance the discussion. She invited a number of hip-hop artists, social commentators and media journalists to engage in a panel discussion on the Imus flap in particular, and the pernicious influence of rap in general. Included in the discussion were Rev. Al Sharpton, journalist Stanley Crouch, rap mogul Russell Simmons, and Simmons's associate and hip-hop advocate Dr. Ben Muhammed (formerly Ben Chavis of NAACP fame, and a personal acquaintance). A central theme of the dialogue was the dehumanizing effect of rap music.

Crouch, a noted jazz historian and columnist for the *New York Daily News* (and no fan of rap music), offered this take on the dehumanizing aspect of rap:

> The point is that Hitler proved what can happen when a group of people is constantly dehumanized, and there are those out there who, rightfully, do not intend for anyone to forget that fact. If the civil rights establishment were as concerned about the depiction of black people as those who look out for Jews are about the treatment of Jews, the rap industry would have been brought on the carpet years ago. In fact, if the industry had been the creation of white people, it would have been snuffed out two decades ago, since no white person could get away with calling black people "niggers," "bitches," "hos" and the rest of it.[14]

Crouch's observations point to the issues of accountability and double standards, issues that too few artists seem willing to confront. When it comes to music, artistic freedom and potential sales trump all other concerns, no matter how salacious or degrading the product. The CEO of a particular media-entertainment conglomerate may personally deplore the effects of rap, or any other dehumanizing art form on the society in which he lives, but their job as a CEO is to make shareholders happy, a scenario that points to a hardcore, bottom-line mentality. However, artists are not exempt from responsibility in their creative endeavors. When pressed on this issue from a member of Winfrey's audience, Russell Simmons defended the right of "the poet" to say what he wanted to say. Simmons would give no quarter to any censorious mindset. I concur, but I would make a distinction between artistic freedom and license—and there is a difference.

There was a telling moment when Winfrey's panelists were asked if any of them would allow *their* daughters to appear in the misogynist videos that they produce. It was interesting to see how they all went mealy-mouthed in trying to find the appropriate spin to justify *their* objectifying of women in *their* creative endeavors. It seemed that exploiting other people's daughters for profit was acceptable, but these producers would think twice when it came to their children. To his credit, Simmons has since called for rappers to drop the "n-word" from their poetry, and his. Don Imus met with the Rutgers's women's basketball team to offer a personal apology. This was a significant "teachable moment" and one hopes the lessons learned will have positive and lasting impact. Too often we miss opportunities to actually assimilate the lessons learned from such circumstances into our common cultural psychology and revert to our bad habits of incivility and offensive behavior.

In an earlier reaction to the increasing misogynist tendencies in popular music and video, *Essence* magazine launched its *Take Back the Music Initiative* in 2005. The crux of their campaign is articulated in *Essence's* mission statement on the topic:

> We at ESSENCE have become increasingly concerned about the degrading ways in which Black women are portrayed and spoken about in popular media, particularly in popular urban music and music videos. Aware that these images may be having a negative impact on our children, we realized that, as Black women, it was up to us to take a stand.
>
> We understand that not all of us see this issue in the same way, and that many of us are card-carrying members of the hip-hop generation. Those of us who aren't, abhor censorship in any form and cherish artistic freedom even when we find the art personally distasteful.
>
> For these reasons, we want to make clear what our initiative is not. It is not a blanket condemnation of hip-hop nor an attack on cultural liberalism. It is not a boycott of any particular artist or venue for artistic expression. It is not a lashing out at Black men in front of or behind the video camera, for we recognize these men as our brothers and understand that we all have a common stake in raising awareness of how we are individually and collectively portrayed.
>
> Indeed, the editors shaping our Take Back the Music Initiative hold complex and diverse views on the subject of popular music, but we all have one thing in common: We're deeply concerned by the pervasiveness of negative images of Black women and its effect on our girls. Each of us is charged with finding our own personal response to the negative imagery, and not all of our responses will be the same.
>
> But respond we must. As Michaela Angela Davis, our campaign spokesperson explains, "We're not trying to tell people what to think about this; we simply want to encourage them to think."[15]

As noble as it was, the *Take Back the Music Initiative* began to fizzle out not long after it started, and perhaps not coincidentally, this was around the same time that Time Warner, the conglomerate the owns and publishes a great deal of popular music, became a majority owner of *Essence*. Was this a muzzling of a badly needed voice of reason and consciousness by a corporate entity that didn't like what that voice was saying?

Artistic License and Social Responsibility

Essence was in effect taking its cue from civil rights pioneer and activist C. Delores Tucker, who along with conservative Bill Bennett, bought stock in Time Warner and Sony as a way to voice her concerns about the dehumanizing influences of rap and hip-hop. I had the opportunity to hear Tucker speak at several conferences on this issue and was always impressed with her determination and passion to take responsibility and try to make a difference. Not everyone shared my admiration. She took major criticism from the hip-hop community, especially the late rapper Tupac Shakur. Tucker was highly critical of the NAACP for its selection of Tupac for one of its Image Awards and she attempted to persuade the organization to reconsider its choice. Shakur was not enamored with Tucker's efforts and made her the subject of his song "How Do U Want It?"

> *C. Delores Tucker, you's a motherfucker,*
> *Instead of trying to help a nigga you destroy a brother.*

And this from rapper Eminem:

> *I'm all for America, fuck the government,*
> *Tell that C. Delores Tucker slut to suck a dick,*
> *Motherfucker ducked, what the fuck? Son of a bitch,*
> *Take away my gun, I'm gonna tuck some other shit.*

So much for enlightened and humane rebuttals. What was it that Socrates supposedly said? "When the debate is lost, slander becomes the tool of the looser." And where were the same voices of indignation that were so quick to besmirch Don Imus and call for his head when Eminem called a much beloved civil rights pioneer who marched with Dr. King a slut? No double standards there, right?

Tipper Gore also became the object of hip-hop laced derision when in 1985 she and other concerned parents established the Parents Music Resource Center (PMRC) with the intent of heightening awareness about the content of certain popular music, especially rap and hip-hop. A result of the PMRC initiative was the so-called "Tipper Sticker," a parental advisory label that was attached to certain albums and CDs, warning of sexually explicit or violent lyrics. Many prominent musicians took issue with Gore and the PMRC for what they viewed as an overt attempt at government censorship; the rapper, Ice-T penned this little ditty:

> Yo Tip, what's the matter? You ain't getting' no dick?
> You're bitchin' about rock'n'roll, that's censorship, dumb bitch.
> The Constitution says we all got a right to speak.
> Say what we want Tip, your argument is weak.

We thank Mr. Ice for illustrating the need for the PMRC. In our current socio-cultural climate this could easily be characterized as "hate speech." Gore's argument notwithstanding, does Ice-T warrant a Tipper Sticker? You be the judge. In an interview for CBS's *60 Minutes* in 2010, Eminem confided that he doesn't allow profanity in his home because he has children, so maybe he should give himself a Tipper Sticker. To be fair, he says he doesn't mind if parents do the job of parenting by limiting what their children listen to or preventing their kids from buying his profanity-laced, dehumanizing product. If that's the case, why all the vituperation levied at the efforts of the PMRC and other decency advocates?

I would hope that the legacy of Ms. Tucker, who passed in 2005, might inspire other advocates of responsibility in the entertainment industry to do the right thing and buck up in the fight for decency and goodwill. Regrettably, but not surprisingly, Tupac was gunned down by his fellow rappers. Perhaps, if rappers heed Tucker's admonitions instead of engaging in derision and contempt, there might be less thuggish behavior in the hip-hop community.

Though the *Essence Magazine* initiative may have been the victim of corporate greed, its *cri de coeur* for raising consciousness is an important starting point in the quest for a culture of peace. And wasn't that the *essence* of what we had hoped for at Woodstock? A world of peace has been the hope of all ages, and idealist souls of every generation have felt that impulse. Yet time and again that impulse is crushed as the dark side of our human nature wins the day. Whatever victories we achieve often seem pyrrhic. Yet to bring light where there is darkness, as C. Delores Tucker and other proponents of altruism and decency have attempted to do, is in a very real sense, a way for each person to contribute to the progress toward social betterment.

Cultural commentator, Martha Bayles, argues that something has gone "seriously wrong, both with the sound of popular music and with the sensibility it expresses," and that the "affirmative spirit" that had been so prevalent in pop music has been "rejected in favor of anti-musical, anti-social antics that would be laughable if they weren't so offensive."[16] If, as Michael Jackson suggested, "we are the world" and the "ones who make a brighter day," then yes, "let's start giving" in the attempt to recover that "affirmative spirit."

In many respects, our Woodstock generation didn't take enough stock in the ethic of living for a higher purpose. We have become agnostics regarding the ideals that we so indignantly accused of others of being bereft of. In the opening chapters of *The Mansion on the Hill*, Fred Goodman chronicles the ascent of Bob Dylan and his legendary manager, Albert Grossman in the early days of the music industry. It's not a pretty picture. Grossman, who also managed Janis Joplin and the Band—and who was instrumental in bringing the Woodstock Festival to upstate New York—was shrewd, visionary, and by all accounts, a brilliant businessman. Grossman (known as "the Cloud") was also cold and calculating and his effect on Dylan about the money aspect of the music business was indicative of how the collision of art and commerce could reduce the most idealistic artists to the type of greedy capitalists that they loathed and railed about in their songs; with serious substance abuse problems to boot.[17] Even before Woodstock, the robber barons, the lawyers, accountants, hustlers and parasitic personal managers were crouching at the door ready to line their pockets on the talent of unsuspecting (or drugged out) musicians in the most dishonorable way.

On issues of social responsibility we became obfuscators and prevaricators, more willing to talk-the-talk than to walk-the-walk—or live the lyric—at least not to the degree that was necessary to actualize the social gospel that we sang about in our songs or protested about in our social and political activism. In fact, by assailing certain foundational enterprises like family, religion and a strong work ethic, things that had instructed us well in the ways of compassion, self-discipline and community cooperation, we unwittingly participated in our own cultural demise. The statistics regarding the results of irresponsible behavior on contemporary society are too veracious to refute, and as we are finding out in our autumn years, that irresponsibility has lasting consequences.

Van Gogh asserted that, "the best way to know God was to love many things."[18] But to love often takes courage, especially on an Aquarian scale. Dr. King instructed that the first thing necessary in any attempt at fashioning a non-violent solution for peace or justice was to be courageous. Echoing Dr. King's assertion, the legendary cellist and humanitarian, Pablo Casals believed that each person has great potential goodness, but it required courage to be good and decent in a world beset by selfishness. For Casals music wasn't just for his personal fulfillment: "I could no longer lose myself in my music. I did not feel … nor have I ever felt that music, or any form of art, can be the answer in itself. Music must serve a purpose; it must be part of something larger than itself, a part of humanity."[19]

Anyone who has been a parent knows that there are times when "tough love" is necessary to get children to behave responsibly. Being willing to get tough in love takes a bit of courage, whether with your children or with your fellow humans, especially when they are not acting in a way that is suited to the well-being of the larger society. The same courage demonstrated by Dr. King and C. Delores Tucker in the 1960s, when the injustice of "man's inhumanity to his fellow man" acted as the carcinogen that begat the horrible scourge of racism in America, is needed more now than ever if we're going to have any shot at cleaning up the mess that our generation created and has been quite derelict in taking responsibility for. Is it too late to make a difference? For those of us who decades ago experienced an epiphany regarding higher consciousness and the fulfillment of the Aquarian ideal of peace and love, doing nothing ought not to be an option.

Recommended Recordings

Woodstock: Original Concert Recording

Hair: Original Soundtrack Recording

Bernstein: *Mass*, Leonard Bernstein, conducting

Stephen Stills: *Crosby, Stills and Nash*

Beatles: *Anthology*

Charles Wright: *The Watts 103rd Street Rhythm Band*

Little Richard: *The London Rock & Roll Show*

Dionne Warwick: *Dionne Warwick's Golden Hits, Vol. 1 & 2*

Tupac Shakur: *All Eyez on Me*

Eminem: *The Eminem Show*

Mozart: Symphonies Nos. 35, 40, 41, Pablo Casals, Marlboro Festival Orchestra

Endnotes

1 M. N. Mukherjee, P. Mukhopadhyay, S. Sinha Roy and U. Dasgupta: *Rudiments of Mathematics, Part I* (Academic Publishers, 2004), p. 750.

2 David Sheff, *All We Are Saying: The Last Major Interview with John Lennon and Yoko Ono* (Playboy Enterprises, Inc., 1981), p. 184.

3 Jonah Goldberg, *Suicide of the West: How the Rebirth of Tribalism, Populism, Nationalism, and Identity Politics is Destroying American Democracy* (New York: Crown Forum, 2018), p. 244.

4 "Hugh Hefner's Desperation," *The Washington Times*, editorial, October 8, 2010.

5 Elbert Hubbard, *Little Journeys to the Homes of the Great Musicians* (London and New York: G. P. Putnam's Sons, 1903), p. 419.

6 Jamie Bernstein, "The Time My Parents 'Took A Knee' For the Black Panthers," *Huffington Post*, October 18, 2017.

7 James Howard Kunstler, "Boomer Elegy," *Clusterfuck Nation*, April 3, 2020.

8 David Brooks, *Bobos in Paradise: The New Upper Class and How They Got There* (New York: Touchstone, 2001), pp. 137-138.

9 Devin Faraci, "The Unwritten Dystopic Ending of Paddy Chayefsky's *Network*," *Birth. Movies. Death,* February 18, 2014.

10 Fred Goodman, *The Mansion on the Hill: Dylan, Young, Geffen, Springsteen, and the Head-on Collision of Rock and Commerce* (New York: First Vintage Books, 1998), p. xi.

11 Hunter S. Thompson, *Generation of Swine: Tales of Shame and Degradation* (New York: Summit Books, 1988), p. 43.

12 Dionne Warwick, "Big Radio's Attacks on Me Aren't Surprising," *Huffington Post*, July 29, 2009.

13 Nikki Schwab, "Smokey Robinson Testifies before Senate for More Streaming Royalties," *New York Post*, May 15, 2018.

14 Stanley Crouch, "Profit Drives Ugly Images of Black Kids," *New York Daily News*, June 25, 2001.

15 Mission Statement, "Take Back the Music," *Essence*, July 16, 2006, http://www.africanamerica.org/topic/ essence-take-back-the-music-campaign-mission-statement.

16 Martha Bayles, *Hole in Our Soul: The Loss of Beauty and Meaning in American Popular Music* (Chicago: University of Chicago Press, 1994), p. 3.

17 Fred Goodman, *Mansion on the Hill*, p. 94.

18 Deborah Silverman, *Van Gogh and Gauguin: The Search for Sacred Art* (New York: Farrar, Straus and Giroux, 2000), p. 166.

19 Pablo Casals, *Joys and Sorrows: Reflections by Pablo Casals* (New York: Simon and Schuster, 1974), p. 51.

25

Music as a Vehicle for Change

What omniscience has music! So absolutely impersonal,
and yet every sufferer feels his secret sorrow soothed.[1]
Ralph Waldo Emerson

Emerson's opinion regarding the ability of music to heal and quiet our innermost distress, and to be an "arch-reformer" of all things negative and injurious, is one that many will readily agree with. Yet music can also intensify feelings of despair, melancholy and sorrow. Emerson's observation with regard to music's capacity to transport one into altered states of mind echoes that of Leo Tolstoy.

> Music makes me forget my real situation. It transports me into a state which is not my own. Under the influence of music I really seem to feel what I do not feel, to understand what I do not understand, to have powers which I cannot have. ... Music transports me immediately into the condition of soul in which he who wrote the music found himself at that time.[2]

As perspicacious as these opinions may be, it has been my contention that the issue of music's moral and ethical power, and how that power affects individuals and society, receives too little attention in our postmodern world.

Assessing art from an axiological, as well as a theoretical and/or aesthetic perspective, is an approach that too few artists seem willing to consider. Indeed, the deconstructionist rationale that refutes the notion that there are meta-narratives or universal truths makes such assessments highly vexatious. The metaphysical aspects of music, as well as the limitations of language to elucidate specifics about it (Mendelssohn's assertion), makes any attempt to ascertain how music effects the soul difficult at best. Understanding the mysteries as to how music affects our being remains highly inscrutable, yet we sense that Emerson's and Tolstoy's intuition about music is essentially correct.

In the Broadway musical *Billy Elliot* (based on the British film by Lee Hall, musical score by Elton John), the narrative is set against the backdrop of the labor unrest between the National Union Of Miners (NUM) and Margaret Thatcher's Conservative Party in 1984. The young Billy is discovered to have extraordinary talent as a dancer, a situation that causes his gruff, working-class family great consternation. His talent is developed by the equally gruff, but warm-hearted ballet teacher, Mrs. Wilkinson, who runs the local dance school. In an early scene when instructing her young charges, the crotchety Mrs. Wilkinson prods her dancers into their daily rehearsal routine by saying in a somewhat sardonic and off-handed manner, "Come along now, children. It's time to transform our tawdry little lives through power of the arts."

As it happens, what seems to be merely a throwaway line is, in fact, a central premise of the play. As Billy's talent becomes more apparent (via the terrific choreography by James Darling), the desire to pursue his dream of becoming a great dancer begins to affect his family and community in uplifting ways. Seeing the passion and beauty of Billy's creative endeavors his family's working-class prejudices gradually subside. His family rallies to support Billy in his attempt to audition for the Royal Ballet Academy, and even a scab laborer who crossed the NUM picket line offers financial support. As the play concludes, Billy's previously recalcitrant father takes him to London for his audition and rejoices in his son's acceptance to the Academy. Mrs. Wilkinson's off-handed remark has come full circle as many lives are transformed by Billy's gift as well as his determination to follow his heart's desire.

Historically, art and music have been viewed as being either uplifting and transcendent, or conversely subversive and deleterious. To be sure, the production of art has consequences simply because it generates a response or reaction by those who come in contact with it. Because of this, there have been numerous attempts to control art and artists going back to antiquity. Whether that control manifests in outright censorship or political correctness, the attempts have been real (re: Nazis, Marxists, Maoists, the Taliban, the Catholic Church, multiculturalists.) Forbearance, as a mode of self-censorship and discipline, ought to be more prudent and noble ways to deal with the consequences of producing art that might be considered provocative or unsettling.

At the outset of the twenty-first century it is undeniable that a good deal of popular culture and the values it engenders has had a significant and in many ways troubling effect on our social reality. In light of the current climate of Western popular culture, "art music" has become increasingly marginalized. Regrettably, the word "art" has been greatly trivialized as the lines between trend and tradition, the profound and the superficial, truth and cliché, have become decidedly indistinct. To this unfortunate situation it must be noted that *though all art may be a form of self-expression, not all self-expression is art.* In the post-World War II era, the quasi-tyrannical and derisive attitudes of modern composers in the academy (and their advocates), reflected a decidedly non-pluralistic condition in which composers who attempted to adhere to more conventional modes of writing were often characterized as being obtuse and/or closed-minded to the idea of change—de facto "reactionaries." In actuality, it was the modernists, whose determinist mindset about what had value in the compositional landscape, who, through their detached arrogance, became the voices of intolerance (e.g., Ligeti's assertions in Chapter 10). This mindset has contributed to the widening of the "cultural gap" between the artist and the public.

In his book on classic literature, *Love and Friendship*, Allan Bloom, argues that having true intellectual openness

> ...consists in trying to understand the writers [or composers] as they understood themselves, which is possible if one is not arrogant about one's own understanding of things. One begins by picking up a story and reading it with the same wonder that one had as a child. The combination of innocent experience and cultivated intelligence is what we seek.[3]

The innocence that Bloom alludes to is often non-existent when experiencing art that is born out of the pessimism and despair of what was perhaps the most brutal and cruel century ever. This is to our collective loss. Contemporary society's increasingly contemptuous view of high art fosters cynicism and a misguided disdain for that which is born out of a spiritual or religious impulse. Genius and intellectual honesty get short-changed along the way. The tenets regarding art as espoused by the civilizations of antiquity—Plato's truth, beauty and goodness paradigm, for example—have been bludgeoned into submission by progressives who view the past as being nothing more than a history of exploitation and the cultural rape of "the other." The idea that tradition is "the corpse of wisdom" or "the enemy of progress" ignores the objective truth that certain traditions exist because they proved to be beneficial to society. Speaking to this mindset, American painter, Jack Beal opined: "The Platonic ideal of truth, beauty and goodness is not a bad set of ideals to live by. But where has that gone? For thousands of years, art was seen as a source of responsible moral and ethical leadership. Today taking that stance is almost seen as being comic."[4]

Multiculturalism, with its disingenuous penchant for deriding Western culture while calling for diversity and mutual respect for all cultures, is a manifestation of this dishonesty. Bloom reminds us that there was a time the European aristocracy aspired to high motives and supported art and artists to degrees that would make any American arts-advocacy organization green with envy. Music and art were seen as being fundamentally transcendent and educational, but modernism, it seems, cannot easily humble itself to that conviction. Even the morally challenged Richard Wagner acquainted himself "with a culture in which people did not merely do things, but lived up to things" by way of his study of medieval German literature.[5] The philosophical evisceration of the "truth, beauty and goodness" paradigm by both the multiculturalists and the post-structuralists has led us precisely to the point where our cultural patrimony has been lost in the abyss of radical egalitarianism and political correctness. Mix in corporate bottom-line concerns with the penchant of instant gratification, and you get a noxious stew of cynical superficiality.

In an article in the *Huffington Post*, Richard Dare (who at the time was the executive director of the Brooklyn Philharmonic), decried the ongoing decline of art and culture as a means to edify society. Yet this kind of lamentation has been going on for decades. Mr. Dare asserted that art, "should instead lead the way in a real community conversation about life. Culture needs to get real ... our future is too important to sit passively by while some of the most important experiences created by humanity fall into shambles."[6] I dare say that culture will "get real" only if the people creating it, producing it, supporting it and appreciating it "get real." The superficiality and commercialism that permeates our increasingly secular society only exacerbates the problem. The dismissal and/or rejection of the humanities as a source of knowledge and enlightenment concerning our cultural patrimony is not encouraging.

Commentators such as Allan Bloom, Camille Paglia, Kay Hymowitz, Dana Gioia, Roger Scruton and Victor Davis Hanson have been sounding the alarm about the dissolution of the humanities since the 1980s, but who's listening? Perhaps a more fundamental question is, "Who reads anymore?"

Our current video-driven culture has rendered reading and contemplation increasingly negligible. As American poet and writer, Larry Woiwode wrote in a 1992 essay, "Television: The Cyclops that Eats Books," that that particular contention is not an exaggeration.

> What is destroying America today is not the liberal breed of one-world politicians, or the IMF bankers, or the misguided educational elite, or the World Council of Churches; these are largely symptoms of a greater disorder. If there is any single institution to blame, it is, to use the cozy diminutive, "TV".
>
> TV is more than a medium; it has become a full-fledged institution, backed by billions of dollars each season. Its producers want us to sit in front of its glazed-over electronic screen, press our clutch of discernment through the floorboards, and sit in a spangled, zoned-out state ["couch potatoes," in current parlance] while we are instructed in the proper liberal tone and attitude by our present-day Plato and Aristotle—Dan Rather and Tom Brokaw.[7]

Mr. Rather and Mr. Brokaw have moved on but the deleterious effect of television on the intellectual condition of America (and the world) is difficult to refute. In his award-winning book, *The Dumbest Generation: How the Digital Age Stupefies Young Americans and Jeopardizes Our Future*, Emory University's Mark Bauerlein cites numerous studies regarding the pernicious effects of the digital age on education and study habits. Bauerlein cites the 2006 *High School Survey of Student Engagement*, which surveyed over eighty thousand students in schools from twenty-six states. The survey found that 90% of the student spent less than five hours per week reading and studying for their classes, while 31% admitted watching television or playing video games at least six hours per week, and 25% spent a minimum of six hours per week surfing the web or chatting online. Bauerlein points to the diminished emphasis on the arts and humanities in our schools as having considerable effects on the dumbing-down of young people. Because the arts are not a significant part of the American household, schools could be an alternative way for young people to gain exposure to great art, literature and music. But to our loss, this is becoming a thing of the past. Bauerlein writes:

> With voluntary (or parent-ordered) involvement in the fine arts so subdued among teens and young adults, for many of them the classroom is the only place they will ever encounter Michelangelo, Mozart, Grandma Moses and Thelonious Monk. Little in their homes and among their friends exposes them to artistic works that have stood the test of time and inspired their forbearers, and so, if they don't become attuned to the fine arts in school, they probably never will.[8]

Becoming "passive servants of the Cyclops" has created the "anti-enlightenment" condition that Theodor Adorno referred to in his *Essays on Mass Culture* (1944), whereby adult sensibilities are fettered in such a way that the "development of autonomous, independent individuals who judge and decide consciously for themselves,"[9] is impeded to such an extent that a truly democratic and pluralistic society cannot be easily sustained. The more we become passive members of society, the more we can be easily dominated or controlled by a particular power elite and thus be conditioned to desire and satiate "false needs." Commenting on the sphere of popular entertainment, Dominic Strinati observes:

> To ignore the nature of the culture industry, as Adorno defines it, is to succumb to its ideology. This ideology is corrupting and manipulative, and underpins the dominance of the market and commodity fetishism. It is equally conformist and mind-numbing, enforcing the general acceptance of the capitalist order. ... The culture industry deals in falsehoods, not truths, in false solutions, rather than real needs and real solutions. ... The masses in Adorno's eyes become completely powerless.[10]

Adorno was wrong about many things, but he wasn't wrong on the issues of control and the fettering of consciousness by the entertainment industry. It's not hard to imagine that the so-called "low information voters" that many have cited as being a bane to our republic, are the by-product of "TV culture." But like all good Marxists (neo or otherwise), Adorno viewed capitalism as the great evil to be vanquished. It's been suggested that Marx was a brilliant diagnostician, but a terrible clinician. Adorno suffers from the same outcome because the "real needs" and "real solutions" have more to do with spiritual, moral and ethical concerns than to purely economic ones. He misses the causal aspect completely. Prioritizing the wrong things, as St. Augustine averred, was what could bring any culture to its demise. Needless to say, our choices with regard to what we prioritize and what we love are elemental to establishing a more humane world.

We should remember that Adorno considered musical aesthetics of nineteenth-century Europe to be expressions of the "bourgeoisie" culture of "the old world." Moreover, he believed that it was desirable "to reduce the magic essence of music to human logic," as well as "the emancipation of the human being from the musical force of nature and the subjection of nature to human purposes."[11] Ironically, the prioritization of process and methodology over the romantic preoccupation with "the idea" in traditional art was what would eventually bring the progressive avant-garde to its demise. How so? The forces of nature are far too powerful and universal to be subjugated by human logic, and the wise among us intuit that. Rather than seek to subject those forces to human will, we should seek to understand them and harmonize with them.

As Jean-Philippe Rameau (known in France as "the Isaac Newton of music") posited in his treatise on harmony in 1722, the "magic" that tonal music invokes results from the harmonization of natural law (physics) and the theoretical logic of the tonal syntax. For Rameau harmony derived from nature was the primary source in "determining the essential character and coherence of musical expression."[12] Even Schoenberg admitted as early as 1923, just two years after he introduced his atonal 12-tone method of composing, that it was the "natural" properties that are intrinsic to the tonal idiom (polarity, tension, resolution, attraction, hierarchy, etc.) that gave tonality its strong sense of "cohesion" and its emotive power.

Manifestation of Goodness

In his immensely popular film *Playing For Change: Peace Through Music*, music producer Mark Johnson takes us on a journey from California to Africa, to Russia, to Europe, to Asia, to the Middle East demonstrating the power and effect of music to create conditions for positive change. Musicians representing various countries and cultures join in several remarkable, global jam sessions ingeniously captured on film and in song by Mr. Johnson and his production team. The film has generated a great deal of attention and has led to the establishment of *The Playing For Change Foundation* that Johnson and his co-producers are now using to bring the art of music to those who might not otherwise have the opportunity to learn and experience the joy of music-making. One of their principal endeavors is the creation of music schools in the developing world. This type of vision, and the initiatives it has spawned, deserves high praise for encouraging us to examine and appreciate the culture and art of "the other" and in so doing affirms the potent effects of music as a force for positive change. (If you have the opportunity to hear the *Playing for Change* band on one of their promotional tours, by all means do so. They are terrific!)

Playing for Change takes a page from the cultural initiative of Venezuelan economist Jose Antonio Abreu, the inspirational figure behind the creation of "*El Sistema*," the music education program that he created in 1975 to provide Venezuelan children the opportunity to live a better, more constructive life through the pursuit of music. Mr. Abreu's initiative, formally known as *Fundación del Estado para el Sistema de Orquestas Juveniles e Infantiles de Venezuela,* has resulted in a model of cultural education that has garnered international acclaim for its highly successful, and greatly needed, social service to the underprivileged youth of Venezuela—young people who might otherwise become victims of poverty, drug abuse and gang-related violence. To those who argue that children cannot or will not respond to high culture, *El Sistema* provides coruscating evidence to the contrary.

With the largesse of the Venezuelan government, there are now youth orchestras throughout the country that act as a training ground for thousands of young musicians to hone their craft and work their way into the professional orchestras that have been established in Venezuela in recent years.

Gustavo Dudamel, the firebrand music director of the nation's premier youth orchestra, The Simon Bolivar Youth Orchestra, and protégé of *El Sistema*, has achieved international attention and has been appointed as the music director of the Los Angeles Philharmonic. The *El Sistema* model is now being duplicated in other South American countries, Asia, and in the United Kingdom. Having heard the young Venezuelans in concert in New York in 2015, it is easy to see why they draw such high praise. To see and hear the young Venezuelans perform Beethoven, Tchaikovsky and Bernstein with such infectious panache can cause serious horripilation.

The *El Sistema* project does have its critics, however. Geoffrey Baker's book, *El Sistema: Orchestrating Venezuela's Youth* (2014), takes a swipe at Abreu, Dudamel and the *El Sistema* franchise for the hyperbolic tone of its public relations posture. Like any large-scale operation, there will be tales of disappointment and disillusion. Some have questioned the expense of maintaining such an ambitious project when the overall economic condition of Venezuela remains bleak. However, as Mark Swed, writing in Los Angeles Times observes, "Abreu is clearly no saint. But accusing him of promoting empty spectacle is gross oversimplification. ... *Sistema's* achievement of excellence gives the country one thing it desperately needs at the moment: something to feel good about. That excellence, after all, is what drew Baker to Venezuela in the first place."[13]

While living in New York City I have numerous opportunities to collaborate with gifted artists who are mentoring inner-city children in the arts. The fine work of the directors and teachers at the Harlem School for the Arts (HSA) has provided talented youth with the necessary resources to pursue musical studies in a setting that is as supportive as it is impassioned. My partnership with Kelvin Mack and other teachers at the Harlem School of the Arts and the New York City Symphony at our Apollo Theater benefit concert in 2006 aptly demonstrated an innocence and wide-eyed enthusiasm that is often present when working with young artists, regardless of their social circumstances or cultural circumstances.

Choreographer and producer, Marcus Knight, who has worked with luminaries such as Prince, Janet Jackson, and Paula Abdul, has established a non-profit arts development entity to mentor young performers with the intent of guiding them toward a socially responsible lifestyle. Through his organization, Global Entertainment Rhythms (GER) he has trained young dancers and musicians including several who appeared in the Sony Pictures's Screen Gems film, *Stomp the Yard*. Marcus's passion and conviction in mentoring young people is infectious. One of his protégés is a gifted, teenage, female singer from Haiti, Sheimyrah Mighty, who in the aftermath of the devastating earthquake in her nation, desired to use her abilities to help raise funds for those who were affected by the disaster through her *Hope for Haiti* initiative.

In his experiences with young, talented kids, Marcus sees too many adults willing to cash in on the talents of youngsters for personal gain. Producers often line up "with dollar signs in their eyes and greed in their hearts" to unabashedly pitch the dream-life of celebrity and fame, completely obtuse to the well-being and innocence of the children they seek to exploit. This scenario has resulted in far too many unfortunate and sometimes tragic accounts of young people being sold up the river for the almighty dollar. Regarding this untoward mindset, Marcus succinctly observes, "The idea that kids are just commodities is just wrong. How many kids are we going to lose to this stupidity?" How many, indeed?

Manhattan Institute Fellow and author Kay Hymowitz points out in her arresting book *Ready Or Not: Why Treating Children as Small Adults Endangers Their Futures, and Ours* that there is a pernicious attitude among many contemporary educators and child psychologists that young children think and act in the same way as adults and should be treated as "autonomous actors" who can make moral and ethical distinctions without adult supervision or guidance. The spuriousness of this assertion seems self-evident. Yet, the over-emphasis on "being cool" and acquiescing to commercial-driven peer pressure is inescapable. Hymowitz writes:

> The teening of those we used to call preadolescents shows up in almost everything kids wear and do. In 1989 the Girl Scouts of America commissioned a new MTV-style ad with rap music in order to, in the words of the organization's media specialist, "get away from the uniformed, goody-goody image and show that Girl Scouts are a fun, mature, cool place to be." … The seduction of children with dreams of teen sophistication and tough independence, which began with Barbie and intensified markedly in the last decade, appears to have had the desired effect: it has undermined childhood by turning children into teen consumers.[14]

Hymowitz contends that one of the troubling outcomes of this mindset is that our society, with its penchant for instant gratification and materialism, has become less effective in producing mature and responsible people who are willing to be accountable for their behavior. It's obvious that we're being called upon to recognize that children need nurturing from those who know better, otherwise, we unwittingly create a culture where immaturity breeds more immaturity and our society will continue to fall prey to the proclivities that we seek to ameliorate. In this scenario arrested development becomes commonplace. A key to making our planet a better place for our children is to make better children for our planet. Inculcating children with adult sensibilities too early in their lives can be counterproductive in achieving that particular goal. Inspiring examples like *Playing for Change*, the *El Sistema* and Global Entertainment Rhythms point to the importance of music as a sociological factor in contributing to the betterment of the human condition.

In his novel *War and Peace*, Leo Tolstoy posits: "To study the laws of history we must completely change the subject of our observation, must leave aside kings, ministers and generals, and study the common infinitesimally small elements by which the masses are moved."[15] In a climate where any advocacy of utopian ideals is seen as being highly suspect, even invidious, I believe it is important to celebrate folks like the administration and faculty at the Harlem School of the Arts, Mark Johnson, Kelvin Mack and Marcus Knight for their visionary entrepreneurship, for they are among the "small elements" who are making and impact on the masses. It would be very gratifying to see national and local governments (ministers and kings) follow the lead of Abreu, Mack and others and support arts initiatives to greater degrees.

Any art form that can move us towards altruism and unselfishness should be viewed as inherently beneficial. If saving our children from the ravages of the cruel world in which we live, and in turn protect their innocence as the valuable attribute that it is, it would seem that greater support for arts education and cultural endeavors would be a favorable proposition—one that might assist the Billy Elliots of the world to realize their potential as great artists and altruistic citizens. Developing better children for our planet will ensure that our planet will be well taken care of in the future. Music education ought to be considered germane to that process.

Postscript

In a *Washington Post* opinion piece published on May 27, 2021, Geoff Baker and William Cheng report disturbing revelation of sexual abuse within the *El Sistema* sphere. According to their report, a former musician in the program, Angie Cantero, posted a Facebook message alleging that *El Sistema* has been "plagued by pedophiles, pederasts, and an untold number of people who have committed the crime of statutory rape." Cantero alleged that there are many "disgusting people" who used their power and influence to deceive young girls and proposition them for sexual favors. Others confirmed the practice of systematic grooming for sexual favors.[16]

This scenario points yet again, to the need for a universal moral code to be identified and adhered to in all human endeavors. The idea that our better angels will always rule the day has no historical precedent. Laws are meant to mitigate bad behavior, but people still violate laws and engage in various forms behavior that result tyranny and immoral conduct. As I have argued throughout this book, there is a need to find God-centered solutions in our quest for socio-cultural betterment. Governance, education, journalism, commerce, the arts and sciences ought to be guided by the idea God needs to be in the equation if we are to become the best we can be.

Recommended Recordings

Beethoven: Symphony No. 5, Gustavo Dudamel, Simon Bolivar Youth Orchestra

Mendelssohn: Concerto for Violin, Itzhak Perlman, violin, Daniel Barenboim

Mahler: Symphony No. 1, Gustavo Dudamel, Los Angeles Philharmonic (DVD)

Playing For Change: *Songs Around the World*, CD & DVD

Elton John: *Billy Elliot*, Original Cast Album

Thelonius Monk: *Monk's Dream*, Thelonius Monk Quartet

Mozart: *Coronation Mass*, K. 317, Peter Schreier, Leipzig Radio Chorus, Dresden Staatskapelle

Endnotes

1   Ralph Waldo Emerson, *Journals of Ralph Waldo Emerson* (Boston and New York: Houghton Mifflin Company, 1914), p. 42.

2   Leo Tolstoy, *The Kreutzer Sonata* (West Valley City, UT: Waking Lion Press, 2006), p. 70.

3   Allan Bloom: *Love and Friendship* (New York: Simon and Schuster, 1993), p. 32.

4   Jack Beal, *Artist to Artist: Inspiration and Advice from Visual Artists Past and Present*, compiled by Clint Brown, (Corvallis, OR: Jackson Creek Press, 1998).

5   Roger Scruton, *Understanding Music: Philosophy and Interpretation* (New York and London: Continuum, 2009), p. 125.

6   Richard Dare, "The Scandalous Failure of Art and Music," *Huffington Post,* August 8, 2012.

7   Larry Woiwode, "Television: The Cyclops that Eats Books," *Imprimis,* February 1992, http://www.roca.org/OA/119/119k.htm.

8   Mark Bauerlein, *The Dumbest Generation: How the Digital Age Stupefies Young Americans and Jeopardizes Our Future (Or, Don't Trust Anyone Under 30)* (New York: Penguin Group, 2008), p. 5.

9   Theodor Adorno, *The Culture Industry: Essays on Mass Culture* (London and New York: Routledge Classics, 2001), p. 106.

10 Dominic Strinati, *An Introduction to Theories of Popular Culture* (London and New York: Routledge, 1995), pp. 58-59.

11 Theodor Adorno, *Philosophy of Modern Music* (New York and London: Continuum International Publishing Group, Inc., 2003), p. 65.

12 Lawrence M. Zbikowski, *Conceptualizing Music: Cognitive Structure, Theory, and Analysis* (Oxford: Oxford University Press, Inc., 2002), p. 132.

13 Mark Swed, "El Sistema founder, Gustavo Dudamel are Targets of a Scathing New Book," *Los Angeles Times,* December 6, 2014.

14 Kay S. Hymowitz, *Ready or Not: Why Treating Children as Small Adults Endangers Their Future—and Ours* (San Francisco: Encounter Books, 2000), pp. 125-126.

15 Leo Tolstoy, *War and Peace,* translated by Aylmer and Louise Maude (New York: W. W. Norton, 1966), pp. 919-920.

16 Geoff Baker and William Cheng, "The 'Open Secret' of Sexual Abuse in Venezuela's Famous Youth Orchestra Program is Finally Exposed," *Washington Post,* May 27, 2021.

26

The Wagner Conundrum

The crisis of the modern age is principally one of faith, as it is premised upon Nietzsche's declaration of the 'death' of God. With God's 'death,' there was no transcendent left to make perceptible. ... Also, the loss of the transcendent eliminated beauty as the object and goal of art.[1]
Robert R. Reilly

The most abstract idea conceivable is the spirit of sensuality. But in what medium can it be represented? Only in music. It cannot be represented in sculpture, for in itself it is a kind of quality of inwardness. It cannot be painted, for it cannot be grasped in fixed contours; it is an energy, a storm, impatience, passion, and so on, in all their lyrical quality, existing not in a single moment but in a succession of moments, for if it existed in a single moment it could be portrayed or painted.
Søren Kierkegaard

My first encounter with the music of Richard Wagner was by way of the fine recording of his *Rienzi Overture* by George Szell and the Cleveland Orchestra while a budding music student in high school. The noble and majestic theme of Rienzi's prayer moved me to tears. The brilliant brass fanfares that punctuate the score thrilled me to my core (and still do.) I thought that this was great music and I eagerly sought to know more about the composer's work. This led me to other Wagner recordings; the instrumental music of the Ring cycle, the overtures and preludes, the *Liebestod* from *Tristan und Isolde*. Before long I was purchasing recordings of these compositions by other great orchestras and conductors and getting my hands on the scores to study their music in greater detail.

At the time I knew little about Wagner the person and his proclivities, and how as an individual he was reprehensible on many levels. I knew nothing of his relationship with Friedrich Nietzsche, his anti-Semitic screeds, his adulterous and megalomaniac behavior, the influences of Feuerbach and Schopenhauer on his art, or how Adolph Hitler viewed his music in the context of Aryan supremacy. In fact, I understood little about the personal lives of the composers whose music I enjoyed. Like many other students in the nascent stages of their musical discoveries, I was oblivious to the biographical aspects of the composers whose music moved me.

Conflating the artist's life with their art personal lives and worldviews wasn't a concern for me at the time. It mattered little to me that Beethoven could be an anti-social lout, or that Schumann went insane, or that Richard Strauss and Carl Orff had Nazi associations, or that Paul Hindemith was considered a "cultural Bolshevik" by the arbiters of culture in the Third Reich, or that many of my pop music idols had severe addictions and were social miscreants. Their music was all that mattered. It was only when in college, as I began to study music history and the lives of these artists did I begin to see the larger picture. I could then understand the reasons why Jews might not be enamored with the Israel Philharmonic performing the *Rienzi Overture*, or why Jascha Heifetz playing the music of Richard Strauss in Israel might cause serious consternation.

In his early years, Wagner was influenced by the atheistic leftist philosophies of Hegelian philosopher, Ludwig Feuerbach. Feuerbach's critique of Christianity would have profound effects on Wagner and Nietzsche, who together would become among the more notable assailants of the Christian ethos of "the old world." Later in his life, Wagner was introduced to the writings of Arthur Schopenhauer and this had a profound effect on his life and work. According to Schopenhauer, music possessed far greater emotional power than other art forms due to its metaphysical properties. Paintings and sculpture, for example, are representational arts forms, whereas music offers a direct phenomenological experience with the primal, metaphysical reality, which Schopenhauer called "the will." Joyful music isn't a representation of joy. Joyful music is joyful—the thing in itself. Schopenhauer's philosophies regarding music and sexuality ("copulation ... as the true essence and core of all things, the aim and purpose of all existence." e.g.) would play heavily into Wagner's view of life and his creative endeavors.[2]

All of this begs several questions: What effect does a person's morality play on one's creative endeavors? Does enjoying Wagner's music mean one is giving tacit credence to his questionable worldviews, or that one is either anti-Semitic, or anti-Christian, or adulterous? Theologian, Dr. Young Oon Kim, posits that art possesses a "transmoral" dimension, and as such, the aesthetic qualities of a Ming dynasty vase or a Wagner opera stand apart from the morality of the artists who did the creating. As Dr. Kim posits:

> It is in the transmoral dimension of aesthetic experience that beauty approaches God. All the laws from and within God—give and take, polarity, harmony—connect beauty from all cultures. And to the extent that they clearly amplify and substantiate God's nature they evoke a response of love and appreciation from man. Since God represents absolute love and freedom, beauty is never confined.[3]

In Dr. Kim's view, imagination, combined with considerable talent, technique and discerning taste are the fundamental elements that determine the aesthetic qualities of a particular artwork regardless of an artist's moral, ethical and political inclinations. In this respect, it is not easy to overlook the deep humanity of Wagner's music, regardless of what we may feel about his moral proclivities, his life choices, his politics, or Hitler.

A central theme in the libretti of several of his operas is the redemptive power of love. This narrative is present in most of his mature works. The paradox of the man, his music, his narratives and the extra-musical associations continues to create many cognitive dissonances more than a century after his death, perhaps none as disquieting as the idea of a highly gifted artist who expounded on the power of love in such brilliant musical fashion, being a vile and reprehensible person, a person for whom many people (Jewish or not) found to be unlovable.

Some have argued that there is something within Wagner's music and mythic libretti that foster racial superiority and bigotry, especially of an anti-Semitic bent. Theodor Adorno attempted "in his tortured and tortuous way" to identify Wagner corruptions in the actual musical materials that Wagner employed. Roger Scruton points out there have been numerous unscrupulous attempts to denigrate Wagner's art based on his political and racial beliefs, including Barry Millington's suggestion that because the composer's anti-Jewish thought is "somewhere near the top of Wagner's musical and intellectual agenda," these unsavory connotations "should be constantly borne in mind as we study his works."[4] But Scruton is keen on the idea that Wagner's discovery and celebration of myth was "not merely a matter of one person's moral and artistic credo," but something much more significant on a purely artistic basis. As Scruton notes:

> It is also one of the greatest intellectual advances of modern times, the ancestor and inspiration of comparative anthropology, symbolist poetry, psychoanalysis and many aesthetic and theological doctrines that are now common currency. ... He transformed ancient myth into quintessentially modern art.[5]

The temptation to derogate an artwork because of the moral failings of its creator puts us in the position to censure any artwork composed since the fall of Adam and Eve. Speaking to the issue of Wagner's "fallen" condition, composer Matthew Guerrieri proffers that profound ideas, "don't automatically lose their validity just because unscrupulous people try and assimilate them into their own distasteful worldviews—and it's an awfully tenuous assumption that, by listening to a composer's music, we automatically perceive and accept that composer's philosophy."[6] Many of us have listened to and performed Wagner for years without succumbing to the malevolence of rabid anti-Semitism, fascism, racism or adultery. Think of the Jewish conductors who have delivered convincing performances of Wagner's music; Gustav Mahler, Georg Solti and Daniel Barenboim. Jewish conductor Hermann Levi who knew Wagner personally and frequently conducted the composer's music, said, "Wagner is the best and noblest of men. ... I thank God daily for the privilege to be close to such a man. It is the most beautiful experience of my life."[7] Go figure.

Having traveled to Israel on many occasions I now possess a deeper understanding of the underlying sensitivities about Wagner among many in the Jewish community. Yet, that has not diminished my appreciation for his music on purely musical grounds.

In his book, *Wagner: The Terrible Man and His Truthful Art*, Catholic priest, M. Owen Lee offers several important insights into the Wagner paradox. Speaking to the issue of religious associations accorded to music, he offers a decidedly theocentric perspective on the issue of art's metaphysical veracity.

> God speaks to us through works of art. What is it that we have a right to expect great art to say to us, to do to us? To delight us, of course, but also to open our awareness of the things that matter, to enable us to accept darkness and pain, to tell us what we might not have wanted to know but needed to know, to make us into something more than we were before, more human, more compassionate. And most of all I think, to enable us to see into ourselves.[8]

For Father Lee and many others who profess a strong religious conviction, the idea of redemptive love has powerful and deeply spiritual connotations. The Judeo-Christian tradition sees God as a loving parent, the epitome of unconditional love and compassion. Without compassion, forgiveness would be impossible. Nietzsche, an early admirer of Wagner, turned against the composer and came to view Wagner's obsession with the idea of redemptive love in a derisive way. In his 1888 essay, "The Case Against Wagner," Nietzsche writes:

> The problem of redemption is certainly a venerable problem. There is nothing about which Wagner has thought more deeply than redemption: his opera is the opera of redemption. Somebody or other always wants to be redeemed in his work: sometimes a little female—this is his problem. ... I was capable of taking Wagner seriously. ... Ah, this old magician, how much he imposed upon us![9]

Nietzsche's early admiration of Wagner was due in large part to the composer's contumacious attitudes regarding Christian virtues, especially as they pertained to sexuality. For Nietzsche, the Christian ethics of self-denial and sacrifice were exercises of negation and morbidity, whereas his concept of "master morality" (saying "yes" to oneself) was life-affirming, ascending, beautifying, transfiguring and rational. Nietzsche's abnegation of Christianity wasn't merely aimed at Christian hypocrisy, but Christianity *itself* due to its preoccupation with Paulian attitudes about sin and guilt. He believed that Christian values were detached from the real world and part of a "fictitious" reality, quite apart of the world of reason and scientific fact. By critiquing Christianity's epistemological roots he was striking at the heart of the Christian faith.

Alex Ross notes that after the Revolution of 1848 in which Wagner was involved, German idealism became the basis of "a new intellectual faith" that prioritized the individual and one's thinking for oneself rather than relying on any supernatural influences or religious-based moral guidelines. The Young Hegelians of the era "took aim at religious pieties" in their Marxist views. Wagner "especially prized Feuerbach's notion of the philosophy of the future," and the revolutionary idea of liberating individuals from the chains of traditional authority, especially religious authority.[10] Feuerbach was of the opinion that Christian dogma placed "placed virtue in a heavenly sphere and therefore find no virtue in themselves."[11] Nietzsche's early admiration of Wagner eventually diminished due to the composer's infatuation with Christianity later in the composer's life.

Some have argued that Wagner's increased use of chromaticism in his later works (with its departure from accepted theoretical rules of functional harmony), was a musical revolution against the "common practice" of tonality; a theoretical system predicated upon strict adherence to syntactic rules and customary musical grammar. Certain Wagner critics view this musical development as Wagner's spiritual alignment with Nietzsche's revulsion of Christian values vis-à-vis sexuality and family, and that chromaticism was a very effective musical device in evoking sensuality. Moreover, this was concomitant with Nietzsche's intellectual attack on a stable sexual morality and his advocacy of sexual liberation.

Though Nietzsche had become an apostate to the Wagnerian ethos long before the composer's final opera, *Parsifal* (with its overt Christian narrative), he nonetheless found Wagner's score beguiling in the extreme. In a letter from

1877 to his friend, composer Johann Heinrich Koselitz, Nietzsche's impressions of the *Parsifal* prelude were highly laudable.

> Speaking from a purely aesthetic point of view, has Wagner ever written anything better? The supreme psychological perception and precision as regards to what can be said, expressed, communicated, here, the extreme of concision and directness of form, every nuance of feeling conveyed epigrammatically; a clarity of musical description that reminds us of a shield of consummate workmanship; and finally an extraordinary sublimity of feeling, something experienced in the very depths of music, that does Wagner the highest honor; a synthesis of conditions which to many people, even "higher minds," will seem incompatible, of strict coherence, of "loftiness" in the most startling sense of the word, of a cognizance and a penetration of vision that cuts through the soul as with a knife, of sympathy with what is seen and shown forth. We get something comparable to it in Dante, but nowhere else. Has any painter ever depicted so sorrowful a look of love as Wagner does in the final accents of his Prelude?[12]

Nietzsche's effusive praise of the *Parsifal* prelude echoes the observations of Søren Kierkegaard who posited that music is akin to "an energy … existing not in a single moment but in a succession of moments" in which "the spirit of sensuality" can be realized and then transmitted to the listener in a supremely efficacious way.[13]

Despite his admiration of the music, Nietzsche repudiated Wagner's dalliance with a Christian narrative. "*Parsifal*," he would say," is a work of perfidy, of vindictiveness, of a secret attempt to poison the presuppositions of life—a bad work. The preaching of chastity remains an incitement to anti-nature: I despise everyone who does not experience *Parsifal* as an attempted assassination of basic ethics."[14] The paradox for Nietzsche is not unlike that of many of us who may love the music, but loathe the musician, albeit for different reasons. If one is oblivious to the extra-musical associations that play into so much of the Wagnerian reality, one finds music of immense emotional power, sublime compositional skill and the effulgent "loftiness" that Nietzsche alluded to. Rienzi's prayer, the Pilgrim chorus in *Tannhauser*, the *Parsifal* Prelude, the final act of *Gotterdammerung*, this is indeed lofty music—music that approaches the aesthetic condition that Dr. Kim considers to be "godly."

Father Lee believes that Wagner, like many great artists, possessed the gift of being able to understand the human condition despite his own human failings: "Let me suggest that the god of music—call him Apollo, if you will—gave Wagner. a wonderful, powerful gift, and then visited on him characteristics many have thought loathsome, so that he hated and was hated."[15] These characteristics, according to Lee, had the effect of allowing Wagner to obtain profound understandings regarding human weakness and corruption, good and evil ("the conflicting forces within the human psyche"), thus allowing him to identify and come to terms with these forces, and in the process convey the importance of redemptive love in his libretti and the transcendent music that accompanies it.

Allan Bloom would seem to agree with Lee's assessment, but he views it from the perspective of the poet. Bloom writes:

> Above all, [the poet is] a skilled observer of human beings without any necessary prior commitment to theory. Everything, of course, depends on how good his eyes are. ... [Poets] take seriously what they see and are, in a profound sense, phenomenologists. If love is indeed the highest expression of the soul, the recognized link between love and the poetic muse further fortifies their claim. And so does the fact that love is primarily love of the beautiful, for although it is perhaps difficult to remember today, art more than any other human endeavor was dedicated to the beautiful. The artist depicting the soul of lovers is also experiencing the genius of the artist himself. He must observe what goes on in his own soul as he creates the souls of the lovers.[16]

Leonard Bernstein reminds us that to the extent that music is a language it is a metaphorical language and as such is suggestive rather than literal. Any portrayal of love in musical terms requires the use of apposite musical materials to make the poetic image or "suggestion" convincing. If love is a condition in which the harmonization of souls, minds and hearts is manifest as an expression of beauty in the internal or spiritual sense, then employing pitch sets, chords and rhythms that resemble or reflect a harmonized reality become a fundamental necessity. Wagner's use of the requisite musical materials to realize an expression or "suggestion" of love in an aesthetically pleasing fashion, results in his music fulfilling both internal/subjective and external/

objective purposes. Wagner was able to accomplish this to a great extent due, in all likelihood, to what Bloom might ascribe to the composer's phenomenological instincts—his personal failings notwithstanding.

Art as a Facilitator of "Godliness"

Wagner's music exhibits great aesthetic beauty due to his wonderfully poetic use of musical materials. Even in the more chromatic passages of his compositions, his music is deeply affecting as a result of its embodiment of certain "godly" attributes and principles that suggest and/or convey the feelings or emotions associated with the poetic narrative of love and its redeeming aspects. Like Mozart (especially in his G-minor Symphony), Wagner's use of chromaticism remains rooted in diatonic modality, resulting in music that is alluring, even beguiling. Sensuality, in and of itself, may not be out of the sphere of "godliness." (Think of the alluring sensuality of a beautiful sunset or majestic mountains.)

The diminishment of the spiritual function of art music in the latter half of the twentieth century has been due in large part to the dissolution of religious faith and practice. This can be traced to the aforementioned German idealism that detached intellect from any religious connotations. Citing Nietzsche's "God is Dead" supposition, cultural commentator, Robert R. Reilly views this correlation as being central to the crisis of life—and art—in modernity.

> The crisis of the modern age is principally one of faith, as it is premised upon Nietzsche's declaration of the "death" of God. With God's "death", there was no transcendent left to make perceptible. This loss of purpose is the source of exhaustion in modern music, not some supposed depletion of tonal resources. Also, the loss of the transcendent eliminated beauty as the object and goal of art. The ugliness of twentieth century art is a reflection of a spiritual problem, not of a horror that has surpassed, for instance, the Black Death. Composers did not write atonal, cacophonous music after the plague wiped out nearly half of Europe, because they did not lose their faith. It was only in the twentieth century that a composer like Schoenberg could declare himself "cured of the delusion that the Artist's aim is to create beauty."[17]

This lack of faith gave rise to a plethora of justifications for the atonal compositional rationales of the post-World War II era and has resulted in a climate where the pursuit of aesthetic beauty has been lost in the abyss of secular reason and theoretical intellection.

Because religion and mythology played heavily into the romantic ethos, even the "progressive" Wagner did not entirely reject the importance of mythology as it pertained to establishing the basis of a humane cultural reality. Scruton observes that is was through Wagner's study of medieval German literature that he acquainted himself "with a culture in which people did not merely do things, but lived up to things," a culture that possessed "a distinct category of human thought, as open to us ... in a world of scientific skepticism, as it was open to the inhabitants of ancient Greece or Iceland." Scruton suggests that "myth dawned on Wagner as a form of social hope," and that it was "a way of thinking that could restore modern man the lost sense of the ideal, without which human life is hopeless."[18]

In his observation of the music of French twentieth century composer, Olivier Messiaen, Alex Ross avers, "The Lord could manifest Himself in consonance and dissonance alike, though consonance was His true realm."[19] This view does not seem at all in concordance with the laws of nature, nor does it give much credence to the idea that in tonal music polarity is ontologically intrinsic to its syntax. The "nature of Nature" has a great deal to do with attraction and achieving balance and harmony between polar opposites as the way to attain and sustain productive energy in the pursuit of progress and development. Religious and philosophical viewpoints dating back to ancient China posited that nature reflects God's image in substance. It is the interaction between correlative aspects of male and female (or consonance and dissonance in music) that results in making God's deity evident (Romans 1:20). Moreover, the creative/sexual act is the union of two equally important aspects, where if one aspect were missing, procreation could not occur. In tonal music, dissonance plays a significant role. It is intrinsic to the tonal syntax since dissonant intervals exist in the acoustic spectrum of the overtone series—the sonic etymology of all music. In a very real sense, it is the amalgamation of consonance and dissonance that gives tonal music its profound emotive poignancy, as well as its aesthetic soulfulness.

Arnold Schoenberg acknowledged that "relatedness" and the subsequent "binding together" of polar "opposites" was intrinsic to the natural "ebb and flow" of key-centered, tonal music, and it was these very properties that gave the tonal syntax its "tonal cohesion" and emotional impact.[20] He admitted that atonal music, in which the polarity paradigm was either conspicuously absent or not perceptible to the listener, would be deficient in its ability to evoke or convey emotion in a meaningful way. Moreover, he believed that the handling of atonal materials with the intent of producing an emotional satisfaction would be the essential trial for any composer working in atonal idioms. Schoenberg nonetheless considered assigning any universal or cosmic law to a particular musical theory to be "superfluous." Consequently, he could not make the leap of faith that the "secrets of the cosmos" could be ascertained or comprehended by anything other than "the human brain available to me."[21] Intellection became the basis of Schoenberg's compositional rationale.

From this perspective, it would seem that any compositional theory or system that is not predicated on having a spiritual or cosmic aspect to its causal dimension would not be wholly effective in its ability to express, convey, or evoke spirituality or manifest the aesthetics that we acknowledge was being beautiful. If, as Schoenberg suggested, beauty is no longer the desired goal for musical composition, then perhaps atonality can eventually find its justification. However, our intuition tells us that seeking beauty in our lives is both necessary and desired. It is part of the human instinct. To be attracted to beauty is natural. Denis Dutton, professor of philosophy at New Zealand's University of Canterbury, contends that great works "seldom make overt assertions of fact or instruct people on how they must behave," however they "possess a relentless capacity to arrest attention and excite the mind, generation after generation. Their nobility and grandeur also flow from their ability to address deep human instincts."[22] Dutton supports the contention that the aesthetic beauty manifested via music is the result of how music materials are utilized.

> Works of music are not beautiful because they arouse emotions in us as a drug might; they are beautiful because of how emotions are created by the total structure of the music itself. … The emotional tone of art reaches deeply into the mind, not by manipulating general moods or kinds of feelings, but by creating the highly individual work of art from which unique feelings emerge.[23]

Dutton's observation comports with Schopenhauer's metaphysical belief that music "is as *immediate* an objectification and copy of the whole *will* as the world itself is, indeed as the Ideas are."[24]

It is an immutable fact that our instinct to seek beauty is a fundamental aspect of our humanity, individually and collectively. It becomes apparent that beauty is achieved when the process of how art is created (the objective reality) is in balance or in accord with the purpose, motivation and intent (the subjective reality) of creating. When a composer is utilizing musical materials in such a way that embody the godly laws and principles that Dr. Kim cites, the beauty that is manifested stands apart from the character of the individual creator.

Wagner, Israel and Redemption

When, in 2001, conductor Daniel Barenboim* performed Wagner's music at an Israel Festival concert with the Berlin Staatskapelle Orchestra in Jerusalem, the uproar that followed, with the inevitable denunciations and condemnations, stoked the Wagner/Jewish debate yet again. There had existed an unofficial ban on performing Wagner's music by the Israel Philharmonic dating back to the *Kristallnacht* pogrom in 1938 and Barenboim's action elicited charges of arrogance and insensitivity.[†]

The scenario: At the end of the concert when he returned to the podium for what was to be a second encore, Barenboim asked the audience if they would like to hear music by Wagner. Addressing the audience, Barenboim cited the trepidation of the festival's organizers views about performing Wagner and acknowledged that this could be problematic for some. He then suggested that there might be many in the audience for whom listening to Wagner's music would not necessarily summon Nazi associations. After a 30-minute debate between Maestro Barenboim and members of the audience, a number of people walked out of the auditorium, some shouting "fascist" and "concentration camp music" as they left, but most of the audience remained and

---

* In 2008 Daniel Barenboim became the first person to hold both Palestinian and Israeli passports.

† The Palestine Symphony Orchestra was founded in 1936 by Bronislaw Huberman. The ensemble was comprised exclusively of Jewish musicians. Arturo Toscanini became the orchestra's first conductor. In 1948 the ensemble changed its name to the Israel Philharmonic.

gave Barenboim's performance of Wagner's prelude to *Tristan und Isolde* an enthusiastic ovation.

Not everyone was enthralled. Israel's prime minister, Ariel Sharon, commented after the concert: "I would rather it hadn't been played. There are a lot of people in Israel for whom this issue is very hard." Ehud Omert, the mayor of Jerusalem, opined that Barenboim's decision was "arrogant, uncultured and unacceptable." He added that Israel would likely review its relationship with Maestro Barenboim. "It's not his job to determine whether the state of Israel decides to allow Wagner to be heard or not. As a musician he is great, but as a human being I could say a few other things."[25]

One can surely empathize with those for whom Wagner's music evokes the legacy of Nazi perfidy, yet an open society provides for the engaging in pluralistic discourse. Barenboim's actions, in not an insignificant way, may have initiated the reclaiming of Wagner's music from the evil legacy that it has been somewhat spuriously linked. Those who walked out of the auditorium that night were fortunate to live in a free society where public dissent is not met with tyrannical retribution, and by making their choice to leave were exercising their democratic right as free citizens.

Barenboim is seen by some as a grandstanding provocateur possessing a naïve political outlook. Yet, in this particular instance, he was providing an opportunity to make a choice based on certain moral convictions. In so doing he was demonstrating the power of free individuals to do what they believe to be good in a most civil fashion, even when it may be unpopular to do so. This is hardly being fascist.

Redemptive love, be it the progeny of a religious conviction or not, may be that which can save us from ourselves. Wagner's music, free from the troubling, extra-musical appropriations that accompany it, reminds us of humankind's immense capacity for truth, beauty and goodness. These attributes would seem to be necessities in the pursuit of a truly liberated, and enlightened existence—an existence where love is celebrated in its highest expressions. Without freedom, love remains an impossibility. Freedom is necessary for human development, for without it, there is no truth, beauty or goodness, nor forgiveness and compassion born out love's redemptive power.

Forbearance in any relational circumstance requires all parties to make concessions to "the other." The result of Maestro Barenboim's actions in Israel was an affirmation of music's ability to heal and assuage even the most intractable differences. In this particular instance, Wagner's music contributed to a moment of transcendence and harmony among those who chose to remain at the concert. In that moment of communication, the greatness of art as the embodiment of beauty passes directly from artist to appreciator unmediated by other human concerns. Wagner's fallen proclivities were no longer a concern as art fulfilled its ultimate purpose on this occasion. As music journalist, Michael Walsh observes, in this era of political correctness and illiberal cancel culture activism, it is very easy "to trump up a series of latter-day charges against almost any dead individual, exhume his corpse, and, like a Cadaver Synod run by a grad-school Nuremberg court … cut off his head mount it on a pike, and chuck the body into a ditch."[26] This has been the case with Wagner for well over a century.

Noted author and former member of the English Parliament, Bryan Magee, recalls a story handed down from the family of Jewish writer, Rudolph Sabor about Wagner, his failings and his troubled legacy with the Jewish people. Sabor's uncle Abraham, who had actually loaned Wagner money, shared this bit of "transmoral" insight:

> I gave him a lot of money. He hardly said thank you. I told him I couldn't help being a Jew, and he called me Shylock. You see, my friends, the world is full of people who borrow and don't repay; who steal other men's wives, daughters and sweethearts. But only one of them wrote *Tristan und Isolde*. … I only hope my children will not listen to me when old age might make me bitter, but will listen to his music.[27]

This perspective might not sit well with those who posit that we must not assess an artwork from only an aesthetic viewpoint. If we commit to that rationale, then all art becomes susceptible to a kind of moral condemnation born of guilt by association. Since all music is a product of a flawed human reality in one way or another, are we going to stop listening altogether? I prefer Sabor's perspective, for obvious reasons.

Recommended Recordings

Wagner: Orchestral Music and Overtures, George Szell, Cleveland Orchestra

Wagner: *Der Ring Des Nibelungen*, James Levine, Metropolitan Opera

Wagner: *Parsifal*, Daniel Barenboim, Berlin Philharmonic

Hindemith: *Der Schwanedreher*, Daniel Benyamini, viola

Beethoven: *Egmont*, Op. 84, Otto Klemperer, Philharmonia Orchestra

Shostakovich: *Lady Macbeth of the Mtsensk District*, DVD, Mariss Jansons, conductor

Copland: *The Tender Land*, Kirk Trevor, Bohuslav Martinu Philharmonic Orchestra

Orff: *Catulli Carmina*, Franz Welser-Möst, Munich Radio Orchestra

Strauss: Violin Sonata, Op. 18, Jascha Heifetz, violin

Riegger: *Music for Orchestra*, Op. 50 Alfredo Antonini, Oslo Philharmonic

Adams: *Nixon in China*, DVD, Metropolitan Opera Orchestra and Chorus

Schoenberg: *Moses und Aron*, Daniel Gatti, Vienna State Opera (DVD)

Tchaikovsky: Symphony No. 5, Daniel Barenboim, West-Eastern Divan Orchestra

Mahler: Symphony No. 5, Gustavo Dudamel, Simon Bolivar Youth Orchestra

Chopin: Mazurkas for Piano, Robert Casadesus, piano

Hindemith: *Mathis der Maler*, Simone Young, Hamburg State Opera Orchestra and Chorus

Endnotes

1   Robert R. Reilly, "Reaching the Transcendent," *World & I Magazine* 5/1, January 1990. Online edition, article #17368.

2   Arthur Schopenhauer, *Manuscript Remains, Vol. III*, as cited by Bryan Magee, *The Tristan Chord: Wagner and Philosophy* (New York: Henry Holt and Company, 2000), p. 170.

3   Young Oon Kim, *Unification Theology and Christian Thought* (New York: Golden Gate Publishing, 1975), p. 181.

4   Roger Scruton, *Understanding Music: Philosophy and Interpretation* (London and New York: Continuum International Publishing Group, 2009), p. 120.

5   Ibid., p. 125.

6   Matthew Guerrieri, "The Censures of the Carping World, October 26, 2007, http://sohothedog.blogspot.com/2007/10/censures-of-carping-world.html.

7   Derek Strahan, "Was Wagner Jewish?" *Limelight*, February 2012, p. 59.

8   M. Owen Lee, *Wagner: The Terrible Man and His Truthful Art* (Toronto, Canada: University of Toronto Press, 1999), p. 91.

9   Friedrich Nietzsche, *The Writings of Nietzsche: The Case Against Wagner*, translated by Walter Kaufmann (New York: Random House, 1967), p. 616.

10 Alex Ross, *Wagnerism: Art and Politics in the Shadow of Music* (New York: Farrar, Straus and Giroux, 2020), p. 25.

11 Roger Scruton, *The Ring of Truth: The Wisdom of Wagner's Ring of Nibelung* (UK: Penguin, 2016).

12 Friedrich Nietzsche, *The Case Against Wagner*, as cited by Magee, *The Tristan Chord*, p. 320.

13 Søren Kierkegaard, *Either/Or: A Fragment of Life* (UK: Penguin, 2004), p. 27.

14 Lucy Beckett, *Richard Wagner: Parsifal*, Cambridge opera handbook (New York: Cambridge University Press, 1981), p. 115.

15 Lee, *Wagner: The Terrible Man*, p. 27.

16 Allan Bloom, *Love and Friendship* (New York: Simon and Schuster, 1993), p. 263.

17 Joseph Henry Auner, *A Schoenberg Reader: Documents of a Life* (Yale University Press, 2003), p. 93.

18 Scruton, *Understanding Music,* p. 125.

19 Alex Ross, *The Rest is Noise: Listening to the Twentieth Century* (New York: Farrar, Straus and Giroux, 2007), p. 447.

20 Arnold Schoenberg, *Style and Idea* (Los Angeles: University of California Press, 1984), p. 207.

21 Ibid., p. 212.

22 Denis Dutton, *The Art Instinct* (New York: Bloomsbury Press, 2009,) p. 10.

23 Ibid., p. 234.

24 Arthur Schopenhauer, *The World as Will and Representation, Vol. I* (New York: Dover Publications, 1969), p. 257.

25 Ewen MacAskill, "Barenboim Stirs Up Israeli Storm by Playing Wagner," *The Guardian*, July 9, 2001.

26 Michael Walsh, *The Devil's Pleasure Palace: The Cult of Critical Theory and the Subversion of the West* (New York and London: Encounter Books, 2015), p. 139.

27 Magee, *The Tristan Chord*, p. 357.

The Case for Tonality—Part 1

Despite the skillful ruses we have cultivated in our desperate effort
to make the world of the past serve our present-day needs,
we can no longer elude the essential trial: that
of becoming an absolute part of the present,
of forsaking all memory to forge a perception
without precedent, of renouncing the legacies of the past
to discover undreamed-of territories.[1]
Pierre Boulez

n 1986 I was asked to write reviews and commentary for *World & I* magazine after attending the New York concerts presented by the Paris-based Institut de Recherche et de Coordination Acoustique/Musique (IRCAM). Several essays that appear in this book are the progenies of that article. This essay, and the two that follow (including a slightly edited version of the original article, "A Case For Tonality in the Twentieth Century-Part II"), constitute a tripartite summation of the compositional landscape of late twentieth-century and early twenty-first century art music as seen from the perspective of hindsight. Historical hindsight provides us with clarity of perspective, however, as we age our vision can become blurred and the resulting fuzziness can have the effect of making things look different than they are. The polemics that have become so pervasive in our discussions regarding culture can be vexatious, but hopefully wisdom, conjoined with the refined intuitive sense that accrues with age, can be like a good pair of reading glasses that allows us to view the past with greater clarity and with a better understanding of where we stand culturally.

The IRCAM concerts in New York featured new works by composers from the institute as well as the celebrated composers of the Second Viennese School.* Pierre Boulez, who at the time was considered the leading exponent of modern music, was the artistic director of IRCAM and the music director of the outstanding Ensemble InterContemporain, the institute's resident orchestra.† Maestro Boulez conducted the concerts, one of which featured his "work in progress," *Repons*, a composition that features the interfacing of traditional instruments with computers and electronic media.

The IRCAM Tour-1986

At the time of the IRCAM concerts in New York in 1986, the atonal, serial compositions of the post-World War II era composers, with their attendant indeterminacy, complexity and intellectual constructs that had been championed by most mid-century modernists, was still very much in favor—especially within the academy. Change, however, was in the wind. The legion of Schoenberg/Varèse/Boulez acolytes, whose music was viewed as being devoid of an appealing aesthetic, had been firmly ensconced as the arbiters of style in the "new music" arena for decades. In addition, and perhaps more importantly, the voices of the academy who espoused the atonal rationales became rigidly dogmatic in promoting the ideological premises for composing according to the strictures of formulaic serial methodologies.

---

* The Second Viennese School refers to a group of early twentieth-century composers, most notably Arnold Schoenberg, Anton Webern and Alban Berg who pioneered the compositional syntax of atonality that was a radical departure—in both method and aesthetics—from the traditional compositional methods of the European "common practice."

† The quote at the beginning of this chapter appeared in the IRCAM United States tour program in 1986 (p. 10). The tour program in its entirety could be considered a manifesto for the IRCAM project.

In the mid-1980s the compositional landscape was evolving and the hegemony of atonal serialism was being challenged with the ascendancy of minimalist composers such as Terry Riley, Steve Reich, John Adams and Arvo Pärt, as well as the works of composers influenced by non-Western and non-European influences, including Tan Dun*, Osvaldo Golijov, Lou Harrison and Roberto Sierra. Neo-romanticism, with a renewed emphasis on "accessibility," also found earnest adherents for the music of Lowell Lieberman, George Rochberg, Ellen Taaffe Zwillich, Stephen Albert and Lee Hoiby. The emergence of these diverse styles of composing, styles that exhibit quasi-tonal properties, contributed to the increased desuetude of the formulaic and serial techniques that dominated much of the second half of the twentieth century. By the 1990s, formalism, as practiced by the purveyors of mid-century modernism, was seriously on the wane.

Though Arnold Schoenberg is credited with inventing and promulgating the atonal idiom of 12-tone music (he objected to the term "atonal," preferring the term, "pantonal"), and breaking away from the long-accepted practices of key-centered music, others had been experimenting with non-traditional approaches as well, most notably, Austrian composer/theorist, Josef Matthias Hauer and the American iconoclast, Charles Ives. Hauer was an extreme antipode to the romantic ethos of the late nineteenth century and as such detested any "extra-musical" underpinnings in music, believing that music should be composed according to impersonal formulas and laws. Hauer viewed Wagner's chromaticism and the modern Wagnerian orchestra as being hyper-sensual and believed that its "sweet swamp of sound" needed to be purged "of its noise and sensuality."[2] For Hauer, the individual notes in the 12-tone system "led a spiritual, higher life rather than a sensual one."[3] His early works, *Nomos*, Op. 1 and 2 (from the Greek, meaning *laws*) were based on the twelve semitones within the octave and represented, in his view, art that "liberated itself from the coarse imitations of nature." It was Hauer's contention that complete and absolute lawfulness was "the highest state of spirituality in music."[4]

This viewpoint became the underlying rationale by which many avant-garde composers carried out their work in the ensuing decades. The vestiges of

---

* I conducted the world premiere performances of Tan Dun's Third Symphony and his Violin Concerto at Lincoln Center on February 7, 1988 with the New York City Symphony and violin soloist, Vera Wei-ling Tsu.

romanticism were decidedly anachronistic to the modernists of Schoenberg's and Hauer's ilk and were to be eschewed at all costs. Though initially favorable to Hauer's 12-tone ideas, Schoenberg eventually became skeptical of Hauer's methodology (known as *Tropen*), saying that it was "mystically unproven."[5] Schoenberg considered his version of the twelve-tone method to be more "natural" than Hauer's and his new method eventually became the principal syntax that many avant-garde composers embraced with great alacrity. Both Hauer and Schoenberg became preoccupied with formalism rather than aesthetic or axiological concerns. Not all musicians were in accord with Schoenberg's ideas. Citing Schoenberg's methods in his Norton Lectures at Harvard, Leonard Bernstein asserted:

> The trouble is that the new musical "rules" of Schoenberg are not apparently based on innate awareness, on the intuition of tonal relationships. They are like rules of an artificial language, and therefore must be learned. This would seem to lead to what used to be called "form without content," or form at the expense of content—structuralism for its own sake.[6]

Though Schoenberg and his early disciples, most notably Anton Webern and Alban Berg, became staunch advocates of atonal/serial composition (the aforementioned Second Viennese School), other prominent composers of the early twentieth century did not embrace atonality with the same enthusiasm. Though decidedly more adventurous than their late nineteenth-century counterparts, prominent composers of the early twentieth century, including Igor Stravinsky, Paul Hindemith, Benjamin Britten, Sergei Prokofiev, Béla Bartók, Ralph Vaughan-Williams, Aaron Copland, Darius Milhaud, Samuel Barber, Leoš Janáček, Dmitri Shostakovich, Frank Martin, Gustav Holst, Claude Debussy, Maurice Ravel, Boris Blacher, Ottorino Respighi, Karol Szymanowski and William Walton, continued to demonstrate that tonal and quasi-tonal syntaxes remained viable means of musical expression. Moreover, Stravinsky, Hindemith, Mihaud, Shostakovich, Copland, Ravel and Blacher were influenced more by American jazz than by Schoenberg's atonal concepts in the era immediately after World War I. Stravinsky and Copland would eventually embrace serial methodology later in their careers, but up until World War II the tonal idiom held its own against the encroaching specter of Schoenbergian conventions. As Vit Roubíček, a recording producer for the

Czech Republic's *Supraphon* recording company aptly put it, the compositional landscape of the first half of the twentieth century was an "intricate web of styles and evolutionary trends." There was no single "triumphant" style or idiom. To state otherwise is revisionist history. The evolutionary trends of Stravinsky alone prove that to be the case.

It's been said that that if you tell a lie often enough people eventually believe it to be true. The two big lies that Schoenberg, Theodor Adorno and their acolytes propagated were that tonality was "exhausted" as a viable musical idiom, and that the emergence of atonal serialism was a historical inevitability—it had to happen. The music of the aforementioned composers (Prokofiev, Barber, et al.) demonstrates that these were spurious contentions. Adorno's frequent use of the term "bourgeoisie" in his evisceration of the tonal syntax, whether in art music or pop music, should have been an indication that there was an ideological aspect to his perspectives regarding music; one rooted in a decidedly neo-Marxist dialectic rationale. Cold War attitudes regarding composition vis-à-vis the narratives of historical determinism, radical egalitarianism, anti-capitalism, the emancipation of dissonance, etc., began to find credibility among a growing number of composers and theorists who sought creative "purity" by way of a scientific and impersonal approach to their creative endeavors. But there was a cost. As contemporary German composer, Hans Werner Henze observed:

> Everything now had to be stylized and made abstract … Discipline was the order of the day. Through discipline it was going to be possible to get music back on its feet again, though nobody asked what for. Discipline enabled form to come about; there were rules and parameters for everything … The audience at whom our music was supposed to be directed, would be made up of experts. The public would be excused from our concerts; in other words, the audience would be the press and our protectors.[7]

As mentioned previously, Schoenberg's observations regarding Hauer's atonal principles regarding their "natural" attributes, or lack of such, put him at odds with his fellow Austrian. In several articles from 1923 (published in his anthology of essays, *Style and Idea*), Schoenberg suggests that Hauer's renunciation of extra-musical associations tended to deny music's "cosmic," "occult," and spiritual attributes—attributes that Schoenberg acknowledged as having an "inkling" of being real—and natural. Ontologically, natural law is manifested in the tonal syntax in a number of significant ways and Schoenberg does not argue this. In fact, he conceded that the "the ebb and flow" of polar opposites (yin/yang) is what gave tonality its "strong effect of cohesion"[8] and emotive power. He considered this to be "natural."

Conversely, he acknowledged that the lack of harmonic cohesion, especially with regard to the tone rows that are germane to dodecaphonic methodology, made it difficult to comprehend and understand this type of music at first hearing. He believed that this was due in large part to the lack of "the external rounding-off and self-containedness" that the "simple and natural principle of (tonal) composition brought about better than did any of the others used alongside it."[9] He admitted that rhythmic, structural and motivic repetition in the atonal idiom, regardless of the tight organizational structuring of such, did not easily supplant the "cohesive" properties and the resultant emotional impact of key-centered music born of the polarity paradigm. This begs the question: If tonality really was the superior manifestation of nature in musical composition, why try to supplant it with something that was seemingly unnatural? The "combinatorial" democratization of pitches in Schoenberg's tone rows seemed deficient as a vehicle of communication and in this regard, the essential trial of twelve-tone music became the attempt to find greater efficacy as a musical syntax possessing communicative capabilities. To this day that search continues and in many cases the dodecaphonic method has been abandoned precisely because music born of this method doesn't "speak" to people in a cogent or meaningful fashion.

Music theorist and composer René Leibowitz was a supreme advocate of the Schoenbergian aesthetic stating that the advance of the dodecaphonic syntax was the "symbol of incorruptible purity" in musical composition because it eschewed extra-musical associations in favor of "absolute" musical properties. An enthusiastic advocate of Anton Webern's music, Leibowitz averred that 12-tone music "was the only genuine and inevitable expression of the musical art of our time."[10] However, the weight accorded to the idea of "inevitability" was seen as being dogmatic, fanatical and deterministic (in the Marxist sense) to many composers of the Cold War era in Europe and the United States. Richard Taruskin notes that Leibowitz and Boulez could be guilty of "coercive and intolerant rhetoric" and targeted composers for not adhering to the new paradigm of composing. After Bartók's death in 1945, Leibowitz accused him of being "a moral failure" in exactly the way that "passive collaborators" were besmirched for allegedly compromising with Nazi perfidy. So what was Bartók's crime? Simply, composing in a stylistically accessible syntax (*Concerto for Orchestra* and his third piano concerto), and seeking approval rather than taking up the cause atonality. As Taruskin suggests this kind of assault "was the undisguised language of political denunciation, a cruel insult to Bartók's principled antifascist commitment and the sacrifices it entailed.[11]

Was Schoenberg actually interested in musical communication, or were other motives at work? The irony is that in Schoenberg's attempts at avoiding consonances and "simpler dissonances (diminished triads and seventh chords)—almost everything that was used to fashion the ebb and flow of harmony,"[12] he was, like Hauer, rejecting several fundamental principles of nature; namely polarity, hierarchy, harmonization and correlation. In 1961 Adorno acknowledged that the atonal utterances of the Cold War era created the condition where "it was difficult to avoid the sense of a certain monotony, of an excessive similarity in the numerous works composed from pitch particles and discrete individual sounds," music that "frequently seemed all too mechanical and lacking in tension."[13] This tension—and its correlative resolution—is in large part what gives tonality its cohesiveness, its emotional richness and its aesthetic *raison d'etre*. Most importantly, *we can hear it* and upon hearing it we are affected psychically. Beauty and meaning in tonal music are the direct results of phonology and syntax that are predicated on nature, polarity and relational constructs—tonic/dominant, major/minor, consonance/dissonance, for example. Although Schoenberg attempted to deny individual pitches "the privilege of supremacy," the forces of nature were against him *and* his determinist rationale.

It is not at all implausible to suggest that tonality as a musical syntax is akin to natural languages in that it possesses an underlying "deep structure" born out of the primal, subconscious desire for communication and relationship, and as such is a "natural" phenomenon. Atonal, formulaic music, on the other hand, music predicated primarily on intellection, as well as the avoidance of any harmonic "ebb and flow" (tension and resolution) may be ontologically outside of nature's archetypes and therefore does not possess the ability to move the heart in the ways it may stimulate the mind, thus resulting in soulless music. Schoenberg's famous supposition of 1948, in which he stated that all that was needed for "the emancipation of dissonance"[14] and atonal music to be accepted by the larger public was greater exposure, has not materialized. In actuality, the opposite has transpired as the un-lovely aesthetic of atonality has given way to the aforementioned minimalism (the emancipation of consonance?), neo-romanticism and styles derivative of ethnic, folk, New Age and pop influences. Interestingly, and somewhat ironically, a renewed interest in spirituality and religious conviction has once again found favor as sources of inspiration for composers in recent decades, as evidenced by the music of Arvo Pärt, Giya Kancheli, Eric Whitacre, Ola Gjeilo and Morten Lauridsen. As a result, the crabbed mannerisms of serial/formulaic music have fewer and fewer advocates among modern composers—and audiences.

It would seem that the increased accessibility to new music via copious recordings, would have been a godsend for the advocates of atonality. Yet, this is clearly not the case. If, as Schoenberg (and Adorno) supposed, greater exposure to atonal music would eventually lead to its greater acceptance, the hardcore *avant-garde* might be more widely accepted by now, but in reality it continues to be viewed as being arcane and increasingly subsidiary. American, Pulitzer Prize-winning composer Stephen Albert (1941-1992) commenting on the atonal/serial movement stated, "Once you brought the cultural bolshevism of the time, you were down the mindless trail of the *avant-garde*. Twenty-five years down the line I suspect that one will look back with mystification as to how people took the fifties to the seventies seriously except as some kind of sociological aberration."[15] Now, several decades since his untimely passing, Mr. Albert's supposition has been proven to be quite prescient.

Towards the end of the twentieth century, a great deal of research regarding music and cognition has provided new insights into the realm of psychoacoustics. Based on his studies in this area, composer Fred Lerdahl of Columbia University posits that certain musical syntaxes have "cognitive constraints." Echoing Bernstein, Lerdahl argues that compositional grammar is not unlike the grammar of language in that "natural grammar" is born of a spontaneous impulse within a culture whereas artificial grammar is "a conscious invention." He differentiates between a musical syntax that is complex as opposed to one that is complicated; one in which cognitive processes are challenged well beyond their natural, biological and psychological capacities.

Lerdahl asserts that complex music based on "hierarchical structural richness," results in a perceptible, communicative syntax, whereas complicated music tends to neutralize (or obfuscate) hierarchical properties due to "numerous non-redundant events per time unit."[16] Complicatedness has the effect of short-circuiting the cognitive process in ways that prohibit certain psychoacoustic phenomena to occur. If listening and comprehension capacities are confused or compromised by complicated pitch sets, obtuse chord grammar and indistinguishable rhythmic properties, indeterminacy rules the day and "nature" no longer calls the tune. Music then is no longer distinguished by its "pleasantness" (as Immanuel Kant described it in his *Critique of Judgment*).

Moreover, the idea that hierarchies were considered suspect by the purveyors of Marxist thought, the democratization of pitches in the 12-tone method in which no pitch within the octave could be repeated until the other eleven tones had been heard, was viewed as an egalitarian compositional mode—democratic art in its fullest iteration. Because hierarchical power issues played heavily into the Marxist narrative, dominant hierarchies of any kind were viewed as being suspect; the result of "a secondary consequence of a socio-political economic structure" that uses power to control or oppress. But as Jordon Peterson correctly notes, certain hierarchies of dominance in the natural world are millions of years old, therefore these hierarchies are natural and organic and there's no blaming them on capitalism or any other human construct or proclivity. Though Schoenberg has become (somewhat unfairly) the all-purpose whipping boy of modern music's failure to attract significant numbers of devotees, the claim that his "discovery" of the twelve-tone system would "ensure the supremacy of German music for the next hundred years" has not materialized.[17]

Having recently listened again to Boulez's *Repons*, some thirty years since my first exposure to the piece in 1986, my impressions of this music have not changed much. It is aurally fascinating, yet I find it to be emotionally unsatisfying. I don't begrudge others the contentment of experiencing this type of music, but I suspect that like many music lovers, I seek far more than intellectual interest or aural excitement (ear candy) from what I listen to. I wish to be moved, inspired and emotionally engaged by music. *Repons* and music of this ilk often fail on all three counts for me, despite its vaunted intellectual and aural properties, claims of historical determinism aside.

Referring to Boulez's "quasi-scientific" approach to composing, Dutch composer John Bortslap cites the emphasis on "sonicism;" a condition where sound generation supplants other aspects of composition. Bortslap equates those who prioritize these various modes of sonic research to the "inadequate neuroscientists who try to undo the notion of the human psyche as an old-fashioned romantic fairy tale." When "sonicism" overrides other concerns—especially melodic content—we are often left with music that he characterizes as "insignificant decoration without artistry and interest."[18]

In attempting to ascertain why this is so, Lawrence Kramer's perspectives on modern music regarding melody, or lack thereof, offer some measure of elucidation. Acknowledging certain richness of rhythmic complexity, orchestration and timbre, as well as the vaunted structural and organizational properties in new music, he asserts that these components "remain a subplot" in relation to discernable melodic ideas.[19] Kramer and others view various aspects of modernity as being hostile to tradition (and "personhood") and remain counterintuitive in relation to our creative impulses and a more "natural" methodology. Former director of the Voice of America, Robert R. Reilly concurs:

> The source of much 'originality' in modern art has not been in creation, but in destruction: a process of taking away what has been given not only by tradition, but by Nature itself. Of course, the principal premise of modern ideology is that wholesale destruction is the necessary ground for the truly new. True freedom [and] real creation demands the abolition of the past. Then one can create in the same way as God was once thought to have created—ex nihilo.[20]

In Boulez's IRCAM manifesto he asserts that "forsaking all memory" and "renouncing all legacies of the past" was considered a requisite condition for the impact of new music to be fully appreciated. Our intuition tells us that something is amiss here. Instinctively we know that the musical traditions of the past remain important due to their ability to elicit strong emotions and in so doing affect our consciousness in profound ways. What is it about the old, "bourgeois" music, such as the finale of Jean Sibelius' fifth symphony that educes such an emotional catharsis decades after its creation? Is it the arresting "swan theme" or the harmonic suspensions (and their resolutions) that create the emotional catharsis in the final bars? Is there something innately "natural" at work in Sibelius' compositional choices?

In truth, it is the juxtaposing of these elements in the context of the tonal syntax that produces the dramatic and cathartic impact. When, through the genius and labor of the composer, the elements of melody, harmony and rhythm are fashioned in sublime ways in the tonal idiom, these cathartic experiences, according to Roger Scruton, "lift us from time and space and into an ideal time and space, ordered by an ideal causality, which is the causality of freedom. From the ideal time of music it is, so to speak, a small step to eternity."[21] Adorno would likely consider this a counterfeit contention, one born out of a decidedly bourgeois mindset and a "false consciousness." But Adorno's views were decidedly binary and dialectical in the Marx/Hegel sense, and as Taruskin notes, like many leftist thinkers of his generation (and presently), Adorno "turned a blind eye to the actual historical consequences of Marxist philosophy,"[22] not only in the sphere of music, but also with regard to man's inhumanity to his fellow man.

Despite his ideas regarding "disinterestedness" in matters of assessing art, Kant believed there were universal aesthetic qualities intrinsic to all great art and many believe that these qualities allowed for temporal transcendence—a condition that is conducive in the effort of finding the best of who we are, individually and collectively. This, in no short measure, is what makes great art so alluring and important in the human experience. After Max Steiner declared that God was dead in 1845, Nietzsche picked up that torch and rather than shed light on the human condition, he led humanity into the cold-hearted darkness of scientific rationale and existentialist thinking. Our sense of community changed as a result. As Scruton observes, "The death of God really means the death of an old form of human community—a community founded on holiness."[23] This quasi-religious concept was seen as being increasingly *démodé* in *fin de siècle* Europe and Schoenberg's forays into atonality were part of the progressive move away from "the old" and a bold leap into "the new." Worshipping at the altar of science became the new religious practice of the avant-garde.

Psychologically, something else was at work. Taruskin asserts that Boulez's "determination to strip music of its accumulated dirt and give it the structure had lacked since the Renaissance," had the effect of dehumanizing musical composition.[24] The "dirt" that Boulez objected to was the subjective, personal, expressive affectations in music that seemed out of step with impersonal science and technology. This rationale went beyond the realm of composition; it was about the listener as well. There was a disdain for the attitudes of the public and the "skillful ruses we have cultivated in our desperate effort to make the world of the past serve our present-day needs," as Boulez put it.[25] Regarding Boulez's perspective, Taruskin posits:

> After Hiroshima everyone felt like dirt. The only responsible decision left was to face that miserable contingency and find a way of composing that would stamp out the artist's puny person and allow something "realer" to emerge. And what could be realer than number?[26]

Moreover, the history of art music in the post-World War II era has devalued and/or rejected the premises of holiness and community, as absolute standards of any kind were viewed with suspicion or outright contempt in relation to the deconstructionist rationale that became pervasive via Derrida, Foucault, Lyotard, e.g. Religion, mysticism and spirituality, which for so long provided inspiration for artists and composers, were supplanted on one hand by the pursuit of science and empirical truths, and on the other by the postmodern supposition that there are no meta-narratives, or transcendent moral codes, or absolute truths on which humankind can rely upon in order to fashion a culture of mutually agreed upon ideals, values and virtues.

Our entire sense of community has changed due in large part to the distrust for anyone having "deeply held views" or an aura of certainty. Of course, the views that most often come under severe scrutiny in our postmodern era, are those born out of religious conviction—the very thing that inspired many of humankind's most sublime artistic achievements. The abnegation of religious belief combined with a rejection of natural law at the beginning of the twentieth century, led to various occurrences of tyranny as well as the diminution of the tonal idiom in art music. This led to a moral crisis with regard to culture and art in general, for once the "old ideas" of right and wrong were abolished or diminished in the name of "emancipation" or "liberation," or "progress" moral relativism and cultural chaos was a predictable outcome.

Intuition is said to be one of the highest spiritual attributes of the human experience. Bernstein referred to the "intuition of tonal relationships" and inferred that there is something innately humane in the tonal idiom by citing its natural and universal implications. Our intuition leads us to the notion that tonal music rooted in natural law—what Bernstein referred to as "the poetry of the earth"—continues to provide us with the ability to address deep human instincts and in so doing acts as a medium to unfold the untold and mysterious, and in so doing prove the multidimensional aspect of nature as it pertains to the phenomenon of sound and music. This is a significant reason why tonality continues to affect our psyche in such profound ways, and why it continues to be a viable and relevant musical syntax.

Recommended Recordings

Boulez: *Repons*, Pierre Boulez, Ensemble Intercontemporain

Varèse: *Arcana*, Kent Nagano, ORTF National Orchestra

Schoenberg: *Five Pieces for Orchestra*, James Levine, Berlin Philharmonic

Berg: *Three Pieces for Orchestra*, James Levine, Berlin Philharmonic

Webern: *Six Pieces for Orchestra*, James Levine, Berlin Philharmonic

Tan Dun: Violin Concerto, *Out of Peking Opera,** Lin Cho-Liang, Violin

Golijov: *Ayre*, Jamey Hadad, Andalucian Dogs

Sierra: *Sinfonias*, Thomas Sleeper, Frost Symphony Orchestra

Albert: Symphony No. 1, Paul Polivnik, Russian Philharmonic Orchestra

Whitacre: Choral Music, Noel Edison, Elora Festival Singers

Lauridsen: *O Magnum Mysterium,* Noel Edison, Elora Festival Singers

Kancheli: *Silent Prayer*, Kamerata Baltica

Gjeilo: *Northern Lights*, Charles Bruffy, Phoenix Chorale

Harrison: *La Koro Sutro*, William Winant, American Gamelan

Andriessen: *La Passione*, Gil-Rose, Boston Modern Orchestra Project

Vaughan-Williams: Symphony No. 4, Leonard Bernstein, New York Philharmonic

Sibelius: Symphony No. 5, Simon Rattle, City of Birmingham Orchestra

Stravinsky: *Ebony Concerto*, Benny Goodman, clarinet

Shostakovich: Jazz Suites, Mariss Jansons, Philadelphia Orchestra

Copland: Clarinet Concerto, Benny Goodman, clarinet

Ravel: Piano Concerto in G Major, Krystian Zimerman, piano

Blacher: *Orchestra Variations, Op. 26,* Herbert Kegel, Dresden Philharmonic

Mihaud: *La création du monde*, Leonard Bernstein, ORTF National Orchestra

Riley: *Assasin Reverie*, ARTE Quartet

Reich: *Daniel Variations*, Alan Pierson, London Sinfonietta

Adams: *Shaker Loops*, Edo de Waart, San Francisco Symphony Orchestra

Hoiby: *A Pocket of Time*, Lee Hoiby-piano, Julia Faulkner, soprano

Zwillich: Concerto for Violin, Pamela Frank, violin

Lieberman: Concerto for Flute, James Galway, flute

Britten: *Four Sea Interludes*, Sir Neville Marriner, Minnesota Orchestra

Prokofiev: Symphony No. 5, Leonard Slatkin, St. Louis Symphony Orchestra

Bartók: *Miraculous Mandarin Suite*, Jean Martinon, Chicago Symphony Orchestra

Barber: *Adagio for Strings*, Thomas Schippers, New York Philharmonic

Janáček: *Sinfonietta*, Charles Mackerras, Vienna Philharmonic

Respighi: *Pini di Roma*, Eduardo Mata, Dallas Symphony Orchestra

Holst: *The Planets*, Charles Dutoit, Montreal Symphony Orchestra

Martin: *Petite symphonie concertante*, Gunter Wand, NDR Sinfonieorchester

Szymanowski: *Symphonie Concertante*, Antoni Wit, Warsaw Philharmonic Orchestra

Debussy: *Prélude à l'après-midi d'un faune*, Vladimir Ashkenazy, Cleveland Orchestra

Walton: *Variations on a Theme by Hindemith*, George Szell, Cleveland Orchestra

Rochberg: *Caprice Variations*, Eliot Fisk, guitar

Hindemith: *Symphonic Metamorphosis on Themes by Carl Maria von Weber*, Herbert Blomstedt, San Francisco Symphony

Endnotes

1 IRCAM: U.S. Tour Program Notes (Paris: IRCAM editions, 1986,) p. 10.

2 E. Michael Jones, *Dionysos Rising: The Birth of Cultural Revolution Out of the Spirit of Music* (San Francisco, CA: Ignatius Press, 1994), p. 125.

3 Walter Szmolyan, *Josef Matthias Hauer* (Vienna: Verlag Elisabeth Lafite, Vienna, 1965), p. 21.

4 Ibid., p. 23.

5 Arnold Schoenberg, *Style and Idea-Composition with Twelve Tones*, edited by Leonard Stein (Berkeley, CA: University of California Press, 1975), p. 209.

6 Leonard Bernstein, *The Unanswered Question: Six Talks at Harvard* (Cambridge, MA: Harvard University Press, 1976), p. 283.

7   Hans Werner Henze, *Music and Politics: Collected Writings 1953-81*, translated by Peter Labanyi (Ithaca, New York: Cornell University Press, 1982), p. 40.

8   Schoenberg, *Style and Idea*, p. 209.

9   Ibid., p. 207.

10 René Leibowitz, as cited by Richard Taruskin in *Music in the Late Twentieth Century* (Oxford-New York: Oxford University Press, 2010), p. 16.

11 Ibid., p. 19.

12 Ibid., p.16.

13 Theodor Adorno, *Quasi Una Fantasia: Essays on Modern Music*, Verso Classics, London-New York, 1998, pg. 179.

14 Schoenberg, *Style and Idea*, pp. 245-246.

15 Robert C. Reilly, "Reaching the Transcendent," *World & I Magazine*, January 1990, Vol. 5, No. 1, On-line Edition, article #17368.

16 Fred Lerdahl, *Cognitive Constraints on Compositional Systems. Generative Processes in Music: The Psychology of Performance, Improvisation, and Composition*, edited by John Sloboda (Oxford: Oxford University Press, 1988. Reprinted in Contemporary Music Review 6/2, 1992), pp. 97-121.

17 H.H. Stuckenschmidt, *Schoenberg: His Life, World, and Work*, translated by Humphrey Searle (New York: Schirmer Books, 1977), p. 277.

18 John Bortslap, *The Classical Revolution: Thoughts on New Music in the 21st Century*, Revised Edition (Lanham, Maryland, Scarecrow Press, Inc. 2017), pp. 63-64.

19 Lawrence Kramer, *Why Classical Music Still Matters* (Berkeley-Los Angeles-London: University of California Press, Ltd., 2007), p. 70.

20 Robert C Reilly, "Reaching the Transcendent."

21 Mark Dooley, *Roger Scruton: The Philosopher on Dover Beach* (New York: Continuum, 2009), p. 94.

22 Richard Taruskin, *Music in the Late Twentieth Century* (Oxford-New York: Oxford University Press, 2010) p. 89.

23 Roger Scruton, *Philosophy: Principles and Problems* (London-New York: Continuum, 1996), p. 95.

24 Richard Taruskin, *Music in the Late Twentieth Century*, p. 41.

25 Pierre Boulez, IRCAM Program Notes, p. 10.

26 Richard Taruskin, *Music in the Late Twentieth Century* p. 41.

28

The Case for Tonality—Part 2

There can be no justification for music ultimately if it does not convey
eloquently and elegantly the passions of the human heart.
George Rochberg

It has been almost eighty years since Viennese composer Arnold Schoenberg composed his first atonal works and began the march towards what he called "the emancipation of dissonance." By rejecting the tonal syntax of the "common practice" Schoenberg was challenging a system of musical thought and theory that had existed for nearly three hundred years. Schoenberg's twelve-tone technique captured the imagination of a new generation of composers and this new method of composing, and its inherent compositional rationale, eventually became the most significant force behind the evolution of musical composition in the post-World War II era.*

Of all those whose musical lineage can be traced back to Schoenbergian thought and aesthetics, Pierre Boulez stands as a giant among his contemporaries. He is considered the high priest of the musical avant-garde, the "greatest

---

* This chapter was originally a review and commentary written in 1986 after attending several of the Boulez/IRCAM concerts in New York. I've edited the text for this publication but it remains essentially what I wrote—and what I meant—at that time.

living exponent of twentieth-century music" as proclaimed by *The New York Times*. Composer, conductor, administrator and lecturer, Boulez has won high praise from even his most severe detractors as an indefatigable champion of new music. Boulez is currently the director of Institut de Recherche et de Coordination Acoustique/Musique (IRCAM) in France and conductor of the Ensemble InterComtemporain, the institute's resident orchestra.

In 1970, when Boulez was music director for both the New York Philharmonic and the BBC Symphony Orchestra, he was asked by French President Georges Pompidou to become director of a music research institute that was to become part of a national center for contemporary art in Paris, now known as the Center Pompidou. Boulez had long been experimenting in the realm of electronic music and the IRCAM project no doubt seemed to be the most suitable setting in which to continue this work. The relationships between performers and computers, and the synthesis of art and technology, were to be the parameters in which composers, performers, and technicians would carry out their experiments at IRCAM, thereby forging new compositional methodologies in the process.

In 1974 at a world press conference, Boulez stated the philosophy and ideals of the new research center:

> Our age is one of persistent, relentless, almost unbearable inquiry. In its exaltation it cuts off all retreats and bans all sanctuaries; its passion is contagious, its thirst for the unknown projects us forcefully, violently into the future; it compels us to redefine ourselves, no longer in relation to our individual functions, but to our collective necessity. Despite the skillful ruses we have cultivated in our desperate effort to make the world of the past serve our present-day needs, we can no longer elude the essential trial: that of becoming an absolute part of the present, of forsaking all memory to forge a perception without precedent, of renouncing the legacies of the past to discover undreamed of territories.[1]

Certainly a heady statement but one in need of some perspective. The Ensemble InterContemporain has just completed a five-city, fourteen-concert tour in the United States. The programs included several new works by composers who have been active at IRCAM. The tour and the music have generated a great deal of interest along with the attendant controversy and dismay that seems inevitable whenever "new music" is performed. Granted, it is difficult, if not altogether impossible, to draw conclusions about an endeavor as subjective as art and its appreciation; yet history has a way of elucidating even the most inscrutable human experiences.

Of all the phenomena generated by the emergence of modernism and its proponents, the ever-present and continually widening chasm between the contemporary composer and the public remains the most noticeable. This "cultural gap" serves as undeniable evidence that the twentieth-century composer has yet to come to grips with what may be the most essential "essential trial" facing humankind, namely, the ability to communicate effectively, and in so doing avoid alienation and isolation.

Whether intentional or not, modern composers have lost their audience (and in many cases their fellow musicians) in their attempts to be daring, unique, individualistic, and progressive. If the result of composing in such a fashion is alienation and even hostility, one might ask, why embrace such a mode of expression? If, as Schoenberg and his associates believed, dodeca-phonic writing was just the next, most logical step in the evolution of composition, why haven't today's audiences followed along with the same alacrity demonstrated by audiences of the past? In his book, *The Fundamentals of Music and the Human Conscience*, conductor Ernest Ansermet suggests that music produced using the twelve-tone method is based on a "faulty aesthetic," consequently the principles of psychoacoustics are violated in such a way that upon hearing atonal music we experience an unpleasant emotional reaction. While this postulation might explain why many shun *avant-garde* music, it offers little insight as to why some people enjoy modern music and identify with it. Still, Ansermet was not alone in his estimation.

At the first concert presented in New York by the Ensemble InterCon-temporain (EIC), Boulez conducted the New York premiere of his newest work (in progress), *Repons*. The concert was held at the Columbia University Gymnasium where a standing-room-only audience of about three thousand enthusiastically welcomed Boulez and his musicians. *Repons* is a sonically fascinating work that employs a chamber ensemble of about twenty-five instrumentalists and six percussionists, who in this concert were deployed in different corners of the gymnasium. Through the use of computers, the sounds generated by the performers (on traditional instruments) were digitally sampled, synthesized, and amplified through an elaborate loudspeaker system set about the perimeter of the auditorium. The sounds from the instrumentalists were synthesized into new sounds in real time and the result was aurally stunning.

Though the techniques of sound generation and transformation were highly engaging, Boulez's compositional syntax was as expected: atonal, rhythmically complex, indeterminate, and at times cacophonous. The reaction of the audience was what might have been expected for a modern music concert. About half of the audience stood and cheered while the others seemed to join in a collective scratching of heads, not at all sure they understood what had just transpired. It would certainly be an exaggeration to conclude that Boulez had succeeded in alienating half of those in attendance this particular night, yet on my subway ride home I spoke with a painter who had attended the concert and she decreed that she would never go to a Boulez concert again. It was evident that *Repons* simply left many people cold and indifferent. The music didn't speak to them; or if it did, they didn't like what it had to say. Indeed, the most recent trends and innovations in contemporary music seem to be no more successful in setting up channels of communication than were the earlier ones.

Is our essential trial becoming "an absolute part of the present, of forsaking all memory to forge a perception without precedent, of renouncing the legacies of the past," as Boulez claims? Reason dictates that there is much to be learned from the past. Are the philosophical concepts (and the artistic expressions born of those concepts) of composers such as Bach and Beethoven completely alien to modern audiences? If so, why does their music continually "speak" to us? Are there absolute values and ideals with which even the staunchest modernist must eventually come to terms? Is the *avant-garde* still lost in what Stravinsky termed "the abyss of freedom?"

Throughout history artists have been greatly influenced by philosophical and religious thought and their sociological ramifications. Composers have found the freedom to create highly expressive works within the guidelines of certain musical syntaxes—such as tonality—that have their roots in various philosophical and religious beliefs. Johann Sebastian Bach, considered the first master of tonality as we know it, was a church composer. A *kapellmeister* in the Lutheran Church, Bach went as far as to say that for him, "the aim and final reason, as of all music, so of the thorough bass* should be none else but the Glory of God and the recreation of the mind."[2] For Bach, religion and music were one and the same in that both could assist the process of connecting one to the Almighty. Music was an expression, indeed an extension, of his faith in that both religion and music had the potential to connect one with God.

Beethoven, having grown up during the Enlightenment era, was affected greatly by Napoleon and the French Revolution. In a time when it was fashionable to question the rationale behind religion and the relevance of God, Beethoven was nevertheless a believer. He once confided in his friend Bettina von Arnim, "I know that God is nearer to me than to other artists. I associate with Him without fear; I have always recognized and understood Him and have no fear for my music."[3] On the opening page of the score of his great D Major Mass, Beethoven inscribed the words, *Von Herzen. Möge es wieder-zu Herzen gehen.* (From the heart. May it in turn go to the heart.) This certainly could have been a credo for late nineteenth-century artists, for conveying one's innermost thoughts and feelings through one's art was of paramount importance to the artist of that era. Beethoven's music is often an expression of humanistic optimism and confidence for what humankind might achieve once one was free to express their hopes for a better world.

By the end of the nineteenth century, Nietzsche had written God's obituary and proclaimed that it was by engaging in self-transcendence, apart from any supernatural power or deity, that humankind could attain its ultimate fulfillment. Yet the hopes brought forth by the Enlightenment and the French Revolution had turned to disillusionment and uncertainty by the beginning of the twentieth century. The idea of a better world had been tainted by the reality of man's failure to bring that ideal to fruition.

Perhaps no composer expressed the dichotomy between the ideal and the reality to such a great effect as did Gustav Mahler (1860-1911). This may be why Mahler's music continues to speak to us today. As humanity strives for

---

* Thorough bass, also known as Basso continuo or figured bass, is a system of partially improvised accompaniment predicated on a bass line, usually on a keyboard instrument. The use of basso continuo was customary during the 17th and 18th centuries, when only the bass line was written out, or "thorough" (archaic spelling of "through"), giving considerable leeway to the keyboard player, usually an organist or harpsichordist, in the realization of the harmonic implications of the bass in relation to the treble part or parts. [Source: *Encyclopedia Britannica.*]

a better world we are constantly reminded of our individual and collective failures. Mahler's music, like the world in which we live, is filled with anxiety, but along with that anxiety (and the despair which it often engenders) exists some of the most hopeful, glorious, and triumphant music ever written: music of redemption and affirmation. It is self-evident that an intrinsic aspect of the human experience is the desire to attain happiness and fulfillment. Mahler, like Bach and Beethoven, puts us in touch with those desires and aspirations, and in so doing allows us to share something common to everyone. Tonality was Mahler's chosen syntax.

The turn of the century brought about some of the most radical changes humankind has ever witnessed. As Harold C. Schonberg observed, the first two decades of the twentieth century brought us Sigmund Freud and his revelations of the subconscious, Max Planck and his theory of quantum physics, Einstein and his theory of relativity, the inventions of Edison and the Wright brothers, painters Picasso and Kandinsky, and composers Stravinsky, Schoenberg, and Debussy.[4] New ideas, new values, new techniques, new rationales, and new modes of expression were seemingly everywhere. Though it was Stravinsky who set the music world on its ear in 1913 with his score *Le Sacre du Printemps*, it was to be Schoenberg and his disciples Anton Webern and Alban Berg, along with French composers Edgard Varèse and Olivier Messiaen, who were among those who would exert a significant influence on composers of the twentieth century. (Boulez was a student of Messiaen.)

A common tenet that many avant-garde composers espoused was that romanticism and its hackneyed mannerisms must be put to rest. Tonality was considered an exhausted anachronism and new modes of expression had to be developed. Techniques such as serialism (music based on mathematical organization), and *musique concrete* (using tape recordings of any sound and modulating the sounds electronically in various ways) became important compositional devices employed by modern composers of the early twentieth century. Perceptible musical elements such as melody, themes, tonal harmonic progressions, and rhythmic pulsation were often eschewed at all costs in the realm of new music.

Curiously, whether modern composers employed the techniques of total organization (serialism) or total freedom (aleatory), the result is often the same: music that is abstract, incongruous and indeterminate. As a result, music no longer seemed to be a "universal language." Consequently, the concert-going public could not relate to it. Many composers have placed blame for this situation on the shoulders of the public. They consider the public obtuse or just plain obstinate. Still, other composers found this situation rather desirable. Consider Milton Babbitt's commentary on the state of social alienation between artists and the public:

> I dare suggest that the composer would do himself and his music an immediate and eventual service by total, resolute, and voluntary withdrawal from this public world to one of private performance and electronic media, with its very real possibility of complete elimination of the public and social aspects of musical composition.[5]

This can be construed to be a type of creative autism in which social interaction and artistic communication with an audience is considered unimportant. Fortunately, not all composers share this perspective. Another American composer and former atonalist composer George Rochberg, offers a countervailing perspective:

> There can be no justification for music ultimately if it does not convey eloquently and elegantly the passions of the human heart. Who would care to remember the quartets of Beethoven or Bartók if they were merely demonstrations of empty formalisms? Like mushrooms in the night, there has sprung up a profusion of false, half-baked theories of perception, of intellection, of composition itself. The mind grows sterile and the heart small and pathetic.[6]

In dealing with the causal dimensions regarding the state of twentieth-century music as espoused by Boulez and the composers he champions, we must again ask the question; Why compose in a fashion that contributes to more neurosis and alienation? Many composers in the academy argue that the mathematical and quasi-scientific approach to composition merely reflects the technologically oriented environment in which humankind now finds itself. Others, who employ the aleatoric modes of composing, justify that approach by declaring that their music reflects the existential, nihilistic or "anything goes" attitudes that have also become very real aspects of the twentieth-century psyche. Both rationales are at least partially correct. However, it must be apparent to even the staunchest advocate of either argument that people are still, even in this angst-filled, hi-tech world, creatures of heart and emotion who seek beauty.

Since the most basic human impulse is to seek happiness, the composer who refuses to acknowledge that urge is likely to have his music fall on deaf ears and unresponsive hearts and minds. Without communication there is no understanding. Perhaps the "essential trial" facing modern composers is to establish modes of communication that display sensitivity for their audience and its needs: composing music that is accessible, music that actually cares if you listen. In this context, tonality once again becomes relevant to the twentieth-century composer. Some of our most basic emotions, it seems, can only be well expressed via a tonal or quasi-tonal syntax. Intellectualism alone can never be the vehicle to move the heart. Boulez and his contemporaries must accept some responsibility if the chasm between artist and public is to be bridged.

Despite human shortcomings, we still aspire to the ideals of peace and harmony, as well as the end of human suffering and alienation. As with generations past, people still experience the most basic emotions of joy, sorrow, anxiety, and melancholy—and undoubtedly always will. We will continue to experience exhilaration as our unremitting quest for sociological improvement brings us closer to achieving a more humane world. We need not concern ourselves with whether or not a particular compositional style is anachronistic or progressive, passé or innovative. The more essential criterion as to the relevance of compositional style is whether or not it allows for successful "heartistic" confluence.

The twentieth century has brought the music world a plethora of compositional innovations, many of them developed from the application of sophisticated mathematical and intellectual resources from which it is possible to devise infinite varieties of systems for structuring and ordering musical materials. A substantial number of such innovations have contributed in greater or lesser degrees to the state of indeterminacy in which contemporary music finds itself. The issue that remains unaddressed is: What is the relationship between systems developed along these lines and the inner, emotional realities by which people respond to music?

To ask that question is not to deny the validity of applying intellectual processes to music. Richard Norton avers that when examining the "formalist vs.

expressionist" dichotomy, one can experience "a certain cerebral satisfaction in viewing and experiencing a piece of music as a kind of tonal temporary geometry" in the formalist sense.[7] The inner question that must be responsibly addressed by today's composer is one of degree and circumstance, namely: Is the emotional reward imparted by the music, commensurate with the degree of intellectual sophistication invested in its composition? It is a question of priority and balance. The tonal consciousness of the listener is no small matter. Norton admits that "the psychoacoustics of the ear, which, if determined to be inviolate within certain parameters, may indeed prove to be the final court of appeal in explaining why we hear pitches and their incumbent overtones in the fashion that we do."[8] Schoenberg's misunderstanding of the tonal consciousness and the sense organ [ears] of the subject [the listener] in developing his new methodology was his fatal flaw.[9]

Pierre Boulez and others who have embraced a number of these innovations might do well to reevaluate the rationale that has propelled contemporary music into its present condition. Musical progress made on the intellectual front, should it exclude or ignore the existence on the emotional factor, essentially addresses itself to half a person and succeeds in satisfying none of them. This is why most contemporary music fails to find appreciation among the larger segment of the public.

The music born of the "common practice," the music of Bach, Beethoven, Brahms, Ravel and Mahler, for instance, has succeeded to varying degrees in achieving the necessary balances of intellectual sophistication and emotional expression. Any composer who has sat at the keyboard and played the music of these acknowledged masters could never deny that their music represents the most sublime balance of systematic organization *and* emotional expressivity. It is music that speaks to the totality of who, and (ontologically) what we are.

Postscript

In his closing remarks of his Harvard Lectures in 1973, Leonard Bernstein offered his perspective about the viability of the tonal syntax despite the predilection for the atonal modes of composing by many of the mid-century modernist composers of that era. He referred to the lecture a "valedictory moment" and titled this lecture "The Poetry of the Earth," which is a reference to John Keats' poem of the same name. In that lecture, he, like Leonard

B. Meyer, predicted an era of musical composition in which there would be great eclecticism, and that a renewed interest in the tonal syntax would play a significant role in this evolution.[10] Because tonality has its sonic etymological underpinnings in nature via the overtone series, Bernstein believed that this earthly phenomenon would outlast the stoic hyper-intellection and stochastic trends that characterized much of the mid-century modernism that became pervasive in the post-World War II era.

As Keats put it, "The poetry of earth is never dead." Indeed, nature often does call the tune and continues to do so, literally and metaphorically. The tonal implications found in nature remain appealing and alluring precisely because they are ontologically aligned with the poetic aspects of nature, including polarity, ebb and flow, physical and metaphysical, for instance. The phonological "universals" found in the harmonic series are not easily swept away by intellection theories or hypothetical paradigms. Expressive music that retains its roots in earth continues to satiate the innate human desire for aesthetic beauty and pleasure.

Due to the advance of technology, differing styles of musical expression interface with greater regularity resulting in new styles, new modes of expression and new formulations of musical materials. This too is a natural process and the resultant eclecticism ought to be viewed as a welcome circumstance. Diversity in this regard can assist in the process of bringing people together in the spirit of creating a universal brotherhood/sisterhood in which mutual respect, dignity and prosperity can be realized.

Recommended Recordings

Boulez: *Repons*, Pierre Boulez, Ensemble Intercontemporain

Schoenberg: *Moses und Aron*, Michael Boder, conductor (DVD)

Varèse: *Arcana*, Kent Nagano, ORTF National Orchestra

Messiaen: *Chronochromie*, Pierre Boulez, Cleveland Orchestra

Stravinsky: *Le Sacre du Printemps*, Pierre Boulez, Cleveland Orchestra

Bach: Brandenburg Concertos, Nikolas Harnoncourt, Vienna Concentus Musicus

Beethoven: Symphony No 3, Christoph von Dohnanyi, Cleveland Orchestra

Brahms: Symphony No. 3, George Szell, Cleveland Orchestra

Mahler: Symphony No. 5, Herbert von Karajan, Berlin Philharmonic

Ravel: *La Valse*, Christoph von Dohnanyi, Cleveland Orchestra

Strauss: *Thus Spake Zarathustra*, Fritz Reiner, Chicago Symphony Orchestra

Debussy: *La Mer*, Ernest Ansermet, Suisse Romande Orchestra

Bartók: String Quartets, Emerson String Quartet

Babbitt: *Correspondences*, James Levine, Chicago Symphony Orchestra

Berg: *Wozzeck*, Pierre Boulez, Paris National Opera Chorus and Orchestra

Webern: Pieces (6) for Orchestra, Robert Craft, Philharmonia Orchestra

Rochberg: Violin Sonata, Sheppard Skaerved, violin

Endnotes

1   Pierre Boulez, IRCAM: U.S. Tour Program Notes (Paris: IRCAM editions, 1986, p. 10.

2   Johann Sebastian Bach: *Christmas Oratorio*, BWV 246, edited by Walter Blankenburg, as cited by Ignace Bossuyt (Leuven, Belgium: Leuven University Press), footnote, p. 143.

3   Alexander Wheelock Thayer, *Thayer's Life of Beethoven* (Princeton, NJ: Princeton University Press, 1949), p. 494.

4   Harold C. Schonberg, *The Lives of the Great Composers* (New York-London: W. W. Norton & Company, 1981), p. 595.

5   Milton Babbitt, *Who Cares If You Listen: Music in the Western World: A History in Documents*, selected and annotated by Piero Weiss and Richard Taruskin (Schirmer, Wadsworth Group/Thomson Learning, 1984), p. 533.

6   George Rochberg, *The Aesthetics of Survival, On the Renewal of Music* (Ann Arbor, MI: University of Michigan Press, 1984), p. 236.

7   Richard Norton, *Tonality in Western Culture* (University Park and London: The Pennsylvania University Press, 1984), p. 170.

8   Ibid., p. 61.

9   Ibid., p. 236.

10   Leonard Bernstein, *The Unanswered Question: Six Talks at Harvard* (Cambridge, MA: Harvard University Press, 1976), p. 424.

29

The Case for Tonality — Part 3

*I have made a discovery that will ensure the supremacy of
German music for the next hundred years.*
Arnold Schoenberg

*Directing attention resolutely away from content and focusing
entirely on form is hardly an "immediate" response to art.
It is no one's first response.*
Richard Taruskin

So here we are, some three-plus decades since those IRCAM concerts and much has changed in the landscape of art music.* Major American orchestras are facing bankruptcy, the classical recording industry has all but vanished in the United States, the demographic shift of the concert-going public is decidedly younger with wide-ranging tastes. Moreover, the study of the humanities has become, as described by Victor Davis Hanson, "a melodrama of race, class and gender oppression."[1] The diminished importance of

---

* I initially wrote this essay prior to Pierre Boulez's death in 2016 and expanded it in 2020.

the humanities as a repository of moral knowledge and wisdom has "managed to turn off much of the college audience and the general reading public."[2] When I wrote the review of the IRCAM concerts in 1986, I was not fully aware of the influence of the neo-Marxist Frankfurt School (especially the views of Theodor Adorno), and its ideological rationale regarding atonality in modern music. Adorno's tendentious views about formulaic music are infused (some might say "infected") with Hegelian dialectics and large doses of Critical Theory. Nor was I cognizant of the influence of the post-modernism, deconstructionist ideas of Jacques Derrida and Michel Foucault.[*]

Regardless of the ideological position one identifies with, it's clear that Arnold Schoenberg's prediction that his dodecaphonic "discovery" would "ensure the supremacy of German music for the next hundred years," has not come to fruition. In fact, Schoenberg's new idea wasn't actually a "discovery," but rather it was a conscious invention; a systematic way of going about composing music. In the formalist vs. expressionist debate, the issue of expression remains pertinent no matter how many ideological broadsides have been fired at it.[†] Adorno and his acolytes likely experienced severe psychological angina due to the fact that the marketplace was proving to be a significant measure of musical taste and value. Consequently, the indeterminate art music of mid-century modernism has failed to supplant the aesthetic satisfaction elicited by tonal music.

If memory serves, I believe it was American composer, William Schuman, the inaugural Pulitzer Prize winner for music in 1943, who likened the avant-garde composer to an orator who wished to impart an important message to his audience, but used a lexicon that was so specialized and arcane that the message could not be comprehended. All too often this has been the case in modern art music. Schuman, who served as the president of Lincoln Center for the Performing Arts from 1961 to 1969, believed that composers' penchant for issuing explanations regarding "complicated polemics for particular aesthetic creeds or compositional procedures" of a given composition might

---

* My first encounter with Theodor Adorno was as a music student at Ohio State in 1973. My encounters with Foucault and Derrida would not occur until years later.

† Dodecaphonic is a term used to describe the 12-tone method of composing as invented by Arnold Schoenberg (1874-1951); Do (two), deca (ten), phonic (tone).

have value to those in the academy who prioritize intellection over most other concerns, but tend to "confuse laymen." Viewing didactic explanations as being propagandistic, he opined that these "skillfully contrived" justifications were no substitute for "musical clarity."[3] One might ask: Are the "skillfully contrived justifications" put forth by modern composers akin to the "skillful ruses" cited by Boulez in his critique of past traditions?

Schuman, like his American colleagues Aaron Copland and Samuel Barber, embraced modernism to varying extents, yet he was unconvinced that electronic sound production as espoused by Boulez and the IRCAM project could supplant the aesthetic beauty of purely acoustic instruments. As Schuman's biographer, Steve Swayne, observes, despite their dalliances with modernism, Barber and Schuman "aimed for the heart," whereas hardcore modernists continually aimed for the head. In many respects, this has been the 800-pound gorilla in the concert hall in the decades since World War II, for as Goethe reminds us, intellect is important, but understanding the human heart is indispensable.

Sound generation (acoustic vs. electronic) aside, the indeterminacy of atonal serial music does not manifest in musical clarity in which perception, understanding and appreciation are easily attained. Serialism may yield astoundingly well-organized musical formulations, but if one cannot make distinctions due to the cognitive constraints of the idiom, what's the point? George Rochberg's insightful essays in his book, *The Aesthetics of Survival*, speak compellingly to the specious tendency in the second half of the twentieth century to view musical composition as being primarily a scientific or systematic endeavor while regarding aesthetic, spiritual, cosmological and humanitarian concerns as being either irrelevant or inconsequential. Alex Ross also observes that music that is predicated primarily on mathematic (serial) properties yields very little in the way of emotional content satisfaction. As Ross puts it:

> The feeling of delirium wears off after a few minutes, giving way to a kind of objectified, mechanized savagery. The serialist principle, with it surfeit of ever changing musical data, has the effect of erasing at any given moment whatever impressions the listener may have formed about previous passages in the piece. The present moment is all there is.[4]

This, of course, is old news. So old in fact, that in some respects it is hard to fathom that there remains any enthusiasm for this type of soulless music when the public at large voted with their feet—and wallets—long ago. The specious *cri de coeur* of post-World War II modernism, that "new" equates with "significant" rings increasingly hollow, yet more than a few "important" composers don't see it that way. Esa-Pekka Salonen's claim that musical expression is "bodily expression" possessing "no abstract or cerebral expression"[5] indicates a fixation with but one aspect of music—sound, which is its external aspect. Minimizing or ignoring the metaphysical aspects of any art form while fixating on the physical, formalistic and methodological aspects, results in an unsatisfying experience for many who seek more from their encounters with music, old or new. Richard Taruskin considers Thomas Adès a composer who can offer the advocates of serious art music "renewed hope" in the new millennium. Yet for many, it's difficult to distinguish the indeterminate nature of Adès' music from that of the mid-century modernists (Elliot Carter and Donald Martino, e.g.) that Taruskin rails against.

Taruskin suggests that Schoenberg's "emancipation of dissonance ... owes its political vibes to the liberatory rhetoric of the dialectic," and had more to do with emancipating composers than musical style.[6] Additionally, the Marxist narrative of "liberation" is rooted in the leftist Hegelian idea that conflict is necessary for progress. Old too are the aforementioned philosophical ruminations of Adorno, whose neo-Marxist perspectives regarding the abnegation of the natural and the metaphysical aspects of music no longer hold the credibility they once did. Though Adorno was at least partially correct in his belief that art forms can "reflect the history of man even more truthfully than do documents," he nevertheless failed to understand (or, more likely ignored for purely ideological reasons), the fact that nature has been a significant factor in the evolution of musical style, temperament and syntax; not the only factor, but not an inconsequential factor with regard to tonality's expressive viability.*

As Taruskin notes, a "forced dichotomy ... The Great Either/Or" became pervasive in the debates of academically trained musicologists regarding modern music, and this resulted in a "pseudo-dialectical 'method' that cast all

---

* Like many who still embrace Marxism, Adorno seems to have conveniently forgotten the untold human suffering caused by Marxist regimes whenever and wherever they held power.

thought in rigidly—and artificially—binarized terms,"[7] specifically the influence of political or philosophical ideas on the composer. The reasons for this binary outlook was, as Taruskin observes, very much rooted in Cold War psychology, "when the general intellectual atmosphere was excessively polarized around a pair of seemingly exhaustive and totalized alternatives."[8] The offshoot of this binary modality was the all too familiar perspectives of Adorno and his Frankfurt School comrades who viewed the trajectory of twentieth-century music in decidedly Hegelian terms; a struggle between the "heroic resisters"[9] of the *avant-garde*, and the old world "reactionaries" clutching the traditions that were rooted in religious idealism and tonality, not to mention capitalism, the bane of all serious Marxists. The "pure truth" of atonal serialism, with its predilection for impersonal intellection and mathematical certainty, was for Adorno and company, the perfect antidote to any and all remnants of bourgeoisie culture. The neo-Marxist musical liberation movement was gaining steam and Adorno became one of its chief ideological propagators.

It is undeniable that all systems of musical organization are human constructs, but it's also true that sound, or more correctly, pitch production (vibratory energy in motion) is the progeny of physics and nature. Musicologist, Richard Norton considered Adorno "the only effective antidote for Pythagoras," not to mention the concept of the *Klang*, the so-called, "chord of nature" as proffered by Jean-Philippe Rameau and Heinrich Schenker. For Adorno, Norton and others of the neo-Marxist persuasion, the idea of conjoining nature and pitch production in the attempt to justify any system of pitch organization was viewed as a mode of "physical determinism" and was decidedly reactionary. But as Taruskin opines, those who are quick to denounce physical (or biological) determinism, "are often determinists of another stripe, usually historical. When you're convinced that history has a purpose—your purpose—that must inevitably triumph, you can rationalize any means of helping the inevitable along."[10] This mindset was highly evident in the writing of György Lukács, a co-founder of the Institute for Social Research (aka the Frankfurt School) who belligerently asked, "Who will save us from Western civilization?"

Schoenberg would declare that, "tonality is no natural law of music." Although the tonal syntax is a human construct, it's impossible to divorce pitch production from the laws of physics and nature. Moreover, the concept of *Klang* in relationship to how and what we hear is not intrinsically false or without merit.* Norton reminds us that Schopenhauer, in his theory of color, posited that "a real theory should start with the subject," the observer. This is reminiscent of Nietzsche's dictum: "In order for an event to have greatness two things must come together: The immense understanding of those who cause it to happen, and the immense understanding of those who experience it."[11] We readily admit that colors are "physiological phenomenon, 'conditions, modifications of the eye' and we don't debate the specificity of sight in that which we observe."[12] In musical observation and perception the subject's sense of hearing cannot be easily negated or ignored. Any musical system or theory (terms that were uncomfortable to Schoenberg) that is based on "purely objective grounds" without regard to the subject's sense organ (their ears) could be said to be ontologically "unnatural" because it disaffirms the relational modality of subject-object. As well, the abstract and ambiguous nature of music lends itself to a myriad of subjective interpretations depending, not insignificantly, on the state of mind or heart of the listener at a given moment.

Advances in cognitive psychology have yielded important, new considerations about hearing and cognition that simply did not exist in the 1920s. As noted in these essays, Taruskin, Leonard B. Meyer, Fred Lerdahl, Leonard Bernstein and others have offered enlightened perspectives regarding the issues of patterning and familiarization in music as being elemental aspects of the cognitive and appreciative process. The avoidance of such in the pursuit of originality and/or innovation has the effect of shortchanging or undermining the emotive aspect of music.

In my opinion, Bernstein efficaciously argues in his Harvard Lectures, that there is a similarity in the evolution of natural languages and musical language regarding the linguistic concepts of deep structure in the context of their syntactic and semantic development. Just as natural languages evolve through various transformational processes (deletion, augmentation, metaphor,

---

* The concept of *Klang* (German for "sound") in music has been confusing. It sometimes refers to the so-called "chord of nature" that stems from the hierarchical pitches in the overtone series. Not all music theorists agreed with this concept citing Jean-Philippe Rameau's misunderstanding of the experiments of Joseph Sauveur regarding natural harmonics. Rather than a specific "chord," in the syntactical or functional sense of tonality, as Rameau suggested, the idea of *Klang* had more to do with the non-functional sonorities found in the overtone series—a kind of primordial sonority apart from any theoretical of syntactical pretext.

poetics, permutation, embedding, e.g.), music employs similar processes to arrive at a "meaningful" aesthetic—a "surface structure" that has a communicative ability. Though music and language possess these similarities, there are significant differences and perhaps the nearest parallel is music and poetry, both of which have aesthetic surface structures. Whereas natural language has a "literal" aspect to it, music is metaphorical and far less specific in a semantic sense.

The psychology of modernism has led to the condition of music being highly indeterminate and nondescript, which ironically, was one of Adorno's laments about serial music—even as he championed it. Aesthetically, Salonen's *Foreign Bodies* or Adès' *Asyla*, are not unlike the music of Leslie Bassett or Elliott Carter—music composed decades ago. Very little in Salonen's piece is actually new in the mélange of contemporary compositional techniques. He offers some interesting sonic effects, but it's all been done before—many times going back almost one hundred years, in fact.

Taruskin has praised the composer of *Asyla* in the most glowing terms, but as an experiment, I suggest listening to the first several minutes of *Asyla* and then Carter's *Variations for Orchestra*. (Carter considered the *Variations* among his favorite of his compositions.) The aesthetic similarities are striking, yet Taruskin has critiqued some of Carter's works in the most caustic fashion. Many of the "conventional anti-conventionalities" that are common in post-World War II modernism are present in both works.* Aesthetically, they are very much of the same atonal and indeterminate modality. Perhaps professional composers (or professional listeners) can more easily make distinctions between Carter's formalist techniques and Adès's eclectic surrealisms, but then we're arguing against the idea that Adès's compositions can rescue art music from its specialist milieu, not to mention the fixation of how the music is made—the "poetic fallacy" that Taruskin considers a specious strain of modernist rationale—as do I.

---

* Regarding "conventional anti-conventionalities," I suggest that many, if not all of the techniques that are the progeny of the music of Schoenberg or Varèse, for example, have been in use for over a century and have been employed by hundreds of composers in thousands of works. They are very few, if any "new," or "revolutionary," or "innovative" techniques, only modern conventions that appear with regularity in contemporary compositions.

In a concert review of Carter's music for *New York Magazine*, Justin Davidson echoes Alex Ross' observation regarding Carter's music:

> It's often suggested that appreciating Carter requires a special kind of training—that some secret knowledge would make all those vinegary chords and dribbling rhythms suddenly make sense. Actually, the ideal listener would be one who had experienced total short-term memory loss ... After the first minute or so of this maze-like music, I lose all sense of how deeply I have wandered in. Each passage blots out its own past, and at any given moment the possibilities for what the ensuing few bars might hold are virtually infinite. Carter creates no expectations, and so he cannot defy expectations, either. I will accept any dénouement, but I do so without investment in the outcome. A single blinding moment might be worth a standing ovation; a long chain of them gets only an irritated shrug.[13]

Mr. Davidson's critique could be a blanket statement for large portions of the modernist canon and I had very similar feelings while listening to the music of Salonen and Adès. Their music is the stuff of contemporary cinema in that the reliance on special effects is the dominant mode. The onslaught of computer technology in the cinema has rendered techniques such as constructing a cohesive narrative, coherent script writing, character development, acting and social commentary, peripheral, thus resulting in decidedly superficial modes of entertainment and storytelling. (All that green screen stuff—all together boring and totally without magic or mystery—because we know how it's done.)

Igor Stravinsky's sagacious observation that the dilemma for composers was not a paucity of ideas and possibilities to chose from, but rather a profusion of such. As such, limiting choices in the attempt to create a coherent, discernible musical narrative is a necessary aspect of the creative process. The challenge of composing becomes making choices that result in a unified, cohesive and harmonious juxtaposing of musical materials that, in turn, allow for a greater ability to comprehend and appreciate both the aesthetic and semantic attributes of a given composition. Late in his life Stravinsky developed a begrudging respect (or was it jealousy) for Schoenberg's lawful musical methodology. But even Schoenberg warned against over- analyzing his music saying, "I've always been dead set against seeing how it is done; whereas I have helped people see: what it is."[14] The more pertinent issue regarding music is for people to *hear* and *perceive* what is being done, and in this respect most serial music, for all of its vaunted discipline and organization, fails on a basic perceptual level.

Citing the tight motivic organization of *Der Mondfleck*, from Schoenberg's *Pierrot Lunaire*, Taruskin refers to it as "an analyst's delight." Charles Rosen called it "one of most elaborately worked out canons since the end of the fifteenth century."[15] Yet in the final analysis, if one cannot aurally decipher the intricacies of the various motifs and canonic devices due to the cognitive constraints of the atonal idiom, what's the point?

The prioritization of the technical devices utilized in its making over any *perceptible* and *intelligible* musical syntax results in a deficiency of the work's communicative competence and renders the work ultimately unsatisfying. Taruskin avers that this type of complexity "does not make it any more pertinent or available to the listener's experience[16] … it's all about frenzied but pointless activity … a perfect description of an elaborate contrapuntal textures with emancipated dissonance."[17]

Promoting complexity and intellection into a musical value, according to Taruskin, "is the ultimate poietic fallacy … one that led modern music into the *cul-de-sac* where absurdly over-composed monstrosities by Elliott Carter or Milton Babbitt have been reverently praised by critics and turned into obligatory models of emulation by teachers of composition."[18] Taruskin's invective may seem a bit harsh, but Babbitt died a neglected composer in 2011 despite the fact that he was highly regarded and much celebrated among other modern composers in the academy. Forecasts of revivals of Babbitt and others of his ilk seem to be wishful thinking on the part of hardcore modernists because the larger concert-going public doesn't seem to care about music that doesn't "aim for the heart." Merely becoming better listeners doesn't resolve the problem of indeterminacy vis-à-vis emotional satisfaction.

Wonderful Economy

In a recorded interview by conductor George Szell for CBS Records just before his passing in 1970, the acclaimed maestro recalled the insights of his mentor, Richard Strauss regarding the craft of orchestration. Strauss, according to Szell, asserted that if one wished to know how to orchestrate well, studying the scores of Wagner or Mahler was not always the best choice. Strauss, as Szell recalled, suggested that it was far better to study the score of Georges Bizet's opera *Carmen*, noting its "wonderful economy," in which "every note and every rest is in its proper place."

This is an intriguing perspective because as Mark Swed notes, Strauss was a gifted orchestrator "who could accomplish with a symphony orchestra what now requires 3-D Imax, Oculus or, at the very least, recreational marijuana."[19] This is not to suggest that studying the brilliant scores of Strauss, Stravinsky or Ravel is not without merit, but when the relatively tame scores by Tippet or Bartók can still confound many listeners, the opaque utterances of hardcore modernism will have little success in finding audiences beyond the academy or a coterie of "new music" enthusiasts. Later in the interview, Szell was asked if there was any important music being written and he stoically responded, "If it is, it hasn't come to my attention." Like any well-informed musician, Szell was aware of Pierre Boulez (who became the interim music advisor of the Cleveland Orchestra after Szell's death) and the Darmstädt modernists of which Boulez was a high priest. However, being a disciple of the central-European tradition of the late nineteenth-century, Szell obviously didn't give Boulez and his epigones much credibility in matters of composing.

To be sure Carter has his advocates and admirers. However, the collective shrug that a great deal of modern music like Mr. Carter's elicits from many music lovers indicates that there remains a great deal of apathy from the public, and this has been the case for decades. The atonal techniques that Carter and his aesthetic brethren continue to employ have fallen on deaf ears and unresponsive hearts and minds. The tired, determinist claim of historical inevitability by atonal composers and their advocates rings false—more now than ever. At this juncture in history, it seems safe to say that the esoteric and recondite properties of the atonal syntax as introduced by Schoenberg and practiced by Carter have simply failed to express or convey much in the way of what might be considered a truly humane musical expression. As mentioned previously, Taruskin opines that this wasn't because dissonance had been emancipated by Schoenberg, but rather, that it was composers who had been liberated to do just about anything. The giveaway was when Schoenberg said, "Now that I have emancipated dissonance, anyone can be a composer."[20]

The fatal conceit of lineal evolution in musical style, specifically, Schoenberg's contention that "someone had to be him" to liberate musical style from "the straight-jacket of the tempered system" (the aim of Busoni and Varèse) is one that remained entrenched in the minds of mid-century modernists. However, as Taruskin points out, the "central evolutionary" reasoning that has driven modern music is a faulty premise.

> Unlike tonality, atonality (the kind that has survived) has one father. This has given rise to a cult of personality, has intensified polarization, and has lent historiography of twentieth-century music a characteristically post-romantic Caesaristic mode that has long been under siege but will not capitulate until those who have cast themselves as the victorious father's dynastic heirs have relinquished their power bases ... The cast of characters is still divided into sheep and goats, strong and weak, rebels and conformists, and its central myth still hopelessly confuses all these categories by attempting to marry the Permanent Revolution to the Great Tradition.[21]

Over the past three decades, the dialectical divide between the linearist progressives and the historical conservatives (more binarization), has become far less polemical than when Taruskin offered his commentary in 1993. Diversity is everywhere in art music and eclecticism is now taken as a measure of contemporaneity.

In his notable essay, "Tradition and the Individual Talent," T.S Eliot posits that the difference between the present and past is that "the conscious present is an awareness of the past," and for the poet, having a "historic sense" is indispensable. For Eliot, that which is primarily a novelty is like a castle in the sand—something that is easily trumped by the power of tradition.[22] Newness is rarely the best barometer of qualitative assessment in art. Boulez's emphasis on "renouncing the legacies of the past" seems to be an attempt to remove judgment and comparison from any discussion of artistic merit. It is a favorite ploy of modernists for it relegates the Eliotic concept of "tradition" to a subsidiary concern—or entirely irrelevant. By negating the importance of their precursors the contemporary artist is, thanks to Schoenberg, emancipated from such comparisons. Boulez, knowingly or not, sought to do the same in his IRCAM manifesto. Alluding to revolutionary attitudes and methods in contemporary musical composition, American composer Charles Wuorinen queried, "How can you make a revolution when the revolution before last has already said that anything goes?"[23]

The purge of anything and everything in music from the "old world" of romantic, emotional excess, was rooted to a large extent in "neoclassicism," in which "extra-musical" associations were considered anathema to the modernist rationale; a rationale that resulted in a "stripped-down, denuded style and with the same neo-primitivist, anti-humanistic ideals," that were becoming salient characteristics of new music "in the name of a resurgent, reformulated "'classicism.'"[24] Those who purported that neoclassicism was the antidote to romantic excesses viewed the music of Stravinsky's Russian period, and especially *Rite of Spring,* as being something to be emulated. But this assessment is what might be called a "fruitful misrepresentation", one predicated on a determinist premise, as well as "a willed ignorance, a willed blindness" to Stravinsky's decidedly "extra-musical" program of the *Rite.* To the advocates of neoclassicism and "absolute music," formalism was essential because it was seen as the result of a lineal progression from to tonality to atonality, and eventually serialism and the hyper-left-brain intellection that permeated mid-century modernism.

But this is a "quest narrative" with determinist underpinnings, as described by Taruskin, for Stravinsky's own commentary about the programmatic aspects of his music, especially *The Rite of Spring,* belies that particular contention. "In *The Rite of Spring,*" Stravinsky would say, "I wished to *express* (emphasis added) the sublime uprising of Nature renewing itself—the whole pantheistic uprising of the universal harvest."[25] So much for the "new objectivity." That would come later for Stravinsky and other proponents of neoclassicism, but it was *not* the stylistic justification for *The Rite of Spring.* The idea purported by the avant-garde that expression in music was a decadent remnant of the nineteenth century ignores the fact that expressiveness had been in the Western musical equation for a millennium.

The advocacy for prioritizing form over other artistic concerns becomes a self-fulfilling prophecy. In critiquing Pieter van der Toorn's emphasis on formal concerns (vis-à-vis Stravinsky), and the idea that one's immediate response to "absolute music" is primarily "pleasure" and "esthetic rapture," in which "the mind, losing itself in contemplation, becomes immersed in the musical object, and becomes one with the object," Taruskin opines:

Directing attention resolutely away from content and focusing entirely on form is hardly an "immediate" response to art. It is no one's first response. (Why else, after all, is a taste for "absolute music" the most notoriously "cultivated" of all musical tastes?) It is a learned response—learned from Stravinsky. It has its costs.[26]

Becoming "immersed" in contemporary art music on the level that Pieter van den Toorn advocates requires a serious intellectual investment on the part of the listener. Coming to a deeper appreciation of the more sophisticated expressions of the late nineteenth-century tonal utterances of late Brahms or Mahler, or the early twentieth-century works of Bartók or Stravinsky require a focused commitment as well. But with tonal music, even the most advanced in the idiom, cognitive constraints are not nearly as severe as they are when experiencing atonal music. Getting to the point of "esthetic rapture" is rarely an immediate response in the case of atonal serialism. It is a hard-won circumstance. The hindsight of history suggests that it may be futile.

Art Music in the New Millennium

As mentioned in the previous chapters, composers continued and continue to work in pan-tonal, extended-tonal and quasi-tonal syntaxes in the wake of the contra-tonal, Schoenbergian aesthetic of the Second Viennese School (Barber, Britten, Schuman, et al.). Their intention in doing so indicated an understanding that beauty and communication still mattered in an era where modernism was considered progressive and "cutting edge." As James Howard Kunstler opines in his observations about modern architecture, there has been purposeful divorce from nature that is linked to an elitist drive for power in an attempt to compel the public toward utopian fairness and justice. He views this as being a quasi-Marxist rationale and writes:

> Modernism doesn't care about truth and beauty; it cares about power, especially the power to coerce. Many people detect that dynamic, and that is one reason they loathe Modernist buildings. The main imperative of Modernism was to separate us from nature, since it was human nature that brought about all the horrors of the 20th century and so revolted the intellectual elites. The result of that was a denatured architecture of the machine and an animus against what it means to be human located in nature.[27]

The highly mechanized, formulaic, left-brain music born of the same modernist rationale was but another "denatured" art form that was foisted upon the public by elites who believed that they "knew better than others" in an attempt to fashion a society that left the old, "bourgeois" culture in the dust. In 1966 Bernstein suggested that pop music was the realm of invention and "unabashed vitality," while the modernist iterations of "electronic music, serialism, chance music" had become stale and "acquired the musty odor of academicism."[28] One can imagine Adorno's apoplectic reaction to a serious musician of Bernstein's stature "going rogue" with regard to pop culture. A few years hence, Bernstein considered jazz to be the new frontier of musical creativity. But as the avant-garde started to outgrow its academicism in the late 1970s, tonal influences began showing up, "sneakily at first, and then with radical new approaches through which composers have found a way to share again the fruits of the earth."[29] Bernstein spoke to this development accordingly:

> So the crisis turns out after all to be a solution, ironically enough, just as the earlier crisis of the mid-fifties can now be seen in retrospect to have been an occasion for synthesis, the merging of the two previously hostile camps. Thus, what was hitherto seen as the Great Split ... can now be seen as a fusion of extraordinary force ... So all in all things don't look so bad. We are in a position where one style can feed the other, where one technique enriches the other, thus enriching all of music.[30]

When American composer Jennifer Higdon (b. 1962) received a commission to compose a new work for the seventy-fifth anniversary of Philadelphia's Curtis Institute of Music, her thoughts regarding her work reveal a decidedly romantic notion: "Curtis is a house of knowledge—a place to reach towards that beautiful expression of the soul which comes through music."[31] Her resulting composition, *Blue Cathedral*, is a reflection of *l'elan du Coeur*, an impulse of the heart. Stylistically, her music is not the romanticism of Mahler or Strauss, but in spirit, it clearly possesses a romantic soul and is far removed from the extreme atonal utterances that failed to be attractive on the most basic level. As the music of Higdon, Eric Whitacre (b. 1970), Arvo Pärt (b. 1935), Ola Gjeilo (b. 1978) and other composers who revere music's ability to elicit the "beautiful expression of the soul" demonstrates, there now exists a more humane rationale evident among many late-modern composers. I, for one, believe that is a positive thing, and necessary if art music is to make its way out from the margins of contemporary society. Times have changed, and so has art music.

In previous essays I alluded to the diversity of styles and rationales within the sphere of contemporary art music, a diversity that Leonard B. Meyer so presciently prophesied in 1967. Of course, we understand that diversity (the "fluctuating stasis" as Meyer called it) has been a part of the compositional landscape going back at least to Ives and Stravinsky (both were eclectic in their source materials), but the determinist Darmstadt clouds that hung over the post-World War II era blocked the sunny disposition of music written by numerous composers who didn't buy into a *contra*-tonal aesthetic. If, as Boulez suggested, the past cannot meet our "present-day needs," the music of the "neo-spiritualists" provides ample evidence to the contrary.

After the first World War, Claude Debussy—often considered the first "modern" composer—believed that Stravinsky was "leaning dangerously toward Schoenberg" and the international atonal school that prioritized intellection over all other compositional concerns. In a letter from 1893 to entrepreneur Andre Poniatowski, before he established his reputation as a major talent, Debussy opined that music is "not even the expression of feeling, it's the feeling itself."[32] This echoes Arthur Schopenhauer's attitudes regarding musical phenomenology and "the will."

For the advocates of formalism who espoused the idea that neo-classicism was the necessary revolution against romanticism and/or impressionism, Stravinsky's *Rite of Spring* established a new paradigm for literal and "impersonal objectivity" and the "renunciation of sauce," in that it "passed from the sung to the said, from the invocation to the statement, from poetry to reportage."[33] Despite this "fruitful misrepresentation," it could be said that it is the singing, the invocation of the poetics and feeling in music—the non-literal and tonal properties—that puts us in touch with our humanity. It has been said that Stravinsky's music is admired more than it is loved. One can easily extrapolate that this is due in large part to the "impersonal" neo-classic objectivity that is endemic in much of his later work—objectivity that relegates the emotive aspect of music to something subsidiary.

Lincoln Center's *White Light Festival*, initiated in 2010, markets its festival concerts with the promise of a "transcendent," experience. Recent festivals have highlighted music composed and performed by notable artists such as Gidon Kremer and the Hilliard Ensemble, artists who have specialized in liturgical, quasi-New Age, "back-to-the-basics" genres of Sacred Minimalism, *Tintinnabuli* and neo-Spiritualism. The festivities have also included panel discussions featuring an auditory physiologist, a cognitive neuroscientist and an expert on comparative religion, presumably to discuss the religious and spiritual traditions of music and its effects on our psyche.

In recent decades, ascribing the term "conservative" to anything is more often than not seen as being pejorative and decidedly teleological—reactionary, in fact. Conversely, being a "progressive" is viewed as something desirable for its connotations of egalitarianism and liberation. A century ago, Eliot observed that using the adjective "traditional" had become a term of "censure" or opprobrium when assessing art—a condition or state of being anachronistic and to be avoided. Yet Eliot's wisdom concerning the importance of tradition is in itself timeless. The pursuit of artistic excellence is "traditionally" associated as much with genius as it is with industry and developing a focused work ethic (Goethe's contention). Having talent is certainly an important factor, but talent must be molded and developed for it to reach its full potential. "Tradition," according to Eliot, "cannot be inherited, and if you want it you must obtain it by great labour."[34] Artists who are aware of their precursors stand to benefit from comparisons with great artists of the past in their pursuit of excellence.

The emergence of the neo-spiritualist musical genre in the 1980s, with its renewed emphasis on melodic and harmonic simplicity and its predilection for diatonicism is now seen as being a reaction to indeterminacy—the pervasive by-product of atonal syntaxes. Perhaps neo-spiritualism isn't "neo" after all. In his novel, *Doktor Faustus*, Thomas Mann asserts that art music never fully emancipated itself from the influence of "the cultic setting" despite modernism's attempts at dissolving any remnants of supernatural religiosity.* The emotive power and attraction of tonality and pan-tonality were never actually supplanted by the postulates of atonality, but rather were slandered by those

---

* Thomas Mann's use of the term "cultic" in his novel Doktor Faustus, refers to Christianity.

with anti-essentialist ideological leanings and determinist agendas. Some may view the renewed yearning for that which is spiritual and religious with a jaundiced eye, but the impulse for inner fulfillment, whether through religious faith, nature, or great art is fundamentally humane; impulses that were considered universal and valid according to Immanuel Kant. Roger Scruton suggests that Kant hypothesized that aesthetic beauty superseded religion as the "archetype of revelation." As the music of Higdon and other composers who revere music's ability to elicit the "beautiful expression of the soul" demonstrates, there now exists a more humane rationale evident among many post-modern composers and their music. And *that* is a welcome sound.

Recommended Recordings

Schuman: *New England Triptych*, Gerard Schwartz, Seattle Symphony Orchestra

Copland: *Connotations*, Leonard Bernstein, New York Philharmonic

Barber: Concerto for Piano, John Browning, piano, St. Louis Symphony

Salonen: *Foreign Bodies*, Esa-Pekka Salonen, Finnish Radio Symphony Orchestra

Britten: *Simple Symphony*, English Chamber Orchestra, Benjamin Britten, conductor

Ades: *Asyla*, Simon Rattle, City of Birmingham Orchestra

Bassett: *Echoes From an Invisible World*, Sergiu Comissiona, Baltimore Symphony

Carter: *Variations for Orchestra*, James Levine, Chicago Symphony Orchestra

Babbitt: *Around the Horn*, Group for Contemporary Music

Tippett: *A Child of Our Time*, Sir Colin Davis, London Symphony Orchestra

Bartók: Piano Concerto No. 1, Zoltan Kocsis, piano, Ivan Fischer, conductor

Busoni: Piano Concerto, Garrick Ohlsson, piano, Christoph van Dohnányi, conductor

Stravinsky: *Firebird Suite* (1919 version), George Szell, Cleveland Orchestra

Ravel: *Rapsodie espagnole*, Pierre Boulez, Berlin Philharmonic

Varèse: *Ionization*, Pierre Boulez, Ensemble InterContemporain

Bizet: *Carmen*, Carlos Kleiber, Vienna State Opera (DVD)

Wagner: *Götterdämmerung*, Sir Georg Solti, Vienna State Opera and Philharmonic

Higdon: *Blue Cathedral*, Robert Spano, Atlanta Symphony Orchestra

Brahms: Piano Concerto No. 2, Emil Gilels, piano

Mahler: Symphony No. 3, Claudio Abbado, Vienna Philharmonic

Strauss: *Alpine Symphony*, Zubin Mehta, Los Angeles Philharmonic

Schoenberg: *Pierrot Lunaire*, Pierre Boulez, Ensemble InterContemporain

Pärt: *Da pacem Domine*, Andrey Boreyko, Hilliard Ensemble

Whitacre: *Lux Aurumque*, Eric Whitacre, conducting

Gjeilo: *Serenity*, Charles Bruffy, Phoenix Chorale

Wuorenin: *The River of Light*, Oliver Knussen, Contemporary Music Group

Endnotes

1   Victor Davis Hanson, "In Defense of the Liberal Arts," *National Review* On-line, December 16, 2010.

2   Victor Davis Hanson, "How Not To Save the Liberal Arts," *New York Post*, Op-Ed, December 18, 2010.

3   Steve Swayne, *Orpheus in Manhattan: William Schuman and the Shaping of America's Musical Life* (New York: Oxford University Press, 2011), p. 324.

4   Alex Ross, *The Rest is Noise, Listening to the Twentieth Century* (New York: Farrar, Straus and Giroux, 2007), p. 447.

5   Esa-Pekka Salonen, *Full Speed Ahead* (Deutsche Grammophon, CD-B0003965-02, liner notes, 2005).

6   Richard Taruskin, *The Danger of Music and Other Anti-Utopian Essays* (Berkeley: University of California Press, 2009), p. 317.

7   Richard Taruskin, *Music in the Late Twentieth Century* (Oxford-New York: Oxford University Press, 2010), p. xv.

8   Ibid.

9   Ibid., p. xvii.

10 Taruskin, *The Danger of Music*, p. 48.

11 Friedrich Nietzsche, *Richard Wagner in Bayreuth*, as cited by Carl Pletsch (*Young Nietzsche*, New York: The Free Press/Simon and Schuster, 1991), p. 189.

12 Richard Norton, *Tonality in Western Culture* (University Park and London: Pennsylvania University Press, 1984), p. 236.

13 Justin Davidson, "After 99 Years, an Admission; On appreciating but not necessarily enjoying—Elliot Carter's music," *New York Magazine*, February 18, 2008 Issue, http://nymag.com/arts/classicaldance/classical/features/43889.

14 Arnold Schoenberg, *Letters*, edited by Erwin Stein, trans. Eithne Wilkins and Ernst Kaiser (Berkeley, CA: University of California Press, 1987), p. 164.

15 Taruskin, *Dangers of Music*, p. 321.

16 Ibid., p. 311.

17 Ibid., p. 321.

18 Ibid., p. 311.

19 Mark Swed, Review: "L.A. Phil and Semyon Bychkov achieve a musical summit with 'Alpine Symphony,'" *Los Angeles Times*, October 30, 2015.

20 Taruskin, *Dangers of Music*, p. 321.

21 Ibid., pp. 364-365.

22 T.S. Eliot, *The Waste Land and Other Writings-Tradition and the Individual Talent* (New York: Modern Library/Random House-pbk, 2002), pp. 99-102.

23 Taruskin, *Music in the Late Twentieth Century*, p. 353.

24 Taruskin, *The Danger of Music,* p. 423.

25 Igor Stravinsky, *Music in the Western World: A History in Documents*, selected and annotated by Piero Weiss and Richard Taruskin (Schirmer-Wadsworth Group/Thomson Learning, 1984), p. 439.

26 Taruskin, *The Danger of Music,* p. 425.

27 James Howard Kunstler, "Executive Order," *Clusterfuck Nation Blog*, January 10, 2020

28 Leonard Bernstein, *The Unanswered Question: Six Talks at Harvard* (Cambridge, MA-London, England, 1976), pp. 420-421.

29 Ibid., p. 421.

30 Ibid., p. 422.

31 Jennifer Higdon: *Blue Cathedral* (Telarc CD-80596 liner notes, 2002).

32 Taruskin, *The Danger of Music,* p. 197.

33 Jacques Rivière as cited by R. Taruskin, *The Danger of Music,* p. 388.

34 Eliot, *The Waste Land and Other Writings,* pp. 99-100.

Mahler: The Composer Only Conductors Love?

My Time Will Come
Gustav Mahler

n 1988, while preparing to conduct a concert featuring the music of the young, and at the time, relatively unknown Chinese composer Tan Dun, I visited the Park Avenue offices of Beata Gordon, cultural affairs director of the Asia Society to discuss the current state of contemporary Asian music. During our conversation, Ms. Gordon informed me that she was the niece of the esteemed Ukrainian conductor Jascha Hornstein. I made mention of the late maestro's recordings of Gustav Mahler's symphonies, of which I was a great admirer. Ms. Gordon's eyes rolled back, and in somewhat of a disdainful manner, she half-sighed, "Maaaahler; the composer only conductors love."

Her sentiment is shared by many, who for one reason or another, find Mahler's music unapproachable and incommodious.[*] George Szell, a protégé of Richard Strauss, and admittedly a "late convert to Mahler," once referred to Mahler's long symphonic utterances as being "hypertrophic" and "not really capable of salvation." Indeed, Mahler's symphonies have bewildered and confounded for decades. However, increased exposure to his music via the copious recordings that are now available as a result of the digital age has resulted in many new converts. The Mahler cult has evolved into a major religion with zealous devotees flocking to concerts whenever his music is performed.

Although not to everyone's tastes, conductors have long held a fascination with Mahler's music as evidenced by the numerous of recordings of his major works dating back to the earliest years of long-playing albums. Early champions of his music included Bruno Walter and Willem Mengelberg, who was the music director of the Royal Concertgebow Orchestra (RCO) from 1895 to 1945. Mengelberg conducted all of the Mahler symphonies with the RCO in 1920 as part of a Mahler Festival, which surely was unprecedented at the time. Walter, who knew the composer personally, was also one of his earliest champions. In his 2010 chronicle of Mahler's life, *Why Mahler? How One Man and Ten Symphonies Changed Our World*, Norman Lebrecht dispels the popular myth that Mahler's compositions were neglected in the decades following the composer's passing. With over two thousand performances of his music between his death in 1911 and World War II, only the music of Jean Sibelius and Richard Strauss was performed with greater frequency in Europe and the United States.

---

* The predicate of this chapter was a review of two concerts that I wrote for *World & I* Magazine. The concerts took place in 2002, when in successive weeks the Vienna Philharmonic and the Royal Concertgebow Orchestra of Amsterdam appeared in New York. Both orchestras—Vienna under the direction of Riccardo Muti, and the RCO under Riccardo Chailly—performed Mahler symphonies on their programs; Nos. 4 and 5 respectively. Both ensembles have had long associations with Mahler's music going back to the composer's tenure as the director of the Vienna Court Opera from 1897 to 1907. In Amsterdam, Mahler conducted a week of concerts in 1903 with the RCO, including two performances of his Fourth Symphony—in the same concert! The RCO's music director at that time, Willem Mengelberg was a great admirer of Mahler and one of the first serious advocates of the composer's work outside Vienna. He recorded Mahler's Fifth Symphony with the RCO in 1926. With 2011 being the centennial of Mahler's death I felt inclined to offer a perspective as both a conductor and collector of historic recordings. I've included my review of the concerts at the end to this chapter and will reference the performances of 2002 on occasion.

Currently, there are more than 700 recordings of Mahler's nine symphonies (and an unfinished tenth) commercially available with 174 versions of his popular first symphony leading the pack. (I own twenty-two recorded versions of the first symphony, but don't tell my wife.) German conductor, Oskar Fried, was the first to record Mahler's music in 1924. Other recordings by Dmitri Mitropolis, Rafael Kubelik, Eduard van Beinum, Paul Kletzki, Charles Adler, Eduard Flipse and Herman Scherchen date back to the 1930s. Bruno Walter's legendary recording of Mahler's symphonic song cycle, *Das Lied von der Erde* dates from 1938.

Perhaps due to the significant Mahler legacy of the RCO, Holland's Philips recording company (*Philips Phonographische Industrie—PPI*) founded in 1950, was among the first recording companies to take up the Mahler cause with earnest. Among the earliest Philips releases include recordings of Mahler's 6th and 8th symphonies by the Rotterdam Philharmonic conducted by Eduard Flipse, which were recently re-released in 2010 and available via the Rotterdam Philharmonic website. Leopold Stokowski, who recorded the first stereophonic recording for Bell Labs in the 1930s, was one of the first conductors to take a keen interest in the advances of recording technology. He conducted the U.S. premiere of Mahler's 8th symphony and recorded a live performance of the work with the New York Philharmonic and the Westminster Choir at Carnegie Hall in 1950.

Despite the passing of Sir Georg Solti, Leonard Bernstein, Klaus Tennstedt, Lorin Maazel and Claudio Abbado, legendary maestros who were serious Mahler-ites, the Mahler craze has continued unabated. In 2014 I attended a New York Philharmonic concert in which Bernard Haitink, another important Mahler conductor, turned in a brilliant account of Mahler's third symphony. (I enjoyed it so much I took my daughter to hear it the following evening.) The concert hall was packed and maestro Haitink received standing ovations on both nights.

Which begs the question: Who, among the more recent crop of the new "elder statesmen" might be candidates for future distinction as Mahler champions? The names are familiar: Dohnányi, Barenboim, Jansons, Tilson-Thomas, Zander, Levi, Chailly, Inbal, Fischer, Geilen, Rattle. They've all turned out recordings of Mahler's symphonies, but to survey their entire output may not be possible, though for the Mahler fanatics the prospect seems inviting.

Mahler as Measure

Mahler is considered to be the most confessional of composers. It's been said that Mahler looked a rose through world-colored glasses, and that observation is telling. According to his biographer, Deryck Cooke, Mahler was "intensely preoccupied with this discrepancy between human aspiration and human weakness."[1] This was a central narrative in his life and work. Cooke offers this assessment:

> His persistent theme is "The spirit is willing, but ... no, not the flesh is weak; rather the spirit is willing, but it is undermined by its own fatal weakness—faced by life's frustrations, it is prey to discouragement, bitterness, emptiness, despair ... Mahler's inner conflict was the eternal one between innocence and experience, idealism and realism, affirmation and denial.[2]

These dichotomies resulted in a musical style that composer Julian Johnson refers to as having a "plurality of constituent voices," voices that express a vast array of emotions. Though he wrote no operas, he wrote many songs and his symphonies might be considered musical dramas played out on a metaphysical sound stage. For many, Mahler is the ultimate tone poet. His second, third, fourth and eighth symphonies contain texts that are sung by female soloists or choruses.

The Greeks taught us that catharsis could be uplifting and beneficial. They also asserted that the experience of suffering could be the way to attain deeper understandings of truth and the meaning of life. Mahler's music gives us large doses of ebullient catharsis and turbid despondency, often in the same movement of one of his symphonies. Given the horrors of the 20th century, many can identify with Mahler's sullen and pessimistic musical utterances and believe his music is reflective of the tempestuous times in which we live. The decidedly "un-rosy" and melancholic aspects of his music co-exist with the triumphant and effulgent episodes resulting in a profound emotional juxtaposition of the "constituent voices" that Johnson alluded to. As Johnson notes:

> Mahler's music presents itself as a kind of telling. It addresses us directly, demanding to be heard and intimating that it has disclosures to make ... it is romantic in the sense that it demands that we, as listeners, identify subjectively with its musical voice such that it comes to speak powerfully for us

... Mahler himself subscribed to the idea and encouraged others to hear his work this way: "I have written into them everything I have experienced and endured."[3]

Characterizing his experiences as something that he "endured" is revealing in that it suggests a difficult life; one filled with anguish, loneliness, despair and other not-so-pleasant circumstances. Significant aspects of that difficulty had to do with certain personal tragedies—the death of his daughter, his fatal heart disease—as well as the racial tensions that existed in Austria for Jews living as a minority in the Austro-Hungarian Empire. He would say, "I am thrice homeless, as a native of Bohemia in Austria, as an Austrian among Germans, as a Jew throughout the world."[4] Morbidity and death are narratives that play heavily into Mahler's compositions. At eighteen he wrote a letter to a friend in which he expresses the thoroughly conflicting thoughts of suicide and fervent hopes for a bright future. His preoccupations with the dichotomy of life's contradictions, especially as they pertained to the cruelty of life in relation to a supposedly loving God, became the vortex of his creative endeavors, and all of this is expressed via "the schizo-dynamics" of his music, as Leonard Bernstein described it.

At the turn of the twentieth century, the angst expressed in Mahler's music was seen by some as a foretelling of the impending cataclysm of a new dark age and romanticism's last ride into oblivion. Bernstein considered Mahler to be the musical prophet of the century of death, one who foresaw the possibility of the apocalypse and humanity's self-annihilation. This extrapolation has become part of the Mahler religion, and though a leap of faith is required to fully accept that premise, all religions require this kind of faith conviction from their adherents. In his Harvard lectures of 1973, Bernstein suggests that the reason that Mahler's music wasn't enthusiastically received in the decades after his death was because the foreboding pessimism of the composer's prophetic utterances—a pessimism summed up in his final completed symphony—was too true and the public would rather not be troubled by such discomforting thoughts. The baleful history of the twentieth century surely gives Bernstein's extrapolation credence.

Mahler's symphonies are rich in "extra-musical" associations and several of his nine works in the genre feature religious-based texts. Cooke contends that

Mahler was the link between the late romantic era and modernity in much the same way that Beethoven was the link between the classicism of Mozart and Haydn, and the early romantic utterances of Schubert and Schumann. Citing Mahler's progressive harmonic explorations and "disrupting of tonality," Cooke views Mahler as the bridge between Wagner's chromaticism and Schoenberg's atonality, asserting: "Mahler was the focal point of the age: he stepped up the psychological tension of romanticism until it exploded into the violent patterns of 'our new music.'"[5]

Though some view Mahler's progressive tendencies as a contravention with the tradition of nineteenth-century musical style and rationale, his music is deeply infused with the romantic spirit in that it is highly programmatic and often has literary associations, and is decidedly tonal and not at all preoccupied with the kind of intellection and formalism that characterized Schoenbergian modernism of the early twentieth century.[*] In spirit and syntax, he is closer to late Beethoven than Schoenberg. His use of extended tonality in his ninth and tenth symphonies, exemplified by some of the most unconventional harmonic properties in his output, is said to be expressions of his emotional state upon being notified by his physician that he had little time remaining due to his declining health. The romantic notion that music is a communicative art form was part of Mahler's compositional rationale to the end. Taking issue with the notion that Mahler was a "precursor" to the atonal music of the Second Viennese School, conductor Kenneth Woods avers:

> And had Mahler lived another 38 years? I think anyone who contends he would have joined, or even preempted Schoenberg's revolution in doing away with tonality and functional harmony, is either deluded, deluding or ignorant. Yes, Mahler's music may have continued to get more dissonant and complex, and his harmonic schemes more fraught, but tonality and tonal structure were absolutely central to everything Mahler did as a composer. Without a sense of a tonal starting point and a hierarchy and progression of tonal centers, Mahler's whole approach to form couldn't possibly work, and for Mahler, each key, however extended or obscured, had symbolic meaning.[6]

---

[*] Curiously, though somewhat predictably and enigmatically, Mahler suggested that the idea of his music being highly "programmatic" was a counterfeit claim.

His unique style, with its "curiously contrapuntal fabric" and his brilliant command of orchestration, yields music of great communicative power. His music could be banal and "hypertrophic," but as Aaron Copland opined, despite these inherent weaknesses and perplexing characteristics, "there remains something extraordinarily touching" and deeply compelling about his mode of composing. As Copland put it:

> All of his nine symphonies are suffused with personality—he has his own way of saying and doing everything. The irascible scherzos, the heaven-storming calls in the brass, the special communings with nature, the gentle melancholy of a transitional passage, the gargantuan ländler, the pages of an incredible loneliness—all these combined with his histrionics, an inner warmth, and the will to evoke the largest forms and the grandest musical thoughts, add up to one of the most fascinating composer-personalities of modern times.[7]

Copland made these observations in the early 1940s, a mere thirty years after Mahler's death and before many of his post-World War II champions, most notably Kubelik, Abravanel and Bernstein, took up his cause. As Szell reminds us, at the turn of the century, a time when there was tremendous turmoil in the world and the arts, Vienna was very "pro-Mahler" as a conductor but very "anti-Mahler" as a composer due to the confounding nature of his highly personal compositional idiom. The zeitgeist of the early twentieth century increasingly celebrated science and innovation while taking a dim view of religion and stylistic traditions of the past. Extolling the virtues of aesthetic beauty was increasingly considered to be superficial and glib, even hypocritical in the face of humanity's inhumanity towards one's fellow man. The derision directed toward anything "romantic" in the early decades of the twentieth century, especially as it pertained to using "extra-musical" associations in one's compositions, was seen as archaic and completely antipodal to modernity.

Mahler's "communings with nature" and his willingness to acknowledge the spiritual dimension of the human experience, with all the attendant cosmological associations, set him apart from the emerging avant-garde composers (who, by the way, loved to appropriate him as one of their own), in significant ways. It is also a primary reason why his music continues to find converts, even in our postmodern culture. We intuit that there is something authentic in the idea of "otherworldliness" and in this regard, we readily identify with the surreal aspects of Mahler's music (those cowbells, the harp and celesta passages, and the muted trilling violins in the Sixth Symphony!) Though the modernists increasingly considered these associations to be unsophisticated and/or banal, Mahler's sincerity of expression carries the day and inextricably draws us into his sound world. Another twentieth century American composer, George Rochberg, offers this insightful perspective regarding Mahler's cosmology:

> The of the ancients and the primitives, expressed in magic, rites and rituals, which invested the world around them with signs and symbols of the unknown, paradoxically insured the survival of these peoples; for through their seemingly unsophisticated notions they preserved the sense of awe and mystery in the face of a cosmos into which man had seemingly stumbled. And we? Because we have lost that precious sense of the magic and mystery of existence, we have no cosmology—physics and astronomy are poor substitutes … Mahler was the last composer to intuit that music belongs to cosmology and is supported by it.[8]

In our postmodern society, where many have turned to the music of the minimalists such as Philip Glass and John Adams, and neo-spiritualists Arvo Pärt and Henryk Górecki (with their decidedly non-cathartic ruminations), in order to find inner peace and contentment, it's fascinating to observe how Mahler's cathartic laden, histrionic and "schizoid" music continues to find an increasingly cosmopolitan audience willing to embrace its sound world, in spite of its banalities and paradoxes, which are myriad. His symphonies, along with those of Dmitri Shostakovich, Jean Sibelius, Sergei Prokofiev, Anton Bruckner and Sergei Rachmaninoff represent the last of the great symphonic tradition that began with Mozart, Haydn and Beethoven and proceeded to Schubert, Schumann, Mendelssohn, Brahms, Dvořák and Tchaikovsky.

But what a sound world it is. Alluding to an all-encompassing aspect of the symphonic medium, he once told Jean Sibelius that "a symphony should be like the world; it should contain everything,"[9] and in Mahler's sound world it frequently does. The hammer blows in his sixth symphony, guitar, mandolin, large choruses, children's chorus, solo voices, bells, gongs, celesta, harps, alternate violin tunings, posthorn solos, multiple bass clarinets, multiple timpanists, klezmer bands, pipe organ, off-stage brass ensembles, cowbells, sleigh bells—all in service of Mahler's unique creative utterances.

His stylistic mélange included muscular marches and counter-marches, symphonically proportioned dirges and landler, folk melodies, nursery tunes, birdcalls, heaven-storming choruses, stentorian brass fanfares, ultra-romantic melodic writing that incorporated so many "constituent voices." It seems that Beata Gordon's assertion that only conductors love this music was only partially correct as many more have been attracted to this highly compelling music and its creator. Perhaps no composer, save Beethoven, sweeps the listener into a world so personal in its introspection yet so universal its musical, dramatic and poetic visage.

The Mahler Tradition

The Vienna Philharmonic, founded in 1842 by Otto Nicolai, was at one time Mahler's orchestra as he was its Music Director from 1898 to 1901. Mahler was also appointed the General Director of the Vienna Court Opera (at Brahms' urging) in 1897 at the age of 37, a position he held for ten years. Being that the Philharmonic was also the orchestra of the Vienna State Opera, Mahler obviously cultivated an intimate musical relationship with that ensemble.

It's interesting to note that in all likelihood Mahler only heard his music on the occasions in which he conducted it. Cooke observed that the composer heard his Fifth Symphony only eight times in his life and made revisions of the orchestration after each performance. He never heard the ninth symphony and his tenth remained unfinished when he died. He once told Otto Klemperer, "If after my death something doesn't sound right, then change it. You have not only the right, but the duty to do so.[10] Lebrecht observes that an examination of the second symphony undertaken by Viennese scholar Renate Stark-Voit turned up more than three hundred material differences between the published score of 2001 and two of the composer's performing manuscripts—in the third movement alone![11] As Lebrecht notes:

> He conducted with an awareness of immortal perfection and made constant changes to his own works, requiring the Fifth Symphony, among others, to be reprinted with extensive Changes ... a precisionist who tried to leave nothing to chance and, on the other, a dreamer in pursuit of an unattainable perfection ... Everything Mahler said and did about his music implies that there is more than one way to read his work, and that a conductor should follow fantasy rather than literal fidelity.[12]

So much for Toscanini's *con scritto* creed.* The issue of conductors editing scores, commonly known as "retouching," has often been a source of contention. What liberties, ask the dogmatists, can a performer take in editing a score, thus altering the intentions of the composer? In a 1998 New York Times essay on the practice of "retouching" of Robert Schumann's symphonies (works that Mahler himself re-orchestrated), Richard Taruskin cites a survey of these works by English scholar, Brian Schlotel. Schumann's abilities as an orchestrator have been long debated and many esteemed conductors have "adjusted" the scores of his canonical symphonies in an attempt to bring aural clarity to certain passage that otherwise suffer from perceptual opacity. But is this a fool's errand? Schlotel tends to think so. "The sense of striving for high ideals, which the symphonies communicate, is in a way echoed by the orchestra striving for effect in those passages that are difficult to bring off."[13]

Taruskin agrees and portends that there exists "an ethical dimension, endemic to the romantic concept of art,"[14] that is diminished when attempts are made to remove the challenging aspects of a particular orchestration decision in favor of something that may be more easily executed by the musicians. This, in turn, diminishes perhaps the most compelling aspect of romantic music; that is, the realization of the "undreamt" or impossible—the metaphysical. Mahler's music, like Strauss', is technically demanding in the extreme, thus when the execution is brought off with seemingly effortless command and precision, the result can be thrilling. Mahler is said to have been greatly impressed with the technical skill of Mengelberg's Amsterdam orchestra and its ability to perform the most difficult passages of his music effortlessly.

Four of Mahler's symphonies contain texts, however, it is the drama within the music, and the struggle entailed in its realization, that fascinates and fires the imagination of many contemporary audiences. As a result, the ability to penetrate Mahler's emotional world in order to achieve oneness with the spirit and character of his music, and then being able to convey those emotions convincingly, has become a measure of a conductor's (and orchestra's) mettle, and this is why many conductors now take up Mahler's case.

---

* Italian conductor Arturo Toscanini was famously known for his strict fidelity to the printed score of a given work and wasn't concerned with extra-musical associations. The term *con scritto* means "as written."

Although there can be more than a few myths regarding the art of conducting, there is one aspect about conducting that is clearly not mythic; namely, that age and experience are significant assets in the conducting profession. Maturity and experience, combined with solid musicianship, scholarship and a cultivated sense of taste, are necessary elements in the makeup of a truly great conductor. Autocratic dictators who berated musicians and had the power to hire and fire are relics of a past era. Fear of the person standing on the podium can no longer be the motivating factor in attaining musical excellence. Emotional and intellectual profundity, combined with expertise to manifest those attributes into a meaningful musical expression, become the true measure of a successful maestro.

As mentioned at the beginning of this essay, coming to terms with Mahler can be a daunting challenge for any number of reasons. A close friend, who made a serious listening effort to come to terms with Mahler's remarkable Sixth Symphony, came away bewildered, even after listening to the score multiple times, unable to fully comprehend the mammoth structures that Mahler constructed. Lebrecht offers some sage wisdom in the attempt to "understand" this music.

> The symphonies are dauntingly long, and the songs are in German. For those who lack patience in languages, Mahler can be impossibly forbidding, a fortress with no entry point ... Mahler is not an over-the-counter medicine. What works for one person may leave another cold ... Much depends on the interpretation you choose and the mood in which you receive it ... Not every civilized person is susceptible to Mahler, but within the monumental edifice of his works there are chinks that allow a listener to be at one with him-or herself. And those are the points when the Mahler fortress becomes a private refuge.[15]

Coming to Mahler may be for many a step-by-step process. Lebrecht may be a bit hyperbolic when he suggests that Mahler's symphonies have "changed our world," but if one has the patience, determination and discipline to undertake the exploration with vigor, this music can be life changing. It certainly changed mine.

(The following remarks are excerpts from my reviews of the concerts by the Vienna Philharmonic and the Royal Amsterdam Concertgebow Orchestra in 2002, which appeared in World & I Magazine.)

Mahler's Fourth Symphony for soprano and orchestra, which was offered by Riccardo Muti and the Vienna Philharmonic at Carnegie Hall was composed between 1899 and 1901, with the composer conducting the final revised version in New York in 1911, the year of his death. It is undeniably his most pastoral symphonic offering. Its quiet, idyllic character shocked critics at its Munich premiere, undoubtedly due to their expectation of another epic, heaven-storming utterance that was evident in Mahler's earlier works in this genre, especially his "Resurrection" Symphony (No. 2). The fourth's leaner orchestration and chamber-like textures were in stark contrast to the monumental complexities of the first three works of his symphonic output, thus critics considered it a failure. The use of sleigh bells in the signature opening bars, "a celestial sleigh-ride" as described by Cooke, and a solo violin tuned a full tone lower than the standard tuning, sets an aura of rustic tranquility at various junctures in the piece.

Mahler's childhood was far from being a completely happy experience, having lived with domestic discord for much of his youth, thus the sardonic, quasi-cynical expressions that permeate much of his music are never far from the surface. The celeritous shifts of mood, from the ebullient playfulness to the bittersweet, are invariably part and parcel of Mahler's compositional modality. Muti and the VPO played this dichotomic gambit superbly as the adroit Vienna players captured the emotional nuances of Mahler's moodiness with great *élan*, often breathtaking in its realization.

The dance-like scherzo, with its "country fiddle" episodes, is one of Mahler's most ingenious creations. Originally titled, *Freund Hein spielt auf* (Friend Death Strikes Up), the poetic contrast between the music's innocence and querulous characteristics is once again cunningly juxtaposed. Perhaps no orchestra anywhere can realize the ländler-like quality of this music in the manner of the Vienna Philharmonic and on this occasion they executed that especial Austrian inflection to great effect. The tender, "heart-easing" slow movement, "a transfigured cradle song" as described by Cooke, displayed once again the distinctive beauty of the VPO strings. The diaphanous quality of their playing demonstrated the extent to which they are capable of producing a variety of timbres. The delicate and translucent timbres displayed in this movement left little doubt as to why this orchestra has achieved its eminence.

Mahler based the finale of his Fourth Symphony on one of the ten orchestral *lieder, Das himmlische Leben* (The Heavenly Life), which he composed on the folk-anthology *Das Knaben Wunderhorn* (The Youth's Magic Horn). Composed in 1892, he originally intended to it be the finale of his third symphony and parts of this song appear in the fifth movement of his third symphony. He subsequently withdrew that idea and reconstructed the song incorporating thematic elements of the first three movements of his Fourth Symphony, thereby making it cyclical and suitable for its finale. There exists a spirit of unfettered innocence in this angelic music. Mahler creates an evocation of heavenly atmospherics as the final notes from the harp seemed to disappear into the afterlife, and on this occasion, Muti and the VPO achieved a perfect realization of Mahler's intentions.

If Mahler's Fourth Symphony may be considered to be his "pastoral" symphony, his Fifth might be considered his "schizophrenic," as the polar worlds of anguish and exultation exist side by side with little more than Mahler's proficiency for organizing and controlling monumental symphonic structures giving the work any sense of cohesiveness. This seventy-five-minute work may be considered one of his "hypertrophic" compositions, however Riccardo Chailly and the Royal Concertgebow Orchestra made a strong case for it in their Lincoln Center performance.

Like the Vienna Philharmonic, the Royal Concertgebow Orchestra has significant links to Mahler as he was a frequent guest conductor in Amsterdam. Willem Mengelberg, the orchestra's music director from 1895 to 1945, became one of the first conductors to champion Mahler's music and produced a Mahler Festival in Amsterdam in 1920 where Mahler's entire symphonic oeuvre was presented, an unprecedented feat, even by today's standards. The Mahler tradition has continued in Amsterdam as the RCO has produced many highly acclaimed recordings by noted Mahler conductors, including Bernard Haitink, who was the music director of the RCO from 1963 to 1988. Mahler's Fifth, as played by one of the great Mahler orchestras, was a highly anticipated event coming on the heels of the RCO's recording of the work with maestro Chailly conducting.

Presenting a series of "one-nighters" as part of an extended tour might wreak havoc with balances and textural considerations in a lesser ensemble, as acoustical properties change from venue to venue. One never sensed any such difficulty from the RCO. The string tone of the ensemble was rich and dark with exceptionally fine cellos. Given that there is still very little bass response in Lincoln Center's Avery Fisher Hall, the lower strings projected admirably, however in louder passages one could have hoped for more bass sonorities. This wasn't a note perfect performance (there were a few minor problems in the brass and the wind intonation was at times slightly imprecise), but the tension and excitement of the music were quite palpable.

The famous trumpet fanfare that begins the symphony as played by Fritz Damrow, was taut and bracing, and the orchestral *tuttis* that occur throughout the piece were brilliantly realized. Chailly highlighted the work's tripartite structure by playing the first two movements virtually without a pause, resulting in a release of tension at the end of the second movement that was evident throughout the hall as the audience, conductor and orchestra took several moments to gather themselves.

The scherzo was exciting without being histrionic in a superficial or glib manner. Chailly's interpretation didn't impart the wild abandon of Herbert von Karajan or Leonard Bernstein, but his account possessed a dynamic vitality and swagger, nonetheless. One revelatory feature of this performance was Chailly's placing his excellent principal hornist, Jacob Slagter, between the first and second violins thereby highlighting the importance of the horn solos that appear throughout the movement.

Dedicated to his wife Alma, the symphony's fourth movement *Adagietto,* is surely one of Mahler's most tender and intimate creations. Scored for strings and harp, this movement is often a topic of debate among conductors, scholars and Mahler aficionados. An *Adagietto*, technically speaking, should be played at a marginally faster tempo than a full-fledged *Adagio*. Mahler confuses the issue somewhat by assigning the designation *Sehr langsam* (very slow) to the score. Consequently, conductors who opt for the faster *Adagietto* character will perform this movement between eight and ten minutes (Kubelik and Solti), while those who choose to adhere to the *Sehr langsam* designation will take up to twelve minutes or longer to reach the final bars (Karajan, Bernstein). Chailly opted for the slower approach and the lovely sonorities of the RCO strings made for a wholly convincing reading as the poignancy of this music was expressed to its fullest. The capricious rondo finale was presented without pause (*attaca*) as indicated in the score and once again the cumulative effect of the presenting the musical architecture in its triptych form resulted in an overwhelming release of tension; the final peroration bringing the Avery Fisher Hall audience to it feet.

The proficiency with which the Royal Concertgebow Orchestra dispatched this fiercely demanding music was most impressive. Mastering technical demands in the realization of any Mahler symphony is part of the drama that is played out on the concert stage. The catharsis that Mahler summons via the instrument that is his—the orchestra—and the expression of his struggles, are vicariously transmitted by the efforts of the musicians on stage to the listener in very powerful ways. I was struck by this very real phenomenon time and again during the RCO's performance. There was a strong sense of oneness between Chailly and his orchestra on this night, and for anyone who belongs to the Mahler religion, this performance was surely riveting, even spiritual. In this day and age, we tend to get large doses of Mahler via recordings, however, to experience his music in the concert hall is an occurrence that all confirmed Mahlerites surely relish. The psycho-acoustic phenomenon that transpires in the live concert experience reminds us of just how miraculous orchestral music can be.

Needless to say, both Muti and Chailly had their respective ensembles in fine form and the occasion to hear two orchestras of this caliber perform Mahler symphonies in less than a fortnight offered an extraordinary opportunity to assess two of the emerging "elder statesmen" in repertory that an increasingly sympathetic public is finding easier to love.

Recommended Recordings

Gustav Mahler's symphonies have been well served through recordings, as there are numerous accounts of distinction of his symphonic output by many esteemed conductors. It should be noted that while Leonard Bernstein was recording his first Maher cycle for Columbia amid great fanfare in the 1960s, Maurice Abravanel in Utah and Rafael Kubelik in Europe were quietly completing their own recorded cycles. Kubelik's fine Mahler recordings are now available from Deutsche Grammophon as a budget box-set. Georg Solti's epic cycle with the Chicago Symphony is also available as a budget set from London and several accounts in that set are deeply satisfying.

What is fascinating is how much interpretive license various conductors take in the face of the Mahler's copious instructions. It would seem that given Mahler's abundant designations in his scores, there would be a fairly consistent way to present the music. But this is not the case. How many conductors, for instance, completely ignore the designation of *poco ritardando* at bar 628 in the finale of the first symphony (just about all of them), or perform the final bars of the same symphony as a hyper- *stretto* (taking a suddenly faster tempo) while adding a bass drum and or timpani whack on the final note when it's not in the printed score? These are but a small sampling of the variances that you'll hear from one interpretation to another. Compare Sir John Barbirolli's recording of the sixth symphony to anyone else's. It's astounding!

Perhaps we shouldn't fret too much over these interpretive liberties because as Lebrecht reminds us, Mahler stated that his symphonies should be revised every five years and that conductors could be rather free in their realizations of the score. As Mahler would say, "the music is not to be found in the notes."[16]

Recommended Recordings

(Conductor, Orchestra and Record label)

Symphony No. 1, *The Titan*
   Rafael Kubelik, Bavarian Radio Symphony, Deutsche Grammophon, (DG)
   Michael Geilen, Southwest German Radio Orchestra, Hänssler Classic
   Seiji Ozawa, Boston Symphony Orchestra, DG

Symphony No. 2, *Resurrection*
   George Solti,Chicago, Symphony Orchestra, London
   Bruno Walter, Columbia Symphony, SONY
   Ivan Fischer, Budapest Festival Orchestra, Channel Classics
   Riccardo Chailly, Royal Concertgebow, Orchestra, Decca

Symphony No. 3
   Leonard Bernstein, New York Philharmonic, DG & SONY
   Jascha Hornstein, London Symphony Orchestra, Unicorn
   Claudio Abbado, Vienna Philharmonic, DG
   Bernard Haitink, Chicago Symphony Orchestra, CSO Resound

Symphony No. 4
   George Szell, Cleveland Orchestra, SONY (Judith Raskin, soprano)
   Georg Solti, Chicago Symphony, London (Kiri Te Kanawa, soprano)
   Klaus Tennstedt, London Philharmonic, EMI (Lucia Popp, soprano)

Symphony No. 5
   Leonard Bernstein, Vienna Philharmonic, DG

Herbert von Karajan, Berlin Philharmonic, DG
Riccardo Chailly, Amsterdam Concertgebow, London
Gustavo Dudamel, Simon Bolivar Youth Orchestra, DG
Rudolf Barshai, Junge Deutsche Philhamonie, Laurel Records

Symphony No. 6
Herbert von Karajan, Berlin Philharmonic, DG
Yoel Levi, Atlanta Symphony Orchestra, Telarc
George Szell, Cleveland Orchestra, SONY
Benjamin Zander, Philharmonia Orchestra, Telarc
Sir John Barbirolli, New Philharmonia Orchestra, EMI

Symphony No. 7
Michael Geilen, Southwest German Radio Symphony, Intercord
James Levine, Chicago Symphony Orchestra, BMG
Leonard Bernstein, New York Philharmonic, SONY
Valery Gergiev, London Symphony Orchestra, LSO Live

Symphony No. 8, *Symphony of a Thousand*
Georg Solti, Chicago Symphony Orchestra, London
Klaus Tennstedt, London Philharmonic Orchestra, EMI (DVD)
Eliahu Inbal, Frankfurt Radio Symphony, Denon
Antoni Wit, Warsaw National Philharmonic, Naxos (CD & DVD)
Leonard Bernstein, London Symphony Orchestra, SONY

Symphony No. 9
Herbert von Karajan, Berlin Philharmonic, DG
Bruno Walter, Vienna Philharmonic, EMI (1938)
Bernard Haitink, Amsterdam Concertgebow, Philips (1971)
Christoph von Dohnányi, Cleveland Orchestra, London

Symphony No. 10 (Unfinished)
Rafael Kubelik, Bavarian Radio Symphony, DG (Adagio only)
George Szell, Cleveland Orchestra, SONY (Adagio only)
Riccardo Chailly, Berlin Radio Symphony, Decca (Completed reconstruction by Deryck Cooke)

Das lied von der Erde
Reiner-Forrester-Lewis, Chicago Symphony Orchestra, RCA Victor Living Stereo
Walter-Miller-Haefliger, New York Philharmonic, SONY
Klemperer-Ludwig-Wunderlich, New Philharmonia Orchestra, EMI Classics
Oue-DeYoung-Villars, Minnesota Orchestra, Reference Recordings
For more information on Mahler recordings see Tony Duggan's survey at:
www.musicweb-international.com/Mahler/index.html

Endnotes

1   Deryck Cooke, *Gustav Mahler: An Introduction to His Music* (Cambridge-London-New York: Cambridge University Press, 1980), p. 6.

2   Ibid., pp. 7-9.

3   Julian Johnson, *Mahler's Voices: Expression and Irony in the ts and Symphonies* (Oxford-New York: Oxford University Press, 2009), p. 3.

4   Cooke, *Gustav Mahler,* p. 7.

5   Ibid., p. 5.

6   Kenneth Woods, *View From the Podium,* August 11, 2011, http://kennethwoods.net/blog1/2011/08/11/re-rating-richard-part-i-strauss-he-was-no-mahler-he-was-no-wagner.

7   Cooke, *Gustav Mahler,* p. 5.

8   George Rochberg, *The Aesthetics of Survival, On the Renewal of Music* (Ann Arbor, MI: University of Michigan Press, 1984), p. 237.

9   Donald Mitchell, *Gustav Mahler Volume II: The Wunderhorn Years: Chronicles and Commentaries* (London: Faber and Faber, 1975), p. 286.

10   Norman Lebrecht *Why Mahler? How One Man and Ten Symphonies Changed Our World* (New York: Anchor Books, 2011), p. 212.

11   Ibid.

12   Ibid., p. 213.

13   Richard Taruskin, *The Dangers of Music and Other Anti-Utopian Essays*, Chapter 19, *Let's Rescue Poor Schumann From His Rescuers* (Bereley-Los Angeles-London: University of California Press, 2011), p. 127.

14   Ibid., p. 128.

15   Lebrecht, *Why Mahler?,* p. ix.

16   Ibid.

31

Soul Music

I had no idea Beethoven had so much soul.
A Senior Citizen from Harlem

The place: Harlem's historic Apollo Theater.

The date: February 25, 1990.

The occasion: A Black History Month Concert featuring the New York City Symphony.

The Program: Music by American composers Duke Ellington (his *Three Black Kings* Suite), Joseph Schwantner (*New Morning for the World*, based on texts of Dr. Martin Luther King, Jr.), and the not-so-American, Ludwig van Beethoven—his ebullient Seventh Symphony. Yours truly conducting, with the legendary bass-baritone, William Warfield (Narrator) and Eric Person (Saxophone) exhibiting excellence in their respective solo roles.

By all accounts, the concert was a resounding success. The atmosphere in the hall was warm and despite the below-freezing temperatures outside (a faulty heating system nearly sabotaged the dress rehearsal), and the audience was highly enthusiastic in its appreciation of our efforts.

As is the custom at such events, there was a post-concert reception where patrons, sponsors, board members and friends gather to share their opinions and impressions. At the reception, I was asked by a number of the concert's attendees why I chose to close the program with a work by Beethoven as opposed to music by another Black American composer. Certainly, there was much fine music by William Grant Still, Louis Moreau Gottschalk, or Ulysses Kay that could have served as a fitting finale. In responding I expressed my desire to give the audience, many of whom might have never heard a large symphony orchestra, a taste of the great legacy of classical music—music that in all likelihood, inspired the youthful Still, Gottschalk and Kay and fueled their passions to become fine composers in their own right. As the reception was coming to a close an elderly African-American lady approached me, shook my hand, and with a big smile thanked me for bringing the orchestra to Harlem. She expressed what a joy it had been to hear the orchestra in the very auditorium where she had heard so many legendary entertainers over the years. As she was about to depart she looked back at me and said in somewhat of a reflective manner, "You know, I never knew Beethoven had so much soul."

Mission accomplished! This person was touched by music quite that was apart from her usual cultural experience. That's a significant reason why I do music. The power of music to touch hearts and minds in profound and meaningful ways—to inspire, to build bridges, to ameliorate antagonisms, to remove boundaries, and in so doing, allowing us to share in the glory and potential of our collective humanity, is in large measure why we accord music so much importance. Beethoven and Ellington composed music that possesses great soul and passion, though their musical styles are as different as the cultures from which they came. Musical style may be considered akin to a dialect or an accent of a particular language in that it is an external reality. It is the metaphysical dimension of beauty that approaches the transcendent and affects the heart and soul in profound ways; and *that*, as Immanuel Kant asserted, is a universal phenomenon that is common to all people, regardless of their cultural origins.

Much is made of music's transcendent properties, as well it should, for it is through these properties that the potential to find and experience the best of ourselves, including our latent divinity, can be manifested, if only temporarily. In recalling the elderly women's remarks about experiencing the soul of Beethoven's music, I couldn't help but think of the stereotypical view of classical music being music for the well-educated upper-class. Music critic,

Alex Ross notes that this mindset "is planted deep in the cultural psyche" of contemporary society.[1] Lawrence Levine avers in his book, *Highbrow/ Lowbrow: The Emergence of Cultural Hierarchy in America*, that this perception has alienated certain demographics in terms of finding greater enthusiasm for art music in general. Still, the lady at the post-concert reception reminds us that these stereotypes are superficial and often without credence. Great music speaks loudly across those superficialities, whether composed by a son of Germany or a son of Harlem.

In the latter half of the twentieth century there emerged a prevailing attitude that regarded European culture as being elitist, non-inclusive and a product of white privilege. Politically correct, multiculturalist attitudes, though well intentioned in some respects, have had a downside in that they tend to devalue great art and music based on criteria other than aesthetics, craft, or axiological concerns.[*] The recent penchant to examine art based on *a priori* abstractions and politically correct conceits has the effect of diminishing the aesthetic aspect of art. We should remember that the term "politically correct" has been attributed to Marxists Antonio Gramsci and Leon Trotsky. Art historian Camille Paglia has been especially outspoken on this issue, and though she values multiculturalism, she sees how it has become an ideological cudgel that has resulted in a spate of hyper-presentism that ignores historical context.

Regarding this emerging attitude, musicologist Leonard B. Meyer observed: "Making explicit value judgments about individual works of art is considered invidious and elitist ... because privileging any work or style is non-egalitarian."[2] Consequently, making distinctions based on objective standards is too often considered discriminatory. Moreover, developing one's craft through dedication and discipline in order to succeed (meritocracy) is scrutinized by those with politically correct mindsets as being the result of certain unfair or unjust social advantages. Charges of discrimination and privilege are becoming commonplace in every sphere of art.

British composer and author Julian Johnson obverses, "To be discriminating used to mean to be capable of exercising judgment—to be wise, in fact."[3] In our politically correct society making critical distinctions in matters of art and

---

[*] Axiology is the study of the nature, types, and criteria of values and of value judgments, especially in ethics.

creativity has become antipodal to realizing genuine democratic ideals. Instead, we find ourselves in what Johnson calls a "pseudo-democracy;" a situation in which it is no different "to discriminate against" than to "discriminate between." Not seeing the difference between things is, in a sense, anti-pluralistic. Johnson avers that this is a condition "not built on self-respect, but on lack of respect for one another and even ourselves," precisely because it has the effect of diminishing our human individuality and "the inviolable identity of every one of us."[4] This is the underlying rationale of political correctness and groupthink and should be viewed with great trepidation.

Capitulating to the notion that making distinctions is discriminatory in a pejorative sense undermines any attempt at achieving a balanced perspective when attempting to assess art and music. Many things can be demonstrated as being objective in the art of music. Even if a great deal of what goes into aesthetic judgment and criticism is primarily subjective, it is the attempt to apply objective standards which makes any sort of arrival at a judgment meaningful. If our assessments are merely a matter of personal opinion or taste, then any great art form is rendered to be something much less powerful and important than it actually is. In this "pseudo-democratic" condition where *faux* egalitarianism rules the day, we are confronted with the condition where everything could be considered great art, or conversely, nothing is great art. Not all cultures are equal in every sense. Some are superior or inferior to others in a variety of ways, especially with regard to civil liberties, thus surrendering reason to a subjective viewpoint in the attempt be "fair" can have the effect of diminishing the value of a particular culture as well as elevating cultures that are intrinsically unjust and inhumane.

This has resulted in an emergence of a misguided tendency to consider classical art and music, and those who are advocates of "high art," as being elitist. Some scoff at this notion citing a lack of perspective based on a limited or prejudicial view of history. The long history of Western classical music points to a decidedly inclusive attitude by composers who embraced music outside of their provincial circumstances. I recall a conversation with several conducting colleagues at a conference of the League of American Orchestras where the late Maurice Abravanel, the long-time music director of the Utah Symphony Orchestra, was holding court. The conference had included several panel discussions regarding the allegations of elitism in the art world in general, and as the discussion turned to the charges of elitism being directed at those who love classical music, Maestro Abravanel declared somewhat indignantly, "If I'm an elitist for loving the music of the great composers of the past, well then, so be it!" The acceptance and enthusiasm for classical music in Japan, Malaysia, Korea, Taiwan, Viet Nam, Venezuela, China, Brazil and Dubai testifies to its ability to touch the human heart in profound ways. If the music has soul, then people are "down with it," regardless of culture, ethnicity or socio-political circumstances.

Having great talent and craft, and using those attributes to attain sublime artistic and aesthetic results, transcends political concerns. That's not to suggest that artists don't have political views or agendas, or that they will avoid ascribing political views to their art. We all do, albeit to varying degrees. But the claims of those who view art through the politically correct prism of contemporary multiculturalism are rooted in something other than objective assessments about art itself; namely ideology. Charles Rosen considered the idea that all cultures are "equally valid or valuable" to be an "absurd thesis." He was especially contemptuous of multicultural advocates who attempted to "suppress any critical examination of non-Western societies" in the name of political correctness, whether that examination was cultural, artistic or social.[5]

Roger Scruton reminds us that though all civilizations have culture, "not all cultures achieve equal heights."[6] This view is considered deeply offensive to those who champion radical egalitarian perspectives, yet it can't be argued that many cultures and nations continue to hold backward attitudes regarding gender equality, homosexual rights, racism and religious intolerance. Despite the fact that the arts have been historically supported by the wealthy, composers were often destitute and deeply in debt (Schubert and Wagner, e.g.) Most artists are among the 99% demographic that is currently the object of concern of the "occupiers" advocating for redistributive economic justice.

It should be noted, however, that private sector contributions to the arts in the United States remains quite significant. Writing for *Heritage Action for America*, (July 8, 2013), Katherine Rosario cites a *The Washington Post* report that private donors contributed $13 billion to the arts in 2011. This has been the reality for decades. Without the largesse of wealthy individuals and corporate entities, most arts organizations would become insolvent rather quickly. By comparison, yearly federal government appropriation to the National Endowment for the Arts between 2008 and 2014 averaged about $150 million.

After the New York Philharmonic returned from its concert in North Korea in 2009, Zarin Mehta, executive director of the New York Philharmonic addressed the Korea Society in New York City about the orchestra's experience as cultural ambassadors.* As he spoke about the importance of financial support for this type of cultural exchange, he mentioned that the number of households that regularly purchase tickets for the Philharmonic's concerts in a given year amounts to about 40,000. Thankfully, wealthy patrons and corporations that value the arts recognize the need to keep arts organizations afloat. Still, without finding new advocates the financial situation for the arts remains precarious. Sadly, Cristoforo Ivanovich's dire prediction (back in 1681), that diminishing "profits at the door" would lead to the endangerment of "the noble entertainment" of art music remains an enduring problem.

In 2006 I returned to the Apollo Theater with the New York City Symphony to conduct a benefit concert for the Harlem School of the Arts. The school boasts a jazz ensemble, a flute choir and a 25-piece string orchestra, and all the school's ensembles were invited to take the stage. The string ensemble joined the NYC Symphony in a performance of Bach's third *Brandenburg Concerto* and it was evident that the young students relished the opportunity to perform with the professionals. The H.S.A. Jazz Ensemble collaborated with the orchestra in a spirited performance of Duke Ellington's *Sophisticated Lady* in an arrangement by the school's music director and an old friend, Kelvyn Bell. It was a deeply gratifying experience for all, and ten thousand dollars was raised to support the school's educational endeavors.

In addition to having the New York City Symphony at this Apollo Theater concert, I invited David Bratton, composer of the iconic gospel song *Every Praise*, and Mzuri Moyo Aimbaye to perform. Mzuri offered an excerpt from her one-woman show based on the life of civil rights advocate Fannie Lou Hamer. It was in Hamer's impassioned speech before the Credentials Committee of the Democratic National Convention in 1964 that is cited as being the final impetus that propelled Congress to pass the Civil Rights Act. In Mzuri's show

* The Korea Society is a private, nonprofit, nonpartisan, 501(c)(3) organization with individual and corporate members that is dedicated solely to the promotion of greater awareness, under-standing, and cooperation between the people of the United States and Korea.

she performs many of the songs of the Civil Rights movement as well as the song, *Still I Rise*, which is based on Maya Angelou's 1978 poem of the same name.* In a speech at the Williams Institutional CME church in Harlem, New York on December 20, 1964, Hamer uttered her famous remark, "I've been tired so now, I'm sick and tired of being sick and tired, and we want change."[7]

Speaking with the HSA students, they possessed an enthusiastic willingness to explore music that might be viewed as being "un-hip" by their peers. They were beyond that particular cultural limitation and were eager to make music and bring joy to the audience. In their innocence and enthusiasm, they seemed unaffected by any cultural or social stereotyping and only sought to do their best.

Speaking to the transformational power of music in *Politics*, Plato stated that "education in music is the most sovereign because more than anything else rhythm and harmony find their way to the inmost soul and take the strongest hold upon it."[8] Aristotle concurred: "It is plain that music has the power to of producing a certain effect on the moral character of the soul, and if it has the power to do this, it is clear that the young must be directed to music and be educated in it."[9] I'm not sure that the Harlem students could relate to the cosmic influences that the ancient Greeks referred to, yet it was clear to me that on a very fundamental level, the young musicians from Harlem, and the elderly lady at the Apollo Theater experienced the soulfulness of the music Beethoven in significant measure. Though this was music from a different time and culture, it proved yet again the elemental power of music to transcend the external realities in which we live and work. On these two occasions in Harlem music had the effect of connecting all of us to a higher dimension and a greater sense of community, and in so doing, allowed us to relate more soulfully as brothers and sisters.

Postscript (February 2021)

In 1999 Specioza Naigaga Wandira Kazibwe was invited to speak at an event sponsored by the Family Federation for World Peace and Unification in Washington, DC, I was asked to assist in producing an entertainment program for that event. Miss Kazibwe was Vice President of Uganda from 1994 to 2003.

---

* In 2011 I arranged the song "Still I Rise" for Mzuri Moyo Aimbaye and the New York City Symphony for a performance at the United Nations General Assembly Hall commemorating the tenth anniversary of the 9/11 attacks on the United States.

She was the first woman in Africa to hold the position of vice-president of a sovereign nation.

Prior to the event, I was informed about Ms. Kazibwe's initiative in Uganda called *Soulin' the Girl Child*, an empowerment program for young women. I was inspired by her *Soulin'* initiative and I approached the Family Federation directors with the idea of writing a song dedicated to her efforts. I composed a song called *Soulin'* with the idea that we need *Soulin'* to heal the world. The vocalists on the recording, which we recorded at Manhattan Center Studios are gospel singer Mzuri Moyo Aimbaye and Rev. Phillip Thomas of the American Clergy Leadership Conference and the former lead singer with the Brooklyn-based Funk, R & B band, Crown Heights Affair.

In 2020, while going through some of my older (and forgotten music), I rediscovered the song and sent it to Mzuri. She too had forgotten "Soulin'" but was inspired to revive it and in so doing she, and her husband Djehuty Se Hotep, launched a weekly Internet radio program based on the "Healing Power of Music" and decided to use the song as their theme song. Djehuty expanded on the *Soulin'* concept and he offered the following etymological premise for the term *Soulin'* and how it works in the context music and art. Expounding on the "Soulin'" concept, Djehuty explains:

SOULIN' is Expressing compassion towards oneself and others. It is a compound word consisting of the words SOUL and IN use as a verb to denote positive action. The widely accepted definition according to the Merriam-Webster and Cambridge dictionaries follows in which SOUL is used as a noun or adjective.

i.   As a noun SOUL is defined as the spiritual or immaterial part of a human being or animal, regarded as immortal. Also, a person's moral or emotional nature or sense of identity.

ii. Emotional or intellectual energy or intensity especially as revealed in a work of art or an artistic performance.

iii. A strong positive feeling (as of intense sensitivity and emotional fervor) conveyed especially by African "Black" American performers.

iv.   Cultural Consciousness and pride among people of African heritage such as SOUL MUSIC, SOUL FOOD, SOUL BROTHER.

v.   A person that shows affection or pity – compassion which means a sympathetic consciousness for others distress with a desire to alleviate it.

IN, the word IN "I" "N" is to denote being enclosed or surrounded by or in our case to denote direction as to say inner vs. outer, inside vs. outside, etc.

Recommended Recordings

Joseph Schwantner: *New Morning for the World*, James DePriest, Oregon Symphony
Ellington: *Three Black Kings*, Maurice Peress, American Composers Orchestra
Beethoven: Symphony No. 7, George Szell, Cleveland Orchestra
Still: Symphony No. 2, Neeme Jarvi, Detroit Symphony Orchestra
Gottschalk: *Symphonie romantique*, Maurice Abravanel, Utah Symphony
Ulysses Kay: *Aulos*, Kevin Scott, Metropolitan Philharmonic Orchestra
Bach: *Brandenburg Concerto No. 3*, Trevor Pinnock, English Consort
Mzuri Moyo Aimbaye: The Fannie Lou Hamer Project

References

1   Alex Ross, "Cheap Seats: The Affordable Art of Concert-going," *New Yorker Magazine*, February 2, 2009.

2   Leonard B. Meyer, *Music, Arts and Ideas* (Chicago, IL: Chicago University Press, Second Edition, 1994), p. 348.

3   Julian Johnson, *Who Needs Classical Music?: Cultural Choice and Musical Value* (Oxford-New York: Oxford University Press, 2002), p. 26.

4   *Ibid.*

5   Charles Rosen, "Multicultural Correctness," reply to Ralph P. Locke, *New York Review of Books*, January 16, 2003.

6   Roger Scruton, *Culture Counts: Faith and Feeling in a World Besieged* (New York: Encounter Books, 2009), p. 2.

7   Fannie Lou Hamer, *The Speeches of Fannie Lou Hamer: To Tell It Like It Is*, edited by Maegan Parker Brooks and Davis W. Houck (Copyright: University Press of Mississippi, 2011), p. 62.

8   Albert L. Blackwell, *The Sacred in Music* (Louisville, KY: Westminster John Knox Press, 1999), pp. 169-170.

9   *Ibid.*, p. 170.

32

Hierarchy

Power is a fundamental motivational force ("a," not "the").
But the fact that power plays a role in human motivation
doesn't mean that it plays the only role, or even the primary role.
Jordan Peterson

In the final decades of the twentieth century the juxtaposition of political correctness and deconstructionism, along with the residue from the social rebellion of the Woodstock generation, have made all manner of hierarchy highly suspect. To be sure, there is a certain justification for the opprobrium and mistrust directed at authority figures given the copious examples of tyrannical dictatorships, morally depraved aristocracies, corporate malfeasance, political corruption and a spate of immorality and ethical equivocation among members of the clergy of various faith traditions.

Lord John Dalberg Acton's axiom regarding the corrupting aspect of absolute power seems especially apt. It's important to understand that Acton was not only referring to the power held by authority figures, but also how those who *enable* authority figures by turning a blind eye to corruption for personal gain become corrupt as well. As Acton wrote, "there is no worse heresy than that the office sanctifies the holder of it." Heresy of this type is also contributing to our socio-cultural malaise.[1] Merely holding a position of authority is not an indication of virtue, therefore it is important to be wary of being seduced by authority figures for personal gain.

Holding the proverbial moral high ground has become nearly impossible for any "leader" regardless of profession or vocation. As troubling as these circumstances may be, they are not new and the connection between hierarchy, authority and abuse is not easily dismissed. The advent of liberal democracy in Europe and the West was in many ways a reaction to the miscreant behavior of various authority figures who professed to have the best interests of "the people" at heart.

Jean-Jacques Rousseau's idea that institutions and the leaders of institutions are intrinsically corrupt was an idea that held great currency in the years following the French Revolution. Some two hundred years later, postmodernists such as Michel Foucault, touted the idea that power is the fundamental operating principle in societies and a particular society will have its own "truths" based on who wields power, in other words, truth is fungible. Commenting on this perspective, Foucault writes:

> Each society has its regime of truth, its "general politics" of truth: that is, the types of discourse which it accepts and makes function as true; the mechanisms and instances which enable one to distinguish true and false statements, the means by which each is sanctioned; the techniques and procedures accorded value in the acquisition of truth; the status of those who are charged with saying what counts as true.[2]

The practice of democracy on a large scale is relatively new in the context of human history, and according to Winston Churchill a messy and awful type of governance, "except," as he said, "for all those other forms that have been tried from time to time." Despite democracy's messiness, the intent to foster pluralism and to provide power to the people via representative government remains a noble pursuit, for it has allowed freedom and creativity to flourish in unprecedented ways. Yet even in democratic pluralistic societies, there exists a need to govern and in this regard authority and hierarchy are necessary. Regarding the evolution of the messy democratic process, Roger Scruton observes:

In referring to Western civilization we are not, like Spengler, describing some localized and time-bound fragment of human history. We are describing a project, which grew from the great events in the Mediterranean basin two millennia ago, and which now engages the aspirations and antipathies of all mankind. This project, it seems to me, can endure if it can win a place in our emotions.[3]

Scruton posits that America's great gifts of a "viable democracy and masterful technology," though important and praiseworthy, are not central to its achievements because they "do not conquer the heart," and as such, they do not provide the moral or ethical pillars on which "human life and its meaning can stand up to the sarcastic nihilism of the West's internal critics," or other pernicious social and/or ideological agendas born of "the rising flood of the world's resentment." Judeo-Christian values, according to Scruton, provided the moral and ethical convictions that were indispensable for the grand vision of a constitutional republic to flourish, fending off "sarcastic nihilism" and other ideologies rooted in moral relativism in the process. It is this faith conviction and "the shared meanings conveyed to us by our culture—meanings conveyed equally to the one who believes and the one who doubts,"[4] that makes culture so important. In this regard, culture becomes "the repository of moral knowledge." Foucault would consider truths born of the Judeo-Christian "regime" to be nothing more than the attempt by the church authorities to control their congregations.

Regarding the well-being of the society (the "commonwealth"), Baruch Spinoza opined that "men are not born fit for citizenship, but must be made so," thus he believed that "peace is a virtue that springs from force of character: for obedience is the constant will to execute what, by the general decree of the commonwealth, ought to be done."[5] For Spinoza the "highest degree of independence" could best be achieved when *reason* was the prevailing rationale, thus "to assure the utmost self-preservation" men should be free from the dominion for those prone to wickedness, seditions and wars." That which "ought" (*sollen*) to be done in the context of society, is predicated in large part by the moral and ethical precepts that are perceived to be most beneficial to the greater welfare of the community. Unlike Rousseau's myth of "the noble savage," John Locke believed that individuals start their journeys through life as blank slates (*tabula rasa*) and that virtue and nobility "must be taught—and earned.* It is not inherited."⁶ According to Locke humans have freedom and can choose that which defines their character—good or bad. Like Thomas Hobbes, he was well aware of the human propensity for selfishness and understood that our better angels don't always rule the day. The American founders held similar views regarding human "fallen nature and sought to put limits on governmental power via decentralization.

German philosopher Johann Gottlieb Fichte opined that freedom was "double-edged" and could result in inhumane behavior regardless of culture. Locke understood that noble savages were no less fallen than the nobility in the aristocracy. Fichte properly noted that both noble savages and noblemen needed moral standards to mitigate immoral behavior.⁷ Twentieth-century author V.S. Naipaul (who won the Nobel Prize for Literature in 2001) shared similar perspectives and was criticized by liberal progressives for allegedly not being empathetic, but rather judgmental, in his attitude toward cultures of the developing world, as if indigenous cultures were beyond reproach in matters of morality and responsibility. When asked if he thought that empathy precluded judgment, he responded, "Well, I understand that point of view, too … But I think if you try to look at the world through other people's eyes, that act of looking contains a kind of judgment as well."⁸ In matters of morality and ethics judgment is necessarily in the equation.

Scruton points out that what we "ought" to do means that we "can" do things according to moral and ethical principles *if* we choose to. Intentionality is salient in this regard. In the West, and the United States specifically, the precepts of Judeo-Christian thought are those that have assured a beneficial impact on the development of our republic. The idea of our political leaders being "public servants" too often becomes subsidiary to other, not wholly altruistic, concerns. Understanding hierarchy in the context living for "the purpose the whole" and the greater good is fundamental to the process of establishing a society in which the general welfare of the citizenry is prioritized.

Immanuel Kant wrote about how a "perfectly constituted state" would be based on the "secret plan of nature."⁹ Ironically, the nature of Nature is more

---

* The term "noble savage" is usually attributed to Jean-Jacques Rousseau, but it was British poet John Dryden (1631-1700) who first coined the term in his play *The Conquest of Granada* in 1670. The concept of *tabula rasa* can be traced back to Aristotle and certain Persian and Muslim philosophers who expounded on the idea.

hierarchical than egalitarian, and at times predatory. Christian philosophers and theologians put forth the idea of *scala natura* (the Great Chain of Being), whereby God was at the top of the scale followed by angels, humans, higher animals, lower animals, plants, etc. Certain Judeo-Christian doctrines view humans in a higher position than angels; sons and daughters of God, in fact. The family, consisting of grandparents, parents and children possesses hierarchical characteristics. Though there may be times when family members act in egalitarian ways, they are fundamentally hierarchical.

Predation—the concept of attacker and prey—also reinforces the idea of hierarchy in nature. Richard Dawkins, in his book *The Selfish Gene* (1976), argues that we are evolutionarily hard-wired in such a way as to always assure our survival by seeking power and success, thereby ensuring the survival of our genes. Dawkins posits that it is our genes, "the lowest level of all," and not our bodies, "are the fundamental unit of selection ... the unit of heredity."[10] A noted atheist, he nonetheless views this as being an ineluctable and quasi-altruistic attribute. He avers that there exists an innate willingness in humans to sacrifice themselves for the sake of assuring that one's lineage (and genes) will carry on through one's descendants. Dawkins posits that the penchant for sacrifice (from the Latin *sacra-ficio*; to make holy) is an intrinsic part of human DNA. He admits that those who possess religious convictions are more willing to make sacrifices and concedes that this has been a significant matter in the development of certain cultures in which religious belief was a primary aspect of society.*

---

* It should be noted that renowned evolutionary scholar Stephen Jay Gould considers Dawkins' "selfish gene" concept an "impotent meme" due to what he considers a contradictory and "fallacious argument;" namely the belief in "strict gene selectionism" as the primary mode of evolution. In his subsequent book, *The Extended Phenotype* (1982), Dawkins argues against the central premise that he articulated in *The Selfish Gene*; specifically, that genes, not phenotypes (observable physical or biochemical characteristics of an organism—a body, e.g.), are "the exclusive units of selection." In 1976 Dawkins argued "in no uncertain terms" that genes were "the causal agents" in the evolutionary process, and bodies, those "passive lumbering robots" could not play such a role." Yet in *The Extended Phenotype*, Dawkins offers (in his words) "a work of unabashed advocacy," in which he avers that by observing phenotypes (bodies and behavior) we can better understand the causal dimension of the evolutionary process. Gould writes: "I do not know why Dawkins altered his view so radically. But may I suggest that he simply could not— because no one can after a proper analysis of the basic logic of the case—maintain full allegiance to the fallacious argument of strict gene selectionism." Gould admits being "beguiled" by the "unifying power" of selection theory as an undergraduate student, but as evidence mounted

Scruton notes that we are "intentional" beings, not solely, or even primarily, biologically autonomous in an evolutionary sense as Freud or Darwin might have us believe. He points out that altruism is instinctive; "a considered response," based on "complex personal emotions like pride and shame, which are in turn founded on the recognition of the other as another like me.", the emotions that result in compassion, empathy and charity are the expressions of altruism and "the recognition that what is bad for *the other* is something that *I* have a motive to remedy."[11] Why we have these emotions has everything to do with the fact that in our inter-personal relationships, we are both "self and other," and every self has a perspective that in turn, influences our consciousness in relation to "the other." In this regard, Darwinism fails to take human consciousness into account.[*]

Social Darwinism, a concept mistakenly attributed to English anthropologist and eugenics advocate Herbert Spencer, was "often used as an ugly and bastardized Nietzschean racial philosophy of the strong against the weak," and as a way of assigning blame to one's intellectual enemies.[12] Spencer did, in fact, coin the phrase "survival-of-the-fittest," and in the post-World War II era, this concept is often cited pejoratively by progressives as being a rationale used by those in power to exploit the weak and defenseless for their benefit. Social Darwinism is often linked to the proclivities of eugenics, fascism, racism, capitalism and various modes of social engineering. It's interesting to note that many progressive economists in the first half of the twentieth century, Republicans and Democrats (Teddy Roosevelt and Woodrow Wilson, e.g.), were serious advocates of eugenics and were preoccupied with racial issues. Roosevelt would go as far as to say, "He who thinks not of himself primarily, but of his race, and of its future, is the new patriot."[13] In 1911, when Wilson was governor of New Jersey, he introduced eugenics-based legislation to the state's lawmakers.

---

against the universality of Darwin's initial evolutionary theory he has since changed his perspective. Stephen J. Gould, Structure of Evolutionary Theory.

[*] In Ben Stein's documentary film, Expelled, *No Intelligence Allowed* (2008), Dawkins offers the supposition that there is a higher probability that intelligent life forms from another galaxy (a civilization created via evolutionary processes) seeded our planet with intelligence rather than an un-provable Supreme Being.

Though Darwin's theory may explain certain behavior in the chain of survival and evolution, it does not take into account the issue of human freedom and intentionality in relationship to the aforementioned concept of *scala natura* vis-à-vis God's providence, or the idea of purposeful, intelligent design. For if God exists and is a being of love, then surely freedom and love—or the misuse of freedom and lack of love—are significant factors in the equation when assessing humankind's progress as a species. As Arthur Koestler observes in his book, *Sleepwalkers: A History of Man's Changing Vision of the Universe* (published in 1959, the centennial anniversary year of the publication of Darwin's *On the Origin of Species*), the materialist view of science within much of the scientific community had "retained its dogmatic power over [the] mind," and in so doing rejected the concept of "purpose" from nature, even a purpose unrelated to an "anthropomorphic deity" at a time when an "unprecedented spiritual ebb-tide" was increasing.[14] For Koestler, Scruton and the founding fathers of the American society, intentionality remains an important factor in the pursuit of life, liberty and the pursuit of happiness, thus freedom is a *sine qua non* in the intentionality equation. Yes, we have certain instincts—some good, some bad—but the right to choose remains an intrinsic aspect of the human condition and should not be encroached upon by governmental intrusion.

In his essays on romanticism, political philosopher Isaiah Berlin notes that Greek culture in the classical age was based heavily on mathematics and the belief that there were absolute, unbreakable "axiomatic truths ... from which it was possible by severe logic to deduce certain absolutely infallible conclusions."[15] Because numbers don't lie the Greeks believed there could be absolute wisdom and knowledge, which in turn could be used to order society in ways that could alleviate suffering, doubt, ignorance and vice. Though civic virtue is given high priority by the Greeks, their path toward attaining virtue was at odds with the Judeo-Christian ethos; an ethos predicated on faith, parentalism, filial piety, the brotherhood of man, sense of duty, sin, salvation and atonement. Though the Judeo-Christian tradition places importance on numerology, it is not the primary premise on which its moral tradition takes its cue. Supplanting mathematics with a religious understanding of morality and ethics, according to Berlin, would have been totally beyond comprehension to the Greeks.

As social beings we have a reciprocal nature, consequently reciprocity plays an important part in our development, individually and collectively. This becomes a salient issue for those espousing any hierarchical paradigm, for the need to achieve a harmonious balance between exercising authority while preserving individual freedom, requires benevolence and goodwill. Adhering to strict lawfulness can be seen as inhibiting spontaneity. Isaiah Berlin referred to this dichotomy as "value pluralism," a condition in which certain fundamental values can seemingly be "incommensurable," in that both have merit but are perceived as being in opposition or incompatible with each other.* These seemingly disparate aspects need to be harmonized in an efficacious way so that we might have the best of both worlds at our disposal in our attempts to straighten out "the crooked timber of humanity." In modern times it was in England where respect for "dissident or hostile elites and institutions out of power was written into law, and more importantly, into the *culture*," and where there was a "psychological acceptance of the idea that people had the right to be wrong."[16] Regrettably, in the current gestalt of liberal progressivism being wrong is characterized as being immoral or invidious. This is an unreasonable proposition that undermines the concept of pluralism and has the effect of creating enmity.

Musical Hierarchy

In his book, *Tonality in Western Culture: A Critical and Historical Perspective*, musicologist Richard Norton notes that a prevalent theory emerged among modern composers and theorists that proffers that the era of "classic tonality" in the West was something "that had to emerge." He believes that this is a naïve and determinist extrapolation because it doesn't take into account the idea "that tonality appeared as and how it did through economic, social, political, philosophical, cognitive and aesthetic, as well as "natural" means."[17] Early in his book he describing tonality as "a decision made against the chaos of pitch,"[18] By taking this viewpoint, Norton seems not to understand that

---

* In the evolution of harmonic syntax in Western music there existed two seemingly polar opposite acoustic forces at work; diatonicism and chromaticism. It was Johann Sebastian Bach, who through his brilliant method of equal temperament in 1722, was able to codify and demonstrate the way through which these modalities could be harmonized for expressive purposes.

virtually all musical composition, regardless of syntax, genre or style, can be characterized as a decision to order the musical components of melody, harmony, rhythm and form in a manner that provides order over chaos.

Norton admits of having empathy for the ideas of the neo-Marxist philosopher, Theodor Adorno. He considers Adorno's rationale to be "the only effective antidote to Pythagoras" because it rejects the modernist concepts of "logical positivism, scientific empiricism, idealism, and vitalism;" concepts, that in his view, encumbered virtually all speculation on tonality.[19] According to Norton, it wasn't exclusively human intentionality or natural law that spawned tonality and its wider usage, but rather a variety of circumstances, including the pursuit of power and control—all those "authoritative, theoretical, or theological interests" that Adorno and Norton believe restrain consciousness. As Norton suggests:

> Tonality emerged and developed through the human desire for expressive modes of utterance that were not available in spoken discourse. This emergence was largely pre-reflective and relatively unconcerned with its origins other than to place them within the assumed precision of mathematics (as did the Pythagoreans) or in the hands of the gods (as did the Greek poets). Tonality was frequently observed as an activity of consciousness whose explanatory procedures of creativity were already encrusted by authoritative, theoretical, or theological interests.[20]

Because all codified systems of music are human constructs, and humans are affected by numerous circumstances in their life experiences, it's not unreasonable to argue that intentionality and choice played significant roles in the development of the tonal syntax, just as they did in the evolution of natural language, economics, education, politics or agriculture. Referencing Adorno, Norton views tonality as "a societal expression; it is heard and judged as an immediate historical moment." He avers that the use of various musical materials is like natural language in that "all words of a given language may be available, but they are accepted or rejected according to a given society's mores and laws."[21] This argument has some veracity, but Norton is arguing from the Adorno-esque perspective that the human desire for greater "expressive modes of utterance" from music is a result of something apart from nature. For Adorno, the idea that "nature calls the tune," was a decidedly "bourgeoisie" contention; one that preserved the corrupt status quo despite the reality that tonality had certain "natural" predicates and was efficacious in addressing the innate human instinct to seek beauty, not to mention music's communicative aspect. Foucault would consider this perspective to be merely an attempt by whoever was in power to maintain power by citing natural phenomena, such as the overtone series, in order to maintain authority.

The musical syntax of tonality (aka "the common practice") was indeed a human construct, however, the laws of physics regarding pitch production is predicated on inarguable mathematical premises that Pythagoras ascertained long ago. Moreover, the ontological premises of the tonal syntax reflect various phenomena found in nature, most significantly polarity. Consider the various polar opposites (*yang/yin*) found in the tonal syntax: major modes/minor modes, tonic/dominant chord, and consonant/dissonant intervals to name but a few. It is well established that hierarchical premises are fundamental to the Western tonal syntax. The relational modality of tonic and dominant chords, or dominant and secondary dominant chords, being in a subject-object relationship are fundamental to the harmonic grammar of tonality and its ability to evoke human emotions in an efficacious manner.

Taking his cue from Adorno, Norton views the human desire for beauty and the musical syntax that is its progeny, to be something that needed to be deconstructed in the context of power politics. Accordingly, if the interests of the ruling classes were primarily about aesthetics and/or communication, then aesthetic and communicative concerns were considered "subsidiary" by Adorno, precisely because they serve to further empower the ruling class. The Adorno-Norton view that the public has been alienated from the "romantic composer" who utilized the tonal syntax is patently false. It may be true, as Norton argues, that there "never occurred a perfect tonal moment in the history of music, any more than there has appeared a perfect legal, social, economic or linguistic moment in the history of human consciousness."[22] However, as we are now well into the twenty-first century it is apparent that it's the theories of Marx and Adonro, and the atonal music of Schoenberg and his epigones, that the public has become increasingly alienated from. This is due to the fact that human cognitive processes do not easily sort out complicated and abstract aural stimuli that result in indeterminate musical utterances. The music of the "romantic composers" of the nineteenth century is thriving and is well received by emerging audiences in China, Taiwan, Japan, Korea, Viet Nam, Malaysia, Paraguay, Brazil and Venezuela due to the aurally perceptible and discernible characteristics of tonal music and the various hierarchical inclinations that are intrinsic to its syntactic properties.

Tonal Evolution

As composers in Europe during the Middle Ages and the Renaissance began to compose music with greater linear complexity (polyphony) the natural by-product of this process was a vertical alignment of tones (chords) that possessed definite harmonic properties, and perhaps, more importantly, definite grammatical functions. The evolution of harmonic syntax through the fifteenth and sixteenth centuries, along with the experiments in tuning and interval modification (temperament), led to the development of a hierarchical harmonic grammar, which in turn gave rise to a codified system of key centers and chord functionality. The impulse behind the establishment of equal temperament was distinctly intentional and had *everything* to do with composer's desire to discover more varied and profound modes of expressivity.

Diatonic major and minor scales, along with the evolution of chord grammar based on triadic harmony, became the cornerstones of the tonal spectrum. This in turn provided an aural basis for a sonically rooted "home key." In the era of high polyphony, Claudio Monteverdi (1567-1643) introduced monody (a single melody with a harmonic accompaniment) into the musical lexicon, and though it didn't immediately alter the stylistic reality of the time, it nonetheless set the stage for the compositional style that would become the dominant style of the post-Baroque era a century and a half later. The evolution of the tonal idiom was far more organic and far less "determinist" than Adorno and Norton were willing to admit.

As noted previously, modernists who embraced the ideas of deconstruction and/or post-structuralism, viewed universals, absolutes and anything claiming to possess "eternal verities" as being highly suspect; invidious, in fact. Postmodern progressives view any assertion about how the hierarchical facets of the tonal syntax are in accord with nature, and how they reflect metaphysical truths, to be a claim of privilege and superiority. Whether tonality "had to emerge" as it did, is certainly debatable. But the fact that it did emerge in the way that did and became (and continues to be) the dominant musical syntax for hundreds of years is indisputable. Adorno considered the notion that key-centered music was the "historical fulfillment of tonal truth," to be nothing more than a "fetishistic view of the concept as the concept does in interpreting itself naively in its own domain."[23]

It's more than a bit ironic, if not disingenuous (and downright Hegelian), that Adorno considered the fetish of "historic fulfillment" in relation to *tonality* to be determinist, yet he and other advocates of *atonality* used that very premise to justify the emergence of atonal serialism. Atonality was viewed by early modernists as the next logical and rational step in compositional methodology. It had to happen! Though one can argue that certain social, political, philosophical and aesthetic considerations played into the emergence of atonality, it can be safely argued that atonality's indeterminate aural properties lack the "cohesion" born of the natural, hierarchical and polar characteristics that are apparent, and *perceptible*, in the tonal idiom. Even Schoenberg admitted *that!*

Schoenberg readily conceded that the "simple and natural principle" of polarity, which is germane to the tonal idiom—an idiom based on hierarchical pitch and chord relations—is what gave tonal music its "cohesion" and hence, its commanding emotive power.[24] Further duplicity can be seen when we observe those who embraced and championed the compositional methodology of strict adherence to mathematical and/or hyper-intellectual processes in composition, while inveighing the most vituperative critiques against the idea that tonality may be predicated on certain "universals" found in nature. This rationale threatened their most cherished tenets, most notably, that the evolution from the tonal idiom towards chromaticism and "free tonality" (an oxymoron?) was historically inevitable—a tenet that hardcore modernists love to claim. In this context, were the mid-century modernist composers justifying their own power base in championing music that was predicated on the primacy of rationalism dominating chaos?

In his retrospective of John Cage's legacy, Richard Taruskin posits that a significant reason that Cage was a "scary" antipode to mid-century modernists, was because he challenged their most sacred contentions regarding a "controlling intelligence" as it pertained to having "an ear for music;" that which provided a "reassuring evidence" and a "moral accountability" to the contention that serialism and its methodological cousins were justified. As Taruskin puts it:

> But as Cage implied with his mischievous characterization of "the musical ear," the coherence of the serial structure could only be demonstrated conceptually—that is, on paper—to professionals. As increasing numbers of musicians are now willing to concede, there is no possibility of perceptual corroboration; and musical psychologists are beginning to suspect that the mind's structure may actually preclude the cognitive processing—the "understanding"—of non-hierarchical pitch and rhythmic information. Thus Cage's open renunciation of the discriminating, theory-laden "musical ear" in favor of the literal, physical, uncritically accepting biological ear was especially scary to postwar serialists, because it tainted their ostentatious rationalism with a hint of fraud, producing not just musical dissonance, but cognitive dissonance too.[25]

The research of composer Fred Lerdahl of Columbia University and Ray Jackendoff, a linguist at Tufts University, regarding cognitive constraints of various nonhierarchical compositional syntaxes has indicated that there is a difference between compositional grammar and listening grammar. They contend that their hypothesis in this matter "says nothing about the relative value of compositional techniques," in that a composer is free to imagine and compose in ways that "is of value to him."[26] However, they contend that the cognitive processes of sorting out complicated musical acoustic properties— pitch, rhythm, harmony, structures—no matter how well organized, result in aural constraints that yield little in the way of communicative ability and emotional satisfaction due to the indeterminate nature of complicated music.

Lerdahl argues that compositional grammar is not unlike the grammar of language in that "natural grammar" is born of a spontaneous impulse within a culture and that artificial grammar is "a conscious invention." He differentiates between music that is *complex* as opposed to music that is *complicated*. Lerdahl opines that complication produces a condition in which cognitive processes are challenged beyond their natural and physiological capacities. He contends that *complex* music is based on a "hierarchical structural richness," that results in a perceptible, communicative syntax (tonality is ontologically such), whereas *complicated* music tends to neutralize, even obliterates hierarchical properties due to "numerous non-redundant events per time unit" that tend to hinder the cognitive process and violate certain psycho-acoustic realities.[27]

If listening and comprehension faculties are confused or compromised by complicated pitch sets and rhythmic properties, indeterminacy rules the day, and as Taruskin and others suggest, nature no longer calls the tune. The drive for neutrality, especially the democratization of pitch that Schoenberg and the mid-century modernist composers advocated, can be seen as being inherently unnatural. Leonard Bernstein espoused similar views in his Harvard Lectures in 1973, views that were met with a fair amount of derisive commentary at the time. (The academic serialists ensconced in academia at the time couldn't easily take Bernstein's waxing poetic about the poetics of Mozart's G-minor symphony.) Bernstein, like Cage, was challenging the status quo of the academically entrenched, hardcore modernists who viewed intellectualism as the be-all and end-all of musical composition—and they didn't like it!

Internet journalist Nicholas Carr buttresses Lerdahl's assertion by citing the work of educational psychologist John Sweller, who spent decades researching how we process information in relation to our learning capacities. His studies about cognition and memory are highly relevant to our capacity to sort out sonic information in the process of understanding and enjoying music. Current evidence, as cited by Sweller and others in the field, suggests that "we can process no more than about two to four elements at any given time, with the actual number being lower rather than the higher end of the scale ... the more complex the material we're trying learn, the greater the penalty exacted by an overloaded mind." When retention levels get "maxed out" due to information overload, "it becomes harder to distinguish relevant information from irrelevant information, signal from noise."[28] This points to the natural function of our hearing and how any sonic data that is overly complicated will have the effect of not being perceptible or pleasurable. In the end, even Richard Norton concedes that "the psycho-acoustics of the ear, which, if determined to be inviolate within certain parameters, may indeed prove to be the final court of appeal in explaining why we hear pitches and their incumbent overtones in the fashion that we do."[29]

It's interesting to note that tonality, with its distinctly hierarchical aspects, has been embraced in both European and non-European cultures. Ethnomusicologist Bruno Nettl has observed that in indigenous cultures there also exists a type of social hierarchy concerning music. Nettl's findings indicate that in many cultures music that accompanies ritualistic or ceremonial events is usually more intricate and sophisticated than the music that accompanies simple, quotidian tasks. Moreover, the ceremonial music of a given indigenous group, is more often than not, performed by men due to the power relations in societies where women are not given equal status.

> On the surface, it appears that in many societies men engaged in more musical activity than did women; it's certainly the impression one gets from the bulk of [ethnomusicological] field collections and publications. While this impression may be a result of the larger numbers of males field workers in ethnomusic-ology over the years, many collections by female scholars reflect more or less the same tendency ... the belief that some societies are dominated by men and others by women has for many decades ceased to have much credence in anthropology.[30]

If beauty in the natural world can be considered a feminine attribute (Mother Nature!), and truth can be considered to be a masculine attribute, then the harmonization of these two elemental attributes can be the basis for completeness in the human equation, in life and art. The pursuit of equality in gender matters is a worthy cause and one that can ultimately assist in process of bringing our collective humanity to a better place. The nurturing attribute of "the eternal feminine" is a necessary attribute in the development of any human being.*

Commenting on hierarchies and the pursuit of power, clinical psychologist, Jordan Peterson notes, "Power is a fundamental motivational force ("a," not "the"). But the fact that power plays a role in human motivation doesn't mean that it plays the only role, or even the primary role."[31] Peterson has become a vociferous critic of postmodernism, especially the idea that there are no immutable truths or meta-narratives that inform the human condition. In this respect he views postmodernism, combined with leftist progressivism as being inherently at odds with the idea of hierarchies because hierarchies have

---

* It is interesting to note that many prominent male composers in the twentieth century (Aaron Copland, Quincy Jones, Astor Piazzolla, Elliott Carter, Leslie Bassett, e.g.), spent time in Paris studying with Nadia Boulanger (1887-1979), who was considered the *grande dame* of the Western harmonic theory and syntax.

been fundamental to human progress—and they exist in nature. He notes that according to postmodern orthodoxy, even observable phenomenon in the natural world is suspect, including well-established "biological universals," are increasingly viewed as being merely social constructs.

Because power issues play heavily into postmodernism and cultural totalitarianism, dominant hierarchies of any kind are viewed as being suspect; the result of "a secondary consequence of a socio-political economic structure" that uses power to control or oppress. As Peterson notes, certain hierarchies of dominance in the natural world are millions of years old and are pre-homo sapiens, therefore "there's no blaming them on capitalism" or any other human construct or proclivity. Peterson cites his colleague, Dr. Daniel Higgins, who argues that, "human organizations are sufficiently complex so that dominance is an insufficient means to establish hierarchical priority."[32] That may be obvious to some, but those who possess a progressive mindset won't have it because that premise flies in the face of the narrative that issues other than capitalist economics are part of the socio-cultural equation. Peterson acknowledges hierarchies have been problematic. Because dominance plays a role in certain developmental procedures—not least of which has been the evolution of the natural world, there have been instances where dominance has caused injustices.

With this a backdrop, we can more clearly understand why the neo-Marxist perspectives of Adorno and Norton vis-à-vis the tonal syntax, with its predilection for hierarchical harmonic grammar rooted in nature, is seen as being regressive, bourgeois and out-of-step with egalitarian concerns, and possibly an unseemly vestige of capitalist mendacity. Viewed from their reading of history it is a credible argument. However, this determinist rationale completely usurps the idea that humans are intentional beings and volition plays a significant part in cultural development.

Taruskin avers that mounting evidence points to the idea that music is a "human language" that evolved in much the same way as natural languages. Ideas that worked well were kept. Those that didn't were discarded. He posits that those who were quickest "to reject and denounce biological determinism were determinists of a different stripe; usually historical." If you're convinced that history's purpose is on your side, "you can rationalize any means in helping the inevitable along."[33]

In the tonal syntax of diatonic music there are minor triads within major keys and major triads within minor keys. There are also consonant and dissonant intervals in music much the same way that there are consonants and vowels in language. It is via the aural relationship of intervals and triads (phonology) as formulated by composers, that meaning and beauty in tonal music is realized. If the concept of *scala natura* is to be believed, and many who profess religious convictions do in fact believe this, it would seem that tonality, with its hierarchical and polar properties, is a musical syntax that aptly reflects the nature of Nature—and perhaps the invisible nature of the Creator. Tonality may not be the "perfect" musical idiom as Richard Norton suggests. However, it's not all that far-fetched to suggest that it's ontologically in accord with the attributes and characteristics of the Being at the top of the Great Chain of Being in significant ways.

Recommended Recordings

Bach: *Magnificat in D*, BWV 243, Leonard Bernstein, English Bach Festival Orchestra

Boulanger: *Prelude for Organ in F-minor*, Paul Jacobs, organ

Schoenberg: Orchestral Works, Sir Simon Rattle, Berlin Philharmonic Orchestra

Cage: *Bacchanale for Prepared Piano*, Steffen Schleiermacher, Prepared Piano

Carter: Clarinet Concerto, Ensemble Intercontemporain, Jérôme Comte, clarinet

Copland: *Quite City*, Leonard Bernstein, New York Philharmonic

Bassett: *Variations for Orchestra,* Feruccio Scaglia, RAI Symphony Orchestra of Rome

Lerdahl: String Quartet No.1, Daedalus Quartet

Monteverdi: *Missa In illo tempore*, Paolo Da Col, Odhecaton Ensemble for Ancient Music

Endnotes

1   John Dalberg Acton, "Letter to Bishop Mandell Creighton," April 5, 1887, as found in *Historical Essays and Studies*, edited by J. N. Figgis and R. V. Laurence (London: Macmillan, 1907).

2   Michel Foucault: *The Foucault Reader*, edited by Paul Rainbow (New York: Pantheon Books, 1984), p. 73.

3   Roger Scruton, *Culture Counts-Faith and Feeling in a World Besieged* (New York: Encounter Books, 2007), p. vii.

4   Ibid., p. ix.

5   Baruch Spinoza, *Political Treatise*, translated by A. H. Gosset (London: G. Bell & Son, 1883), html edition by the Constitution Society, 1998, Chapter V, http://www.constitution.org/bs/poltr-00.htm.

6   Jonah Goldberg, *Suicide of the West: How the Rebirth of Tribalism, Populism, Nationalism and Identity Politics Is Destroying American Democracy*, (New York: Crown Forum, 2018), p. 141.

7   Isaiah Berlin, *The Roots of Romanticism: W.A. Mellon Lectures in the Fine Arts*, edited by Henry Hardy, (Princeton, NJ: Princeton University Press, 1999), p. 90.

8   Anand Giridharadas, "V. S. Naipaul: The Constant Critic, the Lover of Animals," *The Atlantic*, January 5, 2011.

9   Immanuel Kant, *Idea for a Universal History with a Cosmopolitan Aim*, as cited by Ruth Chadwick, *Critical Assessments* (London-New York: Routledge, 1992), p. 406.

10   Richard Dawkins, *The Selfish Gene*: 30th Anniversary Edition, (Oxford-New York: Oxford University Press, 2006), p. 11.

11   Roger Scruton, *The Face of God*, pp. 30-31.

12   Jonah Goldberg, *The Tyranny of Clichés: How Liberals Cheat in the War of Ideas*, (New York, NY: Penguin Group USA, 2013), p. 103.

13   Charles Richard Van Hise, *The Conservatism of Natural Resources in the United States*, (New York: MacMillan, 1910), p. 378.

14   Larry Witham, *By Design: Science and the Search for God*, (San Francisco: Encounter Books, 2003), pp. 31-32.

15   Isaiah Berlin, *The Roots of Romanticism*, pp. 2-3.

16   Jonah Goldberg, *Suicide of the West*, p. 60.

17   Richard Norton, *Tonality in Western Culture: A Critical and Historical Perspective*, (University Park and London: Pennsylvania State University Press, 1984), p. 17.

18   Ibid., p. 4

19   Ibid., p. 262.

20   Ibid.

21   Ibid., p. 51.

22   Ibid, p. 263

23   Theodor Adorno, *Negative Dialectics*, (New York: The Continuum Publishing Group, Inc., 2007), p. 11.

24   Arnold Schoenberg, *Style and Idea-Composition with Twelve Tones*, edited by Leonard Stein, (Berkeley, CA: University of California Press, 1975), p. 209.

25 Richard Taruskin, *The Danger of Music and Other Anti-Utopian Essays*, pbk. (Berkeley-Los Angeles-London: University of California Press, 2010), p. 265.

26 Fred Lerdahl and Ray Jackendoff, *A Generative Theory of Tonal Music* (Cambridge: M.I.T. Press, 1983), pp. 300-301.

27 Fred Lerdahl, *Cognitive Constraints on Compositional Systems. Generative Processes in Music: The Psychology of Performance, Improvisation, and Composition*, edited by John Sloboda, pp. 231-59, (Oxford: Oxford University Press, 1992), Reprinted in *Contemporary Music Review* 6/2), pp. 97-121.

28 Nicholas Carr, *The Shallows: What the Internet is Doing to Our Brain* (London-New York: W.W. Norton & Company, 2010), pp. 124-125.

29 Norton, *Tonality in Western Culture,* p. 61.

30 Bruno Nettl, *The Study of Ethnomusicology: Thirty-one Issues and Concepts*, (Champaign, IL: University of Illinois Press, 2005), pp. 410-411.

31 Jordan B. Peterson, *12 Rules for Life: An Antidote to Chaos* (Toronto: Random House Canada, 2018), p. 311.

32 Jordan Peterson, "Simulation," lecture, February 21, 2018, https://www.youtube.com/watch?v=j_Y_bQmxcg0.

33 Taruskin, *The Dangers of Music,* p. 48.

Multicultural Wars

If we cannot justify the very concept of the aesthetic, except as ideology,
then aesthetic judgment is without philosophical foundation.
An "ideology" is adopted for its social or political utility,
rather than truth. And to show that some concept —
holiness, justice, beauty, or whatever — is ideological,
is to undermine its claim to objectivity. It is to suggest that
there is no such thing as holiness, justice, beauty, but only the belief in it —
a belief that arises under certain social and economic relations
and plays a part in cementing them, but which
vanish when conditions change. [1]
Roger Scruton

Does the "Culture War" actually exist, or is it purely a myth? In the aftermath of the 2004 presidential election, Morris P. Fiorina of the Hoover Institute, published his book, *Culture War? The Myth of a Polarized America*, in which he contends that the idea of America being a "deeply divided" nation is a specious claim.* Offering copious data, Fiorina makes the case that a high percentage of Americans possess moderate viewpoints regarding social issues and politics, and as such, citizens are not as "deeply divided" as those on the fringes of the political or cultural spectrums (or the news media) would have us believe. According to Fiorina, these fringe elements tend to confer with coteries who reinforce their particular perspectives and do not represent the large, moderate and politically ambivalent demographic that seeks pragmatic solutions to problems. This is a countervailing argument to that of Pat Buchanan, who has long held that America is under siege due to the encroachment of non-traditional religious (or *contra*-religious) influences and not-so-well intentioned multiculturalists. For Buchanan, nothing less than the soul of America is at stake, and being proactive in defense of our national identity is required.

Yet, despite his claim, Fiorina admits, perhaps unwittingly, that there is something to Buchanan's concerns. He writes:

> The culture war metaphor refers to a displacement of the classic economic conflicts that animated ieth-century politics in the advanced democracies by newly emergent moral and cultural ones.[2]
>
> Even mainstream media commentators saw a "national fissure" that "remains deep and wide," and "Two Nations under God." In sum, many contemporary observers of American politics believe that old disagreements about economics now pale in comparison to new divisions based on sexuality, morality and religion, divisions so deep as to justify fears of violence and talk of war in describing them.[3]

By characterizing the idea of a culture war as a "myth," yet admitting that cultural concerns have displaced what heretofore had been conflicts born of economic concerns, is Professor Fiorina conceding that the "culture war" is more than a metaphor or myth.

Relegating the culture war to a fictive invention makes it easy to dismiss it as a spurious and somewhat inconsequential issue. However, a deeper review of the twentieth century reveals that the "emergent moral and cultural" divide is neither mythic nor metaphoric. Buchanan's apocalyptic prognosis may be

---

* It should be noted that the circumstances in the United States regarding political and socio-cultural polarization are quite different in 2021 than they were in 2004.

seen as expressions of paranoia and hyperbole, but few would argue that in the second half of the twentieth century we witnessed various social and cultural upheavals that give credence to the idea that a culture war is well underway. Moreover, the media-based commentariat that too often dominates the shaping of public opinion has been fully engaged in promulgating the idea of the culture war being real.

Fiorina bases much of his data on the American political environment during the 2002 and 2004 elections. Though the Red State/Blue State paradigm has become a common way to portray the political divide that now exists in the United States, it remains a generalization that does little to explain how and why political and cultural fault lines have developed to the degree they have. Fiorina argues that as a nation we are "more purple" than red or blue and making across-the-board generalizations may not be helpful in accurately assessing our current cultural dichotomy. He correctly asserts that party operatives and insiders are more entrenched and strident in their opinions than most citizens.

But that observation seems fairly self-evident. Culture warriors of any stripe are generally more zealous and intensely opinionated than the citizenry at large. Fiorina doesn't argue that political operatives are not heavily engaged in influencing the public, but rampant virtue signaling, gas-lighting and instances of "cancel culture" in contemporary culture—whether perpetrated by politicians, clergy, activists, entertainers or the media, have become so pervasive that the contention that there isn't a culture war in our midst is untenable. Citing "novelty and negativity" as features that enhance news value, he considers the media to be an accelerant of inflammatory rhetoric because vociferous exhortations and denunciations from partisans produce a sense of conflict, which in turn, makes for juicy sound bites and revenue-generating "clickbait." Winning and spinning the nightly news cycle is the new political sport and "narrative journalism" is the preferred tactic among most media outlets.[*]

Not surprisingly, as we approach the third decade of the new century both Congress and the media vie for the lowest approval ratings from most

---

[*] Sharyl Attkisson's book *Stonewalled: My Fight for Truth Against the Forces of Obstruction, Intimidation, and Harassment in Obama's Washington*, published in 2014, is an insightful commentary on the topic of narrative journalism and transactional journalism.

Americans. The general public has growing contempt for both entities. Politics is adversarial by nature. Moreover, politicians have always been guilty of being patently dishonest for political gain, but now news organizations increasingly align themselves with political parties or ideological perspectives, often in irresponsible ways. Since the 2016 election, Camille Paglia, a liberal Democrat, has been chiding the media for colluding with the Democratic party for creating chaos regarding Donald Trump and his administration. (This is not to suggest that Trump's team hasn't been chaotic.) In an interview for the *Washington Examiner* Paglia declared, "I am appalled at the behavior of the media. It's the collapse of journalism ... I feel like the Democrats have overplayed their hand ... I'm looking forward to voting Democrat again ... But the point is I feel that the media has so utterly lost its credibility that I think people are going to vote against the media again."[4] Certain members of the media have accused President Trump of trying to de-legitimize journalists, but in a very real sense, a large segment of the media has de-legitimized itself.

His data notwithstanding, Fiorina's assertions do not take into account how "friendly fire" in various cultural skirmishes affects the general welfare of the nation. It's one thing to contend that by and large Americans are not caught up in culture wars on a daily basis to the same degree as the political and media elites, but it's quite another to suggest that the battles don't exist, or, if they are being fought on the periphery by partisans, that the effects of those battles don't impact our social condition in significant ways. The passing of the Affordable Care Act, for instance, has been both praised and denounced by partisans on both sides of the debate, but the law will affect just about every citizen in one way or another regardless of political affiliation. The firestorm over revelations of Dr. Jonathan Gruber of MIT regarding how the "selling" of the Affordable Care Act to the American electorate was predicated on deception (and that's putting it mildly) further illustrates how far a particular interest group will go advance its cause, no matter what collateral damage the greater public may experience. The volatility surrounding certain "hot button" issues seems rather intense, even to the casual observer. This bifurcation has become especially fractious between religionists and secularists. Fiorina's statistics may indicate that the chasm as being primarily politically driven, but evidence has mounted since 2004 that those "newly emergent moral and cultural" concerns are playing heavily into the psyche of a larger demographic.

Authoritarianism—Countervailing Views

Alan Abramowitz's book, *The Disappearing Center*, and Marc Hetherington and Jonathan Weiler's book, *Authoritarianism and Polarization in American Politics*, offer countervailing evidence to Mr. Fiorina's contentions. Abramowitz's well-researched findings indicate the partisan political divide that simmers in the political arena reflects a more significant division, one that goes beyond the common contention that only political elites and their acolytes are caught up in the fray. Hetherington and Weiler offer a perspicacious view that a significant underlying factor in the battle for the hearts and minds of the populace is the degree of structured "authoritarianism" that we want in our lives. Questions about "who controls who and what," and under what ideological rubric are never far from the surface when social, political and cultural debates occur. The framers of the American Constitution sought to put limits on the power of government, but over time those limits have been eroded (or ignored) and herein lies the basis for the contentious debates about control and authority. A common critique of Presidents Obama and Trump has been that they tend to circumvent the Constitution in the attempt to wield more executive power.

For Hetherington and Weiler this cultural and ideological dichotomy "is not between two groups with the same psychological disposition who merely disagree," but are "animated by fundamentally different dispositions" and "dramatically different world views."[5] Abramowitz, Hertherington and Weiler argue that those worldviews are increasingly connected to issues of morality and as a result, the issue of religion becomes vexatious. The palpable alignment of political parties in the United States with either religionists or secularists makes it difficult to refute this particular contention. It is not merely a myth and Fiorina concedes that there is nothing new about "cultural conflict" vis-à-vis the role of religion in the United States.

In these skirmishes, suspicions regarding authoritarianism call to mind the influence of neo-Marxism and the ideas expressed by Theodor Adorno in his co-authored book, *The Authoritarian Personality*. The malevolent perspectives of Adorno and the Frankfurt School philosophers, with their penchant for deriding those who advocate traditional, conservative religious-based attitudes, have attained widespread credibility among progressives for decades. The perspective of Jonah Goldberg on this topic is worth noting:

The original Marxist explanation of fascism was that it was the capitalist ruling classes' reaction to the threat of the ascendancy of the working classes. The Frankfurt School deftly psychologized this argument. Instead of rich, white men and middle-class dupes protecting their economic interests, fascism became a psychological defense mechanism against change generally. Men who cannot handle "progress" respond violently because they have "authoritarian personalities" [as measured on the F-scale, "F" for fascist.] In effect, anyone who disagrees with the aims, scope and methods of liberalism is suffering from a mental defect, commonly known as fascism.[6]

In what has become a rather heavy assault on religion and "conservative" dogma, merely labeling a person, or an idea, that is antipodal to a progressive, egalitarian world view as being "fascist," now passes as a viable critique. Sophism of this sort gets you only so far. Hazy and lazy invective may help win the 24-hour news cycle (or the hearts and minds of naïve university undergraduates), but as a cogent response to the deeper issues of value, judgment and behavior, it is disingenuous and dangerous. As Goldberg correctly asserts, sophistry of this sort absolves the proponents of the progressive mindset of actually having to mount a serious, intellectual argument as to why their prescriptions provide better and more humane solutions. Goldberg also points to a fatal contradiction in the progressive argument. On one hand, progressives denounce authoritarian control as being fascist or oligarchical while extolling the virtues of bigger and more intrusive government. In fact, progressives seek greater government control so long as it is in accord with their socio-cultural vision as opposed to a "reactionary" conservative perspective.

The COVID-19 crisis in 2020 has been especially revelatory in terms of observing the duplicity of liberal social justice warriors who pontificate about the West's injustices while ignoring injustices in China. This has been especially dismaying in the wake of the COVID-19 outbreak as politicians, business leaders and sports celebrities (Joe Biden, Michael Bloomberg, Howard Schultz, Lebron James, Google and Apple) have engaged in bad faith and astonishing dishonesty in their comments about the political regime in Beijing—a regime that has imprisoned or executed doctors who acted as whistleblowers in the

COVID crisis, not to mention the plights of the Falun Gang religious sect, Christians and the Uighur Muslims.*

As Goldberg often points out, liberals have blind spots for blind spots in these matters. He understands the desire for social betterment but strikes a cautionary tone regarding the role of government:

> The desire for community is deep and human and decent. But these yearnings are often misplaced when channeled through the federal government and imposed across a diverse nation with a republican constitution. The government cannot love you ... ever since the New Deal, liberals have been unable to shake this fundamental dogma that the state can be the instrument for a politics of meaning that transforms the entire nation into a village.[7]

Hetherington and Weiler cite the metaphorical social theories of University of California (Berkeley) professor of linguistics, George Lakoff, who posits that conservatism is the progeny of what he terms "the strict father model," while the liberal view is the progeny of a "nurturant parent model." For Lakoff, a proponent of the Rockridge Institute, a progressive think tank that assists liberal politicians, the "strict father model" is preoccupied with tradition, hierarchical order and structure, whereas the "nurturant parent modal" is concerned with well-being compassion, justice and equality. Lakoff contends that both perspectives have value but acknowledges that the proponents of these divergent outlooks see each other as being threats to their respective agendas.

The opprobrium of the combatants on both sides of the ideological spectrum extends beyond news bites and strident Op-Ed pieces, and according to Hetherington and Weiler, these opposing views "go far beyond disagreements over policy choices and even ideology, to conflict about core self-understandings of what it means to be a good person and to the basis of a good society."[8] Debates about values and appropriateness have long been rooted in moral and ethical perspectives. What we deem to be worthy of our concerns has both a subjective/emotional aspect and well as an objective/intellectual aspect, yet

---

* It has been interesting to observe that as social justice advocates in the USA have denigrated the American flag and the national anthem for being alleged symbols of injustice and various crimes against humanity, the freedom advocates in the Hong Kong protests have been waving the American flag and singing "The Star-Spangled Banner."

judgment in any form has come to be seen as a manifestation of the "strict father" authoritarian model and out of step with progressivism and decidedly anti-egalitarian. However, it can easily be argued that authoritarian and nurturing attributes can be beneficial in the development of a more humane society. It's not an either/or proposition, for both can be beneficial in various contexts. Isaiah Berlin refers to this as "value pluralism;" a condition in which two seemingly contradictory views or values can be correct and beneficial.

Culture Counts

Traditionally, religion has acted as the proverbial "moral compass" in the process of achieving a moral and ethical society in which love and trust were intrinsic to everything—family, community, business, education, arts, media, economics, etc. Judeo-Christian theology instructs that at some point in history there was a deviation away from God and godly behavior, thus restoring the lost ideal by making our way "back to the Garden" became the essential trial for humankind to free itself from the bondage of sin and spiritual darkness. Compromising or violating those foundational elements would be seen as a violation against the common good of the community at large. Hence, moral judgment enters the socio-cultural equation.

As Roger Scruton observes, judgment is implicit in any faith-based community because once ideals and tenets are firmly in place, there is an expectation that good citizens of the community will abide by them in order to realize the "ethical vision." For the religious person, there is an understanding that judgment is our destiny—something we will all face it when we ascend to the incorporeal realm. This concept is deeply rooted in the Judeo-Christian psyche, and though we may live our lives with the intentionality of doing what is morally and ethically correct, how we behave in relation to others is the ultimate measure of our contribution to an ethical society (not to mention where we may find ourselves in the next world). T. S. Eliot believed that the interface between religion and community "cannot be finally divorced from one another" and that religion, poetry and education could foster collaborative efforts towards establishing a more humane society. As the apostle James put it, "faith without works is dead." The Unitarian Universalists echo that sentiment when they say, "More important than the creed is the deed."

Coming to the realization that there are universal, objective truths and not merely interpretations of such, remains a critical step in the process of creating a just and compassionate culture. By accepting such, responsibility—being answerable for our behavior—becomes a significant aspect of our psychological maturation, thus we cannot easily escape the reality of judgment and accountability in our life choices. Refusing to accept responsibility is immature. Ayn Rand averred, "Man is free to choose not to be conscious, but not free to escape the penalty of unconsciousness: destruction."[9] Rand's supposition that altruism is nothing more than a type of "moral cannibalism," is considered to be specious by many. Yet, she could not be more correct in her perspectives regarding the importance of "conscious choice" vis-à-vis "escaping" or avoiding certain life choices that might inadvertently result in "destruction."*

If conscious choices are made along purely ideological lines without ascertaining what values and virtues might be beneficial for socio-cultural betterment, destruction is surely a possible outcome. In his philosophical tome, *On Liberty*, John Stuart Mill asserted that "silencing the expression of opinion" was (among other things) "robbing the human race; posterity as well as the existing generations" of the ability to dissent. In his view, "robbing" of this sort effectually deprived individuals the opportunity to ascertain what was true in the quest for betterment. Accordingly, if a dissenter's opinion was correct it could be verified by comparing to other views. Conversely, if a dissenter's opinion was wrong it would be proven wrong by allowing a "collision" with "the clearer and livelier impression of truth" to take place.[10] The far left's perpetual obsession with shutting down speech it doesn't like (dissent) is "robbery" in this context.

Herbert Marcuse was a big proponent of that thievery. In his essay from 1965, *Repressive Tolerance*, Marcuse contorts Mill's view of dissent and freedom of expression to serve his ideological (Marxist) ends. According to Marcuse, the process of "liberating tolerance" would involve "the withdrawal of toleration of speech and assembly from groups and movements" on the Right, and the aggressively partisan promotion of speech, groups, and progressive movements on the Left

---

* Ayn Rand's oft-cited quote is usually seen as, "You can avoid reality, but you cannot avoid the consequences of avoiding reality."

(*Repressive Tolerance,* p. 81). This is the exact opposite of what Mill was advocating.

We might be fine with the far left espousing the perspectives they find to be beneficial, but more often than not, the left is not willing (as Marcuse's essay demonstrates) to be confronted with "the clearer and livelier impression of truth" because it might prove their views to be suspect, or just plain wrong. This now results in canceling, de-platforming and defenestrating those who dissent from progressive pieties. Mill's advocacy of diverse perspectives colliding in the pursuit of truth challenges this particular mindset and as a society we should give pause to the illiberal demeanor of Marcuse's acolytes.

Avoiding Destruction

In his *New York Daily News* article (July 24, 2011) regarding the untimely death of pop singer, Amy Winehouse, Patrick Huguenin was not unlike many who suspected that her unwillingness or inability to "grow up" and take responsibility for her life choices, likely contributed to her becoming another iconic artist who left us in such a tragic way as another member of the "27 Club."* However, many now take the position that exercising judgment in this fashion is inherently wrong and mean-spirited. The idea of the artist-as-a-tortured-soul has become a shopworn cliché but it still resonates with a segment of the population that views the non-conformist artist, free from the constraints of "bourgeoisie" values, as a measure of artistic authenticity. On this matter, it's worth considering the perspective of American composer, Charles Ives.

> The intensity today, with the techniques and media are organized and used, tends to throw the mind away from "common sense" and towards "manner" and thus to the resultant weak and mental states—for example, the Byronic fallacy—that one who is full of turbid feeling about himself is qualified to be some sort of an artist. In this relation "manner" also leads some to think that emotional sympathy for self is as true a part of art as sympathy for others; a prejudice in favor of the good and bad of one personality against the virtue of many personalities.[11]

Ives (1874-1954), a serious artist in his own right (and one whose music could be "farther out" than most), was of the mindset that pride was a vice that

---

* The "27 Club" refers to musicians who died at age 27: Jimi Hendrix, Janis Joplin, Brian Jones, Jim Morrison and Kurt Cobain.

artists could not easily recover from. He viewed false pride as being a symptom of the Byronic fallacy that portended that an individual's angst should be weighed evenly against the concerns of "the majority." This attitude, that Emerson unflatteringly referred to as the "hog-mind," was "the antithesis of everything called 'soul,' 'spirit', 'Christianity,' truth,' freedom,'" and was antithetical to the "great primal truths," one of which was the idea that "there is more good than evil" among people, and that living for the benefit of the public purpose superseded the concerns of the individual. "God," Ives would say, "has made men greater than man, that he has made the universal mind and the over-soul greater than the individual mind and soul, that he has made the Divine a part of all."[12] Ives' assertion calls us to explore the morality of the individual in the context of community. By doing so we can begin to attain a sense of our Divinity as children of God. This speaks to the importance of virtue, community and the need for artists to be mindful of their position within that community, and how their creative endeavors might affect their fellow citizens. It also speaks to the idea that we possess godly attributes and that by manifesting our latent divinity we can become co-creators with the Almighty in the establishment of a better world. Rome's collapse was the result of the dissolution of civic virtue and the proliferation of self-centeredness.

In a recent political about the tradition of utilizing the filibuster in Congress, Senator James Clayburn claimed that Senator Joe Manchin was like Nero who watched Rome burn because Manchin wasn't caving to the centralization of power that certain members of his political party were advocating. Predictably, Senator Manchin was vilified and characterized as being a racist by his detractors. Victor Davis Hanson, whose background is in the classics and who has studied Roman and Greek history, made the point that Rome survived for hundreds of years after Nero, and the two things that actually destroyed Rome were inflation and tribalism. When Romans started to identify less as Roman citizens and more with their ethnic and racial backgrounds, this division and polarization made Rome vulnerable to invasion.

Another factor was the increasing confusion over sexual identity. J.D. Unwin's anthropological studies (published in 1934) revealed that in the eight-six cultures that he studied going back thousands of years, sexual immorality and confusion led to the dissipation of all of those cultures—every one of them—including Rome! The data is irrefutable and points to the importance of personal morality in the context of creating morally sound communities. By understanding the need to take our portion of responsibility seriously, we can become productive and nurturing citizens, hence, our faith is justified. If we give in to the selfish, "endarkened" aspect of our nature, we collude in our own "destruction," individually and collectively.

Regrettably, offering critiques or making distinctions is considered highly invidious, untoward and elitist in matters of morality and ethics. Scruton observes that our intellectual life has become "one vast commotion" of specialisms where making distinctions between the "virtuous and the vicious, the beautiful and the ugly, the sacred and the profane, the true and the false—is to offend against the only value judgment that is widely accepted, the judgment that all judgments are wrong."[13] Consequently, the quality of our intellectual life declines and becomes lost in the abyss of moral relativism and situational ethics. The suspicion of certainty and having "deeply held views" contributes to a condition that undermines the establishment of a common culture. Scruton writes:

> Now there are no certainties, and no common culture worth the name. Doubt is the refrain of popular communication, skepticism extends in all directions, and philosophy has been deprived of its traditional starting point in the faith of a stable community. A philosophy that begins in doubt assails what no one believes, and invites us to nothing believable.[14]

Some may dismiss the contention of Louis Armstrong (or was it Duke Ellington?) that there are only two types of music—good music and bad music—but the fact is that we make aesthetic judgments regarding literature, architecture, art, cinema and in so doing we discriminate when it comes to our musical and/or artistic preferences. Some may prefer the music of Queen to Dvorák, but is Freddie Mercury's performance of "Somebody to Love" any less expressive or less moving, than say, Lucia Popp's rendition of Dvorák's "Song to the Moon"? (I enjoy both!) Personal tastes are just that; personal, and they require no proof. *De gustibus non est disputandum*; In matters of taste there can be no dispute. Personal taste is easily acquired. It is when our personal tastes are militated by altruistic concerns and informed perspectives that we begin to arrive at a more enlightened understanding regarding life and art, which hopefully can make us more understanding, compassionate and resolute in our pursuit of betterment. Reason dictates that the balance between the concerns of the self and the concerns of the greater public is something we should continually strive for. Turbid self-absorption and the "hog mind" are often inimical to our community.

Educational Concerns and Political Correctness

In the realm of education, there has been an emphasis on making students "feel special" despite academic mediocrity or even failure. Ross Rosenfeld, an educator from New York who runs a tutoring service, contends that "parents and teachers are not doing children any favors by promoting false confidence with ridiculous, incessant flattery," reminding us of Bill Gates' opinion that "success is a lousy teacher."[15] Devaluing merit and academic achievement in the attempt to make students "feel special," or to avoid judgment, is a poor substitute for acumen in the "real world" where one's actual knowledge and abilities will be the measures by which one is judged as being competent, or not. The mindset that Rosenfeld cites can have the effect of instilling a sense of entitlement and it fosters an atmosphere in which judgment is considered unfair, hurtful or racist. In this type of scholastic modality, achieving good grades via testing becomes an affront to students' skewed opinion of themselves for it diminishes responsibility and accountability. Merely "trying hard" is not enough for achieving success after one's student days are finished.

Rosenfeld cites a survey by the National Assessment of Educational Process that found that only 34% of eighth-graders in the United States read at a competent level. Rosenfeld states, "We have a shortage of engineers—but an abundance of egocentric children." Thomas Sowell asserts that the problem is not so much that Johnny can't read, as it is that Johnny can't distinguish between thinking and feeling. The idea that it's important to teach students that the real world doesn't reward failure is seen by many well-meaning but misguided teachers as being preoccupied with "winning" and attaining "superiority" through the process of acquiring knowledge. Earning self-respect through actual achievement has become increasingly associated with the aforementioned "strict father" model as described by Lakoff. Meritocracy is often viewed as "perpetuating privilege." Yet, as any musician who has progressed from being a student-level instrumentalist to the professional ranks knows, acquiring the necessary musical proficiency to work in a professional ensemble is a *sine qua non*. Meritocracy has merit.

Furthermore, professor of comparative literature at Columbia University John McWhorter believes that the emergent "hyper-woke" view that Black or Latino children shouldn't be expected to do well in their scholastic pursuits is a form of racism because it perpetuates false and bigoted notions that minorities are intrinsically inferior and intellectually challenged in comparison to their white counterparts. In an interview with Ben Domenech (Fox News Primetime, April 24, 2021), he characterizes this as stereotyping and an example of "racism in a new guise," something out of the unreconstructed society of the American south of one hundred years ago. He views this trend as fundamentally deleterious and a threat to the education system in the United States.

Multiculturalism and the Arts

During the height of the controversies surrounding the art of Robert Mapplethorpe, Andres Serrano and the National Endowment of the Arts (NEA) in the early 1990s, I was asked to speak at a forum on the issue of artistic censorship at the United Nations. To the dismay of the forum's organizers, I took the stance that I didn't consider it an affront to artists or arts organizations that were receiving taxpayer-funded grants from the NEA to be held accountable, or to be criticized by those who were providing the grant money. It was my contention that taxpayers' rights were every bit as sacrosanct as artists' rights. As someone who believes that art has moral and ethical power and that artists don't create in a vacuum free from accountability, my perspectives on that occasion rankled some in attendance who were of a more progressive mindset.

I made my points without rancor or vituperation (or so I thought), but the invective that was hurled my way after my remarks by a few participants … well … you would have thought that I was speaking to members of the Catholic League having just urinated on a crucifix in the sanctuary at St. Patrick's Cathedral during High Mass. The conference moderator attempted to mollify my detractors by suggesting that I really didn't mean what I said, but I really did mean it! That an artist would somehow hold fellow artists or arts institutions accountable for a questionable decision regarding the issue of public funding caused cognitive dissonance among a number of the conference attendees.

I find it rather hypocritical, if not altogether disingenuous, that many artists who reflexively express animus toward corporate culture, traditional values, religion, the wealthy, the military—all those "reactionary" things that progressives reproach—when in many cases it's those very things that provide for their livelihoods, keep them safe, and conditions their audiences towards a humane world view. I mean, where do artists think those big commissions and tenured professorships that they covet come from? Doesn't the military, for instance, help to ensure national security, and by extension ensure one's right to be controversial? Don't families who go into serious debt to pay for their children's higher education and pay taxes have the right to express their discontent about art that they feel is a slap in the face of their values when they might be paying for it? Could the New York Philharmonic, or the Museum of Modern Art, or the United Nations exist without corporate largesse, tax revenue, or private sector contributions by wealthy patrons? The retreat from common sense and reason in these matters points to a rather myopic and obtuse perspective. I find the indignation expressed by many in the arts community regarding this particular duplicity disturbing.

This is not to suggest that art should be innocuous. In my presentation at the United Nations, I made the point that "pushing buttons" has always been the provenance of artists, but taking shots at the expense of others, especially in this case, when those shots are directed at tax-payers who fund the N.E.A., was at the very least, a questionable proposition. Freedom of expression cuts both ways. Taxpayers are not required to forfeit their freedom of expression and refrain from denouncing what they see as a sleight when they feel that their taxes are being used to have their values trashed in the name of artistic freedom. As Camille Paglia opined, if creating art to get a rise out of the Catholic League when using N.E.A. funds is what now passes for serious artistic intent, it's no wonder that people smell a scam and recoil from that kind of incitement. (Paglia correctly observes that it's rarely Islam or Judaism that artists ridicule in their artistic provocations.

My U.N. experience was my first encounter with progressive-oriented "multiculturalism," though I was not entirely aware of it at the time. In the intervening decades the phenomenon of this ideological perspective, which professes to promote inclusion, has metastasized into a malevolent ideology fraught with totalitarian self-righteousness masking as moral virtue. More recently in the West, we have been entering a post-democratic, post-truth era with more, not less, political and financial corruption in the equation. The advocates of politically correct multiculturalism have been instituting illiberal cultural totalitarianism driven by an ideology that is highly intolerant of any worldview that doesn't comport with progressive orthodoxy. The recent phenomenon of "cancel culture" is analogous to medieval witch-hunts.

Fear has become the weapon of choice for the progressive, neo-Marxist left. As Shelby Steele notes, in their attempt to create a just society, the progressives are using the fear "of being stigmatized with America's old bigotries—racism, sexism, homophobia and xenophobia. To be stigmatized as a fellow traveler with any of these bigotries is to be utterly stripped of moral authority and made into a pariah."[16] Being called a racist makes one feel inferior and fearful—a pariah. Because it is a natural human tendency to seek safety when confronted with fear, it is the hope of the progressive left that people will trade their freedom to speak out against neo-Marxist illiberalism in exchange for safe havens that are free from the possibility of defenestration from their jobs, careers, schools, sports teams, churches or musical ensembles.

At face value, the idea of "leveling" and removing "judgment" from discussions about art, culture and social behavior may seem to be a move toward equality and justice. Canadian political philosopher Will Kymlicka sees multiculturalism as an idea that contests "inherited hierarchies" that have historically resulted in various modes of coercion and paternalism. This seems to be necessary in overcoming cultural prejudices and injustices, but something more pernicious and sinister is at work. Because multiculturalism has become a movement with decidedly "politically correct" features, political correctness now clouds any attempt at arriving at a reasoned, objective outlook in matters of art—especially the values of Western art born of the Judeo-Christian religious sphere. In our postmodern era, multiculturalism, while professing equality, has become hostile to various traditions. Pianist and music historian Charles Rosen puts it this way:

> We owe to various versions of political correctness an improvement in
> the status of women and minorities, a greater tolerance of unorthodox sexu-
> ality, and a more serious examination of the aspirations of classes with little
> political power. There are benefits from multiculturalism, too, but when

combined with political correctness, it has produced the absurd thesis that all cultures are equally valid or valuable, the consistent denigration of Western civilization, and the attempts to suppress any critical examination of non-Western societies.[17]

All civilizations have cultural expressions, but not all cultural expressions rise to the same level of accomplishment or expertise. Even within a particular cultural sphere, there are various levels of accomplishment and expertise. In the history of European music Mozart is considered a better composer than Johann Stamitz, and for good reason. Any critical analysis of the music of these two composers reveals that Mozart's use of harmonic and melodic invention in the service of musical narrative and drama is far more sublime and sophisticated than that of Stamitz (or mine). To make that analysis requires a theoretical understanding of music. Acquiring the necessary expertise to make informed analytical distinctions requires study and objective examination—the heavy lifting that too often is portrayed as just more Western power tripping and "strict father" associations. As Russell Jacoby notes, "The multiculturalists pretend to liquidate false generalizations while trading in them. Even a term like 'Eurocentrism' is objectionable, as if a homogenous European culture existed—as if Adolf Hitler and Anne Frank represented the same Europe."[18] When emotion trumps reason at every turn (Thomas Sowell's assertion) we are inundated with a great deal of inane art. Although we might readily acknowledge that all art is a mode of self-expression, not all self-expression is art.

Making any distinctions in this manner is increasingly viewed in our politically correct society as judgment, the bane of all progressive culture warriors. This rationale has led to a *faux* egalitarianism in which there exists a rather spurious means of evaluating values and creative endeavors in general and music in particular. Richard Taruskin weighs in saying: "Social convention today demands ... that nothing that goes on in 'art' be judged from any standpoint other than the 'esthetic, which is usually just a euphemism for the assertion of one's casual tastes or one's unexamined snobberies."[19]

What is too often overlooked is that Western musical tradition, rather than being intolerant to traditions outside of its own, has embraced musical idioms of "the other" with great alacrity. Ravel, Debussy and Rimsky-Korsakov incorporated Spanish folk elements into their compositions. European composers such as Hindemith, Stravinsky, Blacher and Milhaud embraced jazz and employed its rhythmic properties in their music to great effect. Ethnomusicology (originally called "comparative musicology") is the study and preservation of folk music of different cultures and is a distinctly Western invention. Western musical notation and theoretical analysis provided the means to preserve, examine and appreciate music outside of its own cultural sphere. Jazz is the juxtaposing of numerous ethnic influences—including European harmonic syntax, Latin and African rhythms, Caribbean folk music, field hollers, Blues and Negro Spirituals. Is this "appropriation," or rather finding value and pleasure in the artistic expressions of "the other?" As Edward Rothstein, former cultural commentator for the *New York Times,* notes:

> It is a Romantic view that argues against the dominance of Western rationality, education and culture and praises societies felt to be "closer to nature." But in fact, just those properties of Western culture have made the music of other peoples accessible. Oral cultures ... have not traditionally had the analytical self-consciousness to describe or communicate or even understand their achievements.[20]

In a conversation I had with noted American musician Paul Winter at the United Nations' Interfaith conference in 2012, he spoke of his first visit to Brazil and how Brazilian music affected the direction of his music. He had been playing Bebop in his successful sextet—the first jazz ensemble to perform at the White House—but his encounter with Bossa Nova led to a convergence of cultural influences that spawned new stylistic possibilities. This in turn led to the founding of his iconic band, the Paul Winter Consort, a pioneering ensemble in the realm of world music.

American popular music has a history of being "global and democratic," and as Roger Scruton observes, it was "able to defeat any rival simply by its refusal to believe in rivalry, happily appropriating every sound that could be reissued as a song."[21] Assimilation has been the American way, but European composers of the nineteenth and twentieth centuries were also fairly egalitarian when it came to appreciating the musical styles outside of their cultural sphere.

Perhaps those cultures didn't value analysis, nor did they see the necessity of their art to be studied or understood outside their societies. But the development of ethnomusicology points to the willingness of Western minds and hearts to appreciate and embrace the musical traditions of "the other." The diversity and pluralism in art music that Leonard B. Meyer had presciently predicted in 1967 are in great evidence as the music of Tan Dun, Arvo Pärt, Osvaldo Golijov, Toru Takemitsu, Jennifer Higdon, Bright Sheng and Einojuhani Rautavaara indicates. The diversity found in serious art music belies the claim that there is no "cultural equity" to be found in Western cultural expressions.

But as Mr. Rothstein notes in his perspicacious and controversial essay on the spuriousness of the multicultural mindset regarding Western music, "Roll Over Beethoven: The new musical correctness and its mistakes," (*The New Republic*, February 4, 1991) the purveyors of this attitude have a particular kind of "equity" in mind, and that has everything to do with funding, education and the "prestige" accorded to Western music. Why, they ask, should "any priority be given to European-oriented arts in the midst of ethnic variety?" Rothstein writes:

> The multiculturalist argument about music has three basic steps: (1) No judgment can be made between musics on the basis of intrinsic value because there is no hierarchy in the arts. (2) The tradition of Western music has no essential claim on our attention, particularly as our population becomes less and less European in origin and outlook. (3) Our political democracy should be a host to democracy in education and taste as well. Let a hundred flowers bloom, and let none be given more water than another.[22]

In certain respects, these concerns seem valid and worthy of consideration. But as Rothstein points out, even in indigenous, non-Western cultures, there exists a hierarchical musical stratum based on various functions within those cultures (social, ceremonial, ritualistic, etc.). He cites Bruno Nettl's distinguished work in the field of ethnomusicology in which Nettl argues that not all cultures are alike in that some cultures develop a "high" musical culture and others do not. Additionally, Nettl's research reveals that "nearly every culture—whether or not it has a 'high' tradition—tends to have some kind of hierarchy in its musical system, a continuum from some kind of elite to popular." These findings, according to Rothstein, point to the inherent contradiction within the multicultural mindset, because it "condescends to the very cultures for which it demands 'equity' because it refuses even their own distinctions," and in this respect, "multiculturalism is not just about the equivalence of world cultures; it is also about their equivalence *within* Western culture."[23] (Emphasis is Rothstein's.) Multiculturalism sees Western culture as inherently supremacist and intolerant of "the other," therefore the drive for equity in the arts is "a form of domestic anti-imperialism." And this strikes at what some consider the dark heart of multiculturalism—a darkness with distinct neo-Marxist and progressive implications.

Diversity and pluralism are important and noble pursuits, but contextualization requires that we examine differences from various perspectives—objectively as well as subjectively. Paradoxically, the ongoing politicization of cultural choice has had the effect of creating conditions of intolerance. This is especially evident in the university culture where speech codes become "protective" measures to guard against offending "community values" and "human dignity." But as columnist John Leo observes, these kinds of protective measures, though seemingly altruistic, can have chilling effects on free speech, because "almost any passionate argument or satirical comment on campus can easily be construed as harmful to someone's dignity."[24] Again, who gets to make that call, and under what provisos?

Leo cites an explanation of the Field Museum in Chicago concerning an exhibit of Aztec culture and its attempt to create a non-judgmental perspective. In its official statement, the museum stated: "It is important to remember that there is no best or model culture. All cultures are equally valid to the individuals living in them."[25] As Leo explains, this "defensive crouch" meant "explaining away Aztec human sacrifice," as if ritual slaughter was akin to other cultures that offer sacrifices, such as the Romans who sent Christians to the lions in the guise of state-sponsored "ceremonies."

Another "unsavory" aspect of contemporary sociological criticism, according to Charles Rosen, is the attempt to debunk the idea that there exists true genius in the work of great artists and that the "genius" tag appropriated to the likes of Beethoven or Shakespeare "is entirely due ... to a process of brainwashing by the cultural elite in power." This was the attempt by Michel Foucault and other postmodernists to create the condition where "commonly shared and recognized values can be dismissed since these values are simply a successful imposition by an elite upon society as a whole."[26] In this context, any belief in "certainty" regarding any particular issue quickly leads to charges of extremism, intolerance, and of course, fascist authoritarianism born of patriarchal circumstances.

Camille Paglia concurs with the concerns of Rosen regarding the drive for political correctness under the rubric of multiculturalism. Speaking to the "grandeur of religious history," Paglia, an atheist, considers much of the opprobrium directed at the religious impulse in matters of art to be intransigent, even corrupt. She respects the spiritual dimension of art and is highly suspect of those who ignore the qualitative aspect of great art for purely political or ideological reasons, stating:

> I am for multiculturalism—it's about the great artistic traditions of the world ... Japanese culture, Chinese culture, high culture. That was about quality. But the idea of quality has been divorced in the discussion of the arts in our universities because, "Oh, it's just a mask for ideology. There is no such thing as greatness. These are all completely subjective. For people who want to protect their own power elite—dead, white, European males." This is the garbage that has come out. I can see the point of where the argument started, OK. But what's the end result of it? We are now thirty years, almost forty years down the line. What's the end result? Are we getting better art? Better writing? Better educated people? More knowledgeable people?[27]

No, no, no and no! Paglia, Scruton, Rothstein, Leo and Rosen view the ongoing dissolution of objective, intellectual assessing of art at the hands of politically correct, multicultural ethos as being inherently deleterious. Allan Bloom thought so too, and he gave many in the multicultural camp angina for saying so. Bloom led the early charge in reinforcing the idea that the humanities could and should play important roles in the pursuit of attaining a more enlightened worldview. For Bloom, and many others, great literature could be highly instructive in the process of achieving better personhood by providing glimpses into the human condition, and it didn't matter if it was dead, white, European males who created it. The best books, according to Bloom, could nurture a sense of "human connectedness" and in so doing allow us to share profound experiences and knowledge. He was among the first to see the politically correct assault on the canonical literature and music that had long been a source of what Schiller considered to be a way of providing "aesthetic education." In the conclusion of his book, *Love and Friendship*, Bloom recalls an incident where a group of students at Cornell University unfurled a banner at one of his lectures that read: "Great Sex is better than Great Books." Bloom's rejoinder: "Sure, but you can't have one without the other."[28] Can the same be said about great music? Many people believe so.

Consider Susan McClary's appropriating the stentorian timpani episode in the climax of the opening movement of Beethoven's ninth symphony as an expressive equivalent of rape. This is but another misguided misreading born of the insalubrious pieties of the politically correct, multiculturalist mindset that reactively assigns perfidy to all things European and patriarchal.* McClary revised her initial assertion because there is nothing in the copious research on Beethoven's life that suggests that he harbored any such feelings or intentions. This was McClary's opinion, or her chosen metaphor nothing more, but her original comment was likely informed by a decidedly postmodern, neo-Marxist, feminist perspective—one that Paglia considers odious.

How might we know this? In her book, *Feminine Endings: Music, Gender and Sexuality*, in which the original statement about Beethoven's Ninth Symphony appeared, McClary cites Antonio Gramsci's "empowering correctives," Theodor Adorno's "finely nuanced analysis" of music, and Michel Foucault's "archaeologies of knowledge" as important influences in developing her perspectives on music and history, not to mention the influence of the Frankfurt School.[29] It is not an inaccurate extrapolation, given her influences—a Marxist, a neo-Marxist and a postmodern deconstructionist—to imagine that McClary had a particular ideological inclination in her choice of metaphor regarding this episode in Beethoven's symphony.† She's entitled, but the right to criticize her based on an ideological slant that has resulted in a great deal of inhumane behavior should not be dismissed out of hand as an expression of misogyny.

---

* Camille Paglia contends that the only actual patriarchal culture in Western civilization was in ancient Rome.

† Musicologist, Sir Donald Francis Tovey metaphorically referred to the same passage in Beethoven's Ninth Symphony as, "The heavens on fire."

When contested opinions are passed off as fact for ideological purposes, moral relativism is more often than not the result.

As Roger Scruton reminds us, ideologies that are created under certain social and economic conditions often change when societal conditions change because they are based on utilitarian concerns rather than universal truths. Obviously, our search for truth ought to be guided by a sincere desire for socio-cultural betterment. In the West there has been an attempt to fashion societies in which fairness, respect and dignity are afforded to all people. These attributes need to be rooted in truth and not be held hostage by misguided emotivism that too easily capitulates to illiberal double standards and moral relativism. Volition is essential, however, our choices ought to be guided by truth, therefore the search for truth and meaning is no small matter.

In his discourse on conservatism, Ralph Waldo Emerson acknowledged that there was a certain "meanness in conservatism, but it was superior because it held to facts and truth. It affirms because it holds." Whereas, in his estimation, "reform has no gratitude, no prudence, no husbandry."[30] This assessment may be too binary for some and in need of some nuance. Liberalism and reform are a part of the betterment equation because humankind faces many seemingly intractable problems, thus reformation is necessary. That said, the issues of gratitude and ownership (being accountable) are salient precisely because they are prudent in that there is it appealing aspect to both judiciousness and common sense in the quest for betterment. Too often common sense is defenestrated due to ideological premises that are not predicated on truth, but rather specious theories and don't pass the falsifiability test and are easily discredited. If the truth sets us free, then freedom must be in accord with the truth that there is no freedom without responsibility.

Recommended Recordings

Ives: The Unanswered Question, Michael Gielen, Southwest German Radio Orchestra

Tan: Concerto for Pipa, Yuri Bashmet, Moscow Soloists

Golijov: *Dreams and Prayers of Isaac the Blind*, St. Lawrence String Quartet

Rautavaara: *Book of Visions*, Mikko Franck, Belgian National Symphony

Sheng: *Flute Moon*, Lan Shui, Copenhagen Philharmonic

Takemitsu: *Yume no toki*, Marin Alsop, Bournemouth Symphony Orchestra

Pärt: *Tabula Rasa*, Takuo Yuasa, Ulster Orchestra

Higdon: *On a Wire*, Robert Spano, Atlanta Symphony Orchestra

Chopin: Mazurkas, Arturo Benedetti Michelangeli, piano

Schoenberg: *Erwartung*, Christoph von Dohnanyi, Vienna Philharmonic Orchestra

Dvořák: *Song to the Moon*, Lucia Popp, Munich Radio Symphony Orchestra

Paul Winter: *Icarus*, Paul Winter Consort

Beethoven: Symphony No. 9, Roger Norrington, London Classical Players

Richard Wagner: *The Ring Without Words*, Lorin Maazel, Berlin Philharmonic

Blacher: *Paganini Variations,* Eliahu Inbal, Frankfurt Radio Symphony Orchestra

Stravinsky: *Ebony Concerto,* Ensemble InterContemporain, Michael Arrington, clarinet

Rimsky-Korsakov: *Capriccio Espagnol,* George Szell, Cleveland Orchestra

Ravel: *Rapsodie espagnol,* Pierre Boulez, New York Philharmonic

Debussy: *Iberia Suite,* Pierre Boulez, Cleveland Orchestra

Milhaud: *La création du monde*, Michael Tilson-Thomas, New World Symphony

Endnotes

1   Roger Scruton, *Beauty: A Very Short Introduction*, pbk. (Oxford-New York: Oxford University Press, 2011), p. 53.

2   Morris P. Fiorina, *What Culture Wars? Debunking the Myth of a Polarized America,* Second Edition (New York: Pearson-Longman, 2006), p. 2.

3   Ibid., p. 7.

4   Emily Jashinsky, "Democrats are colluding with the media to create chaos," *Washington Examiner*, May 16, 2017.

5   Marc Hetherington and Jonathan Weiler, *Authoritarianism and Polarization in American Politics* (Cambridge: Cambridge University Press, 2009), p. 42.

6   Jonah Goldberg, *Liberal Fascism: The Secret History of the American Left from Mussolini to the Politics of Change* (New York: Broadway Books, 2007), pp. 227-228.

7   Ibid., pp. 159-160.

8   Hetherington and Weiler, *Authoritarianism and Polarization,* p. 11.

9   Ayn Rand, "The Objectivist Ethics," essay delivered at the University of Wisconsin, 1961 (Source: *Ayn Rand: Her Works and Legacy*, ed. Wikipedians), p. 67.

10 John Stuart Mill, *On Liberty* (London: John W. Parker and Son, 1859), p. 33.

11 Charles Ives, *Essays Before a Sonata, The Majority, and Other Writings* (New York: W.W. Norton & Company, Inc., (pbk) 1970), p. 91.

12 Ibid., p. 29.

13 Roger Scruton, *The Intelligent Person's Guide to Philosophy* (New York: Penguin Books, 1996), p. 12.

14 Ibid.

15 Ross Rosenfeld, "Your Kid Is Not Special," *New York Daily News*, February 9, 2012.

16 Shelby Steele, "The Exhaustion of American Liberalism," *Wall Street Journal*, March 5, 2017.

17 Charles Rosen, "Multicultural Correctness," reply to Ralph P. Locke, *New York Review of Books*, January 16, 2003.

18 Russell Jacoby, *The End of Utopia: Politics and Culture in an Age of Apathy* (New York: Basic Books, 1999), pp. 61-62.

19 Richard Taruskin, *The Danger of Music and Other Anti-Utopian Essays* (Los Angeles-Berkeley-London: University of California Press, 2010), p. 4.

20 Edward Rothstein, "Roll Over Beethoven: The new musical correctness and its mistakes." *The New Republic*, February 4, 1991.

21 Roger Scruton, *Understanding Music: Philosophy and Interpretation* (London and New York: Continuum International Publishing Group, 2009), p. 216.

22 Rothstein, "Roll Over Beethoven."

23 Ibid.

24 John Leo, *Tufts Still Struggling With Free Speech*, December 16, 2009, http://www.johnleo.com.

25 John Leo, *Dark Night at the Museum*, March 5, 2008, http://www.johnleo.com.

26 Charles Rosen, Review: "The Oxford History of Music," by Richard Taruskin, *New York Review of Books*, February 23, 2006.

27 Camille Paglia, Interview with Robert Birnbaum, *The Morning News*, August 3, 2005, http://www.themorningnews.org/article/camille-paglia.

28 Allan Bloom, *Love and Friendship* (New York: Simon & Schuster, 1993), p. 546.

29 Susan McClary, *Feminine Endings: Music Gender and Sexuality*, Kindle Edition (Minneapolis-London: University of Minnesota Press, 2002), Locations 598 and 614.

30 Ralph Waldo Emerson, *The Conservative*. From a lecture delivered at the Masonic Temple, Boston, December 9, 1841. *The Works of Ralph Waldo Emerson,* compiled by Richard Poirier (Oxford-New York: Oxford University Press, 1990), pp. 68-69.

34

Simple Truths

Now I've heard there was a secret chord,
That David played, and it pleased the Lord.
Leonard Cohen

My discovery was a result of musical perception.[1]
Albert Einstein

From time to time I've been asked if I believe in the concept of a "cosmic chord" or a universal "chord of nature"; *Klang*, as Schenkerian music theory defines it. Is there some Aeolian harmony of the spheres that evokes a secret, metaphysical understanding of the laws that govern physics and music? Imagining that cosmic vibrations exist has been a part of the mythology surrounding music for ages.

When Leonard Cohen wrote his iconic song *Hallelujah*, he referenced a "secret chord" that pleased the Lord. Could a single chord please the Almighty? My answer goes like this: In the Bible, Saint Paul states in the book of Romans, chapter 1, verse 20:

For since the creation of the world God's invisible qualities—his eternal power and divine nature—have been clearly seen, being understood from what has been made, so that people are without excuse.

The natural world possesses various dual characteristics that maintain its existence and develop through the polar relationships of complementary opposites: male/female, cation/anion, positive valence/negative valence, e.g. Ontologically, the created world reflects the nature of God's being or essence, as Scripture suggests. We can extrapolate that within the Godhead there exists original masculinity and femininity and original positivity and original negativity. Polar paradigms are intrinsic to the tonal syntax of Western music; consonant intervals/dissonant intervals, major modes/minor modes, major chords/minor chords, tonic/dominant chords, and these can be said to be symbolically reflective of God's nature.

Extrapolating further, it can be suggested that when these polar opposites arrive at a harmonious junction they are a manifestation of godliness. Therefore, I submit that it may not have been when David played an isolated chord that the Lord was pleased, but rather the Lord was pleased when David played several chords (at least two) resulting in a harmonious sonic occurrence, and *that* is what ultimately pleased the Lord. As the familiar axiom goes, "It takes two to Tango."

Historically, the realms of science and philosophy have provided numerous insights into the concept of "the chord of nature." The cosmology of music has been expounded upon by numerous theologians, philosophers and theorists—Pythagoras, Damon, Aristotle, Augustine, Boethius, Rameau, Kepler, Luther, Schopenhauer—hence there are numerous theories regarding this enigmatic topic. Pythagoras' contention that numbers were the primordial constituents of the universe was a revelation in his time. His explications regarding the production of pitches and intervals in Nature (vibratory energy in motion) remain the basis of virtually every important treatise on sound production.[*] Whether one ascribes to the tuning modes of equal temperament, just

---

[*] It should be noted that certain Marxist philosophers, Theodor Adorno in particular, have questioned the idea of nature playing a significant role in development of tonality. Musicologist, Richard Norton considered Theodor Adorno "the only effective antidote for Pythagoras," not to mention the concept of the *Klang*, the so-called, "chord of nature" as proffered by Rameau and Schenker. For Adorno, Norton and others of the neo-Marxist persuasion, conjoining nature and

intonation or any variation of such, Pythagorean theory is always in the equation (no pun intended).

Recently, a friend suggested I read the book, *The Elegant Universe* by theoretical physicist Brian Greene. The book espouses the idea of "string theory" as a basis for understanding the workings of the universe. String Theory posits that there may be as many as eleven dimensions of space and time, as opposed to the common understanding of three for space and one for time. It goes without saying that if one is not well versed in the disciplines of relativity and physics, getting through Greene's book is more than a bit daunting. However, in reading several chapters I was intrigued by two points. According to Dr. Greene, Albert Einstein "was driven by a passionate belief that the deepest understanding of the universe would reveal its truest wonder: the simplicity and power of the principles on which it is based."[2] Greene also asserts (as did Einstein) that it may be through the realm of the arts, where creativity and imagination are paramount, that discoveries and epiphanies regarding the mysteries of the universe might be revealed in greater detail.

It has often been said that the greatest truths are often the simplest truths, and herein lies a conundrum. As Greene and others in the realm of physics seek to understand the deeper aspects of the principles that govern the universe, Einstein seems to have been working under the premise that it may all be rather simple. It's intriguing to note that Einstein possessed a lifelong affinity for music once saying, "If I were not a physicist, I would probably be a musician. I often think in music. I live my daydreams in music. I see my life in terms of music … I get most joy in life out of music."[3] Einstein's mother was a pianist, and he began studies on the violin when he was six years old. He was especially fond of the violin sonatas of Mozart and was given to improvise at the piano in the manner of Mozart.

His son, Hans, amplified what Einstein meant when recounting that "whenever he felt that he had come to the end of the road or into a difficult situation in his work, he would take refuge in music, and that would usually resolve all his difficulties."[4] He continued to play the violin for a good part of his adult life and was an ardent supporter of the Israel Philharmonic. As a

---

pitch production in the attempt to justify any system of musical pitch organization, was viewed as a mode of "physical determinism" and was considered decidedly "bourgeoisie."

physicist, his relationship with the violin must have been especially meaningful due to the instrument's tonal properties vis-à-vis the overtones series and the harmonics that are highly evident in the production of sound on string instruments.

Einstein's assertion that "imagination is more important than knowledge," points to the importance of imagination in relation to cognition and perception in the process of problem-solving. As any artist knows, having an active and probing imagination is necessary to the creative process. One can possess voluminous amounts of knowledge and craft, but imagination is the ingredient that can transform knowledge into art of originality, beauty and meaning.

If we take Einstein's view of simplicity at face value, we might then be able to see the proverbial forest from the trees. Examining the simple truth of polarity, a concept that the ancient Chinese espoused to significant degrees, we begin to understand that polarity lies at the heart of development, progress and existence. This is a fundamental tenet of the *I Ching*. Positive and negative valences, cation and anion, proton and electron, stamen and pistil, male and female—these polar opposites reflect a very simple design paradigm, one that works in powerful ways. Pythagoras too, believed in a "cosmic polarity" as it pertained to complementary opposites. In their book, *The Pythagorean Sourcebook and Library: An Anthology of Ancient Writings Which Relate to Pythagoras and Pythagorean Philosophy*, Kevin Sylvan Guthrie and David Fideler allude to Pythagoras' ideas regarding cosmic polar opposites. They write:

> We have seen that for Pythagoras philosophy represents a "purification," the aim of which is the assimilation to God. The universe is divine because of its order (kosmos), harmonies and symmetries which it contains and reflects … If we are to become like God, then according to Pythagorean philosophy, the soul must become aware of its harmonic origin, structure and content … Moreover, as certainly as the principle of polarity underlies the world of phenomenal manifestation, so to the mind depends on dualistic typologies, such as the Table of Opposites,* in order to make intellectual progress.[5]

* In Pythagorean theory, the "Table of Opposites" is a set of ten pairs of contrary qualities. The earliest reference of the table is in Aristotle, who stated that it was in use among some contemporary Pythagoreans. But Aristotle provided no real information about its function in Pythagorean practice or theory or about its origin. Some scholars have detected possible archaic elements in it, but others have suggested that its originator was in fact Speusippus, Plato's

According to Pythagorean theory, the principle of *resonance* was an important factor in understanding polarity in terms of the "harmonic attunement" of mind and body as well as the incorporeal and corporeal worlds. For Pythagoras "man is a microcosm," therefore the investigation and utilization of the principles of harmony in the corporeal realm could "activate those same principles within."[6]

This concept of polarity was also evident in the "Tao" of music, in which *yang* and *yin* elements formulate a basis for a harmonious musical expression when ordered in a well-balanced fashion.* Consonance/dissonance, major keys/minor keys, tension/resolution, strong beats/weak beats, loud/soft, fast tempi/slow tempi—are the complementary opposites that embody the cosmic laws of *yang* and *yin* in a musical fashion as a means of expressing realms of heart and emotion. In the *Tao Te Ching* of Lao Tzu, we read: "That the musical notes and tones become harmonious through the relation of one with the another; and that being before and behind and give the idea of one following another."[7] As we can see, the concept of relational harmony was fundamental to music, as well as being essential to the philosophies of the cultures of antiquity.

Of course, the artist's imagination is germane in bringing these elements into harmonious order, and in the process of doing so the *yang* and *yin* elements of imagination and technique become essential counterparts in the creative act. Analytical philosopher, Dr. Michael Beaney of York University (UK) asserts:

> In much of Western thought, the imagination has an ambiguous status, seemingly poised between spirit and nature, mediating between mind and body—the mental and the physical—and interceding between one soul and another. For Aristotle, the imagination—or phantasia—was a kind of bridge

---

nephew. Aristotle's table of the Pythagorean opposites is as follows: Limited/Unlimited Odd/Even, Unity/Plurality, Right/Left, Male/Female, At rest/In motion, Straight/Curved, Light/Darkness, Good/Evil, Square/Oblong. [Source: *Encyclopedia Britannica*.]

* In Chinese philosophy, *Tao* ('the Way') is the natural order of the universe. Human intuition must discern its characteristics in order to realize the potential for individual wisdom. This intuitive knowing of "life" cannot be understood merely conceptually, but can be known through one's life experience.

between sensation and thought, supplying the images or 'phantasms' without which thought could not occur.[8]

It's interesting to note the polar opposites mentioned in Dr. Beaney's comments: Spirit and nature, mind and body, mental and physical. In a very real sense, "the nature of Nature" is rooted in polarity, thus it is not difficult to imagine that the concept of polarity is an underlying principle of the intelligent design of the created world.

Descartes did not hold imagination in high esteem due to its abstruse properties, whereas Kant believed that it was an important factor in the harmonization of our sensory and intellectual faculties. Romanticism in the nineteenth century attributed great importance to the idea of imagination and it was seen as having enormous effects on the creative process of musicians, poets and artists. The ability to think of something, or conceive of something that may not yet be real is a primary function of imagination. In this context, it would seem that physicists must rely on imagination in their quest for understanding and truth in much the same way that artists use their imagination to see or hear things not yet realized or fully created.

The science of acoustics, the physics behind sound production (from the Greek, *akoustikos*; "relating to hearing"), tells us that there are mathematical absolutes behind the production of sound—vibrations, frequencies, ratios and intervals. The series of natural harmonics (known as overtones) in nature is the basis of pitch realization; the sonic etymology of all music. In any given overtone series there exists consonant intervals (those that produce aesthetically pleasing sounds) and dissonant intervals (those that produce harsh or acerbic sounds). Within the codified systemization of pitch relations in Western musical theory (tonality), consonant and dissonant intervals are the basic phonetic properties that we are hearing. It is the sonic juxtaposing of these intervals that results in producing the aural phenomena of attraction as well as tension and resolution. It is this relationship of polar opposites that give Western music its highly evocative emotional characteristics. When we hear music our ears are engaged in a mathematical process (*yang*) that transmutes the ratios of pitch relations (2:1, 3:2, e.g.) into an aesthetic condition that imparts an emotional response in a psychoacoustic fashion (*yin*). This is not a new concept, but the underlying polarity is worth noting in the context of Einstein's postulations regarding simplicity.

Regarding the "beauty" of physics, Brian Greene writes, "The elegance of rich, complex and diverse phenomena emerging from a simple set of universal laws is at least part of what physicists mean when they invoke the term 'beautiful.'"[9] Einstein believed there was beauty in the mysterious and that was likely why he gravitated to music. Though the way that music affects our soul and psyche remains somewhat mysterious, the underlying principles (polarity) that govern the relationships of musical components in the realization of musical art are profoundly simple. For Einstein, insight did not come from logic or mathematics. It came, as it does for artists, from intuition and inspiration. "When I examine myself and my methods of thought," he would say, "I come close to the conclusion that the gift of imagination has meant more to me than any talent for absorbing absolute knowledge."[10] Elaborating, he added, "All great achievements of science must start from intuitive knowledge. I believe in intuition and inspiration ... At times I feel certain I am right while not knowing the reason."[11]

But how, then, did art differ from science for Einstein? Surprisingly, it wasn't the content of an idea, or its subject, that determined whether something was art or science, but how the idea was expressed.

> If what is seen and experienced is portrayed in the language of logic, then we are engaged in science. If it is communicated through forms whose connections are not accessible to the conscious mind but are recognized intuitively as meaningful, then we are engaged in art. Common to both is the loving devotion to that which transcends personal concerns and volition.[12]

Einstein worked intuitively and expressed himself logically. Perhaps that's why he considered science and the arts being related.

> All religions, arts and sciences are branches of the same tree. All these aspirations are directed toward ennobling man's life, lifting it from the sphere of mere physical existence and leading the individual toward freedom. Both churches and universities, insofar as they live up to their true function, serve the ennoblement of the individual.[13]

The truth, beauty and goodness paradigm ("the big three" as American philosopher, Ken Wilber calls them) may never have had a more astute advocate than Einstein. Yet it remains astounding that many espouse the postmodern trope that this paradigm is but a power-tripping weapon wielded by dead, white, European males (or living ones like me). My intuition tells me that individual freedom is necessary to achieve the betterment we all desire. Being lost in the abyss of postmodern relativism and its convoluted irrationality can never be a prescription for attaining the "ennoblement of the individual." History tells us that rational truth must be the socio-cultural equation.

The second verse of Cohen's song begins, "Your faith was strong but you needed proof." In our epistemological pursuits the transcendent attributes of beauty, whether experienced through nature or art, can be effective in our attempts to validate various truth claims. I *imagine* that our desire to achieve cosmic order in our chaotic world will require surrendering to the simple truth that without the concept of "loving devotion" in our social equation we'll never transcend the "limitations of our personal concerns" to find our personal, or collective, Elysium. That too is a very simple truth.

Recommended Recordings

Bach: Violin Concertos, Jeanne Lamon, Tafelmusik

Mozart: Piano Concertos, Michiko Uchida, English Chamber Orchestra

Cohen: *The Essential Leonard Cohen*, CD

Endnotes

1   Terry Jamison/Linda Jameson, *Psychic Intelligence: Tune in and Discover the Power of Your Intuition* (New York: Hachette Book Group, 2011) p. 64.

2   Brian Greene, *The Elegant Universe: Superstrings, Hidden Dimensions, and the Quest for the Ultimate Theory* (New York: W.W. Norton & Company, Inc. 1999), p. 1.

3   Albert Einstein as Edited by Alice Calaprice, *The New Quotable Einstein*, Forward by Freeman Dyson (Princeton University Press and The Hebrew University of Jerusalem, 2005), p. 149.

4   Ibid., p. 305.

5   Kenneth Sylvan Guthrie and David Fideler, *The Pythagorean Sourcebook and Library: An Anthology of Ancient Writings Which Relate to Pythagoras and Pythagorean Philosophy* (Grand Rapids, Michigan: Alexandria Books, 1988), pp. 33-34.

6   Ibid., p. 34.

7   Lao Tzu, *Tao Te Ching*: New English Version, translated by Stephen Mitchel (Perennial Classics-pbk, 2006), p. 9.

8   Michael Beaney, *Imagination and Creativity*, (London: The Open University, 2005), p. 1.

9   Greene, *The Elegant Universe*, p. 169.

10   Einstein-Calaprice, *The New Quotable Einstein*, p. 19.

11   Ibid., p. 180.

12   Helen Dukas-Bennesh Hoffman, *Albert Einstein, the Human Side: New Glimpses from His Archives* (Princeton, NJ: Princeton University Press, 1979), pp. 37-38.

13   Albert Einstein, *The Einstein Reader* (New York: Citadel Press, Kensington Publishing Corp., 2006), p. 7.

35

'Tis a Gift

Words make you think thoughts, music makes you feel feelings,
but a song makes you feel a thought.[1]
Yip Harburg

During the inauguration ceremony of President Barack Obama in 2009, there was the presentation of a musical selection, *Aire and Simple Gifts*, composed by John Williams and based on the quintessentially American, Shaker tune, "'Tis a Gift to Be Simple," also known as "Simple Gifts." The arrangement was scored for a quartet comprised of violin, cello, piano and clarinet. Using sing the Shaker tune as the basis of the composition, Williams captured the spirit of the moment in a sublime musical expression.[*]

At the time it struck me that the instrumentation that Williams chose for his new work was the same as Olivier Messiaen's seminal, *Quartet for the End of Time*, composed in 1940 while Messiaen was a prisoner in a Nazi prison camp during World War II. I'm not sure if this was by design, but the instrumental congruity of these two pieces, albeit composed in different styles, in different

---

[*] The BBC reported that due to the cold temperatures, the performers decided to pre-record the piece, and it was the recording that was heard at the Inaugural.

times and under different circumstances, provided a poignant moment to reflect on the meaning of the inaugural day in light of the historical journey that Americans have traveled since "the Great War" and our Civil War.

In fighting against Nazi tyranny, America and the Allied powers fought for world liberation. Yet on the home front, there was still a great deal of liberating to be accomplished as minorities continued to fight for their basic rights as citizens. Minorities who served their country in both World Wars were often denied the civil liberties that they had fought to preserve. Racism was one of the hypocritical realities that Muslim scholar, Sayyid Qutb, wrote about in his 1951 anti-Christian/anti-American tome, *Milestones*, after he visited the United States in the years just after World War II. Many Americans would agree that Barack Obama's inauguration was in no small measure a deeply liberating moment in our history. Reflecting on the quartets of Messiaen and Williams I couldn't help but be affected by the serendipity of the musical and historical connections.

For Messiaen (1908-1992), a fervent Catholic, it was a scriptural text from the Book of Revelations (10:1-2, 5-7), specifically the Apocalypse narrative that provided the inspiration for his composition.

> And I saw another mighty angel coming down from heaven, wrapped in a cloud, with a rainbow on his head; his face was like the sun, and his legs like pillars of fire ... Setting his right foot on the sea and his left foot on the land ... and, standing on the sea and on the land, he raised his right hand toward Heaven and swore by He who lives forever and ever ... saying: 'There will be no more Time; but in the days when the seventh angel is to blow his trumpet, the mystery of God will be fulfilled.[2]

Messiaen stated that he didn't intend his composition to be a musical representation of the Apocalypse, nor a commentary on his detention, but rather a representation of the end of time and the beginning of eternity. He provided a program explaining each of the eight movements with his reverence for God and Christ being a central theme. The description that he provided for the eighth and final movement, *Praise to the Immortality of Jesus,* reveals his deep reverence for his Christian beliefs.

> Long solo for violin, counterpart to the cello solo in the fifth movement. Why this second eulogy? It addresses more specifically the second aspect

of Jesus: Jesus the Man, the Word made flesh, immortality resurrected, to impart us his life. This movement is pure love. Its progressive ascent toward the extremely high register represents the ascension of man toward his Lord, of the son of God toward his Father, of deified Man toward Paradise.[3]

It is interesting to note that Messiaen chose to compose his quartet in eight movements rather than seven, the number referred to in the Bible as the number of "perfection," and in the book of Revelation when the seventh angel was to intone the end of time by sounding a trumpet. As Robert Sherlaw Johnson writes in his chronicle of the composer's life and work, "Seven is the perfect number, the Creation in six days sanctified by the divine Sabbath; the seven of this (day of) rest is prolonged through eternity and becomes the eight(h) of inextinguishable light, of perfect peace."[4]

According to certain numerological theology, the number eight represents "a new beginning," not unlike the eighth pitch in the diatonic scale in which an octave ends and a new one begins. The eighth movement in Messiaen's quartet can be considered symbolic of a new day of eternal peace and the beginning of a culture of true love centered on God—the Kingdom of Heaven on earth.

In hearing the testimonies of those who experienced the hellish realities of war, one can easily imagine that the "end of time" seemed imminent to those caught in the throes of battle or incarcerated in death camps. Writing about Messiaen's quartet in the *New Yorker Magazine*, Alex Ross opined:

> For Messiaen, the end of time also meant an escape from history, a leap into an invisible paradise … Messiaen always took joy in skating between the mundane and the sublime. He loved God in terms that were sensual, almost sexual. Human love and divine love were not opposites, as they are for so many close readers of the Bible, but stages in an unbroken progression.[5]

In some regards, Barack Obama's election was a long-awaited escape from a particularly painful chapter in the American story. In the singular moment of taking the oath of office, a national rebirth occurred, and I'm sure many citizens thought they had witnessed a glimpse of paradise.

The creation of the song "Simple Gifts" is attributed to Joseph Brackett and dates from 1848. Brackett was an elder in the United Society of Believers in Christ's Second Coming, more commonly known as The Shakers. The

Shaker society was originally established in England in the mid-eighteenth century and was known for its emphasis on egalitarian ideals that included women having important roles in the ministry and working towards a communal way of organizing its congregation. Two women, Mother Ann Lee and Mother Lucy Wright, were the leaders of the Shakers at various times between 1772 and 1821. This was quite a progressive scenario for the time.

Though the song is usually attributed to Brackett another narrative is that the song was a "gift from the spiritual world" from a Negro spirit—a musical apparition.* The lyrics are as follows:

'Tis the gift to be simple, 'tis the gift to be free,
'Tis the gift to come down where you ought to be,
And when we find ourselves in the place just right,
'Twill be in the valley of love and delight.
When true simplicity is gained,
To bow and to bend we shan't be ashamed,
To turn, turn will be our delight,
'Till by turning, turning we come round right.[6]

In another instance of cultural serendipity, the Shakers played a significant role in the abolition of slavery in America. Because they believed in equal rights, they were among the first abolitionists in the United States and played a significant role in the formation of the Underground Railroad in partnership with the Quakers, Congregationalists, Reformed Presbyterians, and other religious groups in the Civil War era.†

The tune for "Simple Gifts" is truly simple and uncomplicated, and Yip Harburg's axiom that "a song makes you feel a thought" captures the spirit of the song perfectly.‡ Messiaen's music is far more complex in its rhythmic, melodic and harmonic properties. His avoidance of a perceptible rhythmic pulse gives

---

* American composer Aaron Copland used "Simple Gifts" in his ballet score *Appalachian Spring* composed for choreographer and dancer Martha Graham in 1944. Copland won the Pulitzer Prize for Music in 1945 for this composition.

† The Underground Railroad was a network of secret routes and safe houses established in the United States during the early and mid-nineteenth century. It was used by freed slaves to escape to free states, Canada and Mexico.

‡ Yip Harburg wrote the lyrics for the song *Somewhere Over the Rainbow*.

the music a sense of timelessness and otherworldliness. The mundane rhythms of earthly life are barely perceptible, purposely so. Undoubtedly, the exigencies of war can make life trying and emotionally demanding and Messiaen's music is representative of that reality.

Messiaen's deep religious conviction was likely an essential factor in dealing with his incarceration in much the same way that the civil rights pioneers in America relied on their faith in times of trial and tribulation. In those times of trial, the "coming Kingdom" likely seemed to be a distant dream. Music born in the times of trial and suffering can be depressing and heart-wrenching utterances. They can also offer glimpses into a more promising reality. Richard Taruskin commenting on Messiaen and the hypocrisies that permeate our increasingly shallow contemporary culture, a culture that looks askance at those who profess religious conviction, asserts:

> The Kingdom of Heaven, the object of mankind's most consoling and necessary imagining, endureth—even unto the twenty-first century, thanks to Messiaen ... Classical music may still be doomed by inexorable social and economic change ... But if so, let it die as it lived, affording glimpses of other worlds and other minds.[7]

When we think of the gift of being free and the price that many paid in order to ensure that freedom, we must live with a sense of gratitude. Living in a free society where civil rights are respected and honored may seem like a "simple thing," something we take for granted. However, upon deeper reflection, we understand that there were many sacrifices made in Europe during World War II and in places like Selma, Birmingham and Memphis during the ensuing years for the cause of preserving and attaining freedom and liberty. The price has been steep, and we have a certain moral obligation never to forget those who gave every measure of themselves for a higher cause. Music that honors that sacrificial spirit in a wordless fashion will always find receptive audiences regardless of style, genre or time of its creation.

As Barack Obama was sworn in as the first American President with African American ancestry, the feeling of national pride was intensely palpable, and once again music provided the unspoken narrative of peace and tranquility in the transferal of the immense power of the office. Williams' music was a "simple gift," and a poignant reminder of the faith traditions that lie at the heart of the American experience. Bravo!

Recommended Recordings

Messiaen: *Quartet for the End of Time*, Tashi

Williams: *Air and Simple Gifts*, Yo-Yo Ma, Cello (SONY CD: #770636)

Copland: *Appalachian Spring*, Leonard Slatkin, Detroit Symphony Orchestra

Endnotes

1   Yip Harburg, Lecture given at the New York YMCA in 1970, *Oxford Essential Quotes, Fourth Edition*, edited by Susan Ratcliffe (Oxford-New York: Oxford University Press, 2016).

2   Rebecca Rischin, *For the End of Time: The Story of the Messiaen Quartet* (New York: Cornell University Press, 2003), p. 56.

3   Ibid., p. 131.

4   Robert Sherlaw Johnson, *Messiaen* (Berkeley-Los Angeles: University of California Press, 1989), p. 41.

5   Alex Ross, "The Rest Is Noise, Revelations: Messiaen's Quartet for the End of Time," *The New Yorker*, March 22, 2004.

6   Charles Hoffer, *Music Listening Today* (Schirmer/Cengage Learning, 2005), p. 18.

7   Richard Taruskin, *The Dangers of Music and Other Anti-Utopian Essays* (Berkeley-Los Angeles-London: University of California Press, 2011), p. 299.

36

The Celebrity Industrial Complex

O great creator of being, grant us one more hour
to perform our art and perfect our lives.[1]
Jim Morrison

You'd be forgiven if you had thought that this sacred petition to the Almighty had been made by Luther, Bach, Beethoven or Brahms, but in fact, it was an appeal made by rock singer Jim Morrison of the Doors. Surprised? Me too!

It goes without saying that in the post-World War II ethos where secular materialism and crass commercialism have become pervasive, expressions of religious faith vis-à-vis art and culture have become as rare as the proverbial snowball in hell. Morrison's plea, from the Door's final album, *An American Prayer*, is especially pertinent in that it reflects a traditional religious view that was completely in accord with the views of Luther, Bach, Brahms and other musicians of the past. Jim Morrison as an avatar of traditional religious expressions vis-à-vis art and music? Who knew?

In previous chapters, I have alluded to various artists who have used their celebrity to promote humanitarian causes. Altruism, when directed toward humanitarian efforts is a much-needed virtue in a world where there remains untold human suffering. It is always inspiring to see celebrity endorsements for causes such as AIDS prevention, breast cancer awareness, environmental concerns, education, arts advocacy and a host of other worthy concerns. Generosity in such matters is always deserving of major kudos. Conversely, it is distressing to see celebrities who have been blessed with copious financial resources and influence, behave in selfish and destructive ways. Too many talented artists seem clueless as to what might be accomplished if they could somehow get beyond their infatuations with themselves and adopt a more altruistic mindset. God knows it's needed. (More about God's needs later.)

Growing up in suburban Cleveland, Ohio in the pre-Beatles era, sports figures were the celebrities who became the objects of my admiration. Cleveland was, and remains a big sports town, and its sports stars, Jim Brown, Rocky Colavito, Paul Warfield (who played for Woody Hayes at Ohio State, and later for the Cleveland Browns) and John "Hondo" Havlicek, of Ohio State Buckeye and Boston Celtic lore, were among my boyhood sports idols. Our heroes of yesteryear seemed to be larger-than-life personalities who we tried to emulate—at least in their sports accomplishments. When one of our heroes fell from grace it caused severe anxiety. I remember being deeply distressed as a young football player when Cleveland Browns defensive end, Paul Wiggin, came to speak at a post-season CYO banquet and I saw him light up a cigarette after his speech. He smokes? Wasn't he in training?

I'm just old enough to remember the final seasons of fireball pitcher, Bob Feller, whose eighteen-year career with the Cleveland Indians was the stuff of legend. "Rapid Robert," who passed away in 2010, wasn't all that big in terms of his physical stature, but he could regularly throw a baseball over 100 miles per hour and was the dominant right-handed pitcher of the era. What endeared Feller to many of his fans was that while in the prime of his career he became the first major league baseball player to enlist in the armed services after the bombing of Pearl Harbor in 1941. During his four-year stint in the Navy, he was decorated with thirteen awards for commendable military service. Feller is one of many players in the Baseball Hall of Fame who served in the military, many during wartime. Other military veterans in the Hall of Fame include Bob Lemon, Phil Rizzuto, Yogi Berra, Larry Doby, Stan Musial, Jackie Robertson, Pee Wee Reese, Joe DiMaggio, Willie Mays, Ernie Banks and Ted Williams.

In the 1940s there were far differing attitudes about serving in the military then than there are now. Love of God and country were considered virtues that more than a few contemporary celebrities now consider a sign of being "unhinged," while patriotism is often looked at askance by certain elements in our society. The "blame-America-first" crowd that views America's intentions and motivations as inherently suspect often seems to have little regard for the religious values that the Founding Fathers and patriots of the past found to be so efficacious in creating a better, more humane culture. Were the founders perfect? Hardly. But they understood that human proclivities needed to be tempered by adhering to the laws of the land, and those laws, rooted in liberty and the pursuit of happiness, needed protecting.

Power Art

When in 1988 after the Berlin Wall fell and the Cold War came to an end, a friend who had participated in anti-Communist demonstrations in Berlin, returned to New York, and while discussing his experiences in Germany, he exclaimed, "Well, we defeated the Reds in Moscow and East Berlin; next stop, Hollywood!" His gibe is not lost on those who see the influence of the entertainment industry as being at odds with "American values." That view might be considered somewhat prejudicial, but it's undeniable that there currently exists a vigorous leftist tendency among those in the entertainment and cultural arenas. It would be unfair to characterize all those in Hollywood and the entertainment industry adversely in an across-the-board way, and as Steven J. Ross observes, historically the political right has been supremely influential in Hollywood, perhaps more so than the left. In his book *Hollywood Left and Right*, he notes:

> Such fears about radicalism in the movie industry reflect a long-standing conventional wisdom that Hollywood has always been a bastion of the political left. Conventional wisdom is wrong on two counts ... it was the Republican Party ... that established the First political beachhead in Hollywood ... and far more surprising ... the Hollywood right, led by Louis B. Mayer, George Murphy, Ronald Reagan, Charlton Heston and Arnold Schwarzenegger—has had a greater impact on American political life. The Hollywood left has the political glitz, but the Hollywood right sought, won and exercised electoral power.[2]

Electoral successes aside, there are social and cultural issues that cause deep concern among many of the more conservative persuasion. Many liberal tendencies born of the Enlightenment are intrinsically humane, yet the aforementioned disingenuousness that is so pervasive in Celebrity-Industrial-Complex is seen as a pernicious element that causes cognitive dissonance among those of a more conservative/traditionalist perspective. History instructs that freedom apart from responsibility continually puts us in morally compromised situations. Without being more accountable for our choices, artistic or otherwise, we collude in our demise (re: ancient Greece and Rome). In his book *Man's Search for Meaning*, Austrian psychiatrist and Holocaust survivor Viktor Frankl comments on East coast and West coast sensibilities:

> Freedom is only part of the story and half of the truth. Freedom is but the negative aspect of the whole phenomenon whose positive aspect is responsibleness. In fact, freedom is in danger of degenerating into mere arbitrariness unless is it lived in terms of responsibleness. That is why I recommend that the Statue of Liberty on the East Coast be supplanted by a Statue of Responsibility on the West Coast.[3]

Dr. Frankl was clearly on to something in alluding to the West Coast, sometimes referred to as "the Left Coast," in relation to moral and ethical responsibility. The opprobrium that many have toward Hollywood and its apparent disregard for common decency on so many fronts, distresses many Americans, and not just those on the Christian sphere. The Celebrity-Industrial-Complex (in which I occasionally work) seems to be given a pass for questionable behavior in our increasingly voyeuristic culture. The invective hurled at political right by the likes of Jon Stewart and Bill Maher is often as offensive as the right-wing invectives they bemoan, yet their diatribes too often get a pass because it's considered "humor" or "satire." But now, even that scenario is changing as comedians who trade in satire or mockery are coming under attack for being insensitive and engaging in "micro-aggressions" and intolerance. The "woke" agenda has put many comedians out of work.

When looking back on the experience of Woodstock and its ramifications, we see quite a bit of messiness and unfulfilled promise from a generation that seemed to harbor so much hope (and self-righteousness) for a better world. In the post-Woodstock era in which musicians and Hollywood icons became our new cultural heroes, we tend to hear way too much in the way of lip service from those who pine for an end to all the inhumane perfidiousness, yet whose personal lifestyle choices too often typify the hedonist, materialist, self-centered trappings that are antithetical to the ideals they want others to live by. Many celebrities seemed lost in the abyss of superficiality and self-absorption and the public-at-large is seeing though that duplicity. This results in the righteous indignation expressed by moralistic celebrities falling on deaf ears. Prevarication seems a condition that infects many of those who are a part of the Celebrity-Industrial-Complex when confronted with the double standards in which they engage. In circumstances where truth is badly needed, more often than not we get equivocation, obfuscation and moral relativism; none of which advances the prospects for betterment. Whether it be the predilection for the intemperate, overindulgent lifestyle, or the mindless kowtowing to a spurious ideological paradigm, a significant percentage of those in the Celebrity-Industrial-Complex seem wholly out of step with the axiological precepts that are necessary to ameliorate the problems that contribute to the social malaise that plague our society at large.

I'm reminded of C. S. Lewis' exegesis on the influence of popular culture and Madison Avenue in his insightful book, *The Screwtape Letters*. In Letter No. 20, Lewis' protagonist, the senior devil, Screwtape, is explaining to his young nephew, Wormwood, about the type of "physical attributes" that women should have in order to seduce men into the false reality of "falling in love." Screwtape explains that the type of woman that is best suited for this seduction

> ...is a question decided for us by the spirits far deeper down in the Lowerarchy than you and I. It is the business of these great masters to produce in every age a general misdirection of what may be called 'sexual taste.' They do this by working through the small circle of popular artists, dressmakers, actresses and advertisers who determine the fashionable type. The aim is to guide each sex away from those members of the other with whom spiritually helpful, happy and fertile marriages are most likely.[4]

Lewis's *The Screwtape Letters* was published in 1942, and he could not have been more prescient. Surveying the current political and social realities that we face requires a word or two vis-à-vis artistic freedom, responsibility, artistic license, and the "general misdirection" that the demon, Screwtape, was alluding to. If we are to find a way out of our cultural malaise we might do well to begin by sorting out the proverbial wheat from the chaff. The kind of agitprop that is produced by Michael Moore, for instance, does not contribute to any meaningful solutions due to Mr. Moore's distinct disregard for the truth. That Mr. Moore is known as a provocative fabricator goes without saying. What rankles many, is how seemingly intelligent people accept Moore's disingenuous narratives without a hint of objective evaluation. There seems to be little or no outrage about Moore's shoddy ethics from an artistic standpoint and to me, this is a complete abdication of moral responsibility. The abject fawning that goes on by the liberal left about Mr. Moore is hard to fathom. Regarding Moore and the reaction to his films by the Celebrity-Industrial-Complex, Manhattan Institute fellow, Kay S. Hymowitz, observes:

> And you can be sure that the trendy sophisticates in Cannes and Hollywood will once again rise to their feet to honor their mendacious auteur, European intellectuals will bow before his Manichaean simplicities, and the international radical left will cheer the moral obtuseness of the man who has made his fortune turning the documentary into fiction.[5]

It would seem that if those of a liberal persuasion in the Celebrity-Industrial-Complex wish for their concerns to be taken more seriously by those at the other end of the spectrum, rejecting Moore's dishonest, pseudo-populist, cinematic rants would be a good first step. This is not to say that Moore's films don't occasionally make important points, but rather than do the hard work of fashioning persuasive arguments, he lazily resorts to impressionist insinuations. Bashing the capitalism system that he benefits from comes across as whiny petulance, especially when a great deal of the perfidy perpetuated by greedy corporate executives has nothing to do with actual capitalism but rather a bastardization of such (the sub-prime mortgage fiasco, hedge funds, e.g.). Making that distinction is important if the merits and/or demerits of capitalism are to be debated in a cogent fashion.

The duplicity of the Celebrity-Industrial-Complex in its treatment of women is especially onerous. Where is the Hollywood elite when there were politically motivated personal attacks on women such as Sarah Palin, Michelle Bachman, Michelle Malkin or other conservative women? Joy Behar called

Sharron Angle, a politician she disagrees with, a "bitch" on network TV, and Barbara Walters laughs it off. One can imagine the outrage if a conservative referred to Ms. Behar, or Rachel Maddow, or Michelle Obama, or any woman with a liberal/progressive persuasion in a similar fashion. The denunciations would be positively stentorian. Why do hear so little about President Clinton's "war on women" or how Islamic radicals treat the fairer sex?

The brouhaha over Mitt Romney and his association with corporations that "fire people" begs several questions: Don't liberals who run corporations occasionally fire people? Is handing out pink slips solely a conservative proclivity? Is firing someone a proclivity at all, or is the left advocating a socialist model and a government guaranteed job or income? (Cloward and Piven, anyone?)* Is high unemployment strictly the result of conservative economic policies? There is a great deal of opprobrium directed against gun violence in our society, especially by celebrities, yet Hollywood churns out copious films in which violence and gunplay are pervasive. As Jonah Goldberg opines, "It's a safe bet that Hollywood liberals loathe guns. But you wouldn't know that by what they produce. Not many action stars save the day by quoting a poem."[6] Yet, all those "mean-spirited conservatives" are the ones needed to be excoriated at every turn for their obtuse attitudes regarding social justice, and Hollywood is only too happy to pile on.

Citing F.A. Hayek's *Mirage of Social Justice,* Goldberg points out that justice of any type "creates a claim on others," and "assumes rights—social rights, economic rights—that cannot be enforced" without resorting to government coercion, in other words, totalitarianism. Hayek was concerned about the ill effects of social justice because of his disdain for "distributive justice," which treats justice as a feature of outcomes rather than of procedures. He was concerned with the idea of a "merit czar" being appointed to determine "winners and losers," or who's worthy of government largess (healthcare, e.g.) and who's not. In the case of unemployment, who is being unjust? Goldberg asks: "The

---

* The Cloward-Piven strategy is a political strategy outlined in 1966 by American sociologists and political activists Richard Cloward and Frances Fox Piven that called for overloading the U.S. public welfare system to precipitate a crisis that would lead to a replacement of the welfare system with a national system of "a guaranteed annual income and thus an end to poverty." They believed that it would be through Democratic party that their tactic could be implemented due to the Democratic party's predilection to overspend on welfare programs.

employers who cannot afford to hire more workers? The consumers who refuse to create enough demand to justify more workers? The government for not taxing innocent parties to pay for labor that isn't needed and that they didn't vote for?"[7] The contortions of what has become liberal orthodoxy can be dizzying in their justifications. As Goldberg puts it, behind every double standard lurks an unstated single standard; that standard is *power*."[8]

For instance, it's well established that liberal orthodoxy favors developing alternative sources of energy and "green" technology. Fine. So why pummel free-market capitalism, the very economic system that generates the necessary wealth needed for research and development in the creation and manufacturing of the technology needed to accomplish the "green dream?" Those who profess to be environmentally conscientious while opposing the system that makes it possible, become, according to their twisted logic, "objectively" anti-environmental. And how many movies, television programs or music videos would actually get produced *and consumed*, without a thriving, capitalist, free-market economic system humming along.

In the run up to the 2016 Democratic primaries, there was a discussion underway as to which millionaire, Hillary Clinton or Elizabeth Warren, had more populist *bona fides* as if either of these ladies can speak to the struggles of the middle class and the poor with any credibility. Both claimed "the system to be rigged" in favor of the rich, yet both have played the system to their financial advantage. Again, Hollywood looks the other way. The duplicity, situational ethics and virtue signaling here is astonishing. It makes one wonder about the incongruities of these viewpoints. Now, I'll be the first to admit that conservatives have not exactly cornered the market on virtue and good will, or that patriotism is the sole province of conservatives and the Christian right. As a good friend, Bishop Cecil B. Reilly occasionally reminds me, Scripture tells us that we all fall short of God's glory and that church is not so much a museum for saints as it is a hospital for sinners. No argument there.

Political Hollywood

The tendency of celebrities to identify with anti-capitalist ideals dates back to Charlie Chaplin whose impoverished upbringing made him deeply sympathetic to the plight of the underprivileged. Though he became fabulously wealthy he never lost his concern for those who were so adversely affected by the Great Depression. He was accused of being a Communist sympathizer for advocating socialist remedies for the common man. Goldberg, Hayek and Thomas Sowell acknowledge that the desire to use government to remedy social ills has some merit, but in the end, "the government cannot love you," and there is just too much diversity of circumstances in any group to prescribe across-the-board solutions without infringing on individual liberties. We pine for across-the-board fairness, but as Sowell asks, "At what cost?" It's an important question. This is a significant reason why the American Constitution stops and individual rights. For many, the liberal perspective too often seems at odds with common sense, though it continues to see itself as the voice of reason, compassion and righteousness. In this scenario, intellectual honesty is in short supply and political correctness takes center stage (the Juan Williams/NPR flap, e.g.).*

In an essay published in *The Village Voice* in 2008 titled "Why I Am No Longer a Brain-Dead Liberal," American playwright David Mamet makes more than few perspicacious observations regarding the lack of common sense that he viewed as contributing to the myopia of the contemporary liberal mind. Mamet writes, "I took the liberal view for many decades, but I believe I have changed my mind. As a child of the '60s, I accepted as an article of faith that government is corrupt, that business is exploitative, and that people are generally good at heart."[9]

This, of course, is typical liberal orthodoxy. But through his various epiphanies, Mamet realized there was something incoherent in that viewpoint. If governments and corporations are managed by people, and if people are generally good, according to the basic tenets of liberalism, it didn't follow that the government and businesses would be intrinsically corrupt. How could it be both ways? Mamet came to the realization that not all aspects of government and business are inherently bad. We benefit from the protection of the military and certain regulatory agencies. Big business puts people to work and in so doing elevates our standards of living and education in ways that most

---

* Journalist Juan Williams was terminated from his job at National Public Radio for remarks he made that NPR thought were offensive to Muslims. In his book *Muzzled: The Assault on Honest Debate*, Williams argues that his contract was terminated by NPR as part of a larger pattern of the suppression of unwelcome opinions that didn't comport with liberal orthodoxy.

citizens agree are beneficial to the greater community. Limited government has obvious benefits, as does capitalism and the free-enterprise system.

Corporate greed is seen as the absolute bane to the liberal sensibility (and to a few conservatives), but there is a need to make a distinction between blatant greed and free enterprise methodology. In an interview with Phil Donahue, (it can be seen on YouTube) the noted economist, Milton Friedman responds to Donahue's admonitions about the affliction of capitalist "greed" by citing historical facts. Mr. Friedman makes the case that in the only instances in human history where the masses have escaped from the kind of "grinding poverty" that has afflicted the developing world is where the principles of free enterprise and free markets were not hindered or curtailed by excessive government control. Citing Henry Ford and Albert Einstein, Friedman asserted that heavy doses of government interference were not conducive to Ford's or Einstein's creativity and ingenuity, whereas socialist tendencies tend to hamper creativity and personal incentive. Consequently, economic progress is thwarted and large swaths of the populace are never lifted out from their impoverished condition.

This was Adam Smith's contention as well. It seems inarguable, yet progressives impulsively and imprudently attack capitalism at every turn. Smith understood that their existed both a "self-purpose" and a "whole purpose" in any capitalist nostrum and attaining balance between these two purposes was of paramount importance in fashioning a prosperous society. Celebrities like Moore, Sean Penn and Jim Carey may openly rail about capitalism, but they are fundamentally hypocrites. (Penn's schmoozing with Hugo Chavez was especially abhorrent.)

On his changing perspectives regarding liberal orthodoxy, David Mamet comments:

> These cherished [liberal] precepts had, over the years, become ingrained as increasingly impracticable prejudices. Why do I say impracticable? Because although I still held these beliefs, I no longer applied them in my life ... I had been listening to National Public Radio and reading various organs of national opinion for years, wonder and rage contending for pride of place. Further: I found I had been—rather charmingly, I thought—referring to myself for years as "a brain-dead liberal," and to NPR as "National Palestinian Radio."

This is, to me, the synthesis of this world view with which I now found myself disenchanted: that everything is always wrong. But in my life, a brief review revealed, everything was not always wrong, and neither was nor is always wrong in the community in which I live, or in my country. Further, it was not always wrong in previous communities in which I lived, and among the various and mobile classes of which I was at various times a part.[10]

One wonders why so many smart people on the left fail to see the light as Mr. Mamet has. Neither orthodoxies of the political right or the political left provide all the answers, and once we come to that realization bipartisan compromise and conciliation seem to be the best way to proceed in our attempts to find solutions for our seemingly intractable problems. Certain pieties can be beneficial, even encouraged when directed in an altruistic fashion, but inconsistencies that border on the hypocritical need to be challenged. Churchill's assertion that democracy is a messy process goes without saying, yet even in its messiness it gives us the best opportunity to avoid being ensnared by authoritarian tendencies.

After the Great Depression, there existed a rather naïve belief on the part of many artists in the United States in the 1930s that socialism held the promise of actually establishing a Utopian society based on fairness and equality. Yet, as musicologist Richard Taruskin points out, many who promised Utopian societies gave us "gas chambers and gulags," not to mention various inquisitions and jihads. Russian composer Dmitri Shostakovich, a tormented artistic soul if there ever was one, perhaps understood this better than most. Having lived and worked under the repressive conditions of Communism in Russia he experienced first-hand the brutality of a society that rejected the idea that human beings possessed spiritual characteristics and as such should be treated with basic human dignity. The liberal tendencies of American artists of that era (the Great Depression notwithstanding) to identify with the tyrannical socialist model that he knew so well, must surely have created more than a bit of cognitive dissonance for Shostakovich. He might have appreciated Thomas Paine's view regarding any tendency to take civil liberties for granted: "What we obtain too cheap, we esteem too lightly; 'tis dearness only that gives every thing its value. Heaven knows how to set a proper price upon its goods; and it would be strange indeed if so celestial an article as freedom should not be highly rated."[11] Can I hear an "Amen!"

Well, I could if I lived in the United States in the 1960s, but not if I lived with Shostakovich behind the Iron Curtain where expressions of religious faith were often with met with oppression in the most brutal fashion. Of course, in the USA we have had a few bad actors in our midst, and one wonders to what degree covert activities that our government engages in would be tolerated if there was full disclosure on such matters. That said, for a variety of reasons there seems to be a serious blind spot among many on the political left that results in a failure to comprehend that by advocating leftist/socialist policies utopian ideals are never realized, but rather, brutal oppression becomes the norm. Goldberg half-jokingly posits that by ignoring the historical failures of socialist experiments, the coterie of the liberal left "has blind spots for blind spots."

Most people believe in change, but don't want to change what they believe. This sort of intransigence has created the kind of polarization that is evident in our postmodern culture in general, and in America in particular, especially in the political arena where partisan politics has become extremely toxic. Rather than seeing the value in becoming bi-partisan pragmatists we have tended to become rigid ideologues unwilling to compromise for a higher collective benefit, and this is to our collective loss. But again, this is not news and our failings are manifest in this regard. Our political class has neglected the common man in this regard and the presidential candidacies of Donald Trump and Bernie Sanders tapped into the anger and frustration that many Americans were feeling in 2016.

Mamet's commentary points to various realities of our social condition— some good, some not. He observes:

> … lust, greed, envy, sloth, and their pals are giving the world a good run for its money, but that nonetheless, people in general seem to get from day to day; and that we in the United States get from day to day under rather wonderful and privileged circumstances—that we are not and never have been the villains that some of the world and some of our citizens make us out to be, but that we are a confection of normal (greedy, lustful, duplicitous, corrupt, inspired—in short, human) individuals living under a spectacularly effective compact called the Constitution, and lucky to get it.[12]

Lucky indeed. Anyone who has traveled to the developing countries or places that were formerly under totalitarian rule knows all too well what a blessing it is to live in a free and open society where civil liberties are considered sacrosanct. During my first visits to Russia and Ukraine just after the collapse of the Soviet Empire in 1991, I was astounded to see just how impoverished the situation was. In the West we had been led to believe that Moscow was a gleaming metropolis boasting the best of the Soviet "worker's paradise," yet the entire city seemed drab and badly in need of a paint job (except for the hotel where I stayed—previously a KGB haunt). Department stores and marketplaces were without merchandise or basic commodities. The ruble was virtually worthless. Bands of gypsy youths were on the prowl in broad daylight looking to mug unsuspecting victims.

One day after trying to fetch a taxi for about an hour to get to a rehearsal, I was told by one of my hosts that because taxi drivers get paid a wage guaranteed by the state they didn't need to pick up passengers to make a buck/ruble. (Ah, socialism!) The hope of the Communist ideal seemed hopelessly lost in the abyss of disenchantment and diminishing hope for a better future. While in Moscow in 1992 to conduct a concert for the Mozart Bicentennial, the gifted Ukrainian violinist, Oleh Krysa, sardonically said, "David, hope may be good for breakfast, but it makes a lousy dinner." Of course, if you were fortunate to be a high-profile artist, or part of the political *nomenklatura*, or the KGB and had access to U.S. dollars, then having a nice dinner (and all the vodka you could want) was no problem at all. Over a light lunch at his modest apartment outside of Moscow, Krysa offered me some vodka. I told him that I didn't drink. He responded: "How do you survive?"

About God's Needs

Undoubtedly it seems rather presumptuous to those who are not "believers" to engage in any such conversation about "God's needs" or expectations. But as Thomas Aquinas averred:

> Unbelievers are in ignorance of things that are of faith, for neither do they see or know them in themselves, nor do they know them to be credible. The faithful, on the other hand, know them, not as by demonstration, but by the light of faith, which makes them see that they ought to believe them.[13]

But even for believers the understanding of what "God needs," may be guesswork to varying degrees. Still, the inspired guesser can begin to extrapolate that God may not be too thrilled with the "lust, greed, envy, sloth and their pals" that contribute to the malaise that is so much a part of the human condition.

In the aftermath of World War II, there was a misconception that Joseph Stalin and Communists were going to be a part of the solution in dealing with dictatorial tyranny. After all, they were allies with the United States in defeating Germany, and Communism's promise of socialist equality seemed to be an ideology worthy of emulation. The West was soon to realize that this was not to be the case. As the godless ideology of Marxism began to rear its ugly head in the most totalitarian fashion, the claim that Communism would deliver the utopian ideal to the masses was being exposed as a specious contention. The Nazis were gone but there were new tyrants in the neighborhood trading on the resentments of the oppressed while oppressing those who they purported to be liberating in the name of a utopian future.* With the establishment of a large, contented middle class, the idea of pitting the rich against the poor was no longer a viable tactic for Marxists to employ to advance their dialectic methodology. "Oppressed masses" of a different kind were needed to incite revolutionary impulses. In the post-World War II era, ethnic minorities and women became the oppressed groups that neo-Marxists would identify and use to advance their agenda. White males of European descent were now the new "bogeymen" to be labeled as intolerant, reactionary, racist, chauvinist and fascist.

But there was another pernicious mindset at work. The ethos of Judeo-Christian culture also became a target of neo-Marxists and secular progressives because religion, especially fervent religious conviction, could potentially become "fascist" in its zealotry. The "absolutist" tendencies of religious believers made them less prone to the deconstructionist rationale that questioned and distrusted absolutist principles. Moreover, religion's capacity to militate against resentment and anger—emotions that were necessary to

---

* The word "utopia" stems from the modern Latin, literally "nowhere," and was the title of Sir Thomas More's book of 1516, *Utopia*. More, who read Plato's *Republic*, conceived Utopia as an imaginary island that had perfect legal, social and political systems. By the sixteenth century the term was extended to refer to any imagined "perfect" place or an ideal mode of governance.

foment revolutionary urges—acted as a major inhibitor against the proponents of Hegelian dialectics. Perhaps most importantly, religion emphasized the divinity and sacredness of human beings and family. Therefore, treating people as mere objects to be exploited for a revolutionary cause is considered immoral and unethical. If, as Mao opined, religion was "the opiate of the masses," then resentment was surely the opiate of the revolutionary left.

Modern deconstructionist philosophy is attributed to Jacques Derrida (via Martin Heidegger), but it is a progeny of Friedrich Nietzsche's Zarathustrian claim that "God is dead" and religion is unnecessary.* If God was out of the picture "in the great dice game of existence," then individuals could be left to their personal designs regarding morality and their pursuit of happiness and fulfillment. There now could be a reevaluation of all values because he "unmasked Christian morality." For Nietzsche, the restrictive aspects of Judeo-Christian morality severely limited humankind's quest for ultimate liberation, freedom—and most importantly, eternal joy. In his epic philosophical paean, *Also Sprach Zarathustra*, Nietzsche pens the gospel of what he asserts to be humankind's ultimate pursuit:

O man, take care!
What does the deep midnight declare?
"I was asleep-
From a deep dream I woke and swear:-

The world is deep,
Deeper than day had been aware.
Deep is its woe-

---

* Though Nietzsche is usually cited as being the first to declare that, "God is dead," it was the German, anarchist philosopher, Johann Kaspar Schmidt, also known as Max Stirner (1806-1856) who wrote in his philosophical tome, *Der Einzige und sein Eigentum* (*The Ego and His Own*), published in 1845: "At the entrance of the modern time stands the "God-man". At its exit will only the God in the God-man evaporate? And can the God-man really die if only the God in him dies? They did not think of this question, and thought they were finished when in our days they brought to a victorious end the work of the Enlightenment, the vanquishing of God: they did not notice that man has killed God in order to become now – 'sole God on high.' The other world outside us is indeed brushed away, and the great undertaking of the men of the Enlightenment completed; but the other world in us has become a new heaven and calls us forth to renewed heaven-storming: God has had to give place, yet not to us, but to—man. How can you believe that the God-man is dead before the man in him, besides the God, is dead?"

Joy-deeper yet than agony:
Woe implores: Go!
But all joy wants eternity-
Wants deep, wants deep eternity.[14]

For Nietzsche, immortality is our most cherished hope. What could be better than living forever in rapturous joy free from inhibitions and accountability?

Frankl asserted that finding meaning in life was the ultimate healing balm; Logotherapy, as he called it. Those of a religious persuasion argue that it's only by living a life in the embrace of The Almighty, a life committed to the welfare of others, that we can realize meaning and ultimate fulfillment. Nietzsche and his progressive brethren saw it otherwise. As the philosophical tenets of Nietzsche found adherents in the latter part of the twentieth century—Derrida, Foucault, the Frankfurt School critical theorists, e.g., the assault on moral certainty as envisaged by the purveyors of religious beliefs continued in a way that would have warmed Nietzsche's revolutionary, anti-Christian heart.*

In his book *Liberal Fascism: The Secret History of the American Left, From Mussolini to the Politics of Change*, Jonah Goldberg makes the case with coruscating clarity that religion, in general, has always been seen by progressive liberals and those of a leftist mindset as being an obstacle to their agenda because it provided hope in times of despair, and perhaps more significantly, it placed great importance on family. If people have hope and familial support, it becomes difficult to manufacture the kind of hopelessness, rage and resentment against the villain *du jour* that in turn could motivate "the people" to take to the streets and revolt. Allan Bloom asserted that the "safe limitations of family" mitigate the increasingly hedonist/nihilist spirit of our modern age, and this has decidedly anti-progressive connotations. When people feel loved and protected they're less likely to "act out" in fits of rage, rebellion and retribution.

The neo-Marxists of the Institute for Social Research (aka the Frankfurt School)—Theodor Adorno, Herbert Marcuse, Walter Benjamin, Max

---

* What may not be so well known, is that key players of the neo-Marxist Frankfurt School made serious inroads to the arenas of television and radio in the 1950s. Paul Lazarsfeld, an avowed socialist and founder of Columbia University's Bureau of Applied Social Research, was a Frankfurt School advocate. Lazarsfeld's Columbia University project was of the same ilk of the Institute For Social Research in Frankfurt that spawned Critical Theory.

Horkheimer—were the theorists who would fashion the intellectual basis on which the progressive attack on conservative and religious ideals would be made. Working in the protective environment of Columbia University, Adorno and several Cal. State-Berkeley researchers published the book, *The Authoritarian Personality* in 1950, in which Adorno proffered that conservative views were inherently fascist because conservatives view any change or any affront to traditional values (religious, social, political) as being "reactionary." The Frankfurt School neo-Marxists were highly effective in their attempt to influence and infiltrate academia and the media in order to promulgate their ideology, especially with regard to the blatant character assassinations of their ideological foes. Does this sound familiar? Placards depicting George Bush, Dick Cheney, Scott Walker, Sarah Palin, Donald Trump, Tea Party advocates and a host of other critics the left as racist Nazis have become commonplace at liberal/progressive assemblies. We should remember too that constant ridicule and besmirching the character of one's political opponent was one of Saul Alinsky's *Rules for Radicals*.* Alinsky considered Lucifer to be the first radical to rise up against the establishment.

By simply dismissing conservatives as being afflicted with "authoritarian personality syndrome," those of the progressive ilk were relieved of having to do the difficult intellectual work of defending or arguing the merits of their ideological positions. Passing off their propaganda in the guise of scholarly research or journalistic integrity is invidious perfidy. Using artists and entertainers to do their bidding was part of their game plan. As Goldberg explains, during the nineteenth century, "the original Marxist explanation of fascism was that it was the capitalist ruling classes' reaction to the threat of the ascendancy of the working classes."[15] This malevolent distortion now manifests

---

* Saul Alinsky's Rule No. 5: "Ridicule is man's most potent weapon." Hillary Clinton did her senior thesis on Saul Alinsky and this 92-page document, titled *There Is Only the Fight*, was held from public viewing by the White House and Wellesley College during the Clinton administration. The Washington Post's Peter Slevin reported (March 25, 2007), that both Mrs. Clinton and Barack Obama (while Obama was a community organizer in Chicago) were advocates of Alinsky's "power analysis." In his book *Rules for Radicals*, Alinsky refers to Lucifer as "the first radical known to man who rebelled against the establishment." Bill Dedman of NBC News reported (March 2, 2007) "it was the Clintons who asked Wellesley in 1993 to hide Hillary Rodham's senior thesis from the first generation of Clinton biographers, according to her thesis adviser and friend, professor Alan H. Schechter, who describes taking the call from the White House."

itself in the name of multiculturalism, in which any attempt to "preserve" any legacy of the past, especially the European (white) past, is *de facto* imperialism, racism or colonialism. This is the progeny of neo-Marxist critical theory that views any "universal" or self-evident truth as merely a "false, ideological camouflage for the powerful."[16] The legacy of European classical music now finds itself being the target of this progressive, postmodernist, politically correct, multiculturalist rationale.

Clinical psychologist Jordan B. Peterson points out according to Derrida and other deconstructionists, language was the tool by which oppressors controlled the oppressed; something "built into the very categories we use to pragmatically simply and negotiate the world." The idea that language, which for eons was thought to be a very effective way to communicate in order for progress and order to be achieved in human relationships, was now considered something quite pernicious—a tool for attaining and exercising power. Under the rubric of this postmodern narrative, "hierarchies exist because they gain from oppressing those who are omitted. It is this 'ill-gotten gain' that allows various groups to benefit and gain power over others; men over women, rich over poor, Caucasians over everyone else, e.g.[17] As Peterson points out, hierarchies are natural and have been present in nature for millions of years—before there were trees, and long before there was capitalism.

We witnessed this almost daily from 2009 to 2016 when critiques of President Obama's policies and initiatives are reflexively met with charges of racism or fascism. This demonstrated how language had been weaponized to deflect any objective critique that might hinder President Obama's agenda. This type of inflammatory rhetoric made for juicy sound bytes and no doubt heartened liberal coteries, but it was deeply disingenuous and it contributed to the further polarization of our political discourse. On the national holiday honoring Dr. Martin Luther King. Jr. in 2012 (during the presidential election campaign) we were hearing disturbing references of racism by the political left who characterized GOP candidate Mitt Romney as "the whitest of the white." Whatever happened to Dr. King's assertion about the content of one's character being more important than race or ethnicity? That seems to be lost on the very individuals who cite Dr. King as one of their role models. How about they walk-the-walk and not just talk-the-talk? Many liberals tend to admire

Dr. King for his stance on social justice but loathe the religious impulses that fueled his advocacy of such.

Media Matters

What may not be so well known, is that key players of the Frankfurt School made serious inroads to the arena of television and radio in the 1950s, and why not? What better way to propagate their anti-religious and secular ideology than through the use of mass media. As the influence and power of these broadcast mediums cast a wide net on the public, the opportunities to propagate secular progressive attitudes grew exponentially. On several occasions, I have alluded to Adorno's Essays on Mass Culture and his understanding of the "cultural conditioning" capabilities of mass media. In his essays of 1944, Adorno viewed mass culture as having deleterious effects on the public at large due to the "fettering of conscious" and the diminishing of "adult sensibilities;" attributes he considered to be necessary for creating a climate conducive to democratic ideals. Somewhat ironically (and cynically), other leading exponents of the progressive mindset would eventually come to view the "fettering" of critical thought as a favorable disposition among the masses. The idea of creating "low information voters" could be beneficial in the process of indoctrination on order win elections and control power. Voters who thought deeply about issues couldn't have their consciousness easily manipulated or restrained. Free thinkers were problematic for those seeking greater political power.

If television and radio could inure large segments of the population to the pernicious influences of the neo-Marxist construct, one that viewed the secularization of society as an important step toward advancing Critical Theory, all the better. Adorno understood mass media's dialectical potential in the context of "demythologizing" art and removing the aura of "bourgeoisie" spirituality from the creative and experiential aspects of art. He, and his cohort, Walter Benjamin, realized that "the magic power of the media could be used to re-define previous ideas … all legends, all mythologies, all myths, all founders of religions, and the very religions themselves" could be eviscerated and subsequently rendered invalid and inconsequential.[18] In his cautionary *1984*, George Orwell warned: "Who controls the past controls the future. Who controls the present controls the past."[19] By engaging in revisionist history the neo-Marxists sought to gain advantages in their assault on "bourgeois" values.

The progressive revolution needed not to be fought by air, land and sea, but rather through the airwaves, and now through cyberspace. In a very real way, the neo-Marxists were precursors of the idea put forth by Marshall McLuhan that "the medium was the message." The increased secularization of our cultural heritage can be inextricably linked to commercial media manipulation. In his book, *The Mechanical Bride: Folklore of Industrial Man*, McLuhan writes:

> Ours is the first age in which many thousands of the best-trained individual minds have made it a full-time business to get inside the collective public mind. To get inside in order to manipulate, exploit control is the object now. And to generate light is not the intention. To keep everybody in a helpless state engendered by prolonged mental rutting is the effect of many ads and much entertainment alike.[20]

For Adorno and his acolytes, McLuhan may have been the prescient avatar warning the masses about the tactics of fascist capitalists and their incessant "commodity fetishes." To others, he is a sober prophet warning against the secular progressives who would manipulate media and the entertainment industry in order to propagandize their politically correct, liberal agenda, an agenda that disparages traditional values at every turn because it is seen as maintaining an unjust status quo. McLuhan would temper his concerns after the initial publication of his book, but had he lived to witness our current mass media landscape he might have doubled down on his initial critique. To be fair, conservatives in Hollywood, such as Louis B. Mayer, George Murphy and Ronald Reagan, were among the most influential celebrities to use film and television for spreading their political and social agendas. Liberals also used film and their celebrity status to champion progressive causes—Jane Fonda, Harry Belafonte and Michael Moore. Media spin is neither the sole province of the left or right.

Ben Shapiro, who grew up in Hollywood, has been chronicling recent trends in the television industry and has called attention to the Frankfurt School's propagandistic influence in the medium. In doing research for his book, *Primetime Propaganda*, Shapiro interviewed dozens of actors and industry insiders who openly admitted to distinct progressive socio-cultural biases and anti-conservative perspectives. Shapiro's exposé of media bias in the entertainment industry demonstrates how Adorno and other neo-Marxists infiltrated the industry with the intent of promulgating their ideological worldview via television and the cinema.

It goes without saying that since the 1960s the political and sociological biases of much of the mainstream news media had become a *de facto* mouthpiece for progressive liberal viewpoints, though not exclusively so. The New York Times' motto is "All The News That Fit to Print." Some have suggested that a more appropriate motto might be "All the News That Fits the Liberal Narrative." News organizations no longer claim objectivity, and as Sharyl Attkisson tells it, narrative journalism—and its not-so-distant cousin, transactional journalism—has become pervasive aspects of the news business. Combine these unfortunate trends with the ratings game and it's no wonder that the media has lower approval ratings than Congress. Regarding news reporters, editors and the abdication of journalistic integrity, Attkisson writes:

> We're supposed to be the ground-level newsgatherers who have the contacts, sources and editorial judgment to bring unique ideas to broadcasts. But more often than not, that's not what broadcasts want anymore. What they do want infuriates producers and correspondents far and wide. They want what they see on the competition. It's counterintuitive to the whole idea of journalism.[21]

The days of objective reporting seem long gone. (Before there was a legion of cyber-based fact-checkers, what were journalists?) In an astonishing expression of thin-skinned paranoia, we saw President Obama's administration caution the press corps about the veracity of Fox News' reporting, asking the D.C. press corps not to follow any leads that Fox News might break. The specious charges that Fox News "is not a real news organization," or "Fox News lies," are born of the same reflexive mentality that considers any criticism of the progressive agenda as another example of "authoritarian personality disorder." The opprobrium that the liberal establishment regularly hurls at conservative news organizations and politicians (or anyone who effectively challenges the liberal canon) reflects a decidedly non-pluralistic attitude. Some consider this just a case of hardball politics, but it does evoke an axiom attributed to Socrates: "When the debate is lost, slander becomes the tool of the loser."

The demonizing of those who oppose the progressive orthodoxy, as Goldberg notes, is often carried out with a kind of zeal that one usually associates religious fanatics. The Bolsheviks in Russia and Mao's Cultural Revolution gave old institutions no quarter.

> The religious character of modern liberalism was never far from the surface. Indeed, the 1960s should be seen as another in a series of "great awakenings" in American history—a widespread yearning for new meaning that gave rise to a tumultuous social and political movement. The only difference was that this awakening largely left God behind.[22]

> The left has always had an apocalyptic streak. Lenin argued "the worse the better." The revolutionary vanguard has always demanded that destruction come before creation. The Futurists, anarchists, vorticists, Maoists and other modern left-wing avant-gardes believed that hammers were for smashing first, building second.[23]

And herein lies a problem in the pursuit of a humane society. Secularizing culture has the effect of diminishing or negating spirituality in any human endeavor. This in turn allows for increased violations against that which we consider humane and civil. The coarsening of our society continues unabated and we become inured to human suffering that plagues so much of the world's population. This can be seen especially in the realms of art and entertainment where there exists a destructive and hedonistic strain of cultural consciousness that is antithetical to conditions that are conducive to a higher morality and any ethical construct.

On the fifth anniversary of Michael Jackson's death, Josephine Livingstone commented on the secularization of culture and its effects in her essay in *The New Republic*:

> To analyze the phenomenon of Michael Jackson properly would mean taking on the laborious task of figuring out how we—meaning society at large—ended up with the kind of entertainment industry we have. And it would mean admitting that the American dream—a rapid ascent to stardom on the basis of sheer talent—is hollow ... You may well have been lied to your whole life: about Michael Jackson and R. Kelly, yes, but also about the fact that no celebrity is quite what they seem. Famous people are personae,

packaged and sold to you according to whatever standards of desirability are most profitable at that moment.[24]

This is the norm in popular culture and it has little to do with pursuing "higher" virtues. Some will question what "higher" means, or upon whose authority do we implement these "higher" values. The question is often asked: Whose values should we adhere to in creating a more humane culture? The more pertinent question might be: *What* values do we consider to be those upon which we can establish a more caring and compassionate culture? For Nietzsche, Striner, Marx, Richard Wagner and other revolutionaries of the nineteenth century, the destruction of the old order was the first order of business because Judeo-Christian virtues were anathema to their worldview.

In his book, *Culture Counts: Faith and Feeling in a World Besieged*, British philosopher Roger Scruton takes on the hypocrisy and wrong-headedness of progressives and multiculturalists in their advancement of what he calls "a culture of repudiation." As Scruton points out, this "repudiation" is almost exclusively aimed at European culture born of Judeo-Christian beliefs. Citing Oswald Spengler's view that Christian belief was at the heart of Western culture, Scruton asserts that it was the American Revolution rather than the French Revolution that spawned a stable constitutional republic as well as the conditions through which liberty and the reverence for the common man were more readily apparent. That reverence was the progeny of the very Judeo-Christian ethos that progressives continually gainsay in their quest for a secular society—a society free from the restraints of religiously oriented morality and ethics.

David Mamet's recent book, *The Secret: On the Dismantling of American Culture*, a further examination of his "Brain-Dead Liberal" essay, was pilloried in the *New York Times* (June 17, 2011) by Christopher Hitchens for its irritatingly blunt dismissal of certain liberal persuasions. Mamet's conversion to a conservative perspective has made him a traitor to those in the Celebrity-Industrial-Complex who seem to be forever unthinkingly enslaved to progressive orthodoxies. Hitchens, a brilliant polemicist who was no friend of religion, cited Mamet's contention that America is a Christian country and that our Constitution "is the distillation of the wisdom and experience of Christian men, in a tradition whose codification is the Bible,"[25] as being a counterfeit contention.

Most historians would argue otherwise and they would likely acknowledge the reality of our particular religious heritage and its influence on virtually every aspect of our country's social, political and cultural evolution. Even the noted atheistic ethologist Richard Dawkins concedes that religious convictions played a significant role in human evolution noting that the willingness to sacrifice for future generations (the Pilgrims at Plymouth, e.g.) could ensure a better chance of survival. Our "selfish genes," according to Dawkins, make us predisposed to live for the sake of something beyond our immediate concerns and instant gratification. And hasn't this been a central (and noble) ethic of religion?

If, as Hitchens argues, that "religion poisons everything" what is to be said of non-religious impulses and societies that eliminate God from the equation? Hitchens famously opined that non-believers can be just as good and just as compassionate as believers and as such, religion was superfluous to the human condition. Though there is certainly veracity in the claim that "believers" are not the only virtuous folks on the planet, we know too, that godless societies don't guarantee a humane future. Charles Krauthammer put it this way: Imagine the creation of two societies, one holding that the affairs of man are governed by a Supreme Being to whom all will eventually be answerable to, and let's imagine such a society emerged in 1776. Another holds that we are answerable only to each other or the State. Let's imagine the latter emerged in 1917. In the short run, one can assume that one will do as well as the other. But come back in 100 years and it is clear to see that one has managed significantly better and in a more humane fashion.

If Hitchens and others of his ilk cannot see the veracity of Krauthammer's thought experiment, then why should we concern ourselves with their attitudes regarding the counterfeit contentions regarding our religious patrimony vis-à-vis achieving social betterment and our attempts to create "a more perfect union?" Krauthammer makes the salient observation, that despite the many failings in the American experiment, "We could do worse than merge one's destiny with that of a great and humane nation dedicated to the proposition of human dignity and equality.[26]

Moreover, when we consider religious-based charitable organizations such as the Buddhist Tzu Chi Foundation (headquartered in Taiwan), an organization that raises millions of dollars annually for disaster relief and advocates a "green" lifestyle, Mr. Hitchens contentions are highly specious, to say the least. Surely science has made belief in the incorporeal realm a more questionable undertaking, but during the Renaissance religion and science were not viewed as being mutually exclusive. Einstein famously contended that "science without religion is lame, religion without science is lame," and he was no dummy.

Another noted atheist, Camille Paglia, commenting on the fallacious rationale of progressive multiculturalist mindset, points to the insolence of the art world in its disdain for religious experience, especially Christianity.

> The far-right wouldn't have any opinions about art if it weren't for those big incidents in the late `80s to the `90s when some stupid work was committing sacrilege. [Andres Serrano's painting, "Piss Christ, e.g.] ... some 10th-rate thing. It's always Catholic iconography, I might point out ... It's never Jewish. It's never Muslim ... The art world has actually prided itself on getting a rise out of the people on the far right, thinking, "We're avant-garde." The avant-garde is dead. It has been dead since Andy Warhol appropriated Campbell's Soup labels and Liz Taylor and Marilyn Monroe into his art ... 30 years later, 40 years later, people will think they are avant-garde every time some nudnik has a thing about [the] Madonna with elephant dung, "Oh yeah, we are getting a rise out of the Catholic League."[27]

What infuriates here is that the egalitarian ideal of "respect for the other" tends to get no respect from those who advocate that ideal in the most vociferous manner. Duplicity is everywhere. We often see this on college campuses where those who espouse non-liberal views are often the target of the most derisive censure and un-pluralistic prohibitions. Allan Bloom saw this phenomenon taking shape in the 1980s, as did Manhattan Institute Fellow, John Leo. Mr. Leo has written extensively on the issue of free speech on college campuses where universities routinely profess openness but impose "speech codes" in the interest of "fairness." The desire for utopian, egalitarian conditions often results in conditions that are antipodal to individual liberties. Concerning these utopian prescriptions, Mark Levin writes:

Utopianism is irrational in theory and practice, for it ignores or attempts to control the planned and unplanned complexity of the individual, his nature and mankind in nature. It ignores, rejects or perverts the teachings of knowledge that have come before—that is, man's historical, cultural and social experience and development.[28]

Undoubtedly many actors, actresses, producers, directors, screenwriters, cinematographers, composers and financiers possess strong faith convictions—some more demonstrative in their faith than others. We've all seen Academy Award ceremonies where awardees give thanks to God for their good fortune in winning their Oscars, often with great humility and sincerity. There have been many films in which the narratives deal with issues of faith and spirituality, often with great insight and profundity. It would be dishonest to suggest that there exists no appreciation for the great art and music of the European tradition among Hollywood folks. Yet we see many artistic expressions that seem diabolically anti-social and untoward; completely at odds with the cultural sensibilities and attitudes that are born of the Judeo-Christian ethos. David Brooks of the *New York Times* suggests that we shouldn't "shoot for goodness," but rather we should "shoot for rectitude," because we are "unqualified to judge our own moral performances," and as such we should attach ourselves "to some exterior or social standards."[29] I would argue that aligning with a spiritual sovereignty can have great benefit in the pursuit of being virtuous in our creative endeavors.

We shouldn't be shocked that in a society based on the premise of individual freedom that there would be artistic expressions that reflect the dark side of the human experience. Yet when confronted with such dark art we are often astonished and taken aback by the desensitizing cruelty, obscenity and callousness of what is produced. Our innate desire for goodness is often affronted by the drivel that's created in the name of artistic freedom. This is especially true in the realm of television where the bane of reality shows—with their promise of turning no-name/no-talent individuals into Warhol-esque celebrities without needing to shell out seven-figure salaries—and insipid sitcoms cater to lowest-common-denominator tastes. The public's disdain or indifference for such programming is reflected in sagging ratings for network television.

Liberal television personality Bill Maher has taken to making suppositions about the reality of God and continually savages those who have religious beliefs, considering believers to be morons and that religion is actually prohibitive in any humanitarian efforts for peace or general well being. He ignores the faith-based humanitarian work done by countless charitable institutions; hospitals, orphanages, universities, etc. And if believers are morons (and out of their minds), there are more than few whose endeavors in a wide array of disciplines have provided humankind with an abundance of noble accomplishments; Bach, Beethoven, Brahms, da Vinci, van Gogh, Goethe, Einstein, Messiaen, Eliot and Dr. King come immediately to mind.

In 2008, I had the opportunity to view the heartwarming film *Playing for Change* at the Tribeca Film Festival in New York. In an ingenious use of recording technology, producer/director Mark Johnson captured the performances of a wide array of musicians from around the world representing a multitude of cultures and ethnicities performing the same song. Johnson's musical collage of artists from Europe, Israel, Africa and the United States is an inspiring testament to the universal power of music to act as a harmonizing agent when purposely directed in an altruistic fashion. Johnson and his associates have established *The Playing For Change Foundation* with the express intent of fostering music education in the developing world, and in so doing providing a means for disenfranchised peoples to find joy and hope in their lives. Music as a change agent is not a new concept, yet it is always inspiring to see altruistic individuals using their talents for the greater good.

Waging peace instead of war should be our collective goal. Living for the sake of others is a noble paradigm worth exploring in our artistic pursuits, and if religious teaching can help get us to achieve that paradigm, why undermine it? Using our talents and abilities as creative individuals in the process of creating the "global village" that McLuhan spoke of in the 1960s seems to be a goal worthy of our efforts. McLuhan opined that finding solutions to our problems required looking inward. More than a few social scientists and clergy have noted that the key to building a better community or nation begins by building better relationships in the home rather than relying on "the state" for answers. Statistics clearly demonstrate that stable family structure is beneficial in the creation of mature and responsible citizens as well as mitigating against crime, substance abuse, sexual promiscuity and poor academic achievement.

In a free and pluralistic society, we can expect that there be artistic expressions that will offend. Our trial as a civil society (assuming that we value civility) will be to explore and develop ways to come to terms with these incongruities. As conductor Daniel Barenboim observed, dealing with the viewpoint of "the other" requires both careful speaking and "painful listening" if we are to progress in establishing conditions for mutual understanding and cooperation. Regarding Christianity in the process of building a kinder and civil global village, G. K. Chesterton opined that the Christian ideal

> has not been tried and found wanting. It has been found difficult and left untried. It's not that people have got tired of Christianity; they have never found enough Christianity to get tired of. Another idea that has not been found wanting but has not been properly tried is that of democracy ... but the world is full of these unfulfilled ideas, the uncompleted temples ... History does not consist of completed and crumbling ruins; rather it consists of half-built villas abandoned by a bankrupt builder. This world is more like an unfinished suburb than a deserted cemetery.[30]

To complete the building process requires a bit of honesty, some frank and painful dialogue, as well as art that enlightens. Removing God entirely from the discussion, as if religion is a toxin as Hitchens asserted, leaves us incomplete and without the spiritual components necessary for survival. As another pop music icon Bob Marley advised, "Man can't do without God. Just like when you're thirsty, you have to drink water. You just can't go without God."[31]

Recommended Recordings

The Doors: *An American Prayer*

Brahms: Piano Concertos Nos. 1 & 2, Daniel Barenboim-piano

Strauss: *Thus Spake Zarathustra*, Fritz Reiner, Chicago Symphony Orchestra

Beethoven: Symphonies Nos. 4 & 7, George Szell, Cleveland Orchestra

Wagner: *Das Rheingold*, James Levin, Metropolitan Opera

Bach: Brandenburg Concertos, Florilegium Ensemble

Edgard Varèse: *Hyperprism*, Riccardo Chailly, ASKO Ensemble

Bob Marley: *One Love*

Endnotes

1   Jim Morrison, *An American Prayer*, The Doors, Final Studio Album, 1978.

2   Seven J. Ross, *Hollywood Left and Right: How Movies Stars Shaped American Politics* (Oxford-New York: Oxford University Press, 2011), p. 4.

3   Viktor Emil Frankl, *Man's Search for Meaning* (Boston, MA: Beacon Press, 1959), p. 134.

4   C. S. Lewis: C.S. Lewis, *The Complete C.S. Lewis Signature Classics* (Copyright 2002, by C.S. Lewis Pte. Ltd., Harper-Collins, New York), p. 242.

5   Kaye S. Hymowitz, "Michael Moore, Humbug," *City Journal*, Summer-2003, http://www.city-journal.org/html/13_3_michael_moore.html.

6   Jonah Goldberg, "Our Conservative Popular Culture," *National Review Online*, July 9, 2014.

7   Ibid.

8   Jonah Goldberg, *Suicide of the West: How the Rebirth of Tribalism, Populism, Nationalism, and Identity Politics is Destroying American Democracy* (New York: Crown Forum, 2018), p. 213.

9   Jonah Goldberg, *The Tyranny of Clichés: How Liberals Cheat in the War of Ideas* (New York, NY: SENTINEL, Penguin Group-USA, Inc., 2013), p. 142.

10 David Mamet, "Why I Am no Longer a Brain-Dead Liberal," *The Village Voice*, March 11, 2008.

11 Thomas Paine, *Rights of Man: Common Sense, and Other Political Writings* (Oxford-New York: Oxford World Classics (pbk), 2008), p. 63.

12 Mamet, *The Village Voice*.

13 Thomas Aquinas, *Summa Theologiae*, translated by Fathers of the English Dominican Province (New York: Benzinger Brothers); electronic edition produced by Sandra K. Perry, Part II-II, Q. 1, Art. 5, Reply Obj. 1.

14 Friedrich Nietzsche, *Thus Spoke Zarathustra*, edited and translated by Walter Kaufmann (New York: Penguin Books, 1976), p. 339.

15 Jonah Goldberg, *Liberal Fascism, The Secret History of the American Left from Mussolini to the Politics of Change* (New York: Broadway Books, 2007), pp. 227-228.

16 Russell Jacoby, *The End of Utopia: Politics and Culture in the Age of Apathy* (New York: Basic Books, 1999), p. 125.

17 Jordan B. Peterson, *12 Rules for Life: An Antidote to Chaos*, (Toronto: Random House Canada, 2018), pp. 310-311.

18 Michael Minnicino, "The New Dark Age: The Frankfurt School and 'Political Correctness,'" *Fidelio Magazine*, Winter, 1992, http://www.schillerinstitute.org/

fid_91-96/921_frankfurt.html.

19 George Orwell, 1984 (New York: Harcourt. Inc., 1949), p. 33.

20 Marshall McLuhan, *The Mechanical Bride: Folklore of Industrial Man* (Boston: Beacon Press, 1951, pbk. ed. 1967), p. v.

21 Sharyl Attkisson, *Stonewalled: My Fight for Truth Against the Forces of Obstruction, Intimidation, and Harassment in Obama's Washington* (New York: Harper, 2014), p. 80.

22 Goldberg, *Liberal Fascism*, p. 234.

23 Ibid., p. 235.

24 Josephine Livingstone, "With Michael Jackson is Different," *The New Republic*, March 11, 2019.

25 David Mamet as quoted by Christopher Hitchens, "David Mamet's Right-Wing Conversion," *The New York Times*, June 19, 2011, p. BR 11.

26 Charles Krauthammer, *Things That Matter: Three Decades of Passions, Pastimes and Politics* (Copyright by Charles Krauthammer, published in the United States by Crown Publishing Group, 2015).

27 Camille Paglia, Interview with Robert Birnbaum, *The Morning News*, August 3, 2005, http://www.themorningnews.org/article/camille-paglia.

28 Mark R. Levin, *Ameritopia: The Unmaking of America* (New York: Threshold Edition/Simon & Schuster, Inc., 2012), p. 4.

29 David Brooks, "The Moral Diet," *The New York Times*, June 7, 2012, p. A 27.

30 Ian Ker, *G. K. Chesterton: A Biography* (Oxford-New York: Oxford University Press, 2011), p. 267.

31 Dean McNeil, *The Bible and Bob Marley; Half the Story That's Never Been Told*, (Eugene, OR: Wipf and Stock Publishers, 2013), p. 89.

37

Older and Wiser, Hopefully

The Bible is an acknowledgment of human individuality . . .
Those States which have, in the name of productivity,
racial purity, or, indeed, equality, attempted to limit human individuality
have reverted from the civilization of the Judeo-Christian
state to savagery; for they have rejected the teachings of the Bible.
One need not say they died because they rejected God;
they died because they rejected reason.[1]
David Mamet

Friends tell me that sixty is the new forty. So then, is seventy the new fifty? I certainly don't feel that much different now than I did decades ago. Some friends say that I look the same now as I did thirty years ago, to which my standard reply is, "Are you saying that when I was forty I looked seventy?"

To be sure, many folks who are seventy-something, have made and continue to make valuable and important contributions to society. Inspiration and enthusiasm for one's life's work doesn't automatically diminish when one turns sixty, seventy or even eighty. In my profession of orchestral conducting, there are numerous examples of conductors doing their best work in the later stages of their careers. It's a profession that benefits greatly from experience. In a conducting master class I attended in 1977 with the iconic German maestro Herbert von Karajan, he told the young conductors that one really doesn't *know* a composition until one has conducted it. In his estimation, no amount of study and preparation could provide the knowledge and understanding of a piece in the manner that actually rehearsing and performing does. In my conducting life, I have found Karajan's assertion to be absolutely correct. Having experience is obviously a great benefit in many of life's endeavors.

For me, turning seventy meant that there was much to look forward to as I chart the final episodes of my life. It is also a time to reflect on where I have come from and what influences have shaped my life. Like most of us, it is our relationship with our parents that determine so much in what we become—for better or worse. Winston Churchill once quipped that a person who is twenty years old and not a liberal has no heart, but a person who is forty years old and not a conservative has no mind. Though we'd do well to take Churchill's aphorism with a grain of salt, the balance of emotion and intellect in making choices in our personal lives regarding morality and ethics is an issue that should not be taken lightly. Though I consider myself to be relatively "balanced," I know that my thought process and opinions are not static, but evolving.

The ebb and flow between emotion and reason is innately human. Recalling Ken Wilber's cautionary narrative about the disassociation of beauty, truth and goodness concerning the resultant postmodern malaise that bedevils us on so many fronts, it would seem that having a better understanding of the dynamic of the so-called "Big Three" would serve us well. Our judgments are based on rationality and do not simply accompany our emotions inconsequentially. Reason is fundamentally connected to our emotions and cannot be analytically separated from them as if they were only contingently related. Hegel attempted to disassociate emotion and reason in his dialectic method, asserting that conflict was the necessary impetus for progress to occur. The utility of reason, however, is necessary to ascertain either the truth or spuriousness of the judgments that lie at the heart of our emotions and thereby determine an emotion to be appropriate, inappropriate, misguided, imprudent, and so on. When a person commits a crime of passion, we often say that the person was "out of his mind," or they were "not of sound mind," or "she lost her mind." These are metaphors but they allude to the very real problem of reason and emotional disassociation. To act purely on emotion is, in a very real sense, immature.

In other essays, I've often commented on the need for maturity and adult sensibilities to be in greater evidence in our popular culture. I was reminded of this need in an opinion piece by *Washington Post* columnist Richard Cohen, when he wrote:

> The enthusiasm of youth—the impatience with complex explanations, the exuberant energy that obliterate history and mocks the past—is one of life's enduring cliché. So too, is the conservatism and caution of age, often characterized as a gerontological disease, a consequence of arteriosclerosis or some such thing. Both clichés, as is usually the case, contain a measure of truth.[2]

In our current cultural and political climate there has been a tendency to link youth with righteousness (and the righteous indignation at goes with it) and age with corruption and tired, unproductive political processes. The Obama administration was trumpeted as one that advocated "change we can believe in." Yet, even the most optimistic advocates of President Obama have been disappointed and dismayed as the realities of the world in which we live, not to mention "inside-the-beltway infighting," have encroached heavily on the ideals that his administration heralded. The enthusiastic declaration of "Yes we can" morphed into a somewhat skeptical, even pessimistic, "Can we?"

The Occupy Wall Street protestors purported to be a revolutionary voice of the 99% of Americans who feel disenfranchised by the Capitalist, free-enterprise system and the resultant income inequality. When I ventured down to Zuccotti Park in lower Manhattan during the height of the OWS protests, I saw as many Che Guevara flags as I did American flags—probably more. These folks, many of them twenty or thirty-somethings, didn't represent me, but I was grateful to know that there was no equivocation regarding their loyalties to a bigoted thug like Che.[*]

---

[*] After the 1959 Revolution in Cuba, Che Guevara said: "We're going to do for Blacks exactly what blacks did for the revolution. By which I mean: nothing."
Guevara on socialist revolution: "Hatred is the central element of our struggle! Hatred that is intransigent ... hatred so violent that it propels a human being beyond his natural limitations,

The folly of the Occupy Wall Street demonstrations was typified by the participants in the drum circle at Zuccotti Park. The drummers were reportedly making several hundred dollars in donations daily, as reported by *New York Magazine*.[3] When asked by the OWS General Assembly to contribute a higher percentage of their earnings to support the OWS effort, Shane Engelerdt, the "head drummer," expressed outrage: "We're like, what's going on here? They're like the banks we're protesting." Engelerdt indignantly proclaimed that this was exactly what they were demonstrating against. WRONG! This is exactly what they were demonstrating FOR! Not only didn't he know the purpose of the protest, he strongly objected to being taxed at a rate commensurate to his earnings. You make more, you get taxed more; supposedly that was the central thrust of the OWS protests. Yet many of the drummers seemed clueless about the actual purpose of the demonstrations that they were so self-righteously engaged. And when asked to give more, they objected. Lest we forget, pluralism allows for the clueless to be in the mix.

As much as we might want to avoid political realities in our artistic endeavors and productions, it is inevitable that these realities impact our lives as creative people. The conservative/liberal characterizations that play heavily into any political discussion can have debilitating effects in terms of finding workable solutions for our problems. Still, the complexities of our world cannot be easily ignored, and if we do ignore them we do so at our peril. In a pluralistic society, the politics of entrenchment and the politics of reform often collide. Finding common ground becomes a necessary quest.

In his 2008 essay for the *Village Voice*, "Why I Am No Longer a Brain-Dead Liberal," David Mamet cites the basic proclivities shared by all human beings. These proclivities are at the root of our failures, regardless of political or ideological affiliations, and they inhibit our attempts to create the kind of society that we envision as being fundamentally decent, just and humane. Like many of us in our younger days, Mamet had viewed government and big

---

making him violent and cold-blooded killing machine … We reject any peaceful approach. Violence is inevitable. To establish Socialism rivers of blood must flow! The imperialist enemy must feel like a hunted animal wherever he moves. Thus we'll destroy him! These hyenas are fit only for extermination. We must keep our hatred alive and fan it to paroxysm! The victory of Socialism is well worth millions of atomic victims!" [Source: *Che Guevara Reader: Writings on Politics & Revolution*, edited by David Deutschmann (North Melbourne, Australia: Ocean Press, 2003), p. 360.]

business as being the primary sources of the greed, corruption and exploitation that plagued the human condition. He was an advocate of the typical liberal contention that people are generally good at heart and that those who controlled money and political power were the real enemies of humanity and the ones responsible for all that is going wrong in the world. As he pondered his epiphany regarding the fallacy of this view (an epiphany that came with age), Mamet asked himself, "I wondered, how could I have spent decades thinking that I thought everything was always wrong at the same time that I thought I thought that people were basically good at heart? Which was it?"[4] This conundrum is one that I'm sure many of us have wrestled with.

Another insightful perspective on the unpalatable realm of politics comes from Charles Krauthammer. Citing the great advancements in the human condition, Krauthammer contends that it is those very advancements that now threaten us as a species. Our intelligence as applied to science has brought humankind to the brink of nuclear self-annihilation. We can create lethal biological agents in laboratories that in the hands of people with evil intent could wipe out huge segments of the world's population (Covid-19). Regrettably, living with psychopaths is part and parcel of the human condition. Science can save us, but it can also destroy us.*

So then, what mitigates these potentially ruinous circumstances? Politics. As Krauthammer avers, intelligence, ego, power tripping, religious fanaticism, anarchy and nihilism can, and have been tamed by the rubric "of the mundane, frustrating, often debased vocation known as politics ... Everything ultimately rests upon it."[5] This sobering observation may not inspire great optimism on one level, however, it does offer hope for humankind to maintain some semblance of control over external forces that if not controlled, could result in cataclysmic circumstances.

Capitalism is often viewed by those of a progressive-liberal persuasion as the root of many of our problems and it's not difficult to see this as being a viable assertion. Certain corporate executives may have personal moral qualms with producing, promoting and marketing music or movies that contain vile and coercive content, yet it is their responsibility as corporate executives to make their shareholders happy and as such, bottom line, corporate success

---

* This essay was written eight years prior to the COVID pandemic.

becomes the barometer of their success. If sex sells, there is all too often a "sell-out" to use sex for marketing, regardless of other "peripheral" misgivings and ramifications. This mindset results in a type of moral "collateral damage" that often diminishes standards of decency and contributes to society's moral decline.

A Question of Balance

On his being awarded the Bradley Prize in 2013, Ethics and Public Policy Center Hertog Fellow Yuval Levin offered insightful remarks regarding what he views as the basic differences between conservative and liberal political perspectives. Acknowledging that different conservatives and liberals have differing views about their respective worldviews, Levin, a conservative, asserted that gratitude is a defining aspect of the conservative mindset. As Levin put it:

> To my mind, conservatism is gratitude. Conservatives tend to begin from gratitude for what is good and what works in our society and then strive to build on it, while liberals tend to begin from outrage at what is bad and broken and seek to uproot it. You need both, because some of what is good about our world is irreplaceable and has to be guarded, while some of what is bad is unacceptable and has to be changed. We should never forget that the people who oppose our various endeavors and argue for another way are well-intentioned too, even when they're wrong, and that they're not always wrong.[6]

Levin correctly submits that both perspectives have merit, and to defend our cultural inheritance, an inheritance that includes protecting liberty and "America's unmatched potential for lifting the poor and the weak," is inherently decent and should not be considered reactionary. The liberal predilection of having high expectations, "even utopian expectations" is so fervent, that those of a liberal persuasion are often given to outsized outrage born of compassion in their desire for greater progress in ameliorating injustice and human misery. Defending the liberal desire for compassion and progress, Levin nevertheless preaches vigilance, because the legacy of protecting freedom and ensuring liberty for all has been a hard-won proposition.

We should defend freedom and liberty, Levin says, "not because they are triumphant and invincible, but because they are precious and vulnerable, because they weren't fated to happen, and they're not certain to survive." This balanced perspective is refreshing in a time when vituperative in-your-face political diatribes (from both political parties) provide cathartic satisfaction for the opposing political bases. As Jonah Goldberg avers, this kind of invective can be "catharsis masquerading as principle, venting and resentment pretending to be some kind of higher argument."[7]

Mamet, with coruscating clarity, offers a perspective on the importance of our Constitution vis-à-vis dealing with human nature and creating a society in which we might realize our libertarian hopes for a better situation in "promoting the general welfare" for our citizenry. Our Constitution, rather than suggesting that all behave in a virtuous manner, recognizes that, to the contrary, people have many untoward proclivities and will take any opportunity to subvert any agreement to pursue what they consider to be in *their* proper interests. To that end, the Constitution separates the power of the state into those three branches, which for most of us is the only thing we remember from our high school civics classes. We hold out hope that our elected officials will govern as adults with an eye on the larger picture rather than short-sighted, personal goals (getting re-elected, speaking fees, etc.). Because our system of government was created to allow for corrections, it mitigates the inclination of one governmental branch pulling power plays against another—circumventing the legislative process via judicial or executive fiat, for example. In a rather brilliant way, our constitutional republic was created to prevent selfish intentions from dictating policy decisions and in turn foster the noble goal of representative government. The proclivity to connive for personal gain is what leads to the corruption of government. Mamet observes:

> For, in the abstract, we may envision an Olympian perfection of perfect beings in Washington doing the business of their employers, the people, but any of us who has ever been at a zoning meeting with our property at stake is aware of the urge to cut through all the pernicious bullshit and go straight to firearms.
>
> I found not only that I didn't trust the current government (that, to me, was no surprise), but that an impartial review revealed that the faults of this president [Bush]—whom I, a good liberal, considered a monster—were little different from those of a president whom I revered [JFK].[8]

Though Mamet may come across as a bit snarky, he nonetheless offers an honest appraisal in speaking to the reality of human nature on a very basic level. Providing balance, justice and moderation in a pluralistic society is the essence of our Constitution.

Historian Gertrude Himmelfarb (wife of conservative icon, Irving Kristol) reminds us that the Enlightenment movements of France, England and America had differing attitudes about religion. One aspect of the British Enlightenment that was seriously at odds with the brutal violence of the French Enlightenment ("a great moment has found a little people," according to Schiller) was that the British were not hostile to religious tradition, and they cautioned against the tyranny of reason. In the usual "litany of traits" that are considered the progeny of the Enlightenment—reason, rights, nature, liberty, equality tolerance, science, progress—it is "reason" that was considered the most important hedge against supernatural religion.

However, Himmelfarb proffers that for the British, "social virtues—compassion, benevolence, sympathy" were the attributes that "naturally, instinctively, habitually bound people to each other." The British didn't reject "reason," but rather gave it "a secondary, instrumental role" in shaping their philosophical outlooks regarding the creation of an ethical society.[9] A number of British intellectuals of the Enlightenment era were men of religious orders. Consequently, their views were not unlike Augustine's in that they intuited that "civic virtue" was central in developing a moral and ethical society. The American Enlightenment's predilection for religious tolerance, especially Judeo-Christian morality reflects this view as well.

Commenting on social virtues, customs and the attributes that have naturally, instinctively, habitually bound people together (culture), Manhattan Institute Fellow Kay S. Hymowitz, in relation to sexual mores and conservatism, observes:

> [M]any cultures imagine sex as part of an original, sacred, order. Sex, religion and culture form an intricate trinity. In today's multiculturalism, ancient and stern demands have been watered down … In this naïve version of culture, the Irish, for instance, are less identified with Catholicism than with soda bread, jigs and shamrocks.

> Thus multiculturalists who hope to advance the cause of oppressed minorities, face a simple if unwelcome truth: culture is essentially a

conservative force. It binds people to a past laden with powerful traditions and beliefs and often obligates them to strict customary discipline. Ersatz celebrations of diversity ... may ease fears about hatred, but they also subvert a cautious pluralism that soberly recognizes the passions inspired by cultural identities. Without this recognition, we only trivialize those passions and repeat the errors of our melting-pot past."[10]

Hymowitz's point about the "conservative force" is well taken. The removal of commitment in sexual relations undermines the basic structure of a society. Roger Scruton observes that in the scenario where sex is divorced from long-term commitment, sex becomes a simulacrum in which there is "no cost in terms of education, moral discipline, hardship or love ... it shuts out the adult world completely, and replaces it with a cloud of wishful dreams."[11] And now, with the idea of gender being a "social construct" being promulgated by progressives, the very foundation of culture as we know is being questioned according to a decidedly insipid and scientifically unfounded supposition—a contested opinion being passed off as fact.

In the final chapter of his book, *The Secret Knowledge*, Mamet puts forth the not-so-secret premise underlying the American Constitution—one that is decidedly theistic and in accord with the British aspects of the Enlightenment that Himmelfarb described.

America is a Christian country. Its Constitution is the distillation of the wisdom and experience of Christian men, in a tradition whose codification is the Bible. I will not say this Christian country has been good to the Jews, for this suggests an altruism or acceptance, neither of which exist. But America has been good for the Jews, as it has been, eventually, good for every immigrant group whether fleeing oppression, seeking prosperity, or, indeed, brought here in chains. The result of a 230-year-long experiment is the triumph of Judeo-Christian values. We have created peace and plenty for more citizens over a greater period of time than enjoyed by any other group in history. This triumph is not due to altruism, nor to empathy, nor to compassion, but to adherence to those practicable, rational rules for successful human interaction set out in the Bible. These rules and precepts amount, in their totality, as much to a legal philosophy as to a theology.[12]

It's rather easy for all of us, regardless of our faith or political and ideological persuasions, to understand that we all "fall short of the glory of God." That is not a debatable issue. More pertinent is how we can get beyond our untoward proclivities and lead productive and more humanitarian and altruistic lives. Ideally, as we mature we learn from our mistakes and become more responsible people. It's been proffered that insanity is doing the same thing over and over while expecting different results.* Getting beyond our immediate insanity, individually and collectively, requires maturity without sacrificing our enthusiasm (from the Greek: *en theos*, "with God") and passions about creating a culture of peace and prosperity. Our Constitution provides a framework for attaining a "more perfect union," and it is interesting to note that the framers were people of a certain faith conviction and believed that religion could provide a moral compass in fashioning a civil society. The current progressive tendency is to diminish religious conviction in the public square, but it seems clear that the founding fathers had other ideas about this.

It is important to note that political and geopolitical mistakes have been made by leaders of both political parties and by people who professed a variety of faith traditions. The presidencies of Kennedy, Nixon, Carter, the Bushes, Clinton and Obama surely attest to this. Neither conservatives nor liberals can lay claim to a perfect manifestation of their faith—or patriotism.

As I grow older, and hopefully wiser, I find that the wisdom of the founding fathers in their development of our Constitution offers an enlightened means of attaining the conditions for mutual respect and agreement. The brilliance of the Constitution that Mamet alludes to, allows for a diverse and complicated society to function in a relatively civil fashion. That is what many people find appealing in the "American ideal." As Smokey Robinson says in his poem, *A Black American*, "And if you think America is a leader on inequality and suffering and grievin', how come there so many people comin' and so few leavin'?"[13] Smokey has a point and it's well worth our consideration.

In the new century, conservatism has been spuriously linked to racism, bigotry and fascism via the destructive rationales of postmodernism and progressivism. This is both unfortunate and self-defeating. According to Scruton,

---

* This axiom has been attributed to Albert Einstein, Benjamin Franklin, Mark Twain, and ancient Chinese philosophers.

we not only study history, we inherit it and in so doing we are socially obligated to examine history so as the learn from it, for inheritance "brings with it not only the rights of ownership, but the duties of trusteeship. Things fought for and died for should not be idly squandered. For they are the property of others, who are not yet born."[14]

Because our identities are determined by what we love and hold dear, our examination of historical values requires that we see conservatism "as part of a dynamic relation across generations," and *not* merely as static facts having little meaning to us in the here and now. Scruton views it accordingly:

> Conservatism is about beauty, but it is also, for the very same reason, about history and its meaning. Some have astatic conception of history, seeing it as the remains of past time, which we conserve as a book in which to read about things that have vanished … Conservatism should be seen … as part of a dynamic across generations. People grieve at the destruction of what is dear to them, because it damages the pattern of trusteeship, cutting them off from those who went before, and obscuring the obligation to those who come after.[15]

This once again gets us back to the attribute of gratitude, for being grateful for the good things that we inherit—liberty, freedom, protections from authoritarian tyranny, rule of law—allows to us fulfill our human potential to our fullest measure. Patriotism is generally regarded as love of, and devotion to one's country. This means loving one's country despite its flaws, just as we love our spouses, children, parents and colleagues in spite of their flaws. To only love that which is perfect is not really love at all—and is decidedly immature. As always, the issues of balance and maturity, specifically the balance of emotion and intellect in our attempts to realize a society that reflects the best of who we are, remain central, primary and necessary. Growing older should be making us better—and hopefully wiser.

Endnotes

1   David Mamet, *The Secret Knowledge: On the Dismantling of American Culture* (New York: Penguin Books-USA, 2012), p. 222.

2   Richard Cohen, "Baader-Meinhof Complex flaunts the delusion of my youth," *New York Daily News*, January 11, 2010.

3   Alex Klein, "The Organizers vs. the Organized at Zuccotti Park," *New York*

Magazine, October 20, 2011.

4   David Mamet, "Why I Am no Longer a Brain-Dead Liberal," *Village Voice*, March 11, 2008.

5   Charles Krauthammer, "The promise of the pale blue dot: While searching for life out there, let's also keep order down here," *New York Daily News*, December 29, 2011.

6   Yuval Levin, Bradley Prize Remarks, June 12, 2013, Lynde and Harry Bradley Foundation, http://eppc.org/publications/yuval-levins-bradley-prize-remarks.

7   Conor Friedersdorf, citing Jonah Goldberg, "Stalwart Conservative Belatedly Recognizes the Movement's Problems," *The Atlantic*, September 9, 2015.

8   Mamet, *Village Voice*.

9   Gertrude Himmelfarb: *The Road to Modernity: The British, French and American Enlightenment* (New York-Toronto: Vintage Books/Random House, 2004), pp. 5-6.

10   Kay S. Hymowitz: "Multiculturalism Is Anti-Cultural," *New York Times*, March 25, 1993.

11   Roger Scruton, *The Intelligent Person's Guide to Modern Culture* (South Bend, Indiana: St. Augustine's Press, 2000), p. 115.

12   Mamet, *The Secret Knowledge*, pp. 221-222.

13   Smokey Robinson: *A Black American*.
     http://www.slicksno.com/thalookout/the-black-american-poem.html
     https://www.youtube.com/watch?v=iIkNsj6cDGc

14   Roger Scruton, *How to Be a Conservative* (London-New York: Bloomsbury- Continuum, 2014), p. 182.

15   Ibid.

38

The Prescience of C. S. Lewis

Music and silence—how I detest them both.[1]
C. S. Lewis, *The Screwtape Letters*

Pleased to meet you / Hope you guess my name.
But what's troubling you / Is the nature of my game.
The Rolling Stones, "Sympathy for the Devil"

I admit that I'm a latecomer to the work of C. S. Lewis, but through the prompting of my eldest daughter (who holds a bachelor's degree in religious studies), I finally took the plunge. As I was putting the finishing touches on this book I was looking for several religious-based literary references regarding the perils of postmodernism that might support of few of my contentions regarding music, aesthetics, radical egalitarianism, multiculturalism and pervasive influence of woke progressivism. Surprisingly for me, Lewis' work, especially, *The Screwtape Letters* (1942) and its sequel, *Screwtape Proposes a Toast* (1959), provided a trove of coruscating insight in the examination of the whys and wherefores of our "fallen" condition in the context of "right and wrong as a clue to the meaning of the universe."*

Lewis admitted that writing *The Screwtape Letters* was simultaneously the easiest, but least enjoyable work of his career, and went into deep depression after writing it. Given the brilliant exegesis of how the "Lowerarchy" of Satan and his minions effectively infect the human soul, it's not hard to imagine why Lewis may have felt so depressed. The Cold War was the backdrop of his 1959 sequel, *Screwtape Proposes a Toast* with its narrative about how leftist, neo-Marxist thought subverted academia and the intellectual class in the West. The sequel is more ideologically charged than the original and the perspicacious insights are like a punch in the gut that leaves you reeling and somewhat distressed at the condition that we now find ourselves.

The Screwtape Letters depicts a series of 31 letters written by a senior demon, who goes by the name of Screwtape, to his nephew, Wormwood. Because of his youth, the nephew is less experienced and is in need of mentoring from his malevolent uncle. As part of his apprenticeship, Wormwood is charged with the task of guiding a man (referred to as "the patient") toward "Our Father Below" (Satan) and away from "the Enemy" above (God). As Wormwood's mentor, Screwtape explains many tricks-of-the-trade to his young charge in the process of inculcating him with the proven methods of "the Lowerarchy" (Hell).

In the preface to *The Screwtape Letters*, C. S. Lewis states that there are "two equal and opposite errors into which our race can fall" when we contemplate Satan.[2] One is to deny Satan's existence, the other is "to feel an excessive and unhealthy interest" in him. The first error is Satan's greatest ploy; if he doesn't exist, why fret about him? The second error is that we too easily create common bases with the dark side by our "unhealthy interest" in dark things. With regard to the first error, I'm reminded of Mick Jagger's lyric in "Sympathy for the Devil":

Pleased to meet you
Hope you guess my name.

---

* "Right and Wrong: A Clue to the Meaning of the Universe" is the title of the opening chapter of C. S. Lewis's book *Mere Christianity* published in 1952.

What's puzzling you
Is the nature of my game.

The real question (or perhaps it's an incorporeal question) is: How much does the devil, Lucifer, influence our behavior? As Lewis avers, too often we remain blinded and confused about the nature of Satan's games and when that happens we continually find ourselves in hellish circumstances.

Letter No. 1

In the first letter, Screwtape refers to a time past when humans "still knew pretty well when a thing was proved and when it was not; and when it was proved they really believe it. They still connected thinking with doing and were prepared to alter their way of life as the result of a chain of reasoning." In a prescient foretelling of postmodernism, Michel Foucault and Jacques Derrida, in particular, the senior devil declares that that modern man "doesn't think of doctrines as primarily 'true' or 'false,' but as 'academic,' or 'practical,' 'outworn,' or 'contemporary,' or 'conventional,' or 'ruthless.' Hence, "jargon, not argument" is Satan's best aid "in keeping man from church."[3]

A significant aspect of the postmodern mindset is that "universals" or "immutable truths" are "bourgeois" concepts born of the religious beliefs of "the old world." The rejection of religion and meta-narratives is where Marx's idea of "false consciousness," and postmodern ideas intersect. Screwtape understands that reason, and its cousin, argument, can potentially lead "the patient" to truth and/or knowledge, and this is how "the Enemy" (God) maintains control over humankind. In order to usurp that control, it's best to keep one's patient in a state of relativist thinking and "encourage him to think about realities he can't touch or see," and "to give him a grand general idea that he knows it all." A widespread idea that drives the current iteration of progressive political thought, is that "experts" in the various realms of sociology, for instance, know more than the common man and as a result, can be better arbiters in recommending and implementing solutions for social and cultural betterment.

Letter No. 15

In Letter No. 15, Screwtape advises Wormwood that getting the patient "away from the eternal" and into "the present" necessitates producing a preoccupation with forward-looking utopianism, especially "those schemes of thought such as Creative Evolution, Scientific Humanism and Communism, which fixes men's affection of the Future." This gets the patient out of the hidebound connection to religion, especially concerning anything "eternal."[4] The objective is to get one's patient fixated on the "temporal" and the perpetual pursuit "of the rainbow's end, never honest, nor kind, nor happy *now*," but always looking forward to an idyllic, utopian, unsubstantiated nirvana. Screwtape instructs Wormwood saying, "Gratitude looks to the past and love to the present; fear, avarice, lust and ambition look ahead. Do not think lust is an exception. When the present pleasure arrives, the sin (which alone interests us) is already over.[5]

Ridding society of its "hind-bound connection to religion" is characteristic of many academic liberal arts curricula, in which radical moral relativism and situational ethics are linked to various grievances associated with race, ethnicity, gender, etc. Because religion can mitigate resentment—the opiate of the ideological left—it is seen as a barrier to revolutionary urges. Screwtape's aversion to gratitude is telling, because as Yuval Levin posits, "Conservatives tend to begin from gratitude for what is good and what works in our society and then strive to build on it, while liberals tend to begin from outrage at what is bad and broken and seek to uproot it."[6] Resentment against the facilitators of the status quo energizes the revolutionaries who seek retribution and are willing to pursue violent means to uproot what they view as being inherently evil. The abnegation of religion results in the removal of moral strictures regarding sexuality. Lust becomes an important vice for the teleology of the Lowerachy.

Screwtape cautions against the patient pursuing the natural sciences for fear of exposing him to immutable truths. "If he must dabble in science," Screwtape advises, "keep him on economics and sociology," two highly theoretical realms of thought given to subjective, interpretive and politically correct "jargon." At one point Screwtape reminds Wormwood of his nefarious mission, "But remember, you are there to befuddle him."[7] This too is indicative of the current tendency to view the physical sciences and nature as being obstacles in the quest to deny the idea of meta-narratives and universal truths. The invective hurled at Jordan Peterson, for instance, by the progressive left for advocating that biological universals disprove the claim that gender differences are social constructs (a befuddling idea to be sure) points to why "immutable truths" threaten the ideological leftist's assault on truth and reasoned argument. Peterson argues that if gender identity is socially constructed then it can be socially deconstructed (or one can change one's mind or be talked out of one's gender identity), thus relegating that particular claim to be scientifically unproven and in contradiction with nature. Political correctness, however, has had the disturbing effect of putting certain topics beyond the realm of public debate or reasoned analysis, and when this is the case radical relativism becomes the order of the day.*

In yet another warning against the pursuit of reason and argument, Screwtape instructs: "The trouble with argument is that it moves the whole struggle on the Enemy's own ground."[8] For the postmodernist truth is fungible and this points to the postmodern hypothesis that words (discourse) are used, not to arrive at a particular truth, but rather to advance a particular agenda or maintain or exert power. Foucault argued that power and knowledge are inter-related and he connects the role of discourse in wider social processes "of legitimating power, emphasizing the construction of current truths, how they are maintained and what power relations they carry with them."[9]

Music historian Charles Rosen observes that one of the unsavory aspects of contemporary sociological criticism that is the progeny of Foucault's thought, is the attempt to debunk the notion that there exists true genius in the work of great artists and that the "genius" appellation appropriated to the likes of Beethoven or Shakespeare "is entirely due … to a process of brainwashing by the cultural elite in power." This is full-throated Foucauldian discursive methodology in that it creates the condition where, as Rosen observes, "commonly shared and recognized values can be dismissed since these values are simply a successful imposition by an elite upon society as a whole."[10] Removing

---

* In a discussion between Jordan Peterson and Camille Paglia regarding biology and women's studies curriculum in academia, Paglia recalls how she practically got into fist-fights with feminist ideologues who wanted to keep biology out of the discussion regarding feminine characteristics, "Modern Times: Camille Paglia & Jordan B. Peterson," October 2017, https://www.youtube.com/watch?v=v-hIVnmUdXM&ab_channel=JordanBPeterson.

objective analysis from the evaluative process results in a "post-truth" culture.* Moreover, in this type of discursive methodology, any belief in "certainty" on any particular issue quickly leads to charges of extremism, intolerance or fascist authoritarianism. This is right of out the contemporary, progressive, multiculturalist playbook and it's pervasive in liberal arts academia. Lewis saw this trend decades ago.

Letter No. 20

Here, Screwtape explains to his young nephew about the type of "physical attributes" that women should have in order to seduce men into the false reality of "falling in love." The senior devil instructs his nephew that the type of woman "is a question decided for us by the spirits far deeper down in the Lowerarchy than you and I." As Screwtape acknowledges, "It is the business of these great masters to produce in every age a general misdirection of what may be called 'sexual taste.' They do this by working through the small circle of popular artists, dressmakers, actresses and advertisers who determine the fashionable type. The aim is to guide each sex away from those members of the other with whom spiritually helpful, happy and fertile marriages are most likely."[11] Screwtape admits that this is all a sham:

> It is all fake, of course, the figures in the popular art are falsely drawn ... As a result we are more and more directing the desires of men to something which does not exist—making the role of the eye in sexuality more and more important and at the same time making its demands more and more impossible. What follows you can easily forecast!" This is the general strategy of the moment."[12]

How insightful; and that "moment" continues unabatedly. There is, as we know, empirical data that demonstrates that family breakdown results in higher instances of crime, addictions, promiscuity, poor academic achievement, more divorce and a host of other social maladies. Much of this is due to the objectification ("reification" in neo-Marxist parlance) of sex. After all, Screwtape and the Lowerarchy are fully aware that it's not possible to respect and objectify someone at the same time. Objectification of this sort

---

* Oxford Dictionaries selected "post-truth" as 2016's international word of the year. {Source: Amy B. Wang, *Washington Post*, November 16, 2016.]

undermines the carefully crafted ideal of "the Enemy;" namely, that family values and sexual probity are the foundational pillars of a moral society. By diminishing these virtues Wormwood's patient becomes increasingly coarse, superficial and deluded by unattainable sexual fantasies. Values become subsidiary to ego-driven sexual conquest. Notice too, how the artistic profession, the fashion industry and Madison Avenue are cited as being allies in aiding and abetting the devil's delusionary tactics regarding the allure of sexual desire.

Letter No. 22

"Music and silence—how I detest them both." Screwtape prefers noise! "Noise, which alone defends us from silly qualms, despairing scruples and impossible desires. We will make the whole universe a noise in the end."[13]

Screwtape seems to fully comprehend the power of music with its ability to uplift, inspire and edify, thus putting any patient in touch with truth, goodness and their own divinity via the transcendent aspects of beauty. This was the rationale behind Friedrich Schiller's concept of "aesthetic education," whereby experiencing beauty could assist in humankind's pursuit of truth. Moreover, Screwtape intuited that silence affords the patient time to become contemplative and to ponder eternal verities. This, in turn provides the patient a sense of value, which is anathema for Screwtape because despair, resentment and hopelessness are the emotions that give rise to revolutionary impulses—the very impulses necessary to evoke rage and destroy the old world and its ties to the domain of "the Enemy." Accordingly, music must be either avoided or eliminated.

"The melodies and silences of heaven will be shouted down in the end," Screwtape proclaims, "we are not yet loud enough."[14] We might construe this to being the noise of Critical Theory as espoused by the neo-Marxists of the Frankfurt School, including Theodor Adorno, Walter Benjamin and especially Herbert Marcuse, who "shouted down" any and all claims that didn't comport with progressive, neo-Marxist thought. Marcuse's concept of "repressive tolerance" is a testament to Marxist double-speak. In his 1965 essay, "Repressive Tolerance," dedicated to the students of Brandeis University, Marcuse proffered: "The function and value of tolerance depend on the equality prevalent in the society in which tolerance is practiced." As Marcuse put it in his essay, "Today tolerance appears again as what it was in its origins, at the beginning of the modern period—a partisan goal, a subversive liberating notion and practice … serving the cause of oppression."[15] The specious outcome of this premise was that there is no need for debate, argument, discussion or compromise.

Because the ideological right was always seen by the ideological left as protecting its nefarious self-interests, attacking the status quo, whether it has beneficial aspects or not, is justified—called for, in fact. The contortions that Marcuse engages in are manifestly duplicitous. Continuing in "Repressive Tolerance," Marcuse states: "Impartiality to the utmost, equal treatment of competing and conflicting issues is indeed a basic requirement for decision-making in the democratic process—it is an equally basic requirement for defining the limits of tolerance."[16] On face value, the idea of impartiality as a way to safeguard the democratic process appears to be a notion that most pro-democracy advocates would find heartening. Yet, in the same essay, Marcuse says: "Liberating tolerance, then, would mean intolerance against movements from the Right and toleration of movements from the Left. As to the scope of this tolerance and intolerance … it would extend to the stage of action as well as of discussion and propaganda, of deed as well as of word."[17] One might imagine that a "stage of action" would include censorship, canceling and de-platforming those who express or advocate ideas that don't comport with leftist orthodoxy. This, of course, is no way to practice "impartiality."

The incongruity is astonishing—befuddling, actually. Screwtape would be proud. Marcuse is resolutely calling for incivility in both rhetoric and action. (More noise!) Consider the recent incidents surrounding Sarah Huckabee Sanders and Maxine Waters. Calls for civility have been met with derision and allegations that civility and tolerance are, as Marcuse avers, "effective manifestations serving the cause of oppression." This "stage of action" is a chilling scenario and presages Orwellian totalitarianism.

Georg Wilhelm Friedrich Hegel (1770-1831), who could be considered the Frankfurt school's uncle Screwtape, advocated conflict as a legitimate means to revolutionary ends. Adorno was a serious advocate of atonal music— music predicated on what Arnold Schoenberg called, "the emancipation of dissonance;" music bereft of aesthetic allure due to its extremely dissonant properties. Aural indeterminacy (noise, as some might call it) is one if atonality's primary characteristics. The rapturous harmonies of tonal music born of scared intentions and natural sonic phenomenon, were diametrically opposite to all that, hence Screwtape's opprobrium towards it. For Adorno, the atonal aesthetic—and the methods employed to realize it—represented a categorical break from the ethos of Judeo-Christian culture, and he welcomed that. The "dialects of loneliness" that atonal musical syntaxes evoke with great efficacy could have the effect of heightening the patient's anxiety and fear, causing him to be preoccupied with the future rather than the past or the present.

Screwtape Proposes a Toast

There's much to cover here, but I'll focus on but one important point: celebrity. Screwtape opines: "As great sinners grow fewer, and the majority lose all their individuality, the great sinners become far more effective agents for us. Every dictator or even demagogue—almost every film-star or crooner—can now draw tens of thousands of human sheep with him. They give themselves to him … in him, to us … Catch the bell-wether and his whole flock comes after him (or her). This has been our answer—and a magnificent answer it is."[18]

This points yet again to the power of art and music in shaping attitudes and forging cultural identities. The cultural power of the "celebrity industrial complex" cannot be easily dismissed. A central tenet of Christian doctrine is that by creating a common base with Satan we allow our better selves to be diminished by engaging in selfish acts. Ego is the artist's Achilles heel as Screwtape surely understood. For people of faith "celebritism" has added little redeeming value to our society, but it becomes a hook that Satan uses to feed the artist's ego *and* to fetter the conscience of the masses. Madison Avenue and Hollywood became the epicenters of cultural choice and serious accomplices in the development of what *New York Times* columnist, David Brooks refers to as "The Big Me."[19]

The nexus between music, celebrity, ego and sex is easy to spot. Allan Bloom's concerns about popular music in the 1980s were based on how it affected education because "it ruins the imagination of young people and makes it very difficult for them to have a passionate relationship with the arts," which for Bloom was the basis of a substantive liberal arts education. Because music's sensual properties can be extremely powerful, a student's "first sensuous experiences are decisive in determining the taste for the whole of life, and they are the link between the animal and spiritual in us," which in turn "provides premature ecstasy," and "artificially induces the exaltation naturally attached to the completion of the greatest endeavors," including "consummated love, artistic creation, religious conviction and the discovery of truth."[20] Though Screwtape may not have seen how the power of popular music might have aided his cause in the corruption of his patients, Bloom surely did.

Understanding the moral and ethical power of music, or the verities of scared truths, or the true purpose of sexuality and its effects on self and society, is, however, not solely God's province. Screwtape and the central figures of the Lowerarchy understood this as well. It's important that we remember "the nature of their game."

Thanks to the prescient C. S. Lewis for the reminder.

Recommended Recordings

Rolling Stones: *Beggars Banquet*

Schoenberg: Trio for Violin, Viola and Cello, Op. 45, Leopold String Trio

Beethoven: *Fidelio*, Bernard Haitink, London Philharmonic Orchestra, Glyndebourne Festival Chorus (DVD)

Endnotes

1 C. S. Lewis, *The Complete C. S. Lewis Signature Classics, The Screwtape Letters* (New York: HarperCollins, 2002), p. 249.

2 Ibid., p. 183.

3 Ibid., p. 185.

4 Ibid., p. 484.

5 Ibid., p. 228.

6 Yuval Levin, Bradley Prize Remarks, June 12, 2013, Lynde and Harry Bradley Foundation, http://eppc.org/publications/yuval-levins-bradley-prize-remarks.

7 C. S. Lewis, *The Complete C. S. Lewis*, p. 187.

8 Ibid., p. 186.

9 Paul S. Chung, *The Hermeneutical Self and an Ethical Difference: Intercivilizational Engagement* (Cambridge: James Clarke & Co., 2012) p. 168.

10 Charles Rosen, review, "The Oxford History of Music," by Richard Taruskin, *New York Review of Books*, February 23, 2006.

11 C. S. Lewis: *The Complete C. S. Lewis,* p. 243.

12 Ibid.

13 Ibid., p. 249.

14 Ibid., p. 250.

15 Herbert Marcuse, *Regressive Tolerance*, as cited by Robert Paul Wolff, Barrington Moore, Jr., and Herbert Marcuse, *A Critique of Pure Tolerance* (Boston: Beacon Press, 1969), pp. 95-137.

16 Ibid.

17 Ibid.

18 C. S. Lewis, *The Complete C. S. Lewis*, p. 288.

19 David Brooks, *The Road to Character* (New York: Random House, 2015), Chapter 10, "The Big Me."

20 Allan Bloom, *The Closing of the American Mind* (New York and London: Simon & Schuster, 1987), pp. 79-80.

39

The Beatles as Musical Postmodernists

Christianity will go. It will vanish and shrink. I needn't argue about that;
I'm right and I'll be proved right. We're more popular than Jesus now;
I don't know which will go first – rock 'n' roll or Christianity.[1]
John Lennon

I remember in the months preceding January 1, 2000, that there was a great deal of apprehension regarding what might happen as the calendar ushered in a new century and a new millennium. Millennium celebrations and concerts were planned worldwide, yet there was concern that the so-called "Y2K problem" would disrupt digital technology and create chaos and disarray in the realms of geopolitics, finance, energy distribution, supply chains, healthcare services and other essentials of modern life.* Could nuclear war inadvertently break out due to computer error? Would Wall Street crash? Would water supplies or electricity be disrupted? Would we lose our MTV?

---

* Y2K refers to events related to the formatting and storage of calendar data for dates beginning in the year 2000.

The break with established musical tradition that occurred early in the twentieth century had several causes including the emergent philosophical theories of skepticism and irrationalism, political developments that led to catastrophic occurrences (World War I), the advance of science and technology and the abnegation of religion. As Stephen R. C. Hicks avers: "By the turn of the twentieth century, the nineteenth-century intellectual's world's sense of disquiet has become a full-blown anxiety." As a result, artists were no longer interested or enthralled with the "old world" concepts of rationalism, dignity, optimism and aesthetic beauty. The new rationale was, as Hicks puts it: "Art must be a quest for truth, however brutal, and not beauty," because "the world is fractured decaying, horrifying, depressing, empty, and ultimately unintelligible."[2] As composers embraced this perspective art music became seriously marginalized, especially the music of the mid-century modernists. But the hubris of Pierre Boulez and his acolytes regarding the "inevitability" of the modernist rationale taking center stage was seriously mitigated because large audiences for their music never materialized. Their music remained arcane, specialized and in opinion of many, cold-hearted and inconsequential. In hindsight, composer Stephen Albert may have been correct when he referred to the *contra*-beauty phase of composing "as some kind of sociological aberration."[3] The music of the mid-century modernists is largely ignored. When John Lennon made his controversial remark about the Beatles "being more popular than Jesus," in 1966, he might have included how the atonal utterances and influence of the mid-century modernist composers would also "vanish and shrink." He would have been quite prescient.

Leonard B. Meyer's prediction in 1967 regarding the contemporary compositional landscape becoming "diverse and pluralistic," with a "multiplicity of styles" and no "triumphant style" ruling the roost, has born out.[4] Many of the mid-century modernists who were ensconced in academia have seen the succeeding generations of composers turn away from the practices of their immediate predecessors. By the late 1970s the crabbed mannerisms of hyper-formulaic composing were dying a slow and inevitable death. Eclecticism and fusion, spurred by egalitarian and multiculturalist attitudes regarding source material, were becoming increasingly fashionable and popular. Richard Taruskin cites the circumstances surrounding the Beatles *Sgt. Pepper's Lonely*

Heart Club Band album in 1967 as being an early "symptom" of postmodern-ism in music.

As Taruskin puts it, the alternative culture of the 60s that railed against the machinery of big business and big politics in its music (Bob Dylan, the English "invasion", e.g.), its literature (the Beat poets), and alternative press (the *Los Angeles Free Press, The East Village Other, Rolling Stone*) began to take on greater sophistication in an attempt to be taken seriously as cultural commentary. For many in the counter-culture movement, this was seen as an appeal to cultural elites, the very coterie that revolutionary "Bohemian" artists and their fans dis-dained. Taruskin's view of postmodernism in this context, was not necessarily about postmodernism in the philosophical/ideological sense, but rather how there was renewed interest and preference for music that spoke to the heart; music that reconnected the public to the aesthetics that were the by-product of "the common practice" of tonal music, an aesthetic that pop music never abandoned.*

In the mid-1960s, music critics began analyzing music in ways that had been previously reserved for classical music. A number of "serious" composers like Ned Rorem and Luciano Berio wrote flattering utterances about the Beat-les. In a slap at Pierre Boulez and the academic serialists who ruled academic music curricula in the post-World War II era, Rorem wrote, "Our need for them (the Beatles) is neither sociological nor new, but artistic and old, specif-ically a *renewal*, a renewal of pleasure."[5]

Citing the pleasurable aspects of good melodies and the Beatles' penchant for creating such, Rorem wrote glowingly in the "highbrow" *New York Review of Books*:

> WHY are the Beatles superior? It is easy to say that most of their com-petition (like most everything everywhere) is junk. More important, their superiority is consistent: each of the songs from their last three albums are memorable. The best of these memorable tunes—and the best is a large percentage (Here, There and Everywhere, Good Day Sunshine, Michelle,

---

* The so-called "common practice" era in European art music spanned roughly from 1650 to 1900 and is characterized by the evolution and use of the tonal syntax as the basis of composition.

Norwegian Wood)—compare with those by composers from great eras of song: Monteverdi, Schumann, Poulenc. [6]

Comparing Lennon and McCartney to Monteverdi, Schumann and Poulenc was seen as a provocative analysis, but to progressive modernists, it was considered to be "reactionary." Taruskin posits that Rorem's intent was to use the Beatles' music "as a weapon in his own battle of revenge with the academic avant-garde. In effect, Rorem was inviting the concert-going public to defect from the "unlovely" music that Schoenberg, Boulez and their contemporaries had foisted on the public in the guise of progress and historical inevitability.[7] Rorem was emphatically saying "no" to all that arguing that the "old world" musical traditions still had viability and the marketplace proved that to be the case.

This caused serious consternation for the modernists and the ideologues like Theodor Adorno who considered their "determinist" views about contemporary music to be unassailable and thus shielded from the vagaries of capitalism, not to mention lowbrow kitsch. This was not to be the case. Adorno's disdain for popular music is well documented and it surely caused him and other neo-Marxist intellectuals and progressives in the academy serious angst to see popular music relegating their cherished notions of what constituted important music, let alone music that was considered to be the inevitable result of historical progress, to the dustbin of music history.

The ideological bent of modern art was a major thrust in the academy in the decades after World War II. However, American conductor and musicologist Joshua Rifkin, noted that by the late 1980s the ideological grip of post-World War II modernism was abating and he too viewed the Beatles as having a profound effect on that situation. Rifkin in 1987 wrote that the success of the Beatles caused many in the academy "to wonder about the [ideological] paradigms themselves." The paradigms promulgated by the academic elite were being dismantled by "these musically unlettered kids" acting collectively in a way that was diametrically opposed to the notion of "the fearsomely learned individuals" who were steeped in the left-brain intellection of "serious" music; the music that really mattered.[8] The Beatles were antipodal to all that and it caused those in the academy to recoil in smug disgust.

As the Beatles evolved as songwriters and arrangers their music became more eclectic, sophisticated and diverse in its influences. just as Leonard B. Meyer had predicted. Certain critics (Natt Hentoff) tried to write them off, but others (Rorem, Berio and William Mann of *The Times* of London) saw something else at work. Paul McCartney studied the music of Berio and Karlheinz Stockhausen. George Harrison was influenced by Ravi Skankar and Indian *ragas*. George Martin, the Beatles long-time producer, was a music conservatory graduate and could offer his expertise in the process of notating music for classical ensembles and horn sections to accompany the band's tunes. Recording engineer, Geoff Emerick (who won Grammy awards for his work on *Sgt. Pepper* and *Abby Road*) was also a key player in facilitating the experimental aspects of the recording medium for the band.* The advance of recording technology and the Beatles' willingness to experiment in the recording studio led to their withdrawal from touring and public concerts altogether.

Italian composer Luciano Berio was especially taken by the Beatles' use of electronic methods and equipment. The use of electronic media in art music dates back to the pioneering efforts of the early twentieth century when futurist/avant-garde composers and electrical engineers such as Thaddeus Cahill, Leon Theremin, Olivier Messiaen, Ferruccio Busoni and Edgard Varèse (a primary influence on Frank Zappa) explored new attitudes and aesthetics regarding musical expression. The French connection that began in the electronic and futurist compositional methods of Theremin, Varèse and Messiaen continued with the work of Boulez and Werner Meyer-Eppler, who were among the early advocates of electronic music production. Berio believed that "the promise of a true integration of the electronic and acoustic music" was being realized through the progressive rockers in ways that the early modernists had struggled with.[9] The electronic revolution that began in the early

---

* Speaking to the issue of experimentation in the recording studio, George Martin recollected: "I spoke to Geoff Emerick, the engineer, and he had a good idea. He said, 'Let's try putting his [John Lennon's] voice through a Leslie speaker and back again and re-recording it.' A Leslie speaker is a rotating speaker, a Hammond [organ] console, and the speed at which it rotates can be varied according to a knob on the control. By putting his voice through that and then recording it again, you got a kind of intermittent vibrato effect, which is what we hear on *Tomorrow Never Knows*. I don't think anyone had done that before. It was quite a revolutionary track for *Revolver*." [Source: *Anthology*, George Martin.]

twentieth century was being driven, not by the likes of Boulez, but rather Lennon and McCartney.

And here we see how the anti-capitalist ideologues had to surrender, or at least start to "wonder" about the veracity of their anti-free market perspectives, particularly the notion that all things capitalist were untoward and oppressive. Without major financial investments into the research and development of recording technology none of the sophisticated computers, multi-track recording machines, amplifiers, microphones and synthesizers that produced the music that the public was purchasing with great alacrity, would have been produced. The counterculture of the 1960s that pined for uncorrupted, unconstrained and anti-commercial alternatives to the dreaded "plastic" and "bourgeois" culture of previous generations, eventually and inevitably capitulated to the "business" of music, and this was driven in large measure by the artistic aspirations and technological ingenuity of their musical heroes.

The protestations of the 1960s counterculture held to the belief that music was pure and immune to the "disease" of capitalism. Taruskin notes that though the counterculture "celebrated voluntary poverty" and the "high idealism" of being emancipated from materialism and greed, the music of these idealists became "the product and expression of a moneyed and materialist segment of society, as betokened above all by the emphasis it placed on high technology."[10]

Moreover, as concert promoters looked to fill outsized sports arenas and stadiums with tens-of-thousands of paying customers, the rock scene in the early 1970s became, according to British sociologist, Arthur Marwick, "an expression of financial elitism that paid lip service to the counterculture narratives of social amelioration" while enjoying the lifestyles of the rich and famous, with jealously, double standards and resentment in tow.[11] As Fred Goodman chronicles in his book, *The Mansion On the Hill: Dylan, Young, Geffen, Springsteen, and the Head-on Collision of Rock and Commerce*, when the Boston-based alternative newspaper, *The Real Paper* started making real money, "the limits of being an anti-business business became apparent … the knives came out … and the continual prospect of fame without fortune began to rankle.[12]

Additionally, the bands that looked to emulate the high-tech musical wizardry that the Beatles pioneered needed to have serious financial underwriting to accomplish this. The Beatles raised the bar both artistically and financially because they could afford it! As other bands like Emerson, Lake and Palmer (ELP) and Yes attempted to progress toward a more "artistic" trajectory, costs associated with this were steadily increasing. ELP's *Works* album (Volume 1, 1977) for *Atlantic Records* utilized the London Philharmonic Orchestra and the orchestra of the National Opera of Paris for several of its tracks, including a full-blown piano concerto by Keith Emerson (with a photo of Emerson sitting at piano aping Igor Stravinsky's famous piano pose). When ELP toured the United States the costs for hiring local orchestras to accompany the band on these ambitious compositions (no longer three-minute pop songs) were staggeringly high.* The *Works* album was not a commercial success compared to the standard fare of the time, but the attempt to create music that aspired to the "prestige of art" was a significant development in the progressive rock genre. Taruskin again: "Thus the alternative culture became a meeting ground of art and entertainment categories formerly pigeonholed categorically as high and low. This was the first symptom, in the sphere of art and entertainment of what is now called postmodernity."[13] The net worth of many of the top rock icons is in the hundreds of millions of dollars. Bruce Springteen's "blue-collar" persona has taken a real beating.

Past, Present and Future

Some may think that we've given the Beatles too much credit for "saving" music from the clutches of the avant-garde. It's important to remember that many prominent composers continued to compose in tonal, pan-tonal and extended tonal idioms up to and beyond the post-World War II era—Bartók, Shostakovich, Barber, Britten, Prokofiev, Copland, Rorem, Blacher—to name but a few. Broadway musicals, swing, jazz, gospel music, pop reggae, R&B and rock have maintained healthy popularity because tonality more than held its own as a viable musical syntax. The fixation with rejecting the past, or castigating it for its "bourgeois" patrimony now seems decidedly obtuse.

---

* In 1977 I was a member of the New York City Symphony as well as the orchestra's personnel contractor. Our orchestra was approached by the ELP production group about the possibility of accompanying the band for three concerts at Madison Square Garden. We ran the numbers for the rehearsals and shows, including a videotaping fee and the costs were in excess of $90,000.00. Adjusted for current pricing that figure could easily be three times more in 2021.

Unconscionably, Bela Bartók was denounced by hardcore modernists—Pierre Boulez and Rene Liebowitz in particular—for "compromising" his artistry for having composed music that remained reliant on the tonal syntax—his *Concerto for Orchestra* and third piano concerto being prime examples. This was viewed as a "moral failure" by these atonal ideologues who chided him for seeking "social approval rather than facing his lonely historical obligation" to forsake the past, especially the bourgeois idioms that hearkened to traditional views of beauty, pleasure and spirituality.* Any link to, or preference for, the Judeo-Christian culture that spawned the tonal syntax was considered abhorrent to those promulgating the ideal of a "great renewal" of music; music freed from its religious patrimony and its "dead disgraceful past."[14] The "liberatory vibe" of the aforementioned Young Hegelians is quite evident in Boulez's critique of Bartók's latter works, not to mention the Marxist tinge of historical determinism.

The parallels between the evolution of modernism toward postmodernism in contemporary culture and art music are striking. Whereas in the socio-cultural sphere there was a cessation from the past with regard to religious belief and bourgeois values, and the resulting emphasis on science and realism, the new music of the early avant-garde was becoming decidedly enamored with mathematics and formulaic modes of composing—what American composer George Rochberg referred to as "intellection." This was viewed as keeping in step with modernity's preoccupation with science and rationalism, as well as the dissolution of religious influence. "Music-by-the-numbers" was touted by the likes of Boulez and his advocates as the only way to be taken seriously as a composer.

---

* In what might be viewed as blatant hypocrisy, Pierre Boulez is featured in a video titled "Emotion and Analysis" produced by *medici.tv*. The video features Boulez analyzing and conducting Bartók's *Concerto for Orchestra*. Late in his life Boulez also recorded the symphonies of arch-romantic composer, Gustav Mahler. Given his strident advocacy of "renouncing legacies of the past," including Bartók's later compositions, his embrace of Mahler and Bartók seemed quite disingenuous. Could this have been an admission by Boulez that popularity and the free market are significant dictates of artistic tastes—and that aesthetics really do matter, and therefore there was no "clever ruse" being perpetuated by "bourgeoisie" elements in society in an attempt to "make the world of the past serve our present-day needs?" [Source: IRCAM, U.S. Tour Program Notes, Paris: IRCAM Editions, 1986, p. 10.]

Referring to Arnold Schoenberg's 12-tone method, Boulez would say, "Any composer who has not felt—I do not say understand—but felt the necessity of the dodecaphonic language, is USELESS."[15] Boulez's doctrinaire attitudes made him an adversary to many traditionalists, but he nevertheless articulated the prevailing attitude of mid-century modernist composers and their advocates. Adorno and other modernist philosophers who took an elitist view of culture possessed a sneering disdain for tradition and what they viewed as a sell-out to commercial interests and popular tastes. This mindset corresponds to the socio-political idea that elites in government have the expertise to fashion the necessary remedies to straighten out the "crooked timber of humanity." It is clear that political elites do not understand the common man.

Dutch composer and author John Bortslap suggests that modernist thinking is "in its deepest nature, a totalitarian, top-down, structuralized belief system, artificial, anti-humanist, anti-civilizationist, and unintentionally an appropriate expression of the totalitarian societies, which have disrupted Europe in the last century."[16] According to Bortslap, modernism's rejection of the past (our cultural patrimony) doesn't allow for "renewal" or the "development of alternatives" that might help us to contextualize art in terms of its transcendent properties—properties that were viewed historically as important to both composers and their audiences. If art music is about intellection on one hand, or absurdist nihilism on the other, can anyone be surprised that most music lovers have basically said, "no thanks" to music that neither speaks to them nor satiates their innate desire for aesthetic beauty in any meaningful ways?

With the advance of postmodernism in the new century, we now see how radical relativism has turned against reason and truth, as well as the scientific and formulaic modes of composing that had been touted as the way to arrive at those "undreamed of territories" that Boulez fantasized about. The eschewing of science and rationalism in favor of dubious social constructs, political correctness and/or emotivism, has brought us to the point where aesthetic judgments are deemed invidious and possibly immoral. Radical egalitarianism then becomes the way to ascertain artistic merit.

In her book *The Diversity Delusion: How Race and Gender Pandering Corrupt the University and Undermine Our Culture*, Heather MacDonald of the Manhattan Institute references how artistic ability and aesthetics, once considered the most salient of attributes in assessing art, are increasingly subordinated by issues of gender, sexual preference, political persuasion or race. This postmodernist, neo-Marxist view of art is destructive and has nothing to do with what Camille Paglia refers to as the "empathic, emotional, sensory-based" aesthetic experience that great art affords humanity.[17] MacDonald has chides Alex Ross of the *New Yorker Magazine* for advocating identity-based quotas for various positions in artistic institutions as if one's race or gender determines one's artistic or administrative abilities. Gone is the idea that talent transcends a particular gender, race or social status.[18] When the drive for "equality of outcome" becomes the primary objective in art we shouldn't be shocked that mediocrity becomes the norm and audiences refuse attend concerts to experience such.

The search for meaning and beauty in life and art is a stubborn inclination. We pay good money for the opportunity to experience artistic excellence. Making pilgrimages to experience the wonder of natural beauty is for many a way to experience spirituality on a deep reverberating level. As mentioned in previous chapters of this book, if making a distinction about beauty and meaning is purely subjective, or in art predicated on issues other than artistic merit or craft, we've entered an era where a confusion of values takes precedence and no artistic enterprise can be considered better or worse than another. Relativist thinking in this manner renders all art from any era as being less meaningful than it actually is.

When Boulez and Liebowitz castigated Bartók for his alleged proclivity of pandering to popular tastes by utilizing a quasi-tonal harmonic syntax, they were in effect rejecting the right-brain tendency to seek and appreciate aesthetic beauty. By advocating atonality as a historical inevitability they were discarding that basic, primal and innate human instinct to experience joy via that which is aesthetically pleasing. Their specious claims regarding historical inevitability, as well as their contempt for a tradition that continues to provide aesthetic pleasure, has been undercut by the renewal of the tonal tradition as evidenced by numerous composers who've eschewed the hyper-intellectualism of post-World War II modernism in favor of other modes of composing.

Roger Scruton averred that the primary effect of modernism was to make "high-culture" difficult, and "to surround beauty with erudition. The hidden purpose was twofold: to protect art against popular entertainment, and to create a barrier, a new obstacle to membership, and a new rite of passage to the adult illuminated sphere."[19] To a certain extent, this rationale was based on a *faux* concern that high art was being trivialized by popular culture and by an increasingly naïve public; this was Adorno's contention. By taking music down the path toward greater intellection the modernists believed that they were "rescuing" music from the purveyors of kitsch, cliché and lowbrow pastiche. As Bortslap observes, "Music became a caricature of science and what was perceived as progressiveness: a line of history projected into the future, thus reducing an art form that had been 'an expression and representation of the inner life' of humankind to a quasi-scientific exercise of highbrow sophistication."[20] Yet, as we have witnessed the development of art music in the new century, it is clear that composers are looking to the past for inspiration and source materials, including materials with religious connotations. This is why the music of Eric Whitacre, Osvaldo Golijov and Jennifer Higdon has found many enthusiastic listeners.

This book has been largely an attempt to understand our cultural patrimony; the enduring legacy and values of the past vis-à-vis life and art. The current iteration of postmodernism has had the effect of relativizing everything from gender identification, science, aesthetics, language and all manner of social values. The roots of postmodernism, specifically the Hegelian concept of clash and conflict, have not brought civilization any closer to attaining a culture of peace and harmony. Consequently, we continue to seek the ways by which we might get to a place where peaceful coexistence, co-prosperity and mutually agreed upon values can be identified, understood and practiced in the pursuit of a more humane culture.

Every historical period has had its way of observing and interpreting life and art, and though there are many differences there are also many similarities. It can easily be said that humankind possesses intrinsic attributes that transcend historical epochs. The pursuit of beauty, truth and goodness is as old as humankind itself, and music has been in the social equation forever. Moreover, any attempt to use our creativity to discover innovative solutions to remedy our social malaise requires that we look to the past in order to understand what went wrong and what went right. As I've repeatedly noted, making distinctions or value judgments is neither invidious nor intolerant, whereas moral relativism, political correctness and postmodernism have the effect of undermining the pursuit of universal truth in our quest for betterment.

Why does the music of Mozart, Beethoven, Mahler, Debussy, Bartók, Higdon or Whitacre (and the Beatles) continue to move people of different races, genders, ethnicities, or social statuses? Obviously, there are certain universal attributes in the musical materials that evoke an emotional response to those who encounter this music. I maintain that music can put us in touch with our divinity—the spiritual aspect of our being. When Beethoven spoke of the condition of one's soul state (*Seelenzustand*) he was referencing a common characteristic of his culture. It was an acknowledgment of the potential divinity that we share as well as the idea that beauty in nature and art could affect the condition of our soul. Does late, innovative the music of the Beatles strike the same chords, metaphorically speaking? Many music-lovers believe so.

Recommended Recordings

Rochberg: *Ricordanza* for Cello and Piano,Norman Fischer, cello

Rorem: Concerto for Flute, Royal Liverpool Philharmonic, Jeffery Khaner, flute

Bartók: Concerto for Orchestra, Pierre Boulez, New York Philharmonic

Berio: *Folk Songs*, Opus21musikplus, Stella Doufexis, mezzo-soprano

Higdon: *O magnum mysterium*, Grant Lewellyn, Handel and Haydn Society

Whitacre: *Lux aurumque*, Grant Lewellyn, Handel and Haydn Society

Golijov: *Last Round*, Eric Jacobsen, The Knights

Mozart: Piano Concerto No. 27, Mitsuko Uchida, Cleveland Orchestra

Mahler: Symphony No. 3, Claudio Abbado, Vienna Philharmonic

Beethoven: Music from *King Stephen*, Michael Tilson Thomas, London Symphony

Debussy: *Nocturnes*, Leonard Bernstein, New York Philharmonic

Bortslap: *Avatâra* for Piano, Jeroen van Veen, piano

Joplin: *Maple Leaf Rag*, Joshua Rifkin, piano

The Beatles: *Sgt. Pepper's Lonely Hearts Club Band*

Emerson, Lake and Palmer: *Works*, Volume I

Endnotes

1   John Lennon, Interview: "The John Lennon I Knew," by Maureen Cleeve, *The Daily Telegraph*, October 5, 2005.

2   Stephen R. C. Hicks, *Exploring Postmodernism: Skepticism and Socialism from Rousseau to Foucault*, Expanded edition (Roscoe, IL: Ockham's Razor Publishing,

2011), pp. 249-250.

3   Robert R. Reilly, "Reaching the Transcendent," *World & I Magazine*, January 1990, Vol. 5, No. 1.

4   Leonard B. Meyer, *Music, Arts and Idea* (Chicago and London: University of Chicago Press, Second edition, 1994), p. 317.

5   Richard Taruskin, *Music in the Late Twentieth Century, The Oxford History of Western Music* (Oxford-New York, Oxford University Press, 2010), p. 325.

6   Ned Rorem, "The Music of the Beatles," *New York Review of Books*, January 18, 1968.

7   Taruskin, *Music in the Late Twentieth Century*, p. 326.

8   Ibid., p. 331.

9   Ibid.

10 Ibid., p. 327.

11 Ibid.

12 Fred Goodman, *The Mansion on the Hill: Dylan, Young, Geffen, Springsteen, and the Head-on Collision of Rock and Commerce* (New York: First Vintage Books, 1998), p. xi.

13 Taruskin, *Music in the Late Twentieth Century*, p. 327.

14 Ibid., p. 18.

15 Pierre Boulez, "Eventuellement …" in *Stocktakings From an Apprenticeship*, translated by Stephen Walsh (Oxford: Clarendon Press, 1991), p. 113.

16 John Bortslap, *The Classical Revolution: Thoughts on New Music in the 21st Century* (Mineola, New York: Dover Publications, 2017), p. 8.

17 "Modern Times: Camille Paglia & Jordan B. Peterson," October 2017, https://www.youtube.com/watch?v=v-hIVnmUdXM&ab_channel=JordanBPeterson.

18 Heather MacDonald, *The Diversity Delusion: How Race and Gender Pandering Corrupt the University and Undermine Our Culture* (New York: St. Martin's Press, 2018), p. 162.

19 Roger Scruton, *Modern Culture* (London and New York: Bloomsbury, 2013), p. 85.

20 Bortslap, *The Classical Revolution*, p. 16.

40

Can the Humanities Still Humanize?

The humanities are ruined, and the universities are full of crooks.
Art in America is neglected, coddled, and buried under chatter.
The right looks down on artists; the left looks down on everyone.[1]
Camille Paglia

This caustic bit of pessimism by Camille Paglia is the byline of a 2005 interview by the noted art historian conducted by Robert Birnbaum for the online magazine, *The Morning News*. Paglia is one of the great, straight shooters in contemporary academic circles and always a provocative read. She has defended Sarah Palin, praised Madonna, castigated Lady Gaga, and has referred to the early feminist movement as being "Stalinist." I found her perspectives on the arts and humanities in the interview with Birnbaum to be very much in accord with my own on several important issues regarding the value of humanities in the pursuit of a more humane society.

When I wrote this essay in 2012 I wasn't quite the misanthrope Paglia is vis-à-vis the cultural malady in which we now find ourselves. However, over the past several years, I more fully empathize with her derision regarding the perfidy of the "effete literati" (her term) that is now ensconced in academia and the media who consider themselves to be the arbiters of cultural discernments and values. I still tend to be a glass-is-half-full kind of person and remain hopeful that we can find our way out of the malaise of misguided misreadings regarding art, culture and the human condition. Ms. Paglia considers coteries (and their attendant dogmas) to be a serious obstacle in the pursuit of enlightened perspectives, and though she may claim to be completely free from the influences of others and their beliefs, I doubt that anyone can be hermetic to the point of being completely unfettered by such.

Still, the humanities as understood and appreciated by those of a generation or two ago have undergone a radical transformation due to the pervasive and deleterious effects of postmodernism and political correctness. But this is not a new phenomenon. C.S. Lewis cited the trend in 1942 in *The Screwtape Letters*. William F. Buckley, Jr. observed the nascent indications of what would become the postmodern orthodoxies of collectivism, secularism and atheism in 1951 and wrote about them in his first book, *God and Man at Yale: The Superstitions of "Academic Freedom."* At the time, Buckley likened the "duel between Christianity and atheism" to the struggle between individualism and collectivism and he considered it "the most important conflict in the world.[2] In 1977, the Austrian-born, American sociologist Peter L. Berger was despairing over the condition of American universities as they evolved into "vast identity workshops," where "for four years … students sit under trees with their shoes off and engaged in the not so arduous task of finding out who they really are."[3] For Berger, this kind of speculative naval-gazing had the effect of turning students into creatures of comfort rather than inquisitive seekers of higher knowledge. Allan Bloom wrote of similar scenarios in 1987 in *The Closing of the American Mind: How Higher Education Has Failed Democracy and Impoverished the Souls of Today's Students.*

Fast forward to the new century. In his book, *The Victim's Revolution: The Rise of Identity Studies and the Closing of the Liberal Mind*, Bruce Bawer alludes to the stark contrast between John Stuart Mill and his advocacy of free speech as an essential characteristic of university culture and neo-Marxist Herbert Marcuse, who called for "the withdrawal of toleration of speech and assembly" from groups and movements that didn't advocate the leftist, progressive agenda.[4] Bawer views the deceit of Marcuse's "repressive tolerance" regarding identity studies in the American academy, as nothing less than "a betrayal, in the profoundest sense, of the promise of America." Bawer considers Marcuse's ideas regarding intolerance to be a significant factor in the closing of the liberal mind and the ongoing assault on civil liberties. Speaking to the importance of studying the humanities and learning to think analytically and critically, and "to think for oneself" while living in the university environment, Bawer writes:

> It's about experiencing wildly different products of the human mind and spirit and making comparisons, recognizing affinities, deciding what one likes and doesn't like … It's about encountering unfamiliar thoughts, weighing them against one another and against one's own observations of the world … It's about building an understanding of the history of humankind and of human art and thought and culture, so that one develops, bit by bit, a radically heightened sense of how things got to be the way they are. It is about coming to see the world through increasingly sophisticated eyes, and hence experiencing it in a way far richer than one could ever have imagined at the start of things.[5]

Pluralism, assimilation and advocating for civil liberties have been viewed as a sign of a healthy republic, but these attributes have come under scrutiny by the academics of the progressive left. In speaking to the issue of diversity and the "melting-pot" paradigm of American culture, Arthur Schlesinger, Jr. observes that in recent decades that particular narrative has given way to a multiculturalist bent of segregation born of group identity. "The multiethnic dogma, "he writes," abandons historic purposes, replacing assimilation by fragmentation, integration by separatism. It belittles *unum* and glorifies *pluribus*."[6] This results in individualism being commandeered by groupthink, often through peer pressure or outright coercion. Professor Bret Weinstein, of Evergreen College notoriety, stated in a Congressional hearing that "students should be taught how to think, not what to think."*

---

* Professor Bret Weinstein, according to a New York Times report, "had the gall to challenge a day of racial segregation … The biology professor said as much in a letter to Rashida Love, the school's Director of First Peoples Multicultural Advising Services. "There is a huge difference between a group or coalition deciding to voluntarily absent themselves from a shared space in order to highlight their vital and under-appreciated roles," he wrote, "and a group or coalition encouraging another group to go away." The first instance, he argued, "is a forceful call

This spurious mindset ignores (or willfully rejects) the reality that not all people in a particular group think, act or opine similarly; a point that Thomas Sowell has been making for decades. Moreover, Schlesinger contends, "when pressed too far, the cult of ethnicity has had bad consequences too. The new ethnic gospel rejects the unifying vision of individuals from all nations melted into a new race." I'm convinced that the melting-pot vision of America was not about establishing "a new race,"[7] but rather a new culture by creating a society in which diversity was celebrated and respected, and where a sense of community-based on shared ideals could be a vision worthy of pursuing.

In what has become a severe hindrance to that vision is what Alasdair MacIntyre refers to as "emotivism … the doctrine that all evaluative judgments and more specifically, all moral judgments are *nothing but* expressions of preference, expressions of attitude or feeling, insofar as they are moral or evaluative in character … a theory which professes to give an account of *all* value judgments whatsoever."[8] When objective assessments of a particular truth claim are impeded or dismissed by purely emotive rationale in the attempt to preserve or advance the rights of a group, there will likely be infringements of the rights of certain individuals within said group, not to mention heavy doses of moral relativism, situational ethics and hypocrisy.

Postmodern multiculturalists who trade in the claim that truth is fungible, or that there are no absolute truths or meta-narratives, or that knowledge is "merely a construct of unreliable language" (and then write heavily footnoted books to make their points), are often confronted with the inconvenient "truth" that they are extremely duplicitous in their critiques of the very culture they benefit from.[9] Because there is a distinct political goal in the multicultural equation, Stephen R. C. Hicks points out that when attempting to attain political power "one always has a major obstacle to deal with—the powerful books written by brilliant minds on the other side of the debate." Finding the ways to dismiss opposing views becomes paramount for the illiberal postmodernist,

---

to consciousness." The second "is a show of force, and an act of oppression in and of itself." In other words, what purported to be a request for white students and professors to leave campus was something more than that. It was an act of moral bullying — to stay on campus as a white person would mean to be tarred as a racist." [Source: Bari Weiss, *New York Times*, June 1, 2017] There is a fascinating discussion between Professor Weinstein and Jordan B. Peterson on this issue and other related topics: https://www.youtube.com/watch?v=6G59zsjM2UI.

thus engaging in deconstructionist rationale provides a method to miscon-strue the argument of their ideological opponents without having to do the heavy-lifting of fashioning a cogent argument to explain why their perspec-tives are superior or more beneficial in the pursuit of progress.[10] Hicks points to a not-so-irrelevant issue that inexplicitly gets lost in the rationale of post-modernism. As he states:

> Postmodernism often bills itself as anti-philosophical, by which it means that it rejects many traditional philosophical alternatives. Yet any statement or activity, including the action of writing a postmodern account of any-thing, presupposes at least an implicit conception of reality and values. And so despite its official distaste for some versions of the abstract, the universal, the fixed, and the precise, postmodernism offers a consistent framework of premises within which to situate our thought and actions.[11]

This is to say that postmodernism rejects meta-narratives *while acknowl-edging them* to various extents. Another duplicity is at work as well; namely, advocating diversity while engaging in groupthink at the exclusion of diverse opinions and perspectives.

Consider the demonstrations at the University of Missouri in 2015 when members of the university's football team refused to play in any further games in order to call attention to a cause that they felt needed to be addressed; specifically, inaction by the universities directors regarding racial issues on campus. The activism of the players was laudable in its intent and succeeded in accomplishing its objective. However, in a campus protest on November 10, 2015, Melissa Click, an assistant professor in the university's communications department, confronted a student photographer, Tim Tai, and at one point asks for "some muscle" to have him removed from the demonstration, despite Tai's insistence that he had a right to photo-document the event. Ms. Click's "muscle" comment resulted in her resigning and she did offer an apology to Mr. Tai for the "language and strategies" she used in the confrontation. (Mr. Tai accepted the apology.)

What was somewhat lost in the incident was when Ms. Click (on the video that went viral) encourages the students to make their feelings known about Mr. Tai and says, "Students, can you tell him how much you want him to go?" This was "groupthink" in action. Did *all* the students want him to go? Could *some* of them have felt that he had as much a right to take photos as they did to demonstrate? Did *some*, perhaps, *want* the demonstration to be photo-documented to ensure an accurate depiction of the protest? In the video, it's clear that some of the students were rather ambivalent, even sheepish about the ruckus surrounding Tai's being there, and said nothing.

This was an example of what has become all too familiar in academia. The elite professoriate, rather than encouraging students to think for themselves as autonomous individuals, promotes collectivist thinking. Individuality is expected to be sacrificed for a *faux* egalitarian ideal in which diversity of opinion (pluralism) is derided or silenced if one's opinion doesn't comport to the politically correct cause *du jour*. This is *de facto* thought control wrapped in the integument of cultural determinism and is very much the condition of liberal arts academia in contemporary academic culture.

Liberal journalist Kirsten Powers, in her recent book, *The Silencing: How the Left is Killing Free Speech*, provides example after example of how silencing those with conservative perspectives has become a normative method for progressives, especially in academia. She recalls how, when growing up in Alaska, there was never any thought that conservative views were "illegitimate and unworthy of debate." It was upon arriving in New York City that she realized that having an encounter with a conservative was akin to seeing a unicorn.[12] Her initial encounters with the new left created the kind of cognitive dissonance that many, including non-conservatives like Bawer and Paglia, have experienced and written about. Though it might be easy to dismiss Powers' hyperbole about unicorns and conservatives, it would be unwise and dangerous to dismiss the very real threats to free speech that she finds alarming.

The assertion that Western-based humanities studies fail to "humanize" plays heavily into the narrative that Western culture isn't all that it's cracked up to be. The idea that other, non-Western cultures offer more humane alternatives in dealing with human proclivities has far more currency than previous generations could have imagined. Given the pervasive social problems that plague the Western cultural sphere in the new century, even the faintest whiff of idealism born of Western philosophical tenets is predictably met with derision and contempt. The notion of "the family of man" seems like a shopworn platitude at best, or an expression of male toxicity.

Understandably, unbridled utopianism is met with skepticism when we examine the totalitarian regimes that have traded in brutality of the most heinous sort but is idealism of any kind unrecoverable or untoward? Is the impulse, whether religiously motivated or not, to produce and study art, literature and music with altruistic intent being completely "out to lunch" simply because it is the by-product of Western, Judeo-Christian culture? I think not. And we should not forget that non-Western cultures—secular and religious—produced their fair share of vicious tyrants and illiberal societies that thwarted the innate human desire for dignity and freedom.

Recovery

Writing in the *Washington Times* (March 30, 2016), Suzanne Fields reported how students at Stanford University had petitioned for the restoration of courses that would examine Western culture, including its proponents and detractors. Fields reported that the course will include critiques on the Bible, the philosophers of ancient Rome and Greece as well as Dante, Machiavelli, Voltaire, Darwin, Marx and Freud. The student petition declares: "In recognition of the unique role Western culture has had in shaping our political, economic, and social institutions, Stanford University should mandate that freshmen complete a two-quarter Western Civilization requirement covering the politics, history, philosophy, and culture of the Western world."[13]

One wonders how the word "mandate" will be viewed by progressive postmodernists who view Western culture as nothing more than power politics perpetuated by white males of European descent. Still, the petition is an indication that not all students accept the spurious claim that the cultural patrimony of the West is intrinsically and categorically evil and to be eschewed at every turn. As Fields suggests, if one is to advocate for American or Western values as being viable alternatives in the pursuit of a moral and just society, then knowing the whys and wherefores of the antecedents of said values is, or ought to be a *sine qua non*.

The Greeks may have been guilty of many fallen proclivities, but we know that the sins of the Greeks were intrinsic to humanity *en masse*. Cannibalism and tribal conflict in Africa, human sacrifice in Aztec culture, the conquest dynasties of Asia and Islam, slavery and rape (just about everywhere—even today) have all been part of the human condition. These maladies are not the exclusive progeny of Western culture. Though multicultural advocates such as Martha Nussbaum argue that the West cannot lay claim for the initial formulation of human rights and social justice, historical evidence suggests that, in fact, that was the case.

Nussbaum and others of her ilk assert that non-Western cultures offered certain "elements" of egalitarian tolerance and rationalism in their particular quest for social justice. There may be some veracity in her claim but as Bruce S. Thornton avers in his co-authored book, *The Bonfires of the Humanities*, it was in the West where the fundamentals of civil liberties "cohere into a system of abstract *concepts* that could be the subject matter of a *rational* intellectual (as opposed to religious) tradition, and hence develop, be refined and ultimately culminate in the Enlightenment." Moreover, it has become increasingly clear that as non-Western peoples strive for freedom, dignity and respect, that "'the other' is becoming more Western rather than the Westerner is becoming more 'the other.'"[14] And this all started with the Greeks.

It's fair to criticize the Greeks for their failings but to intimate that because of their myriad transgressions, that we must condemn rather than commend them for their contributions in shaping a civilized culture is throwing the baby out with the bathwater. As Thornton acknowledges, if a utopian paradise existed, a place free from racism, bigotry, injustice and classism, millions of folks would want to move there. But you can be assured that as soon as a few dozen of us arrived at that "no place," human proclivities would be in tow and it would quickly degenerate from utopia to paradise lost.

Throughout the late twentieth-century the "effete literati" in academia has continually derided the spiritual and religious aspects of the human experience and in so doing diminished the importance of spirituality as it pertains to the creative impulse. The colliding of worldviews as espoused by the secularists and the religionists (Buckley's "duel") has resulted in a great deal of polarization in our contemporary culture. At one point in her interview with Birnbaum, Paglia makes an astute observation regarding the views of the ideological left and right in this context:

> Most people who are secular humanists have the idea that they are doing fine ... our only enemy is the Bible-based far right. The reason why the real threat is the far right is that they have the Bible. And the Bible is a

masterpiece … Not only do they have a spiritual vision given to them, but artistic fulfillment. They don't even recognize just the pleasure of dealing with this epic poetry and drama. Everything is in the Bible. What does the left have? The left has a lot of attitude.[15]

Of course, those on the right have their share of "attitude" and as Richard Dawkins gladly will tell you, the God of the Old Testament was a vile and nasty deity. Hurling invectives is a two-way street and there are more than a few right-wingers who can be insufferable and malicious in their excoriation of those whom they reprove (the Alt-right crowd, e.g.).[*] But such is life in a society in which free speech is a measure of progress and liberty. As much as we might lament the ongoing rancor, it is, nonetheless, a sign of a healthy pluralism—and we're lucky to have it.

Education Inculcation and Our Cultural Patrimony

Speaking to the issue of the diminishing emphasis on the humanities in the realm of higher education, Manhattan Institute Fellow, Kay S. Hymowitz echoes the concerns of Paglia, Thornton and Bawer regarding multiculturalism in academia vis-à-vis postmodernism.

> All that once ordered higher education requirements, majors, the traditional disciplines, the core curriculum—is vanishing into the chaos of post-modernism … In demolishing the notion of a relatively stable body of knowledge, a traditional set of disciplines to which developing thinkers must apprentice them-selves, [American universities] have invited their students, though half-formed and ill-educated, to indulge in a fantasy of their own extravagant powers.[16]

Multiculturalists in academia believe they are challenging the establishment, but as Thornton asserts, "multiculturalsim *is* the establishment" and the acculturation of this mindset begins early and is pervasive. It is, according to Thornton, "the reigning ideology from kindergarten to university, from

---

[*] The Alt-right movement has no formal ideology or mission statement but tends to reject the agenda of those who adhere to traditional conservative positions as well as all liberal, leftist and progressive positions and those who advocate such. It is largely driven by social media and is generally considered a form of extremist, right-wing populism. The rhetorical tone of the Alt-right is often laced with strident and malevolent invective against the objects of its ire.

television to advertising, from sit-coms to Disney cartoons, from government bureaucracy to the corporate fief, where Diversity Trainers make big bucks schooling white folks on their insensitivity to 'the other.'"[17] It would seem that cultures that continue to practice slavery and human trafficking, or that discriminate against homosexuals, women, or a particular religious group (all those cultures that white folks supposedly fear and loathe), are in greater need of this kind of diversity training than melting pot White Anglo-Saxon Protestants. But the fix is in and this diversity mindset "functions as a secular religion, a sort of Apostles Creed that certifies one's superior social conscience and sensitivity to the "oppressed other."[18] This particular multicultural narrative is a malevolent ruse. Christian virtues based on the tenets of living for the sake of others, sacrifice (from the Latin; to make holy), loving one's enemy, and "do unto others," are seemingly needed more now than ever.

University of Arkansas professor Sandra Stotsky contends that the reading choices of young people, and educators, are not predicated on challenging students but instead are predicated on what they like. The "oppressive" canonic literature of "dead, white, European males" is avoided and replaced by a curriculum based on "easy contemporary young adult fantasies" (Werewolves, vampires, wizards, et al.). Stotsky observes that "challenging students is not the order of the day" because the progressive education model promotes "the damaging notion," that students, not teachers, choose what they want to read.[19]

The evidence is now in. As Professor Stotsky points out in her book, *The Death and Resurrection of a Coherent Literature Curriculum*, the reading choices that students in grade levels 9 through 12 make are on average at fifth-grade reading levels. She holds teachers and school librarians accountable. If students prefer reading *Harry Potter* or *The Hunger Games* on their own time, that's fine. But why allow students to choose when the *evidence* proves that they will almost always choose comfort over challenge. It goes without saying that one does not progress in any endeavor when coddled or shielded from any process that is more intellectually challenging. T.S. Eliot asserted that tradition is not merely inherited or easily acquired, but is achieved "through great labour."

Postmodern multiculturalists will argue that this is but another attempt to maintain political power or white supremacy via intellectual superiority. Allan Bloom (Martha Nussbaum's primary nemesis) averred that the "prideful knower" is a bane to the progressives who trade in undergraduate indoctrination. Those who grasp the value of "aesthetic education" via the humanities and the artistic legacy of Europe as a means to understand the human condition and fashion coherent and efficacious solutions are now viewed as the enemies of progressivism. This is part of the "garbage" that Paglia refers to in her interview with Birnbaum. Bloom's distinction regarding openness in the pursuit of "knowing" via a liberal arts education is important here.

> Thus there are two kinds of openness, the openness of indifference—promoted with the twin purposes of humbling our intellectual pride and letting us be whatever we want to be, just as long as we don't want to be knowers—and the openness that invites us to the quest for knowledge and certitude, for which history and the various cultures provide a brilliant array of examples for examination. The second kind of openness encourages the desire that animates and makes interesting every serious student ... while the former stunts that desire.[20]

If attaining knowledge and perspective by making critical distinctions in the attempt to ascertain the veracity of a particular truth claim is derided as being chauvinist, racist, etc., then students will surely be educationally stunted and ill-prepared to deal with life's challenges with all of its injustices and imperfections, human nature being what it is. Russell Jacoby, like Paglia, understands that multiculturalism in its early incarnation was far more "hospitable" to "a whole range of perspectives" regarding gender, race and ethnicity than we see today. Inclusion was a defining trait of multiculturalism. However, as politics—which is intrinsically adversarial—entered the equation, issues like social justice, economic justice and "the flood of the world's resentments" (as Roger Scruton puts it) came rushing through the gates of academia. As a result, politically correct multiculturalism turned on itself. By integrating anti-essentialism* into the mix, multiculturalism "at its best represents familiar liberalism ... being 'open to new perspectives ... at its worst it represents the conservative's nightmare-mindless relativism."[21] To some, Jacoby and Paglia

---

* Generally, anti-essentialism, sometimes referred to as anti-foundationalism in philosophy, is the non-belief in an essence (from the Latin: *esse* or *essentia*) of any given thing, idea, or metaphysical entity (e.g., God). Philosopher Richard Rorty argued that things don't have intrinsic qualities (essences). They only have qualities when they are brought to us into relation to other things.

may come across as being hyperbolic, but the observations made by Bloom were offered in 1987 and like Buckley before him, Bloom was quite prescient in his concerns regarding the dissolution of the humanities resulting from a malignant strain of political correctness.

While progressives who are the acolytes of the French-Nietzscheans (Derrida and Foucault in particular) assail religion and metaphysical narratives, the cultural totalitarian epigones of the Frankfurt School philosophers utilized reason, pragmatism and historical determinism as their rationale to critique and dismiss the idea of inalienable rights endowed by a Supreme Being. Yet when confronted with evidence that is based on actual data they're given to extreme bouts of obfuscation or prevarication. It's all so Hegelian (or Foucaultian). But damn the torpedoes of reason and data; full speed ahead toward group identity, prohibitions on free speech, rejection of all European culture—as if all European countries shared the same views about everything—and groupthink.* There have been many movements like this in the past and as French essayist Alain Finkielkraut notes:

> Like the racists before them contemporary fanatics of cultural identity confine individuals to their group of origin … they carry difference to the to the absolute extreme, and in the name of multiplicity of specific casualties destroy any possibility of a natural cultural community among peoples.[22]

Musical Patrimony

In the current spate of anti-Western culture, I've had a fantasy. In this fantasy, I would love to see a forum convened in which the members of a university's sociology department, who reflexively deride Western culture and its values as being morally obtuse, and university's music department, those who cherish the grand tradition of Western classical music. It would be fascinating to hear discussions regarding the merits—or demerits—of teaching music that is the direct progeny of European, Christian culture. If, as the multiculturalists would have us believe, that any promotion of Western culture, including its

---

* "Damn the torpedoes; full speed ahead", is a phrase attributed to Rear Admiral, David G. Farragut of the Union Navy during the Battle at Mobile Bay during the American Civil War. It refers to his order to disregard the torpedoes (what we now refer to as mines) that were in Mobile Bay and to go forward with the assault on the Confederate forces at Fort Morgan.

great musical legacy, is just more cultural power tripping and the residue of colonialism and racism, then should we follow the lead of the multicultural-ists and have classical music expunged from university curriculum altogether? Why perform Elgar at graduation ceremonies? Why choose Bach for memo-rial services or Mendelssohn and Wagner for wedding ceremonies?*

The postmodern sociologist's tirades and resultant prohibitions about stu-dents being taught the musical tradition that gave us the music of Beethoven, Chopin, or Bartók might lead us to a place where this music would be consid-ered untouchable—toxic, in fact. This progressive, anti-essentialist idea proffers that there are no common or intrinsic properties that can establish a concrete and logical deduction that there are, or may be, universal attributes that have universal appeal. Michael Foucault would say, "All my analysis are against the idea of universal necessities in human existence."[23] Under this rubric, we are asked (required) to believe that no criteria exist to assess art—aesthetically, intellectually or axiologically—in any meaningful way. This again is based on the "emotivist" rationale that MacIntyre cites—a rationale that provides no objective or moral criterion on which to make its claims.

In his essay, "Roll Over Beethoven: The new musical correctness and its mistakes" (*The New Republic*, August 4, 1991), former *New York Times* music editor Edward Rothstein makes the case that the Western musical tradition, rather than being a musical expression of born of oppressive, "bourgeoisie," European culture, has, in fact, been the vanguard in terms of appreciating and preserving the musical traditions of "the other." He views the progressive iteration of multiculturalism as a pernicious inversion of the very notion of the Western tradition vis-à-vis the study of cultures outside of its own sphere, stating, "Multiculturalism fails to see the Other within us, or us within the Other. This is not an assault from outside. It is disintegration within." Roth-stein sees Multiculturalism as having "no use for the heritage of liberalism ... or the energies of modernism. It is, at bottom, folkish romanticism gone bad. Its calls for equity derived not from recognized unity, but from enforced dif-ference." This perspective may seem rather harsh, but when weighed against

---

* Marxist ideologues Wilhelm Reich and Aleksandra Kollontai considered traditional weddings passé and merely another a type of white, male power-tripping. [Source: Paul Kengor, *Takedown: From Communists to Progressives, How the Left Has Sabotaged Family and Marriage.*]

the evidence it's a view that is creditable. Citing the tradition of Western eth-nomusicology, Rothstein states:

> Western music is far from being monolithic or uniform in its will; it is astonishing how many seemingly incompatible styles and views are repre-sented in the history of Western music, how many folk and religious and courtly and aesthetic traditions coincide. But this impulse to universally helps explain the West has been so open to the possibilities of other cultures. Though almost all cultures have some interest in the Other, no other culture or tradition ... has ever invented something resembling the Western attempt to comprehend the Other through anthropology ... or has asserted the tran-scendental perspective through the political vision like Western liberalism or a rational project like Western science.[24]

If we take the postmodernist orthodoxy about Western/European to its logical conclusion we might ask if any music based on the Western diatonic syntax and equal temperament—music with distinct hierarchical properties and religious underpinnings—should be performed, studied or listen to? After all, hierarchies of any kind run counter to the mindset of multiculturalist egalitarian concerns. Do consonances in music actually oppress dissonances? Is the nexus of the tonic-dominant harmonic progression, which is central to syntactical chord grammar of tonality, antipodal to the idea that all chords are created equal? Why should certain chords have more power and prestige over others in a given key? Isn't that unjust? If so, shouldn't the devoted multicul-turalist stop listening to music based on equal temperament, that distinctly Western invention given to us by J.S. Bach? I doubt if the multicultural purists who incessantly deride Western culture would be willing to give up their Bob Marley, Lenny Kravitz, Rage Against the Machine, Bruce Springsteen, U2 or any Western musician who utilizes the tonal syntax and equal temperament. When it comes to tonal music (not to mention iPods, iPads and iPhones), multiculturalist belligerence towards all things Western seems more like a pose than a conviction.

The Hope of All Ages

Because university culture has become a hotbed for groupthink and the mind-less surrender to political correctness, we've lost our connection to the great traditions that can, and do, provide aesthetic education and spiritual renewal. This scenario contributes to the continual loss of our cultural patrimony. It's amazing how few young people know about the great artistic and musical traditions of the past, whether it's the music of Beethoven or even George Gershwin. Writing for National Review, journalist Jay Nordinger reports:

> As we lose our shared patrimony—cultural patrimony—it gets harder to write. You can assume nothing: no familiarity. Last week, I wrote a little post after Ted Cruz's victory in Texas. I quoted one of the Gershwins' most popular songs: "They all laughed at Christopher Columbus, when he said the world was round. They all laughed when Edison recorded sound." Some of my more clueless critics thought I was quoting the candidate himself: "Cruz is so stupid, he doesn't know that Columbus was not laughed at for thinking that the world was round!"
>
> What can you do? Some editors make you say, "Ludwig van Beethoven, a German composer of Dutch ancestry who lived from 1770 to 1827 ..." You always feel you're insulting the reader. But then—are you?[25]

Alasdair McIntyre posits that when discussing moral philosophy, as opposed to empirical history, we are dealing with more than just facts and data, but rather with problems that all cultures and societies grappled with—problems that are the symptoms of our innately human moral disorder—our fallen nature. He makes the salient observation that too often we continue "to treat the moral philosophers of the past as contributors to a single debate with a relatively unvarying subject matter, treating Plato and Hume and Mill as contemporaries both of our selves and of each other ... Kant ceases to be part of Prussia, Hume is no longer a Scotsman."[26] Music historian Charles Rosen proffers that contextualization—understanding the social, political and economic circumstances surrounding the creation of art (the aura of the era)—is a relevant concern when assessing a work of art *vis-à-vis* its influence and influences. Citing the politics of a given era, he states, "Contextualization is an important tool of the historian, but it is never by itself a complete account of artistic success. Politics will inevitably influence some of our judgments."[27] Beyond politics, other "powerful agents" are in the contextualization equation as well, including "institutions and their gatekeepers, ideologies, patterns of consumption and dissemination involving patrons, audiences, publishers and publicists, critics, chroniclers, commentators" and a multitude of other "external" concerns that mediate and/or militate axiological, aesthetic and methodological concerns.[28]

My focus as an artist has been to promote the edifying aspects of art and music in the process of creating a culture of peace. The idea of a culture of peace has been the hope of all ages, and as I have attempted to demonstrate, many musicians—the famous and not so famous—have had much to offer to the pursuit of that particular ideal. I believe there is something in our "original mind," the mind that is intrinsically idealistic and free from cynicism, the mind that seeks truth, beauty and goodness.

I am not entirely convinced in the epistemological concept of *tabula rasa*, the theory that asserts that we are "blank slates" with no preconceived or preordained dispositions in our soul state. My interface with Oriental cultures has opened my eyes to the distinct possibility that ancestral influences may play heavily into our thought processes and behavior, not to mention our cultural DNA. My understanding is still very much a work-in-progress in this regard, however, my intuition and original mind (and ancestors?) tell me that the pursuit of peace is a noble quest, even in the "fallen" world where so much militates against that quest.

This perspective is undoubtedly troublesome to those for whom the idea that religion, especially the religion of modern Europe, holds any legitimacy as a source of authentic inspiration. As Paglia and others have noted, the politically correct charges against anything connected to "dead, white, European males" are born of ideological conceits rather than artistic merit, as if the actual talent of a Beethoven or Rembrandt is a ruse or merely a power-play masquerading as an artistic accomplishment. This unfortunate mindset has resulted in the current state of the humanities in academia. Again, Paglia to Birnbaum:

> I'm still fighting [deconstructionist philosopher Jacques] Derrida at this point. And also the embattled teachers who are always writing to me saying how they are silenced in their departments when they just want to do literature and art. There has been a tremendous flight from the grad schools of people who wanted to devote their lives to teaching literature and were driven out when they were forced to read post-structuralism. I got letters over the years.

609

But, oh my God, I have been on the road only two weeks but people are coming to the [book] signings and the Q&A, how many people multiplied by hundreds and thousands have left the grad schools, our future teachers. Our future generations, people who are teaching our young people—all these drones who are teaching post-modernism.[29]

Postmodernism's disdain for that which is spiritual, sacred or religious in the arts belies a fundamental aspect of the human experience. This contempt for our cultural patrimony in relation to our spiritual lives has resulted in the profusion of a great deal of third-rate art that passes for something meaningful for simply defying or destroying the "old contracts" (Wagner again) of tradition and morality. When "universals" are derided for being tropes that are employed merely to attain political power, we are no longer engaging in enlightened rationale.

Christopher Hitchens famously proclaimed that "religion poisons everything." However, we need only to point to the great musical traditions born of the Judeo-Christian cultural sphere (chants, classical, gospel, hymns, spirituals, e.g.) to prove that particular supposition to be "garbage," as Paglia would say. A poignant irony regarding Dr. Martin Luther King, Jr.'s legacy is that many of those who advocate secular progressivism venerate him for the causes he championed—civil rights, equality, social justice, the content of one's character as a measure of a person's worth—but loathe the religious faith that fueled his vision and his life's work. They choose to view him in a sociological context rather than a religious one. It's important to see both. For Dr. King, faith in God and living according to godly virtues were necessary for the amelioration of racial injustice and bigotry. His courage stemmed from his faith and this particular manifestation of faith provides proof positive that not all things religious are toxic. Dr. King didn't advocate shooting or looting, rather he taught that learning things was better than burning things. Militancy for militancy's sake is regressive and counterproductive in the quest for justice and goodwill.

There are numerous laws on the books (Federal and State) that are intended to decrease the perfidious aspects of the human heart. There are gun laws, laws against murder, rape, armed robbery, insurance fraud, driving while intoxicated and numerous other malevolent behaviors. Yet people commit these crimes with alarming frequency. We have a law that states that one cannot yell "fire" in a crowded theater. Well, actually, you can. A teenager in Aurora, Colorado murdered people in a crowded theater in direct abeyance to the law. Laws, no matter how well-crafted or well-intentioned, do not have the power to eradicate fallen human proclivities. If one chooses to be free from the "old contracts" of traditional morality there will be consequences.

Purposely ignoring or cutting off from our cultural patrimony results in many of the deleterious social pathologies that confront us on a daily basis. The desire to explore perspectives born of various traditions—religious or secular—as a way to be better informed and make better decisions in establishing a more humane culture, seems inherently beneficial; necessary, in fact. Historically, this has been considered one of the great benefits of getting a "liberal education," but no more. The tyranny of multiculturalism in academia has become hostile to that previously cherished concept.

Speaking to the importance of "freedom of the mind," Allan Bloom asserts, "The most successful tyranny is not the one that uses force to assure uniformity, but the one that removes the awareness of other possibilities, that makes it seem inconceivable that other ways are viable, that removes the sense that there is an outside."[30] That is the *raison d'être* for the humanities and why attacking this noble tradition is reckless, imprudent and fundamentally undemocratic. Jonah Goldberg echoes Bloom's sentiments when he states:

> For all intents and purposes, human nature holds constant as the world changes around us. This truth is better comprehended from literature rather than science. When we read about characters in the distant past or the distant future, what makes them recognizable to us is that they are still us; human beings with all the normal joys, desires, and fears we all experience.[31]

We are now in a climate where calling the perverse aspects of multiculturalism into question is tantamount to advocating bigotry. Being called a "traditionalist" is now a "sly slur" used to discredit those who espouse the significance the humanities. But again, we must remember that it was in the West that appreciation for "the other" and the emphasis on diversity to root. It was in the Christian West that the perfidy of slavery, racism and sexism was exposed as being evil and vigorously combated.[32] The transcendentalist cleric, Theodore Parker was a dedicated abolitionist and reformer within the

Unitarian Church who argued that the injustice of slavery could not continue in America because it was ungodly. Moreover, the Religious Society of Friends (the Quakers) fought against slavery in the United States and the United Kingdom. Many Christians and Jews marched with Dr. Martin Luther King, Jr. during the struggle for civil rights. The Israeli Consulate in New York presents an annual concert to celebrate the relationship between the Jewish community and Dr. King.

Our assessment of past cultural legacies, regardless of the sphere of origin, can and does, provide us with sources of inspiration and guidance in our quest of a better world. In his examination of David Hume's *Four Dissertations* (1757), Denis Dutton reminds us that Hume argued accordingly:

> "The general principles of taste are uniform in human nature." In fact, "all the general rules of art are founded only on experience and on the observation of the common sentiments of nature." For Hume, this has to be so in order to explain the persistence of aesthetic evaluations through history: "the same Homer who pleased at Athens and Rome two thousand years ago, is still admired at Paris and London."[33]

> The works that manage to endure over millennia, Hume thought, do so precisely because they appeal to deep, unchanging features of human nature. Some unique works of art, for example Beethoven's Pastoral Symphony, posses this rare but demonstrable capacity to excite the human mind across cultural boundaries and through history. These epochal survivors of art are more than just popular.[34]

Hume's observations reinforce the idea that there are, in fact, universal "essences" and archetypes that impact the human psyche and behavior. These essences may be ontologically in accord with the invisible nature of God. Commenting on Kant's exegesis on judgment vis-à-vis aesthetics, Roger Scruton opines that Kant "situates the aesthetic experience and religious experience side by side," and goes as far as to suggest that it is the aesthetic experience that is "the archetype of revelation."[35] It could be said that by experiencing beauty via the cultural legacies of the past (or present) we become more conscious of our station in relationship to both God and the natural world, and as well, the true and complete essence of our being is affirmed. Accordingly, the humanities have the potential to "humanize" *and* "divinize," and in so doing, bring us out of our "endarkened" condition and into the enlightened mindset necessary to attain our latent divinity and thereby be better at creating a culture of peace and love.

Recommended Recordings

Gershwin: *They All Laughed*, Patti Austin, Hollywood Bowl Orchestra

Elgar: *Pomp and Circumstance March No. 1*, Georg Solti, Chicago Symphony Orchestra

Bach: Cantatas, Sir John Eliot Gardiner, Monteverdi Choir, English Baroque Soloists

Mendelssohn: *A Midsummer Night's Dream*, George Szell, Royal Concertgebow Orchestra

Wagner: *Bridal Chorus*, Robert Shaw, Atlanta Symphony Orchestra and Chorus

Chopin: *Etudes*, Murray Perahia-piano

Beethoven: Symphony No. 7, Bernard Haitink, London Symphony Orchestra

Bartók: Piano Concertos, Yefim Bronfman-piano, Los Angeles Symphony Orchestra

U2: *The Joshua Tree*

Bob Marley: *Kaya*

Lenny Kravitz: *Five*

Bruce Springsteen: *The Rising*

Endnotes

1   Camille Paglia, *The Morning News* (Interview with Robert Birnbaum), August 3, 2005, http://www.themorningnews.org/article/camille-paglia.

2   William F. Buckley, Jr., *God and Man at Yale: The Superstitions of "Academic Freedom"* (Washington, D.C.: Regnery Publishing, 1951), introduction copyright by William F. Buckley, Jr., 1977, p. xxxii.

3   Peter L. Berger, *Facing Up to Modernity* (New York: Basic Books, Inc., 1977), p. 30.

4   Bruce Bauer, *The Victim's Revolution: The Rise of Identity Studies and the Closing of the Liberal Mind* (New York: Harper-Collins, 2012), p. 334.

5   Ibid., p. 328.

6   Arthur Schlesinger, Jr., *The Disuniting of America: Reflections on a Multicultural Society*, revised edition (New York: W. W. Norton & Co., 1991), pp. 20-21.

7   Ibid.

8   Alasdair MacIntyre, *After Virtue: A Study in Moral Theory* (Notre Dame, IN:

University of Notre Dame Press, 1984), pp. 11-12.

9   Victor Davis Hanson, John Heath and Bruce Thornton, *Bonfire of the Humanities: Rescuing the Classics in an Impoverished Age*, Introduction to the Kindle Edition (Wilmington, Delaware: ISI Books, 2001).

10 Stephen R. C. Hicks, *Explaining Postmodernism: Skepticism and Socialism from Rousseau to Foucault* (Tempe, Arizona: Scholargy Publishing, 2011), p. 191.

11 Ibid., p. 6.

12 Kirsten Powers, *The Silencing: How the Left is Killing Free Speech* (Washington, DC: Regency Publishing, 2015), Kindle Edition-Chapter One.

13 Suzanne Fields, "From 'Plato to NATO' in a dangerous world," *The Washington Times*, March 30, 2016.

14 Bruce Thornton, *Bonfire of the Humanities: Rescuing the Classics in an Impoverished Age* (Wilmington, Delaware: ISI Books, 2001), pp. 14-15.

15 Paglia, *The Morning News*.

16 Kay S. Hymowitz, "J Crew U," *City Journal*, Spring, 1996, http://www.city-journal.org/html/6_2_a4.html.

17 Thornton, *Bonfire of the Humanities*, p. 26.

18 Ibid.

19 Sandra Stotsky, "The 'Twilight' of Real Learning," *New York Daily News*, Op-Ed, April 4, 2012.

20 Allan Bloom, *The Closing of the American Mind: How Higher Education Has Failed Democracy and Impoverished the Souls of Today's Students* (New York, NY: Simon & Schuster, Inc., 1987) p. 41.

21 Russell Jacoby, *The End of Utopia: Politics and Culture in the Age of Apathy* (New York: Basic Books, 1999), p. 61.

22 Alain Finkielkraut, *The Defeat of the Mind*, translated by Judith Friedlander (New York: Columbia University Press, 1995), p. 79.

23 Michel Foucault, *Technologies of the Self: A Seminar with Michel Foucault* (University of Massachusetts Press, 1988), p. 11.

24 Edward Rothstein, "Roll Over Beethoven: The new musical correctness and its mistakes." *The New Republic*, February 4, 1991.

25 Jay Nordinger, "Obama-Reid-Pilosi," *National Review*, August 7, 2012, http://www.nationalreview.com/corner/313270/obama-reid-pelosi-jay-nordlinger.

26 Alasdair MacIntyre, *After Virtue*, p. 11.

27 Charles Rosen, "Music and the Cold War," *New York Review of Books*, April 7, 2011.

28   Richard Taruskin: *Music in the Late Twentieth Century*, (Oxford and New York: Oxford University Press, 2010), p. xvi.

29   Paglia, *Morning News*.

30   Bloom, *The Closing of the American Mind*, p. 249.

31   Jonah Goldberg, *The Suicide of the West: How the Rebirth of Tribalism, Populism, Nationalism and Identity Politics Is Destroying American Democracy* (New York: Crown Forum, 2018), p. 10.

32   Thornton, *Bonfire of the Humanities*, pp. 16-17.

33   Denis Dutton, *The Art Instinct: Beauty, Pleasure & Human Evolution*, citing David Hume, *Four Dissertations: IV. Of the Standard of Taste*, (Oxford and New York: Oxford University Press, 2009), p. 36.

34   Denis Dutton, "What Do You Believe Is True Even Though You Cannot Prove It?", https://www.edge.org/response-detail/10944.

35   Roger Scruton, *The Intelligent Person's Guide to Modern Culture* (South Bend, IN: St. Augustine Press, 2000), p. 31.

41

Too Much Caucasian in My Equation?

Equally clear is the right to hear. To suppress speech is a double wrong.
It violates the rights of the hearers as well as those of the speaker.[1]
Frederick Douglass

There are simply two kinds of music, good music and the other kind.
Classical writers may venture into classical territory, but the only yardstick
by which the result should be judged is simply that of how it sounds.
If it sounds good it's successful; if it doesn't it has failed.[2]
Duke Ellington

In the current social drama that is being played out in Western culture vis-à-vis the ascendancy of progressive postmodern ideology, issues of race, gender and sexual orientation have taken center stage in the discussions about how to create a fair and just society. Whether in politics, commerce, education, journalism, science, sports, medicine, or the arts, it has become impossible to discuss anything without venturing into the realm of "woke" ideology. As Shelby Steele pointed out in his *Wall Street Journal* essay, "The Exhaustion of Liberalism" (March 5, 2017), what now passes for liberalism is decidedly illiberal in that any view that doesn't comport with progressive, "woke" rationale is considered invidious and untoward. No longer are those holding ideas that don't comport with progressive views merely wrong or misinformed, they are considered evil and immoral. Accordingly, they must be defenestrated and silenced; canceled!

I have maintained that if the realms of sports and music fell prey to "woke" ideology that these realms would inevitably collude in their own demise. Meritocracy has been the primary arbiter of value in sports and music. Striving for excellence has been the hallmark of both. Contemporary society has rewarded excellence in music because the innate human desire to experience beauty is atavistic. We never tire of the pleasurable aspects of aesthetic beauty. It is my view that creativity was God's expression of love for humankind. In a sense, God bestowed the gift of creativity to humankind as a way for people to experience the joy of creativity and discover their divinity. Of course, one does not need to be a "believer" to experience or appreciate beauty or athletic excellence. The atheistic communist regimes of China and Russia celebrated the artists and athletes who excelled in their respective disciplines. Though it's a basic human inclination to admire excellence, we might also agree with George Bernard Shaw when he opined, "Hell is full of musical amateurs."[3]

One of the distressing "woke" occurrences that is now plaguing Western society is the assault on classical music due to its Christian European heritage. The current iteration of political correctness views anything that is the progeny of Europe as being intrinsically toxic, hence the justification of its calumny toward all things European. Identity and race are now used as ideological cudgels to besmirch anything that has traces of "white supremacy" in its cultural equation. This begs several questions: Does anyone who composes, produces, performs, or appreciates the music of the European tradition have too much Caucasian in their equation? How do the purveyors of "woke" ideology explain that many black artists attained success in the classical music realm? Leontyne Price, Jessye Norman, Grace Bumbry, William Warfield, Kathleen Battle, Wynton Marsalis, James DePriest, Anthony McGill, Demarre

McGill and Michael Morgan are distinguished black musicians who enjoyed successful careers.

Anthony McGill, the principal clarinetist in the New York Philharmonic, speaks about his love for music, and how the joy of being with other musicians was an important factor in his decision to pursue a career in classical music. Presumably, many of his musician friends were Caucasians, Latinos, or Asians. Speaking to the issue of greater diversity in the classical music sphere. McGill says, "It's not about excluding … It's about including more voices in the story, in the narrative, so that as listeners, as audience members, we can have a full menu to choose from."[4] But as with any particular menu, different people will make different choices, and some people will not choose anything on a given menu and opt for a different experience altogether. The "right to choose" should be respected and it extends beyond any particular issue.

Former managing director of the Brooklyn Philharmonic, Richard Dare, described the highbrow and sophisticated aura of the classical music concert experience that has become the norm as "a contrite response to a totalitarian belief system that no one buys into anymore. To act obediently is to act as a slave. It's counter to our culture. And it is not, I am certain, what composers would have wanted: A musical North Korea."[5] I dare say that Mr. Dare's view is seriously misguided and an indication of how orchestra managers have seriously failed in their managerial duties. Are people in the United States, Japan, or Europe required by the state to attend concerts? Do audiences willingly adhere to what has become concert decorum, or are they coerced into doing so? Are all composers in favor of having a boisterous "beer hall" atmosphere in the concert hall as their works are being performed? My guess is that Dare would be perturbed by a raucous or unruly atmosphere while attending a Broadway show, a theatrical production, a poetry reading, or a movie. I'm a composer and a conductor, and though I don't speak for all of my colleagues, I believe most of them would consider Dare's perspective to be seriously out to lunch—perhaps breakfast and dinner as well.

Classical music, like jazz, has always been a minority taste. The market share for classical and jazz recordings has always hovered around 3%. Neither genre caters to popular tastes or preferences for a number of reasons. There is a mistaken perception that classical music in the eighteenth and nineteenth centuries was the pop music of Europe, but that was not the case. It was largely a specialized realm with limited access. It's important to remember that composers of that era only heard their music when it was performed in a live setting. There were no recordings or videos of their work.

Historically, orchestras in the United States have never been self-supporting and have been reliant on the largesse of patrons—monarchs, the church, aristocrats, and more recently, corporations and government grants. In recent decades, major symphony orchestras in the United States have been experiencing serious financial challenges due to aging audiences and the lack of new adherents. The Philadelphia Orchestra had been running annual deficits in the millions of dollars and filed for chapter 11 bankruptcy protection in 2011. Professional orchestras in Detroit, Baltimore and Minnesota have had financial difficulties with the attendant labor strife as evidenced recently in Chicago, San Francisco and Baltimore. Other orchestras that have shuttered completely or are facing bankruptcy include the Syracuse Symphony, the National Philharmonic Orchestra, the Louisville Orchestra and the Nashville Symphony Orchestra. The Covid-19 issue has exacerbated the problem and many professional musicians are facing personal bankruptcy as a result.

In a 2013 essay for *The New Republic*, music journalist Philip Kennicott shed light on the predicament facing many arts organizations, and particularly the American symphony orchestra. Kennicott points to the late realization of problems within the profession:

> To be fair, orchestras may have few options, and much of the battle was lost decades ago. Orchestra leaders bought a lot of snake oil in hopes of democratizing the concert experience, and now they have an audience that views classical music as just one among many entertainment options, and as not very entertaining compared with bubble-gum pop and action movies. They talk about education but have in many places done away with program notes. Marketing material uses a hyperbolic language of emotional engagement to oversell the concert experience, implying that one has only to pull up a rug and surrender to the music. That musical appreciation takes work, and that its greatest rewards are cumulative over a lifetime rather than immediate, is not much discussed.[6]

Many of Kennicott's assertions remain relevant, but he probably didn't see how the ascendency of "woke" ideology would have nefarious and deleterious effects on the future of classical music. The signs, however, were evident decades ago. Camille Paglia, in an interview with Daniel Richler in 1993 for TVO, cites the cynical, post-structural tendency to view art through *a priori* abstractions based in on contemporary, politically correct conceits that had nothing to do with the context in which the art was originally conceived and created, as being especially problematic.* According to Paglia (she's no right-wing reactionary), by promulgating this mindset the post-structural advocates, most significantly Jacques Derrida and Michel Foucault (and their epigones), separated art from emotion thereby evaluating art according to spurious abstractions about power, patriarchy and other socio-cultural grievances. Edward Rothstein, the former cultural critic for the *New York Times*, also weighed in on the politically correct-based multiculturalist attitude that emerged in the 1980s in his controversial essay for *The New Republic,* "Roll Over Beethoven: The New Multiculturalism and its Mistakes" (August 4, 1991). Rothstein's essay was characterized as a "diatribe" against the emerging multicultural studies programs in academia by ethnomusicologists who had devoted themselves to the study and preservation of non-classical musical traditions from a variety of cultures. What angered those in the field of ethnomusicology was Rothstein's supposition that multiculturalism had become preoccupied with requiring "a submission to the systems of judgment employed by the culture being studied," as well as an "abdication of the West's achievements" in matters of art appreciation, and how this reasoning exemplified the tendency to assess art according to the *a priori* abstractions that Paglia alluded to.[7]

In her essay "Ethnomusicology and Difference," noted ethnomusicologist Deborah Wong describes how the realm of ethnomusicology was influenced by the arrival of multiculturalism in the academy and how cultural studies began to intersect with multiculturalism and ethnomusicology. Wong mentions how it took her years "to acquire the critical language" to address the issues of "identity and subjectivity" in matters of cultural studies vis-à-vis her background in ethnomusicology and the emerging culture wars that viewed the arts from ideological perspectives. She admits that Ethnomusicological scholarship in the 1990s "became increasingly politicized" and that "a lot of smart people were thinking about the death of the canon in terms that were

---

* https://www.tvo.org/video/archive/interview-camille-paglia.

immediately applicable and actionable. Additionally, she cites "provoking writings" in the realm of cultural studies that revealed that, "Marxist theory is alive and well," with a resolute emphasis on "power and cultural movement."[8]

Dr. Wong cites the book *Shadows in the Field: New Perspectives for Fieldwork in Ethnomusicology*, co-authored by Gregory Barz and Timothy J. Cooley, as being noteworthy for its insights regarding the evolution of cultural studies in ethnomusicology. The authors noted the importance of "power relations" in the development of musical practice and observed that, "Neo-Marxists saw society as constituted through practices; this jived well with the new folkloristic emphasis on performance, enactment, and doing. That all action was shaped by social context was a tenet of neo-Marxism as well, and this fit nicely with the emphasis on music's ties to cultural context that was the bedrock of ethnomusicology."[9] No longer were the efforts of ethnomusicologists merely focused on collecting and preserving music of "the other", but there was a decidedly ideological facet that in many cases was progeny of neo-Marxist rationales.*

Wong's essay (originally published in 2006) appears in a collection of essays collected and edited by Bruno Nettl, one of the most prominent figures in the field of ethnomusicology. In the introduction of this collection, Nettl mentions her essay in the context of how ethnomusicology "responded to social and academic change—and itself changed—in its embrace of new approaches such as 'cultural studies' and the increased inclusiveness in its population, its subject matter, and its relationship to various components of the academy."[10] As anyone who has been paying any attention to "various components of the academy" knows, there has been an acute incursion of neo-Marxist indoctrination going on for decades. The assault on "the canon," whether in music, literature or the fine arts," has been a part of "the long march through the institutions" ever since the Frankfurt School philosophers found their way into the institutions of higher learning, politics, journalism and the entertainment industry. Paglia and Rothstein were not alone in their concerns. Notable cultural commentators, such as Roger Scruton, Allan Bloom, Victor Davies Hanson, Bruce Thornton, Robert R. Reilly and Alisdair MacIntyre wrote

---

* I don't know if Deborah Wong, Gregory Barz and Timothy Cooley advocate neo-Marxist ideology, however, they acknowledge that various iterations of Marxism intersect with current trends in multiculturalism and its effects on ethnomusicology in profound ways.

extensively about the attempts to dismantle the humanities studies programs in the universities throughout the United States.

Now, an outsized emphasis on diversity, inclusion and identity politics has resulted in an illiberal "hyper-woke" (John McWhorter's term) attitude regarding art and education. If one objects to the rationale of the "hyper-woke" they are defenestrated and ostracized in the most severe fashion. This, of course, is the *modus operandi* that Herbert Marcuse defined and advocated in his 1965 essay, "Repressive Tolerance." The praxis of silencing opposing views in the academy is pervasive because the desire to silence and force obsequious adherence to particular progressive pieties runs deep in the progressive neo-Marxist consciousness. As Frederick Douglass said long ago regarding the importance of free speech, "Equally clear is the right to hear. To suppress speech is a double wrong. It violates the rights of the hearers as well as those of the speaker."[11] Double wrongs are seemingly everywhere in the academy, and in the current iteration of the culture wars, being a "hearer" of classical music is considered to be an expression of white privilege, and thus makes one explicitly prone to racist attitudes.

Meritocracy, once the measure of excellence in scholarship, artistic achievement and athletics, is also characterized as being a vestige of white privilege and protecting the status quo. As such, it must be dismissed or de-emphasized. Governor Kate Brown of Oregon recently signed legislation that will do away with reading and math requirements in her state. Whatever happen to "no child left behind?" Perhaps Governor Brown can ask the University of Oregon to grant bachelor's degrees to anyone in the name of equity. John McWhorter considers this type of rationale typical of the entrenched racism that was common in the unreconstructed South; the soft bigotry of low expectations.[*] If, as a society that purports to care about those who are disenfranchised or powerless, and wants to create better outcomes for all people, it would seem that providing equal opportunities to gain the necessary skills and abilities to succeed in business, education, or the arts and sciences, should not be characterized as perpetuating white supremacy or an unjust status quo. Would Governor Brown be willing to have a serious medical procedure, or have a

---

[*] John McWhorter made his remarks regarding the "hyper-woke" and the lowering of education standards in an interview with Ben Domenech, co-founder and publisher of *The Federalist*, on April 24, 2021, https://video.foxnews.com/v/6250118042001#sp=show-clips.

serious legal matter be handled by someone who was not an expert in medicine or the law? Would she be willing to live or work in a structure that was designed by a structural engineer who didn't possess proper engineering expertise? Why should music, art or the cinema be any different?

Frederick Douglass is alleged to have said that it's easier to build a strong child than to restore a broken man. To build stronger children often requires that they be challenged to go beyond their limitations. As both an athlete and musician, I learned that competing with those who were better than I was provided me the opportunity to challenge my limitations and become more accomplished in both disciplines. It's inarguable that lowering the bar in scholastics, athletics, or the arts results in mediocrity. We shouldn't want that for our children.

The Caucasian Equation

I was prompted to write this essay after reading two essays by Heather MacDonald in *City Journal*, provocatively titled, "Classical Music's Suicide Pact." MacDonald is a fellow at the Manhattan Institute, a best-selling author, and a contributing editor at *City Journal*. The title of her essays caught my attention because I had been contemplating the same troubling issue for years in my work in New York City as a professional composer, conductor and producer. In several conversations with my colleagues in New York, I could sense an uneasiness regarding the emerging "woke" narrative about classical music and how it might affect the future of art and their careers—careers that they had spent decades developing.

In her detailed analysis on this issue, MacDonald cites the current narrative that the classical music tradition perpetuates privilege and supremacy and has been "culpably white." In the aftermath of the George Floyd demonstrations, the League of American Orchestras (LAO) issued a statement "confessing that, for decades, it had 'tolerated and perpetuated systemic discrimination against black people, discrimination mirrored in the practices of orchestras and throughout the country.'"[12] As MacDonald reveals in her essay, this is a specious narrative and doesn't hold up to scrutiny when examined by the facts. It is virtue signaling of the worst kind because it perpetuates a false reality, not to mention how it "fits nicely" with the neo-Marxist stratagem cited by Barz and Cooley. She cites numerous programs and initiatives by

American orchestras to be inclusive in their attempts to widen their audiences and encourage minority communities to explore the classical music tradition. As anyone in the profession knows, minority outreach has been a key issue for audience development for arts organizations of every kind. Regrettably, these well-intentioned initiatives have been characterized by the progressive leftists in academia as being the continuing efforts of the "dominant culture" to perpetuate the *status quo* of white supremacy because it gives the appearance of legitimacy to this unseemly enterprise. The neo-Marxist/Hegelian rationale regarding race is unmistakable. If arts organizations don't make efforts to be more inclusive they are racist, if they do make efforts to be more inclusive they are doing so to perpetuate and protect their power base; damned if they do, damned if they don't.

MacDonald cites Hunter College professor Phillip Ewell's attempt to take down the classical tradition (and Beethoven) via racial grievances. She writes:

> During the Floyd riots, Ewell compiled a glossary of music-related euphemisms for whiteness: "authentic, canonic, civilized, classic(s), conventional, core ('core requirement'), European, function ('functional' tonality), fundamental, genius, German ('German' language requirement), great ('great' works), maestro, opus (magnum 'opus'), piano ('piano' proficiency, skills), seminal, sophisticated, titan(ic), towering, traditional, and western." Since everything is about race, according to Ewell, any time you seem not to be talking about race—referring to someone's piano skills, say—you are actually talking about race by dint of ignoring the topic. (Connoisseurs of deconstruction will recognize the rhetorical technique here of turning an "absence" into a supposed "presence.").

The deconstructionist technique that MacDonald mentions is right out of Robin DiAngelo's playbook. It's also a tactic of Michel Foucault's discursive methodology. According to Foucault's power analysis, ascribing the term "genius" to Beethoven or any other artist who has been admired for their achievements, is but a devious scheme to ensure the supremacist power structure. This type of aesthetic relativism renders any attempt at objective assessment about art to be meaningless. Is there no qualitative difference between, say, a help-wanted ad in the Sunday newspaper or the novels of John Steinbeck or Ralph Ellison? After all, both use English words and employ the same grammatical syntax. In the classical music sphere (and jazz, gospel, Broadway, rock, Motown), there are qualitative distinctions made between various artists all the time. Not all European composers or performers achieve the same level of compositional or performative prowess. That is an accepted fact. According to its website (September 2021), the Boston Symphony Orchestra is auditioning candidates for the position of concertmaster. In their request for candidates, we find this: "The Audition Committee of the Boston Symphony Orchestra reserves the right to dismiss immediately any candidate not meeting the highest professional standards at these auditions. EQUAL OPPORTUNITY EMPLOYER." A perusal of job opening announcements by top-tier orchestras in the American Federation of Musician trade magazine, reveals similar disqualifying remarks. Meritocracy is a huge factor for orchestras in maintaining artistic standards. Are these organizations guilty of perpetuating systemic racism and privilege by accentuating expertise and experience? For the purveyors of "wokeness," the BSO would certainly be considered guilty for doing so.

Any pushback against this type of "woke" perfidy is reflexively, and spuriously, construed as racist by the cultural totalitarians who are committed to the takedown of what they see as the expression of an inherently unjust cultural tradition. Julian Johnson, professor of music at Royal Holloway University of London, makes an insightful point: "To be discriminating used to mean to be capable of exercising judgment—to be wise, in fact." In our increasingly politically correct society making critical distinctions in matters of art and creativity has become a hindrance in attaining genuine democratic ideals. Instead, we find ourselves in what Johnson calls a "pseudo-democracy;" a situation where it is no different "to discriminate against" than to "discriminate between."[13]

Richard Taruskin strenuously objected to Johnson's perspectives in an essay for *The New Republic* ("The Musical Mystique," October 21, 2007) and referred to the term "politically correct" as being "the discredited euphemism through which privileged people have gone on the offensive in defense of their privileges." A "discredited euphemism?" It's become quite apparent that those doing the "discrediting" these days are those trying to protect their politically correct conceits by taking Western culture down a peg. The pursuit of egalitarianism is not intrinsically bad, but neither is the pursuit of excellence. One wonders what Taruskin would say about Sting when the pop music icon offered this take on classical music: "I think it's really about the higher emotions, about the heart and the intellect at a very high level … classical music does tend to be higher in this sense. What it wants to achieve or what it wants to say about the human condition is, I think, rarefied—and I'm attracted to that."[14] Many people of different races, ethnicities and cultures agree with Sting's assertion. But one wonders too, if Sting still holds this view, or if he does, would he be as publicly forthcoming in his admiration as he was in 2009 when he offered his perspective on classical music.

Music historian and pianist Charles Rosen observes that one of the "unsavory" aspects of contemporary sociological criticism of this kind is the attempt to debunk the idea that there exists true genius in the work of great artists, and that the "genius" appellation appropriated to the likes of Beethoven or Shakespeare "is entirely due … to a process of brainwashing by the cultural elite in power." This is the attempt to create the condition where, as Rosen notes, "commonly shared and recognized values can be dismissed since these values are simply a successful imposition by an elite upon society as a whole."[15] Accordingly, any belief in certainty on any particular issue quickly leads to charges of extremism, intolerance and, of course, racism. From this perspective the esteemed youth orchestra project in Venezuela (*El sistema*), the Harlem School of the Arts and Jessica Garand's Opportunity Music Project in Manhattan should be considered nothing more than vehicles to propagate more white power and privilege.

Another salient point that MacDonald makes, is that by besmirching the European classical music tradition as being racist, supremacist and the cultural residue of colonialism and privilege, those who desire to see more musicians of color in the ranks of orchestras, opera companies and chamber ensembles, are undermining their objectives.[16] The desire to have more minorities in orchestras requires greater exposure to the art form in the hopes of inculcating young students with an appreciation for this particular art form. If classical music is an expression of a detestable racist culture, why would any self-respecting person of color want to be part of such an odious enterprise? This incongruity escapes those who defame the tradition but lobby for more diverse inclusion. That shouldn't be surprising considering that the entire postmodern view of the French Nietzscheans is based on the incongruous idea that there are no objective truths but merely interpretations of truth, which is in itself an objective statement. This is but another Hegelian fiction being passes off as fact.

The Transformative Power of Music

In 2015, I conducted the New York City Symphony in a concert in the General Assembly Hall of the United Nations as part of the U.N.'s 70th Anniversary activities. The theme of the concert was, "The Transformative Power of Music" and artists representing Asia, Europe, Africa, the Caribbean and North and South America were invited by the Office of the President of the General Assembly to participate. At the time the president of the General Assembly was H.E. Mr. Sam Kahamba Kutesa from Uganda. The performers for this historic concert included Ky-Mani Marley (the son of Reggae legend, Bob Marley), Geoffery Oryema (Uganda), Seiko Lee, (Japan), Hervé Coeur (Haiti), Jihae Kim (Korea), Kaïssa (Cameroon), Angelo Mazzone (Italy/USA), the Watoto Children's Choir (Uganda), Bakithi Kumalo (South Africa), Csaba Szegedi (Hungarian State Opera), Robin DiMaggio (USA) and Ahmad Gamal (Egypt). It was truly a multicultural array of talent.[*]

Two weeks prior to the rehearsals I received a call from the executive producer of the concert, Jean-Victor Nkolo, informing me that when these artists were informed that the New York City Symphony was going to be on the program, several of them asked if I could arrange their songs so they could perform with the orchestra. I was able to arrange the music of Ky-Mani Marley, Geoffery Oryema, Seiko Lee and Hervé Coeur, and all of the performers joined the orchestra and the Watoto Choir in singing Kevin Pickard's moving anthem, "One World of Peace" as the concert's grand finale. It was apparent that none of these artists harbored any ill will towards me, or the orchestra; the type of artistic institution that leftist progressives might condemn for being an artistic institution of a malevolent and repugnant culture. I was happy to accommodate the requests of the various artist. For these artists, an opportunity to sing with an orchestra was enticing, and on this occasion, they were enthusiastic collaborators in the spirit of "the transformative power of music."

---

[*] Israeli singer Yasmin Levy and Arab-Israeli singer Miriam Toukan were to perform a duet, but due to diplomatic issues, the proper visas for travel to New York were not granted.

Unfortunately, multiculturalism has become a movement with decidedly "politically correct" features, and political correctness now clouds any attempt at arriving at a reasoned, objective outlook in matters of art—especially the art born of the Judeo-Christian religious sphere. In this postmodern gestalt, multiculturalism, while professing equality, has become hostile to various traditions. As Charles Rosen notes:

> We owe to various versions of political correctness an improvement in the status of women and minorities, a greater tolerance of unorthodox sexuality, and a more serious examination of the aspirations of classes with little political power. There are benefits from multiculturalism, too, but when combined with political correctness, it has produced the absurd thesis that all cultures are equally valid or valuable, the consistent denigration of Western civilization, and the attempts to suppress any critical examination of non-Western societies.[17]

MacDonald echoes this view by pointing out that many teachers and artists "have been mute before calls to eliminate their entire field if it cannot be purged of its alleged racism and misogyny," and the humanities, in general, are "being hollowed out with similar charges," because "any tradition that comes out of Europe is racist because its contributors will have been overwhelmingly white. It matters not that the demographics of Europe until the last 50 years made that racial composition inevitable." As she notes, the non-European cultural expressions of Asia, Africa, Indonesia and Latin America "have been as racially monolithic, without falling afoul of the diversity monitors. Only Western civilization is under attack for its traditional racial homogeneity." Progressive multiculturalists ignore history in the attempt to shield non-Western cultures, as if these cultures never engaged in the same "sins" as their European counterparts. Slavery, misogyny and oppression have occurred in just about every culture known to humankind, and it still occurring in many non-Western societies—Afghanistan as I write this, for example. The neo-Marxist ideology of oppressed vs. oppressor is the underlying rationale in all this.*

---

* The etymology of the word "slave" stems from "Slavic." In the ninth century the Arab Muslim pirates of northern Africa (the Barbary coast) enslaved more than one million Slavs.

Deborah Wong's findings that "Marxism is alive and well" in the academy, is the smoking gun here. A defining aspect of Marxism is to rid society of supremacy and establish a more fair and equitable culture. The reality in Marxist regimes, however, is that a new supremacist regime emerges that merely supplants the old regime. At heart in the drive of equality, there is the overt attempt to use the power of government via "the extreme of legal frames," (Aleksandr Solzhenitsyn's term) to compel obsequious adherence to state mandates. Volition becomes the victim in these authoritarian modalities. Now, however, it's not only governmental power that is being sought to achieve equity, but also social outrage and vituperative accusations via social media and the mainstream media are doing the bidding for these cultural tyrants. The pressure to comport with "wokeness" is overwhelming. University of Columbia professor of linguistics and English comparative literature John McWhorter revealed that he receives phone calls from colleagues on a daily basis (an "epidemic" as he put it) who tell of harrowing cancel-culture experiences and threats of job termination if they stray from the "woke" narrative *du jour*.

What is especially disheartening in MacDonald's reportage is how many esteemed artists in the field—conductors, performers and company managers—refused to comment or ignored requests to weigh in on the issue. One music educator admitted that there was a danger in the "suicide pact" that was being forged, saying, "If conservatories start admitting by race and ethnicity, close them down. As soon as standards are modified, the game is over. Mediocrity is like carbon monoxide: you can't see it or smell it, but one day you're dead."[18] I disagree somewhat with this evaluation because mediocrity in music is noticeable, and once it becomes normalized, who will pay steep prices to attend an orchestra concert (or a movie, Broadway show, or rock concert) when the quality is compromised? As noted previously, arts organizations are already facing severe financial circumstances, therefore, offering up a mediocre product in the name of diversity only exacerbates their financial dilemma. Market forces are real and those who detest capitalism face the unwelcome truth that without a quality product the public simply won't buy-in. Furthermore, ideology has a limited market.* Arts organizations and careers will simply die away and the pain will be real and lasting.

MacDonald notes too, that the so-called "sacralizing" of the concert-going experience in the symphony orchestra realm was not the doing of the smug, upper-class aristocrats of the seventeenth and eighteenth centuries, but rather the more "diverse" audiences of the nineteenth century.

> The present-day scourges impugn concert protocols as a classist means of excluding a "diverse" audience. But it was the bearers of inherited privilege during the ancien régime who treated music as a mere backdrop to be gambled and flirted through. The non-aristocratic classes started attending to music with silent devotion, as it became ever more complex and demanding.[19]

This observation points to how classical music satiated the spiritual longings of people who sought to be elevated through a deeper experience of heart and intellect (Sting's acknowledgment) rather than experiencing music as an entertaining *divertissement*. Some lovers of music are intrigued and attracted to the "more complex and demanding" aspects of classical music. Some not. Some jazz aficionados prefer Charlie Parker's style rather than the free jazz of Albert Ayler. Miles Davis was criticized by jazz purists for his album *Bitches Brew* (1970) for venturing into the realm of pop music by using electronic instruments and studio effects. *De gustibus non est disputandum*; In matters of taste there can be no dispute. Citing a Latin axiom may be a bit too highbrow for some (a display of superiority?), so let's go with "different strokes for different folks."† Duke Ellington also had something to say about all this when he averred:

> There are simply two kinds of music, good music and the other kind. Classical writers may venture into classical territory, but the only yardstick by which the result should be judged is simply that of how it sounds. If it sounds good it's successful; if it doesn't it has failed." [20]

---

* Television ratings for the Tokyo Olympic Games were abysmally low. Many have speculated that the politicization of sports had a great deal to do with the downturn in ratings.

† The axiom, "different strokes for different folks" was made popular in 1968 by the soul/funk band Sly and the Family Stone in their song *Everyday People*.

Ellington's assessment may be too simplistic for some, but we should remember that he ventured into the realm of classical music by way of several orchestral suites, including a classical-jazz version of Tchaikovsky's *The Nutcracker* ballet that he recorded in 1960.* In 1965 he began composing large-scale works for his jazz orchestra for several *Sacred Concerts* that jazz historian Gary Giddins characterized as "bringing the Cotton Club revue to the church."[21] Ellington considered these concerts in San Francisco (1965), New York (1968) and London (1973) to be among the most important performances of his career. The London performance featured the John Alldis Choir, one of the United Kingdom's most distinguished vocal ensembles. Ellington's embrace of liturgical leitmotifs in quasi-symphonic musical forms and a classical choir must surely create cognitive dissonances for the purveyors of anti-European and anti-classical music, music that is the direct progeny of Christian faith. Because Marxism, neo-Marxism, cultural Marxism—whatever we might call it—have distinct aversions for the "false consciousness" of religion, we shouldn't be shocked at the attempts to vilify traditions that are born of such.

The attempts to take down art and family by the progressive left are intertwined. The idea that governmental elites (experts) are best suited to solve socio-culture problems, especially inequality, is paramount in the mindset of progressives, thus religious belief and family values are considered mitigating factors in that pursuit. However, the idea of experts, commonly referred to as "elites," shouldn't be dismissed out of hand, as if expertise in medicine, law, politics, sports and music is an attribute that isn't desirable, sought after and admired. In this respect, meritocracy matters. With regard to political or socio-cultural concerns, such as social justice and equality, the overriding issue is whether or not experts have the proper understanding of a particular problem in order to fashion the most efficacious solutions. It is my contention that racism has been a scourge on the human condition for thousands of years, and as such, it is not endemic to a particular culture, but has been a universal

* The jazz interpretation of Tchaikovsky's *The Nutcracker* ballet score was a collaboration between Ellington and his long-time arranger, Billy Strayhorn. It was Strayhorn who conceived the idea. Ellington also composed several other orchestral suites including *Three Black Kings*, a piece that I conducted with the New York City Symphony at the Apollo Theater in 1990 as part of a Black History Month concert.

proclivity of humankind's "fallen nature." Accordingly, experts who wish to create conditions for equality and fairness in the attempt to mitigate injustices should avoid the falling into the trap of an ideological canard that perpetuates more acrimony, discontent and segregation by way of the oppressor vs. oppressed paradigm.

The current iteration of neo-Marxist thought that is being pushed by certain political "elites," requires pushback precisely because it doesn't deal with root causes. Though many progressives reject religious-based solutions, it may be that by examining our "fallen" tendencies through the prism of religious belief, that we can ascertain the root causes of racial strife, economic disparity and the lack of respect for "the other." Once we identify the causes we can better inculcate future generations in the ways to remedy such. As the old song by Crosby, Stills and Nash goes, "Teach your children well."

MacDonald argues that "home transmission" may be the best option in the hopes of developing a scenario whereby black children might explore classical music as a career option, or a pleasurable *divertissement*. But as MacDonald notes:

> The antiracism advocates have said little about that imperative, however. It's easier to extract racial quotas from compliant organizations than it is to engineer a change as profound as exposing students to a vanishing musical aesthetic. Packing off every opera and orchestra administrator to implicit bias training will not produce a single competitively qualified black musician. Nor will potential students be inclined to pick up the violin after learning that its repertoire belongs to a white supremacist tradition. But more power is to be gained by pushing the racism line than by pursuing the unlikely rebirth of public school music training. So the search has been on to find racial scapegoats.[22]

Again, the pursuit of power is a driving force behind the forced mandates that progressives like Ewell seem to be aiming for in their quest for justice and equality. Government coercion is not the way forward. We might all agree that justice and equality are worthy goals, but how best to achieve those goals remains our essential trial. The canard that classical music—or the pursuit of excellence—is essentially racist, and thus thwarts our efforts in these matters, should be debunked as spurious and unhelpful, precisely because "the right to choose" is sacrosanct. Not all Blacks, Asians, Latinos, or even Caucasians, choose classical music as their preferred musical contentment. Respecting musical choices, whether jazz, gospel, pop, rock, r&b, folk or world music, ought to be considered an expression of democratic pluralism. "Different strokes for different folks" is not a bad axiom to live by in matters of musical choice.

Recommended Recordings

Duke Ellington, Billy Strayhorn, P.I. Tchaikovsky: *The Nutcracker Suite*

Leontyne Price: *Leontyne Price at the* Met, The Metropolitan Opera

Neilsen: Clarinet Concerto, Anthony McGill, clarinet, New York Philharmonic

Haydn: Trumpet Concerto, Wynton Marsalis, trumpet

Grace Bumbry: *The Art of Grace Bumbry* (DG)

Mozart: *Exsultate, jubilate*, Orchestra of St. Luke's, Kathleen Battle, soprano

Mahler: Symphony No. 7, Gustavo Dudamel, Simon Bolivar Symphony Orchestra

Bach: *Goldberg Variations*, Charles Rosen, piano

Miles Davis: *Bitches Brew*

Ky-Mani Marley: *Many More Roads*

Geoffery Oreyama: *Exile*

Dowland: *Come Again*, Sting, Lute

Ellington: *Three Black Kings*, Maurice Peress, American Composers Orchestra

Schwantner: *New Morning for the World*, William Warfield, narrator

Shostakovich: Symphony No. 5, James DePreist, Helsinki Philharmonic Orchestra

Feldman: *Coptic Light*, Michael Morgan, Deutsches Symphonie, Orchester Berlin

Ellington*: Sacred Concerts:* The Duke Ellington Centennial Edition: The Complete RCA Victor Recordings (1927-1973) collection

Endnotes

1   Frederick Douglass, *Great Speeches by Frederick Douglass,* edited by James Daley (Mineola, NY: Dover Publications, Inc., 2013), p. 50.

2   Duke Ellington, *The Duke Ellington Reader*, edited by Mark Tucker (New York-Oxford: Oxford University Press, 1993). p. 326.

3   George Bernard Shaw, *Don Juan in Hell* (New York: Dodd, Meade & Company, 1952), p. 7.

4   Kyle MacMillan, "Anthony McGill determined to add voices to the classical music narrative," experience.cso.org., July 15, 2021, https://experience.cso.org/article/4340/anthony-mcgill-determined-to-add-voices-to-th.

5   Richard Dare, "The Awfulness of Classical Music Explained," *Huffington Post*, May 29, 2012, updated December 6, 2017.

6   Philip Kennicott, "America's Orchestras are in Crisis: How an effort to popularize classical music undermines what makes it great," *The New Republic*, August 26, 2013.

7   Edward Rothstein: "Roll Over Beethoven: The New Multiculturalism and Its Mistakes," *The New Republic*, August 4, 1991.

8   Deborah Wong, "Ethnomusicology and Difference," cited in *Following the Elephant: Ethnomusicologist Contemplate their Discipline*, edited by Bruno Nettl, (Champaign, Il: University of Illinois Press, 2016).

9   Gregory F. Barz and Timothy J. Cooley, *Shadows in the Field: New Perspectives for Fieldwork in Ethnomusicology*, Second Edition (Oxford-New York: Oxford University Press, 2008), p. 67.

10   Bruno Nettl, *Following the Elephant: Ethnomusicologist Contemplate their Discipline*, edited by Bruno Nettl, (Champaign, Il: University of Illinois Press, 2016.)

11   Ibid., Frederick Douglass, *Great Speeches by Frederick Douglass*, p. 50.

12   Heather MacDonald, "Classical Music's Suicide Pact," (Part 1), *City Journal*, Summer, 2021.

13   Julian Johnson: *Who Needs Classical Music? Cultural Choice and Musical Value* (Oxford-New York: Oxford University Press, 2002), p. 26.

14   Sting, "A Rock Star in Winter," interview by Ben Finane, *Listen*, November/December 2009, https://www.listenmusicculture.com/interviews/sting-interview.

15   Charles Rosen, Review: "The Oxford History of Music," by Richard Taruskin, *New York Review of Books*, February 23, 2006.

16   MacDonald, "Classical Music's Suicide Pact," (Part 1).

17   Charles Rosen, "Multicultural Correctness," reply to Ralph P. Locke, *New York Review of Books*, January 16, 2003.

18   Heather MacDonald, "Classical Music's Suicide Pact," (Part 2), *City Journal*, Summer, 2021.

19   Ibid.

20   Duke Ellington, *The Duke Ellington Reader*, p. 50.

21   Gary Giddins, *Visions of Jazz, the First Century* (Oxford-New York: Oxford University Press, 1998), p. 491.

22   MacDonald, "Classical Music's Suicide Pact," (Part 1).

42

Cultivating Multiculturalism

Indignation is the soul's defense against the wound of doubt about its own;
it reorders the cosmos to support the justice of its cause. It justifies putting
Socrates to death.[1]
Allan Bloom

In the aftermath of the 2020 presidential election, there was a spate of articles, essays and blog posts that focused on the "whiteness" of America and the need for greater diversity in American culture. The importance of diversity, equity and inclusion (DEI) was seemingly everywhere. Of particular interest to me was the interest in the racial demographics of American symphony orchestras, opera companies and ballet troupes. To be sure, there has been a preponderance of Caucasians in orchestras, ballet troupes and opera companies in Europe and the United States. After all, classical music and ballet are artistic inventions of European culture. I've conducted concerts with orchestras and ensembles in Taiwan, South Korea, Viet Nam, Guatemala, Brazil, and Paraguay and there were no Caucasians in those ensembles. Moreover, the most distinguished youth orchestra initiative in the world since 1980 has been the Venezuelan youth orchestra project known as *El sistema.* It should be noted that in addition to the orchestras I've conducted in Taiwan, Korea and Viet Nam, there are fine orchestras and talented opera singers and virtuoso instrumentalists from Japan, China, Turkey and Malaysia. A quick perusal of the rosters of American symphony orchestras reveals a healthy number of Asians in their ranks. Alumni of *El sistema* are now members of orchestras throughout the world.

It may be a little-known fact, but going back several decades when major American orchestras hold auditions to fill job openings, the applicants play behind screens, thus the jury who assesses the abilities of the applicants have no idea about the race, ethnicity, gender or age of those auditioning. Women applicants are told not to wear high heels to the auditions so as not to tip off the jury about the gender of the musician in question. This particular process was to ensure that there would be no extra-musical bias in the audition process. The instrumentalist's musicianship was all that mattered in the selection process.

The original intent of multiculturalism was seen as a way to create an environment conducive to mutual respect of various cultures and their traditions. However, in the 1980s multiculturalists began to denigrate Western culture in the pursuit of fairness and justice and this penchant to take Western culture down a peg now lies at the heart of the multicultural agenda. A truly pluralistic solution would be to honor and respect all cultural expressions for their intrinsic value. Postmodern multiculturalists fail to acknowledge that the Western musical tradition has a long history of being open to cultures outside of itself. As Roger Scruton observes, artistic tradition "is a constantly evolving system of conventions, allusions, cross-references and shared expectations," thus various musical components "can be inherited and invented and the inheritance is part of what makes invention possible. This speaks to the West's valuing "the other" by way of assimilation and this remains an enduring legacy of the Western democratic experiment. Regrettably, this is now seen in a negative light and is considered a form of "cultural appropriation."

---

* According to its website, the El sistema project has trained over 700,000 young musicians since its founding in 1975 and now boasts of over 400 music centers internationally.

Samuel P. Huntington, in his ruminations concerning the so-called "clash of civilizations," considers assimilation to be problematic due to the acute differences between various cultural spheres. This is especially true when discussing culture from a geopolitical perspective. Huntington avers; "The survival of the West depends on Americans reaffirming their Western identity and Westerners accepting their civilization as unique [and] not universal and uniting to and preserve it against the challenges from non-Western societies." This would seem to be at odds with the neo-Conservative attitude that purports that the democratization of all cultures is a universally desired outcome. To the Western mind, it is hard to imagine that non-Western cultures wouldn't embrace the civil liberties that are cherished in the West. Consider the view of Scruton who suggests that our views of democracy have universal currency and need not be limited to parochialism. He instead subscribes to a universal vision of democracy stating that:

> We are not, like Spengler, describing some localized and time-bound fragment of human history. We are describing a project, which grew from the great events in the Mediterranean basin two millennia ago. This project can endure ... only if it can win a place in our hearts.

Christian values, according to Scruton, provided the moral and ethical conviction that is indispensable in order for the grand vision of constitutional democracy to flourish. It is this faith conviction and "the shared meanings conveyed to us by our culture—meanings conveyed equally to the one who believes and the one who doubts," that makes culture so important for us. In this context, culture becomes "the repository ... of moral knowledge." But can there be a transmission of these "shared meanings" across such acutely diverse religious and cultural spheres in a harmonious fashion? More importantly, do they find common currency among such disparate faith traditions? Though Scruton seems optimistic, Huntington is not convinced that this can, or should happen.

Because music, especially liturgical music born of the Christian faith, has been a significant aspect of Western culture, it might be a vehicle to facilitate greater respect and understanding between Western and non-Western cultural spheres. Because classical music has been embraced in Asian and Latin cultures, as well as Turkey and Egypt, there is reason to believe it could be an effective facilitator in this regard. Though Latin America has a long history with Christian idealism, Asian and Middle-Eastern countries do not. Yet many non-Western countries have found value and enjoyment in the Western classical music tradition.

Various religious traditions may indeed have similarities, but as the violence born of Islamic extremism grows exponentially, it is clear that "shared meanings" and shared values between the Judeo-Christian tradition and radical Islam have been commandeered by those with perfidious intentions. Consequently, finding common ground has been challenging. After the Taliban took control of Afghanistan in August of 2021, one of its first orders of business was to put prohibitions on music. Historically, Islam has had misgivings about music due to its sensual and possibly corrupting influences. Anyone familiar with St. Augustine or Roman philosopher Boëthius and their examinations of music, understands that they were fully aware of music's ability to either ennoble or corrupt individuals and society. Still, personal choice is an essential aspect in the pursuit of dignity and respect for all people.

Pluralism

David Brooks, writing in the *New York Times*, cautions that the drama in the Middle East and elsewhere, should not be viewed as a geopolitical chessboard on which the West can impose its will. Brooks views the malaise as "a generational drama … a contest between the forces of jihadism and the forces of pluralism." Brooks correctly asserts that though we can neither predict nor direct the outcome, we can, "promote pluralism—steadily, consistently, simply" by supporting those who share the concepts of pluralism and civil liberties. It would seem that advocating for pluralism would be in the interests of those who value multiculturalism. Regrettably, this has not always been the case.

The controversy over Brandeis University reneging on its offer to confer an honorary degree to woman's rights advocate Ayaan Hirsi Ali is yet another example of the misguided multiculturalism to silence critics of Islam by using the false premise of religious intolerance; a curious, if not disingenuous claim considering that Ali is a vociferous advocate of fairness and justice for women, a sacred cow of academic elites and progressives. We shouldn't forget that Ali was a collaborator on Theo van Gogh's film, *Submission*, which dealt with the subjects of female genital mutilation in African cultures and the abusive treatment of women in Muslim countries. Mr. van Gogh was murdered by a Dutch Muslim in 2004 in an apparent retaliation for the film.

Is any critique of any religious-based perfidiousness *de facto* bigotry? I think not, but those who advocate Herbert Marcuse's precept of "repressive intolerance" might think otherwise. Repressive tolerance, according to Marcuse (who taught a Brandeis from 1958 to 1965), encourages expressions of intolerance for anything that runs counter to the progressive worldview and contributes to maintaining the status quo—socially, economically, politically and culturally. Repressive tolerance has become the norm on many liberal arts campuses that preach diversity and openness, yet shun, defenestrate and prohibit those who advocate countervailing views to progressive orthodoxy. The demonstrations in Chicago against Donald Trump during the 2016 election campaign were a prime example of this perfidy. "Cancel culture" of this sort is anathema to democracy and pluralism.

Let's not equivocate. This is the stuff of totalitarianism, re-education camps, a threat to civil liberties and sadly, very much the psyche of the leftist elites throughout academia. It is advocacy for the prohibition of free speech and freedom of peaceful assembly. We may decry double standards or trade-offs in our pursuit of social justice, but in a pluralistic society there exists an intrinsic paradox that we can either choose to accept or reject.*

A pluralistic society can, and does, empower people with selfish and oligarchic intentions. However, in a republic we have laws, a judiciary and enforcement procedures that act as hedges against human proclivities

---

* In his 1965 essay, "Repressive Tolerance," Marcuse states: "Impartiality to the utmost, equal treatment of competing and conflicting issues is indeed a basic requirement for decision-making in the democratic process—it is an equally basic requirement for defining the limits of tolerance." In the same essay he contradicts his call for "equal treatment," and "impartiality" saying: "Liberating tolerance, then, would mean intolerance against movements from the Right and toleration of movements from the Left. As to the scope of this tolerance and intolerance: ... it would extend to the stage of action as well as of discussion and propaganda, of deed as well as of word."

that are not in the best interests of the greater community. Not everyone acts criminally, but fallen human nature necessitates laws and law enforcement within a constitutional republic. The debate regarding freedom and democracy dates back to Plato and *The Republic*. Indignation towards those who

Offering a disparate perspective to Marcuse, Austrian-British philosopher Karl Popper would go as far as to say:

> We should therefore claim, in the name of tolerance, the right not to tolerate the intolerant. We should claim that any movement preaching intolerance places itself outside the law, and we should consider incitement to intolerance and persecution as criminal, in the same way as we should consider incitement to murder, or to kidnapping, or to the revival of the slave trade, as criminal.

Former American ambassador to the United Nations, Jeane Kirkpatrick, averred that it generally takes several generations to acquire the "necessary disciplines and habits" for the realization of a truly democratic and pluralistic society. The American republic is a relatively young enterprise when compared to most other social/political paradigms, and one that could easily be characterized as a work in progress. That said, the tradition of acceptance and assimilation in the United States is far ahead of the acceptance curve on a number of fronts.

As a society we have made significant strides in the pursuit of respecting and accepting "the other." Goethe's supposition that mere tolerance of the "the other" is not enough in creating conditions for unity seems inherently correct. For Goethe, acceptance needed to be a part of the assimilation process. Acceptance, however, should not result in the across-the-board rejection or disrespect of the very traditions, and customs that define a particular cultural sphere. Multiculturalism needs to be a two-way, or perhaps more accurately, a multi-way street.

Graeme Wood points out in his perspicacious essay on rise of ISIS in *The Atlantic* (March 2015) that fundamentalist Muslims (of which ISIS considers itself), view any fraternizing with non-believers—politically, culturally, economically—as a betrayal of the tenets of the Islamic faith. Hamas' lobbying for a seat at the United Nations, for instance, is seen by

ISIS fundamentalists as yet another sell out to Western-based diplomatic processes. The U.N. does not represent Allah's wishes for the caliphate, therefore submitting to its charter and/or its representatives is the stuff of apostasy. This type of fundamentalism is fundamentally at odds with democratic processes as well as seeking diplomatic solutions in order to counter religious triumphalism.

Daniel Philpott of the Kroc Institute for International Peace Studies optimistically suggests in his recent book, *Just and Unjust Peace: An Ethic of Political Reconciliation*, acceptance and reconciliation are possible when we choose to seek the commonalities among various cultures and faith traditions. This was a contention in the concluding pages of Huntington's book as well. Like maestro Daniel Barenboim, Dr. Philpott contends that painful listening to the other "is required to build the necessary trust that can allow for reconciliation to occur." He contends that this kind of "soulcraft" must be part of any equation in the attempt to ameliorate historical resentments.

As daunting and difficult as it may be, "addressing the full range of wounds" is essential in "the restoration of the right relationship." Philpott, however, is leery that any cultural/religious reconciliation can be successfully accommodated via political process, stating that when government attempts to "steer selves away from such emotions as anger, resentment and fear, and promote forgiveness, repentance and healing," it engages in form of "illicit soulcraft." Philpott offers this perspective:

> Put more precisely, do governmental efforts to promote transformations of emotions and judgments unjustly stomp on values like autonomy, pluralism, and democratic deliberation that the liberal critics of reconciliation stress? The most direct response to these critics is that the ethic at hand, while it overlaps with the liberal tradition of thought, does not share all of liberalisms commitments.

History instructs that "the state" hasn't always been the best arbiter or protector of human rights. Nor can the "the state" legislate morality. Philcott correctly asserts that the issue of human rights is a "global ethic" and one that "seeks consensus from Judaism, Christianity, Islam and other traditions, such as Confucianism or tribal cultures, that might potentially join a consensus on it." Karen Armstrong reminds us, according the early prescriptions of Islam, neither Jews nor Christians were invited or required to join the new religion of Islam. Yet the Qur'an instructed Muslims "that they must treat the *ahl-al-kitah*, 'people of an earlier revelation' with respect and courtesy. The Qur'an instructs:

> Do not argue with the followers of earlier revelation otherwise that in the most likely manner—unless it be such of them as are bent on evildoing— and say: "We believe in that which has been revealed to us from on high, as well as that which has been bestowed upon you; for our God and your God is one and the same, and it is unto him that we all surrender ourselves.

As it is with any doctrine, it's always about living up to the ideals of said doctrine, in other words, "walking the walk." Multiculturalism in the West has often betrayed its own commitment to a liberal society where pluralism and diversity are celebrated. Multiculturalism too often sinks into politically correct narrow-mindedness and then seeks legal remedies as a way to compel a specific behavior thereby violating the rights of those who might have differing viewpoints. This too can be construed as an example of "illicit soulcraft."

Again, it seems to be a question of finding commonality and shared values that can be the basis for a meaningful dialogue and social action. Perhaps it is too much to ask that the fundamentalists of any religious sphere to accelerate the process of moderation in the hopes creating a culture of peace. However, it would seem that in order to avoid the cultural clashes that are causing the convolutions that we are now witnessing, choosing to proceed down the path of moderation is our best option—perhaps our only option. Though fundamentalists will sniff creeping syncretism, the consequences of not seeking a balanced perspective might doom us all. Allan Bloom's observation that, "Indignation is the soul's defense against the wound of doubt about its own," results in the lack of self-reflection that is necessary in examining our soul—individually and collectively—in the process of trying to attain moral clarity.

There is no guarantee that the proverbial "moral arc of the universe" will inevitably bring is to a better place without taking responsibility as free and moral individuals. As Popper asserts:

Democracy and freedom do not guarantee the millennium. No, we do not choose political freedom because it promises us this or that. We choose it because it makes possible the only dignified form of human coexistence, the only form in which we can be fully responsible for ourselves. Whether we realize its possibilities depends on all kinds of things—and above all on ourselves.

Truer words have rarely been spoken. For those of us who have the good fortune of living in a free and open society, our trial will be how best to use our freedoms, imagination and talent in the most intelligent and humanitarian fashion. Discovering and agreeing upon what moral precepts are best suited to that goal remains our quest. F.A. Hayek, referencing the situation prior to World War II, opined that it was "lamentable" that democracies "had shown an inner insecurity and uncertainty ... about their own ideals and the nature of the difference which separated them from the enemy." This confusion, according to Hayek, contributed to a false sense of security among leaders in the democratic world because they mistakenly believed that many of the aims of Hitler's National Socialist Party were sincere and in accord with their own. This misreading of intentions proved catastrophic.

Attaining moral clarity requires that our emotions be examined in the context of the common good. Baruch Spinoza's assertion that peace is not merely the absence of conflict is rooted in the idea that citizens in a particular commonwealth *ought* to identify and pursue the values that could create a moral and ethical culture in which all citizens could benefit. Multiculturalism that respects the rights and dignity of "the other" and avoids indignation should be informed by principles that comport with tenets of that which is virtuous and godly.

References

1   Allan Bloom, *The Closing of the American Mind* (New York: Simon & Schuster, 1987), p. 71

2   Roger Scruton, *The Roger Scruton Reader* (London-New York: Continuum International Publishing Group, 2009), p. 147.

3   Samuel P. Huntington, *The Clash of Civilizations and the Remaking of World Order* (New York: Touchstone, 1997), pp. 20-21.

4   Roger Scruton, *Culture Counts: Faith and Feeling in a World Besieged* (New York: Encounter Books, 2007), p. vii.

5   Ibid., p. ix.

6   David Brooks, "Being Who We Are," *New York Times*, January 30, 2015.

7   Karl Popper, *The Open Society and Its Enemies* (Princeton, NJ: Princeton University Press, 1945), p. 581.

8   Daniel Philpott, *Just and Unjust Peace: An Ethic of Political Reconciliation* (Oxford-New York: University Press, 2012), p. 84.

9   Qur'an 29:46, translated by Muhammad Asad, *The Message of the Qur'an*, Gibraltar, 1980, as cited by Karen Armstrong in *The Great Transformation: The Beginning of Our Religious Traditions* (New York: Random House, 2006), p. 462.

10 Karl Popper, *All Life Is Problem Solving: On Freedom*, translated by Patrick Camiller (New York: Routledge, 2001), p. 92.

11 F.A. Hayek, *The Road to Serfdom*, edited by Bruce Caldwell (Chicago, IL: The University of Chicago Press, 2007), p. 60.

43

Making Distinctions

> *The ideal of humanity on which we have based our greatest*
> *religious, ethical, philosophical and political thinking is not defined*
> *by our outward, material surface but by our capacity*
> *to exceed the limits of our material existence.*
> *Great art expresses this ideal in every work. In rejecting it*
> *to embrace the ideal of a blank and depthless surface*
> *embodied in contemporary culture, we reject the ideal*
> *of humanity and instead embrace a simulacrum---*
> *a synthetic and hollow substitute.* [1]
> Julian Johnson

Julian Johnson, professor of music at Royal Holloway University of London, created a bit of a firestorm when he published his book, *Who Needs Classical Music?: Cultural Choice and Musical Value* in 2002. Richard Taruskin was especially critical of Johnson's perspectives. I found Johnson's book to be insightful, but I understood why he ruffled some feathers given the socio-cultural climate that has been evolving in academia and the arts in recent decades, especially regarding the issues of multiculturalism, political correctness and diversity.

Johnson makes an interesting observation concerning the issue of judgment: "To be discriminating used to mean to be capable of exercising judgment—to be wise, in fact." In our increasingly politically correct society, making critical distinctions in matters of art and creativity are often viewed as hindrances in attaining genuine democratic ideals. Instead, we find ourselves in what Johnson calls a "pseudo-democracy;" a situation where it is no different "to discriminate against" than to "discriminate between." Not seeing the difference between things is in a sense, anti-pluralistic. Johnson writes:

> And that pseudo-democracy is built not on mutual respect, but on lack of respect for one another and even for ourselves. Because discrimination (being aware of the difference between things) is a corollary of our fundamental insistence on our own individuality and that of others, recognition of differences is a confirmation of human individuality, of the inviolable identity of every one of us.[2]

This is akin to Edward Rothstein's observation regarding the refusal to make distinctions within a particular cultural sphere for fear of offending. Capitulating to the notion that making distinctions is discriminatory in a pejorative sense undermines any attempt at achieving balanced perspectives when attempting to assess art and music, for many things can be demonstrated as being objective in the art of music. Even if a great deal of what goes into aesthetic judgment and criticism is primarily subjective, it is the attempt to apply objective standards which makes any sort of arrival at a judgment meaningful.

Immanuel Kant's *Critique of Judgment* regarding aesthetics speaks to the issue of how our imagination informs our tastes in the process of "discriminating and estimating," yet he proffered that there is a logical, even empirical aspect in assessing art objects (which he termed "disinterestedness"), especially music, which he considered "the most pleasurable of the arts." If assessing art becomes largely a matter of personal opinion, then any art form can be rendered to be something much less powerful and important than it is. In a "pseudo-democratic" condition where *faux* egalitarianism rules the day, we are confronted with the condition where everything could be considered great art, or conversely, nothing rises to the level of greatness.

In an eleven thousand-word essay published in *The New Republic* titled, "The Musical Mystique," Richard Taruskin castigated Julian Johnson for what he considers to be a specious and immoral comparison of "high art" and popular culture.* One of the primary reasons for Taruskin's opprobrium is Johnson's contention that classical music "functions" as art rather than merely entertainment, and as such, we can become better people for preferring high art to pop culture. "To cast esthetic preferences as moral or ethical choices at the dawn of the twenty-first century," Taruskin bristles, "is an obscenity." He considers this type of thinking to be an expression of sanctimonious vainglory and moral exhibitionism. (Full disclosure: I have composed for, and have performed in symphony orchestras, rock bands, jazz combos, hip-hop and gospel ensembles. I believe that I have a certain degree of egalitarian "cred."

Having read Johnson's book (and several of Taruskin's), I'm not fully in agreement with this particular critique. As often in the case, the highbrow vs. lowbrow comparison of music often produces fire and ire in the context of egalitarian concerns, especially regarding the sacralizing of art. Taruskin asks the not-so-rhetorical question: Can classical music be defended without "recourse to pious tommyrot, double standards, false dichotomies, smug nostalgia, utopian delusions, social snobbery, tautology, hypocrisy, trivialization, pretense, innuendo, reactionary invective, or imperial haberdashery?"[3] Not surprisingly, his answer is "no." Citing San Francisco's classical radio station KDFC's program known as "Island of Sanity," Taruskin concedes that this type of advertising resonates with a certain demographic that prefers classical music for that particular contentment. I'm not sure what he would think of WXQR's (New York City's only surviving classical radio station) advertising slogan: "Classical music elevates everything." It would seem that WQXR is doubling down on the idea that there is something to be gained or desired by listening to classical music. Was this merely a marketing ploy to attract listeners (and ad dollars) by making listeners feel good about their musical tastes? Perhaps.

---

* Richard Taruskin's essay, "The Musical Mystique: Defending Classical Music Against Its Devotees" first appeared in *The New Republic* on October 21, 2007, and was subsequently included in his book, *The Dangers of Music and Other Anti-Utopian Essays*, published in 2009.

Any genre of music can potentially "elevate" our consciousness, and vice versa, yet Taruskin opines: "Before romanticism raised the stakes, the purpose of art was always described as that of 'pleasing.' All pretenses notwithstanding, other purposes, and especially Johnson's, are secondary."[4] "Always described as that of 'pleasing?'" J.S. Bach wouldn't necessarily agree with that assumption given his assertion that the purpose of music was to praise and glorify God and to recreate one's mind.

Even if the "purposes" that Johnson cites are, in Taruskin's estimation secondary, does that make them completely irrelevant—or immoral? On what basis are they immoral? Kant believed that art was "purposive" and in his estimation, aesthetics in art transcended utilitarian concerns. T.S. Eliot opined that art could provide a perception of order and purpose in life, as did Confucius. Artists in Confucius' time took the idea of order and relatedness vis-à-vis societal concerns very seriously. Pleasure *may* have been a subsidiary concern for them. In *The Republic,* Plato asserted that music wasn't merely a neutral amusement. It would seem that there is a bit of a double standard here. If one is going to argue that there is more to art than "esthetic" concerns, as Taruskin often does when he cites the "poietic fallacy," cannot the axiological aspects of art and music be a legitimate concern as well? If that disposition is a primary concern to certain individuals, so be it. That may be an incidence of "value pluralism" in which two seemingly contradictory purposes can be valid and have equal value. In a diverse society, people create, perform and listen to music for a variety of purposes, aesthetic pleasure being but one.

Bach certainly viewed the pleasurable aspect of music to be secondary to ecclesiastical concerns given that he believed that the ultimate purpose of music—specifically, figured bass—was a way to minister to the "glory of God." Yet I know many music lovers who find listening to Bach's music to be rather arduous and prefer music by composers whose pleasure is not so hard-won. Listening to Bach's *Musical Offering* with an analytical ear, for example, requires a certain discipline and focus for one to appreciate the intricacies of the composer's innovative techniques and his mastery of dissonance treatment. Listening to pop music, even the best of its kind rarely requires the same kind of listening attentiveness. Why is making that particular distinction invidious or untoward? In matters of architecture, is making the distinction that the Taj Mahal is a greater architectural achievement than the local Starbucks down the street an indication of elitism or smug snobbery? Is a great novel or poem different than a perfunctory news report about someone's lost pet?

In response to Taruskin's supposition that "the purpose of art was always described as that of 'pleasing,'" J.P.E. Harper-Scott (a colleague of Johnson at Royal Holloway) offered this rebuttal:

> 'Always' is a big word, and it suggests a historical blindness to the centuries of influential writing on music that made intellectual engagement with music one of the central and most basic responses to it ... Taruskin even defines 'pleasure' with such expansiveness that Johnson's project can easily be accommodated under headings such as "spiritual pleasures ... the pleasure of worthy accomplishment, of self-improvement, or self-possession and so on." On Taruskin's definition, then, Johnson is as much a pleasure-seeker as Taruskin, so why the grumbling?[5]

The answer, according to Harper-Scott, is that Taruskin believes that market forces are that which determine value in our contemporary culture. We buy what is pleasurable "having been taught what to desire" by the purveyors of mass culture. (This was Adorno's lament in his *Essays on Mass Culture*.) Other concerns—ideological, axiological, spiritual, for example—may "conflict with the needs of producers to extract profit from consumers," and that is seen as being at odds with the "purpose" of those in the business of music. This cost-benefit narrative vis-à-vis composers who are shielded from the vagaries of the marketplace (by way of tenured positions and incestuous commissioning procedures, e.g.) runs through a number of Taruskin's essays on modern art music and is a reason that he offers as to why serious art music has become marginalized or ignored by the general public.

In certain respects, Taruskin is not altogether wrong given the fact that a large segment of a particular "collective" (a term that he has ascribed to ticket-buyers who attend concerts) has refused to support music characterized by aesthetic properties of the Second Viennese School and the Darmstadt composers. Lack of "capital" often relegates certain art to the dustbin. Who, among the most prominent conductors, program the music of Milton Babbitt or Ralph Shapey? (And by the way, whatever happened to the Starland Vocal Band?) Market forces aside, there are those who prefer Beethoven, Bach and Tchaikovsky to Lou Reed, Toto or Queen.

But as Harper-Scott puts it: "On Taruskin's view, 'art' is … the preserve only of elites, entertainment the preserve of the rest of us. And rather than being composed of listeners and composers, the great mass of humanity is composed of consumers and producers, their ontologies fixed by their mediation through Capital."[6] Though there is some veracity in this perspective, it is in no way the entire picture. It is not *always* the case.

According to Johnson, "Elitism as willful, snobbish exclusivity stinks. It should be opposed and shown for what it is." Citing its "inflammatory" connotations, he argues that "elitism" can result in giving license to "anything carried out under its banner and thus becomes a dangerous form of political correctness."[7] And herein lies the real offense for Taruskin. Citing what he views as the flagrant disingenuousness of Johnson's assertions regarding "political correctness," he writes:

> "Distinct from" is a transparent euphemism for better than, and Johnson's recourse to euphemism betrays his guilty consciousness that his argument carries politically unacceptable baggage. He is arguing for privilege, not equality; and that is why his index predictably contains seven entries under "political correctness," the discredited euphemism through which privileged people have gone on the offensive in defense of their privileges.[8]

Political correctness a "discredited euphemism?" Discredited by whom exactly? Charles Rosen? Edward Rothstein? Camille Paglia? Roger Scruton? John McWhorter? Recall Rosen's citing the penchant for examining art according to decidedly politically correct conceits being an "absurd notion." Paglia considers the practice of assessing art according to some *a priori* politically correct abstraction to be "garbage." That said, it is *flagrantly disingenuousness* for Taruskin, a historian, not to take into account how the application of political correctness (the term has been attributed to Leon Trotsky) led to body counts in numbering in the tens of millions in the "utopian" experiments under communist regimes in Russia, Cuba, North Korea and China.

Johnson is correct in citing the dangers here. In political regimes where dissent from the party line could get you sent to a *gulag* or *laogai*, it was vitally important to be "politically correct." Those who might consider political correctness to be primarily a protection of privilege are clearly in bed with the far-left progressive socialists who now rail at anything that is the progeny of Western, Judeo-Christian, "patriarchic" culture. This is the *cri de coeur* of leftist activists. For the "anti-utopian" Taruskin to be so blithely dismissive of Johnson's concerns, and utterly obtuse regarding the bloody legacy of political correctness, is astonishing.

Alluding to Plato's perspectives on music, Roger Scruton avers that music can have "moral effects" and though "we don't forbid music idioms by law … we should remember that our laws are made by people with musical tastes," and, "in modern democracy … changes in musical culture go hand and hand with changes in law, since changes in law so often reflect pressures from the culture."[9] That might be a bit too "Republican" (in the Platonic sense) for some, but when we consider the social significance of folk and gospel music during the civil rights protests, or how rock music became a social force during Czechoslovakia's Velvet Revolution, the Cold War and the Viet Nam era, or Lady Gaga singing "Born This Way," we can easily see that music can and does affect the citizenry, including those who seek votes in to attain political power.

Scruton acknowledges that to criticize another's musical taste is an expression of judgment and any judgment can easily be construed as an imposition of one's views or values on another. But again, is this *always* the case? Sometimes it's just offering an opinion. We all do it and we're all polemicists in one way or another. Moreover, who can argue with a straight face that Scruton's assertion regarding art's effect on the law isn't spot-on? The United States government (via the FCC) used to implement decency laws in response to "inappropriate" content and language. No more. It's undeniable that pop culture has contributed a great deal to the liberalization of moral codes in the broadcast medium. The ongoing normalization of profanity can be directly attributed to its pervasive use in certain pop music genres.

Taruskin views Johnson's characterization of popular music as being shallow and preoccupied with "surface" concerns, being "one dimensional" and generally lacking in spiritual and intellectual profundity. He refutes the idea that listening to classical music can make one a better person. Art and the humanities often fail to "humanize," as evidenced by abhorrent behavior and attitudes of Wagner, Hitler, or any number of rock stars. Still, the potential for betterment via "aesthetic education" shouldn't be dismissed out of hand. One wonders if Taruskin might be in agreement with other, "tommyrot" PC-multiculturalist contentions that claim, for instance, that Bach really wasn't a genius but was merely characterized as such for political advantage and obtaining power by the elites in Europe, or that having the ability to read or notate music is a indication of privilege.

In his essay, Taruskin suggests that anyone who might agree with Johnson's disagreeable viewpoints should read Leo Tolstoy's short story, "Father Sergius." The implication here is that by reading literature that provides a moral lesson, those who are morally obtuse might be enlightened and perhaps be saved from their reprehensible selves. Is Taruskin suggesting that we read Tolstoy because "it's pleasurable," or rather that it might affect our consciousness in a moral fashion? Finding truth and insight in art has been considered a primary virtue of the humanities and it would seem that Taruskin's recommendation validates that claim. If, as Taruskin (and Allan Bloom) believes, that reading literature can be beneficial in the process of recreating one's mind and spirit, can the same be said of music as Bach alleged? If music, like literature, can be conscious altering, then we should acknowledge the potential benefits. Conversely, can certain art or music be anti-social or inhumane? Yes, it can. Regardless of genre, music can function in ways that are moral as well as aesthetic. Instead of a literary recommendation for Taruskin, I suggest he watch Isaac Stern's documentary film, *From Mao to Mozart.**

Looking back on another Taruskin essay that alludes to the problem of anti-Semitic references, "Only Time Will Cover the Taint," Taruskin states:

> As long as some music somewhere is considered tref [not kosher], we have not forgotten that music is a powerful form of persuasion that does work in the world, as serious art that possesses ethical force and exacts ethical responsibilities.[10]

Well yes, ethical responsibilities matter. Some people might *enjoy* classical music because, in their opinion, it moralizes and raises their consciences. I believe that Johnson's argument is more nuanced than Taruskin seems willing

---

* Isaac Stern's documentary film *From Mao to Mozart: Isaac Stern in China* won the Academy Award for "Best Documentary Film" in 1981. The film chronicles Stern's visit to China in 1979, just three years after the end of Mao Zedong's Cultural Revolution. The film includes Stern giving masterclasses to young Chinese musicians as well as presenting concerts and recitals. The film also features first-hand accounts about how those who violated governmental dictums were subjected to imaginable harassment, torture and death for being politically incorrect.

to concede, for there are a number of reasons why people compose and listen to music, including to be entertained, to be put into a different mood, to be inspired, to attain a devotional state, to tap into a higher (or lower) consciousness, for example. Augustine and Luther considered music to have a similar purpose as prayer; a way to connect to God and find truth, "a sermon in sound," as Luther described it. Many ascribe to that notion, yet Luther had anti-Semitic attitudes.

That said, I don't subscribe to the notion articulated by Johnson, David Tame and others who assert that there is *no* redeeming value in the sphere of pop culture. As mentioned previously, many examples of socially and politically relevant pop music belie that particular contention. On the other hand, it's hard to argue with Adorno or Johnson that there has been a concerted effort on the part of the advertising industry to fetter consciousness in the attempt to "condition" the public into a lowest-common-denominator mindset in the attempt to market music (or anything) to a larger demographic. Even a cursory look at the pop industry reveals that the more sophisticated and intelligent pop artists don't sell as well as their less sophisticated counterparts. The pop music industry is just that—an industry, one driven almost exclusively by bottom-line concerns. It is silly to suggest, as Johnson does, that all pop music fails the test of time and becomes "the object of derision in a matter of years."[11] There is a great deal of classical music that has failed in that regard as well. How many composers were working in the courts and in the churches in the time of Mozart and Haydn whose music has not survived in any measurable way? Hundreds? Thousands? Yet it's quite possible that the music of a relatively obscure composer such as Antonio Cartellieri, a contemporary of Haydn, provided spiritual nourishment, pleasure and inspiration to those who encountered it.

Jazz historian and political commentator Stanley Crouch has been especially critical of the "clownish" and unenlightened attitudes of those in the hip-hop realm that views anything of an intellectual bent as being the product of an elitist culture and an affront to black "authenticity." His scorn for this type of thinking is warranted because hip-hop often perpetuates the worst kind of stereotyping that has become pervasive in urban society. *Essence* magazine's "Take Back the Music" initiative was a response to the pernicious effects of rap and hip-hop. Crouch, Oprah Winfrey, Thomas Chatterton Williams,

Thomas Sowell, Anthony B. Bradley, C. Deloris Tucker and other prominent black Americans have forcefully spoken out about the deleterious effects of certain Rap music and the culture it glorifies as an expression of authenticity. They unequivocally assert that by listening to a specific type of music, one can be prone to anti-social and inhumane behavior, especially when market forces are involved and inhumane behavior is aggressively marketed as being "cool," "hip" and "off the hook." In the face of the evidence before us, those condemnations are not entirely without merit. The celebrity industrial complex has power and brazenly uses it to promote values it considers morally acceptable in the pursuit of profit.

Were Crouch, Tucker and the editors at *Essence* guilty of "utopian delusions" or "social snobbery" for not placing the "pleasurable" aspect of music at the forefront of their listening experiences? If so, why? If not, why not? I know a few people who consider the free jazz of Albert Ayler to be anti-social and self-absorbed.* Are people who don't find pleasure in classical music (tonal or atonal), free jazz or gangster rap guilty of bigotry and intolerance? What about those who enjoy the music of Chopin but consider the music of Mahler or Carter incommodious? Taruskin's pleading on the basis of what's aesthetically pleasurable could be considered a preoccupation with surface and/or aesthetic concerns and one that is curiously at odds with his own outlook regarding the aforementioned "poietic fallacy;" the idea that the only thing that matters in a work of "is the art of making it, the maker's input," or his aforementioned belief that art can be a powerful form of persuasion that can exact "ethical responsibilities," while all other concerns are negligible. Was pop icon, Sting, being morally obtuse when he made this reference to classical music?

> I think it's really about the higher emotions, about the heart and intellect at a very high level. It's not about the lower charkas, it's not about humping your girlfriend—and there's nothing wrong with that, there's a place for music in that. But classical music does tend to be higher in this sense. What it wants to achieve or what it wants to say about the human condition is, I think rarefied—and I'm attracted to that."[12]

---

* Albert Ayler committed suicide after recording his final album in 1969, ironically titled, *Music Is the Healing Force of the Universe.*

Sting's appropriating "higher" attributes—emotion, heart, intellect—to classical music may seem untoward and moralizing to some. But racist or anti-Semitic? I think not.

I have no qualms in attempting to know if "universals" exist and if they do how they factor into life and art. Certainty has become anathema to post-modern, multiculturalist sensibilities because it suggests that there may be an ordering principle, an authority, or a creative force that is contrary to the notion of a non-judgmental, feel good, "we're-all-special" mentality. I don't believe that Johnson is necessarily inaccurate when he opines that the emphasis—and that's a key issue—on surface and superficial concerns in popular culture "fetishizes the materiality of the human experience and denies the spiritual personality that vivifies it from within."[13] There is good reason to believe that.

Considering that many songs from the pop canon confine to a static tempo based on an unchanging "beat," rarely modulate or use altered chords while remaining at the same dynamic level, one can easily make the case from an objective viewpoint that pop music is not as sophisticated and nuanced as classical music. Of course, there have been exceptions—Laura Nyro, Joni Mitchell, Radiohead, Imogene Heap, Emerson, Lake and Palmer, Pentatonix for instance. That's not to say that one cannot derive pleasure from popular culture, including hip-hop or rap. But not all things pleasurable are necessarily good, moral and decent? Not to see, nor be willing to make that distinction, results in the enabling of a radical egalitarian mindset. On this score, Johnson is correct. Taruskin acknowledges that many types of pleasure provide satisfaction (guilty pleasure, spiritual pleasure, animal pleasure, etc.) and he concedes that that not all things pleasurable are morally upright.

In commenting on Taruskin's "Musical Mystique" essay, Boston-based composer and music journalist, Matthew Guerrieri observed, "Certainly some pleasures are morally reprehensible, but that means that other pleasures (even if just the pleasure of avoiding the morally reprehensible) are, by comparison, morally advantageous. Taruskin wants it both ways."[14] And wanting it both ways (all ways) smacks of radical egalitarianism as well as a quasi-utopian mindset—something that Taruskin has emphatically cautioned against. As another cyber critic put it: "The biggest giveaway for me (in Taruskin's critique) was this amazing declaration: 'Distinct from' is a transparent euphemism for 'better than.' If you believe that, then ontological egalitarianism is the only normative residue. It's all good."[15]

But again, this is not the entire picture, and Taruskin's viewpoint regarding the "poietic fallacy," calling out Schoenberg and others for German chauvinism, misogyny and other moral lapses, point to a willingness to make judgments about musical expressions that are deserving of contempt because they do not edify, regardless of their pleasurable characteristics. As Guerrieri correctly notes, if certain music can be bad for us, certain music can be good for us. The process of establishing the proviso or criteria of assessment is the central issue. Is any attempt at defining or seeking "universals" intrinsically evil? Again, if one makes the claim that some pleasures are in fact morally reprehensible, then the self-evident correlation is that there are some that are morally advantageous.

Our greatest religions, philosophies and social ideals have been predicated on principles that seek to connect us to a divine reality and in so doing give us the means to achieve dominion over our external realities by transforming our consciousness. A central aspect of the artist's role in that quest, as composer Paul Hindemith stated, is "essentially a victory of external forces and a final allegiance to spiritual sovereignty" and as such, must be "a life of humility, of giving of one's best to one's fellow man."[16] Charles Ives, perhaps the *ur*-multiculturalist composer of his generation, would undoubtedly agree with Hindemith's call for "a life of humility" in the face of the prideful turbidity that too often passes for authenticity in contemporary art. One of Ives' early influences was Brahms, a good Lutheran, and like Brahms, Ives believed that if "wholesomeness" along with "humility and deep spiritual, possibly religious feeling" took a back seat to "manner" and other subsidiary concerns, that music was not fulfilling its edifying purpose.[17] Historically, Ives was not alone in his view.

Edward Rothstein observed that multiculturalism "takes other cultures seriously only as representations of the merely particular," and as a result, it is decidedly illiberal because it, "fails to see the Other within us, or us within the Other … it undoes the very notion of Western culture."[18] Camille Paglia makes no bones about "waging war" against the "toxic trends in academia … that assesses art in a reductively ironic or overly politicized way," in our attempt to properly contextualize the very real enchantments that great art of every culture can elicit.[19] Why might the music of Beethoven be of relevance if toxic masculinity and all things European are vile according to the current advocates of political correctness? Johnson again:

> Beethoven may yet be relevant to the modern age because our age is bound up with his. In particular, some of our most central concepts (of society and art) derive from the period in which he was working: ideas of the autonomous individual subject, authentic self-expression, a society of free individuals, and a reconciliation of nature with human society. Beethoven's age, like our own, wrestled with these ideas despite society's tendency toward their opposites ... No art worth the name is entirely "politically correct." Art reworks and reformulates its social materials, and while it may reinforce dominant ideologies, it may undermine them and critically reconfigure their terms.[20]

The original sin of political correctness, going back centuries—even before Marx and Lenin—was its refusal to acknowledge the "autonomous individual." The revolution of 1789 was the occasion that proclaimed that individual liberty was an inviolable right. Beethoven was nineteen at the time. Identity politics assails individual autonomy. According to Jordan Peterson, identity politics that's rooted in political correctness, "presumes that group identity is paramount. That's the fundamental philosophy that drove the Soviet Union and Maoist China, and it's the fundamental philosophy of the left-wing activists. It's identity politics. It doesn't matter who you are as an individual, it matters who you are in terms of your group identity."[21] Moreover, it was Adorno, in the 1930s, who seized upon the ideas of group "identity" and "victimhood" and fashioned the neo-Marxist narrative of "oppressor vs. oppressed."

In this context, political correctness is *way more* than the "discredited euphemism," because historically speaking, Peterson is correct. Predictably, the far-left activists who Peterson alluded to want him silenced because he dares to offend their sensibilities, and by exposing the original sin of not seeing individuals as autonomous individuals, his argument renders political correctness to be a specious and dangerous claim. Writing in *The Guardian*, Matthew d'Ancona calls for more, not less, of the kind of tough, honest exchange of ideas that Peterson (and John Stuart Mill) advocates in the hopes of avoiding the road to the dystopia that banning speech of his kind would lead to.[22]

Celebrating diversity is noble, but we ought to reject the spurious contention that the humanities as they have been taught or promoted in the West, are inherently prejudicial and imperialist; "toxic trends," as Paglia contends. If all humans are autonomous individuals who possess certain universal traits and attributes, then all humans can potentially benefit from the instructive aspects that great art and culture provide, regardless of its sphere of origin, or its genre. Some may choose not to go that route. The right to choose ought to be sacrosanct. And isn't that the more genuine multiculturalist raison d'etre? The process of gaining a deeper understanding of the human condition is not confined to one particular culture. Western culture has benefited from interfacing with "the other." It can work the other way as well.

Postscript

In September of 2021, Professor J.P.E. Harper-Scott announced his decision to leave Royal Holloway University in London citing the pervasive influence of "woke ideology" in the study of music. Commentators and journalists such as Heather MacDonald, Edward Rothstein, Camille Paglia, Charles Rosen and Frank Furedi have been citing the increasing trend to view European art through the prism of identity politics. Writing for the British online political magazine, *Spiked*, Furedi cites an all-too-familiar narrative: "In the past, opponents of classical music would insist that it was too elitist. Now they insist classical music is too white, or racist, or colonial." He goes on to report that, "Academics at Oxford recently denounced musical notation as 'colonialist' and have attacked the classical repertoire for focusing too much on 'white European music from the slave period.'"[23] This is now a familiar refrain in academia.

It now seems that Richard Taruskin has ceded to this perspective. This is especially ironic, if not duplicitous, considering his long-standing disdain for utopian prescriptions of any stripe. I've cited Taruskin many times due to his erudite perspectives on many topics. Yet, I'm in accord with Lester Hunt (former professor of philosophy at the University of Wisconsin) who posted on his blog in response to Taruskin's condemnation of Julian Johnson's book: "I just think it's amazing that the ongoing egalitarian revolt against the very idea of 'high' or 'fine' art has gone so far that the Chair of the Berkeley music department is actually a partisan of the revolution."[24] Amazing, indeed!

We have come to the point where musical literacy (notation, transposing, reading in multiple clefs) is now considered untoward and the residue of white supremacy by the progressive "woke left." One is left to wonder if the talented young musicians in the Venezuelan Youth Orchestras are now to be considered white supremacists, or, as Michael Eric Dyson might suggest, the Latino voices of white privilege. What about Quincy Jones who to went to Paris to study with Nadia Boulanger? Are Jazz and Gospel artists who can read or notate music to be chided for their "privilege" as well?

Interestingly, in the same month that Harper-Scott announced his decision to leave the bastions of wokeness in academia, Jazz trumpeter and composer, Terence Blanchard had his opera, *Fire Shut Up in My Bones*, staged by the Metropolitan Opera in New York. In an interview for ABC Television, Blanchard said that the reason he loves opera is "because I get a chance to tell our stories."[25] This was not Blanchard's first operatic venture and presumably many, if not all, of the musicians involved in these productions could read music.

Rather than leave the fray, one might hope that Harper-Scott would reconsider his decision and re-engage in the pursuit of truth and common sense. I'm reminded of a quip by Jonah Goldberg who opined that rather than creating five more Hillsdale Colleges to counter the pervasive influence of progressive postmodernism in academia, it would be better to see five conservatives on the faculty of the sociology department at Harvard. I'm not holding my breath on that one.

Recommended Recordings

Bach: The Musical Offering, Jordi Savall, Les Concert des Nations

Beethoven: The *Leonore* Overtures, George Szell, Cleveland Orchestra

Shapey: *Interchange*, Talujon Percussion Quartet

Haydn: String Quartets, Emerson String Quartet

Mozart: Symphony No, 34, George Szell, Royal Concertgebow Orchestra

Hindemith: *The Four Temperaments*, Ruth Laredo, piano, Oregon Symphony Orchestra

Toto: Toto IV

Laura Nyro: *Eli and the Thirteenth Confession*

Joni Mitchell: The Complete Geffen Recordings (2003)

Imogen Heap: *Speak For Yourself*

Carter: *Boston Concerto*, Oliver Knussen, BBC Symphony Orchestra

Mahler: Symphony No. 6, Yoel Levi, Atlanta Symphony Orchestra

Cartellieri: Symphony No. 3, Gernot Schmalfuss, Evergreen Symphony Orchestra

Blanchard: *A Tale of God's Will*, Terence Blanchard, conductor

Stamitz: Symphony in D Major, *La chasse*, Matthias Bamert, London Mozart Players

Albert Ayler: *Music Is the Healing Force of the Universe*

Babbitt: *Paraphrases*, Gil Rose, Boston Modern Orchestra Project

Lou Reed: *Best of Lou Reed & The Velvet Underground*

Queen: *Greatest Hits I & II*

Endnotes

1   Julian Johnson: *Who Needs Classical Music? Cultural Choice and Musical Value* (Oxford-New York: Oxford University Press, 2002), p. 58.

2   Ibid., p. 26.

3   Richard Taruskin, *The Dangers of Music and Other Anti-Utopian Essays* (Berkeley and Los Angeles: University of California Press, 2009), p. 332.

4   Ibid., p. 340.

5   J.P.E. Harper-Scott, *The Quilting Points of Musical Modernism: Revolution, Reaction, and William Walton* (Cambridge-New York: University Press, 2012), p. 16.

6   Ibid., p. 14.

7   Johnson: *Who Needs Classical Music?*, p. 88.

8   Taruskin, *The Danger of Music*, p. 344.

9   Roger Scruton, "Music and Morality," *The American Spectator*, February 11, 2010.

10 Taruskin, *The Danger of Music*, p. 23.

11 Johnson, *Who Needs Classical Music?*, p. 14.

12 Ibid.

13 Taruskin, *The Danger of Music*, p. 23. Johnson, *Who Needs Classical Music?*, p. 59.

14 Matthew Guerrieri, *The censures of the carping world*, October 26, 2007, http://sohothedog.blogspot.com/2007/10/censures-of-carping-world.html.

15 Lester Hunt, Blogspot: "Richard Taruskin, Pottymouth," October 25, 2007, http://lesterhhunt.blogspot.kr/2007/10/richard-taruskin-pottymouth.html.

16 Paul Hindemith, *A Composer's World-Horizons and Limitations*, Harvard University Press, Cambridge, 1951, p. 220.

17 Ives, *Essays Before a Sonata,* p. 73.

18 Edward Rothstein, "Roll Over Beethoven," *The New Republic*, August 4, 1991

19 Camille Paglia, "Is the rise of secularism behind the general malaise in the fine arts?" *Smithsonian Magazine*, November, 2012, http://www.smithsonianmag.com/arts-culture/why-camille-paglia-is-alarmed-about-the-future-of-art-79905670/?no-ist.

20 Johnson, *Who Needs Classical Music?,* pp. 93-94.

21 Jordan Peterson, Interview With Cathy Newman, BBC Channel 4, https://www.youtube.com/watch?v=aMcjxSThD54.

22 Matthew d'Ancona, "Banning people like Jordan Peterson from causing offense—that's the road to dystopia," *The Guardian*, January 21, 2018.

23 Frank Furedi, "Cancelling classical music: The identitarian set wants to jettison the gains of Western civilization." *Spiked*, September 20, 2021. https://www.spiked-online.com/2021/09/20/cancelling-classical-music/

24 Ibid., Lester Hunt, Blogspot.

25 Terence Blanchard, Interview: ABC's *Good Morning America*, September 27, 2021.

44

It's a Long Road to Freedom

Democracy and freedom do not guarantee the millennium.
No, we do not choose political freedom because it promises us this or that.
We choose it because it makes possible the only dignified form
of human coexistence, the only form in which we can be
fully responsible for ourselves. Whether we realize its possibilities
depends on all kinds of things—and above all on ourselves.
Karl Popper

If names be not correct, language is not in accordance with
the truth of things. If language be not in accordance
with the truth of things, affairs cannot be carried on to success.
When affairs cannot be carried out with success,
proprieties and music do not flourish.
Confucius

Beneath every society where self-interest pays off,
lies a foundation of self-sacrifice.
Roger Scruton

It has often been said that freedom is a dicey proposition; a proverbial double-edged sword. Plato perspicaciously stated in *The Republic*, "The excess of liberty, whether in States or individuals, seems only to pass into slavery. And so tyranny naturally rises out of democracy, and the most aggravated form of tyranny and slavery out of the most extreme form of liberty."[1] Plato's discourse on the paradox of freedom—and the pluralism that is germane to a free society—continues to spark debate, often in vituperative tones. Often the word "freedom" means different things to different people. As English author and social critic, Os Guinness notes, "We all declare for liberty, but in using the same word we do not all mean the same thing."[2]

Guinness' book *Last Call for Liberty*, published in 2018, includes the subheading, *How America's Genius for Freedom Has Become Its Greatest Threat*. A primary narrative that Guinness' emphasizes is the difference between the American Revolution and the French Revolution and how now there exist conflicting views on just what freedom means and how to go about protecting and restoring the ideals of a Constitutional Republic. The expansion of government into many aspects of American life in the pursuit of equality or social justice is problematic and gives currency to Lawrence W. Reed's assertion: "Free people are not equal, and equal people are not free."* Reed's assertion echoes Thomas Sowell's contention (one he's been stating for decades), that any process to ascribe any status to any group of people by way of governmental evaluation—equality, inferiority, superiority—must necessarily reduce freedom because in any assemblage of people there is too much diversity of circumstances to ascribe across-the-board remedies to achieve equity without infringing upon the freedom of certain individuals with the assemblage.

This infringement will occur regardless of how well-intentioned the creators of government policies may be. We are witnessing an ever-expanding government bureaucracy with intellectual elites leading the charge in the name of social justice. Joel Stein, author of the book, *In Defense of Elitism: Why I'm Better Than You and You're Better Than Someone Who Didn't Buy This Book*, admits that he's from the "deepest blue" part of California where the Democratic elites have been in charge for decades. His book, in which he uses humor

---

* Lawrence W. Reed's comments were made in the context of economic policies but apply to political and ideological realms as well.

and satire to make his points, defends the need for "experts" to be shaping socio-political policies. He decries the emerging populism in the USA and views it as a threat to progressivism and a return to the bad-old days when the populist attitudes of "deplorables" were in the main. He also asserts that there are only about twenty universities in the United State worth attending.

In his book's introduction, he ascribes the "horrifying destructive power of populism" in America to that which occurred in the Dark Ages, China's Cultural Revolution and North Korea.[3] This assertion is neither humorous nor accurate because it is a fabrication. You could hardly find less populist societies than in the Dark Ages when there was "a virtual disappearance of urban life,"[*] or Mao's China and Kim's North Korea, in which brutal regimes oppressed the citizenry, and continue to oppress the populace in the quest for complete and total control by political elites. There is a reason that these regimes are called "totalitarian," but Stein seems to have missed that point. This type of dishonesty, whether willful or due to ignorance, renders the premise of his argument to be inconsequential.

This begs the question for Stein and others of his ilk: Given the near- catastrophic circumstances of California, with a governmental budget deficit of over $1 Trillion[†], failing schools, unaffordable housing, drug-infested streets in Los Angeles and San Francisco, power outages, water shortages, forest mismanagement, and an over-budget and uncompleted high-speed rail project, why should anyone buy into the narrative that the so-called "elitist experts" who have essentially ruined California be listened to anymore? Perhaps Thomas Sowell gave us the answer when he quipped, "The road to hell is paved with Ivy League degrees." In an address to the Foundation for Economic Education in 2015, Lawrence Reed offered these cautionary remarks regarding the continual quest for governmental power by elites like Joel Stein:

> People obsessed with economic equality do strange things. They become envious of others. They covet. They divide society into two groups: villains and victims. They spend far more time dragging somebody down than they do pulling anybody up. ... And if they make it to a legislature, they can do real harm. Then they not only call the cops—they are the cops.[4]

---

* *Encyclopedia Britannica.*

† Thomas del Beccaro, Forbes, April 19, 2018.

Confucius' prescient insights regarding truth and the "rectification of language" points to the current condition in which language has been convoluted to such degrees that many believe that we are living in a "post-truth" era in which certainty is no longer a viable notion.[5] Consequently, arriving at consensuses about how we understand freedom—and how to protect it—in the context of attaining social betterment has become increasingly challenging. Is there now a "clash between competing freedoms" as Guinness opines? It is easily recognizable that the concept of freedom that animated the American experiment regarding *individual* civil liberties is at odds with the *collectivist* version of freedom as promulgated by postmodernists and identity politics activists.[6] The original impulses of liberalism regarding freedom of speech, religion, association, et al., are greatly hindered by the expansion of the state and the preponderance of postmodernist groupthink, not to mention the subversion of language. Jonah Goldberg expounds on this deceit vis-à-vis totalitarianism:

> The disconnect between names and the named becomes most pronounced in totalitarian societies where words become weapons of the State. When language ceases to be a tool for labeling reality and higher truths and becomes one for upholding the agenda of a regime, the society rots and invites revolt. ... I think there's something very profound about the Chinese idea that revolutions are primarily an effort to bring about the rectification of names; that the demand for justice is first and foremost a demand that words and reality come back into alignment. Nothing is more infuriating than to be told not to believe your lying eyes—or your empty stomach. Take a moment to ponder various revolutions around the globe throughout history and ask yourself if there isn't something to that.[7]

I have several friends who were born, raised and educated in China during the Mao Tse-tung era. After Mao's Cultural Revolution ended in 1976 they came to the United States to further their education and pursue their careers as classical musicians, something they could not easily do in places like Beijing or Shanghai in the 1960s and 1970s when most Western art was deemed subversive and degenerate. It was clear that the freedom my friends enjoyed in America was a condition that they didn't take for granted.

In 1988 I worked with the Academy-Award-winning composer Tan Dun (*Crouching Tiger, Hidden Dragon*). In a concert at Lincoln Center's Avery Fisher Hall, I conducted the world premiere of Tan's Violin Concerto, with Vera Tsu as the soloist, and his third symphony. Both Vera and Tan told of how when growing up in China they had to conceal their interest in Western music for fear of reprisals. Vera told me that simply owning a violin or a recording of a Mozart symphony could result in a prison term or execution. Nothing of Western influence or origin was permitted in Mao's China from 1966-1976. Mao's "Great Leap Forward" was "horrifyingly destructive," resulting in millions of deaths in his attempt to purge China from all Western and capitalist elements, including art and culture. The Cultural Revolution was not a populist uprising and is remembered as one of the darker episodes in human history.

Richard Nixon's gambit to forestall a potential alliance between Beijing and Moscow was predicated on the premise that by encouraging China to engage in free-market economic policies and trade with the United States and the West, the threat of a Sino-Soviet alliance could be mitigated. Regrettably, the plan failed. Though the situation in China may seem far better and more liberal than during Mao's brutal reign, it nevertheless remains a state-controlled society, and certain music and cultural content is not considered appropriate for public performance. Vera Tsu recently informed me over lunch in New York City that YouTube and Facebook remain forbidden in China. (The Great Firewall of China?) When my good friend and collaborator, Israeli vocalist, David D'Or was in China to perform with the Beijing Opera Orchestra in 2007, he related how the Chinese cultural authorities prohibited any songs that had references to God or religion. David lamented, "I had to cut half of my repertory." Moreover, the persecution of Christians, Muslims and members of Falun Gang at the hands of the regime in Beijing continues.

History provides copious evidence that the greatest progress in the realms of technology, art, business, finance and science have occurred in societies that are free of oppression; societies where personal incentive was not inhibited by the state. F. A. Hayek, Milton Friedman, William F. Buckley, Jr., Lawrence Reed and Thomas Sowell have written extensively about the power of the free market and its effect on economic progress and liberating the masses from economic hardship. They understood that the diversity of circumstances in a given social group (a family, a community, an ethnic minority, a nation) made prescribing a single policy or remedy problematic because a single remedy would not be completely fair to everyone without resorting to coercion or authoritarian modalities. When arguing for fairness, justice and economic opportunities, Sowell asks the pertinent question that often goes unasked by those demanding complete and total equity: At what cost?

Moreover, we should remember that the original Marxist grievance against the establishment and capitalism was based on resentment and envy—Reed's observation. Michael Novak and Paul Adams point out in their co-authored book, *Social Justice Isn't What You Think It Is*, that poverty was considered shameful prior to the Industrial Revolution and this impacted the emergence of a large and relatively contented middle class. As Novak and Adams tell it:

> Marx had described it [poverty] as a disgrace, precisely because it stood out in contrast to the unprecedented wealth created by capitalism, but he had overlooked the widespread movement out of poverty in America. Worse still, he had failed to grasp the genius by which new wealth is created from the bottom up. ... For the United States presented to the world not only a new model of a republican polity. ... It also presented a new model of a dynamic economy. It displayed unparalleled upward mobility. Few in Europe grasped America's inspirations, methods and practices.[8]

Novak and Adams cite Pope Leo XIII's thirteen reasons why socialism was problematic and why it will ultimately fail to bring about the desired utopian conditions that it promises. Chief among them is that the underlying rationale behind socialism in the late nineteenth century was envy. "In summary, socialism is not a livable system for humans, for it incites envy, the most evil of social passions ... socialism would incite envy, encourage invective and disturb creative order."[9] For students of the Bible, it is fairly well-known that one of the motivating impulses in Lucifer's temptation of Adam and Even in Eden was his jealousy of their relationship as God's son and daughter, a position/relationship that Lucifer coveted.

Is there unfairness in a free market economy? Yes. But as Friedman often pointed out, history proves that there is no alternative economic model for improving the financial circumstances of people that rivals the productive activities that are unleashed by a free enterprise system. Author Naomi Klein takes a derisive swipe at Friedman and other "free market fundamentalists" in her book *This Changes Everything* (2014), blaming them for the Wall Street meltdown in 2008. Yet anyone who understands the "fundamentals" of capitalism knows that the nonsense that preceded the subprime mortgage scandal and the ensuing economic malaise, was in fact, a bastardization of capitalist rationale; aka "crony capitalism."

As *New York Times*, Pulitzer-Prize-winning author Gretchen Morgenson reveals in her book *Reckless Endangerment* (2011), Democrats Chris Dodd, Barney Frank, Franklin Raines and Jim Johnson were as guilty as any member of the Republican party in the scam that skirted free-market principles at every turn (unless accounting fraud is a now considered a tenet of capitalism). It was, after all, a Democrat president, Bill Clinton, who signed legislation that rescinded the Glass-Steagall Act of 1933 that was passed in the wake of the Great Depression to prohibit the kind of perfidy that wreaked economic havoc in 1929. To be fair several prominent members of the GOP were complicit in this legislative perfidy; Phil Gramm and Jim Leach were among them. Morgenson points out that though much of what happened in the subprime mortgage meltdown was illegal, no one went to prison and some of the perpetrators remain involved in government and various lobbying enterprises.

In the context of the social groups that we belong to (families, churches, etc.), we exact various measures of social justice according to the relationships that we cultivate in those groups, more often than not, without government interference. The term "social justice" was coined in the nineteenth century by an Italian priest, Father Luigi Taparelli d'Azeglio, who averred that it was important to make the distinction between legal justice as implemented by the State, and social justice as implemented in the context of family or other private institutions. Remedying relational conflicts *without* state intrusion was his concern. For Taparelli, the intermediary institutions that existed as buffers between the State and individuals—families, churches—needed to be free from State control or coercion. Father Taparelli's distinction is important. Keeping "the state" at bay was essential to protect the autonomy and spiritual authority of the Church. He was highly suspect of Jean-Jacques Rousseau's views regarding the State as the primary arbiter of justice, thus his concept of "social justice" was a mitigating factor in protecting the various societal organizations within the larger, public society.[10] Taparelli's concept of social justice is a far cry from the current iteration of social justice in which redistributive justice holds center court.

Herbert Croly, considered to be the father of modern liberalism, and Richard Ely, who along with Croly founded *The New Republic*, were both of the mindset that "rugged individualism" and the nineteenth-century notion of "the American Dream" were outdated and a new social paradigm needed to be explored. Their new American vision was rooted in what became known as "Christian Socialism," whereby the government would act as the great equalizer as well as the cure for the "sinful and cruel" aspects of *lassez-faire* economics. As Ely put it: "God works through the State in carrying out His purposes more universally than any other institution ... it is religious in essence ... a mighty force in furthering God's kingdom and establishing righteous relations."[11] For some, this seems like a noble endeavor and a fulfillment of Christian idealism; to others, it's a violation of the separation of Church and State, or worse—the invitation of government interference and overreach. In a very sinister way, Croly's and Ely's brand of liberalism has morphed into a decidedly anti-religious mode of progressivism that now threatens religious liberty—not to mention free speech and freedom of peaceful assembly—in ways that were hardly imaginable a few decades ago.

The right to choose is being encroached upon with great regularity by those who willfully ignore the founding principles of the republic in pursuit of an imagined utopia that can only be realized through control, coercion or intimidation. Currently, Joel Stein's elitist colleagues seem to be everywhere in government. Fortunately, Yuval Levin notes that there exists an alternative to "the pernicious mix" of governmental centralization and hyper-individualism and it begins "in loving family attachments." This family-based modality of relating can "spread outward to interpersonal relationships, neighborhoods, schools, workplaces, religious communities," and even into the work of local governments, businesses and professional affiliations. In so doing this modality can provide a basis for a national identity "that among its foremost attributes is dedicated to the principle of the equality of the entire human race."[12]

In Judeo-Christian culture there exists a prevalent idea that we are meant to be co-creators with God in creating a civilized, humanitarian society. We accomplish this by making choices in the context of the teachings of scripture that act as the proverbial "moral compass" in guiding us in the process of becoming moral and ethical people. In this respect Croly and Ely were correct. But as scripture reminds us (I Corinthians 6:12), though everything is permissible, not everything is beneficial. Our choices have consequences. Philosophers such as Confucius, Spinoza, Kant, Hume, Smith and Sartre had a great deal to say about human nature, freedom and what we "ought" to do regarding morality, ethics and the various circumstances that affect our choices. Rather than get into an exhaustive exegesis on the topic, let me make but a few observations of these noted philosophers that are pertinent to the discussion of freedom and creativity in our current cultural reality in relation to art and music.

In citing Confucius (551-479 BCE) at the beginning of this essay with regard to the rectification of language in the pursuit of truth, I sought to emphasize the importance of honesty in the process. When in his Analects, Confucius refers to "names" being correct or incorrect, he is addressing the necessity of avoiding falsehood and deception. Without a proper understanding of words, meaning can be skewed and societies cannot arrive at a moral or just modality of governing, or carrying out business transactions, not to mention education, artistic creativity, journalism or science. Of particular interest is Confucius' referencing music as something that can be debased if the truth is subverted. Further on in *The Analects* (13:3) we read:

> When proprieties and music do not flourish, punishments will not be properly awarded. When punishments are not properly awarded, the people do not know how to move hand or foot. Therefore, a superior man considers it necessary that the names he uses may be spoken appropriately, and also that what he speaks may be carried out appropriately. What the superior man requires is just that in his words there may be nothing incorrect.[13]

It's interesting to note the concept of "punishment" vis-a-vis music, for that implies that there were moral or ethical standards in the socio-cultural equation and that people (and artists) were to be accountable for their behavior. This is in accord with the idea that responsibility is part of the freedom equation. Furthermore, the etymology of the word "responsibility" stems from the Latin: *respondere*, which means "answering." Therefore, in the context of relationships it takes on the meaning of "being answerable to" or "accountable for" one's actions. Freedom without responsibility results in licentiousness, anarchy and eventually, destruction.

Baruch Spinoza (1632-1677) asserts: "In the nature of things nothing contingent is admitted, but all things are determined by the necessity of divine nature to exist and act in a certain way."[14] Spinoza was making the case that all things are the embodiment of the "divine nature" that religious people often attribute to the characteristics of God. Ontologically, the "nature of Nature" is neither random nor accidental, but rather, lawful, relational and orderly. Believers contend that this is in accordance with the attributes of the deity. St. Paul refers to this in Romans 1:20 when he suggests that the invisible nature of God can be perceived in that which the Creator has created.

As such, these attributes are considered "godly" and causal in that they represent God, the causal being. This would seem to indicate a certain determinist attitude, but in reality, Spinoza is arguing that for God to be perfect, God must adhere to the same principles through which the universe was created and continues to function, and because love is central to the equation, God is seeking objects of love who choose to reciprocate in kind. This is disputed by Friedrich Hegel and Alexander Kojève who postulated that it is via conflict between a subject and object, rather than harmonization, that self-created individuals attain freedom and are emancipated from the alienation and despair caused by "the other." Isaiah Berlin notes that Hegel "supposed that the divine harmonies could be made only by sharp clashes, by violent disharmonies, which from a great height would have been perceived as contributory factors to some enormous harmony."[15]

According to Christian thought, God is a loving parent—an idea that was amplified through the teachings of Jesus and his disciples. Consequently, love and compassion are significant attributes of the Supreme Being, thus for love to be manifested freedom is a *sine qua non*. God loves us, but God loves in complete accordance with what is moral and ethically principled. Humankind, as children of God, *ought* to do likewise, but due to our "fallen nature" our choices are often flawed or misguided, thus resulting in deleterious behavior and human suffering. In this circumstance, God suffers as well because as a loving parent, God feels pain in seeing humankind in various states of distress and misery.

Jean-Paul Sartre (1905-1980) famously opined: "Either man is wholly determined (which is inadmissible, especially because a determined consciousness-i.e., a consciousness externally motivated-becomes pure exteriority and ceases to be consciousness) or else man is wholly free."[16] Sartre, who had serious Marxist leanings, was not a determinist and believed that we were responsible for our actions. "For I am responsible for my very desire of fleeing responsibilities. To make myself passive in the world, to refuse to act upon things and upon others is still to choose myself."[17] Sartre's existential argument was that there was no position from which he could be judged other than his own, and that only thing that could legitimize or authenticate his moral judgments was his choice to act according to his personal view of morality. This can be interpreted as having an extremely self-centered moral outlook, for it doesn't take into account the issue of community and the commonwealth—the other.

As Roger Scruton extrapolates, with this perspective a moral person is one who "wills his own desires as commitments, whereas the immoral person is someone who just has those desires. On that view, the authentic, existentialist rapist is the one who should be praised, not the one who is simply tempted by his sexual appetites." That may seem hyperbolic, but it points to the distorted outcome of a purely existentialist perspective that excludes any absolute perspective with regard to an axiological frame of reference in relationship to others. Scruton avers:

> For Sartre there is no God to provide the reason for my existence; hence it is I who must provide it, and in doing so I lean on the interpersonal intentionality that points in a religious direction, but to which Sartre gives quite another and infinitely bleaker and more solitary slant.[18]

The result of choosing to abdicate our responsibility in our relationships can lead to anarchy, licentiousness, nihilism and moral relativism. As previously noted, the etymology of the word "responsible," is rooted in the concepts of obligation and answerability, both of which infer our relationships with others; literally, the *ability* to *respond*. The quality of our responses is salient. Ideally, our responses should be moral and ethical in context of the communities in which we live. Spinoza would surely see this as being beneficial to one's society and the way to create peace—something we *ought* to do. Implicit in that necessity is being responsible in our relationships because we can choose to be either selfish or selfless.

Scottish economist Adam Smith (1723-1790) writes: "If a nation could not prosper without the enjoyment of perfect liberty and perfect justice, there is not in the world a nation which could ever have prospered."[19] Yet history also instructs that the misuse of freedom can lead to social and cultural upheaval and dissolution (Rome, e.g.). Hence, the essential trial remains: How do we best use our freedom? This becomes a central question in the pursuit of an ideal that embodies an altruistic and godly vision. Before Smith had become an economic theorist of note, he was a philosopher who argued that the imperfections of human nature were a fact of life, and as such, should not be lamented nor regarded as something to be transformed—especially by government. Moreover, Smith viewed "the fundamental moral and social challenge was to make the best of the possibilities which existed within that constraint, rather than dissipate energies in an attempt to change human nature."[20]

Of course, this fatalistic view of life runs counter to any utopian vision or any ideology born of such—religious or non-religious. Yet Smith believed that true capitalism had both a "self-purpose" and a "whole-purpose" and these dual purposes needed to be harmonized and balanced. Freedom to choose in the context of economic concerns could have deleterious effects on one's community if one chose greed over charity and restraint. The aforementioned subprime mortgage fiasco was a direct result of greed and selfishness being out of balance with the "whole purpose." Scruton posits that Smith was quite altruistic in his economic views vis-à-vis morality and ethics, stating:

> In the Theory of the Moral Sentiments, Smith emphasized that trust, responsibility and accountability exist only in a society that respects them, and only where the spontaneous fruit of human sympathy is allowed to ripen. It is where sympathy, duty, and virtue achieve their proper place that self-interest leads, by an invisible hand, to a result that benefits everyone. And this means that people can best satisfy their interests only in a context where they are also on occasion moved to renounce them. Beneath every society where self-interest pays off, lies a foundation of self-sacrifice.
>
> A market can deliver a rational allocation of goods and services only where there is trust between its participants, and trust exists only where people take responsibility for their actions and make themselves accountable

to those whom they deal. In other words, economic order depends on moral order.[21]

The Artist's Role

In taking these various views of freedom into account as they pertain to God, the phenomenal world, relationships, ethics and creativity, we can deduce that the task of creating a culture guided by religious-based moral and ethic precepts in the establishment of a benevolent society, where the ideals of a culture of peace could blossom, requires that those of us who have been accorded the gift of artistic talent, *ought* to use that talent in an altruistic fashion. Human nature being what it is, we know that that hasn't always been the case, but should we ignore Smith's contention that we shouldn't preoccupy ourselves with the transformation of such?

In his amazing (and amazingly long) novel, *Doktor Faustus*, Thomas Mann refers to the paradox of how setting limits can be liberating, especially in the art of composition as it pertains to expressing emotion in music. Describing a composition by Adrian Leverkühn, the fictional protagonist in his novel, Mann asserts that musical expression is a product of "the dialectic process by which strictest constraint is reversed into the language of emotion, by which freedom is born out of constraint."[22] As any composer who has labored in the studies of harmony, counterpoint and form will attest, it is by fully understanding both the potentialities and limits of the tonal syntax that one attains their creative liberation and in so doing can express the widest range of emotions in the most efficacious manner in the context of that particular codified musical syntax.

Conversely, when musical materials (pitch sets, rhythms, chords, etc.) become overly complicated and/or cacophonic due to arcane compositional processes—or if there is a complete abandonment of syntax and process—the result is cognitive overload and imperceptible musical utterances. The resulting indeterminacy yields little in the way of communication, appeal or satisfaction with listeners. Art music of the "modernist project," according to Scruton, "survives in the archive, the last pressed flower in the book of modernism, a *memento mori* (a reminder of mortality) which we study from time to time and then wistfully return to its grave."[23]

Intuitively we understand that any society in which there are no laws or restrictions can quickly devolve into a condition where licentiousness can create conditions in which anarchy, chaos and violence become more evident. Lawfulness is not undesirable in this context because violence begets more violence. Due to a decidedly self-centered and materialistic mindset, we have witnessed a pervasive dissolution and diminishing of artistic standards in relation to art and music in our popular culture. In our desire to be free in our cultural expressions, we have seemingly lost our way regarding that which we create and produce. By being "lost in the abyss of freedom" (Stravinsky's well-known axiom), our contemporary culture has undergone dramatic, and not necessarily favorable changes.

British composer and author Julian Johnson offers an insightful perspective on the condition of art and popular culture and how it affects us individually and collectively.

> What might seem harmless in relation to cultural practices, fashion, cars or even music, is clearly invidious in relation to people. The ideal of humanity on which we have based our greatest religious, ethical, philosophical and political thinking is not defined by our outward, material surface but by our capacity to exceed the limits of our material existence. Great art expresses this ideal in every work. In rejecting it [intentionally or not] to embrace the ideal of a blank and depthless surface embodied in contemporary culture, we reject the ideal of humanity and instead we embrace a simulacrum—a synthetic and hollow substitute. Human potential is not well expressed by the fashionable, the glossy, or the chic, and yet we allow ourselves to be dominated by a culture defined almost exclusively in these terms. In doing so, we collude in our own reduction to objects.[24]

That says quite a bit, but not everyone agrees with Johnson's assertions. Some feel that this type of assessment is the view of a Philistine (or an acolyte of Theodor Adorno). Yet how and what we share via our talent remains an important consideration in cultivating a just, benevolent and altruistic society. The hyper-commercialized condition of our society too easily transforms even the most transcendent aspects of humanity, in this case, great art, into objects or commodities. This tendency is essentially inhumane. Johnson acknowledges:

Because just as music can awaken this sense of exceeding the physicality of our being, it can also have quite the opposite effect. Music can deny those qualities that define a humanist culture, insisting instead on the absence of freedom and capacity for self-improvement, obliterating the differentiating of elements that are the hallmark of thought and substituting them with repetition. It can become a celebration of inanity.[25]

To be sure, the twentieth century has given us a great deal of inane art. The trajectory of a great deal of popular culture is increasingly bound in commercial concerns that trade on the incessant desire for instant gratification. This situation when juxtaposed to a capitalist rationale has the effect of assessing music, not from the perspective of its innate spiritual attributes, but that for its commercial value. Both Johnson and Scruton view this condition as being analogous to pornography, where the divine and spiritual attributes of human sexuality are compromised (or removed altogether), thereby objectifying sexuality (reification) in the attempt to turn it into a commodity to be bought and sold and in so doing, diminishing its intrinsic—and some would say—its godly attributes.* This is not to suggest that artists shouldn't be compensated for their work, but rather that a balance, based on factors other than purely bottom-line considerations be in the societal equation. As Johnson asserts, "Art's apparent refusal of the everyday is not a refusal of the 'human' as such: it is the refusal of the idea that the sum of what it is to be human is found [only] in the everyday."[26]

Art music has also suffered as a result of a myopic view of its role in contemporary society where there exists a widening cultural gap between serious artists and the public. In academia, specialization, rather than commercialization, is the problem. Richard Taruskin observes:

> In the West, a century-long tradition of reckless, socially irresponsible, and self-absorbed avant-garde behavior, supported by the dogma that art is the concern of artists only and coupled with an ever-increasing passivity on the part of an audience that is deprived by its education and by the growth of the recording industry of participatory skills in music, has led to extreme apathy that threatens the continued existence of art music in our culture.

---

* In philosophical terms, "reification" means treating something abstract or immaterial as a material thing.

And yet, anyone who questions the dogma of autonomy, harmful though it has become, is immediately and unthankingly branded as an enemy of art.[27]

Obviously, the issue of censorship vis-à-vis freedom and responsibility comes into play in any discussion about art, creativity, and any moral "obligation" on the part of artists. American educator and playwright Michael Erikson avers that the only censorship we should be willing to tolerate is "self-censorship" which is based on our personal moral and ethical perspectives. Our priorities in terms of what we value remain an individual choice, therefore government censorship is decidedly illiberal. However, as artists it is important to have an understanding that we don't create in a vacuum, therefore, that which we put before the public can have profound social ramifications as philosophers from Confucius to Scruton attest.

The 1979 documentary film *From Mao to Mozart* chronicles violinist Isaac Stern's travels to China in the years just after Mao's Cultural Revolution. (Vera Tsu appears in the film as an eleven-year old prodigy.) Many musicians who had Western musical training were placed in *laogai* (forced labor camps) as all traces of Western influence were expunged from Chinese society and culture. What Stern found in his journeys throughout China was that there was a profusion of young talent emerging in the music conservatories that had been reopened after the demise of Mao's nefarious reign.

The famed "Class of '78" (the first students to enter the Beijing Central Conservatory after Mao's reign of terror) produced a number of important musicians who achieved significant successes in their careers. Stern's visit played a key role in bringing attention to these gifted artists and the film is a moving testament to the power of the human spirit and the transformational impact that great art and music can have on individuals and societies. It is also an affirmation that great art possesses the capability to inspire and energize, and in so doing, can assist in the process of developing our fundamental human aspiration for peace and prosperity. Intrinsic to all that is "the right to choose."

Hegel may have been wrong in many respects, but he nonetheless believed that the purpose of art was to "unveil the truth in the form of sensuous artistic configuration."[28] It was his contention that art was not a means to an end but an end in itself. Though we may view art merely as an object to be appreciated as an end in itself, we know that art can serve other functions. As Stern's film demonstrates, art can function in the promotion of freedom, discipline, liberty and goodwill. Due in large part to its healing and inspirational attributes, music can assist in achieving a humane society in which we use our freedoms in a responsible and humanitarian fashion. The allure of great art, and classical music in particular, as it pertained to the situation in post-Mao China, points to its power as a change agent due to its transcendent potentialities. And this is why a free society is supremely important, despite the messiness that is endemic to the democratic process. The freedom to choose remains vital. To cite Karl Popper, whether we realize freedom's potentialities "depends on all kinds of things—and above all on ourselves."[29] A great deal has been said and written about "a woman's right to choose," but the right to choose extends beyond reproductive issues.

Regrettably, the penchant for state control in China remains a puissant reality as evidenced by the government crackdown on Uighur separatists in Xinjiang, the Tibetans, Falun Gang, Christians, the activist artist Ai Weiwei and the pro-democracy demonstrations in Hong Kong. Freedom of expression and speech are feared by authoritarian regimes because dissent and skepticism are regarded as being inherently subversive and threatening to the status quo—all of those "elites" that Joel Stein cites as necessarily vital for societal improvement. The assertions of Confucius, Plato, Aristotle, Boethius and Isaac Stern regarding the ability of music to act a catalyst for positive social change when one's motivation and intent are inherently ethical, suggest that music possesses significant moral and ethical power. If artists choose to use that power (assuming that they have the freedom to choose) with a sense of moral responsibility in developing a moral and ethical society, a society in which the ethic of "true love" is realized for the continual betterment of the human condition, then perhaps we can become free in the truest sense. How liberating.

Postscript—July 2, 2020

Today as I celebrated my 71st birthday with friends and family, I reflected on some of my past experiences performing and conducting music steeped in Americana; the marches of John Phillip Sousa, Broadway show tunes and the orchestral suites of Aaron Copland and William Schuman. Much of this music is now being vilified by those who consider the American experiment and its culture as being nothing more than an expression of racism and bigotry—the cultural residue of colonialism. But is it?

There is something rather Maoist going on now as our past culture, history and beliefs are being assessed according to current "woke" standards. The Maoists purged all intellectuals and artists in the Cultural Revolution in 1966 for having views that didn't comport with the ideological view-of-the-day. As mentioned in this essay, merely owning a violin or a recording of Mozart's music could land you in a labor camp—or worse. In the same manner of the Maoists, the "hyper-presentism" that has become so pervasive rejects historical context altogether. Conservatives and liberals find this to be seriously at odds with the principles of democracy, freedom and pluralism.

David Hume observed long ago that liberty is seldom lost all at once. The erosion of liberty, more often than not, is a long-term affair. Art historian Camille Paglia has for several decades been strenuously objecting to the practice of assessing art through *a priori* abstractions rooted in contemporary iterations of PC-oriented multiculturalism. She detests this rationale because it ignores historical context *in toto*. This trend has been developing since the end of World War II. Edward Said's book *Orientalism* (1977), and Howard Zinn's book *A People's History of the United States* (1980), and the *New York Times's* "1619 Project" are rooted in this type of post-structural ideology that supports narratives that paint the United States and the West in completely nefarious tones with little or no redeeming value.

The influence of the French Nietzscheans, particularly Michel Foucault, is quite evident in their work. This isn't history, it's historicism—weaponizing historical data for ideological purposes and power. In this context there is virtually no Western art (or artist) that can escape the stain of racism or colonialism. As Michael Walsh puts it in his deconstruction of Marxist Critical Theory, "In his era of political correctness, it is very easy to trump up a series of latter-day charges against almost any dead individual, exhume his corpse, and, like a Cadaver Synod run by a grad-school Nuremberg court, cut off his head mount it on a pike, and chuck the body into a ditch."[30]

Context, however, is important. As University of California political scientist Max Neiman points out, humankind has a long and baleful history with regard to slavery, racism and supremacy. Slavery is not the invention of Europeans. He writes:

> There was a time when Asia and the Near East were dominant and indulged in subjugation, slavery, and inflicted pillaging on other societies. It happened in Africa and South America as well. The process of rationalizing one's advantages over others has been the practice since the beginning of time. Is the West's and the U.S.'s time past? Perhaps. Will Asia, via China prevail? Probably. And then they'll have their own justification for their supremacy. If the planet is around long enough the cycle will start all over again. Blame, Self-worship, Blame and some more Self-Worship. Sanctimony and selective memory are universal practices."[31]

Slavery has been around for ages; think of the Egyptians enslaving the Hebrews some four thousand years ago. The etymology of the word "slave" is derived from "Slavic." During Barbary slave trade along the north African coast during the ninth century, slave traders from Tunis, Algiers, Morocco and Tripoli enslaved over one million Europeans, many of them from Slavic territories. This practice went on for centuries and extended as far north as Iceland.

Alluding to freedom vis-à-vis the Hebrews, the nineteenth-century German poet, Heinrich Heine remarked, "Since Exodus freedom has always been spoken with a Hebrew accent."[32] Most Americans will agree that there ought to be a greater emphasis on social justice, equality and fairness because they honor the idea that all people are created equal. However, an accurate reading of history tells us that totalitarianism, state control or anarchy provide no reasonable solutions for many of our societal ills and often result in greater injustices and greater human suffering. Shelby Steele reminds us that despite our troubled past, "Freedom is still our mother tongue."[33]

As Aleksander Solzhenitsyn cautioned in his controversial commencement address at Harvard in 1978, in these various attempts at using state control to exact equality and justice, "Voluntary self-restraint is unheard of; everyone strives toward the further expansion to the extreme of legal frames."[34] Solzhenitsyn knew full well—as did the rest of the world in 1978—that the revolutions of 1917 and 1966 unleashed unimaginable terror and misery on humankind, all in the name of a utopian ideal based on illiberal modes of state control and dictatorial machinations. Echoing Solzhenitsyn, Jordan Peterson was absolutely correct when, in his famous interview with Cathy Newman, he asserted that the politically correct attitudes of today's social justice warriors are of the same impulses and ideological tenets that were advocated and practiced by Stalin and Mao. There is no denying that when politically correct attitudes and policies go to the extreme—as they did in the Soviet Union and China—we get gulags and huge body counts. Confucius' warning about truth (words) becoming fungible and thus leading to socio-cultural confusion and failure still rings true.[35]

Freedom is essential, for it allows creativity and inventiveness to be in the process of fashioning a better socio-cultural environment. Increased state control, not to mention cancel culture, de-platforming and political-correctness, is antithetical to all that. That said, if we detach freedom from personal responsibility, as well as a belief in a transcendent morality, we really have no right to expect that humankind's better angels will be able to make straight "the crooked timber of humanity."[36]

Recommended Recordings

Tan Dun: *Out of Peking Opera*, Helsinki Philharmonic, Cho Liang Lin, violin

Korngold: Concerto for Violin, Vera Tsu, violin, Yu Long, conductor

Isaac Stern: *From Mao to Mozart*, DVD (New Video Group)

Copland: *Rodeo*, Atlanta Symphony Orchestra, Louis Lane, conductor

John Phillip Sousa: *Marches*, Eastman Wind Ensemble, Frederick Fennell, conductor

David D'Or: Concert with the Israel Philharmonic

William Schuman: *New England Triptych,* Seattle Symphony Orchestra, Gerard Schwartz, conductor

Endnotes

1   Plato, *The Republic* (Edinburgh, UK: Black & White Classics, 2014), p. 166.

2   Os Guinness, *Last Call for Liberty: How America's Genius for Freedom Has Become Its Greatest Threat* (Downers Grove, IL: InterVarsity Press, 2018), p. 10.

3   Joel Stein, *In Defense of Elitism: Why I'm Better Than You and You're Better Than Someone Who Didn't Buy This Book* (New York, NY: Grand Central Publishing, 2019), eBook.

4   Lawrence W. Reed, "Liberty Still Has a Fighting Chance," *Nevada News and Views*, July 28, 2015.

5   *The Analects of The Analects of Confucius: An Online Teaching Translation*, translated by Robert Eno, (Robert Eno, 2018), p. 66, https://chinatxt.sitehost.iu.edu/Analects_of_Confucius_(Eno-2015).pdf.

6   Guinness, *Last Call for Liberty*, p. 10.

7   Jonah Goldberg, "The Rectification of Names," The Goldberg File, *National Review*, September 12, 2014.

8   Michael Novak and Paul Adams, *Social Justice Isn't What You Think It Is* (New York and London: Encounter Books, 2015), p. 97.

9   Ibid., pp. 101-102.

10   Jonah Goldberg, *The Tyranny of Clichés: How Liberals Cheat in the War of Ideas* (New York: Penguin Group USA, 2012), pp. 137-138.

11   Ibid., p, 83.

12   Yuval Levin, *The Fractured Republic: Renewing America's Social Contract in the Age of Individualism* (New York: Basic Books, 2016), p. 4.

13   *The Analects of Confucius*, p. 66.

14   R. J. Delahunty, *The Arguments of the Philosophers: Spinoza*, edited by Ted Honderich (London and New York: Routledge, 1999), p. 161.

15   Isaiah Berlin, *The Roots of Romanticism* (Princeton, NJ: Princeton University Press, 1999), p. 112.

16   Jean-Paul Sartre, *Being and Nothingness* (New York: Citadel Press, Kingston Publishing Group, 2001), p. 418.

17   Ibid., p. 556.

18   Roger Scruton, *The Soul of the World* (Princeton, NJ: Princeton University Press, 2014), p. 188.

19   Adam Smith, *Critical Assessment*, Volume I, edited by John Cunningham Wood (London and New York: Routledge, 1993), p. 335.

20   Adam Smith, *Theory of Moral Statements*, as cited by Thomas Sowell, *A Conflict of Visions: Ideological Origins of Political Struggles* (New York: Basic Books, 2007), p. 12.

21   Roger Scruton, *How to Be a Conservative* (New York: Bloomsbury Publishing, 2014), pp. 19-20.

22   Thomas Mann, *Doktor Faustus*, translated by John E. Woods (New York: Alfred A Knopf, 1997), p. 510.

23   Roger Scruton, *An Intelligent Person's Guide to Modern Culture* (South Bend, IN: St. Augustine's Press, 2000), p. 83.

24   Julian Johnson, *Who Needs Classical Music?: Cultural Choice and Musical Value*

(New York and Oxford: Oxford University Press, 2002), p. 58.

25 Ibid., p. 113.

26 Ibid., p. 49.

27 Richard Taruskin, *The Dangers of Music and Other Anti-Utopian Essays* (Berkeley and Los Angeles: University of California Press, 2009), p. 5.

28

29 Karl Popper, *All Life Is Problem Solving: On Freedom*, translated by Patrick Camiller (New York: Routledge, 2001), p. 92.

30 Michael Walsh, *The Devil's Pleasure Palace: The Cult of Critical Theory and the Sub-version of the West* (New York and London: Encounter Books, 2015), p. 139.

31 Max Neiman, "The (True) Origin of Wealth," response to Umair Haque, *Medium Daily Digest*, March 1, 2020.

32 Heinrich Heine, as cited by Jonathan Sacks, *The Jonathan Sacks Haggadah* (New Milford, CT: Maggid, 2003), p. 76.

33 Shelby Steele, *Shame: How America's Past Sins Have Polarized Our Country* (New York: Basic Books, 2015), p. 198.

34 Aleksandr Solzhenitsyn, as cited by Patrick J. Deneen, *Why Liberalism Failed* (New Haven and London: Yale University Press, 2018), p. 83.
    35 Confucius, *Confucian Analects*, Translated by James Legge (London: Trübner, 1893), Chapter 13, verse 3. https://china.usc.edu/confucius-analects-3

36 *Kant's Idea for a Universal History with a Cosmopolitan Aim: A Critical Guide*, edited by Amelie Oksenberg Rorty and James Schmidt (Cambridge, UK: Cambridge University Press, 2009).

45

Unequal Temperament

Ideas don't automatically lose their validity just because
unscrupulous people try and assimilate them into their own
distasteful worldviews—and it's an awfully tenuous assumption
that, by listening to a composer's music, we automatically
perceive and accept that composer's philosophy.[1]
Matthew Guerrieri

If you cannot achieve equality of performance among people born
to the same parents and raised under the same roof,
how realistic is it to expect to achieve it across
broader and deeper social divisions.[2]
Thomas Sowell

As mentioned in the preface of this book, a pitfall in conflating any artist's personal morality in relation to their art can result in disconcerting paradoxes and conundrums that are difficult to unravel without falling prey to self-serving double standards, virtue signaling and duplicity. In my attempts to disentangle these seemingly intractable issues in order to ascertain what might be the most effective way to facilitate social and cultural betterment, I'm sure some readers might argue that I haven't managed to avoid my own duplicity. Because our better angels don't always win the day, we all fall short of God's glory and expectations.

That said, in several chapters of this book I have alluded to the pervasiveness of deconstructionist, postmodern rationale that has resulted in a growing contempt for art and culture with Christian and/or European derivations. Multiculturalism, combined with left-leaning political correctness and postmodernism's rejection of meta-narratives, has made all manner of European culture suspect in the eyes of the ideological left. In recent years a number of cultural commentators predicted that it would be only a matter of time before Western classical music, with its deep religious underpinnings, would find itself in the crosshairs of the purveyors of progressivism and other far-left ideologues. The conflating of a particular artist's morality with the aesthetic aspect of their art—the essence of the Wagner conundrum—is now a common and troubling occurrence with many other artists who have become the targets of decidedly illiberal, politically correct-oriented multiculturalist activists.

On June 26, 2018, the *Toronto Star* ran a column by John Terauds titled "'Ode to Joy' has an odious history. Let's give Beethoven's most overplayed symphony a rest." Among the offenses that Terauds attributed to this symphony, was that Hitler "adored" this music and how, "Musicians waiting for their deaths in Nazi concentration camps were ordered to play it, metaphorically twisting its closing call to universal brotherhood and joy into a terrifying, sneering parody of all that strives for light in a human soul." Let's be clear: The Holocaust and Nazi concentration camps were Hitler's sin, not Beethoven's.

Mr. Terauds makes the dubious claim that "Western music usually thinks of itself as being apolitical." He probably could have articulated that better because music doesn't think (but we get the point). Richard Taruskin reminds us that from its earliest incarnations, opera libretti often traded in political narratives. As he states, opera was "a world of where satyrs romped and Eros reigned, where servant girls chastised their masters, where philandering counts were humiliated, and where, later and more earnestly, rabbles were roused and revolutions abetted."[3]

Beethoven was greatly affected by the French Revolution and some of his music has political overtones (*Egmont, Fidelio*, e.g.). Paul Hindemith experienced run-ins with the Nazis. Dmitri Shostakovich was ensnared in conflicts with Stalin. Aaron Copland had distinct political intentions in some of his music. Several of John Adams' operas have serious political and ideological overtones. Many popular musicians have used their music to lambast and lampoon politicians regardless of political party or persuasion. Music's linkage with politics is as old as the day is long and will likely continue to be so.

If Terauds was trying to make the point that Western music (regardless of genre) is, or thinks of itself as being apolitical, one must question his understanding of music history. His view is akin to that of the PC-oriented multiculturalists who trade in cultural totalitarian perspectives that have decidedly illiberal and anti-pluralist orthodoxies. I wonder if he'd consider this poem by a communist sympathizer, Alfred Hayes (1911-1985),[4] to be apolitical:

> *Into the streets May First!*
> *Into the roaring Square!*
> *Shake the midtown towers!*
> *Shatter the downtown air!*
> *Come with a storm of banners,*
> *Come with an earthquake tread,*
> *Bells, hurl out of your belfries,*
> *Red flag, leap out your red!*
> *Out of the shops and factories,*
> *Up with the sickle and hammer,*
> *Comrades, these are our tools,*
> *A song and a banner!*
> *Roll song, from the sea of our hearts,*
> *Banner, leap and be free;*
> *Song and banner together,*
> *Down with the bourgeoisie!*
> *Sweep the big city, march forward,*
> *The day is a barricade;*
> *We hurl the bright bomb of the sun,*
> *The moon like a hand grenade.*
> *Pour forth like a second flood!*

Thunder the alps of the air!
Subways are roaring our milllons—
Comrades, into the square!

Hayes' poem was set to music by the iconic American composer Aaron Copland. An article titled "Marching With a Song" by Ashley Pettis, published in the communist magazine *New Masses* (May 1, 1934), reported that Hayes' poem was sent to the Composers' Collective of the Pierre Degeyter Club in New York as well as other prominent American composers, including Wallingford Riegger, with the intent of using music to advance the communist agenda. In the article, Pettis states the following regarding music and its importance in politics.

> One of the most significant developments within the revolutionary movement has been the growth of music and music-making of a nature which helps to unite and inspire masses of workers. The necessity for this kind of music as a weapon in the class struggle daily becomes more apparent. As in Russia, the idea: "We must develop our musical resources for the building of socialism" has made music both a unique power and an integral part of the lives of the people, so we are witnessing in America the gathering together of groups of workers for the making of music which is expressive of their lives and aspirations.[5]

Both Riegger and Copland (who campaign for Communist Party-USA candidate for president, Earl Browder in 1936) landed in front of the House un-American Activities Committee in 1953.*

Western art has been increasingly targeted by those holding politically correct conceits for quite some time. Teraud's slam of Beethoven's Ninth is on the same trajectory as the twisted, down-with-the-humanities rhetoric that Camille Paglia, Victor Davis Hanson and Allan Bloom warned of decades ago. If we are going to assess all Western music in the context of political correctness and skewed multicultural conceits, will rock, jazz, Broadway or gospel music be castigated by multiculturalists as well? Certainly, there are artists

---

* Full disclosure: I have conducted several of Aaron Copland's compositions, including his Clarinet Concerto, *Fanfare for the Common Man, Variations on a Shaker Melody* and *Quite City.*

working in those genres who are given to political motivations and intent, not to mention ideological predilections.

Will the multiculturalist's rebukes only be levied against artists whose ideological slant is deemed to be politically incorrect according to their criterions? Is art created by individuals of European ancestry now considered illegitimate simply because it *may* offend people from non-Western cultures? Are all non-Western people offended by Beethoven's Ninth or Wagner's music? The young Venezuelans in the Simon Bolivar Symphony Orchestra, or the Arab and Israeli musicians in the West-Eastern Divan Orchestra, or the musicians in orchestras through Asia seem not to be at all disturbed.

We shouldn't forget that most Western music created after 1722 is based on equal temperament, the tuning scheme coalesced by J.S. Bach—a dead, white, Christian, European, heterosexual male. Should we do away with the music of Miles Davis, Stevie Wonder, Sting, Yolanda Adams—music created in the equal temperament mode—because it was a white, Christian male who fashioned the tuning system that facilitated musical creativity in the West for the past three centuries? Until the PC-oriented, social justice warrior ideologues give up listening to music predicated on equal temperament I can only surmise that their protestations are more of a pose than a conviction.

Guilt by association is a ploy used with great effectiveness by those who advocate politically correct attitudes to denigrate ideas, thoughts and people who don't comport with progressive orthodoxy—and this is the essence of the Wagner conundrum; conflating aesthetics with the morality of artists. Matthew Guerrieri's observation that profound ideas "don't automatically lose their validity just because unscrupulous people try and assimilate them into their own distasteful worldviews" is salient. Composers may, in fact, have odious worldviews. Wagner and Chopin certainly did, and it's likely that Shostakovich and Solzhenitsyn may have had serious contempt for Copland and Riegger for their odious dalliances with Marxism-Leninism. One can easily understand why those who lived under the yoke of a regime predicated on the abhorrent political machinations of Stalin would have considered Copland to be seriously daft in this instance. I certainly do on this score, but I still enjoy much of his music on purely aesthetic grounds.

One of the disquieting aspects of a society that is predicated on democratic and free-market ideas, is the there will inevitably be various instances of inequality that cannot be easily remedied or done away with altogether. The Pareto principle, also known as the "80/20 rule," or "the law of the vital few," makes the case that in the business sector, there is a disproportional relationship between inputs and outputs in business dealings. The Pareto Principle, named after the Italian economist, Vilfredo Pareto, is an observation that things in business are not always distributed evenly. Though this principle was initially an economic paradigm it can be applied to many endeavors and disciplines.

For example, in the United States between 2016 and 2019, there was an average of 550,000 boys who annually played basketball on their high school teams. According to NCAA data, only 3.5% of those go on to play at the collegiate level. The thirty teams in the National Basketball Association (NBA) draft 150 players per year and not all of them do well enough to sign contracts and make the team. NBA teams are allowed fifteen players per squad and a smaller percentage of those players are paid top dollar. The average salary for an NBA player in 2019-2020 was $8.2 million, but superstar players like LeBron James or Kevin Durant earn five times more than the average. Additionally, star players earn tens of millions more in endorsement deals. In the case of James, the *Audacity* website reports that he is earning $32 million annually from Nike. According to *Forbes*, Michael Jordan's net worth is $1.6 billion.

Very few NBA players attain this level of financial success. This inequality is an example of the "80/20 rule." Because a small percentage of NBA players have significant name recognition and "marketability," they are rewarded accordingly. Moreover, it's their prowess as basketball players that attract paying customers to watch them play, either in arenas or on television and the Internet. These superstars are the cash cows that generate income for the NBA franchises, their teammates, their coaches, television networks, apparel companies, news organizations and various cottage industries associated with the NBA—bars, restaurants, the travel industry, etc. Meritocracy matters and it generates huge profits in the realm of professional sports. Recently the NBA has taken a highly visible stand in matters of social justice, but it seems highly unlikely that the league or its players would be willing to succumb to the calls for economic justice if it meant reducing or relinquishing their opportunities to earn as much as they can in the free-market. Given the fact that the average NBA salary is more than ten times the average household income of Americans, it would seem that there would be a severe outcry over such income inequity, yet most sports fans are fine with the idea of athletes making these enormous sums and are willing partners in this particular financial arrangement.

Former college football player and commentator for ESPN, AOL Sports, Outkick and Foxsports.com, Jason Whitlock, has been addressing the social justice issue with an emphasis on how the NBA has ignored the human rights violations of the Chinese regime regarding the Uyghur Muslims, the Falun Gang sect and Christians while attempting to build its brand in China. He has been especially outspoken on the Marxist ties to Black Lives Matter and how Big Tech companies view BLM as "a sacred cow" and will "cancel" anyone who criticizes BLM. Whitlock's comment that BLM is "the antithesis of Dr. Martin Luther King's civil rights movement," resulted in Twitter account being temporarily interrupted.[6] A fearless defender of free speech, Whitlock cited Dr. King's Christian faith as being an essential aspect of his activism and did not amend his comments in order to seek approval from Twitter.

Financial inequity is not intrinsic to professional sports. Basically, every profession is subjected to the Pareto in some way. However, when the political process is affected by so-called "dark money," we begin to witness the emergence of a plutocracy whereby a wealthy ruling class becomes entrenched and increasingly impervious to sanctions, much to the detriment of citizens and civil liberties. In this respect, the political left has a valid point when it cites crushing financial inequities. The problem, however, is that many of the political left are gaming the system and have become part of the 1% that they love to criticize for being bereft of compassion and concern in matters of distributive justice. California's governor, Gavin Newsom, raised $80 million to stave off a recall challenge in his state while thousands of citizens have had their lives and livelihoods ruined by some of his political decisions. If you declared, "Not fair!," you'd be correct. Is Marx's prediction that capitalism would collapse due to its inherent flaws coming to pass? Perhaps so, but something else is at work.

Neo-Marxism

In an arresting essay by Israeli Biblical scholar and political theorist Yoram Hazony titled "The Challenge of Marxism," published in *Quillette* (August 16, 2020), Hazony cites how the current proponents of Marxist ideology continue to pursue power by aggressively commandeering various enterprises—the media, academia, the entertainment industry, the arts and the political sphere. The "long march through the institutions" is entering its final phase and even long-time liberals such as Naomi Wolf and Bill Maher have expressed concern for what they view as being regressive and illiberal attitudes and practices concerning race and authoritarian inclinations by the government. Wolf's Twitter account* was suspended when she objected to President Biden's COVID-19 policies. Maher cited various examples of increased segregation including black college students wanting black-only dormitories and black-only commencement exercises. Rather than debating these issues in a public forum, the progressive left seeks to silence any and all dissenting perspectives that don't align with its outlooks because power, not truth, is its ultimate objective.

Hazony points out that these neo-Marxists are just another "class or group, using the power of the state to exploit and oppress other classes in the most extreme ways," with the aim of "reconstructing society" in increasingly aggressive fashion. As a result, liberalism, "is being expelled from its former strongholds, and the hegemony of liberal ideas, as we have known it since the 1960s, will end." As mentioned, traditional liberals are now finding themselves in similar circumstances as conservatives and Christians in that they are being targeted as the "opposition" to the progressive neo-Marxist agenda. Hazony predicts that "brave liberals will soon be waging war on the very institutions they so recently controlled."[7]

The paradigm of "oppressor vs. oppressed" has become the ideological weapon of choice that is being used to take down the "exploiting" class, along with its customs, traditions and laws. As such, "a revolutionary reconstruction of society at large" that destroys the oppressor class is viewed as necessary, justified and noble. Hazony notes that Marx promised, "that after the oppressed underclass takes control of the state, the exploitation of individuals by other individuals will be 'put to an end' and the antagonism between classes of individuals will totally disappear. How this is to be done is not specified."[8] Citing the influences of Antonio Gramsci, Michel Foucault and the neo-Marxist philosophers of the Frankfurt School, Hazony speaks to the issue of how democratic processes mitigate the tendency to resort to violence and coercion as a

---

* Wolf's Twitter episode was cited in *The Hill* on June 7, 2021 for "spreading misinformation." Maher made his comments on HBO cable show *Real Time with Bill Maher* on September 10, 2021.

means to create social betterment. This, of course, is antithetical to the Marxist mindset, as Hazony avers:

> Simply put, the Marxist framework and democratic political theory are opposed to one another in principle. A Marxist cannot grant legitimacy to liberal or conservative points of view without giving up the heart of Marxist theory, which is that these points of view are inextricably bound up with systematic injustice and must be overthrown, by violence if necessary. This is why the very idea that a dissenting opinion—one that is not "Progressive" or "Anti-Racist"—could be considered legitimate has disappeared from liberal institutions as Marxists have gained power. At first, liberals capitulated to their Marxist colleagues' demand that conservative viewpoints be considered illegitimate (because conservatives are "authoritarian" or "fascist"). This was the dynamic that brought about the elimination of conservatives from most of the leading universities and media outlets in America.[9]

I doubt that President Biden, or Nancy Pilosi, or various celebrities and sports figures view themselves as being aligned with Marxists, but actions speak louder that words and judging by their actions and attitudes in matters of achieving equity—racial, economic, gender—they seem closer to the illiberal progressives who tout the neo-Marxist views than their democratic and libertarian counterparts. All the "New Dealism" that is being discussed concerning climate change, economics and social progress is predicted on more government reliance and control, not less. Jonah Goldberg notes that early progressives in American politics were advocates of the idea "that the society could be molded to the will of experts." Sound familiar? The idea that experts, many of whom are unelected bureaucrats, should somehow be influencing and determining various political decisions is but another mode by which the progressive left could attain power by circumventing representative government in order to dictate policy. The European Union also suffers from the same scenario in which nameless, faceless unelected bureaucrats assume greater influence over societal and governmental procedures. Goldberg asserts:

> Philosophically, the New Deal drew on—or at least reflected—John Dewey's and Woodrow Wilson's contempt for the outdated vision of the Founders. The Founders "lacked," Dewey wrote in Liberalism and Social Action, "historic sense and interest." The Burkean and Madisonian vision

of government simply serving to protect liberties and enforce fair, neutral rules was inadequate next to what could be accomplished with a sufficient application of will by experts given the power to provide meaning to every individual.[10]

Dewey would say, "Natural rights and natural liberties exist only in the kingdom of mythological social zoology,"[11] and that rights can only be properly secured through "social control of economic forces in the interest of the great mass of individuals."[12] This is the same mindset behind Hillary Clinton's concept of "the politics of meaning" whereby the ushering of government resources in order to dictate or compel societal change was a viable and necessary methodology. Goldberg views Clinton as a "representative figure, the leading member of a generational cohort of elite liberals who (unconsciously of course) brought fascist themes into mainstream liberalism … a direct descendant of the Social Gospel movement of the 1920s and 1930s."[13]

The notion that Hillary Clinton was an advocate of fascism will undoubtedly seem hyperbolic and an expression of unfounded, right-wing paranoia. I used to be of the mindset, as were many of my friends and colleagues, that communism was leftwing totalitarianism and fascism was rightwing totalitarianism. I began to modify my views after reading an essay in *Forbes* by economist Bill Flax. In his essay titled "Obama, Hitler and Exploding the Biggest Lie in History" (September 1, 2011), Flax makes an important observation and asks the following question:

> In Argentina, everyone acknowledges that fascism, state capitalism, corporatism—whatever—reflects very leftwing ideology. Eva Peron remains a liberal icon. President Obama's Fabian policies (Keynesian economics) promise similar ends. His proposed infrastructure bank is just the latest gyration of corporatism. Why then are fascists consistently portrayed as conservatives?[14]

Calling this observation "biggest lie in history" may seem to be hyperbolic, yet Flax's question is pertinent. Upon further research into the realm of geopolitics, I came to the understanding that all regimes that engage in state control (authoritarianism), whether communist, fascist, or tyrannical monarchies, are leftist. The polar opposite on the far right is where there is little or no governmental control—anarchy. Flax contends that fascism is to the right of communism, but only by a few feet, not a few miles. I agree. When any regime asserts authoritarian control over commerce, banking, academia, the media, healthcare, the arts, travel rights, property rights, etc., it is a *de facto* leftist operation. The idea that conservatives are touting fascism is nonsense, but it's nonsense being used as an ideological cudgel to justify and advance a leftist drive for power. Besmirching conservatives with the "fascist" tag is a smear tactic being used to undermine conservative values in the pursuit of power.

So how did we get here? Theodor Adorno, one of the early Frankfurt School ideologues, has been credited with bringing the issue of "identity" in to the neo-Marxist ideology. As a young Jewish man in Germany in the 1930s he, like other Jews, became the target of the Nazi's opprobrium towards Jews in general. Suddenly, he was the victim of an "oppressor" class based on his "identity" as a Jew. Because the Nazis were fascists, Adorno's ideological enemies were always labeled as "fascists." William Haines, Director of the International Education Foundation (UK) points out, the injustice, pogroms and discrimination that Jews in Russia experienced in the eighteenth and nineteenth centuries led to non-religious Jews becoming politically active. Those who did not believe in God but still experienced this discrimination tended to become socialists and communists.

When the Frankfurt School philosophers emigrated to the United States after World War II, they encountered racism and anti-Jewish sentiment in much the same way as they did in Europe. As it was in Europe, much of the enmity that they experienced in America was at the hands of Christians. Haines notes that most of the members of the Frankfurt School were atheists, and although still ethnically Jewish, they feared that they and other Jews would suffer the same fate in Christian America as did the Jews in Europe. Hence, Adorno's analysis of the "authoritarian personality" as being rooted in the patriarchal Christian family became a defining aspect of his identity politics dogma. Accordingly, the origin of "critical theory" was rooted in the idea of unmasking the ideologies of oppression.

In his book, *BLM: The Making of a New Marxist Revolution*, Mike Gonzales of the Heritage Foundation writes about how "a group of self-avowed Marxists, which openly seeks to overturn society, made use of one man's tragedy and has so far largely succeeded in its goal." The co-founders of Black Lives Matter, particularly Alicia Garza, claim to use Marxist tactics and this can be traced to

Adorno's thoughts on identity politics vis-à-vis race and white, Christian culture.[15] During the height of the demonstrations and riots in the aftermath of George Floyd's death, I surveyed the BLM website to understand the genesis of the organization. I was told by several of my friends that BLM was an extension of Dr. Martin Luther King, Jr.'s civil rights activism and that it emerged out of the basements of black churches across America. My survey found no mention of Dr. King, but it did reveal a decidedly anti-nuclear family slant and this statement: "When we gather, we do so with the intention of freeing ourselves from the tight grip of heteronormative thinking, or rather, the belief that all in the world are heterosexual (unless s/he or they disclose otherwise)."[16] Not surprisingly, this is at odds with traditional Christian views of family and sexuality. Like many social activists in the current drive for racial justice, there tends to be an admiration of Dr. King's activism, but a disdain for the religious convictions that propelled his activism. Identity politics is clearly the front line in the current iteration of the cultural wars, whether it's labeled "cultural Marxism," or "cultural totalitarianism," or "progressive postmodernism."

In another essay published by *Quillette* titled "Unspeakable Truths about Racial inequality in America," Glenn Loury[17] of Brown University makes several provocative points regarding the issues of identity politics in relation to white supremacy, the legacy of colonialism, and the culture of dead white men of European heritage. He imagines what white people might say in response to the unending vituperation being levied at European culture, saying:

> I well might begin to ask myself, were I one of these "white oppressors," on exactly what foundations does human civilization in the 21st century stand? I might begin to enumerate the great works of philosophy, mathematics, and science that ushered in the "Age of Enlightenment," that allowed modern medicine to exist, that gave rise to the core of human knowledge about the origins of the species or of the universe. I might begin to tick-off the great artistic achievements of European culture, the architectural innovations, the paintings, the symphonies, etc. And then, were I in a particularly agitated mood, I might even ask these "people of color," who think that they can simply bully me into a state of guilt-ridden self-loathing, where is "their" civilization?[18]

A thought-provoking comment, indeed, but Loury goes on to say that he would never say such a thing, characterizing it as supremacist and racist rhetoric. Yet, his comment acknowledges a particular set of truths about European Christian culture, and it's not all untoward and wicked. I've conducted numerous symphonies and concertos by Vivaldi, Mozart, Haydn, Beethoven, Brahms, Chopin, Schumann, Dvorak, Tchaikovsky, Shostakovich and Hindemith, and I know a number of Black, Latino and Asian musicians who share my opinion that this is music of great beauty and profound meaning. I've worked with Chinese and Russian musicians living in the United States who grew up in under the thumb of communist regimes in their homelands. They have no desire to return and they consider Marxist sympathizers in the West to be seriously daft, as did the iconic Russian composer, Dmitri Shostakovich when he visited the United States in 1949. Have we learned nothing? The values of The Enlightenment that emphasized individual rights, human dignity and rationalism made the socio-economic condition of many much better than had been previously been the case, but to the purveyors of neo-Marxism, these attributes are subordinate to the progressive agenda that prioritizes power above all else. Marxism, on the other hand, has produced untold human suffering and staggering body counts, all in the name of progress and equity, of course. Marxism's history is one of death and destruction. The idea of "the dictatorship of the proletariat" is more a myth than a reality.

Loury asks another pertinent question: "How can we make 'whiteness' into a site of unrelenting moral indictment without also occasioning it to become the basis of pride, of identity and, ultimately, of self-affirmation?" He goes on, "One risks cancellation for saying this, but the right idea is the idea of Gandhi and Martin Luther King: to transcend our racial particularism while stressing the universality of our humanity."[19] What is telling here, is that merely alluding to the idealism of Gandhi or Dr. King as being possible remedies to our socio-cultural malaise, is now considered an offense to the progressive left, and thus being "canceled" or defenestrated is to be expected. The price of being courageous and forthright has become quite steep, precisely because there has been little reasoned pushback on this illiberal and duplicitous ideological creed.

In a peace conference that I attended in Tel Aviv, Israel in 2007, Dr. King's son, Dr. Martin Luther King, III, spoke of his father' guidance regarding non-violent solutions for social justice, and the first necessary attribute was courage—the willingness to take a stand for your beliefs in the face of brutal oppression. There was a great deal of "canceling" going on in the United States since its founding, especially regarding the race issue. The opprobrium that BLM or Adorno express is warranted, given the injustices that occurred in the United States. We cannot ignore the "original sin" of slavery. The civil rights movement that produced righteous leaders such as Dr. King, Joseph Lowery, Robert L. Woodson, C. Delores Tucker and Fannie Lou Hamer was a testament of how pushing back on unrighteous and unscrupulous attitudes and actions could yield progress in the face of unremitting hatred ...."man's inhumanity to man."[*]

Woodson has pushed back against what he sees as revisionist history with regard to the telling of America's story. It's clear that he doesn't consider any iteration of Marxism to be the answer to our racial problems. In his book, *Red White and Black: Recusing American History from Revisionists and Race Hustlers*, Woodson admits that discrimination exists but takes the position that the progressive-oriented view of those who engage in "contemporary groupthink," is not the way forward because it "defames our national heritage, divides our people, and instills helplessness among those who already hold within themselves the grit and resilience to better their lot in life."[20] Woodson is a tireless advocate of personal empowerment and taking responsibility for one's course in life. He doesn't view meritocracy as being inherently a symptom of privilege or supremacy.

The concluding lyrics of "The Star-Spangled Banner," "land of the free and home of the brave," couldn't be more relevant in the context of the threat upon civil liberties by the illiberal edicts being advocated by the progressive leftists who are the progeny of Marxism. It's also an apt lyric for those who have fought to end racism and injustice. We might imagine "one nation under God," or the realization of "a universal brotherhood," or acting as if we were part of "a global family," but without freedom (the right to choose), this is impossible. Forced compliance violates the basis of negative rights—freedom of speech, freedom of religion—the right to freely do something or obtain

---

[*] Dr. King used this phrase in several of his speeches, however it was originally from a poem by Scottish Poet Robert Burns published in 1784 titled, "Man Was Made to Mourn, A Dirge."

something without interference from outside forces. These rights are free from the interference of another person or a group of people. Putting limits on government in order to secure liberty was the essential premise of the U.S. Constitution. It's been said that a society that prioritizes equality over freedom will get neither. It's one thing to argue for equal opportunity but quite another to force equity.

Historian Will Durant reminds us that freedom and equality are not compatible and nature proves that. Thomas Sowell cites how identical twins who grow up in similar circumstances have different talents, opinions, beliefs and affinities. Within any family there will be a variety of circumstances. I have eleven siblings; some are religious, some not. Some are conservative, some liberal and some are agnostic about politics. Some are married, some are divorced and some never tied the knot. Some are artistic, some not. Some are naturally athletic and some are not. Some had substance-abuse problems, some didn't. This reinforces Sowell's contention that it's "unreasonable to achieve equality of performance among people born to the same parents and raised under the same roof, and therefore it is unrealistic to expect to achieve equality across broader and deeper social divisions."[21] This doesn't mean as a society we shouldn't be proponents of justice and fairness, but we ought to be vigilant in the practice of using government and rely on "extreme of legal frames" to attain various outcomes. Emotions do not supersede facts, and though we might *feel* that achieving "cosmic justice" is, or should be a primary goal of government, history informs us that the overreach of government leads to tyranny and an erosion of freedom, and when that occurs, civil liberties are diminished.

Conversely, being vigilant about governmental overreach shouldn't be construed as promoting "rugged individualism." Seeking balance in the pursuit of fairness requires a nuanced approach. Sowell often speaks of "trade-offs" and "costs" in his remarks regarding the pursuit of fairness. Economist Adam Smith posited that there are self-interests and public interests in the free-market paradigm, and there needed to be a balance of these constituent interests. Smith was pointing to an ethical premise that was necessary to fashion fair economic conditions. In this regard, compromise, compassion, conciliation and harmonization—attributes that healthy and stable marriages and families rely on to achieve successful outcomes—ought to be considered in the quest of creating a fair and just society. If we wish for our homes to be dwellings in which we all can get along harmoniously, it is imperative to examine the various trade-offs and compromises that are required to ensure that we can achieve that goal. Compelled conformity is not the way. Adults who insist on having their way at all times, become bullies and tyrants.

In her eulogy of Roger Scruton who passed in 2020, Barbara Kay offers this evaluation on one of his central philosophical outlooks:

> Compelled conformity—not legislated, God forbid, but enforced by social pressure—looks stifling to progressives, but in its own way it can be a great comfort, knowing the rules of what is and isn't decent, and, through them, belonging. We all want to belong, but healthy belonging is sensitive to scale. We're not made for globalization. We're made for homes and homelands. If people don't have homes to keep them rooted, feeling they belong in a good way, they will find fake homes that are tethered to ideas and theories, and then they often belong in a bad way. These are Scrutonesque musings.[22]

In addition to being a thoughtful philosopher, Scruton was also a pianist and composer who wrote extensively and insightfully on the art if music. His musings on classical music and pop music, and the cultures that spawned this music, are astute and wise. His observations of the atonal composers that Adorno exalted (Schoenberg, Webern, Berg, e.g.) in relation to pop music are especially perspicacious. Scruton noted that progressive neo-Marxists who are so enamored with Adorno's theories of identity politics are quite uncomfortable with Adorno's disdain for jazz. Because jazz was largely the invention of black composers, especially the Ragtime composers and their precursors—Louis Moreau Gottschalk, Scott Joplin, Will Marion Cook, James Reese Europe, to name but a few—Adorno's contempt for this genre caused serious consternation for those who view art and culture through the prism of racial identity. Joplin and Cook studied with classical music teachers but eventually took different musical paths and pioneered a new musical style and became among the first Ragtime composers. They were the forerunners of what would become "America's classical music," jazz. Scruton proffered that Adorno was perturbed that jazz and America pop music were styles invented by "the common man" and by-passed the opinions of musical "experts" and academicians—all the "high priests" who thought they knew better than "the people" in matters of musical taste and knowledge.

The life stories of these musicians point to Sowell's contention that within any group of people there will be those who choose paths that don't comport with expected conformity in pursuit of happiness and fulfillment. To expect equality of outcome—economically, artistically, academically, athletically—is to expect the unreasonable. As a young student Thomas Sowell was a Marxist. He cited other conservatives who had been Marxists or socialists, including Ronald Regan, Milton Friedman and F.A. Hayek. When asked by Dave Rubin why he changed his ideological stance, Sowell simply replied, "facts." And the facts tend to support the claims of Durant, Sowell, Whitlock, Friedman and Scruton that in nature there is an unequal temperament in the equation and that our best chance to attain fairness and justice is to protect freedom from the deleterious effects of control and tyranny.

Endnotes

1   Matthew Guerrieri, "The Censures of the Carping World," October 26, 2007, http://sohothedog.blogspot.com/2007/10/censures-of-carping-world.html.

2   Thomas Sowell, *The Quest for Cosmic Justice* (New York: Simon and Schuster, 2001), p. 67.

3   Richard Taruskin, *The Dangers of Music and Other Anti-Utopian Essays* (Berkeley-Los Angeles: University of California Press, 2010), p. 222.

4   Alex Harvey, "Writer's Brains: The Lasting Worth of Alfred Hayes," *Los Angeles Review of Books*, July 6, 2018.

5   Ashley Pettis, "Mayday: Marching with a Song," *New Masses*, May 1, 1934, https://www.marxists.org/subject/mayday/articles/song.html.

6   Emma Colton, "Jason Whitlock Reposts BLM Tweet He Was Suspended for Vowing to 'Never Apologize,'" *Washington Examiner*, April 14, 2021.

7   Yoram Hazony, "The Challenge of Marxism," *Quillette*, August 16, 2020.

8   Ibid.

9   Ibid.

10 Jonah Goldberg, "The Newest Deal: Biden Has Overshot LBJ's Legacy and Gone Straight for FDR Instead," *The Dispatch*, April 10, 2021, https://gfile.thedispatch.com/p/the-newest-deal/comments.

11 John Dewey, *The Later Works of John Dewey, 1925-1953* (Carbondale, IL.: SIU Press, 2008), p. 15.

12   Ibid., p. 27.

13   Jonah Goldberg, *Liberal Fascism: The Secret History of the American Left, from Mussolini to the Politics of Meaning* (New York, NY: Crown Publishing Group, 2008), pp. 317-318.

14   Bill Flax, "Obama, Hitler and Exploding the Biggest Lie in History," *Forbes*, September 1, 2011.

15   Mike Gonzalez, "Marxism Underpins Black Lives Matter Agenda," *The Heritage Foundation*, September 8, 2021, https://www.heritage.org/progressivism/commentary/marxism-underpins-black-lives-matter-agenda.

16   "What We Believe," Black Lives Matter, https://blacklivesmatter.com/what-we-believe/, since removed.

17   Glenn Loury, "Unspeakable Truths about Racial Inequality in America," *Quillette,* February 10, 2021.

18   Ibid.

19   Ibid.

20   Robert L. Woodson, Sr., *Red White and Black: Recusing American History from Revisionists and Race Hustlers,* Kindle Edition (New York-Nashville: Post Hill Press, 2021).

21   Ibid., Sowell, *The Quest for Cosmic Justice,* p. 67.

22   Barbara Kay, "Remembering Roger Scruton, Defender of Reason in a World of Postmodern Jackals," *Quillette*, January 14, 2020.

46

Coda

Since men love freedom, and the freedom of individuals in society
requires some regulation of conduct, the first condition of freedom
is it limitation; make it absolute and it dies in chaos.[1]
Will and Ariel Durant

As for myself, I experience a sort of terror when,
at the moment of setting to work and finding myself before
the infinitude of possibilities that present themselves,
I have the feeling that everything is permissible to me. ...
Will I then have to lose myself in this abyss of freedom?[2]
Igor Stravinsky

Everything is permissible, but not everything is edifying.
1 Corinthians 6:12

I n the opening chapters of this book I often referred to "romanticism" and the "romantic spirit." Among the composers of the classical tradition, Beethoven is seen as the revolutionary who broke with the past and forged a compositional path toward what would become known as "romanticism" in music. But what do we really mean and what are the historical underpinnings of the term?

On several occasions, I've alluded to Isaiah Berlin's celebrated Mellon lecture series presented at the National Gallery of Art in Washington, D.C. in 1965. In those lectures, Berlin set out define romanticism by tracing the important historical figures, circumstances, attitudes and philosophies that impacted the evolution of romanticism in Europe and beyond. Berlin asserts that the development of the romantic spirit emanated from Germany between 1760 and 1830 and was in large part a reaction to the influence of the French in social, philosophical and political matters.

Germany was suffering from an inferiority complex of sorts and was seeking to establish its own philosophical worldview. The German reaction, according to Berlin, was in effect "a very grand form of sour grapes," but it was also in his view, "the largest recent movement to transform the lives and the thought of the western world."[3] According to Berlin that transformation continued to exert a significant influence on Western psychology throughout the twentieth century and into the twenty-first. Berlin posits that the central narratives found among the romantics of nineteenth-century Europe include, "minorities were more holy than majorities," that sincerity and the "readiness to sacrifice one's life to some inner light" was a high priority, that heroism (even failed heroism) was noble, that selling out to anything less than you personal convictions was a sign of weakness, and that knowledge, reason and the advance of science—those salient Enlightenment memes—were subsidiary to one's personal idealism and one's dedication to that idealism.[4] In his *New York Times* review of Berlin's lecture compilation, Douglas A. Silva writes:

> Berlin revels in the romantics' embrace of irrationalism and their rejection of the cold calculations and rigid categories of philosophy; he lauds the romantics' acceptance of irreconcilable conflict and their denial of the tidy, reasonable solutions promised by Enlightenment thinkers; he endorses their mystical vision of all that is above humanity and out of our reach, of what we are powerless to change.[5]

Berlin notes that the zeitgeist regarding the notion of idealism that the romantics celebrated in the late nineteenth century, was not idealism in the philosophical sense, but rather a contemporary and "ordinary" sense of the term, whereby "the state of mind of a man who is prepared to sacrifice a great deal for principles or for some conviction ... who is prepared to go to the stake for some something which he believes" was to be admired and emulated. This disposition towards "sincerity, purity of soul, the readiness to dedicate yourself to your ideal" was the prevalent ethos of the romantic spirit,[6] according to Berlin.

With this attitude as the underlying rationale of romanticism, the arts, especially musical composition, adopted a correlative mindset, or perhaps more fittingly, a correlative "heart-set." Musical composition became much more than a commissioned work for a specific occasion (liturgical or secular), as was often the case in the eighteenth century. In this new psychological zeitgeist, music became the expression of personal feelings and one's convictions became the sources of inspiration resulting in the idea that "art is the expression of somebody, it is always a voice speaking. A work of art is the voice of one man addressing himself to men—the expression of the attitude to life, conscious or unconscious, of its maker.[7] In its more extreme countenance the idea of the artist as, "prophet and priest" became a new, and somewhat self-important (or self-aggrandizing) way in which artists viewed themselves in the circles in which they lived and worked.

Freedom of expression and the exploration of new modes to express oneself through one's art became a significant rationale in artistic endeavors. Moreover, the intentions of artists from a moral, political and ethical perspective began to take on greater importance as artists became keenly aware of the idea that they were often viewed as purveyors of insight and wisdom. An emergent narrative was that artistic genius corresponded to genius in other spheres. Arthur Schopenhauer famously averred, "The person endowed with talent thinks more rapidly and acutely than the rest; on the other hand, the genius perceives a world from different from them all."[8] However, if artists, despite of their talent and genius became morally licentious in their behavior, conversely, there was the danger of artists becoming deleterious influences. Will and Ariel Durant cautioned that unbridled freedom and actions that were not constrained would result in behavior and emotional excesses that might be harmful and injurious to self and society. Being accountable and responsible—having to answer for one's behavior—is a hedge against chaos, destruction and ruin.*

By the late eighteenth century instrumental music, once eschewed by the early church fathers due to its pagan associations, begins to take prominence over vocal music due to its unmatched power of suggestion and allegory. Beginning with late music of Mozart and the music of Beethoven, heightened emotional expression and drama became highly prevalent. This decidedly romantic rationale would influence composers and artists well into the twentieth century despite the emerging stylist trends of dodecaphonic formalism (Schoenberg), new objectivism (Hindemith) and neo-classicism (Stravinsky). The romantic spirit in music was evident well into the twentieth century (Barber, Britten, Copland, Kodály).

Religion vs. Reason

In an essay for the *Wall Street Journal*, Irving Kristol opined, "It is ideas which rule the world, because it is ideas that define the way reality is perceived; and in the absence of religion, it is out of culture—pictures, poems, songs, philosophy—that these ideas are born.[9] This is another way of saying that politics is downstream of culture. When Damon of Athens asserted that if you change the songs of a nation the nation's laws will change, he wasn't far off the mark. As noted in my earlier essays, the diminishing of religious belief has led to a spate of pathologies—secularism, nihilism, hedonism, to name but a few—that have had deleterious effects on society. G. K. Chesterton is said to have opined, "When men choose not to believe in God, they do not thereafter believe in nothing, then they'll become capable of believing in anything."[10]

Too often there is a common misconception that the Enlightenment was a lightning bolt that abruptly ended all religious belief and the reliance on supernatural phenomenon resulting in the immediate supplanting of religious beliefs with reason and logic. In fact, there was no immediate rejection of religion and as we know, many people—composers included—remained "believers" well into the twentieth century—Stravinsky, Ives and Messiaen

---

* The etymology of the word "responsibility" stems from the Latin *respondere*: answered, often in return; to be answerable.

among them. Melanie Phillips observes that history is a complex process whereby seemingly conflicting ideas are evolving concomitantly. As she puts it: "The seismic struggle between reason and irrationality well predated the Enlightenment; and the ideas generated by the Enlightenment created historical feedback loops of reaction and counter-reaction that continue to this day." The ideological debates that have erupted in the late twentieth century are largely predicated on these same "feedback loops." Phillips avers that the current iteration of culture wars and the subsequent "unraveling of the Enlightenment" is the result of the spurious rationale, "that reason can exist detached from the civilization that gave it birth ... the fundamental error of thinking that to be 'enlightened' necessarily entails a repudiation of religion."[11] Many of America's founders, for instance, remained "believers."

Jean-Jacques Rousseau, considered by many to be the father of romanticism, argued that *"getting right with yourself,"* was the creed to live by, "because you, your conscience, your inner lantern, lit the path in this world."[12] Rousseau's idea that religion was just one more oppressive construct that alienated humankind and kept one in chains, was in many ways a precursor to Nietzsche's concept that one's personal view of morality trumped all other considerations. A significant aspect of "the romantic spirit" is the idea of rebellion and the desire to break free from the status quo—culturally, politically, socially—that is perceived as being out of tune with the natural order of things. This was the idea behind Rousseau's vision of "the noble savage" who was always living in harmony with nature in its purest, unadulterated state.[*]

For many in the Enlightenment era, it was not unreasonable to maintain their religious convictions in the face of reason and logic. We should remember too, that the Enlightenment in Britain and America exemplified far different attitudes about the role of religion in fashioning a moral and just society than their French counterparts. The Brits and young Americans avoided the vilification of religion (and the clergy), whereas the French detested religion and embraced the idea that reason was a form of civic religion that could be detached from spirituality. Berlin cites the highly influential philosopher Nicolas de Condorcet who argued (much like the Greeks) that mathematics,

---

[*] The concept of "the noble savage" is often attributed to Rousseau, but it was first used in the seventeenth century by the English poet John Dryden in his 1672 play, *The Conquest of Granada.*

statistics and empirical data could be the basis on which to establish the necessary virtues and truths by which a moral and ethical society could be attained. For Condorcet the "perfectibility of man" and the disappearance of evil was inevitable if society adhered to statistics and empirical data. Any notion of obligation, duty, or one's portion of responsibility is conspicuously absent in this particular narrative.

Religious thought is generally based on the idea of attaining self-betterment by overcoming our proclivities by aligning ourselves with God's purpose and principles. In doing so believers believe they can change for the better if they make the effort to change. (God helps those who help themselves.) It is in this covenant that believers find hope, comfort and ultimately, salvation. Reason would seem to suggest that numbers and statistics are incapable in explaining emotions, morality, behavior and creativity. Martin Luther would go as far as to suggest reason is "a whore and must be avoided."[13] Luther's view aside, reason plays a significant role in our pursuit of goodness.

I've argued throughout this book that the metaphysical aspects of the human experience point to idea that the attributes of reason and emotion, mind and heart, and truth and love ought to be conjoined in a harmonious fashion in order to create the conditions necessary to achieve betterment in ourselves, our families and our societies. This is not a new idea and theologian Joseph Campbell reinforces this view, saying, "Thus in total view of the medieval thinkers there was a perfect accord between the structure of the universe, the canons of the social order, and the good of the individual."[14]

Currently, there has been an emergent perspective that religion can be replaced by pure rationality in our attempt to make the world a more humane and ethical place; that reason and rationality are the paths to greater equity, compassion and goodwill. Atheist author, Sam Harris is a leading exponent of this view. However, as Jordan Peterson posits, the presupposition of religious belief in the West and the culture it spawned cannot be dismissed out of hand, as if hasn't had a serious effect in creating the conditions for attaining an ethical culture. Peterson explains:

> I think the universe that people like [Richard] Dawkins and [Sam] Harris inhabit is so intensely conditioned by mythological presuppositions that they take for granted the ethic that emerges out of that, as if it's just a given—a

rational given—and this is precisely Nietzsche's observation, as well as Dostoevsky's. ... The ethic you [they] think is normative is the consequence of its nesting inside of this tremendously lengthy history, much of which was expressed in mythological formulation. [If] you wipe that out you don't get to keep all the presuppositions and just assume they're rationally axiomatic.

To make a rational argument you have to start with an initial proposition. Well, the proposition that underlies Western culture is that there is a transcendent morality. ... The ethic that drives our culture is predicated on the idea of God, and that you can't just take that idea away and it expect that it will remain intact mid-air without any foundational [metaphysical] support.[15]

This was a major critique of Nietzsche's regarding the attempt to use pure reason to define morality and live accordingly. As noted previously, Immanuel Kant intuited that the intelligible order found in nature pointed to the idea of a "supreme intelligence" and "divine purpose," something that was transcendent and beyond rational explanation or pure scientific analysis that could be a factor in the process of becoming more humane—individually and collectively. Kant argued that there exist three ways in which one could experience pleasure: through that which was agreeable, good and beautiful. He also acknowledged that the conjoining of objective and subjective realities—truth and imagination—is what allows us to make aesthetic judgments concerning art and music in the most efficacious way.

Because Kant ardently believed in freedom and that volition is what distinguished humankind from other creatures, he was faced with a certain dilemma that a person could choose to believe in God, or the incorporeal realm, or myths, mysticism and all of those seemingly unreasonable or irrational aspects of religion. By readily acknowledging the transcendent and metaphysical realities of the human experience Kant (who was a cosmologist) left the door open for the romantics to engage in using myths, legends, mysticism and fantasies as sources of inspiration. Yet, Isaiah Berlin points out that Kant "detested every form of extravagance fantasy, what he called *Schwärmerei*, any form of exaggeration, mysticism, vagueness, confusion. Nevertheless, Kant is justly regarded as one of the fathers of romanticism—in which there is a certain irony."[16]

Berlin suggests that if humans were only beings of reason, lawfulness or in a mode of "slavery at the hand of nature ... then indeed there would be no morality," for determinism of any kind results in a scenario that is "incompatible with any freedom and any morality must therefore be false."[17] Our choices and values determine our identities. To be co-creators in the process of charting our destinies requires the ability to choose, and if one chooses a life of faith in the pursuit of meaning and spiritual fulfillment, the sincerity of that belief can be viewed as a heroic undertaking, especially in an environment where religious belief is under siege.

Our self-interests and our quest for betterment are not easily assuaged. Richard Dawkins attributes this impulse to our "selfish genes;" those evolutionary impulses that propel our innate human desires towards progress, gratification *and survival*. Thomas Hobbes' view that human nature is intrinsically selfish led to his highly influential concept of "the social contract theory" by which the moral, ethical and political obligations of individuals within a given community needed to be predicated upon a mutual agreement in order to assuage selfishness. This is in accord with Spinoza's advocacy of individuals being willingly obedient to the virtues that benefit the commonwealth. The Preamble of the American Constitution references the formation of "a more perfect union" whereby promoting the "general welfare" of the people is viewed as an ongoing process—an evolution of virtuous behavior in which freedom and choice are the necessary attributes to create a moral culture.

Granted, that process can seem to be an exercise in futility given the onerous circumstances that we now face. The aforementioned rationale of postmodernism in the West is antipodal to what had been the accepted norm dating back to the early Christian philosophy and the Renaissance, a time when creating art and music based on religious convictions and scientific principles was celebrated as a reflection of humankind's ability to realize its fullest potential. Because religion and science in the Renaissance were not considered mutually exclusive entities but rather as correlative facets of the human experience, there existed an understanding that when harmoniously integrated into artistic endeavors, these seemingly polar opposite truth-seeking modalities could yield sublime artistic expressions of great beauty and meaning.

Political scientists of the Enlightenment proffered that material interests and concerns such as survival, security and prosperity were the rational concerns of humankind and should be the prime consideration in the pursuit of happiness and fulfillment. (Ayn Rand's concept of "rational egoism" was also rooted in this view.) But this wasn't breaking news. As American economist and author, David P. Goldman points out, Cicero in first-century Rome, was a leading exponent of the idea that a healthy republic would be "an assemblage associated by a common acknowledgment of law, and by a community of interests. Cicero's 'community of interests' is the ancestor of all secular concepts of the state offered by modern political scientists," from Hobbes to Montesquieu, to Leo Strauss.[18]

Saint Augustine, however, would reject Cicero's premise stating that the success of a community is not based on "common interests" but rather, on "higher virtues." Political states and nations fail because the "fallen" proclivities of the people charged with determining what has value is the Achilles' Heel that ultimately prevents a truly benevolent society from coming to fruition. Alexander Hamilton correctly observed that flawed people create flawed systems of governing and as a result when he stated that "all human institutions, even those of the most perfect kind, have defects as well as excellencies—ill as well as good propensities."[19] Personal corruption lead to public corruption. As Goldman notes, "Augustine argued that ... people fail because they love the wrong things. A nation defines itself by what it loves, and the wrong kind of love condemns it to eventual ruin."[20] Max Stirner, Ludwig Feurebach, Nietzsche and Frankfurt School alumni (György Lukács, Theodor Adorno, et al.) viewed religion as being illusory and oppressive. Yet the impulse to give of one's best for the greater good and to sacrifice for that cause is an ideal espoused by virtually every religion and remains a singular virtue in the pursuit of a humane society. This is, at heart, a distinctly romantic characteristic. To love the idea of loving others would seem to be a decidedly Augustinian concept, and one worth abiding by, for both secularists and religionists.

Religion, Politics and Music

As noted previously, this attitude had significance for artists as well, especially the German Romantics. Moreover, Bach, Brahms and other composers for whom religious conviction was more than a peripheral concern intuited that the truth-beauty-goodness paradigm as articulated by the Greeks and the philosophical forbearers of Christian culture in Europe was rooted in the idea of a divine order created by a loving God. As the various perspectives of that paradigm demonstrate, there is quite a bit from the past that remains instructive for contemporary society if we chose to remain open to these ideas.

In Ludwig van Beethoven's development as both a musician and person, we find that "he was to be unfailingly guided by a conscious adherence to the principles of political liberty, personal excellence and ethical action." The composer's biographer, Maynard Solomon observes that Beethoven's "devotion to art and beauty and the acceptance of the main notions of the Enlightenment—virtue, reason, freedom, progress, universal brotherhood," would become defining aspects of his worldview.[21] In his later years he "railed imprudently—but with impunity" against German aristocracy and his fallen hero, Napoleon.[22] Beethoven could not have known it, but the promise of a just and benevolent society in which the hopes and needs of the common man would eventually come to fruition did not occur in France, but in the "New World," albeit not without severe growing pains, including a brutal Civil War in the process of creating "a more perfect union."[*]

German historian Oswald Spengler viewed Christianity as being "the heart of Western culture," but expressed concern about how "our rich and living culture has been replaced by the lifeless precepts of a mere 'civilization.' When culture gives way to civilization … we enter an age of decline."[23] The significance of culture guided by religious-based moral and ethic precepts in the establishment of a benevolent society where the ideal of a "universal brotherhood" could blossom, was central to Spengler's worldview. Spengler, however, did not appropriate the American Revolution much significance in his historical treatise, *The Decline of the West*, yet it was to be in the "New World" where the establishment of a constitutional republic guided by Judeo-Christian principles would give birth to the altruistic and just culture he envisioned.[†]

---

[*] Beethoven initially dedicated his third symphony to Napoleon Bonaparte but withdrew the dedication when he learned that Bonaparte declared himself emperor. The composer had mixed feelings about Napoleon throughout his life. Early in his career, Beethoven sought the favor of the European aristocracy in order to secure commissions for his work. His more "republican" attitudes developed later in his life as he gained greater acceptance, especially in Vienna.

[†] In his two-volume book *The Decline of the West*, published in 1918 and 1922, Spengler predicted that the West's decline would begin around 2000 and one of the signs of its decline would be the attempt to centralize power by the executive branch of government, thereby usurping the democratic process and diminishing representative government.

Political theorist Alan Woods, a British Trotskyite and supporter of Hugo Chavez, has attempted to ascribe Beethoven's "revolutionary" attitudes about music, culture and politics to the same impulses that induced the political upheavals that fostered the rise of Marxist revolutions. Yes, Beethoven was a proponent of universal brotherhood and egalitarianism; and yes, he composed revolutionary music that challenged his audiences. But to appropriate Beethoven's psychology to the godless and brutal tyrannies born of dialectical materialism is one of the most unfortunate and dishonest misreadings you could imagine. This is akin to calling Jesus a proto-Marxist.

Beethoven can be considered to be a child of the French Revolution and advocated for the ideals of independence and liberty, but he would have expressed disdain for Lenin, Stalin, Mao, or any other Marxist dictator in the same manner he did towards Napoleon when *Le petit Caporal* went off the rails into his authoritarian conquest mode. Charles Krauthammer observes that the hyper-mythologizing of the French Revolution resulted in both deifying and popularizing the very idea of revolution. This has given a spurious kind of legitimacy to any insurgency and legitimization of the most brutal and heinous behavior regardless of the moral underpinnings, or lack of such, in a given rebellion. The arbitrariness of many *faux* revolutions is often detached from any objective morality and are largely predicated on "fallen" impulses and emotions; namely resentment, jealousy, vengeance and retribution, especially it the revolution is directed against Western-European culture.

We shouldn't forget that performing Beethoven or owning a violin in China during Mao's Cultural Revolution was an offense that put many intellectuals in a *laogai* (forced labor camp), or sent them to their deaths. In the grand historical context, the traditions and values of the American founders (values that we now identify as "conservative" but were quite "liberal") remain among the most novel and creative ideas in human history. Progressives such as Woods are actually regressive in that they wish to turn back the clock to the dark days of tyranny before 1776 when the notions of inalienable human rights endowed by a Creator were hardly imagined, let alone discussed as a credible political theory of governance.

Beethoven's call for a God-centered, universal brotherhood in his monumental and oft-criticized Ninth Symphony seems the more accurate representation of his psychology. This music continues to resonate with those

712

whose idealism has not been entirely squelched by the nihilist and inhumane circumstances that have been so pervasive throughout the twentieth century and into the twenty-first. His setting of Schiller's *Ode to Joy* (composed in 1824) has represented the hope of a better world generation after generation.

In his coruscating essay on Beethoven's last symphonic work, "Resisting the Ninth," Richard Taruskin suggests that coming to terms with the narrative of its positive and altruistic tone in the "fallen twentieth century" is problematic for some. A century that witnessed such extreme measures of violence, cynicism, repudiation and doubt make contending with the kind of idealistic optimism that Beethoven attempted to express in his Ninth symphony almost impossible. Roger Scruton notes that the current iteration of postmodern psychology invites us to believe in nothing, hence those of a postmodern mindset will resist such an unabashedly hopeful artistic utterance, especially one with implicit religious overtones.

In the symphony's finale, the movement that confounded Beethoven's contemporaries, the solo baritone asks us to imagine something more pleasing (*angenehmere*) after the second "terror fanfare" (Wagner's description). The ensuing "Joy" theme bursts forth in the spirit of hope and ebullient optimism with its vision of Elysium and universal love. Taruskin explains how the dichotomy of a hopeful future as envisioned by the composer, and a disturbing present in which contemporary listeners dwell, can cause some serious cognitive dissonance.

> And the pleasure, as the nature of the Joy theme at once announces, is to be an eminently public pleasure, annulling the private pain Beethoven had previously disclosed to us. ... In this Elysium to which our noble quest has delivered us, the realm glimpsed mistily through visionary modulations amid the crags and ravines of earlier movements? And who are these riffraff, with their beery Männerchöre (male choir) and sauerkraut bands? Our brothers? And the juxtaposition of all this with the disclosure of God's presence "above the stars?" No, it's all too much![24]

This eclectic symphonic concoction was too much to take for some in 1824 and remains so for others today. In Beethoven's time the juxtaposition of these wildly diverse elements in a movement of a symphony was unprecedented—revolutionary, in fact. These heterogenic components elicited confusion and charges of banality (if not insanity) from the composer's friends and colleagues. Alluding to the composer's unabashed egalitarianism and his choice of multi-stylistic influences and the symphony's constituent elements in the symphony's finale, Taruskin opines, "Beethoven apparently took his democracy straight." It's important to remember that Beethoven's Elysium was not a secular, humanistic realm, but an environment in which God's presence was prominent and where love embraced all. The composer implored his listeners to search for God; "Seek Him beyond the starry canopy." This is undoubtedly why "the Ninth" causes cognitive dissonances for some and inspires others. In our time Beethoven's optimism seems misplaced and unjustified, yet this "heroic" music continues to inspire us to imagine something "more pleasing."

A century after Beethoven's death, another German composer, Paul Hindemith, seized upon Beethoven's vision and spoke perspicaciously to the importance of altruism as it pertained to one's creativity. The "moral responsibility" of artists" and "a final allegiance to spiritual sovereignty" in the spirit of humility were, according to Hindemith, important considerations in the pursuit of a better world. Though some have chided Hindemith for his late, and some would argue politically convenient arrival at moral clarity, I believe that it's never to late to have epiphanies regarding one's mistakes and how to rectify them. Shooting the messenger is often unwise and unwarranted, especially when the message is worth noting. Speaking to the issue of humility before the divine, Hindemith asserts:

> The ultimate reason for this humility will be the musician's conviction that beyond all the rational knowledge he has amassed and all his dexterity as a craftsman, there is a region of visionary irrationality in which the veiled secret of art dwell, sensed but not understood, implored but not commanded, imparting but not yielding. He cannot enter this region, he can only pray to be elected one of its messengers, If his prayers are granted and he, armed with wisdom and gifted with reverence for the unknowable, is the man whom heaven has blessed with the genius of creation, we may see in him the donor of the precious [gift] we long for: the great music of our time."[25]

Perhaps Hindemith needed to seek divine counsel during his pre-World War II career with greater alacrity. That said, implicit in Hindemith's commentary is the acknowledgment of the subconscious and metaphysical aspects of art and creativity. The "visionary irrationality" he speaks of is in accord with the "romantics" embrace of irrationalism" that Isaiah Berlin alluded to in his perspicacious essays. In this regard, the Platonic ideal of truth, beauty and goodness remains germane with regard to aesthetic and axiological concerns.

Final Chords

Donald J. Grout's assertion that "all art may be said to be Romantic ... it creates a new world which is necessarily, to a greater or lesser degree, remote from the everyday world" due to its transcendent potentialities, rings true even in a postmodern culture where anti-essentialist and deconstruction-ist mindsets have become dominant philosophical propositions.[26] If, as the deconstructionists tell us, that any and all dialogue is merely a ruse or a form of power-grabbing without actual meaning, then we must conclude that there is no such thing as an enduring moral order, let alone objective truth from which any moral order can be ascertained and thus be a praxis for betterment. But the logic here is deeply skewed. As Melanie Phillips avers:

> For if all knowledge were worthless, why should anyone believe or take seriously a word that Derrida, Foucault or Lyotard ever wrote. Derrida said that texts had no meaning—and wrote so in a text. Fittingly perhaps for the theorist whose raison d'être was the denial of reason, this logical objection cut no ice at all. The irony that was their stock-in-trade abruptly stopped at their own work.[27]

Hear! Hear! We need not give the deconstructionist rationale any credence. If truth is fungible then there is no objective standard by which any ethical society can emerge—ever. Hopelessness and despair then become our eternal companions. Why go there? It should be fairly obvious that there exists an inherent contradiction in the postmodern narrative regarding truth. Phillips notes the obvious: Postmodernism argues that there are no absolute truths, which is in itself a truth claim. The idea that gender is a social construct rather than a biological premise is also a truth claim. The idea that capitalism is the root of all problems, or that all white people are racist (Robin Di Angelo's sup-position), are contested opinions that postmodernists pass off as being "true," all the while arguing that there are no "truths" on which we can establish a moral and ethical culture. It's all rather Orwellian.

In several previous chapters, I have alluded to the importance of balance and harmony in both our human and artistic pursuits. Attaining balance in life and art requires coming to terms with a myriad of relational opposites. How we manage and maintain those relationships harmoniously determines our fate and shapes our creativity. In art, the relationship between knowledge and emotion is central to the creative process. Ayn Rand eschewed religion and that which was beyond pure reason, but in matters of art she embraced the concept of "romantic realism." This is somewhat paradoxical since so much of what constitutes romanticism in art is predicated on that which is beyond pure reason, metaphysical, in fact. Echoing Jordan Peterson's commentary on mythological formulations, American composer George Rochberg offers a sagacious assessment of the importance of understanding this point in the context of out cultural patrimony.

> The cosmology of the ancients and the primitives, expressed in magic, rites and rituals, which invested the world around them with signs and symbols of the unknown, paradoxically insured the survival of these peoples; for through their seemingly unsophisticated notions they preserved the sense of awe and mystery in the face of a cosmos into which man had seemingly stumbled. And we? Because we have lost that precious sense of the magic and mystery of existence, we have no cosmology—physics and astronomy are poor substitutes. Because we have no cosmology, we are faced with the problem of whether man can survive his own thoughtlessness and arrogance, his collective hubris. Mahler was the last composer to intuit that music belongs to cosmology and is supported by it."[28]

Schiller argued that it was through experiencing cultural expressions such as music and art that we could be connected to the "sense of awe" and that this was important to the process of developing one's contemplative faculties. This "aesthetic education" would potentially allow us to more fully understand the intrinsic human values necessary for attaining complete and humane personhood. In this context, Pierre Boulez's contention that "forsaking all memory" of past philosophical, religious and artistic traditions becomes self-defeating. Do the tenets of religious belief have absolutely nothing to offer to a world rampant with conflict, wanton selfishness and self-absorption? Beethoven and Schiller would have us "imagine" a better, "more pleasing" world and I imagine that they would not reject the legacies of the past out of hand.

With the emphasis on technology and science becoming increasingly pervasive in contemporary culture, technology has become dominant in our pursuit of knowledge and the process of how we formulate and articulate ideas. Many see this as being beneficial and inevitable, yet Taiwanese artist, Tsing Fang Chen perspicaciously suggests, that for artists, more important than computer hardware or software, is our "soulware;" the condition of our heart and spirit—our soul state, (*Seelenzustand*—as Beethoven would have called it). Having concerns about the condition of our hearts is something that is beyond time and a particular worldview.

Taruskin suggests that being a modernist "is more than to be modern. Modernism is not just a condition, but a commitment. It asserts the superiority of the present over the past (and, by implication, of the future over the present), with all that it implies in terms of optimism and faith in progress."[29] As of this writing, not everyone would necessarily be optimistic about the condition of our "fallen" world and having faith in humankind to do the right thing. Science can provide amazing benefits, but it can also destroy us. The moral imperatives necessary to guide science towards the establishment of an altruistic society are determined outside the realm of pure science. Social sciences, too, when improperly understood and implemented, can lead to moral confusion and needless human suffering.

Citing the well-known anecdote of a conversation between Johannes Brahms (the traditionalist) and Gustav Mahler (the progressive), and Brahms' speculation that the wave of new music was headed to a "swamp," Taruskin alludes to the penchant of celebrating innovation "as a mark of vitality" and urban sophistication as a reaction against "romanticism as originally defined—in terms of … spirituality, sincerity, naturalness, spontaneity, naïveté, authenticity, pastoralism and transcendence of the worldly, all being the aspects or echoes of the original revolt against the militant optimism of Enlightenment."[30] All those "romantic" attributes are not merely vestiges of a bygone era. They remain central to the human experience. History has provided a clear vision, and it is not an exaggeration to suggest that Brahms may have been extremely prescient in his supposition regarding modernism in music. When Pulitzer Prize-winning composer, Stephen Albert referred to the "innovative" atonal music of the mid-century modernists as being a "sociological aberration," and those who vociferously championed it as being guilty of "cultural bolshevism,"[31] he wasn't all that wrong in his assessment.

Having a belief in God and the incorporeal realm doesn't presuppose that all rational thought is immaterial and should be discarded. Attaining a culture of peace will be predicated on attaining the proper equilibrium of heart and mind—a condition necessary to guide our behavior and our creative impulses in the most godly and humane fashion. Spinoza's assertion that "peace is not mere absence of war" suggests that there are many other factors that play into the pursuit of peace. A renaissance of cosmological understanding vis-à-vis the truth, beauty and goodness paradigm as articulated by artists and philosophers of all eras will undoubtedly be a significant factor in that pursuit, as well as the reclaiming of our cultural patrimony.

In his novel *Doctor Faustus: The Life of the German Composer Adrian Leverkühn as Told by a Friend* (1947), Thomas Mann's ruminates perspicaciously on the influence of the Enlightenment and its effects on music, religious belief, and modern political thought. The setting of the novel takes place at the time when European society was moving decidedly and forcefully away from the "cult" (Christianity) and towards contemporary cosmopolitan "culture." In *fin de siècle* Europe science was becoming a new deity and the influence of Nietzschean thought was pervasive. Adrian Leverkühn, the tragic hero in Mann's novel, is a composer and former theological student who agonizes over the myths encompassed in early religious convictions and the anachronistic musical style of a "bourgeois epoch", as well as the myth of a superior race as embodied in the rationale of the Third Reich. But the propagation of the myth of the superior race has a deeper meaning than racial purity or national pride. Mann expounds on Leverkühn's profound distress as a German citizen and a composer:

> The real reason lay far deeper down, in the renunciation of all the human softness of the bourgeois epoch; in an instinctive preparation for harsh and sinister times which mocked our human ideals; for an age of over-all wars and revolutions which would probably take us back far behind the Christian civilization of the middle ages; in a return to the dark era before it arose after the collapse of the classic culture.[32]

This bleak scenario provides the poetic narrative for Leverkühn's final composition, *The Lamentation of Dr. Faustus*. This composition is referred to in the novel as the "anti-9th Symphony" in which all thoughts of Elysium and universal brotherhood are obliterated in a rush of despair and hopelessness brought on by the tragic passing of the composer's beloved nephew. Influenced by the atonal musical syntax of Arnold Schoenberg, Leverkühn's compositional style becomes increasingly formalist, the zenith of total organization with a serious bow to serialism and a detachment from the pleasing utterances of two other German icons, Beethoven and Richard Wagner.

As Germany, the land of immense musical genius and artistic triumph sinks into the abyss of moral wretchedness, Leverkühn's *The Lamentation* becomes a metaphor for the "dark soul of Germany," a nation that has traded its artistic greatness and religious patrimony for something seemingly more desirable—racial purity and world domination. The effects of "the stupid power of war" (Gustav Holst's term) were still very much in the national psyche of the Germans who were humiliated in World War I. The prospect of more conflict and human suffering in pursuit of another "cultural revolution" played heavily into Leverkühn's distressed emotional condition.

In the novel's conclusion, Leverkühn, who has been suffering from a brain disease, eventually reveals to his friends and associates that he has made a pact with the devil which included his voluntarily contracting syphilis. As he attempts to play his final composition in a gathering of his friends he suffers a stroke and collapses at the piano. He lives for ten more years but in an infantile state cared for by his relatives. No longer a heroic figure, Leverkühn, tragically, is the ultimate sellout.

Ironically, it is the music Beethoven and Wagner, music born of the soft "bourgeoisie" epoch that survives and thrives well beyond Schoenberg's, despite the latter's infamous prediction about his formalist methods ensuring German supremacy in music for one-hundred years. The redemptive power of love, the poetic narrative in many of Wagner's operas, still finds willing believers and his music continues to summon this particular emotional sensation to great effect. Moreover, Beethoven's heroic quest for Elysium still resonates even as we experience an increasing materialist and nihilist reality.

Were Schoenberg's forays into atonality the devil's work? Were the rejection of aesthetic beauty and the utter lack of concern for one's audience an expression of arrogant indifference? Is the desire for beauty merely superficial, or does beauty put us in touch with that which is sublime, transcendent and divine? Arrogance, pride, lack of empathy, and the presumption of being superior are surely attributes of a self-centered mind; malignant narcissism in psychiatric terms. Regrettably, Germany, the nation that birthed the "romantic" movement and in so doing gave the world some of the most transcendent music ever written, also sold its soul and committed a form of cultural suicide.

In an attempt to rally America's support against the advancing threat of fascism in his homeland, Mann delivered a series of lectures under the title *The Coming Victory of Democracy*. The lecture series took place over a four-month period in 1938 and was broadcast throughout the United States. In these lectures, Mann stated: "I must regretfully own that in my younger years I shared that dangerous German habit of thought which regards life and intellect, art and politics as totally separate worlds." Having realized that intellect, art, morality and politics were intricately part of life and the innate human desire for freedom and happiness, Mann set out to make his case in one of the most formidable novels ever written. Critics who objected to Mann's "digressions into frank editorializing" about art, politics and life missed the instructive aspect of his narrative. There were lessons to be learned and utilizing art as a way to enlighten and elucidate remains a significant aspect of our cultural patrimony.

Many narratives in Mann's allegory are still being played out in the current iteration of the culture wars. The influence of the Frankfurt School neo-Marxists and calls for "revolution" seem as stentorian as ever. The weaponization of race, sexuality, gender or ethnicity for ideological or revolutionary purposes is now used as a cudgel against the virtues that have been traditionally thought to be necessary to create a more enlightened society. We may wish to believe that "the moral arc of history" bends toward justice, fairness and benevolence, but without human beings acting in a just, fair and benevolent fashion that wish will remain a dream rather than a reality. As Rich Lowery of *National Review* puts it:

> The notion that History takes sides is a distant cousin to the Marxoid idea that we are on an inevitable path to socialism, and borrows heavily from the (genuine and very hard-won) moral capital of the abolitionists and

civil-rights movement. … Whoever is considered on "the wrong side of history" by the Left is always loosely associated with the opprobrium of slavery and Jim Crow. This means that progressives wield History as a weapon, and make it an occasion for constant self-congratulation.[33]

Calls for "revolution" will always be with us, but as Charles Krauthammer suggests, these revolutionary exhortations are often "without reference to any other human value." Some of the worse atrocities in human history have been the result of well-intentioned but wrong-headed and wrong-hearted "revolutions."

In his book chronicling the French Revolution, *Citizens: A Chronicle of the French Revolution*, Simon Schama points to the seemingly incompatible relationship between "liberty" and "patriotic state power," which in 1789 resulted in revolutionary violence of the worse kind; specifically "brutal competition between the power of the state and the effervescence of politics."[34] Citing Simon Schama, Krauthammer posits that, "the American Revolution succeeded because it chose one, liberty. The Russian Revolution became deranged because it chose the other, state power."[35] Without freedom and liberty being in the equation, there can be no love. Perhaps the real heroes in our contemporary society are not the revolutionaries on the barricades of the culture wars, but the ordinary folks who strive to live in love, even in the most challenging circumstances.

The persistent allure of the "cult" and its attendant myths remains ensconced in our psyche because it *imagines* love, redemption and hope as being a path toward fulfillment—spiritually and physically. The redemptive power of love is a powerful narrative, but secular love has limitations. Our cultural patrimony informs us that without seeking God and godly virtues—especially true love born of a parental heart—we cannot achieve the culture of peace predicated on the concept of the universal brotherhood nostrum that Beethoven and other idealistic artists imagined. That revolution still awaits us and can only be realized when we decide to "Seek Him beyond the starry canopy!"

Recommended Recordings

Stravinsky: *Firebird Suite*, Ivan Fischer, Budapest Festival Orchestra

Mozart: *Missa Brevis*, Andrew Lucas, Sinfonia Verdi, St. Alban's Cathedral Choir

Beethoven: *Symphony No. 9*, Osmo Vänskä, Minnesota Orchestra and Chorale

Brahms: *Alto Rhapsody*, Jard Van Nes, San Francisco Symphony Orchestra

Mahler: Symphony No. 3, Bernard Haitink, Amsterdam Concertgebouw Orchestra

Kodály: *Peacock Variations*, Istvan Kertez, London Symphony Orchestra

Britten: *In Memory of Dennis Brain*, Thomas Zehetmair, Northern Sinfonia

Copland: *Billy the Kid*, Leonard Slatkin, Detroit Symphony Orchestra

Barber: *Second Essay for Orchestra*, Thomas Schippers, New York Philharmonic

Debussy: *Nocturnes for Orchestra*, Pierre Boulez, Cleveland Orchestra

Wagner: Orchestra Excerpts and Overtures, Yuri Simonov, Philharmonia Orchestra

Schoenberg: Chamber Symphony No. 2, Robert Craft, Philharmonia Orchestra

Albert: Symphony No. 2, Paul Polivnick, Russian Philharmonic Orchestra

Hindemith: *Nobilissima Visione*, Herbert Blomstedt, San Francisco Symphony Orchestra

Endnotes

1   Will and Ariel Durant, *The Lessons of History* (New York: Simon and Schuster, 2010), p. 68.

2   Igor Stravinsky, *The Poetics of Music in the Form of Six Lessons,* revised edition (Cambridge, MA: Harvard University Press, 1970), pp. 63-64.

3   Isaiah Berlin, *The Roots of Romanticism* (Princeton, NJ: Princeton University Press, 1999), p. 1.

4   Ibid., p. 9.

5   Douglas A. Silva, Review: "The Root of Romanticism" by Isaiah Berlin. *New York Times*, May 2, 1999.

6   Berlin, *Roots of Romanticism*, p. 9.

7   Ibid., p. 59.

8   Arthur Schopenhauer, *The World as Will and Representation, Volume 2*, translated by E. F. J. Payne (Indian Hills, CO: The Falcon's Wing Press, 1958), p. 376.

9   Irving Kristol, "On Conservatism and Capitalism," *Wall Street Journal*, September 11, 1975, p. 20.

10 G. K. Chesterton, as cited by Jonah Goldberg in *The Suicide of the West: How the Rebirth of Tribalism, Populism, Nationalism, and Identity Politics Is Destroying American Democracy* (New York: Crown Forum, 2018), p. 334.

11 Melanie Phillips, *The World Turned Upside Down: The Global Battle Over God, Truth, and Power* (New York: Encounter Books, 2010), pp. 261-262.

12 Goldberg, *Suicide of the West*, p. 138.

13 Berlin, *Roots of Romanticism*, p. 38.

14 Joseph Campbell, *Myths to Live By* (London: Penguin Compass, 1972), p. 5.

15 Jordan Peterson, Lecture, https://www.youtube.com/watch?v=QcU27Y26tqM
    16 Berlin, *Roots of Romanticism*, p. 68.

17 Ibid., p. 73.

18 David P. Goldman, *How Civilizations Die: And Why Islam is Dying Too* (Washington, D.C.: Regnery Publishing, 2011), p. 249.

19 Alexander Hamilton, *Selected Writings and Speeches of Alexander Hamilton*, edited by Morton J. Frisch (Washington, D.C.: American Enterprise Institute, 1985), p. 390.

20 Goldman, *How Civilizations Die*, p. 250.

21 Maynard Solomon, *Beethoven*, revised edition (New York: Schirmer Trade Books, 2001), p. 57.

22 Ibid., p. 118.

23 Roger Scruton, *Culture Counts: Faith and Feeling in a World Besieged* (New York: Encounter Books, 2007), p. vii.

24 Richard Taruskin, *Text and Act: Essays on Music and Performance* (New York and London: Oxford University Press, 1995), p. 249.

25 Paul Hindemith, *A Composer's World: Horizons and Limitations* (Cambridge, MA: Harvard University Press, 1951), p. 220.

26 Donald J. Grout, *A History of Western Music* (New York: W. W. Norton & Company, 1960), pp. 493-497.

27 Melanie Phillips, *World Turned Upside Down*, p. 275.

28 George Rochberg, *The Aesthetics of Survival: On the Renewal of Music* (Ann Arbor, MI: University of Michigan Press, 1984), p. 237.

29 Richard Taruskin, *Music in the Early Twentieth Century* (Oxford and New York: Oxford University Press, 2005), p. 1.

30 Ibid., p. 2.

31 Robert R. Reilly, "Reaching the Transcendent," *World & I Magazine*, January 1990.

32 Thomas Mann, *Doctor Faustus: The Life of the German Composer Adrian Leverkühn, Told by a Friend* (New York: Alfred A. Knopf, 1947), p. 369.

33 Rich Lowery, "Its Arrogance and Condescension Finally Catches Up with the Left," *National Review*, November 18, 2016.

34 Simon Schama, *Citizens: A Chronicle of the French Revolution* (New York: Alfred A. Knopf, Inc., 1989), p. xv.

35 Thomas Mann, *The Coming Victory of Democracy* (New York: Alfred A. Knopf, 1938).

Afterword

Music without a cosmology will not move the soul;
nor will it illumine the heart. ... Because we have lost that
precious sense of the magic and mystery of existence,
we have no cosmology—physics and astronomy are poor substitutes.
Because we have no cosmology, we are faced with
the problem of whether man can survive his own thoughtlessness
and arrogance, his collective hubris.[1]
George Rochberg

Who controls the past controls the future.
Who controls the present controls the past.[2]
George Orwell

It's been over a decade since I first had the impulse to write this book and though there have been circumstances and scenarios too numerous to mention that have taken center stage in the interim, it remains my contention that music and art are as relevant as ever in terms of raising consciousness and assisting in the process of social betterment. The social, political and cultural chaos that continues to make arriving at any mutually agreeable consensuses about solutions or "best practices" that might ameliorate various antagonisms seems unending. "Wokeness" is now a significant social narrative, especially to younger people. The novel Coronavirus has had the effect of providing us different perspectives regarding life, liberty and the pursuit of happiness, not mention government's role and its effects on people's lives.

There is change in the wind and though there is uncertainly blowing our way, Nietzsche's observation about Beethoven's revolutionary musical expressions being "something that happens between an old crumbling soul which is constantly breaking up and a very young soul of the future which is constantly *coming*,"[3] is an apt metaphor as we imagine a socio-cultural scenario where injustices, intolerance and resentments are supplanted by mutual respect, understanding, empathy, kindness and love. We imagine a better situation for all people, but in our attempts to fashion something better we should be wary of mob rule and vigilante justice, for when societies cower and submit to lawlessness, civilizations die.

In 2007 I attended an interfaith peace conference in Tel Aviv, Israel at which Dr. Martin Luther King III was a keynote speaker. In recalling his father's advice regarding non-violent solutions for peace, Dr. King spoke of how his father would advise that the first attribute necessary in any non-violent social justice activism was to be courageous. Without the courage to stand and "speak truth to power" the necessary conversations for social betterment die in a mode of silent acquiescence. On the 57th anniversary of his father's iconic speech at the Lincoln Memorial, Dr. King III referenced his father's advocacy of non-violent activism and said, "If you're looking for a savior, get up and find a mirror. We must become the heroes of the history we are making." Questions remain as to how we ought to go about attaining social justice and mutual respect, dignity and prosperity, but it should be apparent that without civility and courage non-violent modes of attaining those objectives human suffering will continue, for violent lawlessness only begets more violence and weakness invites aggression.

As we soldier on in the hopes of finding our way out of the "endarkened" circumstances that confound our individual and collective realities, our hopes ought not to be frustrated by the proclivities that are the result humankind's fallen nature. Because we all fall short of our idealistic yearnings, it's incumbent on all of us to engage in the restorative process. Everyone has a portion of responsibility in this quest for betterment, therefore we are obligated to invest in whatever way we can. It's the responsibility of citizens "to get up and find a mirror" and become the change we want to see in ourselves, our families, our communities and our nation and world.

My observations regarding how the ideological divide that has gripped the West since the turn of the new century has compelled me to view the past and the present in ways that I hadn't fully imagined when I began writing this book. If the art of writing is the art of discovering what you believe, as Gustav Flaubert asserted, then my discoveries, reflections and epiphanies over the past decade have served to reinforce my initial contentions about music and art and how we might make the planet a better place for our children, and how we might help our children to become better stewards for our planet. There is a reciprocity of influence in this equation.

The elections of Barack Obama and Donald Trump to the United States presidency surely attest to the wildly diverse social and political circumstances that we now find ourselves in. The rise of ISIS, the #metoo movement, the emergence of Jordan B. Peterson, Antifa and Black Lives Matter points to the ongoing need for "painful listening and sensitive speaking"[4] in our attempts to ameliorate antagonisms on any number of issues. The North Koreans have seemingly made a step toward nuclear non-proliferation after decades of recalcitrance, and it was the oft-described "rogue/fascist/racist" American president who finally stopped kicking *that* can down the road. Only time will tell if the Kim regime will take the necessary steps towards a lasting peace. China's aggression, however, remains a serious concern in the realm of geopolitics.

Much of mainstream media continues to de-legitimize itself and Camille Paglia has been one of its most outspoken critics for its continual journalistic demise.* President Trump's approach to dealings with China raised concerns, but as China expert Michael Pillsbury points out, Trump was the first in decades to stand up to Chinese perfidy on a number of issues. Some view this as necessary while others (Joe Biden, Michael Bloomberg, Howard Schultz,

---

* Consider how during the *Unite the Right* rally in August of 2018, members of Antifa attacked and assaulted members of the media, including some of their CNN colleagues, and attempted to destroy their cameras, only to have CNN's Chris Cuomo and Don Lemon defend those criminal actions against the media on one hand while condemning Donald Trump for his anti-media stance with the other. The duplicitous hypocrisy seemed craven and it further justified Paglia's claim of media malfeasance. [Source: *Real Clear Politics*: "CNN's Chris Cuomo Defends Antifa: Attacks On Police, Journalists 'Not Equal To Fighting Bigots,'" Ian Schwartz, August 14, 2018.]

e.g.) see it as problematic. Tellingly, Bloomberg News admitted that it has been less than objective in its reporting on the regime in China on a host of issues. Kowtowing to the nefarious regime in Beijing rather than reporting the truth is counter to the obligation of the Fourth Estate.

The presidential elections of 2016 and 2020 have been characterized as being a choice between crony capitalism and crony fascism. To some, that might seem too binary but many do view our political reality through this particular prism. This perspective is not all that far-fetched and the partisans who stand at the ideological battle lines are quite impassioned and entrenched in their outlooks. Though everyone believes in change, no one wants to change what they believe. As a result truth becomes a casualty and honest journalism seems hopelessly lost in the abyss of partisanship.

The years since I started writing this book, the classical music scene witnessed the passing of notable artists including Lorin Maazel, Claudio Abbado, Pierre Boulez, Jessye Norman, Joan Sutherland, Aaron Rosand, André Previn, Elliot Carter, Charles Rosen, Neville Marriner, Peter Serkin and Mariss Jansons, to name but a few. We also witnessed a hip-hop artist, Kendrick Lamar win the Pulitzer Prize for music. Regrettably, Hollywood hasn't been the only place where the problems of sexual harassment and abuse have surfaced. Prominent musicians from the classical music realm have been named as abusers as well.

One of the more troubling scenarios that have come to pass is the increased polarization in our social discourse. The advent of postmodernism, combined with progressivism and social media has led to the situation where speech, sexuality, race, ethnicity, history and the arts, have been weaponized and used as cudgels to attack and take down what is viewed by the hardcore left as an intrinsically immoral, racist and oppressive society. As mentioned in the chapter on the Celebrity-Industrial-Complex, the melee over Democratic Congresswoman Maxine Waters' calls for civil disobedience against Donald Trump's cabinet members, resulted in calls for moderation and getting back to "civility" in the hopes of allaying tensions. Yet a writer for TBS's *Full Frontal with Samantha Bee*, Ashley Nichole Black, posted on Twitter that [5]"Civility is a tool of white supremacy." Former Attorney General Eric Holder famously stated that Democrats when their opponents go low "we should kick them." The point being that society may need less civility to facilitate social change and challenge "white normativity." Georgia politician Stacy Abrams has advocated for more identity politics to be in the political equation as the way to obtain political power. In our pursuit of betterment, we need to be careful not to replace one form of supremacy with another. Historically, dictatorships of every stripe (fascist, communist, tyrannical monarchies) usually end badly for "the people."

Nichole Black's mindset recalls Herbert Marcuse's idea of "repressive tolerance" and his view that "what is proclaimed and practiced as tolerance today, is in many of its most effective manifestations serving the cause of oppression."[6] Marcuse's contorted views in his essay "Repressive Tolerance" have an Orwellian tinge and are easy to spot when he writes:

> Impartiality to the utmost, equal treatment of competing and conflicting issues is indeed a basic requirement for decision-making in the democratic process—it is an equally basic requirement for defining the limits of tolerance.[7]

In the same essay he says:

> Liberating tolerance, then, would mean intolerance against movements from the Right and toleration of movements from the Left. As to the scope of this tolerance and intolerance ... it would extend to the stage of action as well as of discussion and propaganda, of deed as well as of word.[8]

These incongruities shouldn't be surprising. We can see many similar modes of duplicitous thinking that accompany progressive rationales everywhere. As mentioned in a number of chapters in this book, this mindset is rooted in the postmodern rationale of Michael Foucault and Jacques Derrida in which truth becomes fungible and language is weaponized to obtain power. When postmodernists claim that there are no objective truths they are making an objective truth claim, yet they don't see the inherent contradiction in that. If language is merely a tool in the quest for power and control we shouldn't be surprised double standards and moral relativism abound. Something else is at work and Jonah Goldberg puts it this way: "Behind every double standard lurks an unstated single standard, in virtually every identity politics campaign that standard is *power*."[9] It should be evident that the views of either side of the ideological spectrum are not always right or wrong. If you believe the progressives on the ideological left you would think they are never wrong *about anything.* Even worse, if one disagrees with certain tenets of progressivism one is considered to be morally challenged and in need of re-education or punishment. It's all very Maoist.

Contextualizing the left's penchant for dialectic duplicity, Goldberg cites Marxist playwright Bertolt Brecht's play *The Decision,** in which Brecht wrote:

> All those who fight for Communism must know how to fight and not to fight; how to tell the truth and not to tell the truth; to be servile and also how not to be servile; to keep one's promises and not to keep them; how to confront danger, how to avoid danger; to be known by sight and unknown. All those who fight for Communism have just this to be said in their favour: that they are fighting for Communism.[10]

The hypocrisy of the ideological left is completely in line with Brecht's suppositions. Considering that the postmodern narrative is that there are no universal truths we shouldn't be surprised that progressives advocate for women's rights while besmirching conservative women who don't share their political views (Sarah Palin, Michelle Malkin, Ann Coulter, Candice Owens), or ignore the plight of Muslim women who are abused or killed, or that they advocate for gay rights yet say virtually nothing when members of the LGBT community are tortured or murdered by certain totalitarian regimes. The controversy over the allegations of sexual abuse by Supreme Court nominee Bret Kavanaugh was but another display of this duplicity. Why were similar allegations about Corey Booker, Justin Fairfax and Keith Ellison (all Democrats) basically ignored by the media? Tara Reade's accusations regarding Joe Biden's sexual abuse have been largely ignored by the liberal press. And what of the sexual trysts of Presidents Kennedy and Clinton? Regrettably, the American Civil Liberties Union has become decidedly partisan in these matters as well.

---

* Bertolt Brecht's play *The Decision* premiered in 1930. Hanns Eisler, a life-long communist, composed musical scores for several of Brecht's plays, including *The Decision.* He also composed the national anthem of East Germany, "Auferstanden aus Ruinen" ("Risen from Ruins"). Eisler became a Hollywood film score composer and co-authored the textbook, *Composition for the Film,* with Frankfurt School philosopher Theodor Adorno. He was among the first of the artists who appeared before the United States House Un-American Activities Committee and was described as "the Karl Marx of music."

As Michael Goodwin points out in an op-ed piece in the *New York Post,* what we witnessed in the Bret Kavanaugh hearings, and what we have witnessed since the 2016 election,

> is not a case of mere political differences, which the Founders recognized as inevitable and even desirable. ... Instead, we face something more akin to the combustible climate that historian Christopher Clark described as the origins of World War I. In his book The Sleepwalkers: How Europe Went to War in 1914, Clark illustrates how none of the great powers wanted war, but all felt free to escalate the buildup in the certainty that the other side would back down."[11]

Some are predicting another civil war in the United States due to the vitriolic invective that gets spewed on a daily basis. President Barack Obama's advice when he addressed students at Howard University ought to be taken seriously: "There will be times when you shouldn't compromise your core values, your integrity, and you will have the responsibility to speak up in the face of injustice. But listen. Engage. If the other side has a point, learn from them. If they're wrong, rebut them. Teach them. Beat them on the battlefield of ideas."[12] This is surely wise and necessary counsel in a society based on pluralism and free speech. But as he endorsed Joe Biden for president, Mr. Obama referred to FOX News as a propaganda arm of the GOP, ignoring the fact that CNN and MSNBC could easily be characterized as media organs of the Democratic National Committee. Double standards abound.

Progressives often rail against censorious behavior, but then say next-to-nothing when dissident rappers, artists or pop musicians are oppressed and imprisoned in Russia, Cuba or China. Where is their outrage over the treatment of religious minorities like Falun Gang in China, or Buddhists in Tibet, or Coptic Christians in Egypt? Liberals carp about the unfair treatment of the press while engaging in narrative journalism and transactional journalism—the practice of promising favorable coverage in exchange for access and a kind of journalistic agitprop. The list of hypocrisies and blind spots goes on. As Goldberg often opines: the left has blind spots for blind spots. It could be said that rather than drinking Kool-Aid, the progressive left in the media are now drinking Woke-a-Cola.

Given the influence of the French-Nietzscheans, Derrida, Lacan and Foucault in particular, we shouldn't be all that astonished at how language has been weaponized for ideological purposes. George Orwell and C. S. Lewis were quite prescient in that regard. The divide-and-conquer modality in which resentment contributes to the "us vs. them" rationale is seen as an essential aspect of revolutionary activities *and has decidedly anti-religious connotations.* Rooted in left-wing Hegelian thought as espoused by the so-called "Young Hegelians" of the nineteenth century, this modern iteration of social and political revolution views any governmental agency or apparatus that has religious underpinnings—legislative, judicial, executive—to be illegitimate and in need of replacing. As such, their aim was to undermine what they believe to be a corrupt and despotic state apparatus, and this necessitates the evisceration of the philosophical basis of religion, hence the opprobrium about religion, certainty and meta-narratives that has become pervasive in academia and the media. Discourse that removes any idea regarding "absolutes" expedites the upheaval.

Stephen R. C. Hicks observes in his highly informative book, *Explaining Postmodernism: Skepticism and Socialism from Rousseau to Foucault,* that contemporary postmodernists fully adopt the four major theses of Hegelian thought:

> Reality is an entirely subjective creation. Contradictions are built into reason and reality. Since reality evolves contradictorily, truth is relative to time and place, and the collective, not the individual, is the operative unit. ... Whatever the variations, the metaphysical themes of clash and conflict, of truth as relative, of reason as limited and constructed, and collectivism are dominant ... postmodernists adopt all four of these theses.

The Hegelian premise of "clash and conflict" is an especially troubling postmodern narrative in that it undermines attempts at building bridges in the pursuit of bi-partisan, harmonious solutions in our increasingly polarized and divisive culture.

I've cited Roger Scruton on many occasions in this book for his erudite observations on music, art, culture, religion and philosophy, and I shall do so again. In *A Political Philosophy: Arguments for Conservatism*, Scruton examines how the manipulation of language has been co-opted by the purveyors of cultural totalitarianism,* (also known as "cultural Marxism") and how this "facilitated the Communist enterprise and its myriad evils." As Scruton explains:

> Who and what am I? Who and what are you? Those are the questions that plagued the Russian romantics, and to which they produced answers that mean nothing in themselves, but which dictated the fate of those to whom they were applied: ... bourgeoisie and proletariat; capitalist and socialist; exploiter and producer: and all with the simple and glorious meaning of them and us![13]

This pernicious juxtaposing of left-wing Hegelian thought with postmodernism has produced what Scruton refers to as "a culture of repudiation" in which any vestige of the Judeo-Christian West is viewed as inherently corrupt. Paglia goes further calling it "radical relativism" and condemns the likes of Foucault (who she characterizes as "a joke ... ignorant, untalented as a researcher ... who knew nothing of antiquity") and his academic, postmodern, Marxist epigones as being "mal-educated ... embarrassingly so ... with little or no understanding of cultural history." Citing the specialized and arcane contortions of language and jargon that's part-and-parcel of postmodernism, Paglia calls the entire enterprise in academia "one of the biggest frauds ever practiced."[14] Her contempt is warranted. The drive for equality of outcome in the guise of compassion and justice can be and has been, inhumane in its consequences as I've stated throughout this book. Without reason and truth being in the socio-cultural equation any emotion, no matter how well intentioned, can be misguided, inappropriate and injurious. The forewarnings that Paglia, Scruton, Peterson and Goldberg have voiced should be a wake-up call for those who understand how the ascendancy of totalitarian movements can result in the most undesirable and inhumane circumstances. Reading the opening chapters of Aleksandr Solzhenitsyn's *The Gulag Archipelago*, or Jean-Francois Revel's *The Totalitarian Temptation* should be required reading for all college students. As Solzhenitsyn pointed out in his speech at Harvard

---

* The term "cultural Marxism" has taken on an anti-Semitic connotation because many of the Frankfurt School neo-Marxists were Jewish—Max Horkheimer, Erich Fromm, Theodor Adorno, Herbert Marcuse, e.g. Melanie Phillips, who is Jewish, uses the term "cultural totalitarianism" in her critique of the Frankfurt School and I believe this to be an apt description.

in 1978, that in their quest for equality the Soviet Marxists merely replaced one supremacist regime (the Czars) with another (the *nomenklatura*) in the name of "equity."

Peterson is correct to state the current iteration of politically correct-based identity politics is the same rational behind the brutality and oppression of the regimes of Stalin, Mao, Castro and the Kims. The attempt to whitewash history—control the past, as Orwell noted—via revisionist history must be identified for what it is; dishonest and pernicious. When as a Senator in California, Kamala Harris took issue with the critique of identity politics that's often levied at liberal progressives at the 2018 New Roots Nation convention in New Orleans, she was echoing President Obama's speech in Montreal (June 6, 2017). In that speech, President Obama called for an end of "tribalism" in order to make the democratic process function more efficaciously. He also reiterated his views on avoiding intolerance of those with whom we disagree.

Fine thoughts, indeed, but thoughts that ignore the facts (and history) that it has been the Democrat party that has traded heavily in duplicitous identity politics and political correctness (a.k.a. tribalism) as a way to energize voters and attain political power.* It has been largely the progressive left that has attempted to curtail free speech and open debate; "repressive tolerance" in action. Professor Michael Rectenwald of New York University observes in his book, *Springtime for Snowflakes: Social Justice and Its Postmodern Parentage*, that it has been on college campuses where speech codes, safe spaces, trigger warnings, bias reporting hotlines and "no-platforming" strictures have had the effect of abridging first amendment rights.[15] Cancel culture is now encouraged in the pursuit of equality of outcome. Vice-president Harris and other progressives are guilty of revising or re-imagining the past, and the very recent past at that. Perhaps they think we'll not notice this Foucaultian sleight-of-hand. Any attempt to give credibility to their view of the past—a fallacious view—in order to justify their specious nostrums for the future should be met with extreme caution. *Caveat emptor!* Stephen Hicks's assessment of postmodern vis-à-vis leftist political rationale is worth noting:

---

* It should be noted that in the 1960s Republicans in the U.S. Congress voted in favor of the Civil Rights Act, the Fair-Housing Act and the Voter Rights in higher percentages than their Democrat counterparts.

The nasty political correctness as a tactic makes perfect sense [to advance political power]. Having rejected reason, we will not expect ourselves or others to behave reasonably. Having put our passions to the fore, we will act and react more crudely. ... Having lost our sense of selves and individuals we will seek our identities in our groups (groupthink). Having little in common with different groups, we will see them as competitive enemies. Having abandoned recourse to rational and neutral standards, violent competition will seem practical [and justified]. And having abandoned peaceful conflict resolution, prudence will dictate that only the most ruthless will survive.[16]

Lamentably, Hicks's account of this postmodern narrative has been playing out in our current political climate to humankind's great detriment. Marx's predicted decline of capitalism failed to materialize. Yes, capitalism made the rich richer, but a rising tide lifts all boats and the emergent, contented middle class became allergic to resentment-based revolutionary impulses because the ascendency of liberal capitalist countries exposed the fallacy of Marxist social-ism. Marx predicted that feudal societies would progress toward capitalism, but the capitalist model would collapse under the weight of its own inherent faults and thus the communism would be the inevitable solution. But this determinist perspective was undermined in Russia and China because in both instances the societies skipped the capitalist phase and proceeded directly from feudalism to communism—at gunpoint! No longer able to justify the ideolog-ical premises of collectivist-based, Marxist socialism (the body counts were too staggering), the political left could no longer convince the working class that socialist/collectivist rationale was the most advantageous economic model to raise the standard of living of the proletariat.

Hicks points out with coruscating clarity, that the leftist intellectuals of the post-World War II era were confronted with a similar crisis of faith that the religious thinkers of the Enlightenment experienced. Religious arguments in the late eighteenth century were increasingly viewed as being wanting of rational answers to many of humankind's problems—economic or otherwise. Reason, science and intellection were seen as providing far more convincing understandings and solutions to social issues, hence religion was being viewed with greater skepticism. Yet, as the iconic historian Will Durant observes, many Enlightenment thinkers remained "believers" (Goethe and Locke, e.g.) but realized that they didn't have a belief system that could effectively replace the moral codes of Christianity. The American founders certainly believed in the importance of Christian morals being foundational tenets upon which to establish and govern a nation. As George Washington asserted in his farewell address in 1789, "Of all the dispositions and habits which lead to political prosperity, religion and morality are indispensable supports." Washington was referring to the tenets of Christianity.

For the political left of the 1950s, the brutal evidence of the socialist nostrum had exposed it as being morally bankrupt. Consequently, an irrational "leap of faith" was needed to justify their beliefs. The canard of postmodernism, according to Hicks, is the progeny "of the marriage of left politics and skeptical epistemology. ... Confronted by harsh evidence and ruthless logic, the far left had a reply ... logic and evidence are subjective; you cannot really prove anything; feelings are deeper than logic; and our feelings say socialism."[17] This became the "rhetorical weapon" that would find currency among academics and ideologues in their continual quest for their utopian vision. Hence, we are living in a post-truth era, much to our societal and cultural detriment.

Understanding the best practices of the past surely can assist us in dealing with the confusion of values that has become so pervasive. In an era when time-tested and scientifically provable universals can be simply discarded in favor of a dubious claim of socially constructed gender identity, for instance, indicates that value confusion is a very real problem—one that postmodernism cannot address with truth since truth is considered fungible in the gestalt of postmodern thought. In this scenario, beauty becomes relative as well. In the post-Holocaust, post-Hiroshima and post-9/11 era, it has been difficult to remain optimistic and get beyond the idea that the ugly aspects of our world require artists to express ugliness in their work. That perspective is not entirely without merit, however, the entirety of the world is not entirely without goodness or beauty.

Moreover, the past informs us that there has been authentic beauty from a variety of cultures to be experienced and enjoyed. The cynicism that has permeated much of the human condition and art in the modern world is largely the result of a lack of love, the loss of emotional innocence, the rejection of nature, and a willingness to become vulnerable. Any "rebirth," or "renewal," or redefinition of what has value in the attempt to reclaim what has been lost in the realm of art in general, and music in particular, requires that we restore a sense of reason and make a commitment to finding the balance between our heart and our intellect. Consciousness transcends race, gender, ideology, ethnicity and economic circumstances. As Paglia avers, the "beautiful cascading tradition of influence" that has been fashioned by the greatest of artists has provided humanity with abundant examples of music, painting, literature, dance and the cinema that can assist in the elevating of our consciousness if we choose to engage in the appreciation of their art.[18]

Hicks considers the groundbreaking, iconic artists of the past to be like gods; gifted individuals "who create a world in their work, and then contribute to the creation of our cultural world."[19] Rather than being "gods," it might be more correct to suggest that artists are co-creators with God as they engage in the creation of art.

Political philosopher, Hannah Arendt, opined that even in the midst of our most despairing and hopeless circumstances, "we have the right to expect some illumination," and this "flickering light" would likely come from people striving for a better life rather than a particular political theory or ideology. Finding our way out of the "post-truth" circumstances that all too often result in despair and hopelessness remains our essential trial. If there is one thing that my conversion to Unificationism has taught me, it's that having a parental heart ought to be a high priority in how we go about ameliorating the seemingly intractable problems that continue to plague the human condition. Living in a perpetual state of the present, with no connection to the past, is the realm of children. In any family, there will be squabbles and disagreements, but allowing the past to be mischaracterized for political gain is fundamentally dishonest, unreasonable, and an expression of bad faith. Having adult sensibilities requires that we have an awareness of our cultural patrimony, for without that our children will likely suffer. No responsible, loving parent, or artist, should want that.

Endnotes

1   George Rochberg, "Reflections on the Renewal of Music," *Current Musicology* 13, p. 80, https://doi.org/10.7916/cm.v0i13.4259.

2   George Orwell, *1984* (New York: Harcourt, 1949), p. 33.

3   Friedrich Nietzsche, *Beyond Good and Evil: Prelude to a Philosophy of the Future,*

translated by Walter Kaufmann (New York: Random House, 1966), p. 180.

4 Daniel Barenboim, *Music Quickens Time* (London and Brooklyn, NY: Verso, 2008), p. 103.

5 Kyle Perisic, "Samantha Bee Writer: 'Civility Is a Tool of White Supremacy,'" *The Daily Signal*, June 27, 2018.

6 Herbert Marcuse, *The Essential Marcuse: Selected Writings of Philosopher and Social Critic,* edited by Andrew Feenberg and William Leiss (Boston: Beacon Press, 2007), p. 33.

7 Ibid.

8 Ibid.

9 Jonah Goldberg, *Suicide of the West: How the Rebirth of Tribalism, Populism, Nationalism, and Identity Politics Is Destroying American Democracy* (New York: Crown Forum, 2018), p. 213.

10 Berthold Brecht, *The Decision: Berthold Brecht Collected Plays*, Vol. 3, annotated and edited by John Willett and Ralph Manheim (New York: Vintage Books, 1970) p. 67.

11 Michael Goodwin, "Hillary Clinton Is Still Finding Ways to Denigrate Democracy," *New York Post*, October 6, 2018.

12 Barack Obama, commencement address at Howard University, May 7, 2016.

13 Roger Scruton, *A Political Philosophy: Arguments for Conservatism* (London and Oxford: Bloomsbury, 2006), p. 161.

14 "Modern Times: Camille Paglia & Jordan B. Peterson," October 2017, https://www.youtube.com/watch?v=v-hIVnmUdXM&ab_channel=JordanBPeterson.

15 Michael Rectenwald, *Springtime for Snowflakes: Social Justice and Its Postmodern Parentage* (Nashville, TN: New English Review Press, 2018), Kindle Edition, Preface.

16 Stephen R. C. Hicks, *Explaining Postmodernism: Skepticism and Socialism from Rousseau to Foucault* (Ockham's Razor Publishing, 2011), pp. 82-83.

17 Ibid., pp. 89-90.

18 Camille Paglia, "Modern Times."

19 Hicks, *Explaining Postmodernism*, p. 265.

20 Hannah Arendt, *Men in Dark Times* (Boston: Houghton Mifflin Harcourt, 1968), p. ix.

Acknowledgements

This book could not have been accomplished without the support of various patrons, editors and friends who have influenced and supported me in my musical journey. They include Susan Osmond (World & I Magazine), Dr. Andrew Wilson, (Journal of Unification Studies), Diego Bellavotti and Dirk Anthonis (Peace Music CommUNITY), Dr. Thomas Walsh and Tajeldin Hamad, Dr. Michael Jenkins, Rev. Joong Hyun Pak, Dr. Tyler Hendricks, Dr. Michael Balcomb, Rev. Hod Ben Zvi (Universal Peace Federation), Dr. Mark Barry and Dr. Michael Mickler (Applied Unification Blog), members of the Seiko Lee Project, Dr. Young Ho Yun, Yeunhee Chang and Eriko Kubo (Hyo Jeong Cultural Foundation), Markus Karr (Manhattan Center), Jonathan Gullery, Peter and Phyllis Kim, Marquis van Demark, and my family. A special note of gratitude to Rev. Sun Myung Moon and Dr. Hak Ja Han Moon for their continued support of the artistic projects that I've been blessed to be part of.

Of course, there have been many musicians, producers, managers and lyricists who've assisted me in my creative endeavors for over the past five decades including Kevin Pickard, David D'Or, Seiko Lee, Laleh Nader, Elizabeth Quinones, Mara Milkis, Matt Ishizuka, Rebecca Keiko Zinke, Jenny Ayako Hughes, Raoul Joseph, Bill Miho, Richie Clarke, Joziah and Tink Longo, Sasha Mishnaevski, Steven Santiago (Opera Steve), Saga Legin, Masahiko Harigai, Roy Clark, Linda Eisenberg Tate Hamasaka, Hyo Jin Moon, Julia Moon, Brian

Hardgroove, Linda Feher, Kenny Muhammad, Mzuri Moyo Aimbaye, Caroline Betancourt, Scott Avery, Marquis van DeMark, Reggie Woolridge, Oji Behian, Jamie Baer-Peterson, Tan Dun, Miyuki Harley, Woo Ahan, Gil Young Lee, Incheol Kim, Sheila Vaughn, Ken Hendricks, Marco Rodriguez, Gloria Criscione, Leonid Fleishekar, Vera Tsu, Eun Hye Kim, Yasuko Sakata, Mark Beaudoin, Eric Holt, Benal Tanrisever, Asaf Cohen and the Little Angels of Korea. There were several teachers who provided guidance along the way as well, especially Wayne Miller, Barbara Rankin and Janos Kiss. Many thanks to all of you.

Index